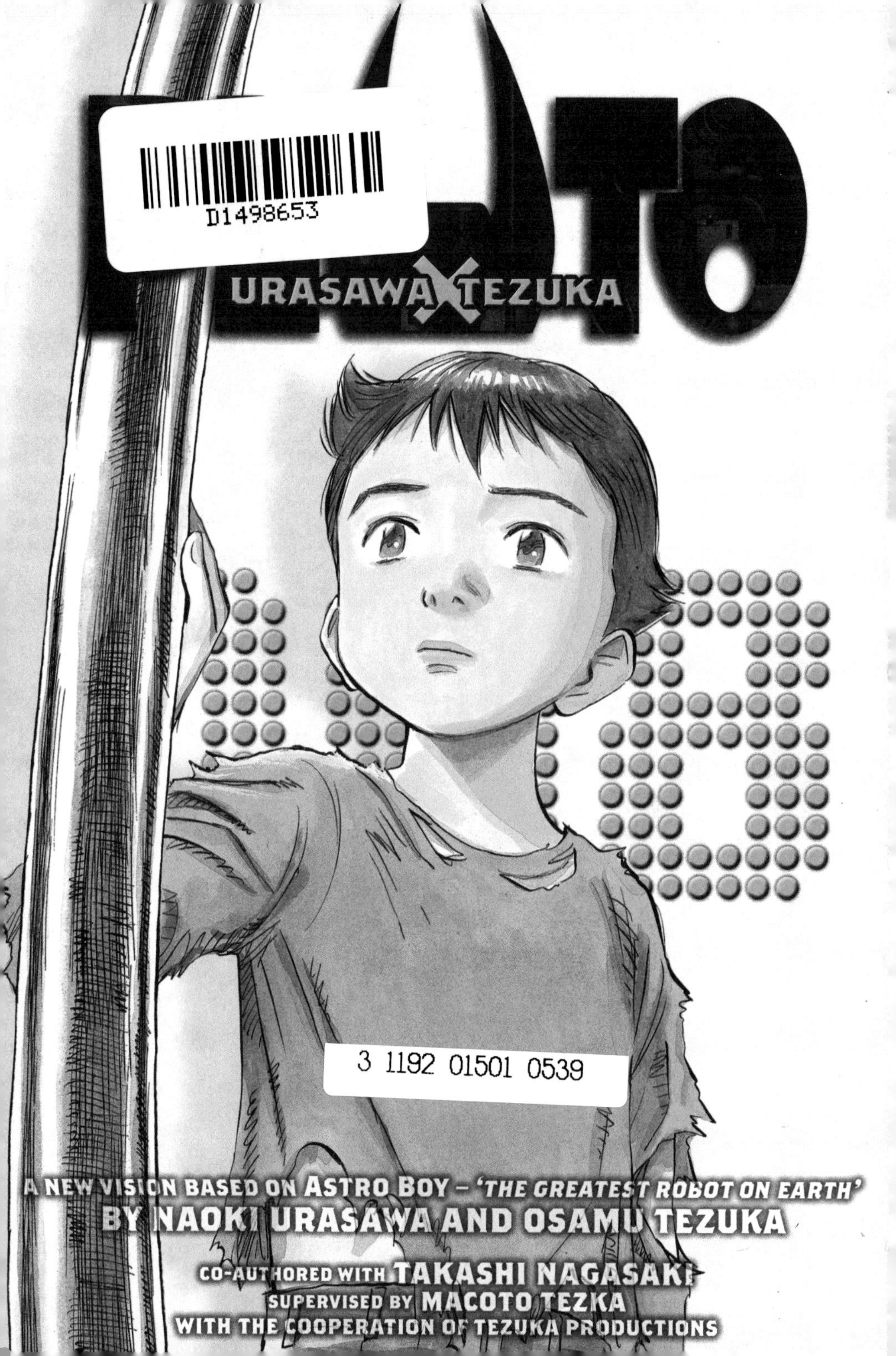
URASAWA X TEZUKA
A NEW VISION BASED ON ASTRO BOY – 'THE GREATEST ROBOT ON EARTH'
BY NAOKI URASAWA AND OSAMU TEZUKA
CO-AUTHORED WITH TAKASHI NAGASAKI
SUPERVISED BY MACOTO TEZKA
WITH THE COOPERATION OF TEZUKA PRODUCTIONS

Act 56 FORMULA FOR DESTRUCTION

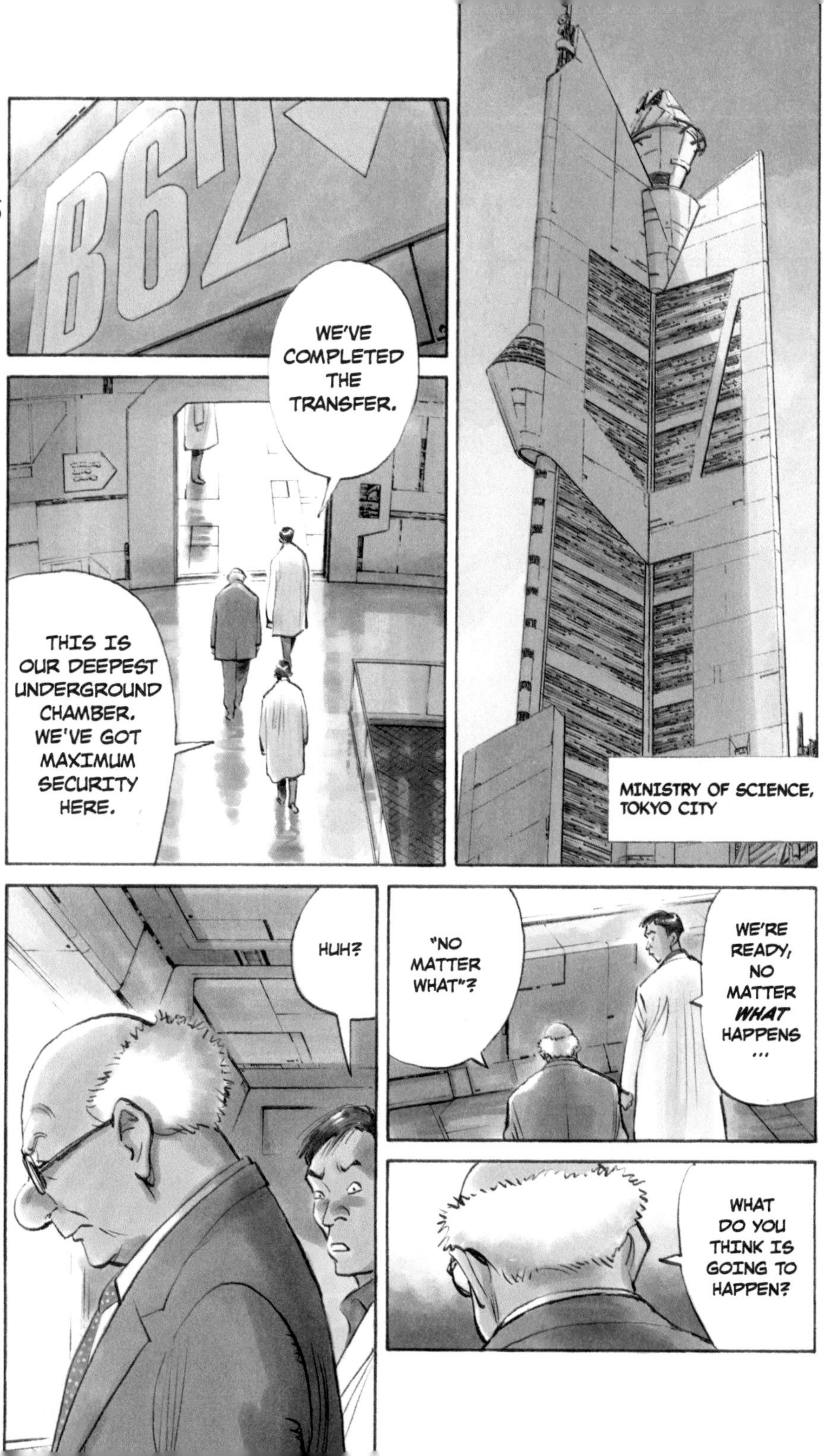
MINISTRY OF SCIENCE, TOKYO CITY
WE'VE COMPLETED THE TRANSFER.
THIS IS OUR DEEPEST UNDERGROUND CHAMBER. WE'VE GOT MAXIMUM SECURITY HERE.
WE'RE READY, NO MATTER *WHAT* HAPPENS...
"NO MATTER WHAT"?
WHAT DO YOU THINK IS GOING TO HAPPEN?
HUH?

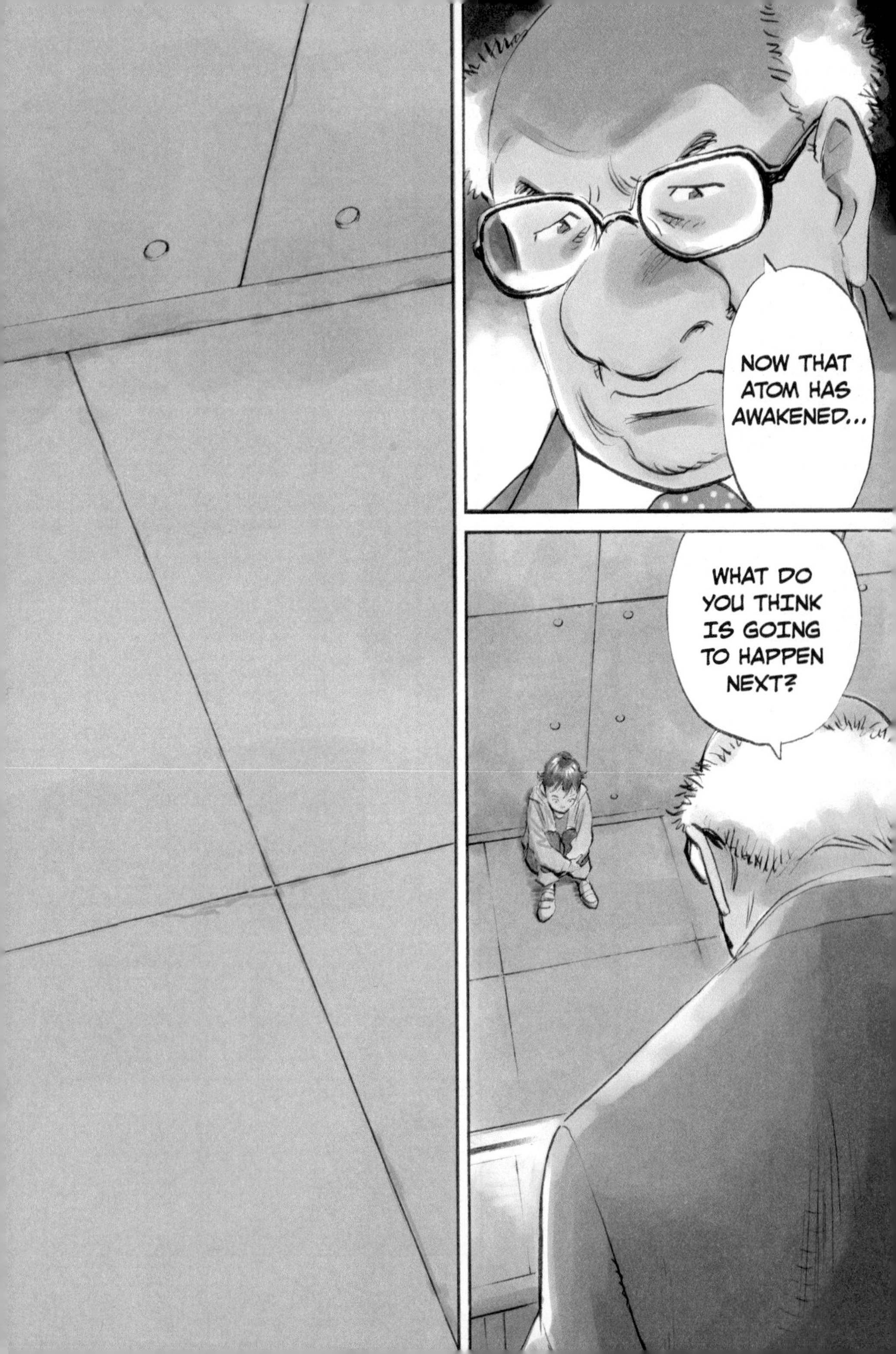
NOW THAT ATOM HAS AWAKENED...
WHAT DO YOU THINK IS GOING TO HAPPEN NEXT?

Act 56
FORMULA FOR DESTRUCTION

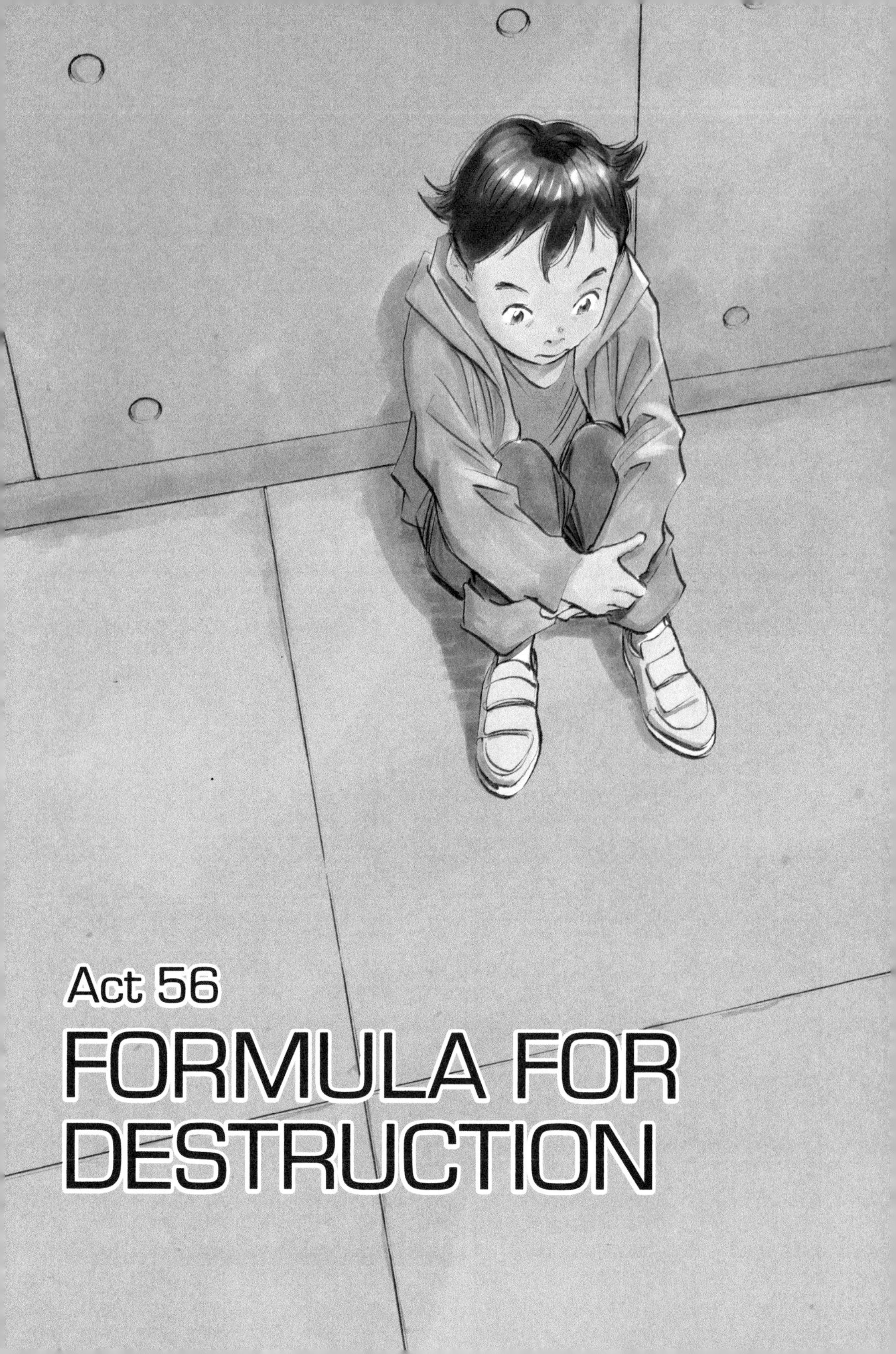

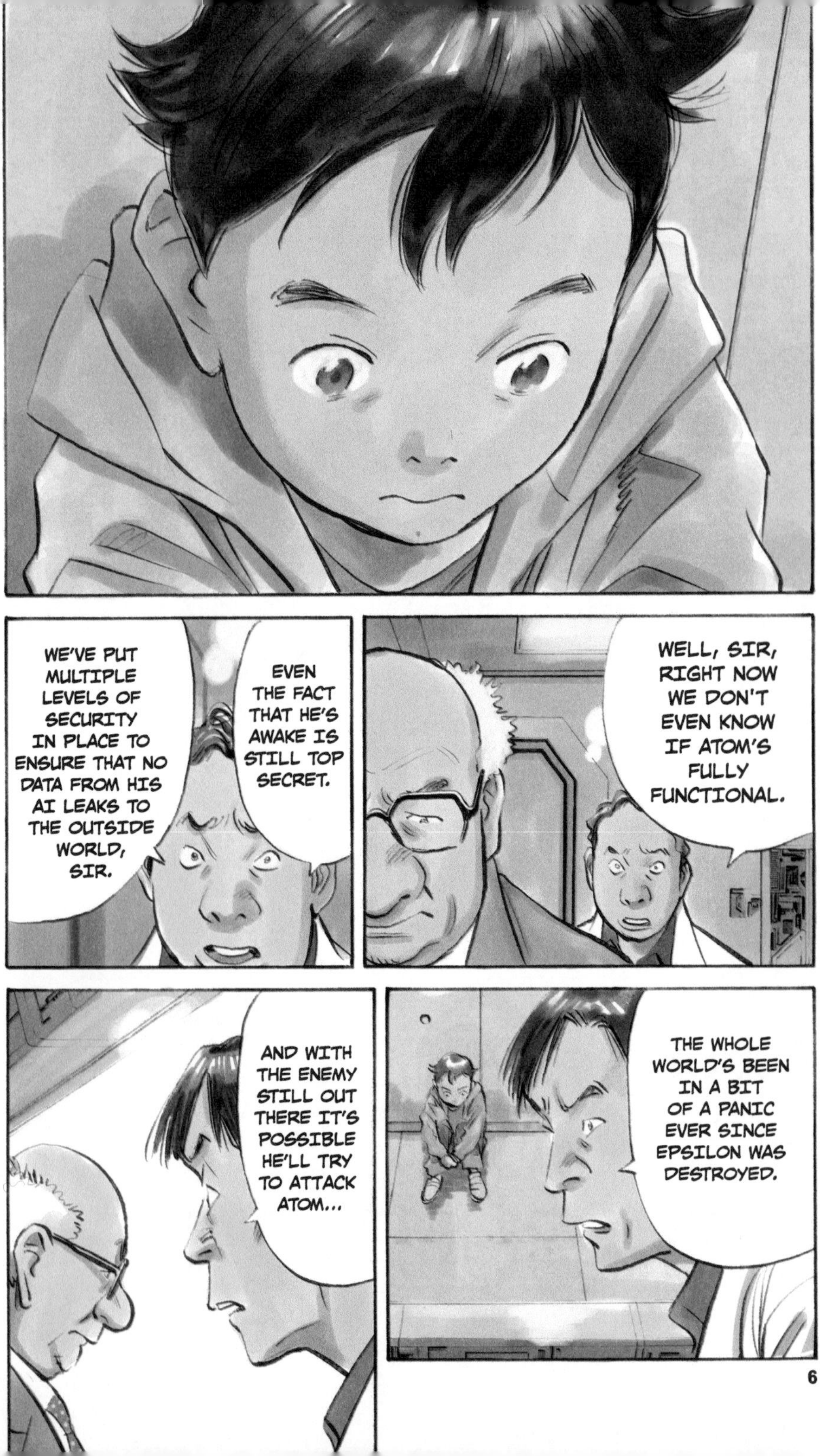
WELL, SIR, RIGHT NOW WE DON'T EVEN KNOW IF ATOM'S FULLY FUNCTIONAL.
EVEN THE FACT THAT HE'S AWAKE IS STILL TOP SECRET.
WE'VE PUT MULTIPLE LEVELS OF SECURITY IN PLACE TO ENSURE THAT NO DATA FROM HIS AI LEAKS TO THE OUTSIDE WORLD, SIR.
THE WHOLE WORLD'S BEEN IN A BIT OF A PANIC EVER SINCE EPSILON WAS DESTROYED.
AND WITH THE ENEMY STILL OUT THERE IT'S POSSIBLE HE'LL TRY TO ATTACK ATOM...

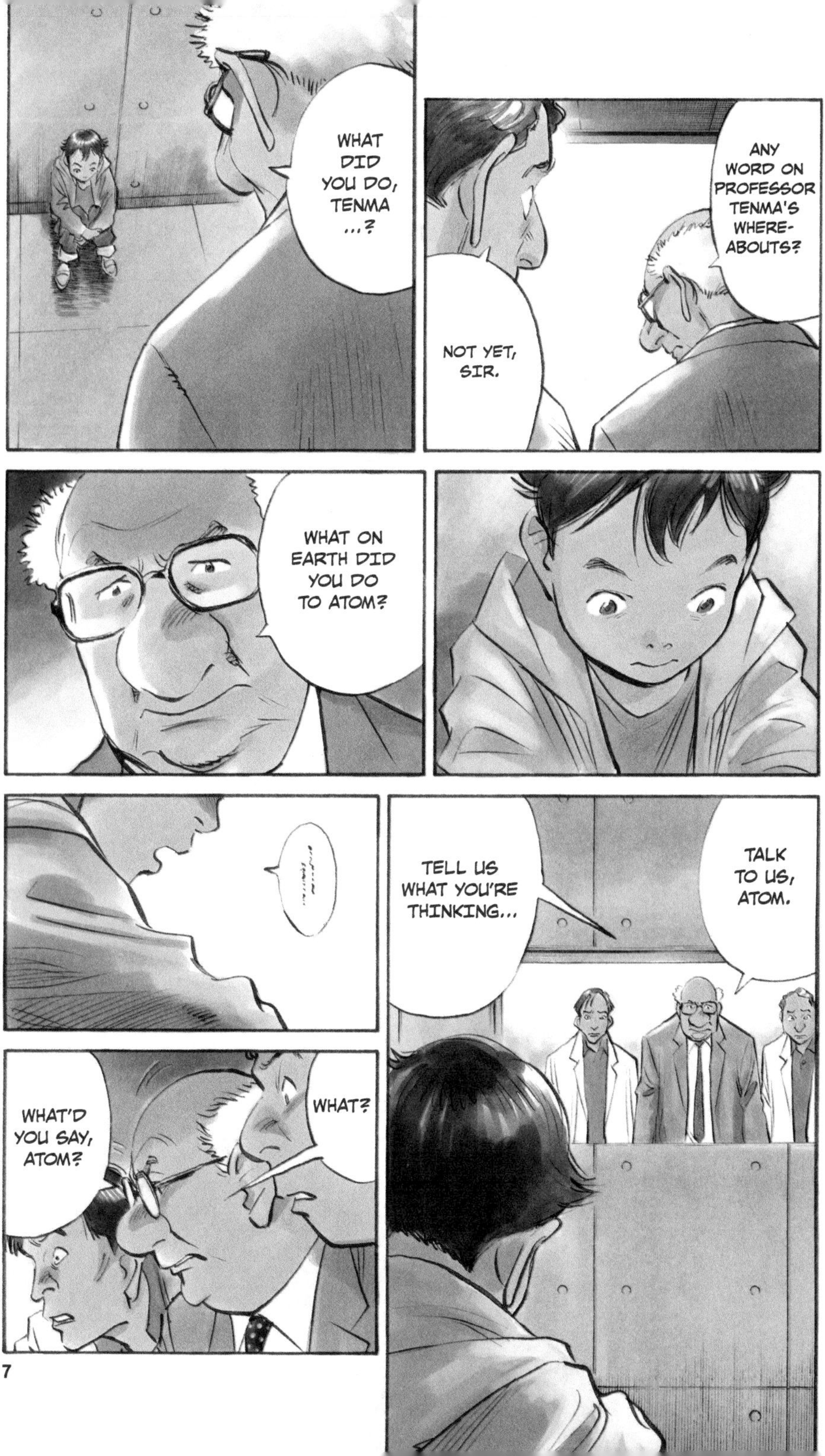

ANY WORD ON PROFESSOR TENMA'S WHERE-ABOUTS?
NOT YET, SIR.
WHAT DID YOU DO, TENMA ...?
WHAT ON EARTH DID YOU DO TO ATOM?
TALK TO US, ATOM.
TELL US WHAT YOU'RE THINKING...
WHAT?
WHAT'D YOU SAY, ATOM?

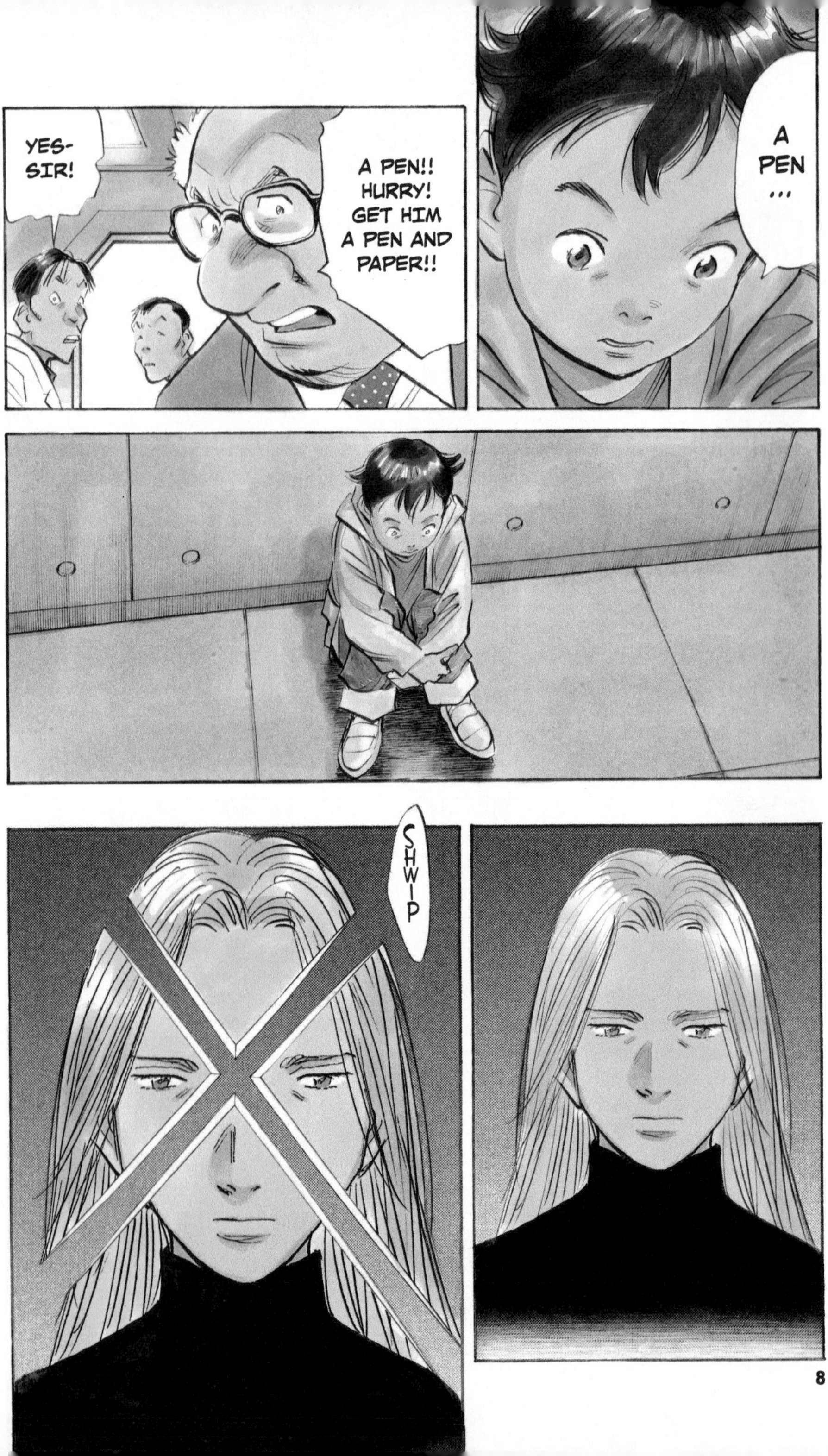
A PEN ...
A PEN!! HURRY! GET HIM A PEN AND PAPER!!
YES-SIR!
SHWIP

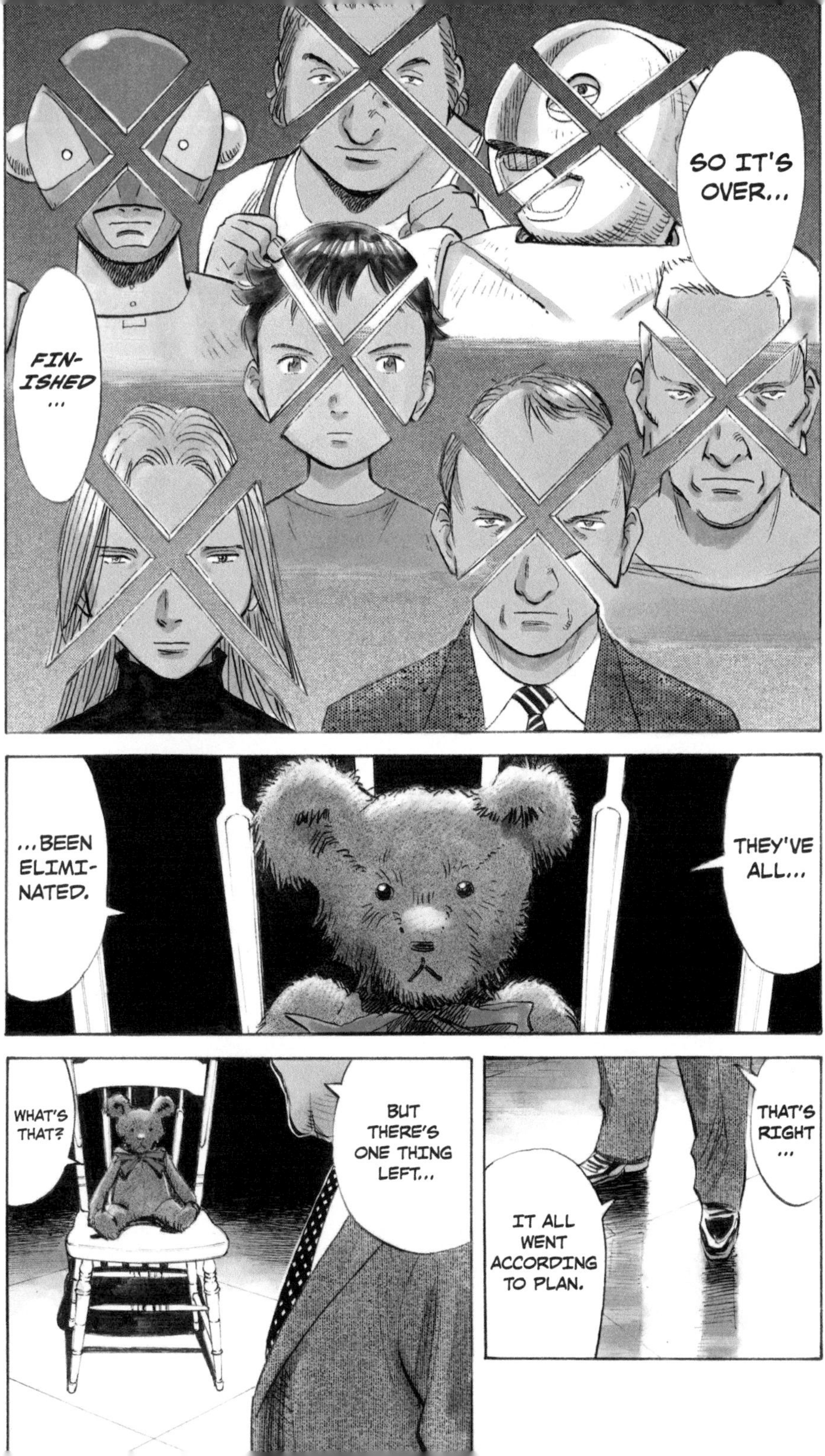
SO IT'S OVER...
FINISHED ...
THEY'VE ALL...
...BEEN ELIMINATED.
THAT'S RIGHT ...
IT ALL WENT ACCORDING TO PLAN.
BUT THERE'S ONE THING LEFT...
WHAT'S THAT?

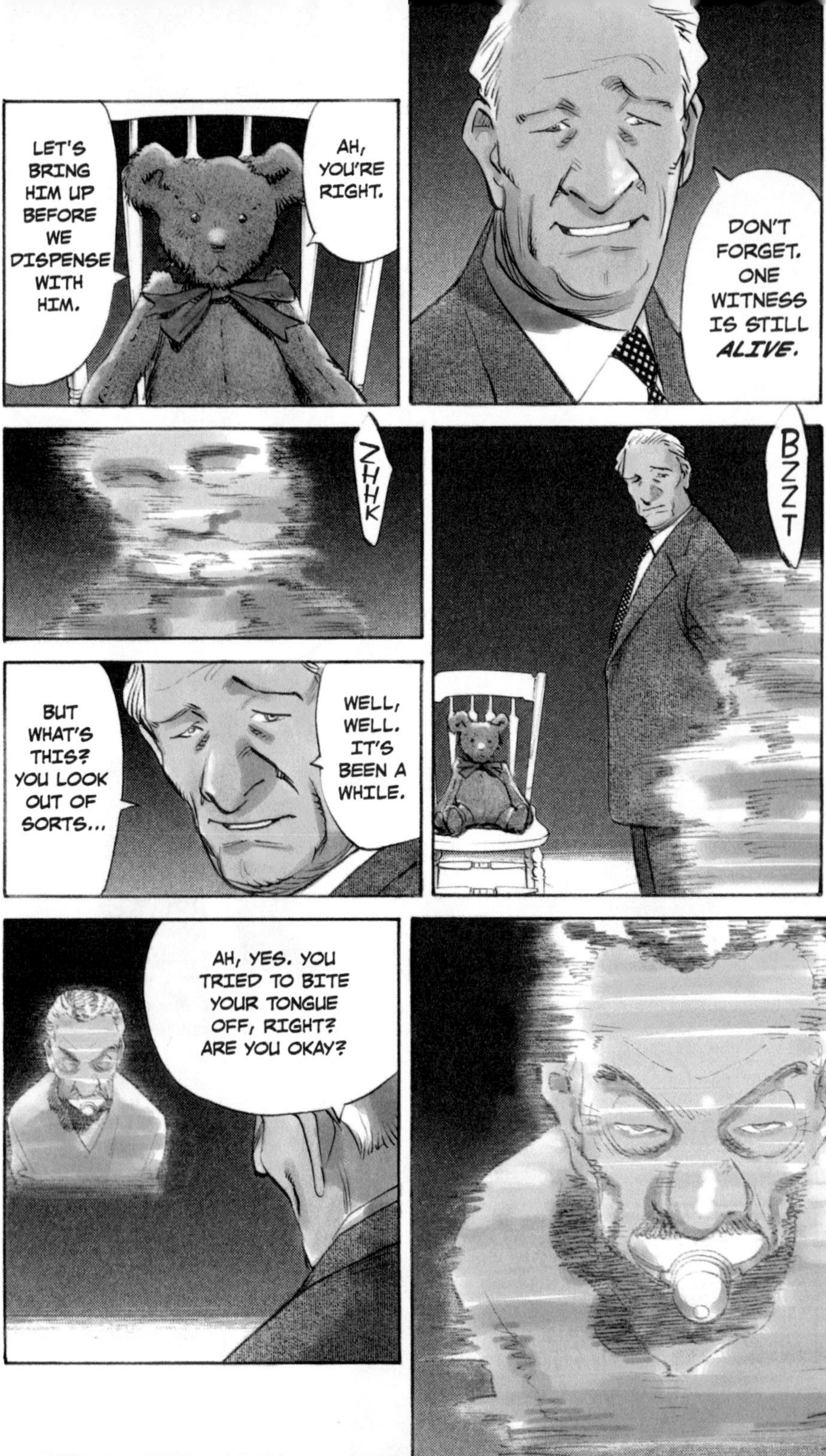
DON'T FORGET. ONE WITNESS IS STILL *ALIVE*.
AH, YOU'RE RIGHT.
LET'S BRING HIM UP BEFORE WE DISPENSE WITH HIM.
BZZT
ZHHK
WELL, WELL. IT'S BEEN A WHILE.
BUT WHAT'S THIS? YOU LOOK OUT OF SORTS...
AH, YES. YOU TRIED TO BITE YOUR TONGUE OFF, RIGHT? ARE YOU OKAY?

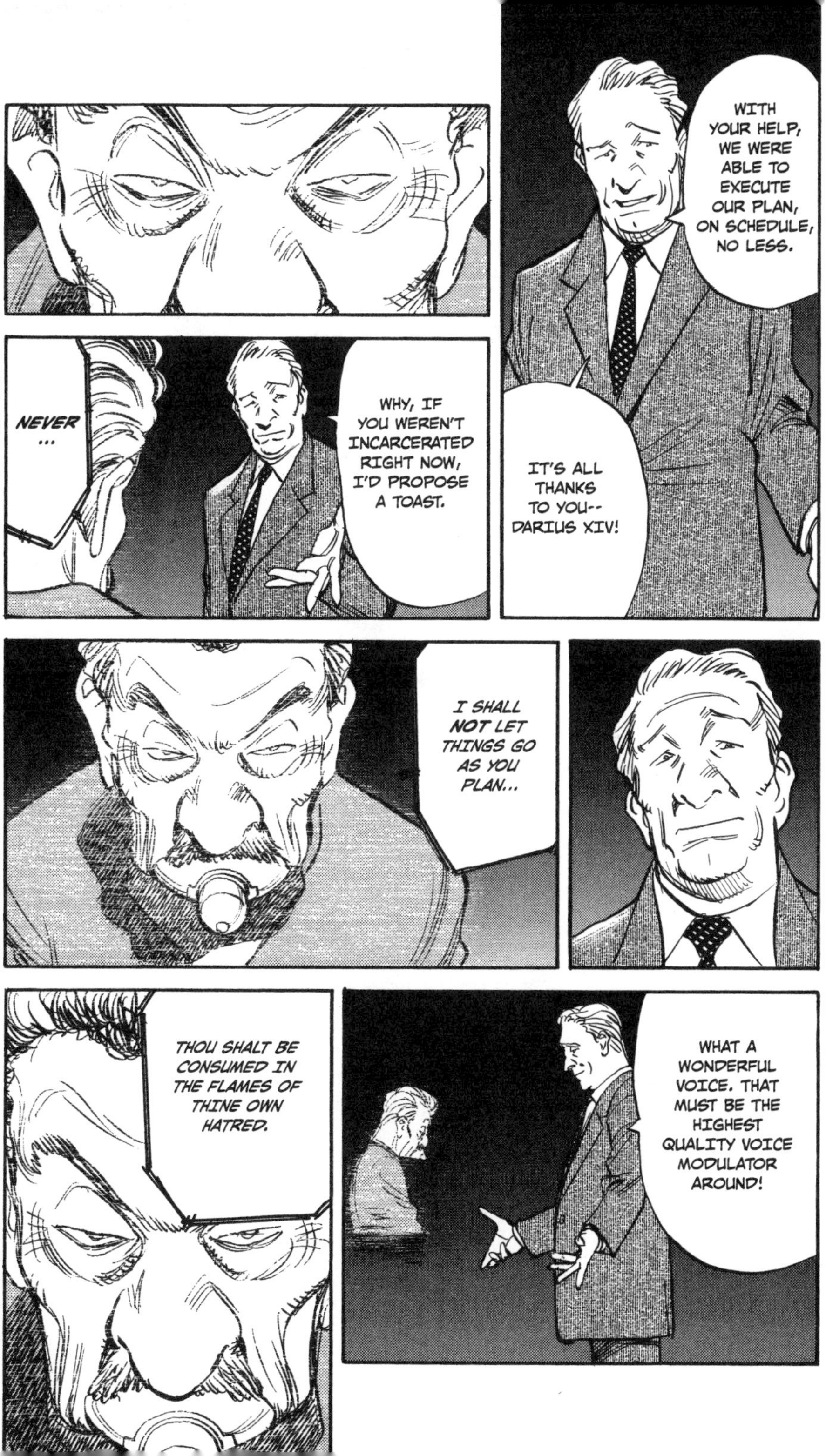
WITH YOUR HELP, WE WERE ABLE TO EXECUTE OUR PLAN, ON SCHEDULE, NO LESS.
IT'S ALL THANKS TO YOU--DARIUS XIV!
WHY, IF YOU WEREN'T INCARCERATED RIGHT NOW, I'D PROPOSE A TOAST.
NEVER ...
I SHALL NOT LET THINGS GO AS YOU PLAN...
WHAT A WONDERFUL VOICE. THAT MUST BE THE HIGHEST QUALITY VOICE MODULATOR AROUND!
THOU SHALT BE CONSUMED IN THE FLAMES OF THINE OWN HATRED.

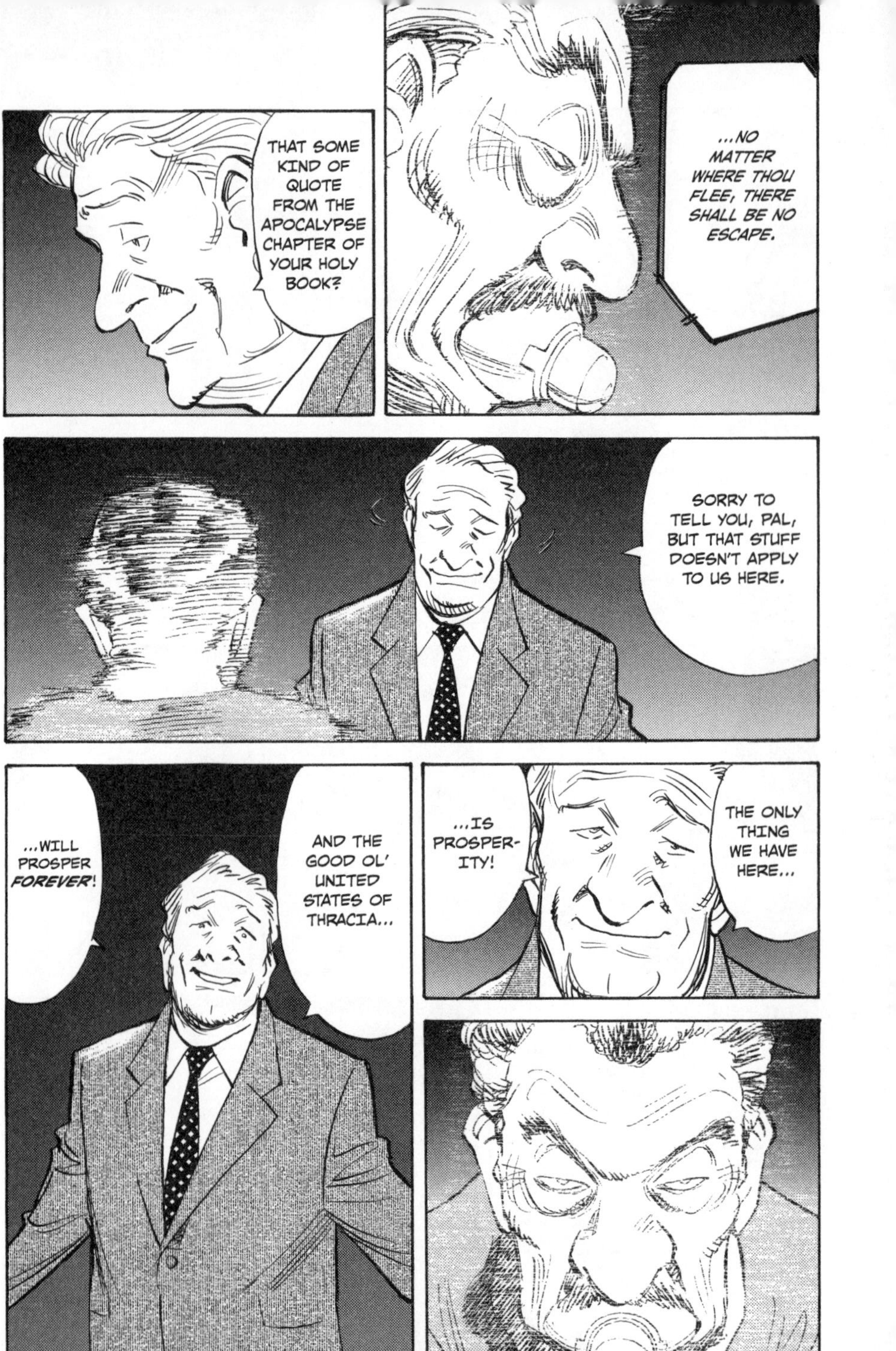
...NO MATTER WHERE THOU FLEE; THERE SHALL BE NO ESCAPE.
THAT SOME KIND OF QUOTE FROM THE APOCALYPSE CHAPTER OF YOUR HOLY BOOK?
SORRY TO TELL YOU, PAL, BUT THAT STUFF DOESN'T APPLY TO US HERE.
THE ONLY THING WE HAVE HERE...
...IS PROSPER-ITY!
AND THE GOOD OL' UNITED STATES OF THRACIA...
...WILL PROSPER *FOREVER*!

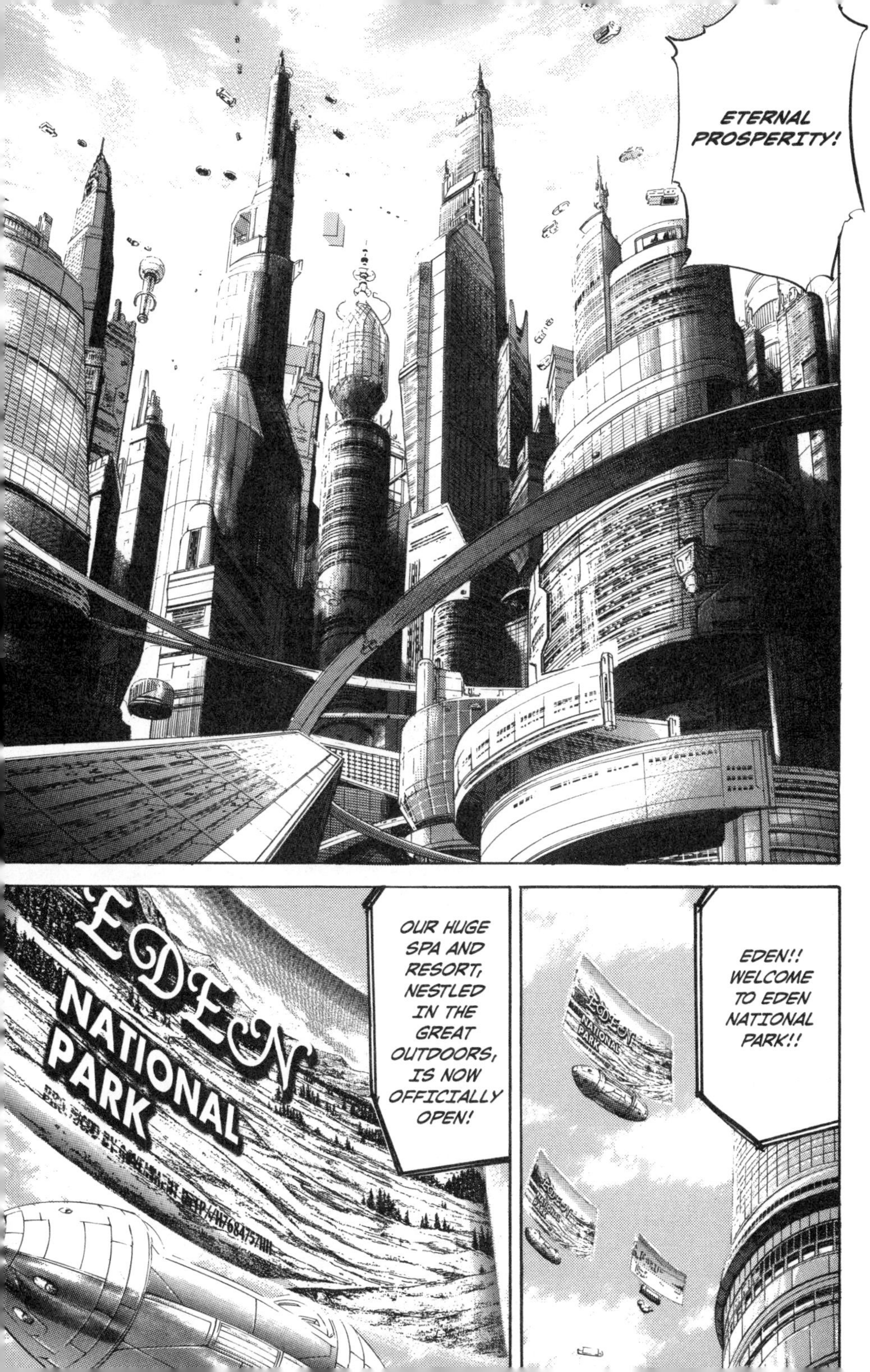
ETERNAL PROSPERITY!
EDEN!! WELCOME TO EDEN NATIONAL PARK!!
OUR HUGE SPA AND RESORT, NESTLED IN THE GREAT OUTDOORS, IS NOW OFFICIALLY OPEN!
EDEN
NATIONAL PARK

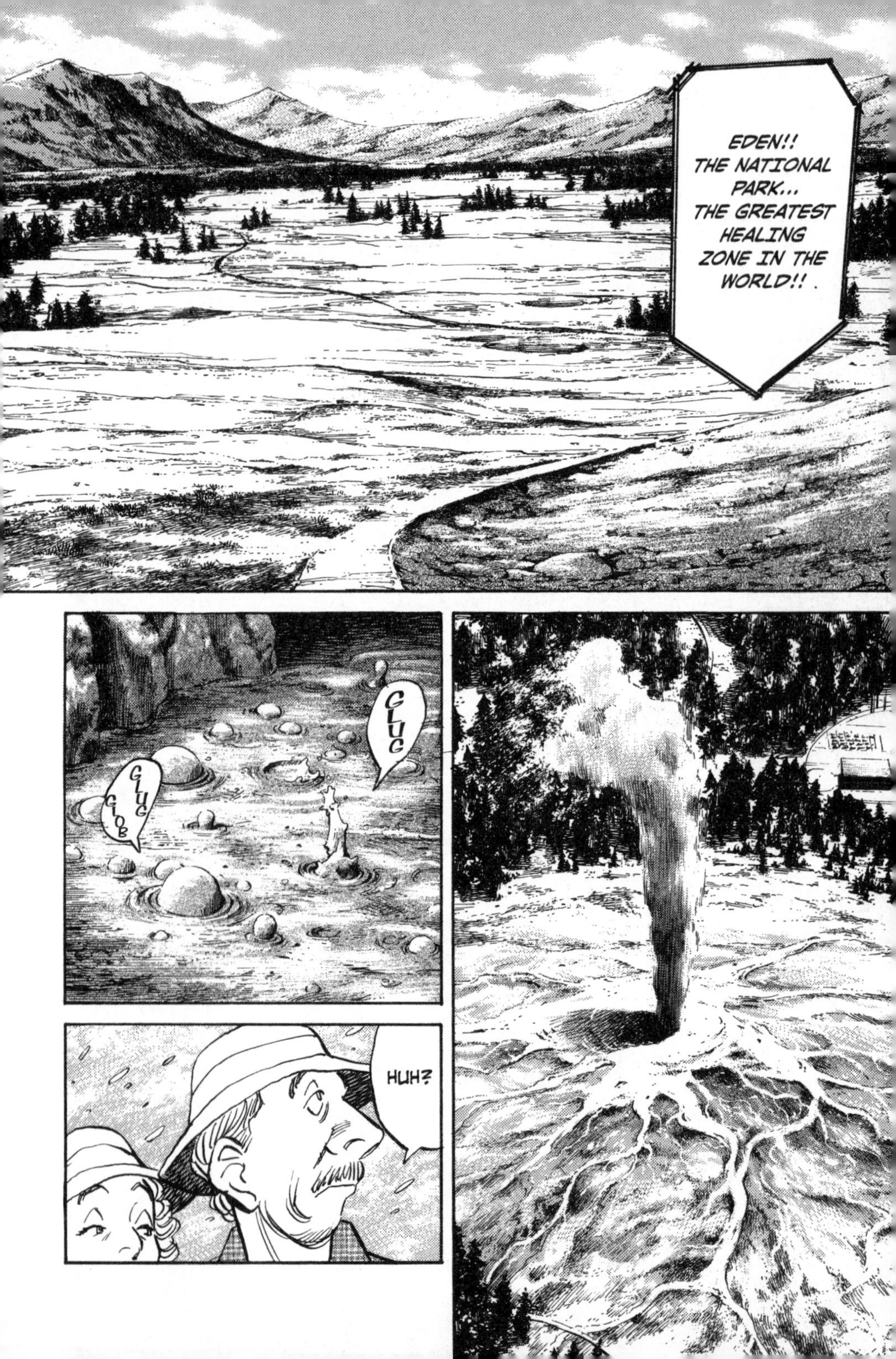
EDEN!! THE NATIONAL PARK... THE GREATEST HEALING ZONE IN THE WORLD!!
GLUG
GLUG GLOB
HUH?

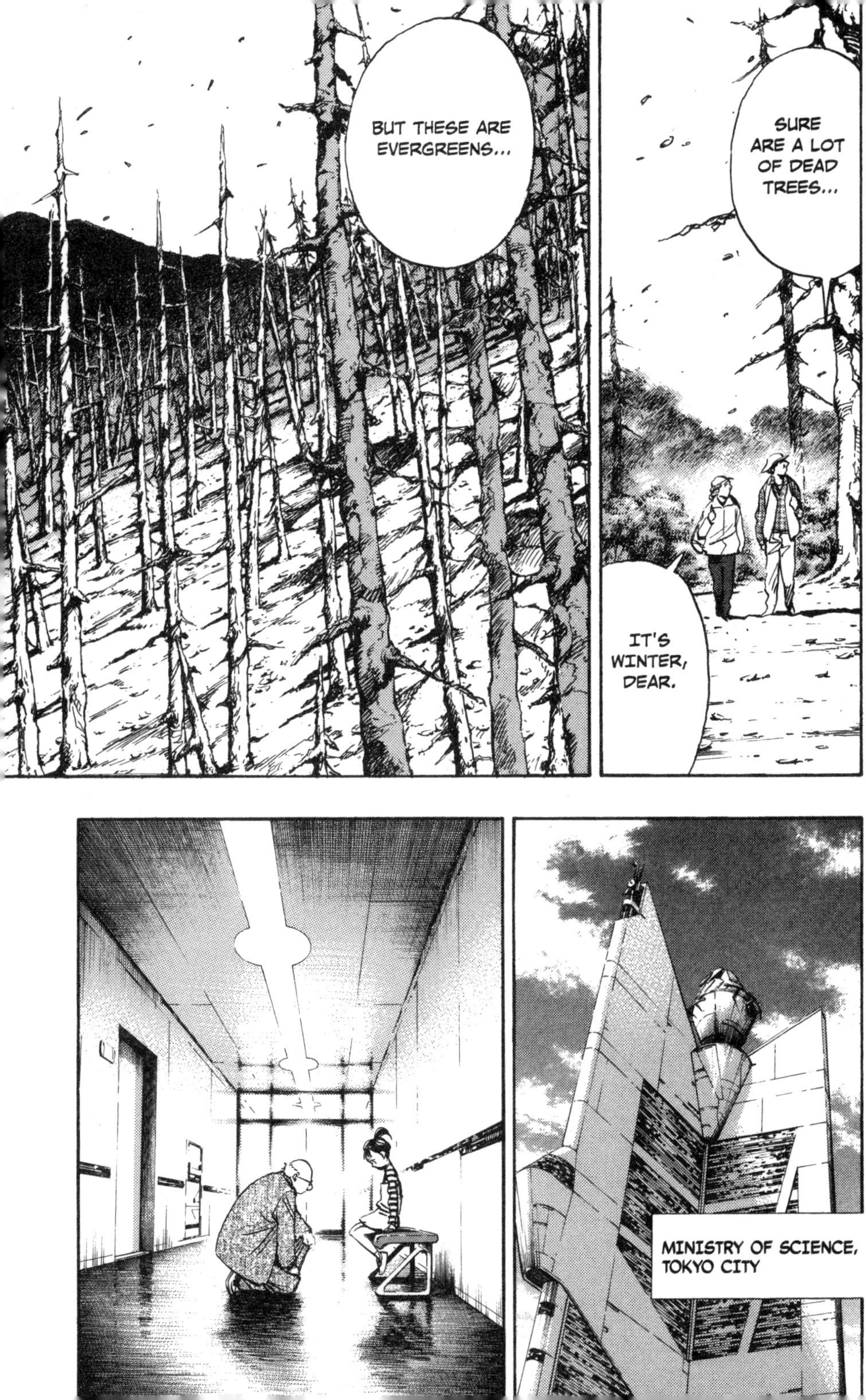
SURE ARE A LOT OF DEAD TREES...
IT'S WINTER, DEAR.
BUT THESE ARE EVERGREENS...
MINISTRY OF SCIENCE, TOKYO CITY

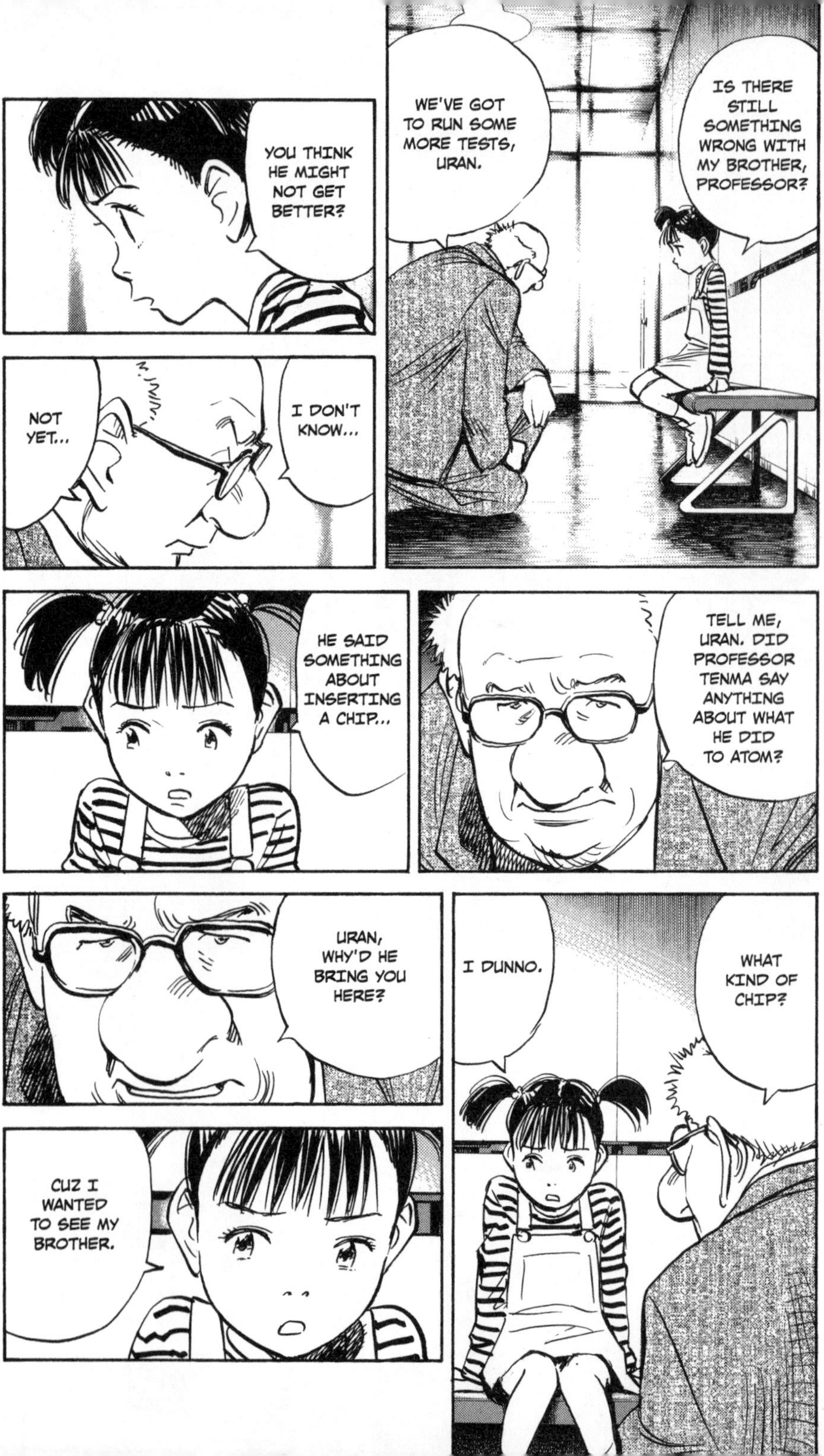
IS THERE STILL SOMETHING WRONG WITH MY BROTHER, PROFESSOR?
WE'VE GOT TO RUN SOME MORE TESTS, URAN.
YOU THINK HE MIGHT NOT GET BETTER?
I DON'T KNOW...
NOT YET...
TELL ME, URAN. DID PROFESSOR TENMA SAY ANYTHING ABOUT WHAT HE DID TO ATOM?
HE SAID SOMETHING ABOUT INSERTING A CHIP...
WHAT KIND OF CHIP?
I DUNNO.
URAN, WHY'D HE BRING YOU HERE?
CUZ I WANTED TO SEE MY BROTHER.

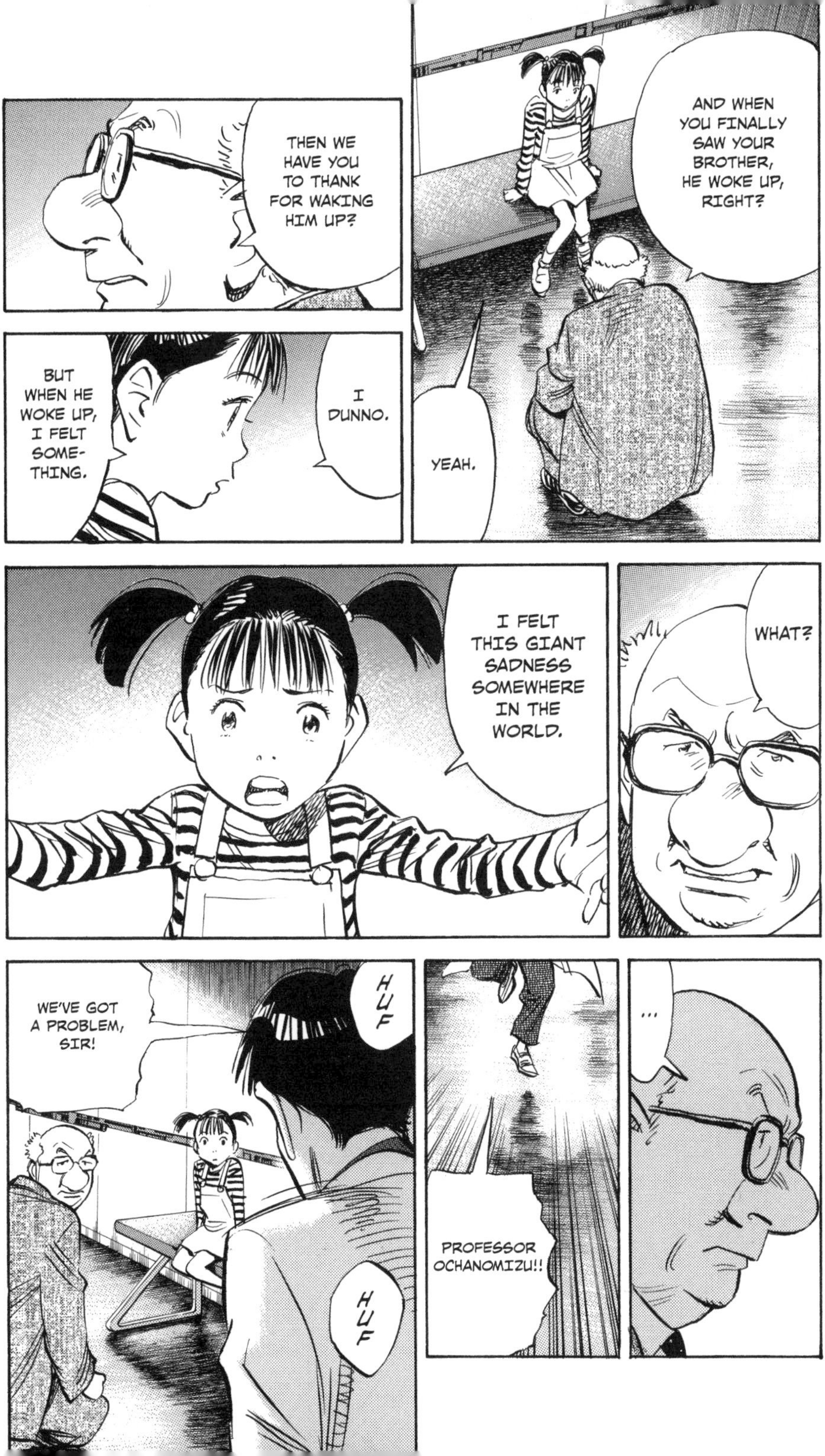
AND WHEN YOU FINALLY SAW YOUR BROTHER, HE WOKE UP, RIGHT?
YEAH.
THEN WE HAVE YOU TO THANK FOR WAKING HIM UP?
I DUNNO.
BUT WHEN HE WOKE UP, I FELT SOME-THING.
WHAT?
I FELT THIS GIANT SADNESS SOMEWHERE IN THE WORLD.
...
PROFESSOR OCHANOMIZU!!
HUF
WE'VE GOT A PROBLEM, SIR!
HUF

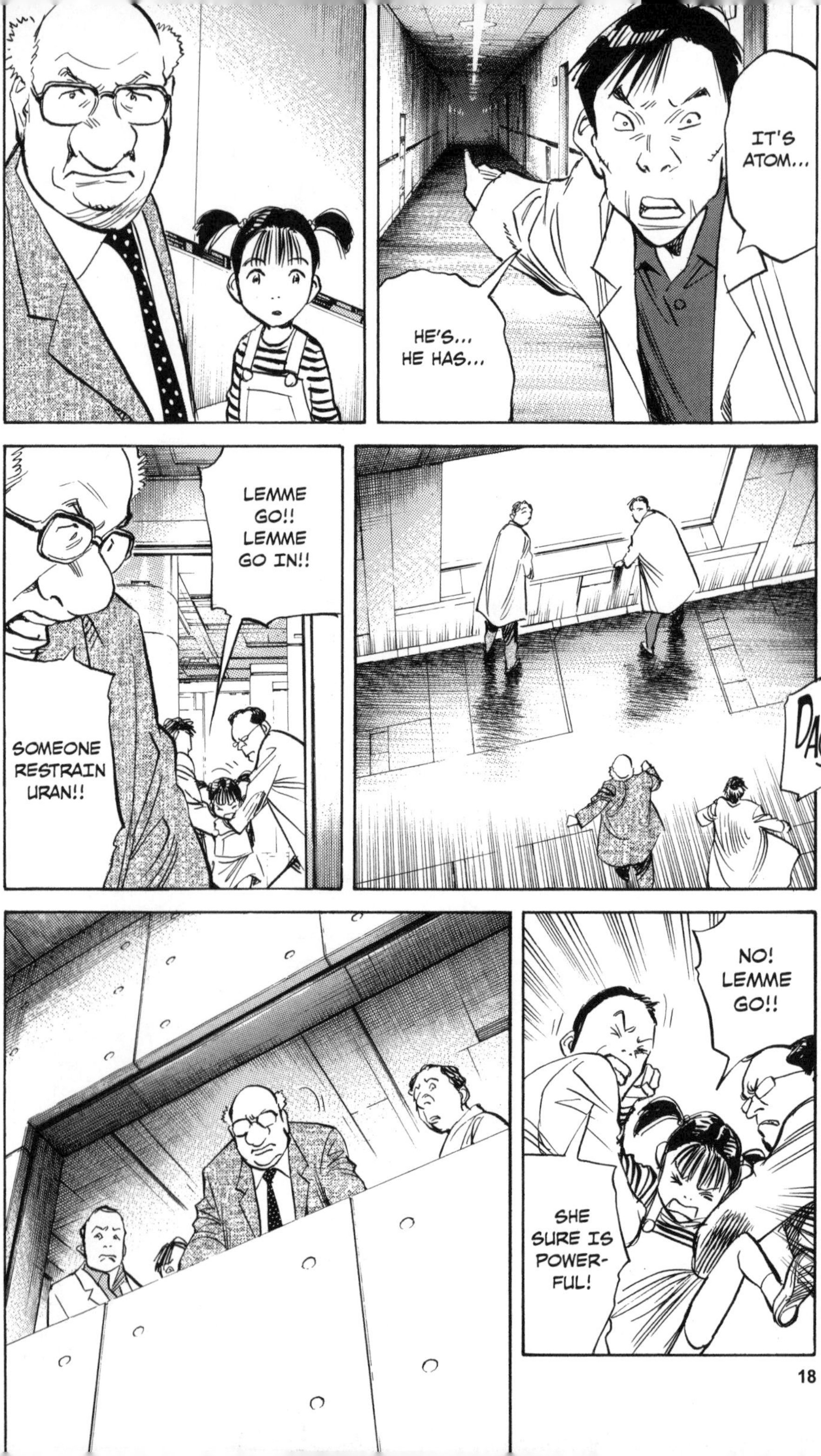
IT'S ATOM...
HE'S... HE HAS...
DASH
LEMME GO!! LEMME GO IN!!
SOMEONE RESTRAIN URAN!!
NO! LEMME GO!!
SHE SURE IS POWER-FUL!

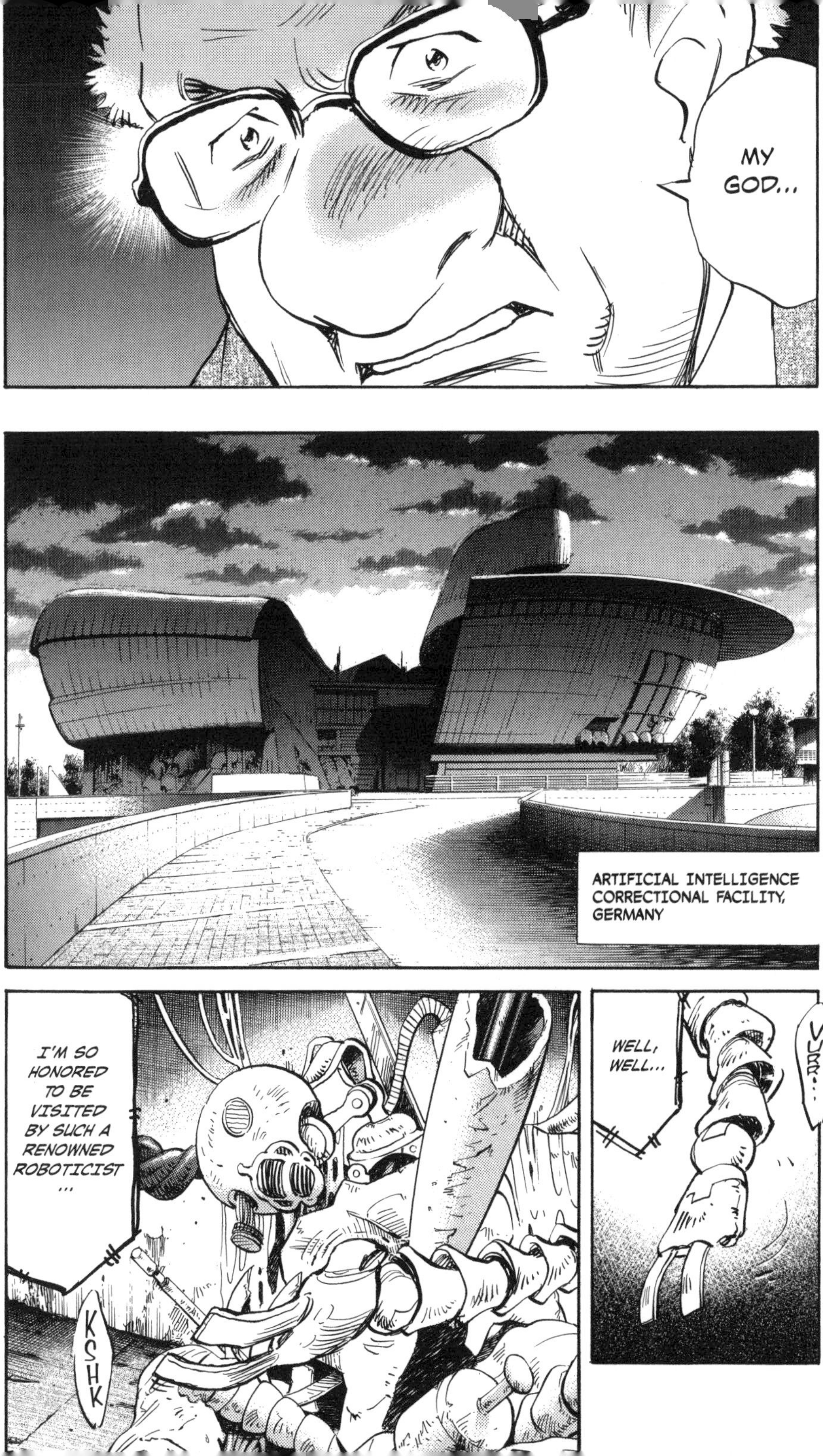
MY GOD...
ARTIFICIAL INTELLIGENCE CORRECTIONAL FACILITY, GERMANY
WELL, WELL...
VURR...
I'M SO HONORED TO BE VISITED BY SUCH A RENOWNED ROBOTICIST...
KSHK

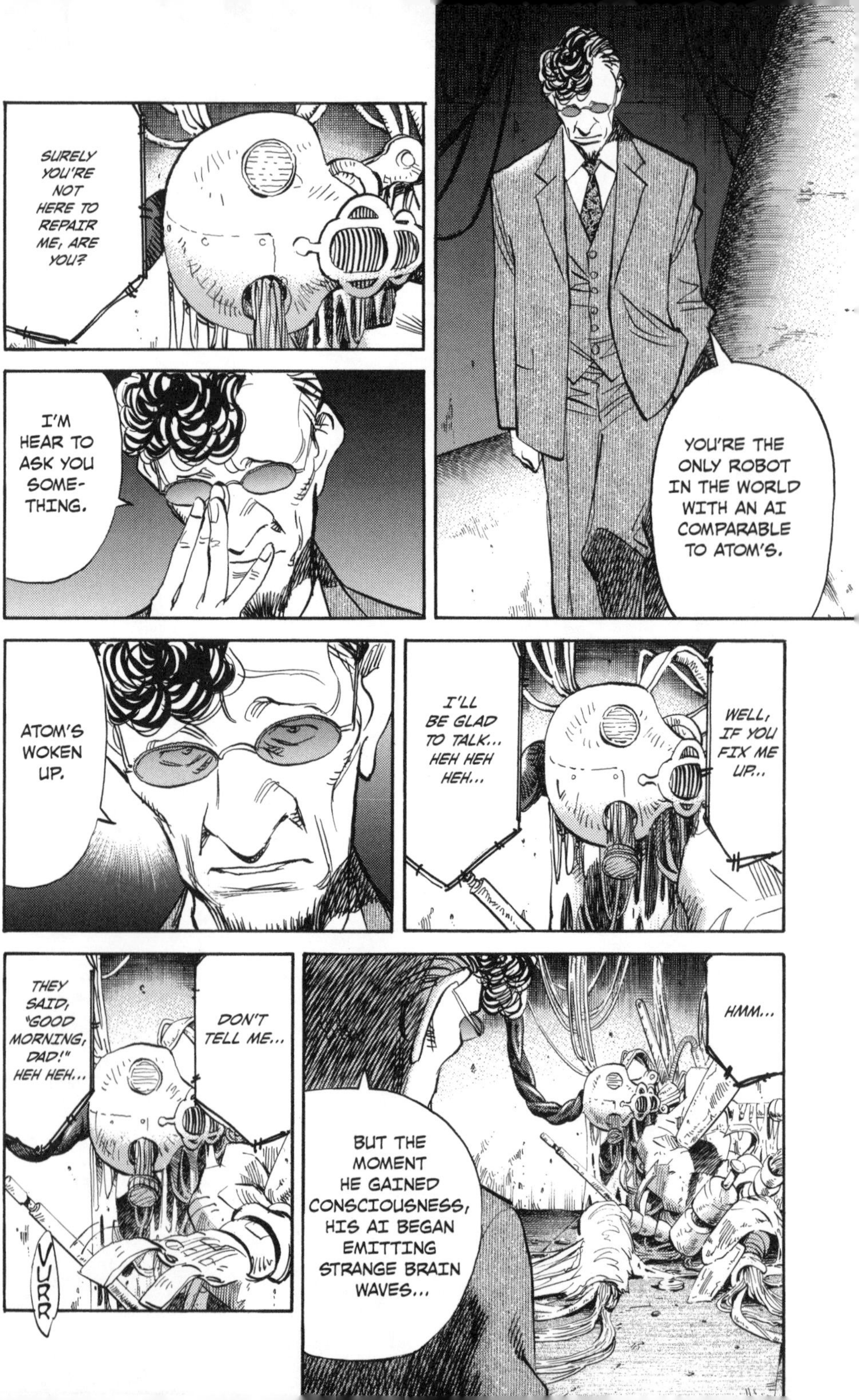

YOU'RE THE ONLY ROBOT IN THE WORLD WITH AN AI COMPARABLE TO ATOM'S.
SURELY YOU'RE NOT HERE TO REPAIR ME, ARE YOU?
I'M HEAR TO ASK YOU SOME-THING.
WELL, IF YOU FIX ME UP...
I'LL BE GLAD TO TALK... HEH HEH HEH...
ATOM'S WOKEN UP.
HMM...
BUT THE MOMENT HE GAINED CONSCIOUSNESS, HIS AI BEGAN EMITTING STRANGE BRAIN WAVES...
DON'T TELL ME...
THEY SAID, "GOOD MORNING, DAD!" HEH HEH...
VURR

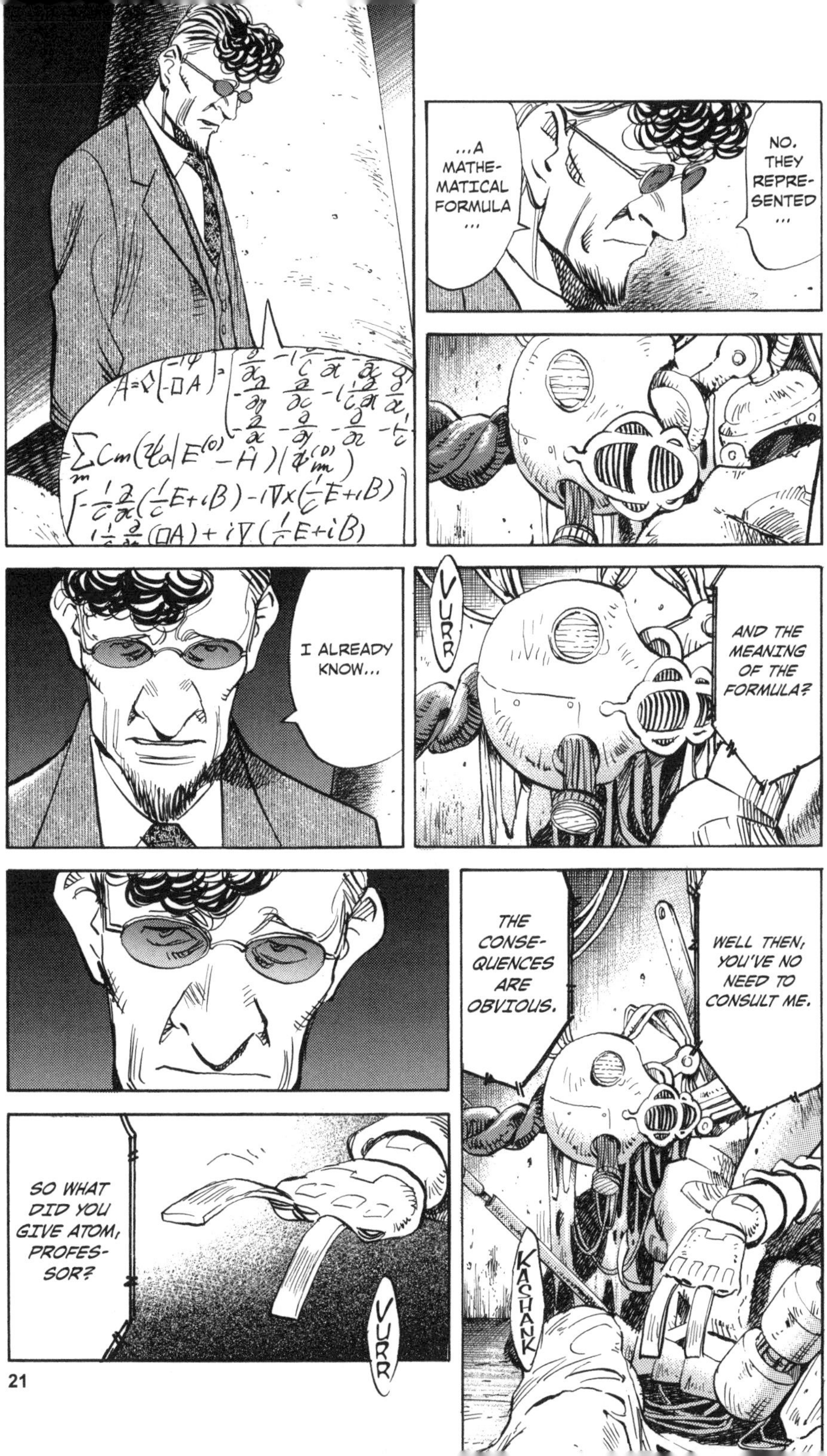
NO. THEY REPRESENTED...
...A MATHEMATICAL FORMULA...
VURR
AND THE MEANING OF THE FORMULA?
I ALREADY KNOW...
WELL THEN, YOU'VE NO NEED TO CONSULT ME.
THE CONSEQUENCES ARE OBVIOUS.
KASHANK
SO WHAT DID YOU GIVE ATOM, PROFESSOR?
VURR

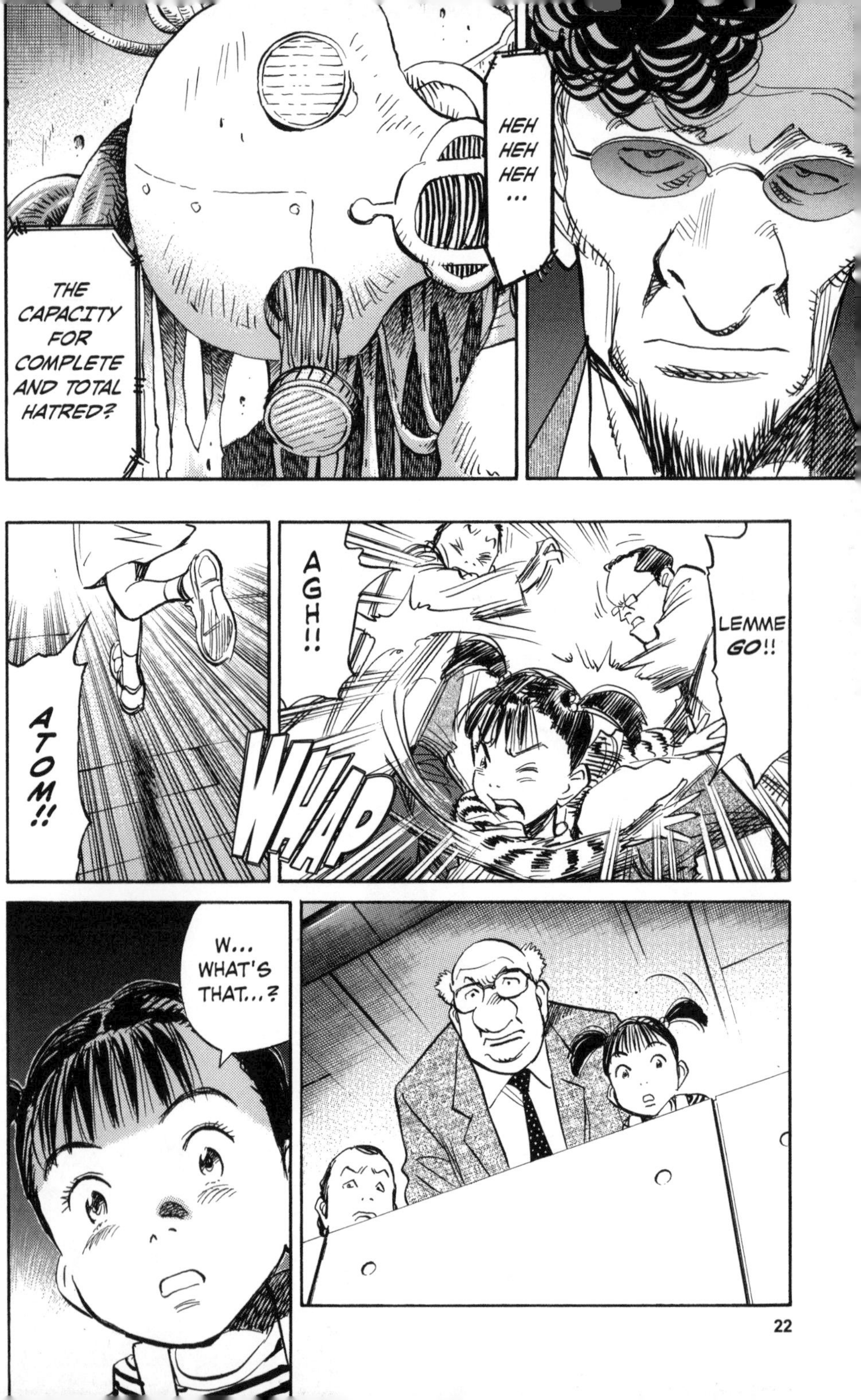
HEH HEH HEH ...
THE CAPACITY FOR COMPLETE AND TOTAL HATRED?
LEMME GO!!
AGH!!
WHAP
ATOM!!
W... WHAT'S THAT...?

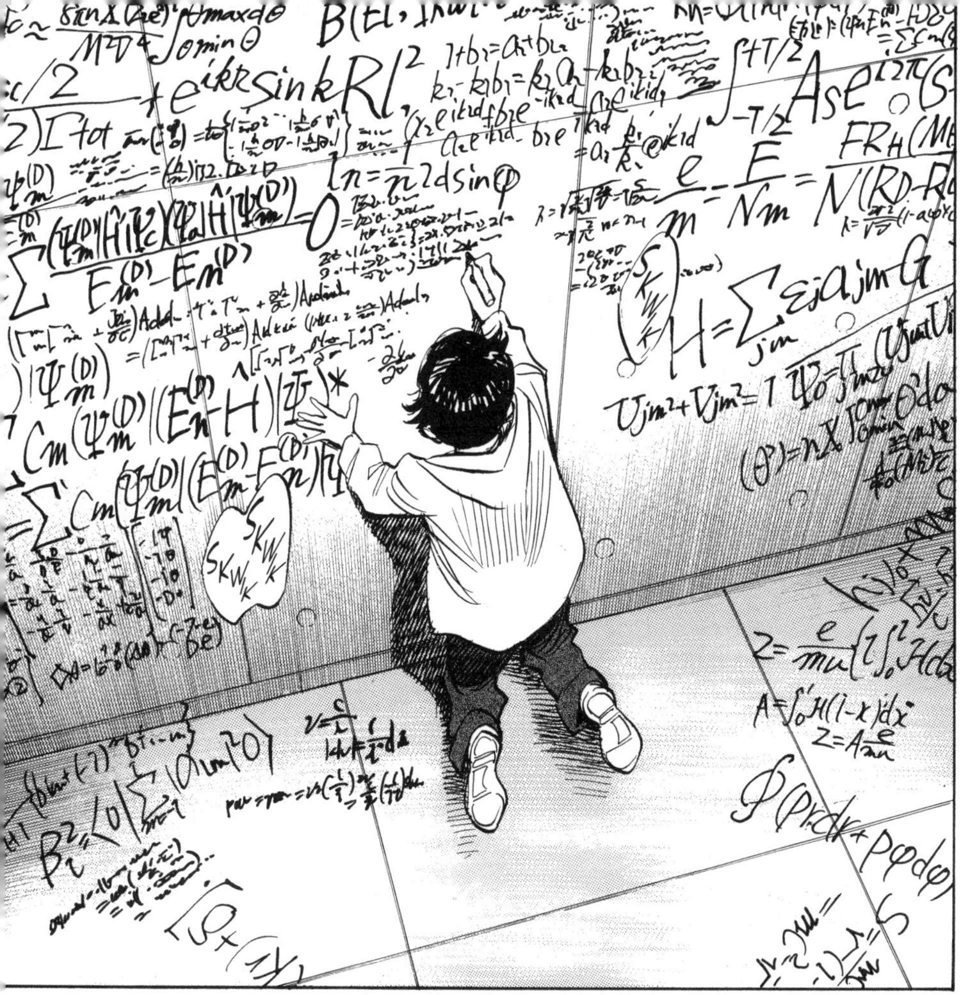
SKWIK
SKWIK
SKWIK
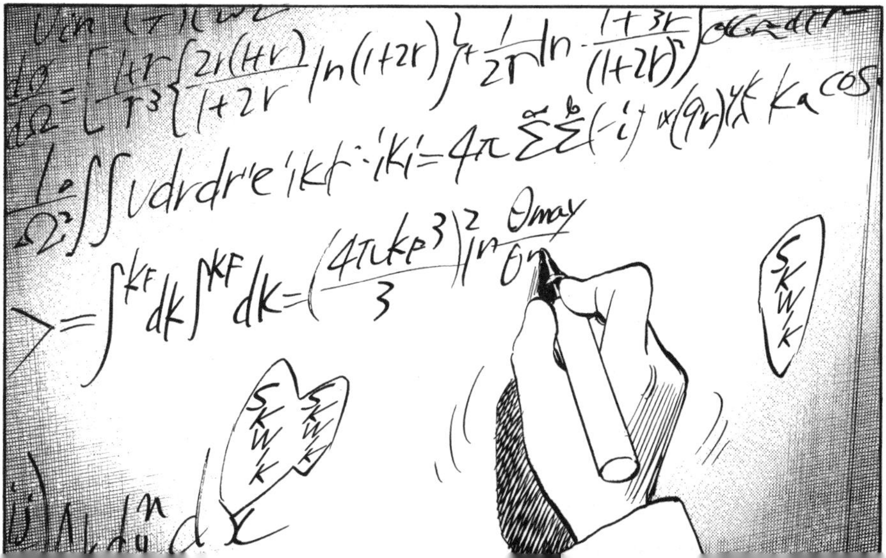
SKWIK
SKWIK
SKWIK

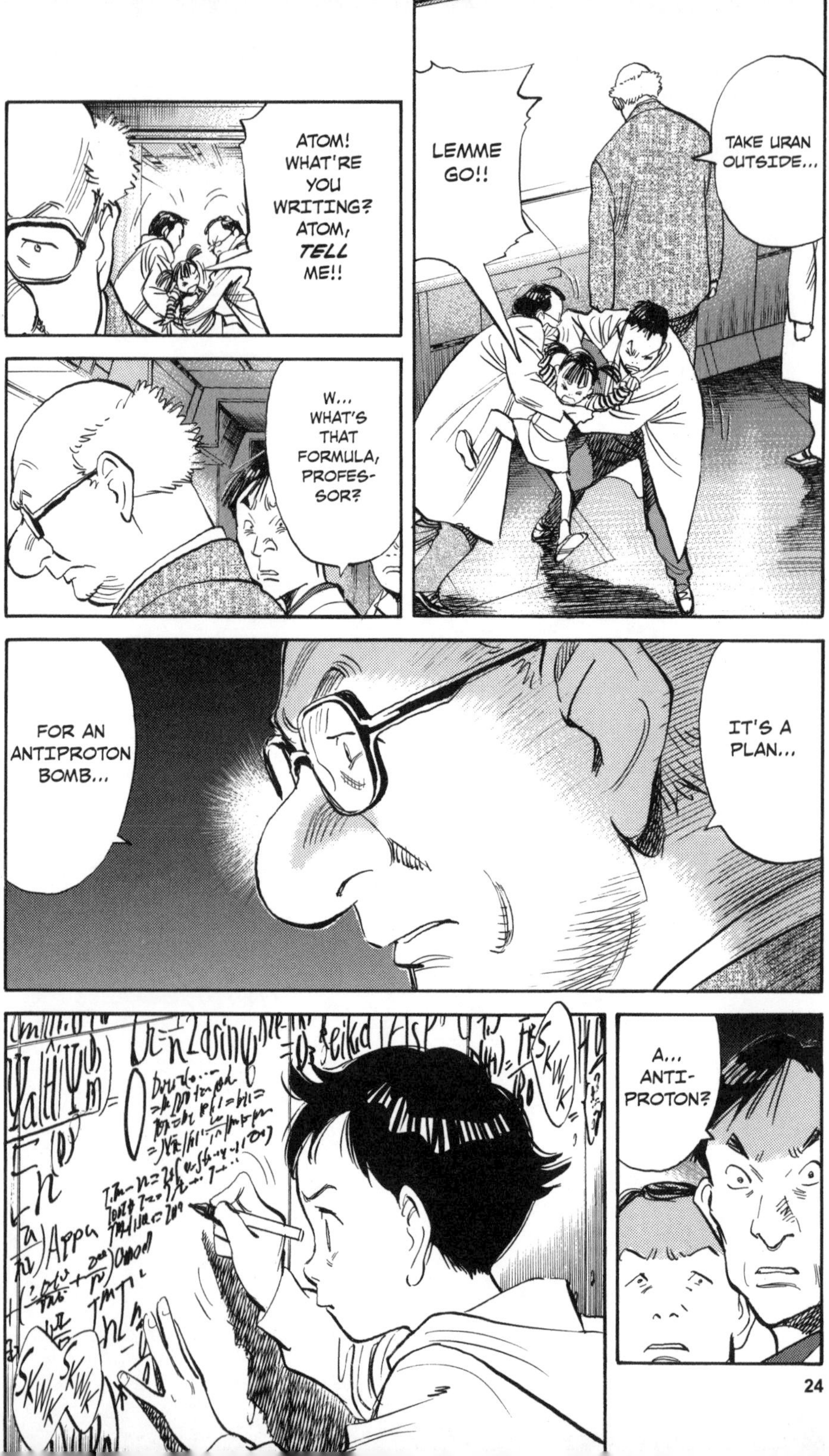
TAKE URAN OUTSIDE...
LEMME GO!!
ATOM! WHAT'RE YOU WRITING? ATOM, *TELL* ME!!
W... WHAT'S THAT FORMULA, PROFES-SOR?
IT'S A PLAN...
FOR AN ANTIPROTON BOMB...
A... ANTI-PROTON?
SKWK
SKWK
SKWK

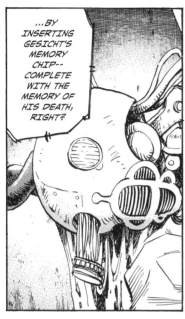

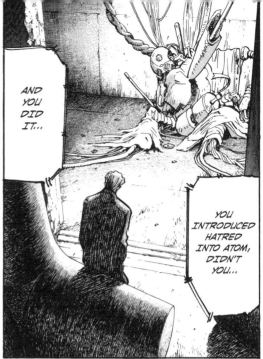

AND YOU DID IT...
YOU INTRODUCED HATRED INTO ATOM, DIDN'T YOU...
...BY INSERTING GESICHT'S MEMORY CHIP-- COMPLETE WITH THE MEMORY OF HIS DEATH, RIGHT?
SO, THE MOMENT ATOM AWOKE...
...HE STARTED TO REPRODUCE A CERTAIN FORMULA.
BZZT
THE FORMULA FOR AN ANTIPROTON BOMB...
BZZT
VURR
YES... HEH HEH HEH...
VRRT

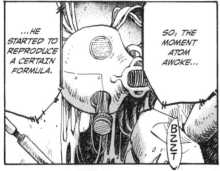

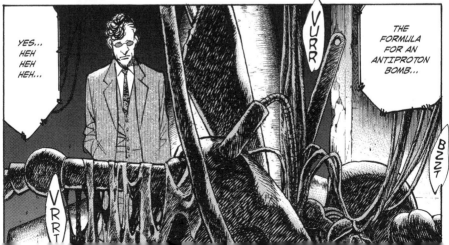

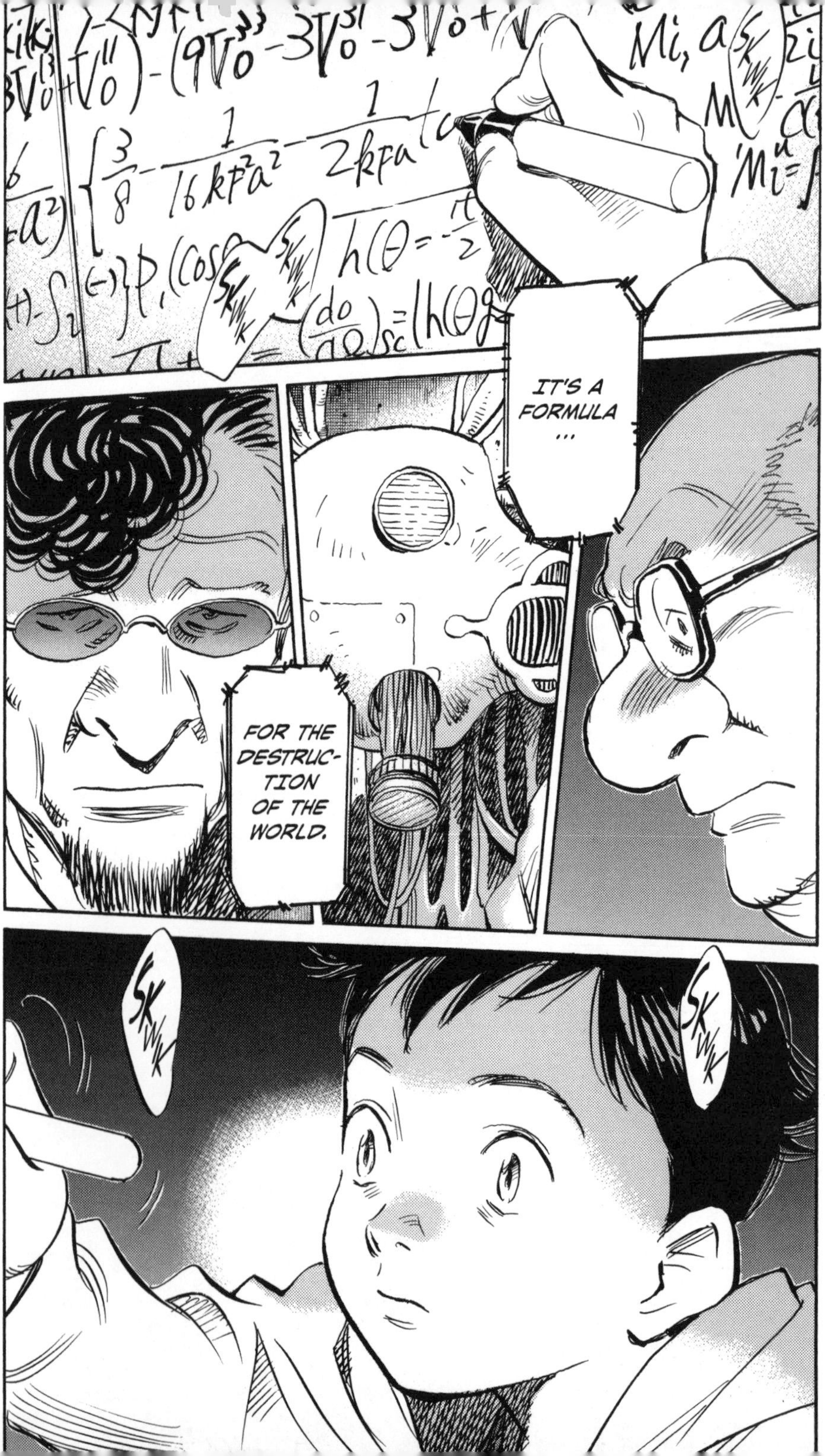
SKWK
SKWK
SKWK
IT'S A FORMULA ...
FOR THE DESTRUCTION OF THE WORLD.
SKWK
SKWK

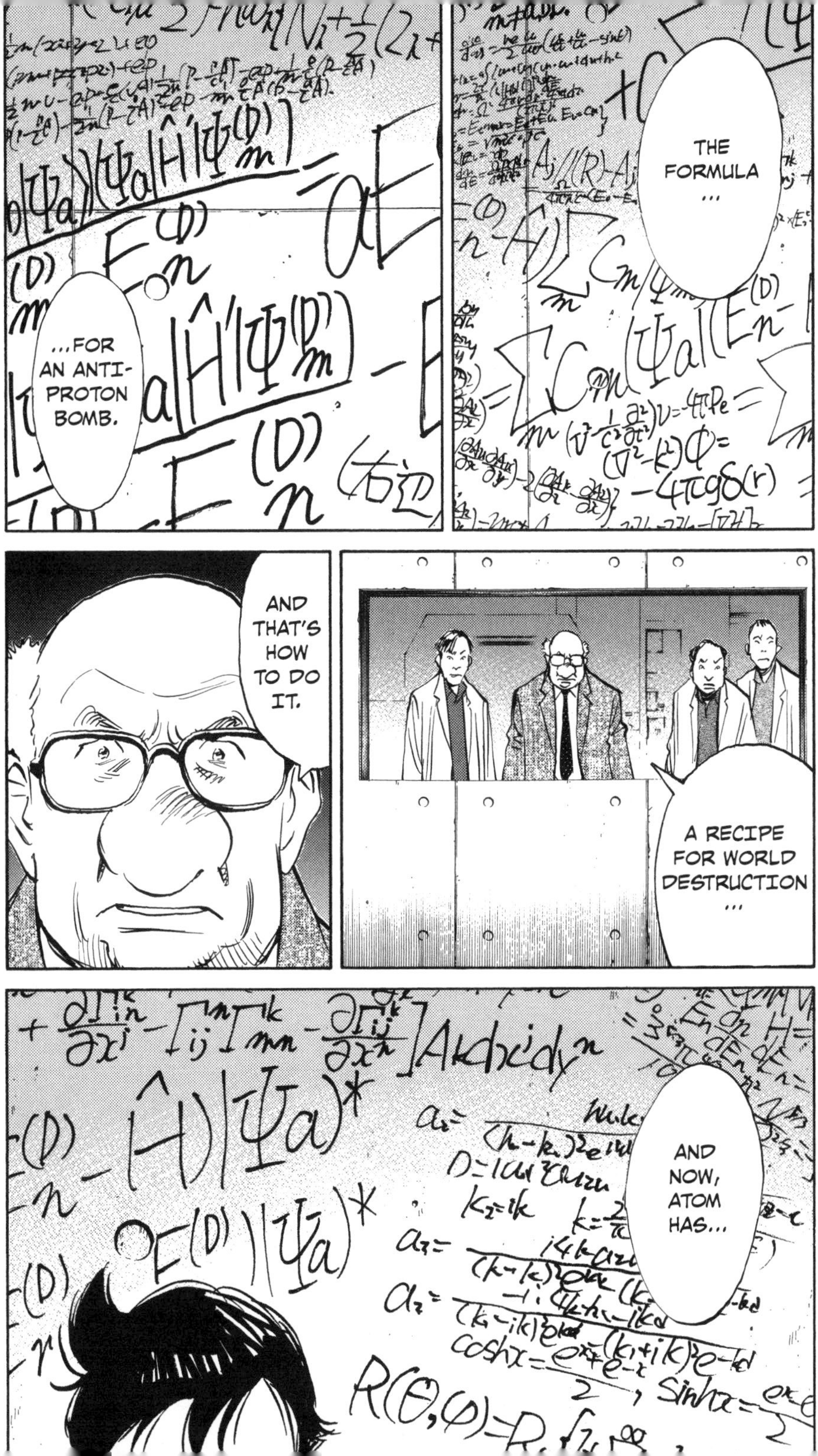
THE FORMULA ...
...FOR AN ANTI-PROTON BOMB.
A RECIPE FOR WORLD DESTRUCTION ...
AND THAT'S HOW TO DO IT.
AND NOW, ATOM HAS...

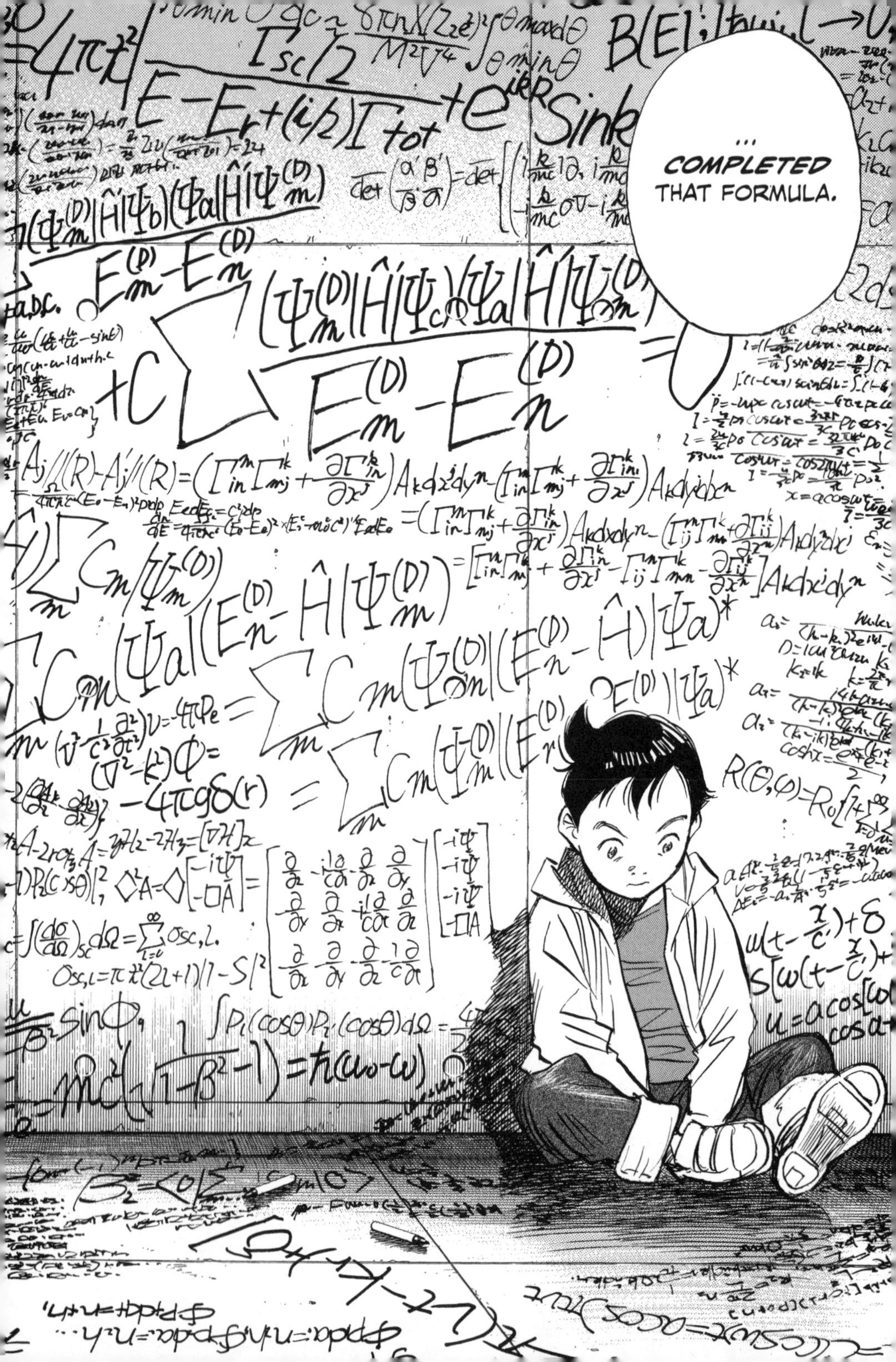
... COMPLETED THAT FORMULA.

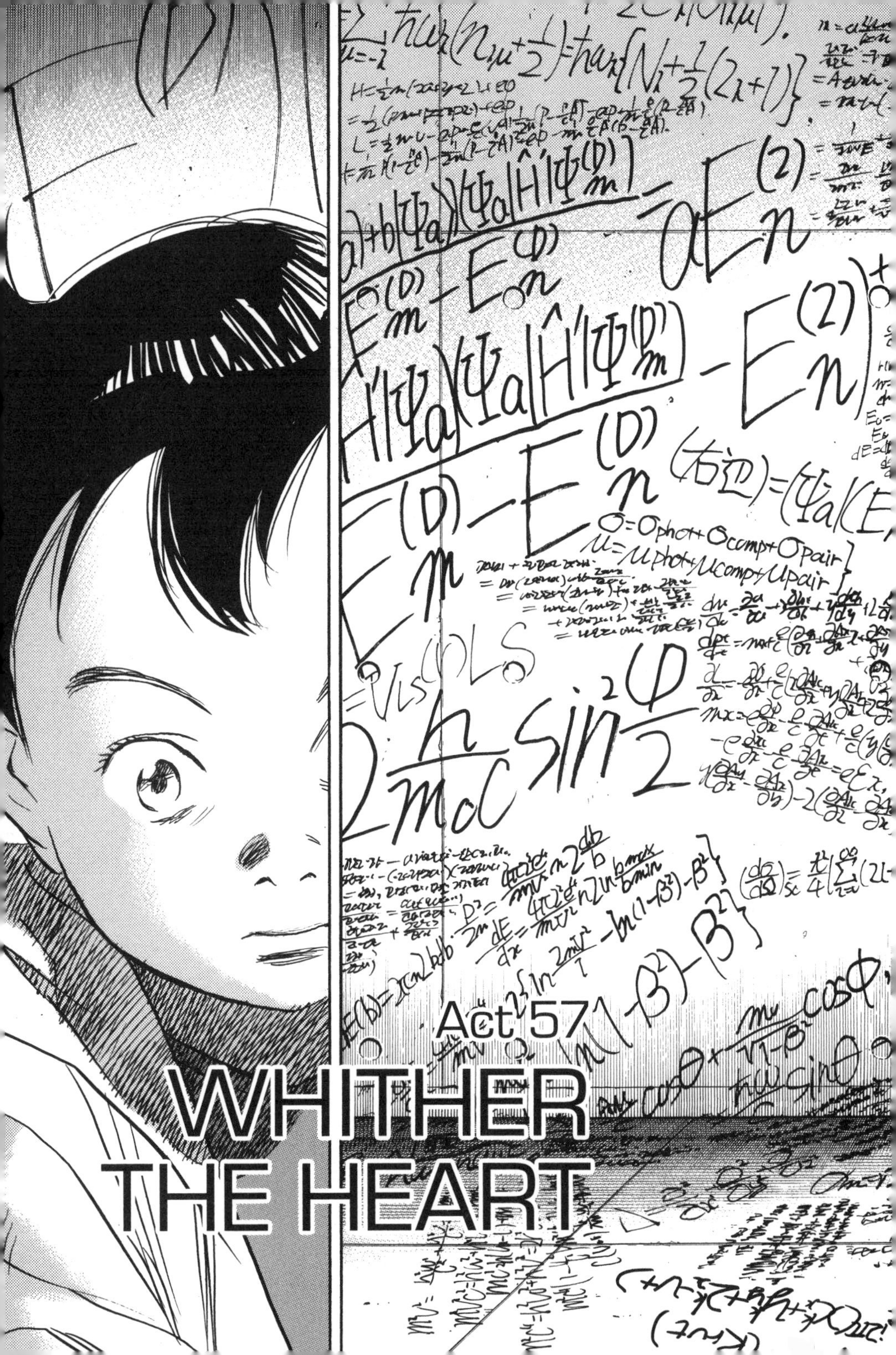
Act 57
WHITHER THE HEART

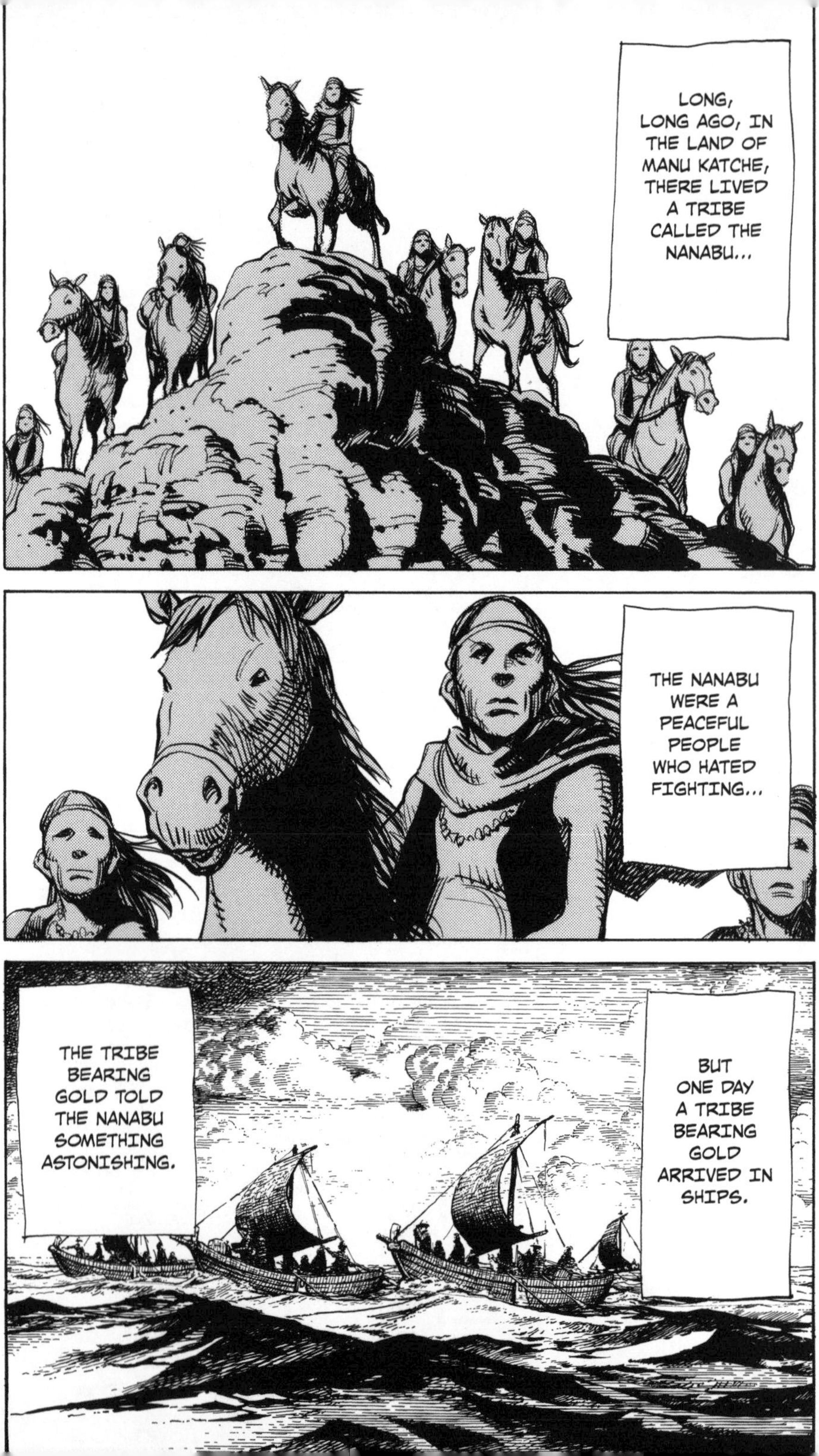
LONG, LONG AGO, IN THE LAND OF MANU KATCHE, THERE LIVED A TRIBE CALLED THE NANABU...
THE NANABU WERE A PEACEFUL PEOPLE WHO HATED FIGHTING...
BUT ONE DAY A TRIBE BEARING GOLD ARRIVED IN SHIPS.
THE TRIBE BEARING GOLD TOLD THE NANABU SOMETHING ASTONISHING.

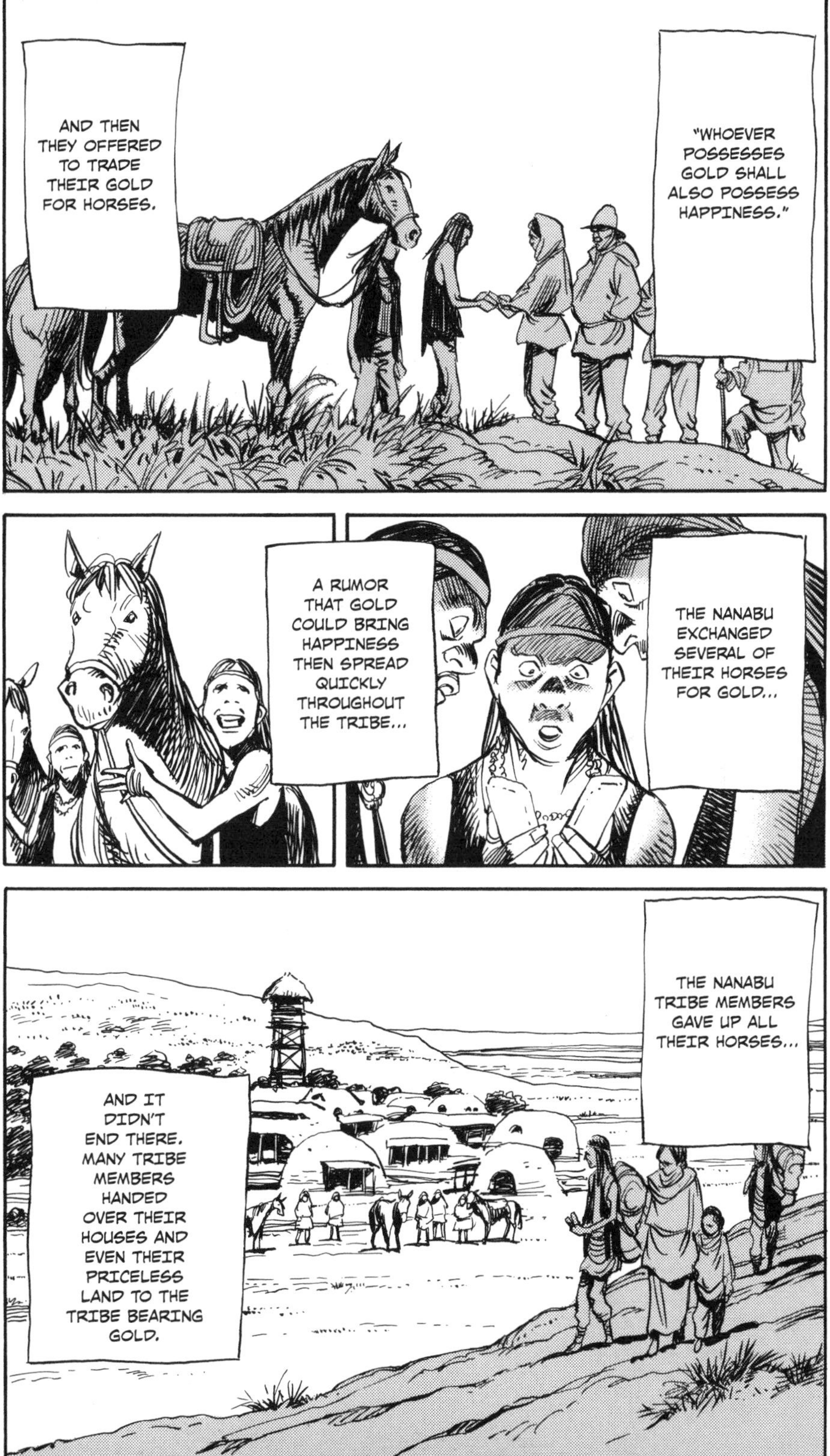
"WHOEVER POSSESSES GOLD SHALL ALSO POSSESS HAPPINESS."
AND THEN THEY OFFERED TO TRADE THEIR GOLD FOR HORSES.
THE NANABU EXCHANGED SEVERAL OF THEIR HORSES FOR GOLD...
A RUMOR THAT GOLD COULD BRING HAPPINESS THEN SPREAD QUICKLY THROUGHOUT THE TRIBE...
THE NANABU TRIBE MEMBERS GAVE UP ALL THEIR HORSES...
AND IT DIDN'T END THERE. MANY TRIBE MEMBERS HANDED OVER THEIR HOUSES AND EVEN THEIR PRICELESS LAND TO THE TRIBE BEARING GOLD.

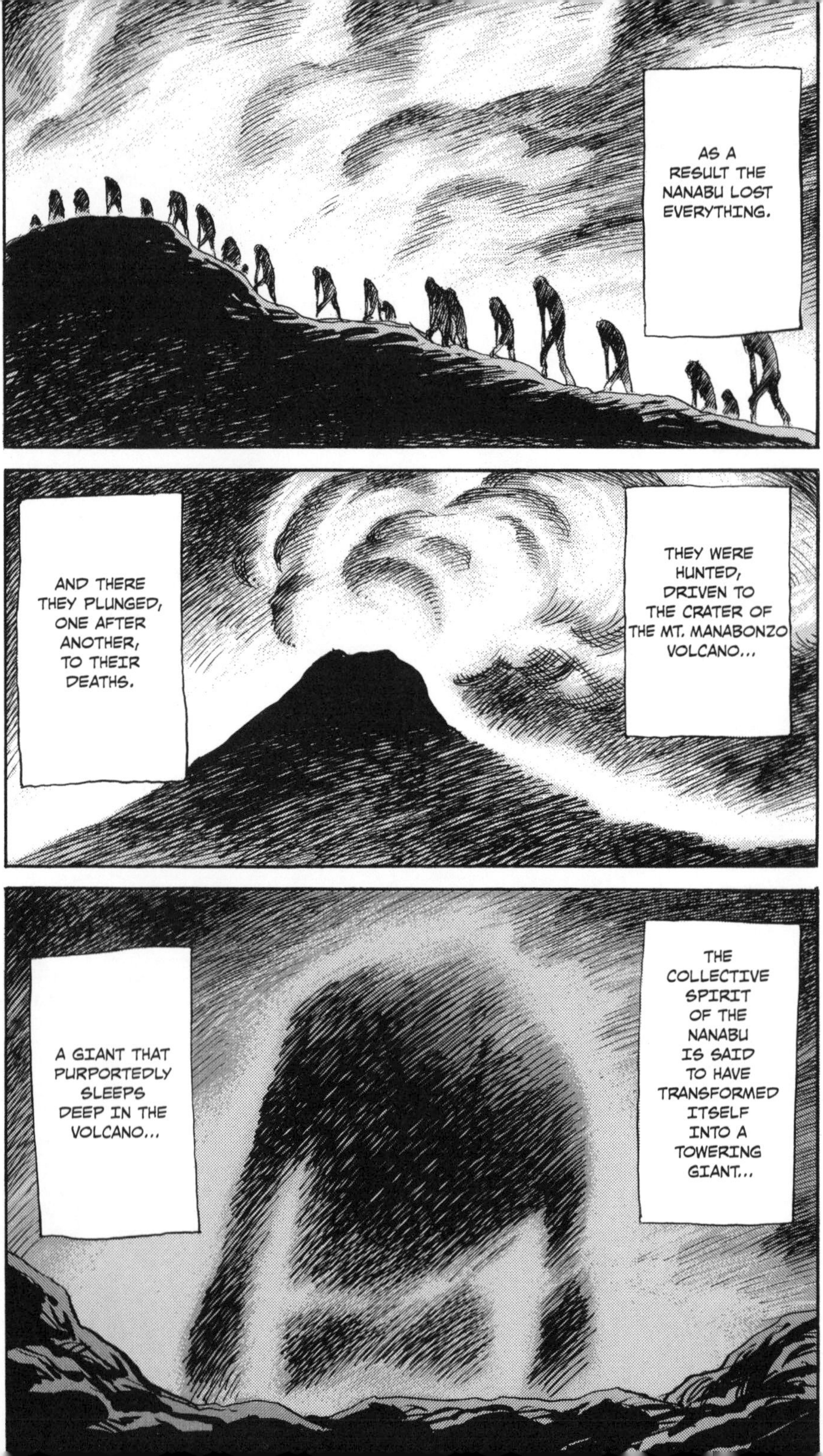
AS A RESULT THE NANABU LOST EVERYTHING.
THEY WERE HUNTED, DRIVEN TO THE CRATER OF THE MT. MANABONZO VOLCANO...
AND THERE THEY PLUNGED, ONE AFTER ANOTHER, TO THEIR DEATHS.
THE COLLECTIVE SPIRIT OF THE NANABU IS SAID TO HAVE TRANSFORMED ITSELF INTO A TOWERING GIANT...
A GIANT THAT PURPORTEDLY SLEEPS DEEP IN THE VOLCANO...

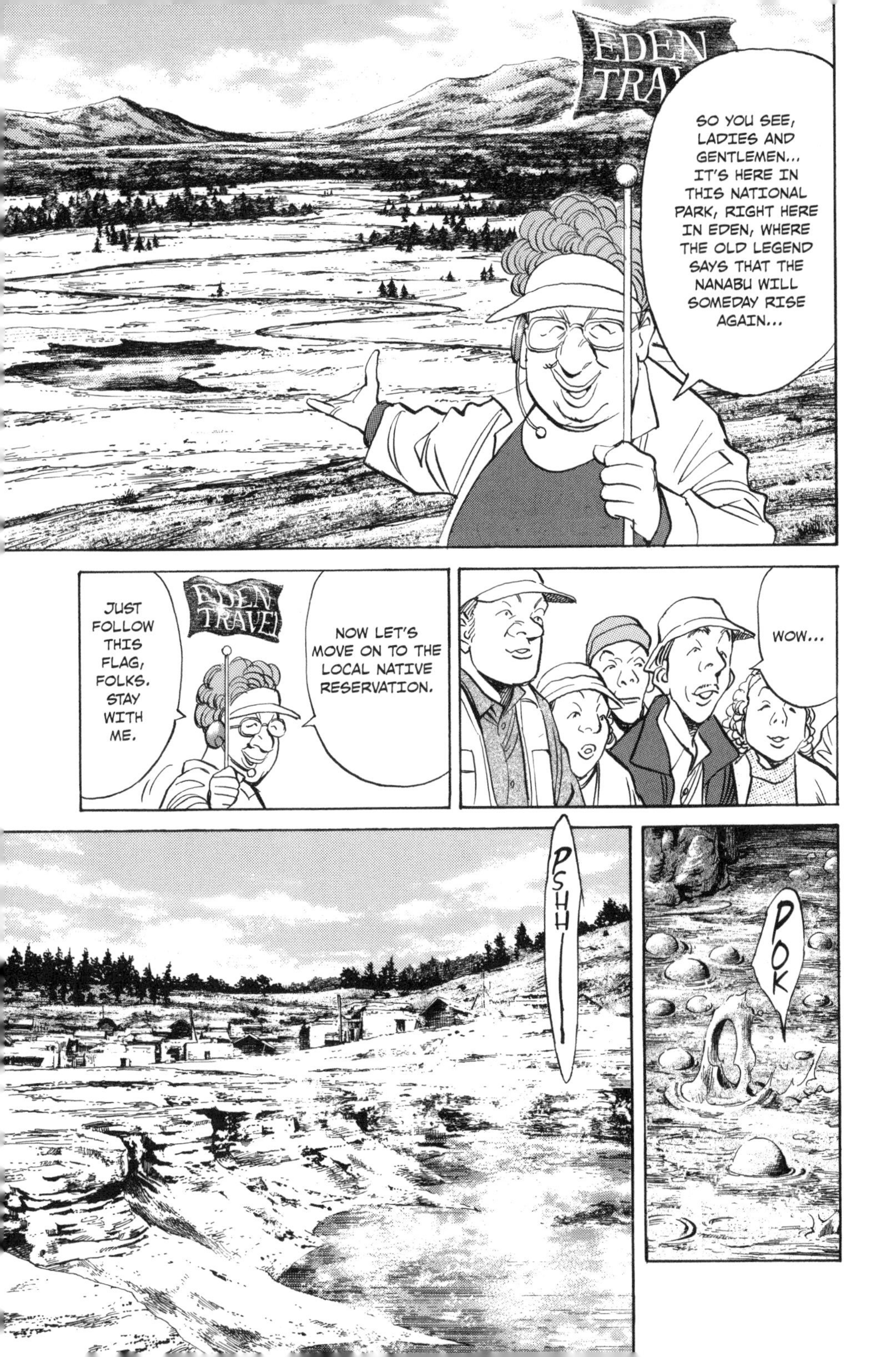
SO YOU SEE, LADIES AND GENTLEMEN... IT'S HERE IN THIS NATIONAL PARK, RIGHT HERE IN EDEN, WHERE THE OLD LEGEND SAYS THAT THE NANABU WILL SOMEDAY RISE AGAIN...
WOW...
NOW LET'S MOVE ON TO THE LOCAL NATIVE RESERVATION.
EDEN TRAVEL
JUST FOLLOW THIS FLAG, FOLKS. STAY WITH ME.
POK
PSHH

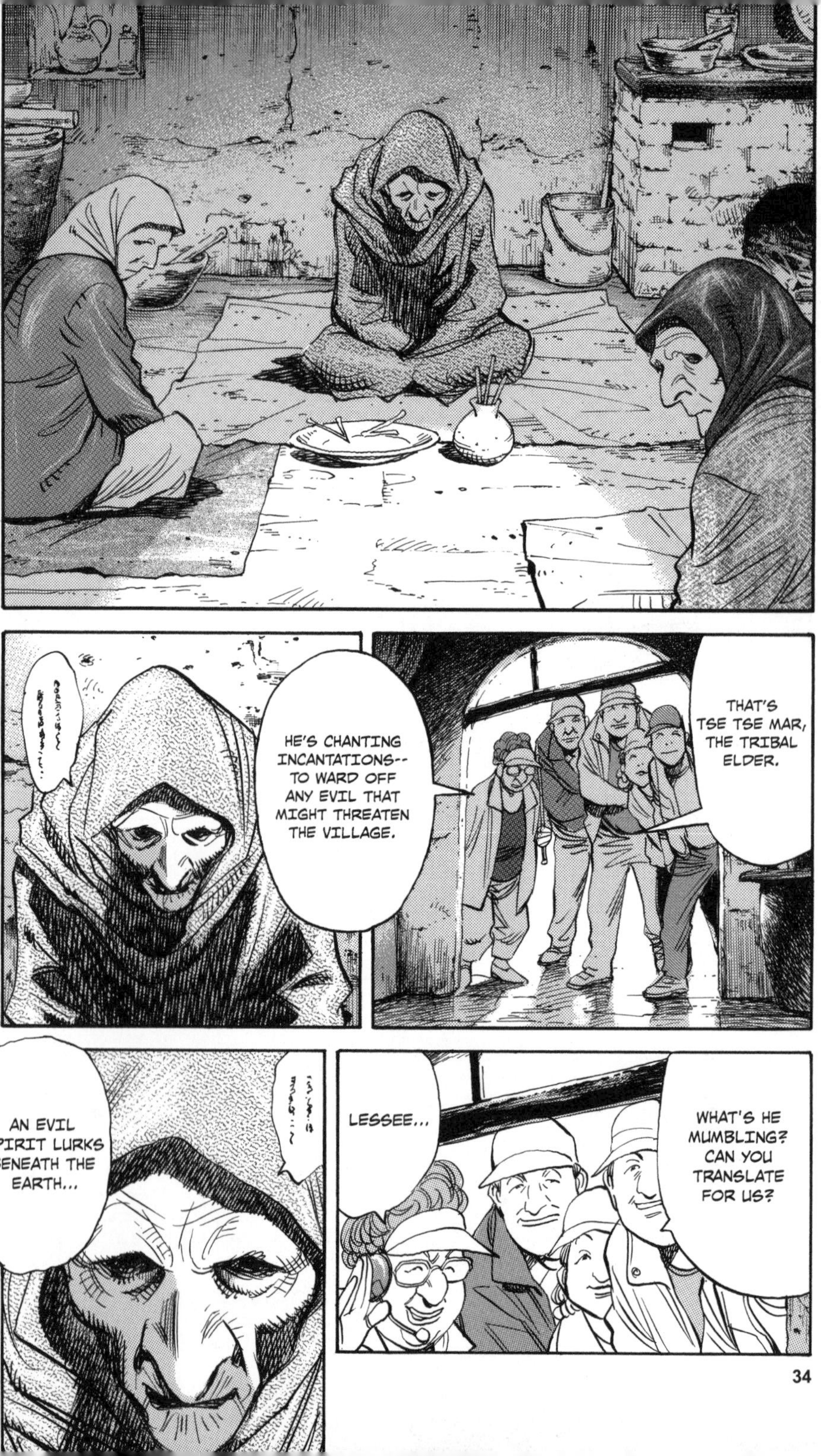
THAT'S TSE TSE MAR, THE TRIBAL ELDER.
HE'S CHANTING INCANTATIONS-- TO WARD OFF ANY EVIL THAT MIGHT THREATEN THE VILLAGE.
WHAT'S HE MUMBLING? CAN YOU TRANSLATE FOR US?
LESSEE...
AN EVIL SPIRIT LURKS BENEATH THE EARTH...

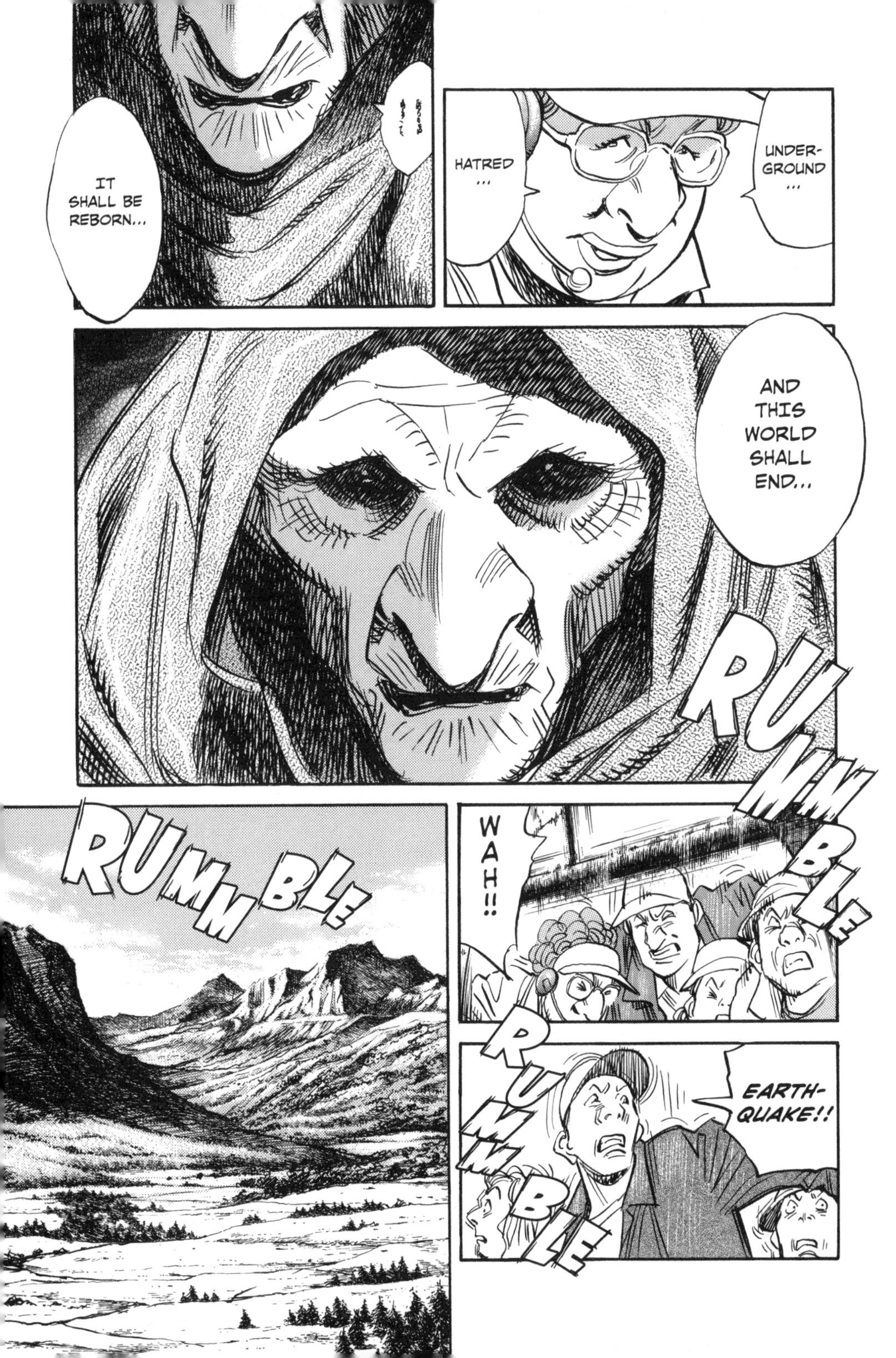
UNDER-GROUND...
HATRED...
IT SHALL BE REBORN...
AND THIS WORLD SHALL END...
RUMMBLE
WAH!!
RUMMBLE
EARTH-QUAKE!!
RUMMBLE

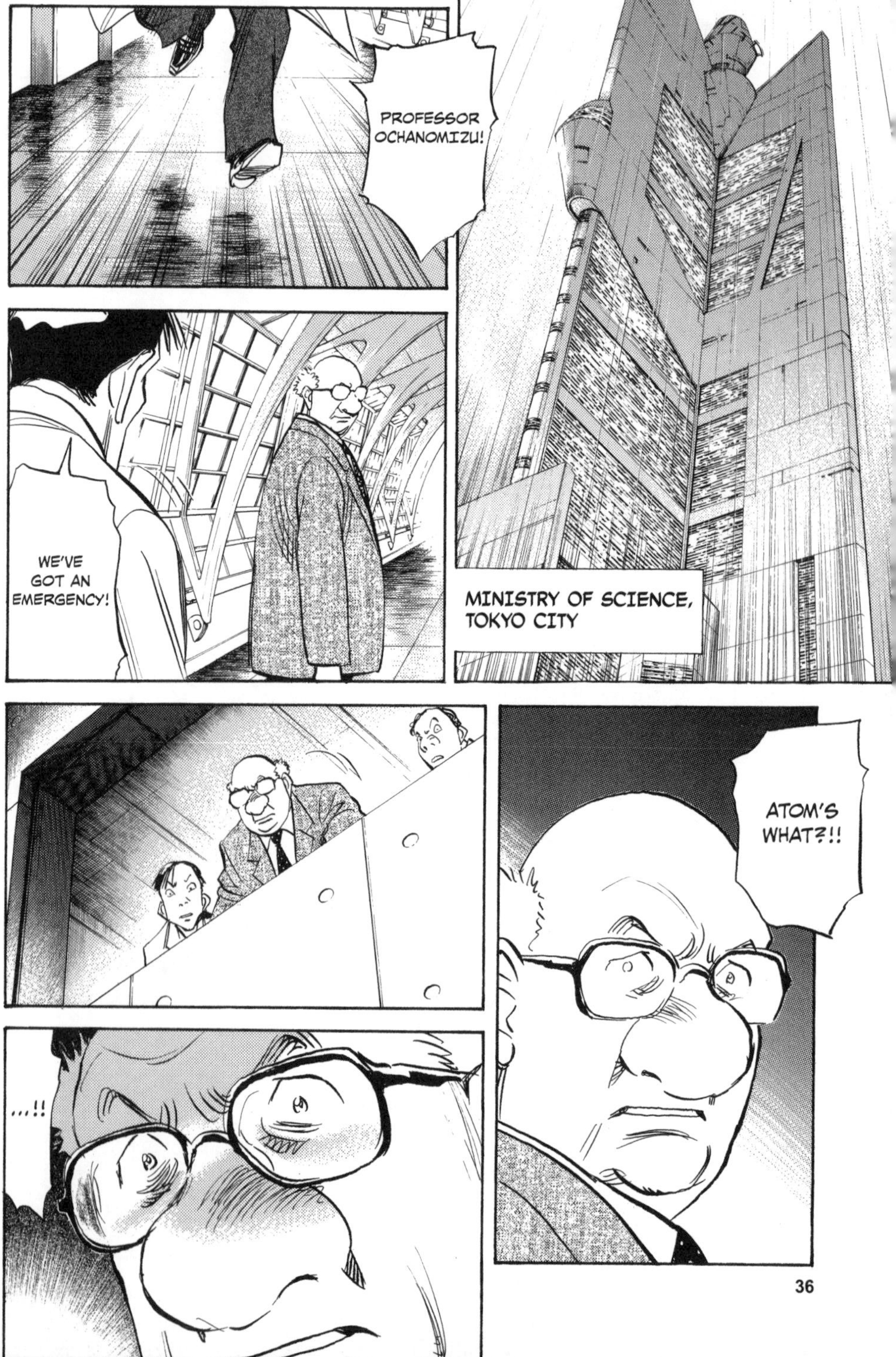
MINISTRY OF SCIENCE, TOKYO CITY
PROFESSOR OCHANOMIZU!
WE'VE GOT AN EMERGENCY!
ATOM'S WHAT?!!
...!!

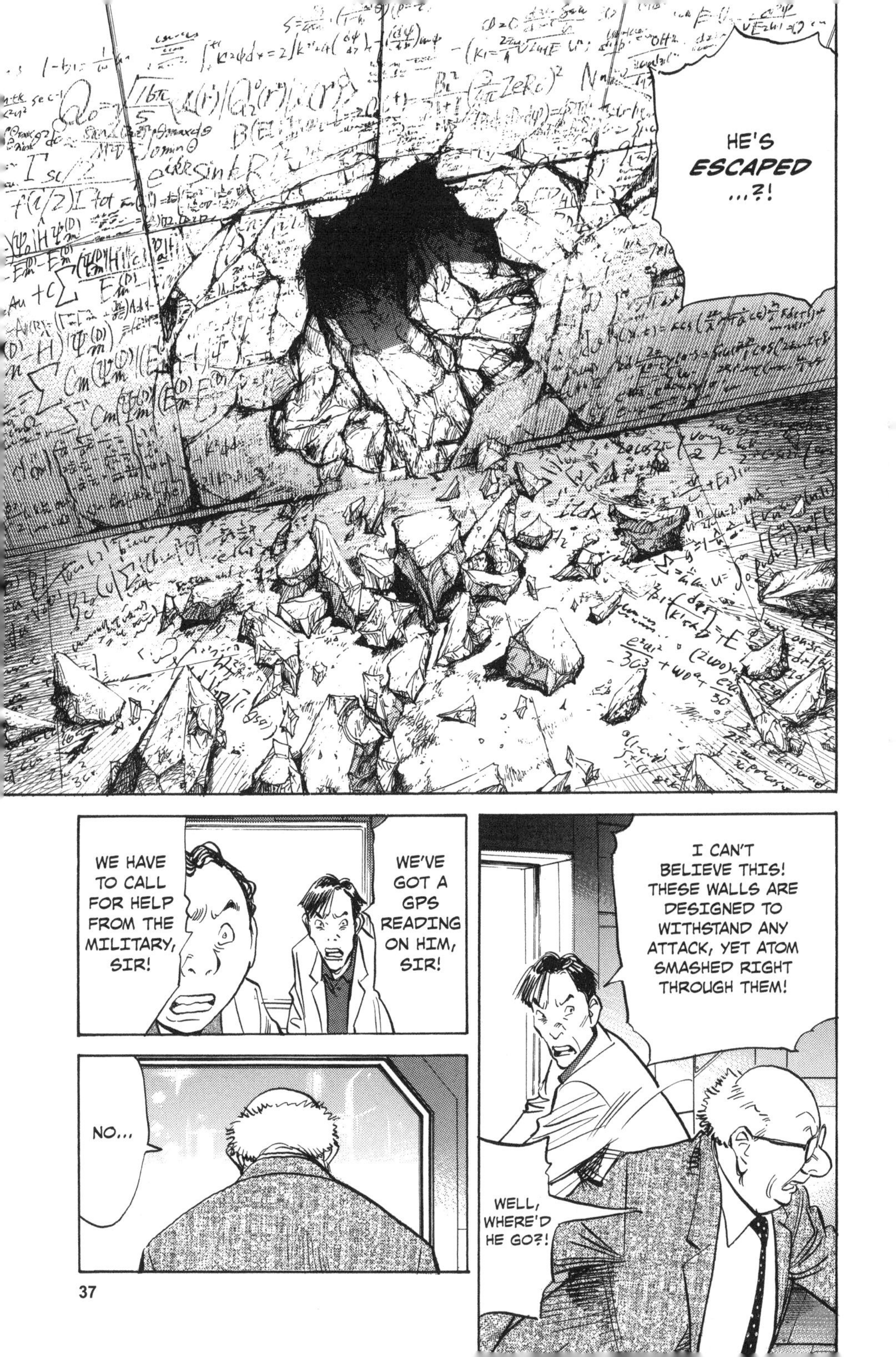
HE'S *ESCAPED* ...?!
I CAN'T BELIEVE THIS! THESE WALLS ARE DESIGNED TO WITHSTAND ANY ATTACK, YET ATOM SMASHED RIGHT THROUGH THEM!
WELL, WHERE'D HE GO?!
WE'VE GOT A GPS READING ON HIM, SIR!
WE HAVE TO CALL FOR HELP FROM THE MILITARY, SIR!
NO...

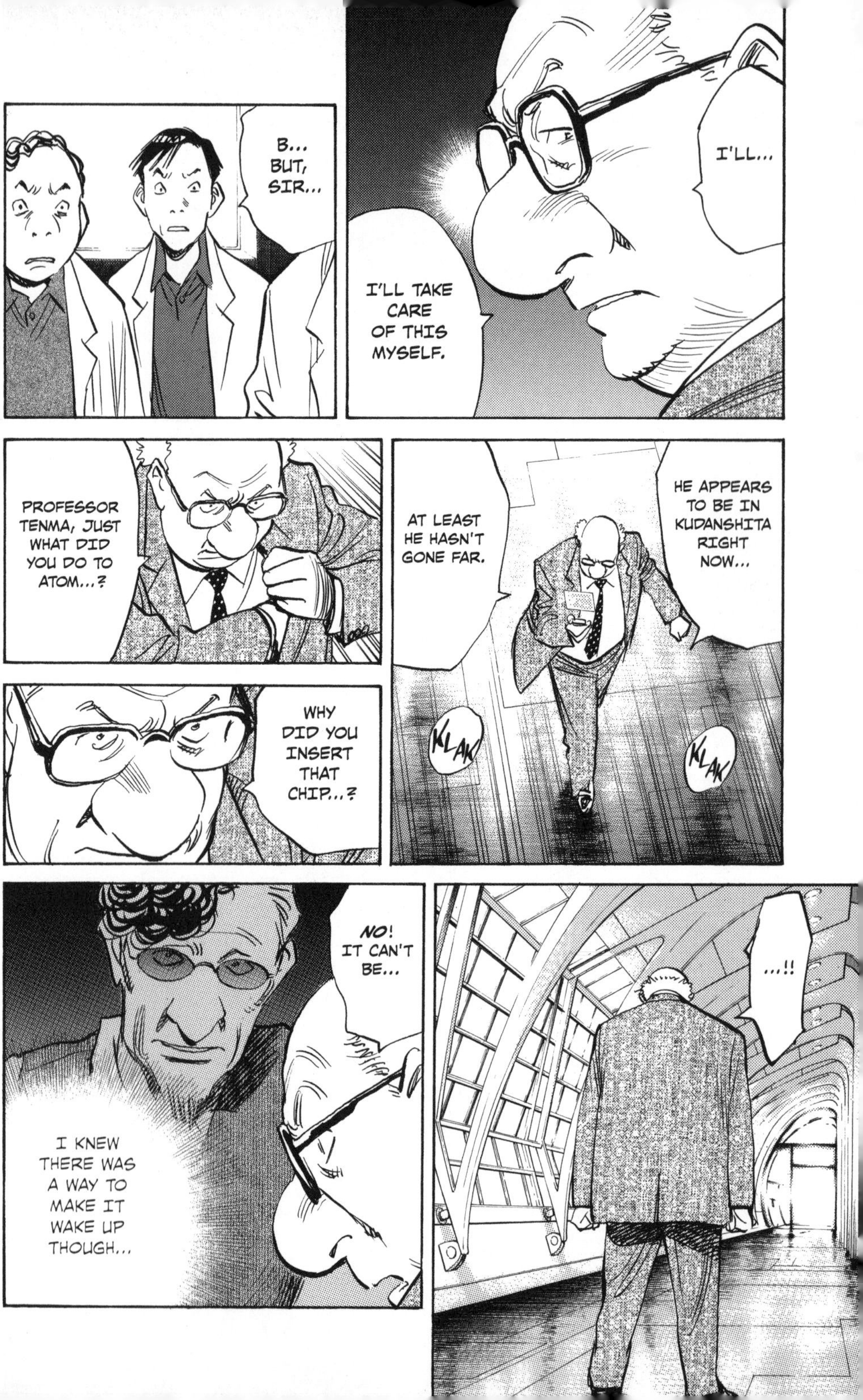
I'LL...
I'LL TAKE CARE OF THIS MYSELF.
B... BUT, SIR...
HE APPEARS TO BE IN KUDANSHITA RIGHT NOW...
AT LEAST HE HASN'T GONE FAR.
KLAK
KLAK
PROFESSOR TENMA, JUST WHAT DID YOU DO TO ATOM...?
WHY DID YOU INSERT THAT CHIP...?
...!!
NO! IT CAN'T BE...
I KNEW THERE WAS A WAY TO MAKE IT WAKE UP THOUGH...

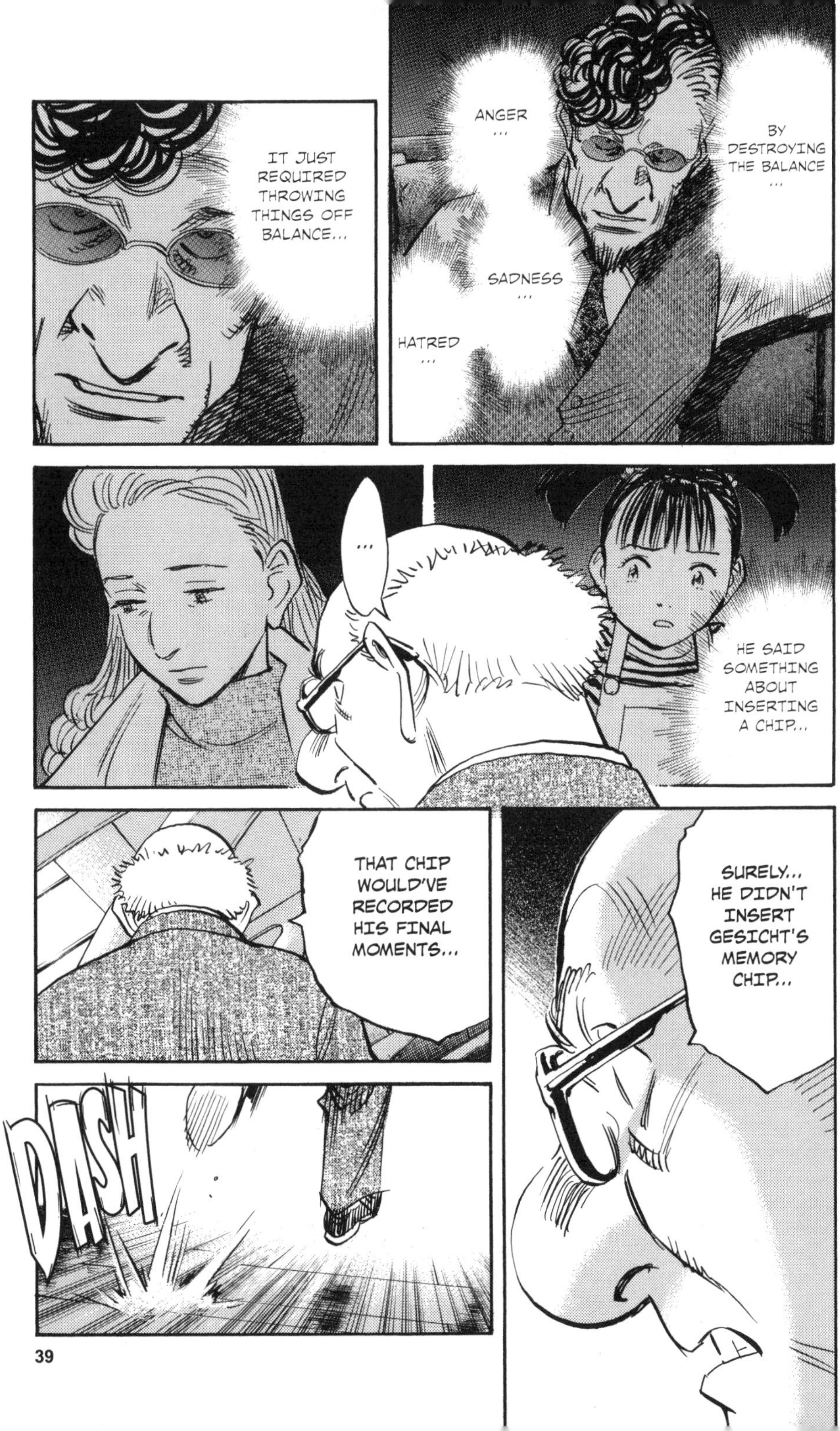
BY DESTROYING THE BALANCE...
ANGER...
SADNESS...
HATRED...
IT JUST REQUIRED THROWING THINGS OFF BALANCE...
HE SAID SOMETHING ABOUT INSERTING A CHIP...
...
SURELY... HE DIDN'T INSERT GESICHT'S MEMORY CHIP...
THAT CHIP WOULD'VE RECORDED HIS FINAL MOMENTS...
DASH

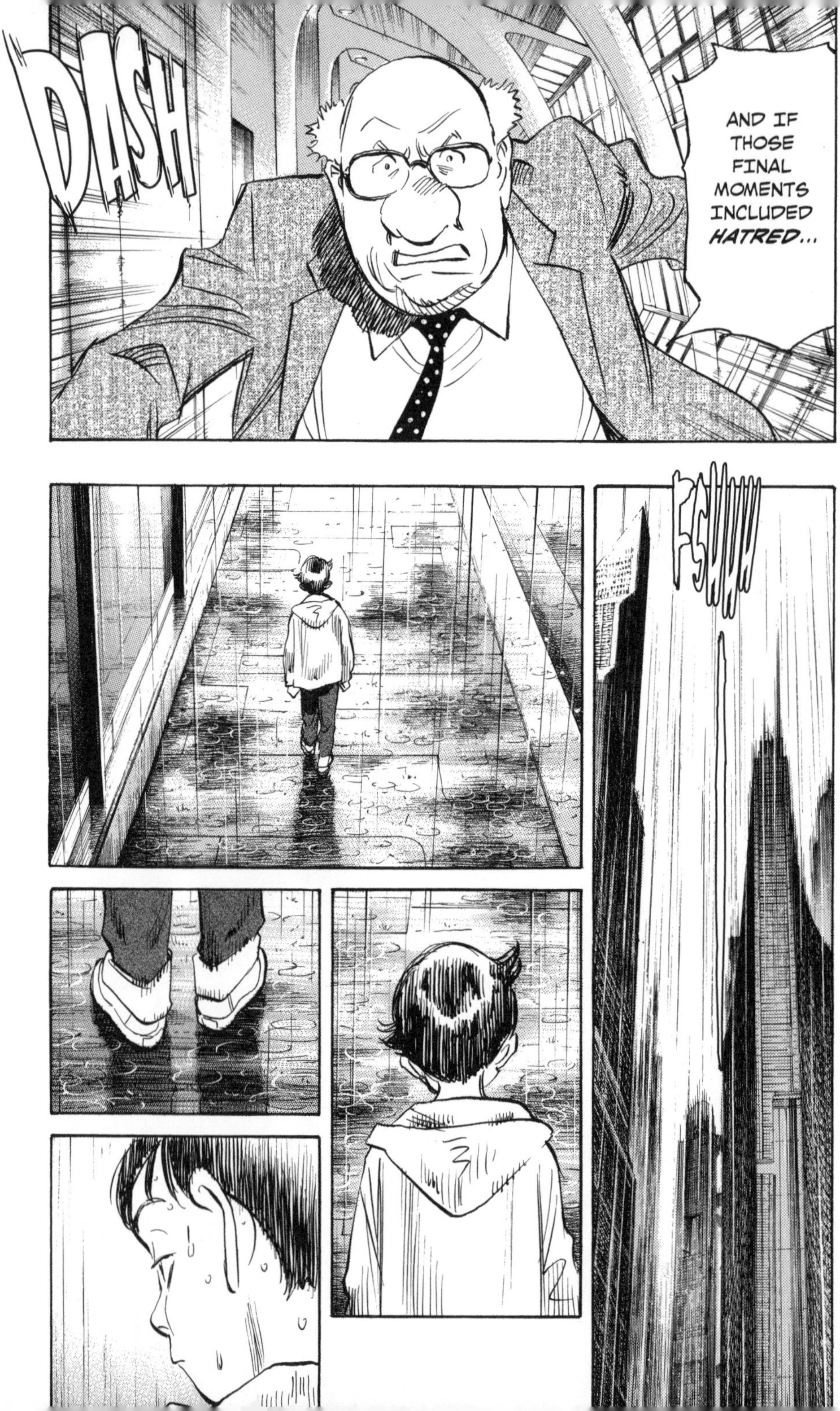
AND IF THOSE FINAL MOMENTS INCLUDED *HATRED*...
DASH
FSHHH

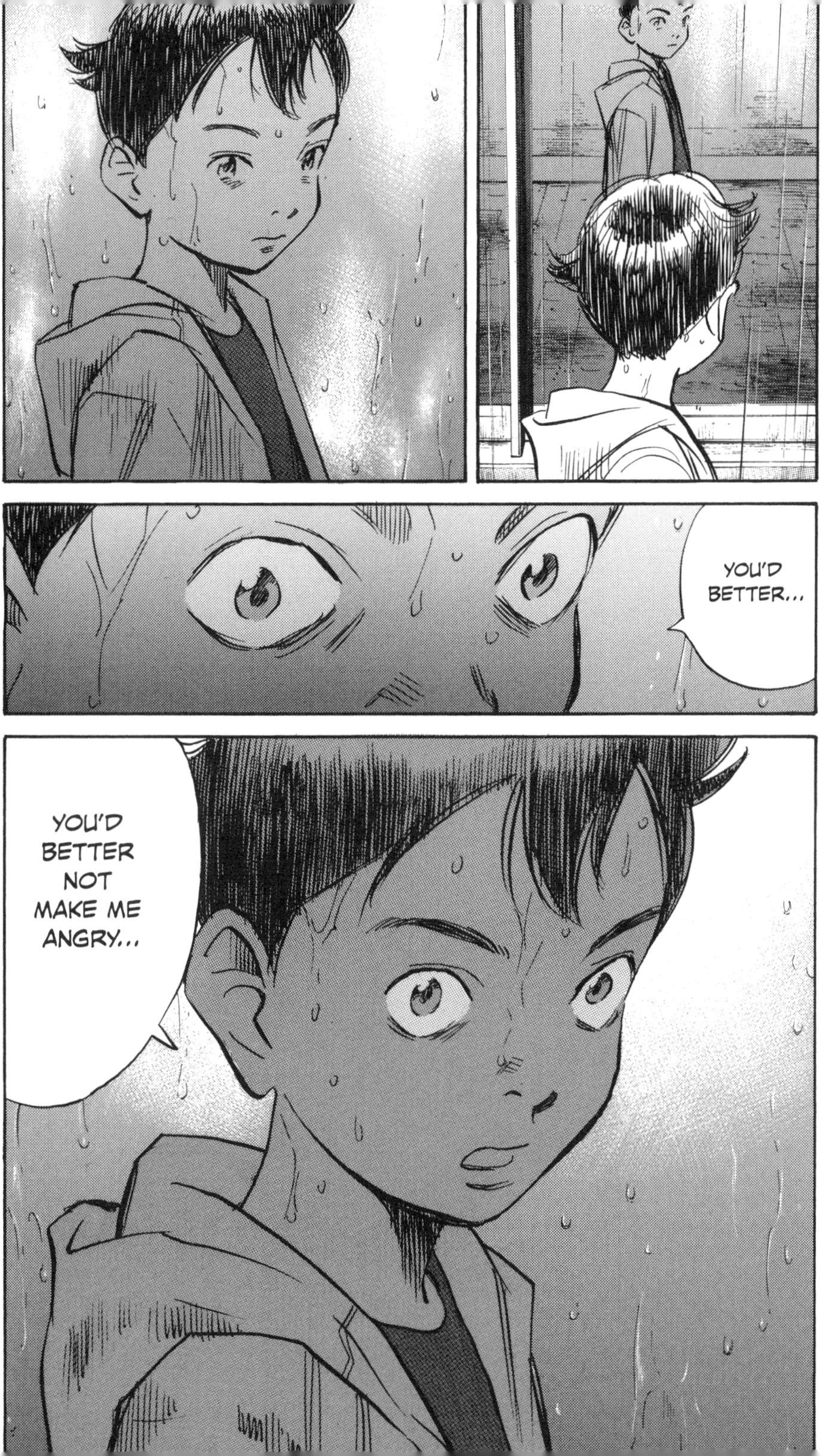
YOU'D BETTER...
YOU'D BETTER NOT MAKE ME ANGRY...

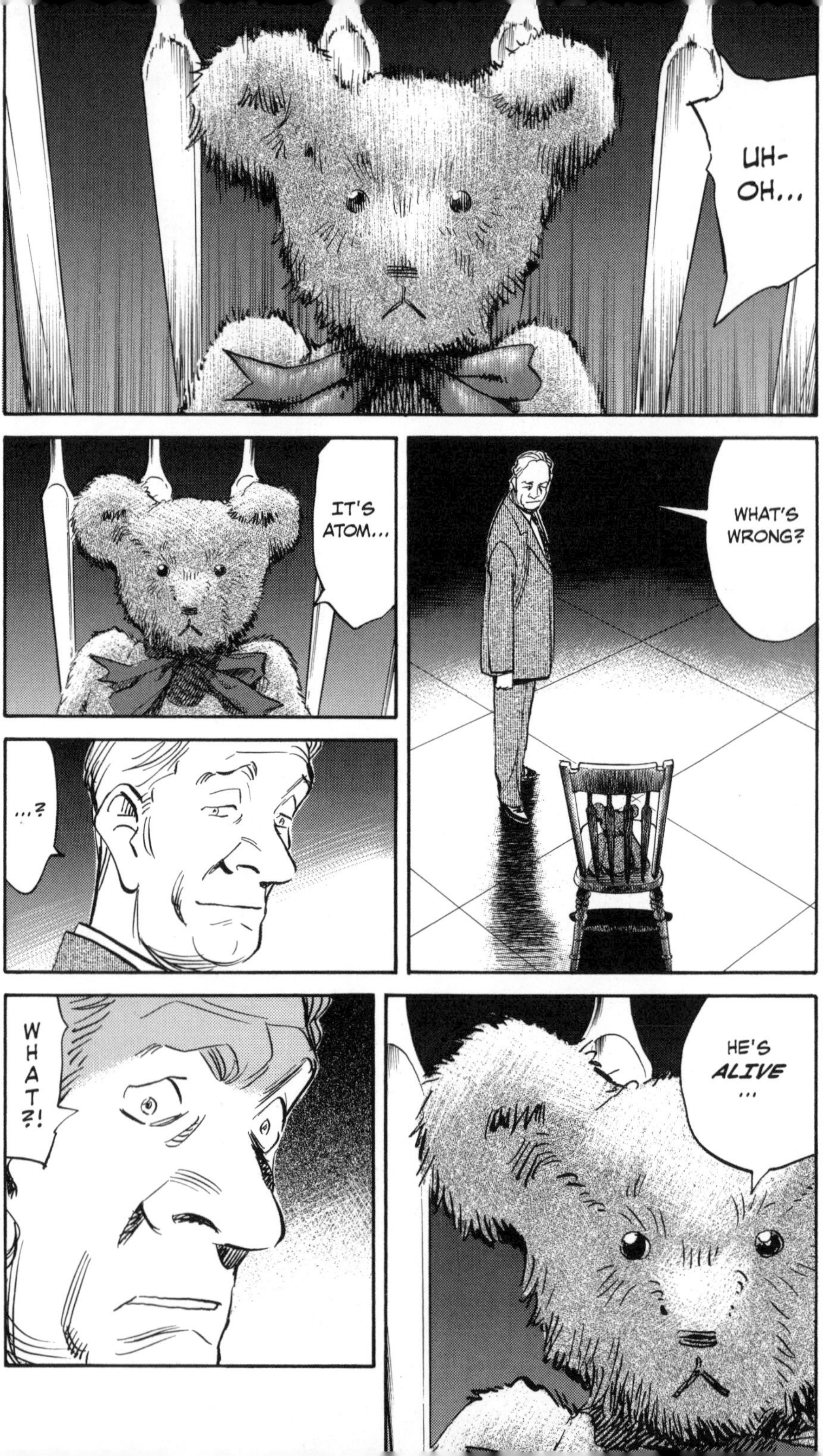
UH-OH...
WHAT'S WRONG?
IT'S ATOM...
...?
HE'S *ALIVE* ...
WHAT?!

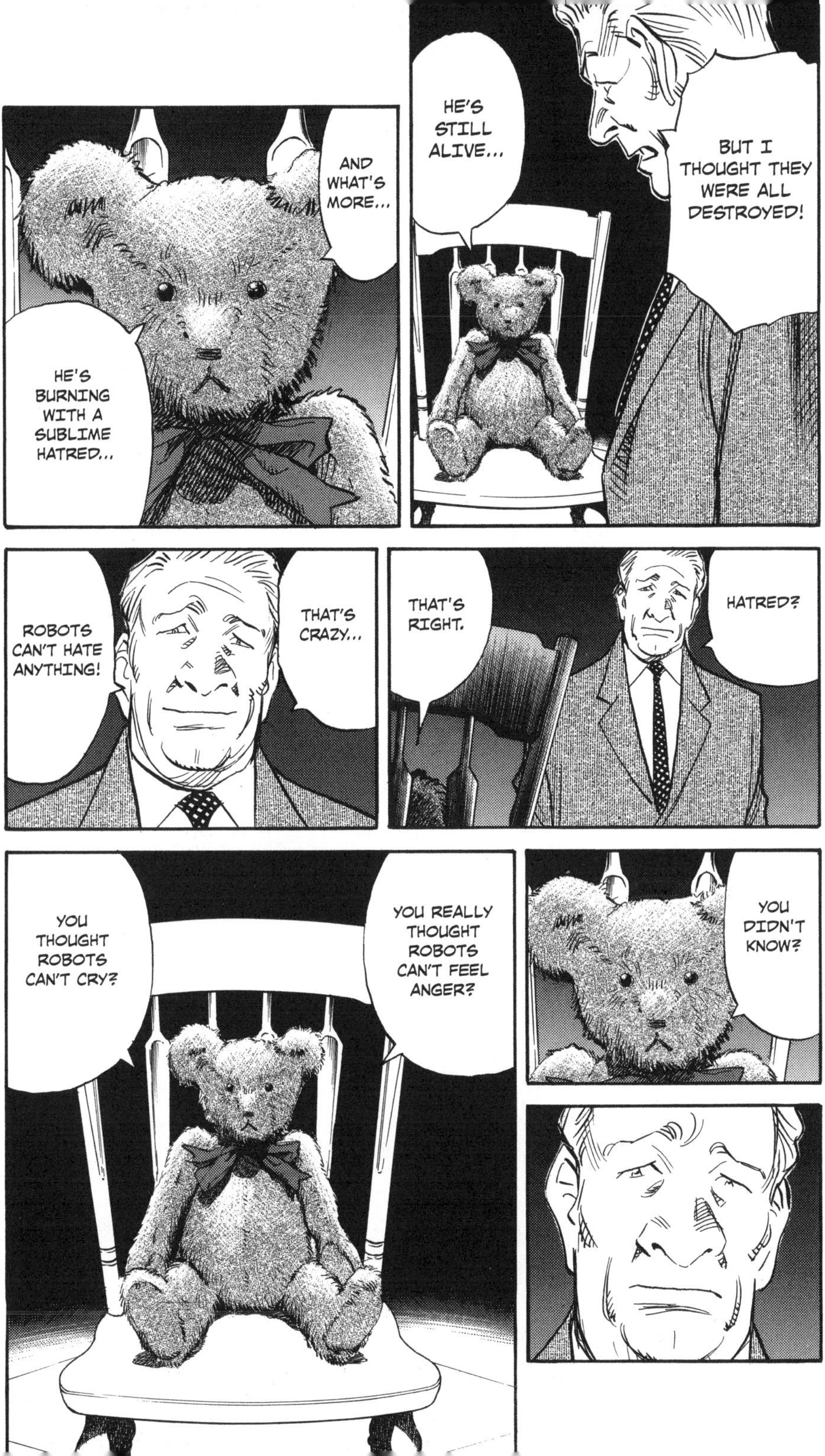
HE'S STILL ALIVE...
BUT I THOUGHT THEY WERE ALL DESTROYED!
AND WHAT'S MORE...
HE'S BURNING WITH A SUBLIME HATRED...
HATRED?
THAT'S RIGHT.
THAT'S CRAZY...
ROBOTS CAN'T HATE ANYTHING!
YOU DIDN'T KNOW?
YOU REALLY THOUGHT ROBOTS CAN'T FEEL ANGER?
YOU THOUGHT ROBOTS CAN'T CRY?

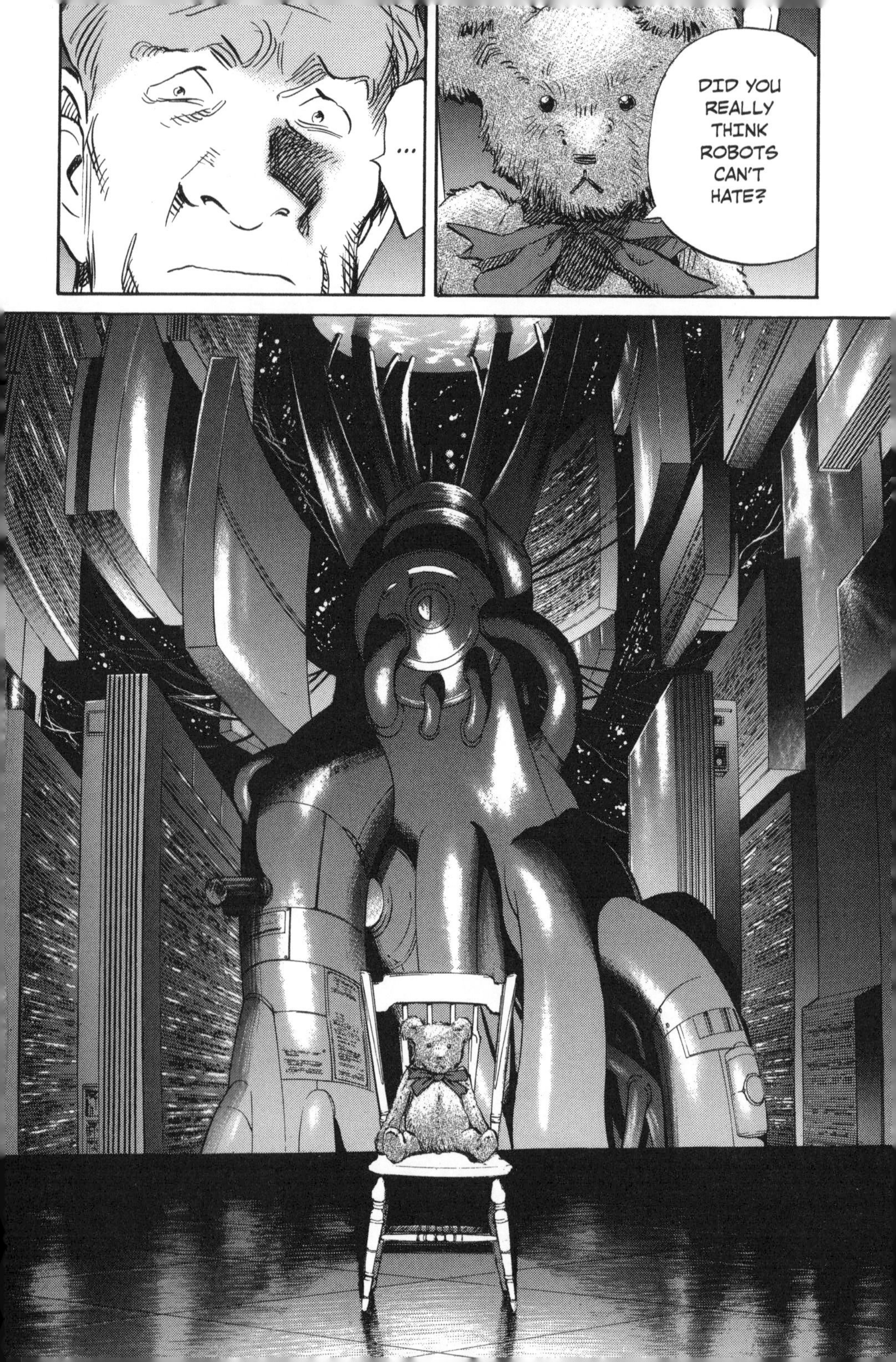
DID YOU REALLY THINK ROBOTS CAN'T HATE?
...

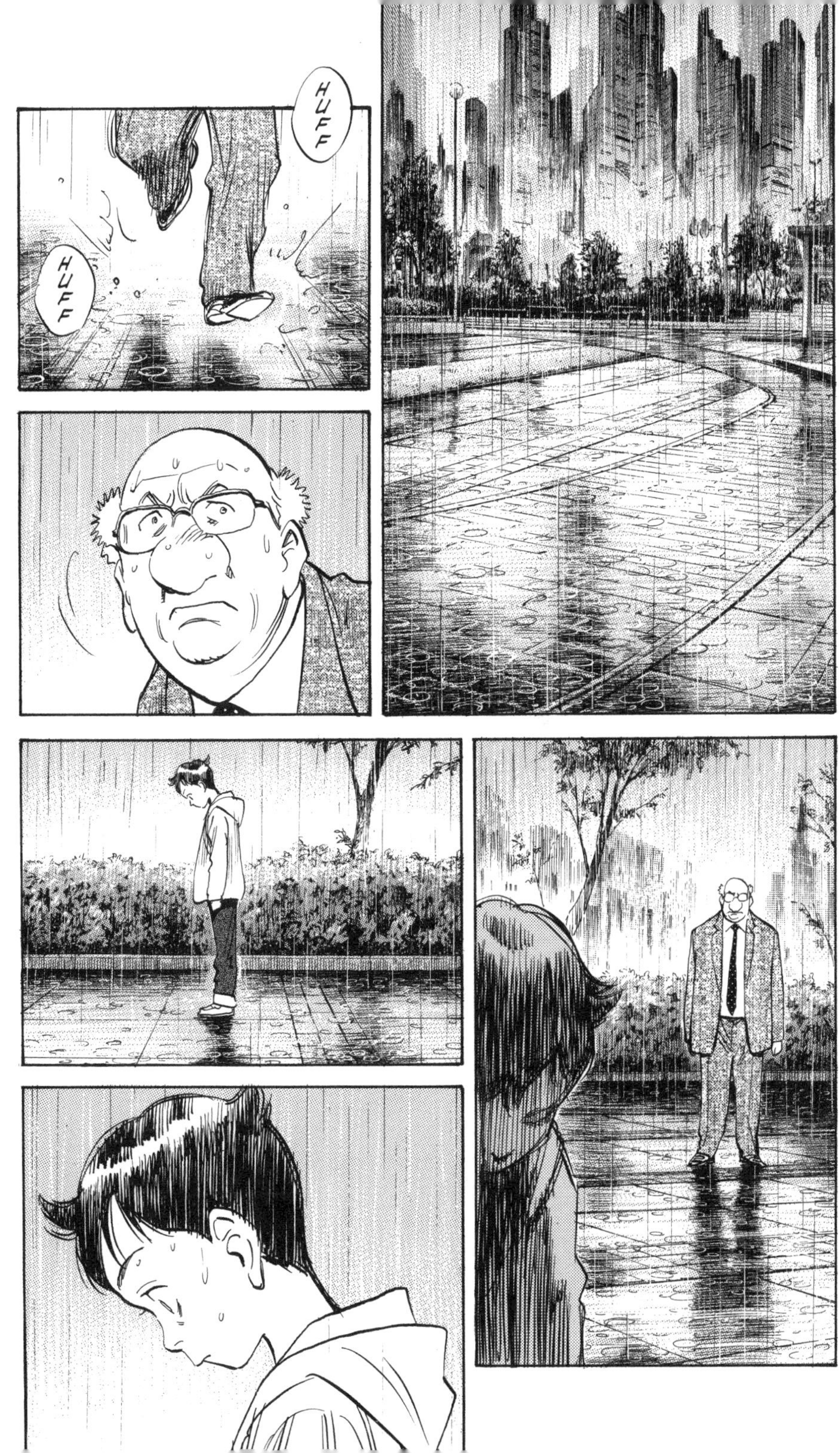
HUFF
HUFF

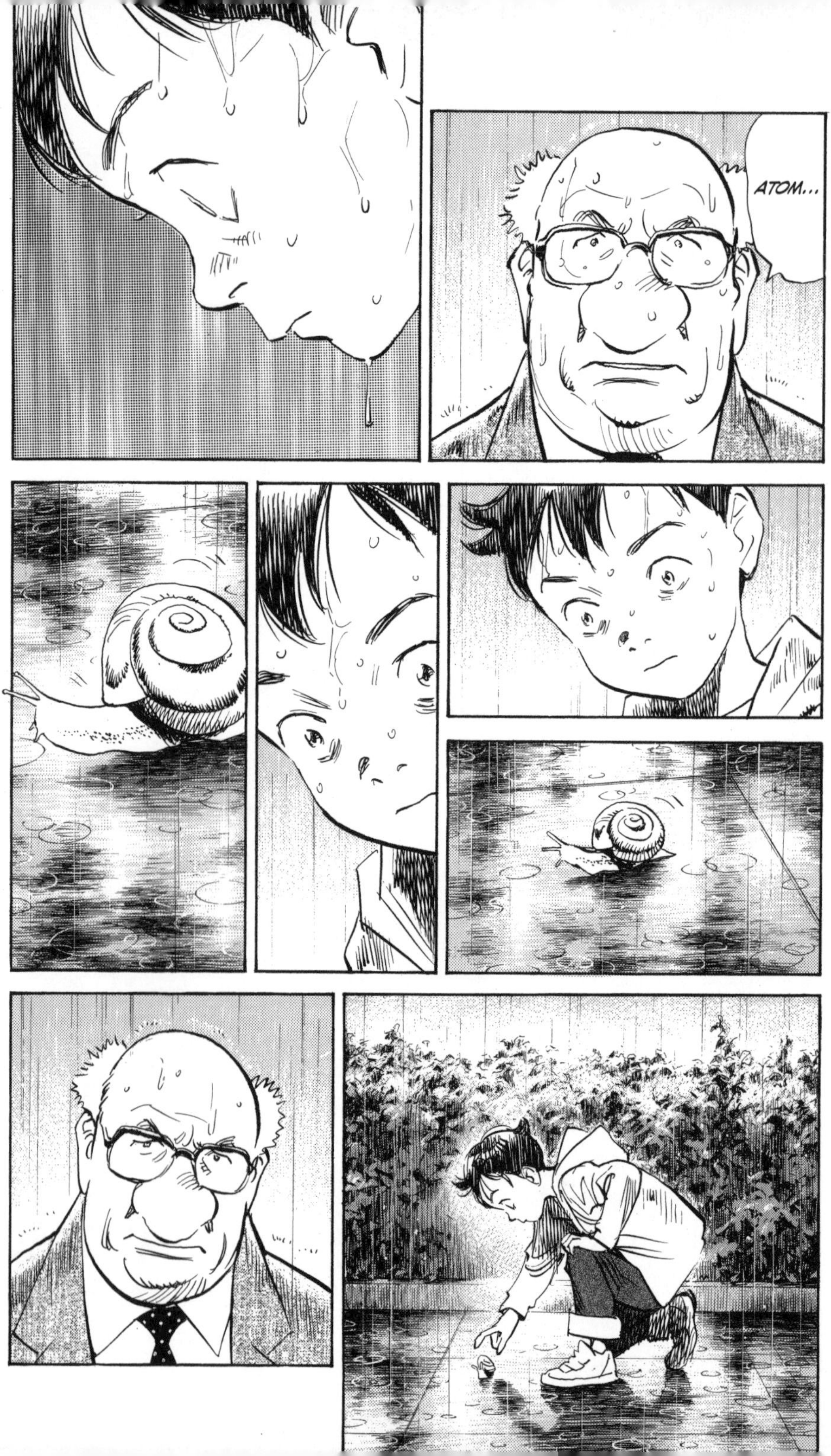
ATOM...

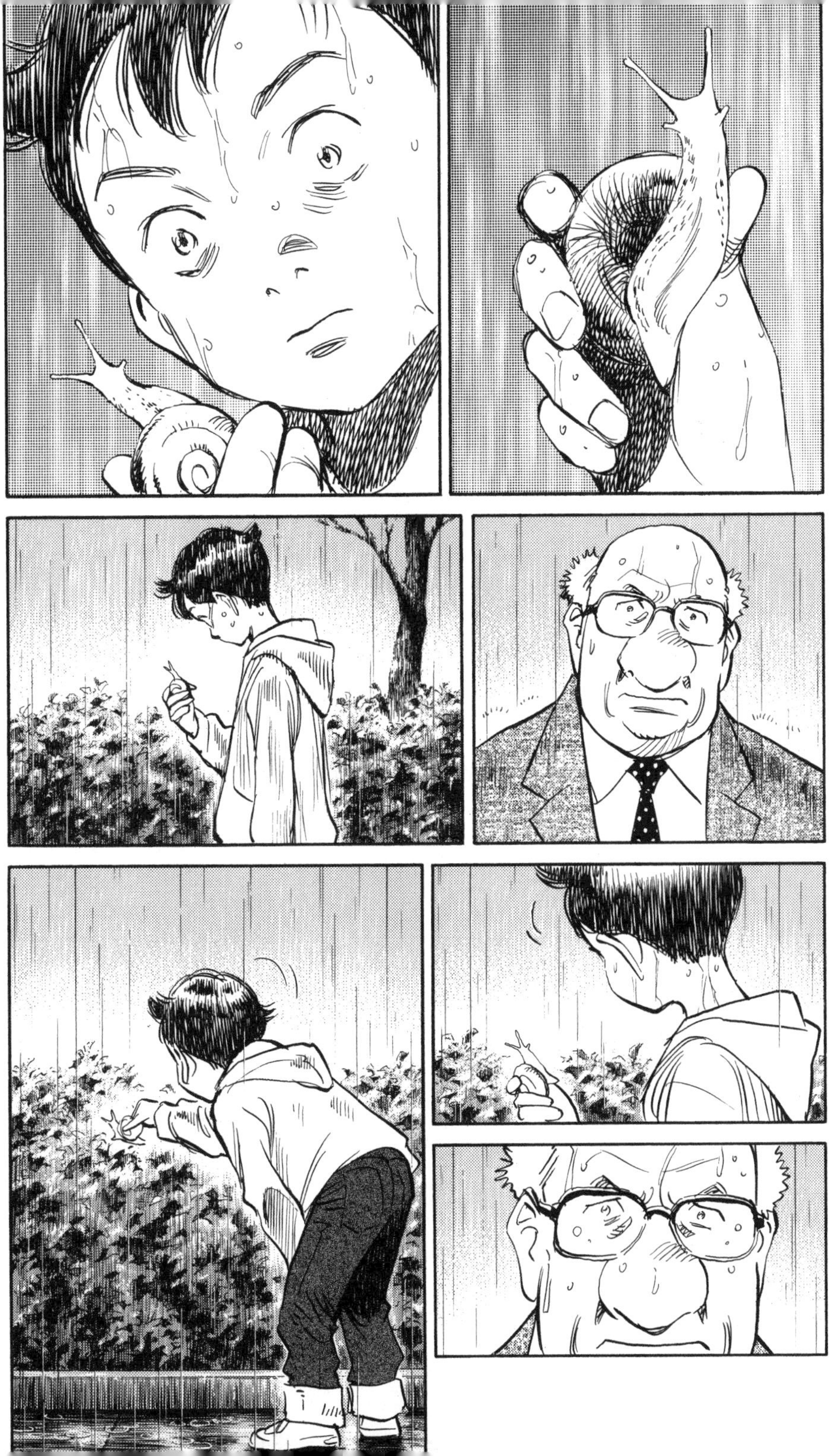

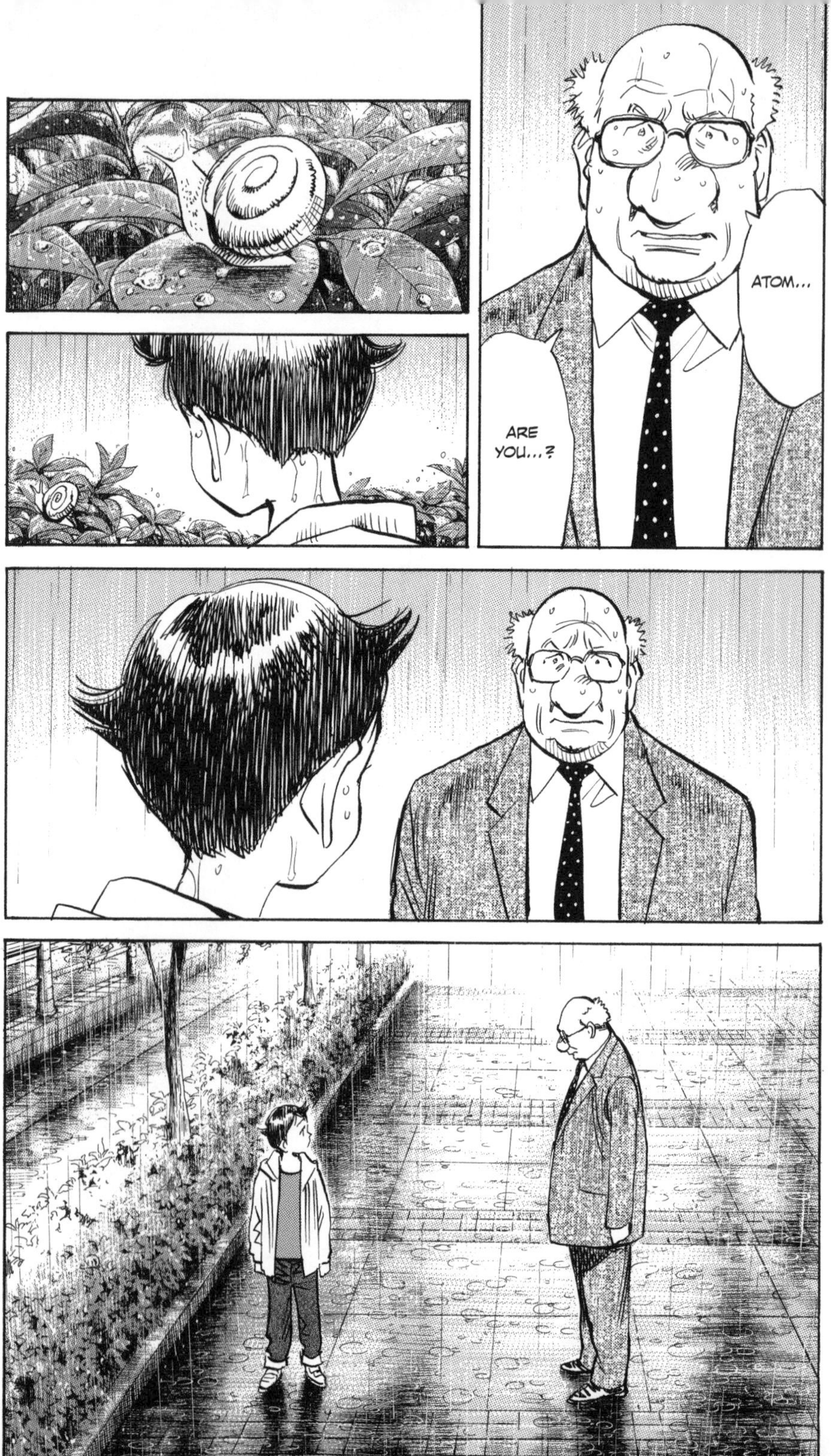
ATOM...
ARE YOU...?

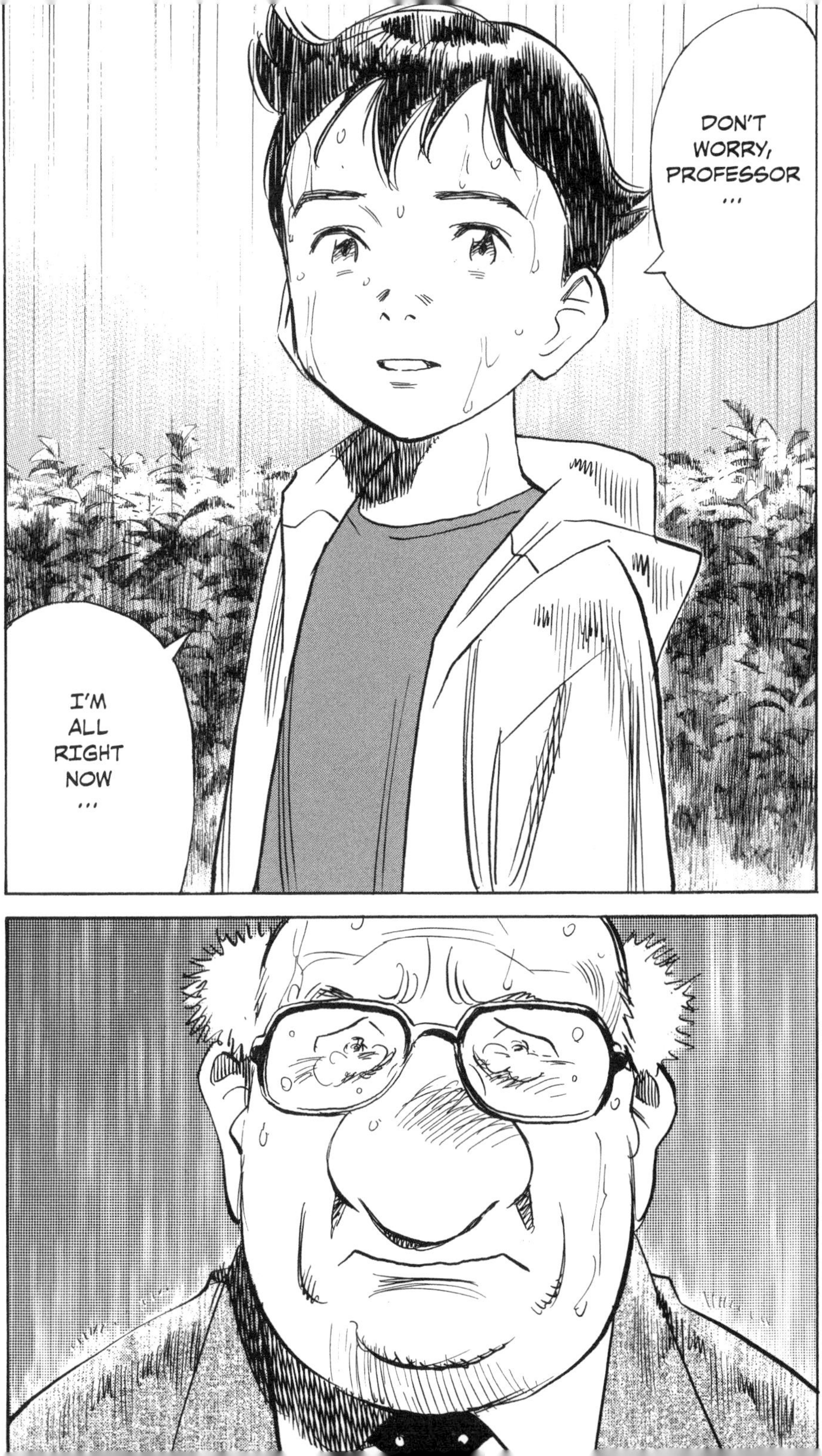
DON'T WORRY, PROFESSOR ...
I'M ALL RIGHT NOW ...

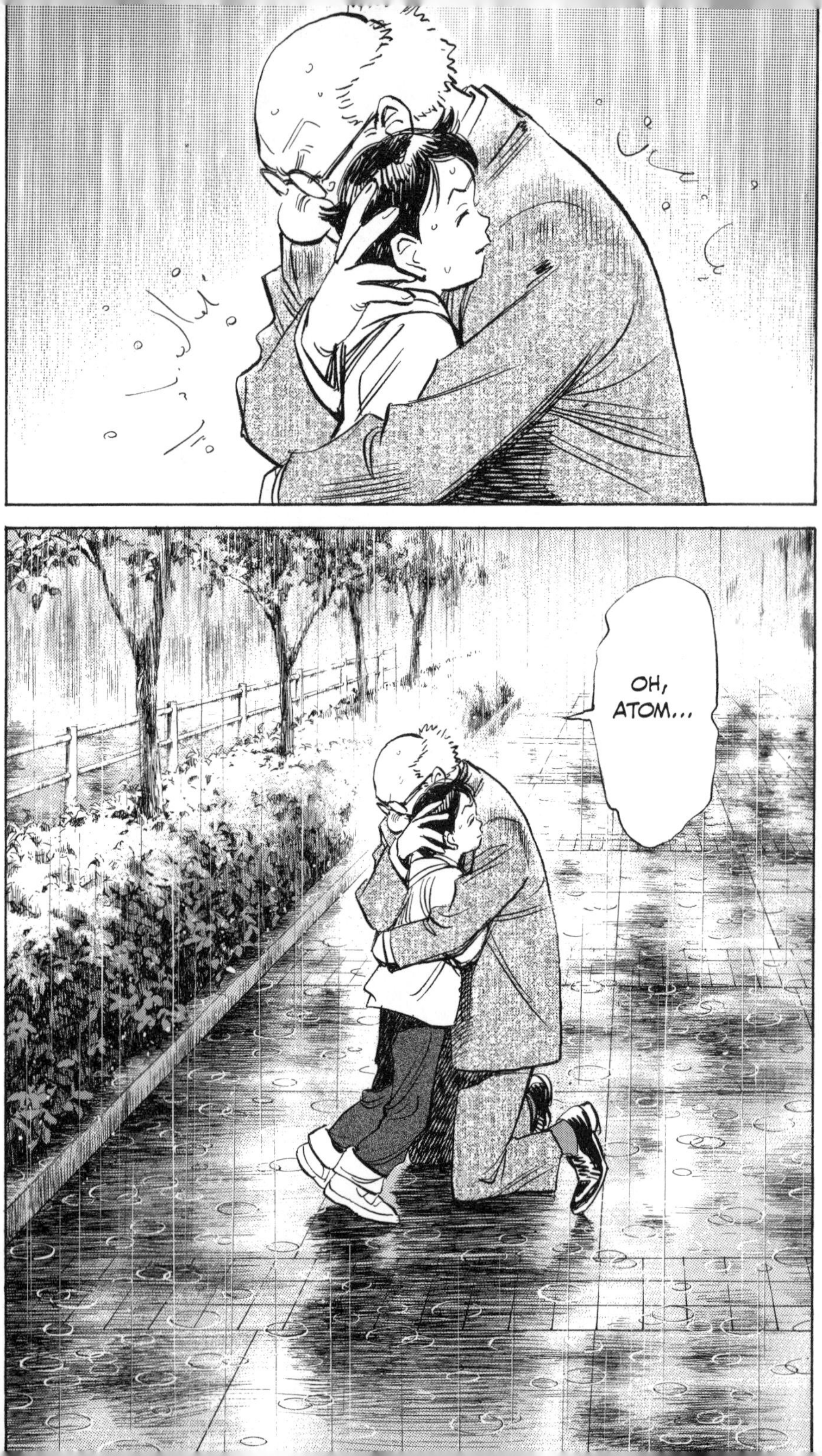
OH, ATOM...

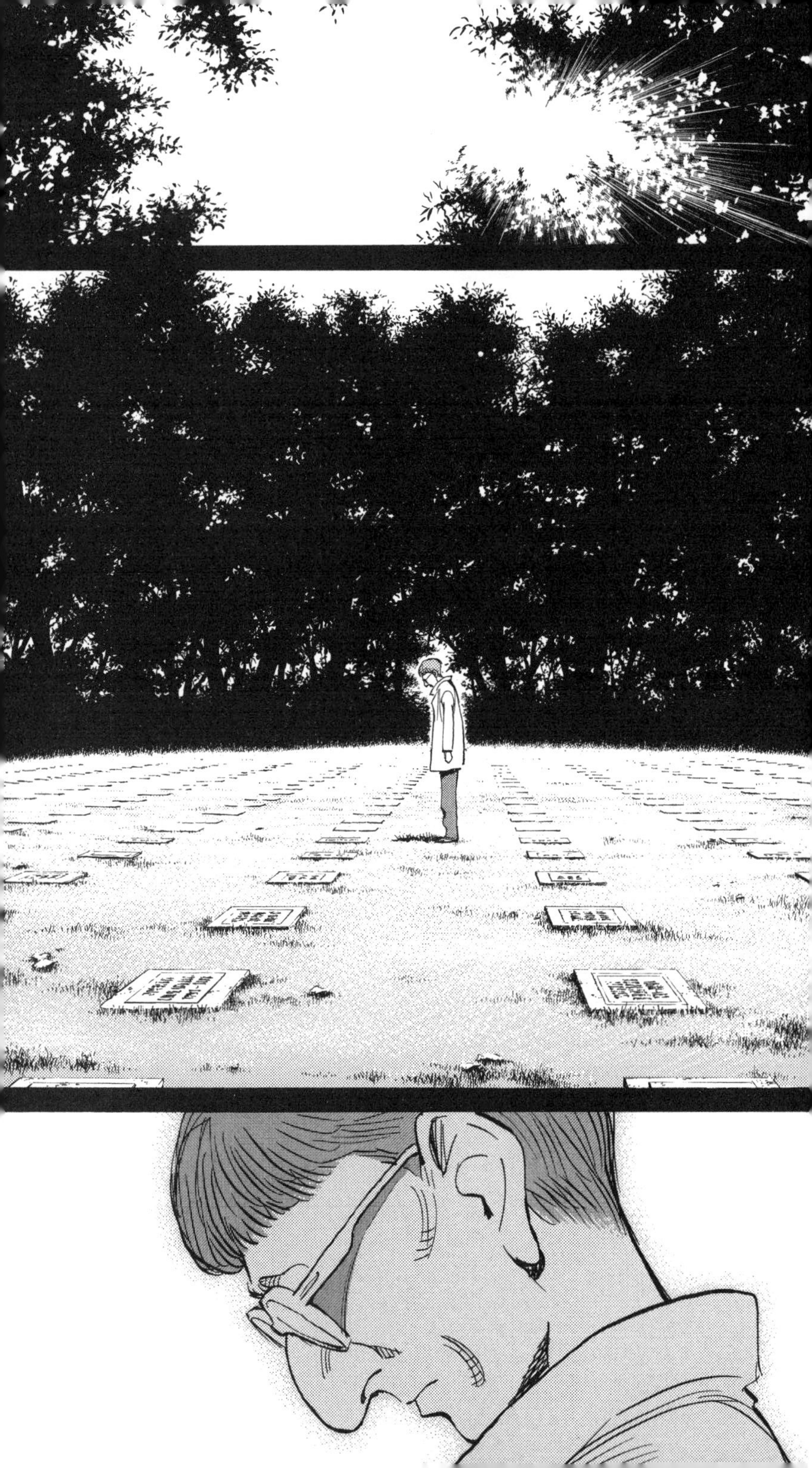

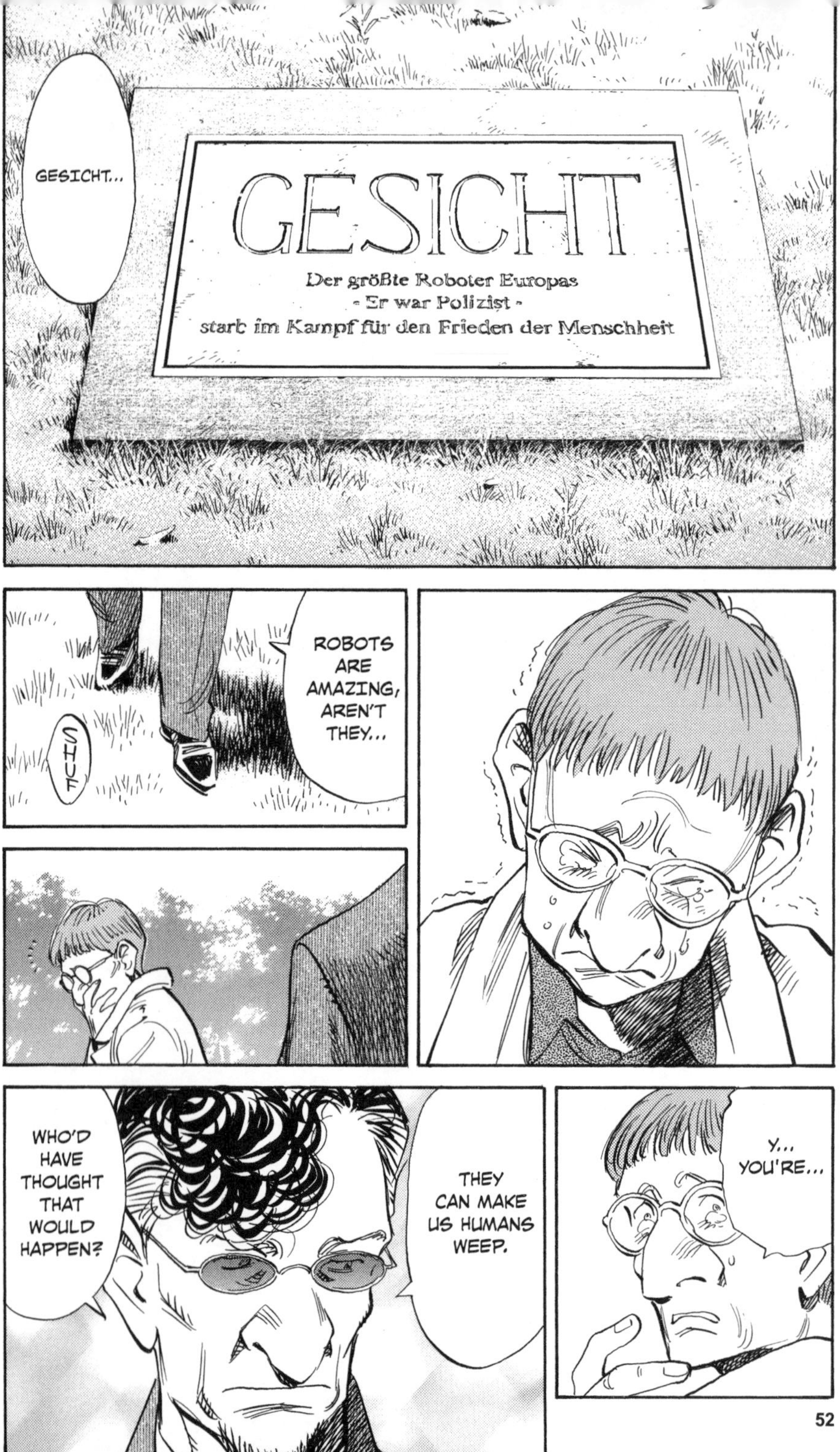
GESICHT
Der größte Roboter Europas
- Er war Polizist -
starb im Kampf für den Frieden der Menschheit
GESICHT...
ROBOTS ARE AMAZING, AREN'T THEY...
SHUF
Y... YOU'RE...
THEY CAN MAKE US HUMANS WEEP.
WHO'D HAVE THOUGHT THAT WOULD HAPPEN?

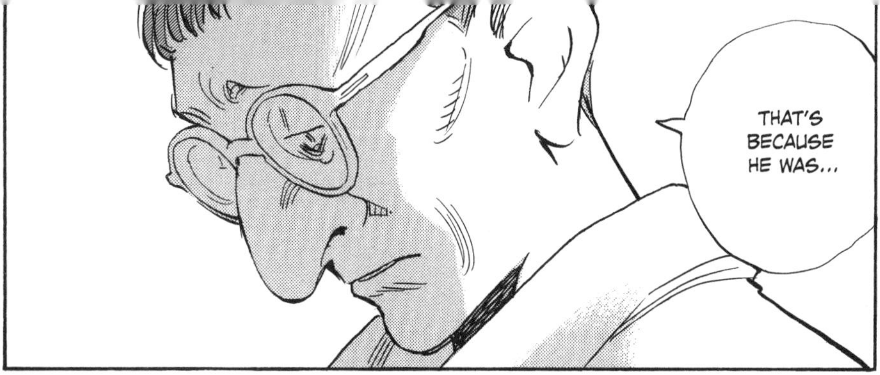
THAT'S BECAUSE HE WAS...

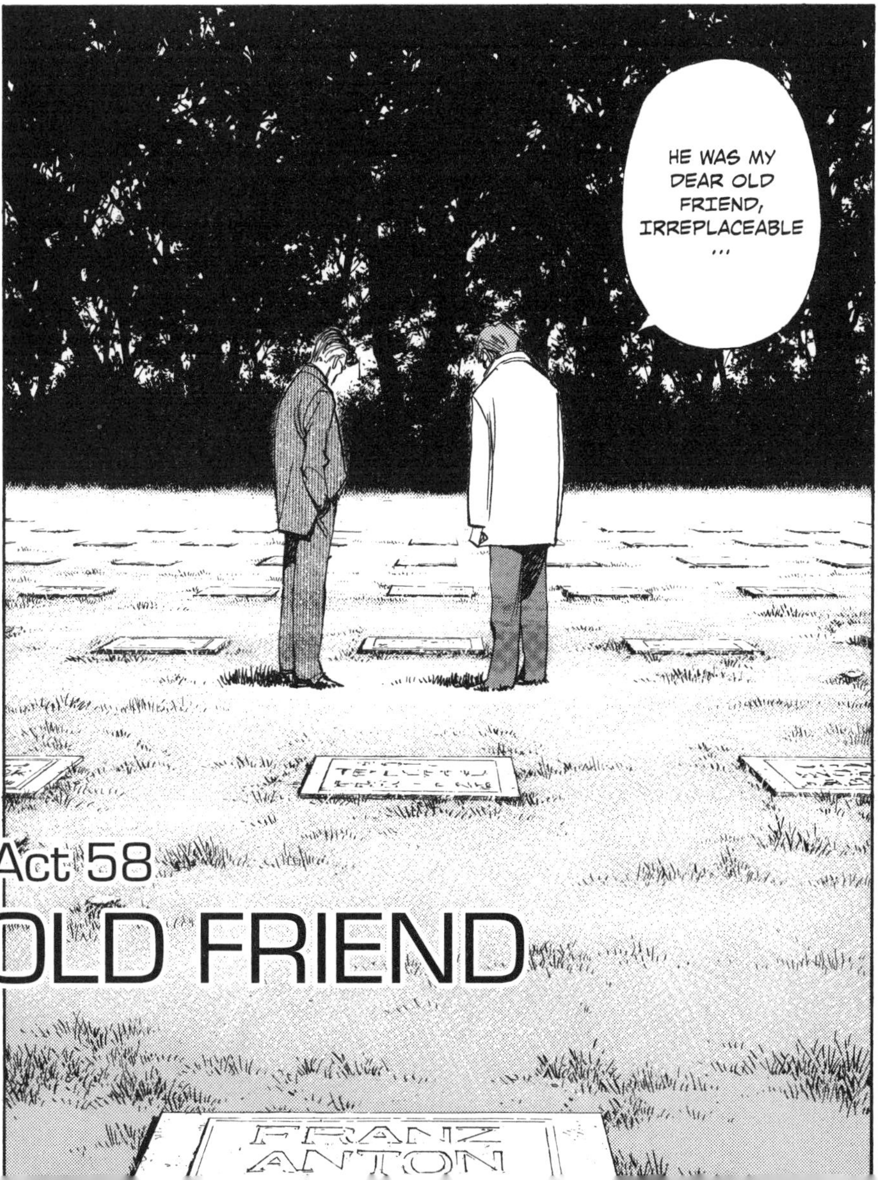
HE WAS MY DEAR OLD FRIEND, IRREPLACEABLE ...
Act 58
OLD FRIEND
FRANZ ANTON

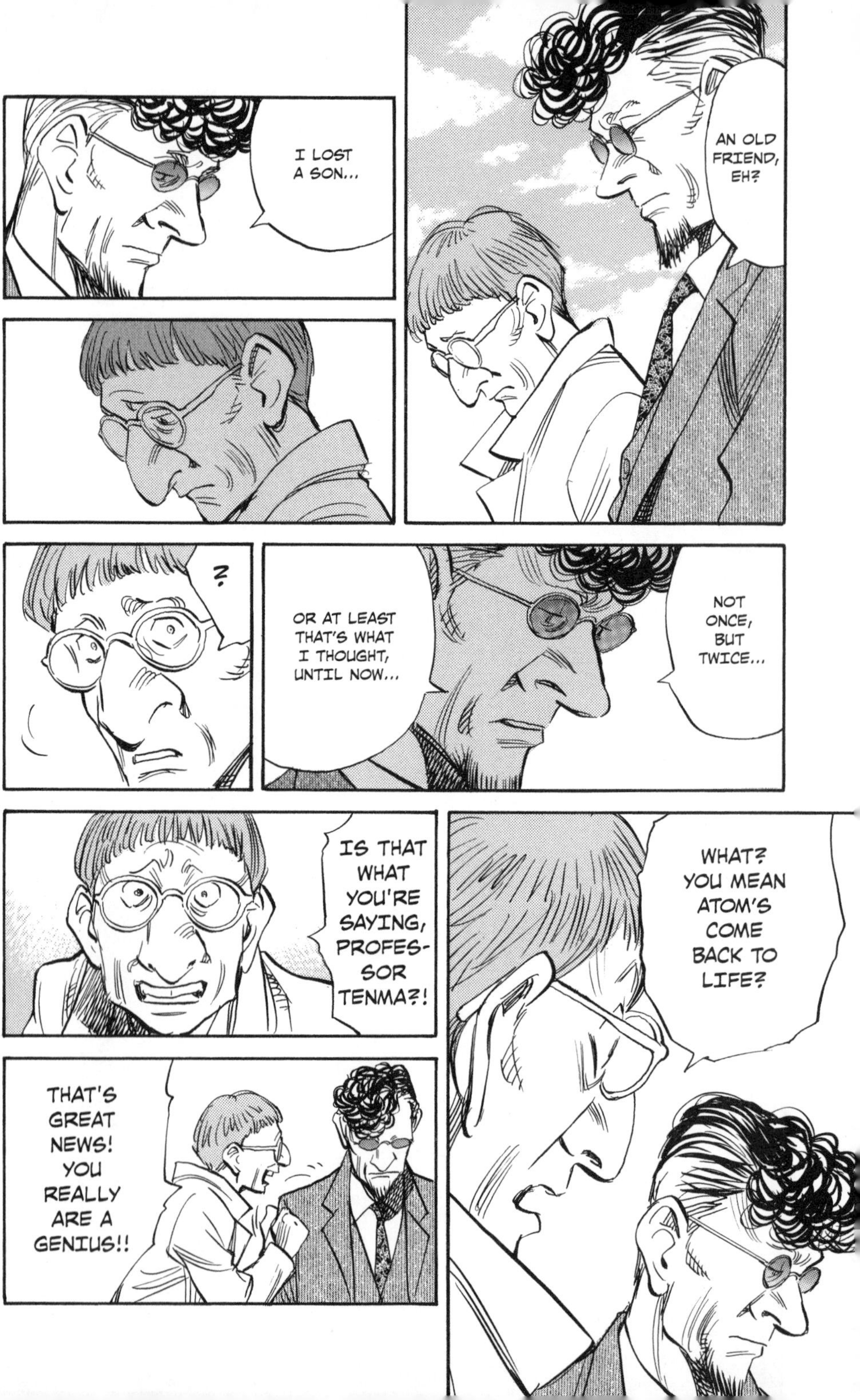
AN OLD FRIEND, EH?
I LOST A SON...
NOT ONCE, BUT TWICE...
OR AT LEAST THAT'S WHAT I THOUGHT, UNTIL NOW...
?
WHAT? YOU MEAN ATOM'S COME BACK TO LIFE?
IS THAT WHAT YOU'RE SAYING, PROFES-SOR TENMA?!
THAT'S GREAT NEWS! YOU REALLY ARE A GENIUS!!

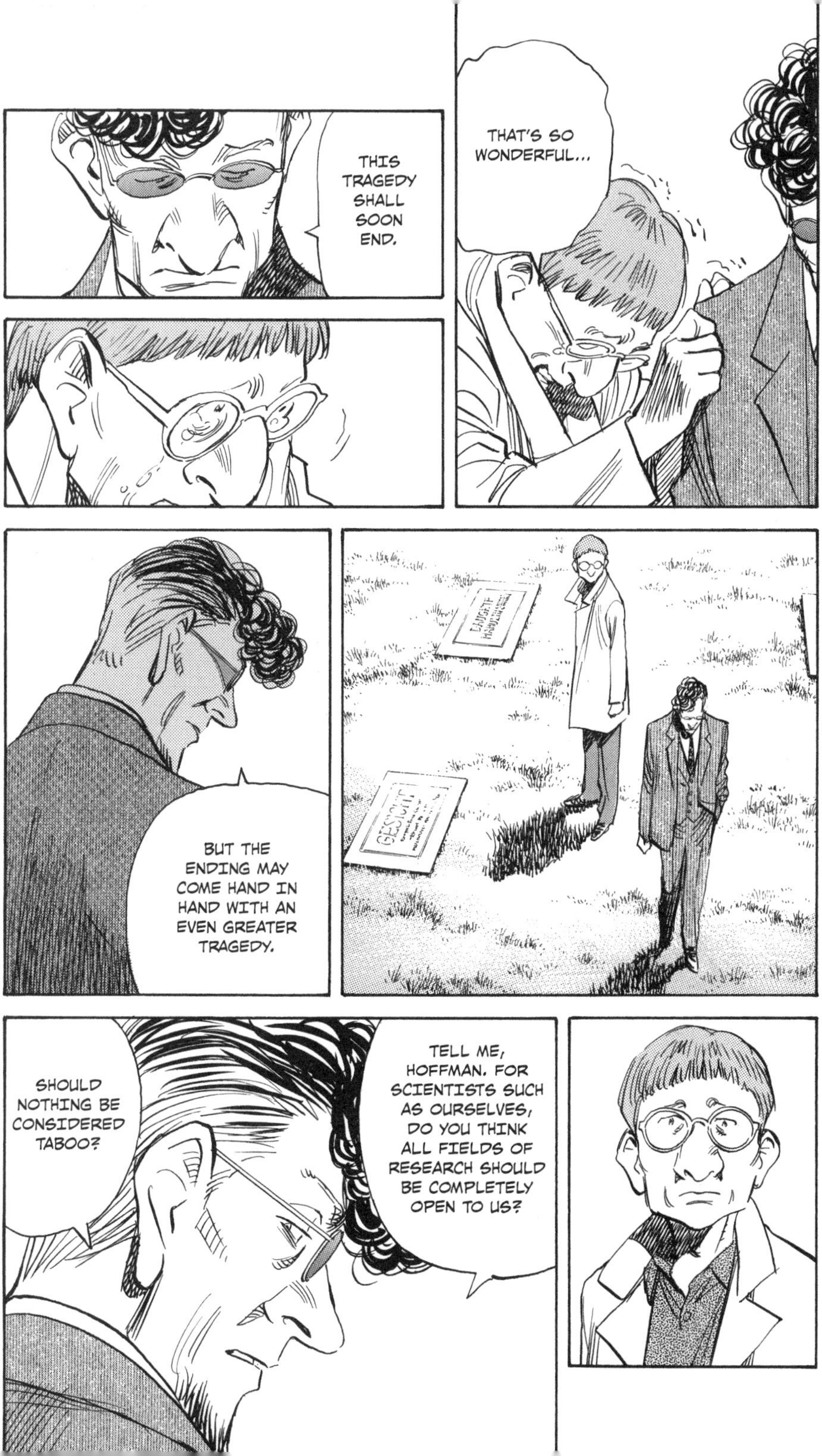
THIS TRAGEDY SHALL SOON END.
THAT'S SO WONDERFUL...
BUT THE ENDING MAY COME HAND IN HAND WITH AN EVEN GREATER TRAGEDY.
TELL ME, HOFFMAN. FOR SCIENTISTS SUCH AS OURSELVES, DO YOU THINK ALL FIELDS OF RESEARCH SHOULD BE COMPLETELY OPEN TO US?
SHOULD NOTHING BE CONSIDERED TABOO?

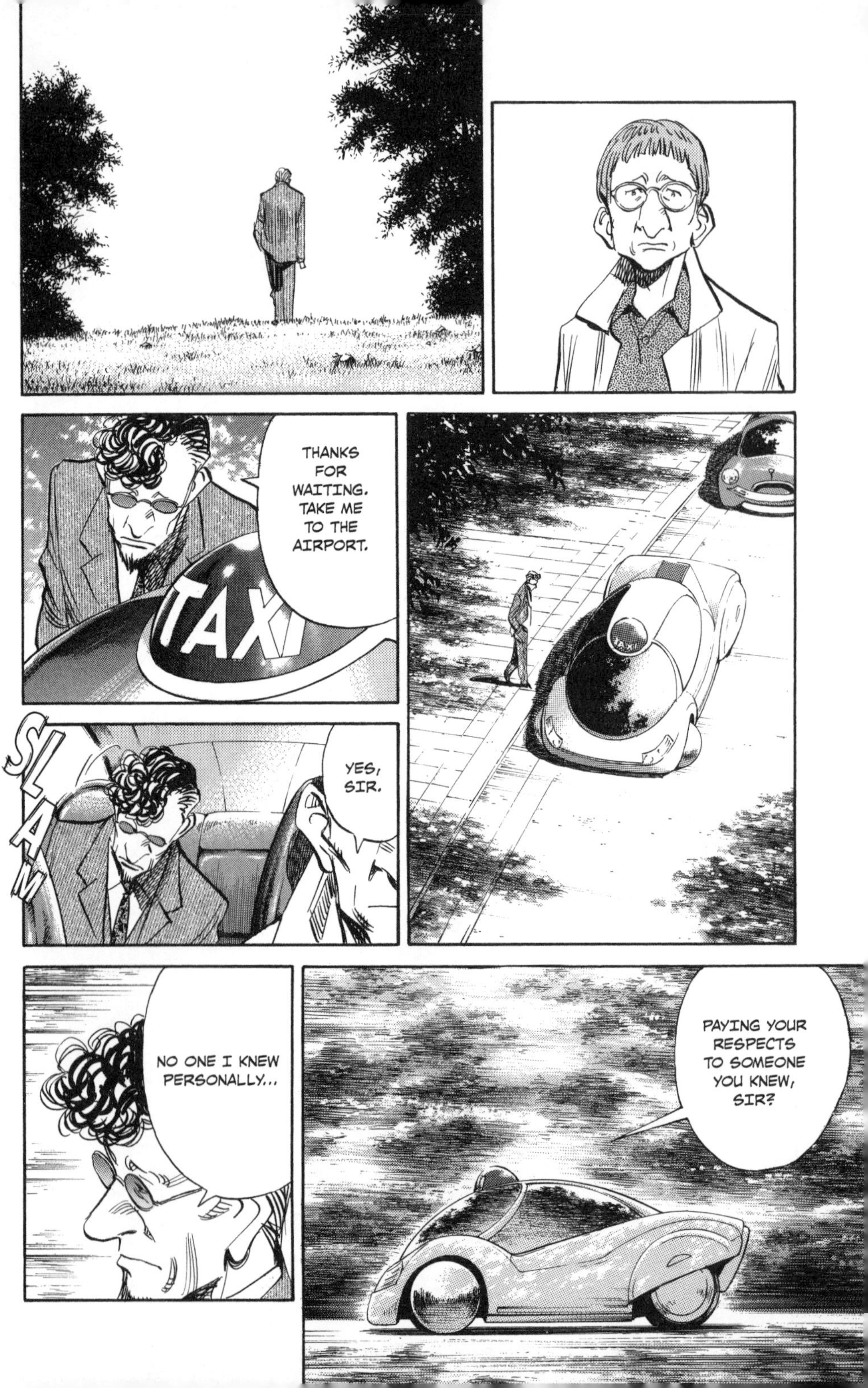
THANKS FOR WAITING. TAKE ME TO THE AIRPORT.
YES, SIR.
SLAM
PAYING YOUR RESPECTS TO SOMEONE YOU KNEW, SIR?
NO ONE I KNEW PERSONALLY...

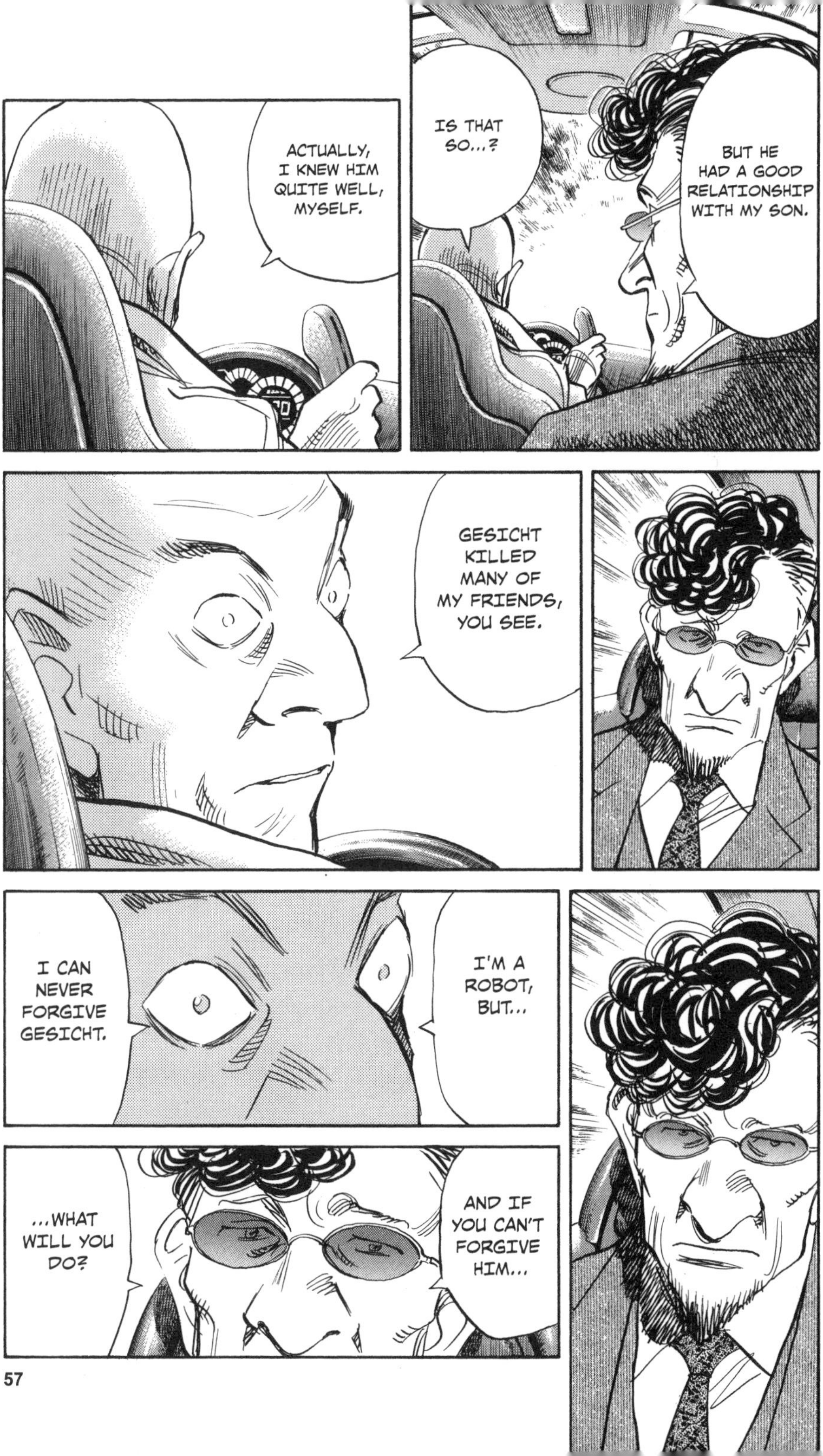
BUT HE HAD A GOOD RELATIONSHIP WITH MY SON.
IS THAT SO...?
ACTUALLY, I KNEW HIM QUITE WELL, MYSELF.
GESICHT KILLED MANY OF MY FRIENDS, YOU SEE.
I'M A ROBOT, BUT...
I CAN NEVER FORGIVE GESICHT.
AND IF YOU CAN'T FORGIVE HIM...
...WHAT WILL YOU DO?

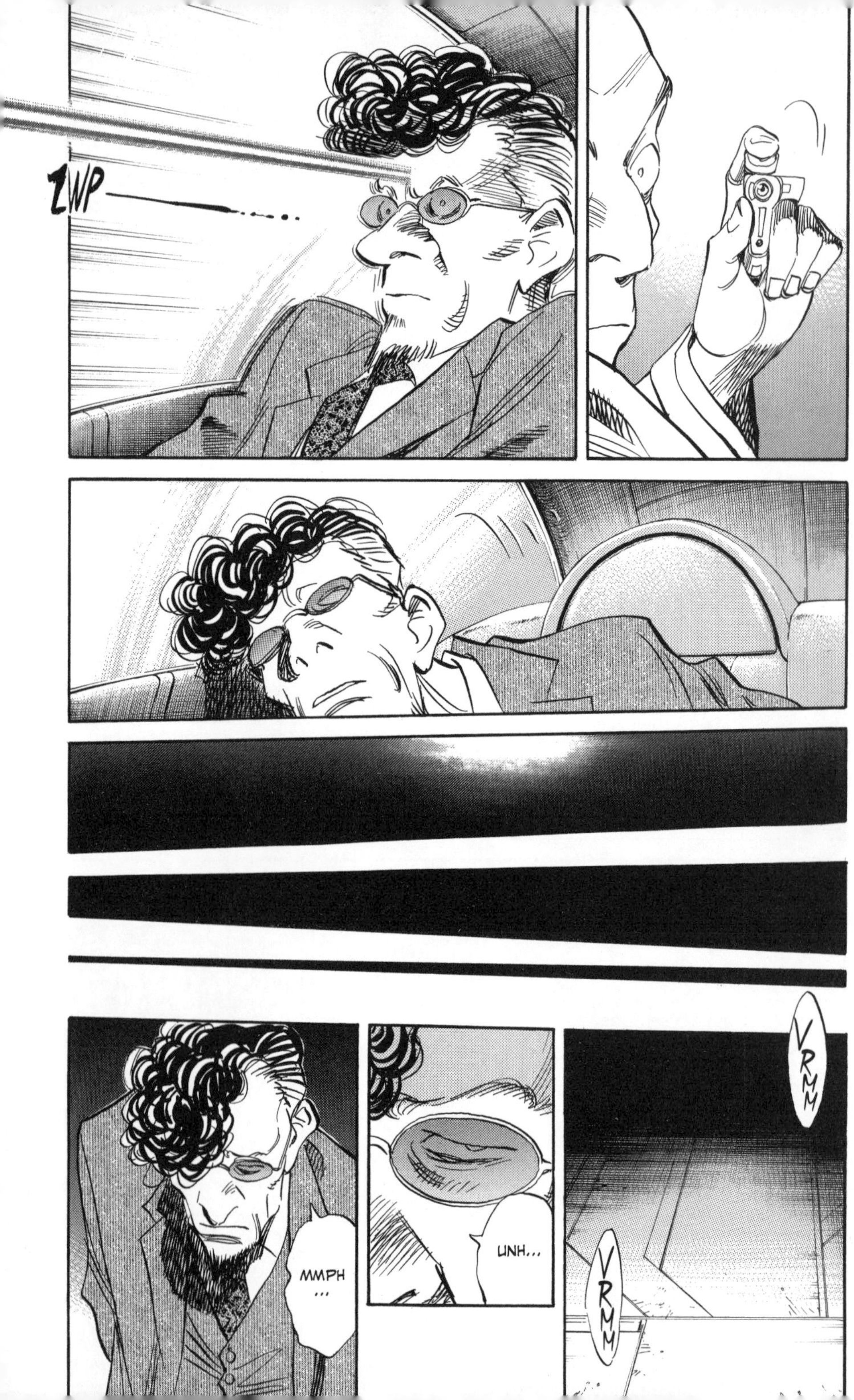
ZWP
VRMM
VRMM
UNH...
MMPH...

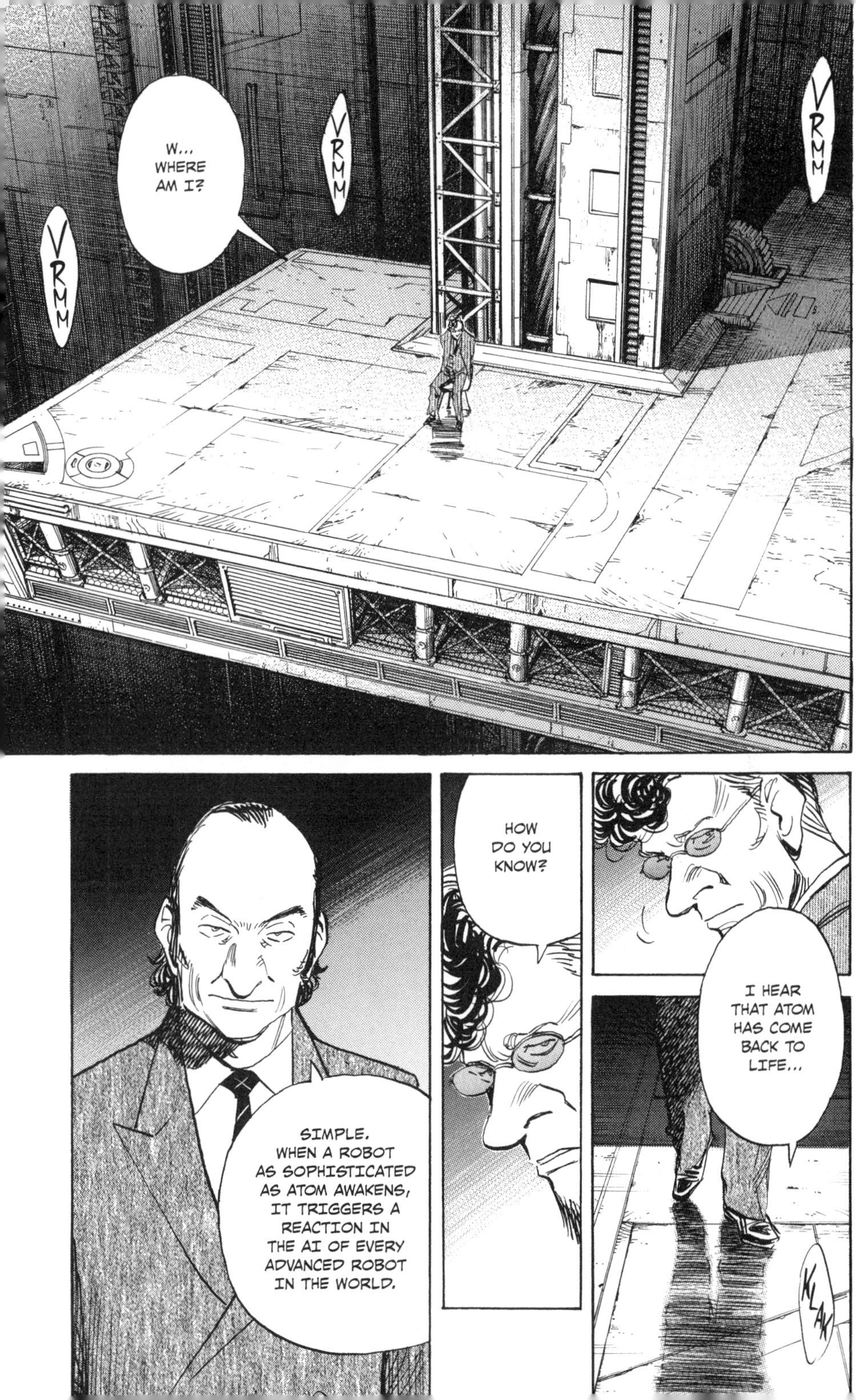
VRMM
VRMM
W... WHERE AM I?
VRMM
I HEAR THAT ATOM HAS COME BACK TO LIFE...
KLAK
HOW DO YOU KNOW?
SIMPLE. WHEN A ROBOT AS SOPHISTICATED AS ATOM AWAKENS, IT TRIGGERS A REACTION IN THE AI OF EVERY ADVANCED ROBOT IN THE WORLD.

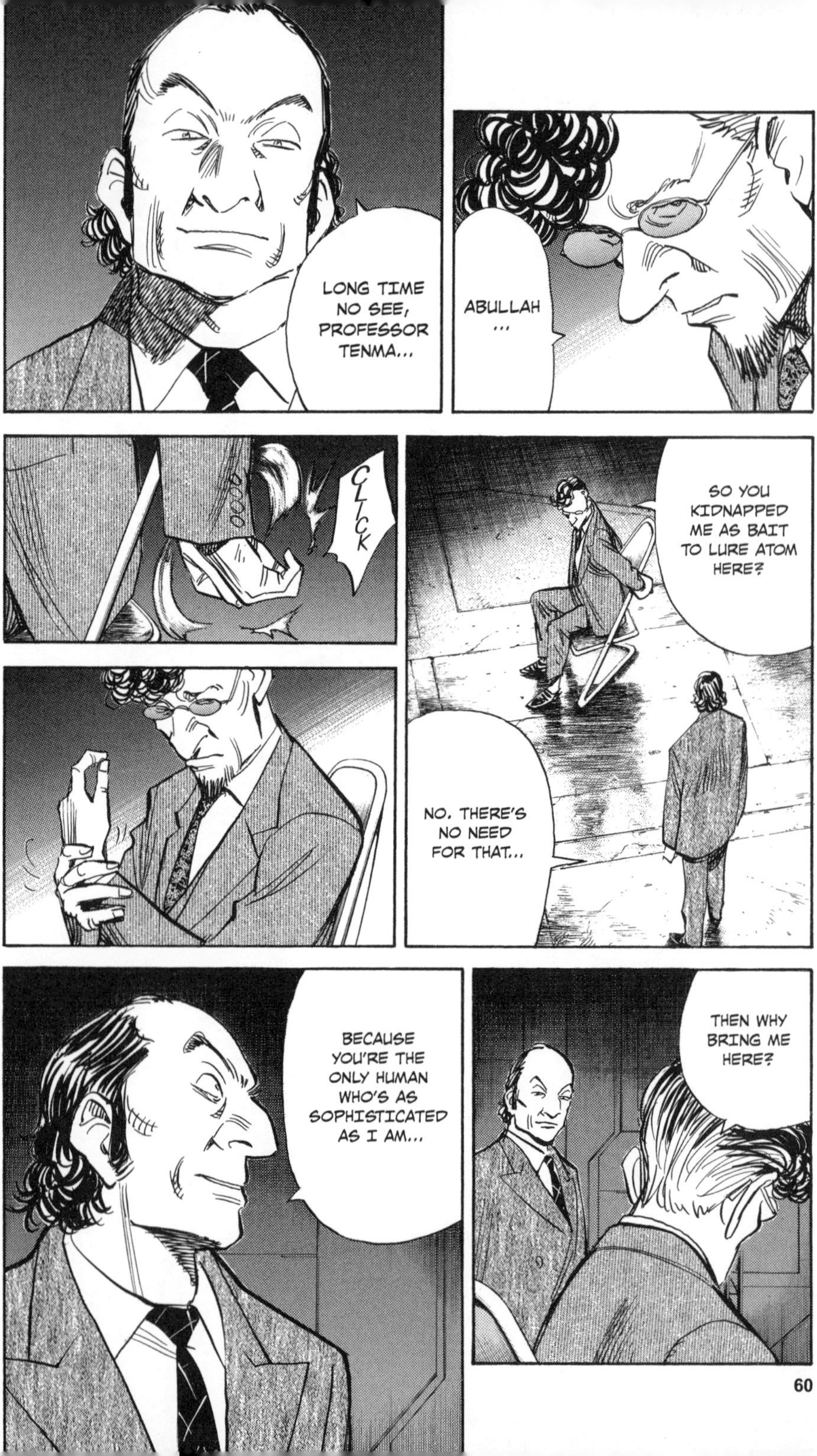
ABULLAH ...
LONG TIME NO SEE, PROFESSOR TENMA...
SO YOU KIDNAPPED ME AS BAIT TO LURE ATOM HERE?
NO. THERE'S NO NEED FOR THAT...
CLICK
THEN WHY BRING ME HERE?
BECAUSE YOU'RE THE ONLY HUMAN WHO'S AS SOPHISTICATED AS I AM...

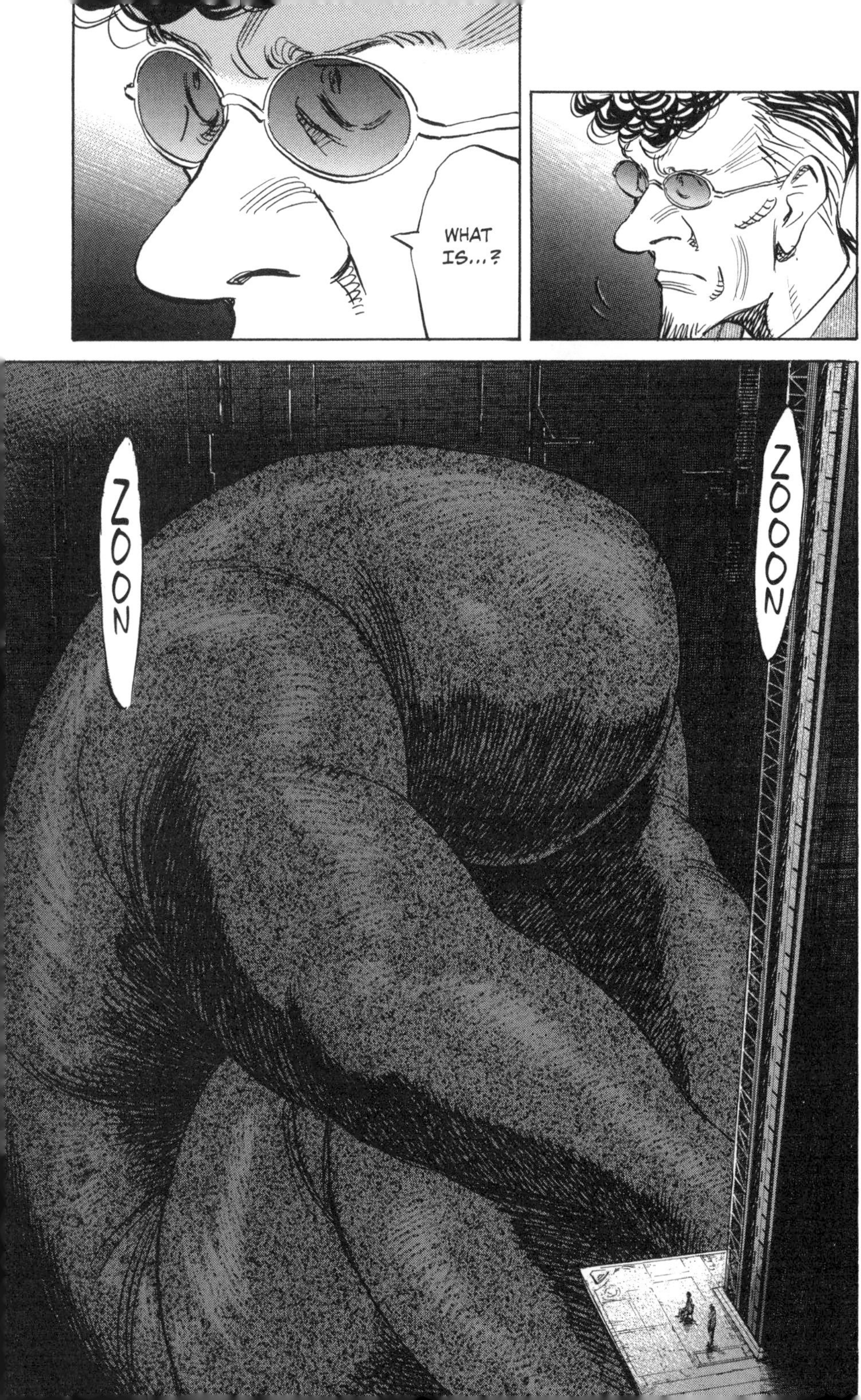
WHAT IS...?
ZOOOON
ZOOON

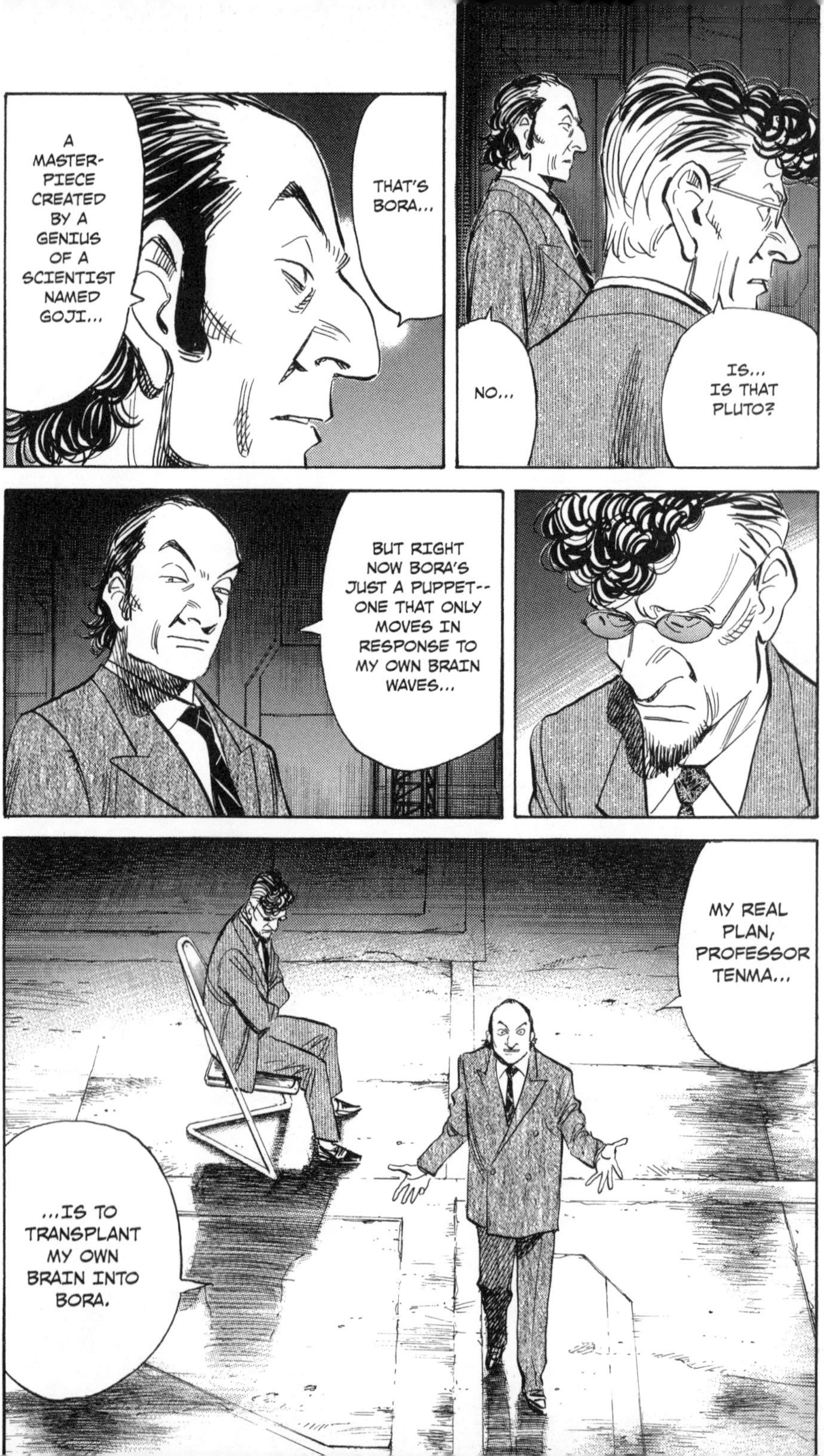
IS... IS THAT PLUTO?
NO...
THAT'S BORA...
A MASTER-PIECE CREATED BY A GENIUS OF A SCIENTIST NAMED GOJI...
BUT RIGHT NOW BORA'S JUST A PUPPET--ONE THAT ONLY MOVES IN RESPONSE TO MY OWN BRAIN WAVES...
MY REAL PLAN, PROFESSOR TENMA...
...IS TO TRANSPLANT MY OWN BRAIN INTO BORA.

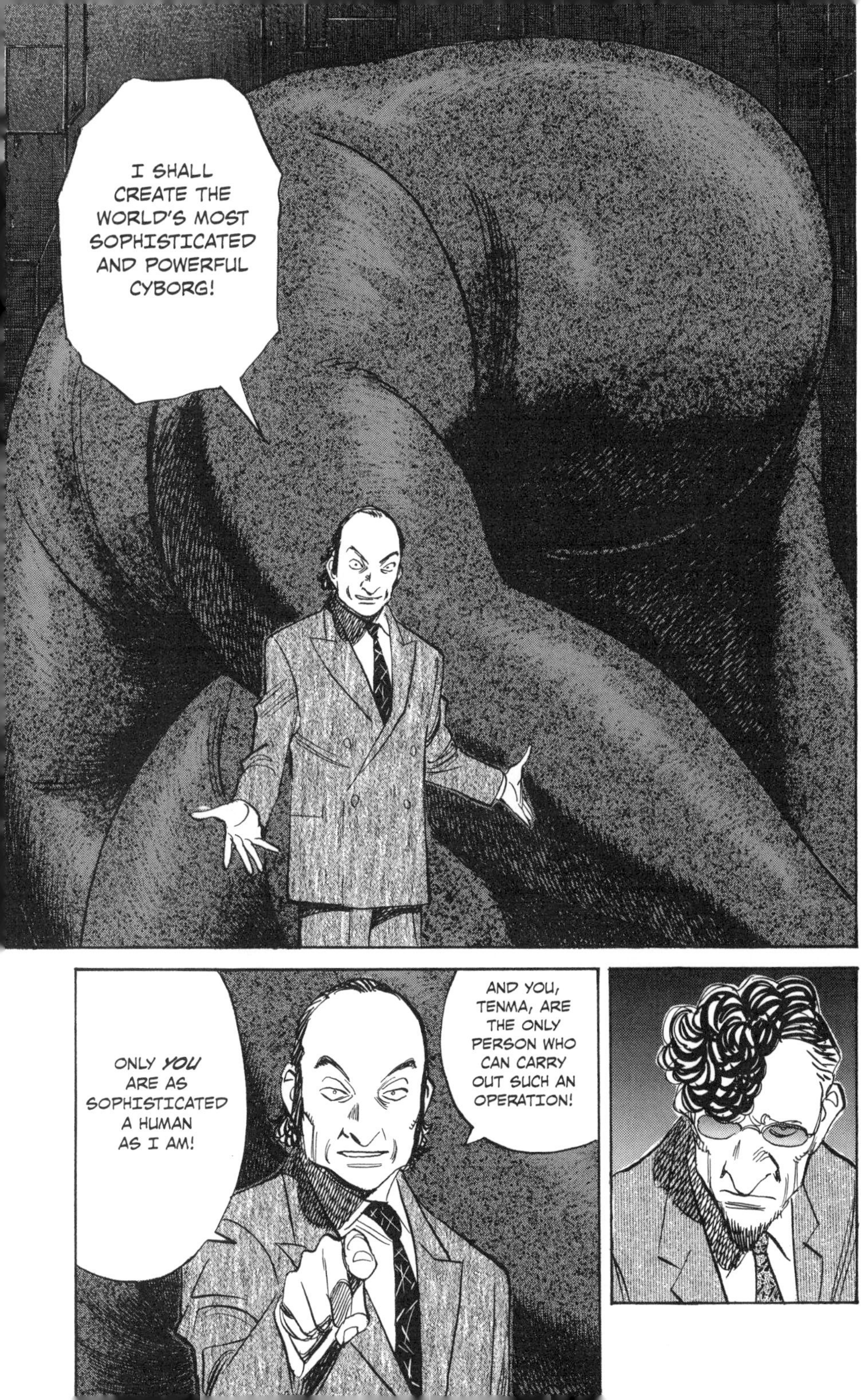
I SHALL CREATE THE WORLD'S MOST SOPHISTICATED AND POWERFUL CYBORG!
AND YOU, TENMA, ARE THE ONLY PERSON WHO CAN CARRY OUT SUCH AN OPERATION!
ONLY *YOU* ARE AS SOPHISTICATED A HUMAN AS I AM!

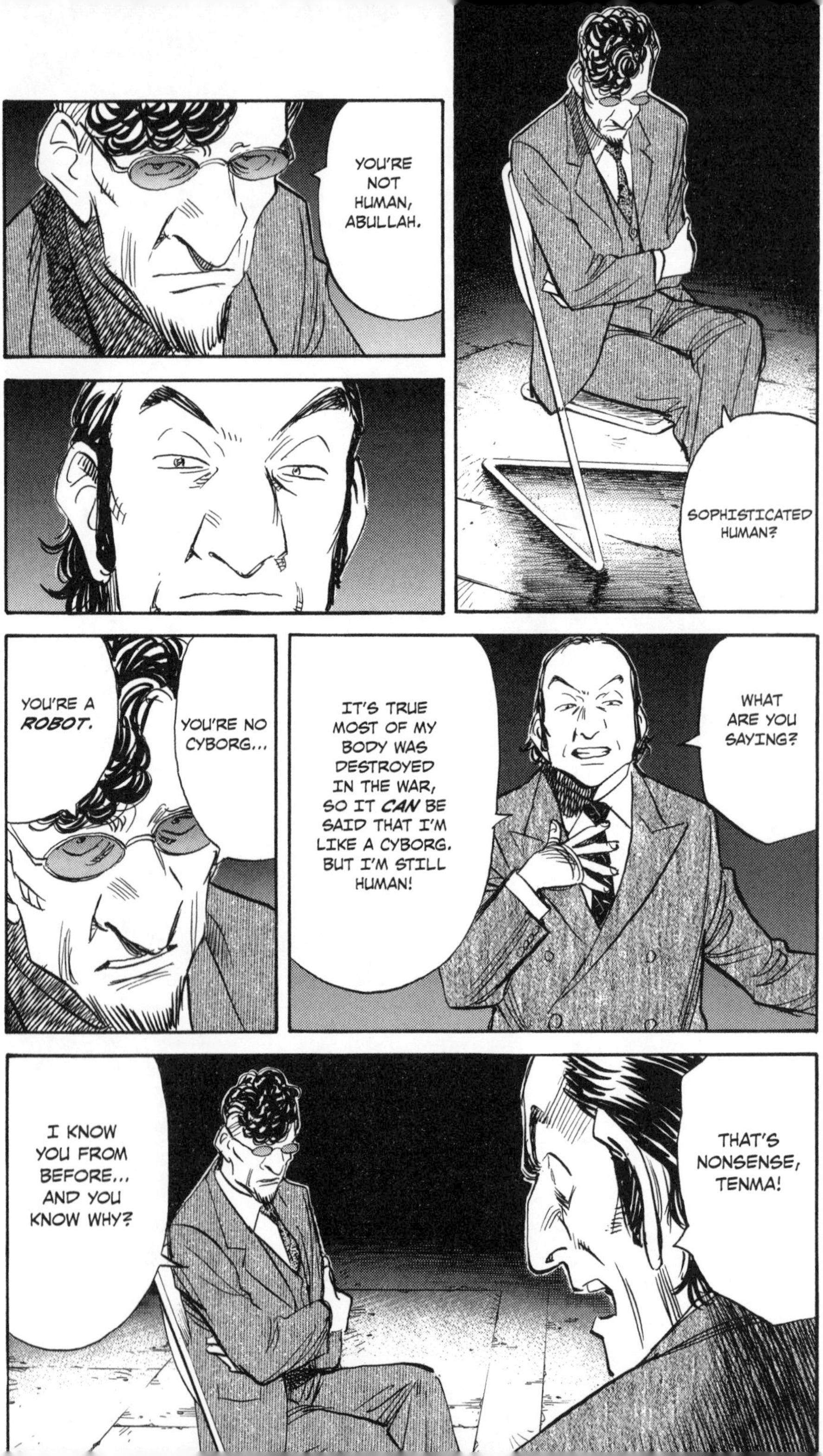
SOPHISTICATED HUMAN?
YOU'RE NOT HUMAN, ABULLAH.
WHAT ARE YOU SAYING?
IT'S TRUE MOST OF MY BODY WAS DESTROYED IN THE WAR, SO IT *CAN* BE SAID THAT I'M LIKE A CYBORG. BUT I'M STILL HUMAN!
YOU'RE NO CYBORG...
YOU'RE A *ROBOT*.
THAT'S NONSENSE, TENMA!
I KNOW YOU FROM BEFORE... AND YOU KNOW WHY?

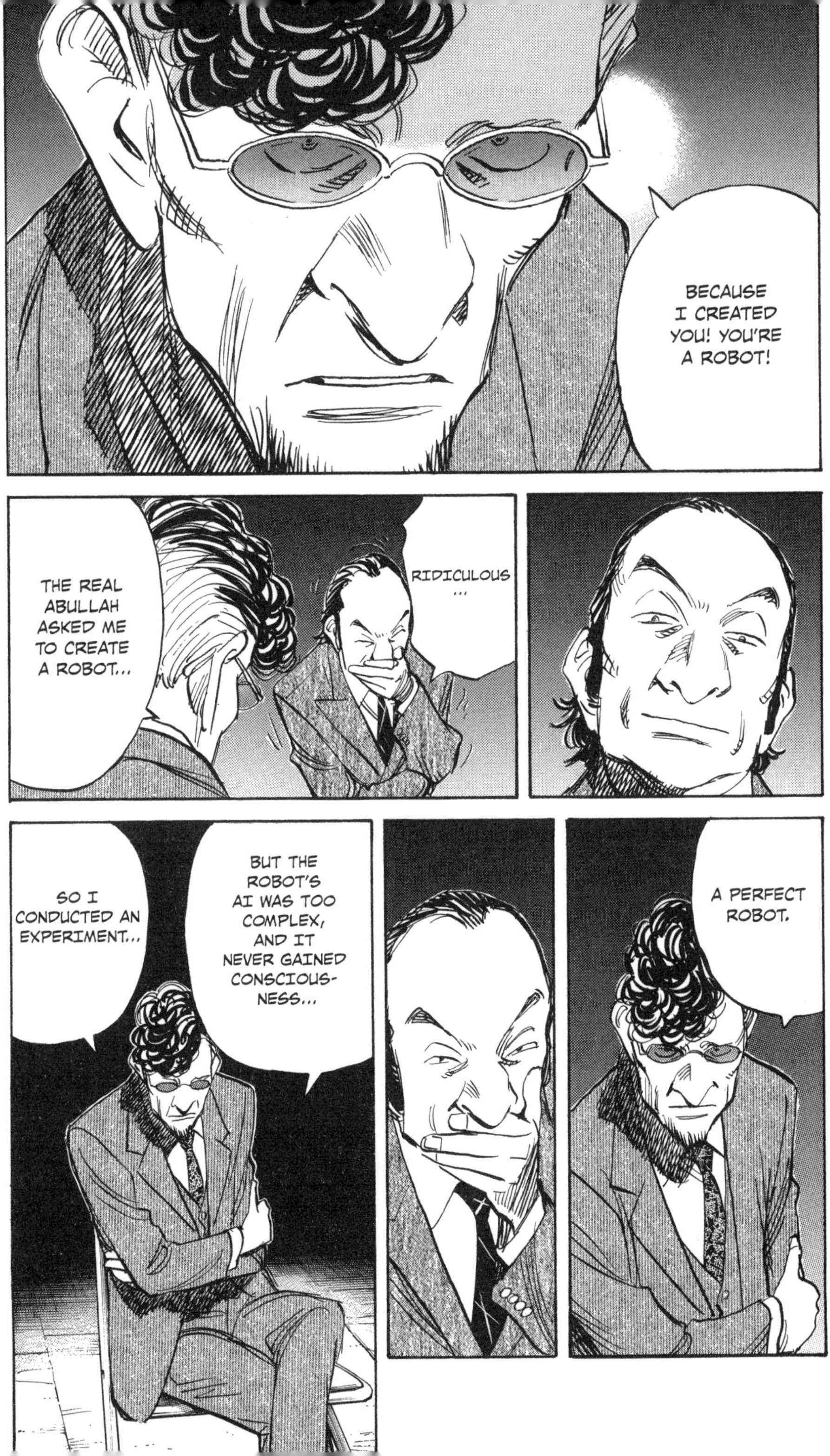
BECAUSE I CREATED YOU! YOU'RE A ROBOT!
RIDICULOUS...
THE REAL ABULLAH ASKED ME TO CREATE A ROBOT...
A PERFECT ROBOT.
BUT THE ROBOT'S AI WAS TOO COMPLEX, AND IT NEVER GAINED CONSCIOUS-NESS...
SO I CONDUCTED AN EXPERIMENT...

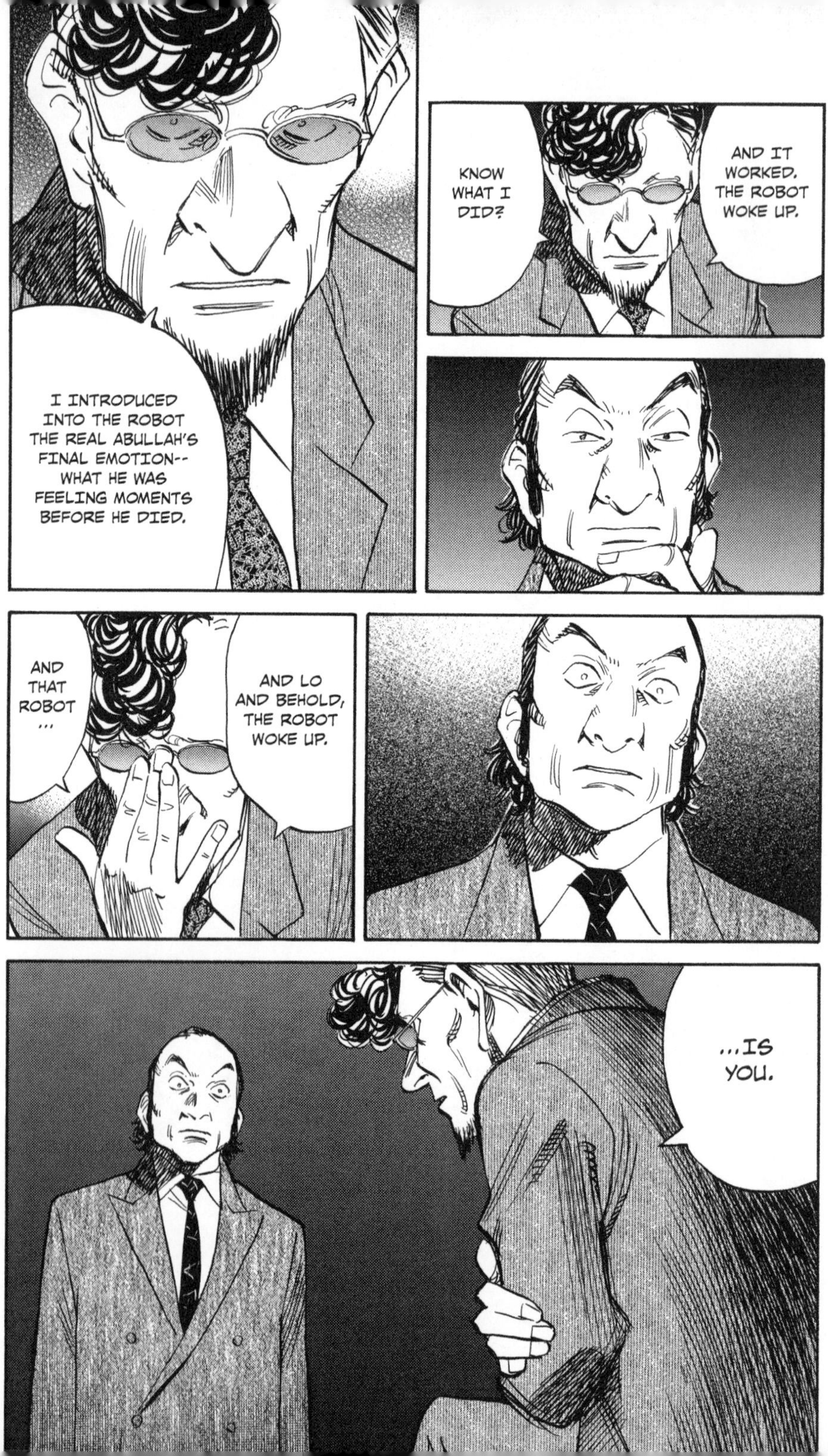
AND IT WORKED. THE ROBOT WOKE UP.
KNOW WHAT I DID?
I INTRODUCED INTO THE ROBOT THE REAL ABULLAH'S FINAL EMOTION--WHAT HE WAS FEELING MOMENTS BEFORE HE DIED.
AND LO AND BEHOLD, THE ROBOT WOKE UP.
AND THAT ROBOT ...
...IS YOU.

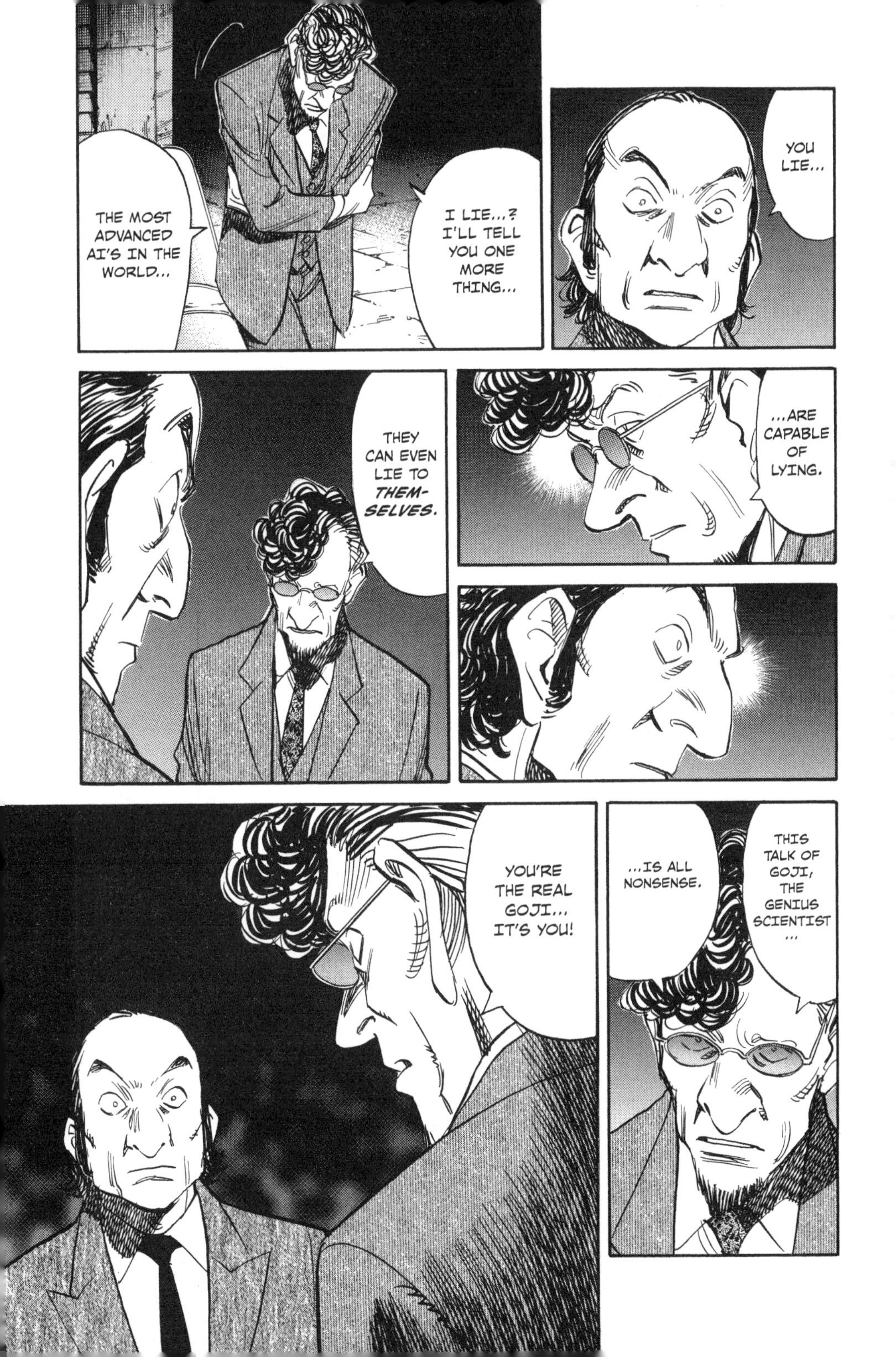
YOU LIE...
I LIE...? I'LL TELL YOU ONE MORE THING...
THE MOST ADVANCED AI'S IN THE WORLD...
...ARE CAPABLE OF LYING.
THEY CAN EVEN LIE TO *THEMSELVES*.
THIS TALK OF GOJI, THE GENIUS SCIENTIST...
...IS ALL NONSENSE.
YOU'RE THE REAL GOJI... IT'S YOU!

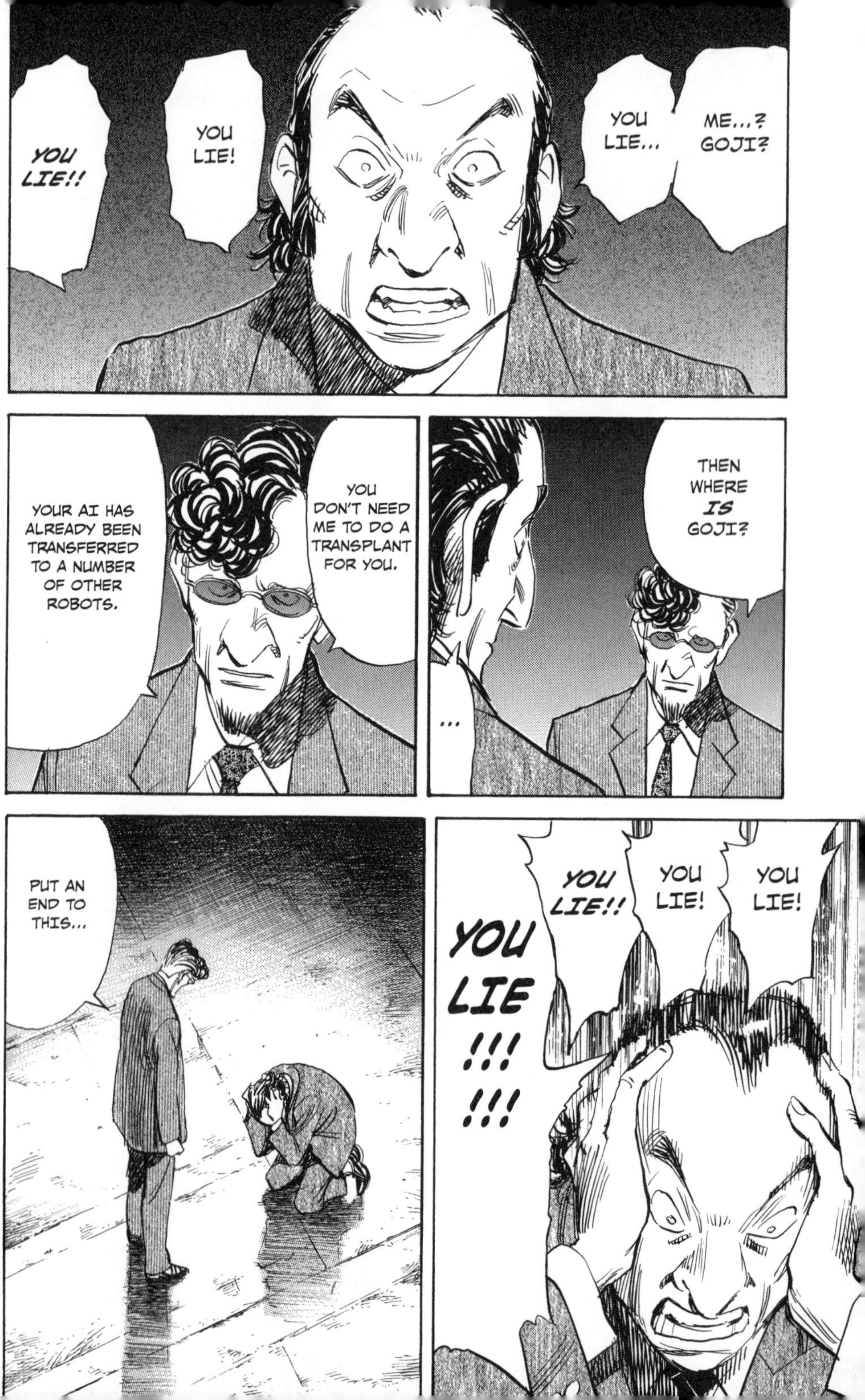
ME...? GOJI?
YOU LIE...
YOU LIE!
YOU LIE!!
THEN WHERE IS GOJI?
...
YOU DON'T NEED ME TO DO A TRANSPLANT FOR YOU.
YOUR AI HAS ALREADY BEEN TRANSFERRED TO A NUMBER OF OTHER ROBOTS.
YOU LIE!
YOU LIE!
YOU LIE!!
YOU LIE !!! !!!
PUT AN END TO THIS...

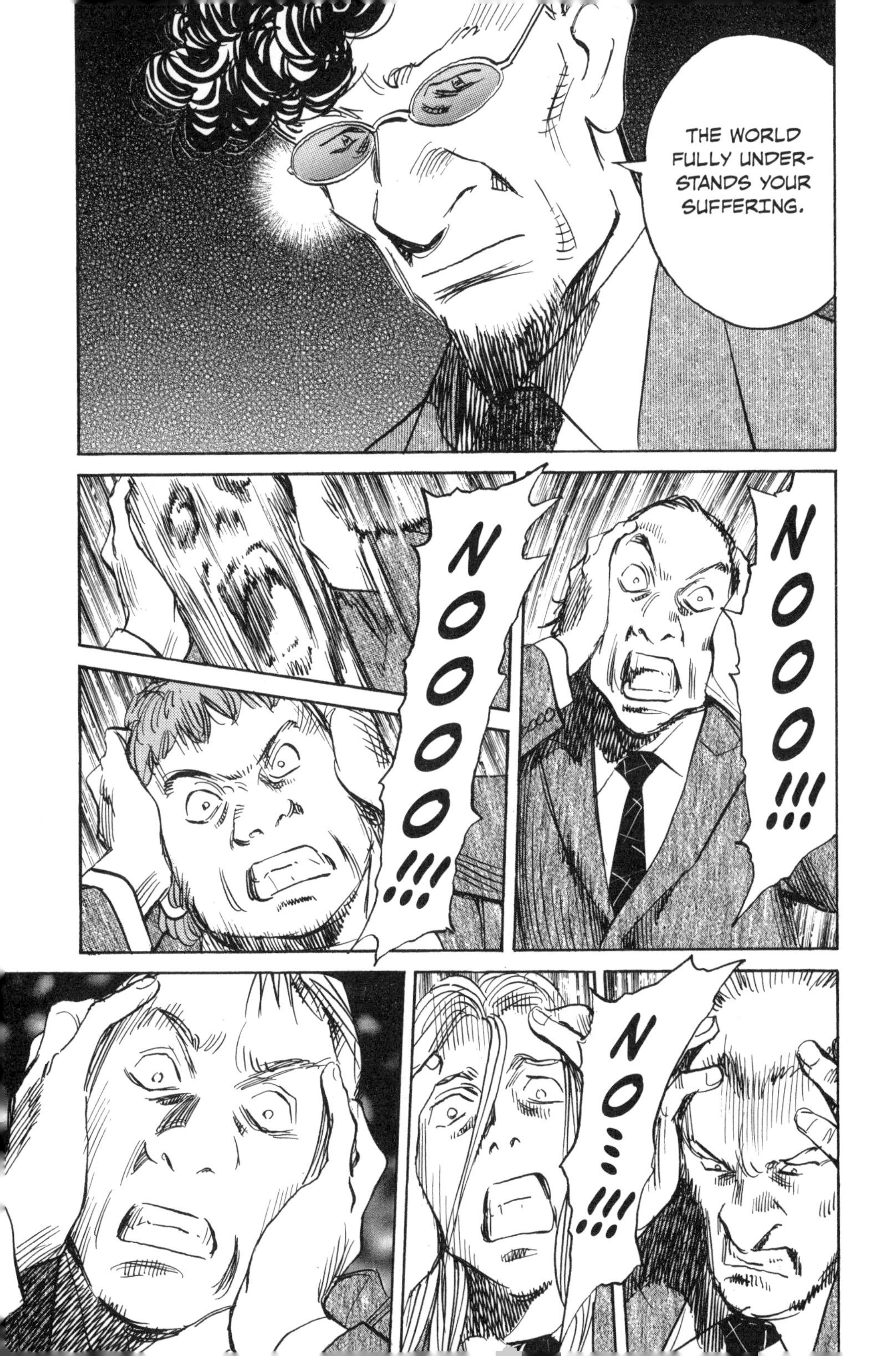
THE WORLD FULLY UNDER-STANDS YOUR SUFFERING.
NOOOO!!!
NOOOO!!!
NO...!!!

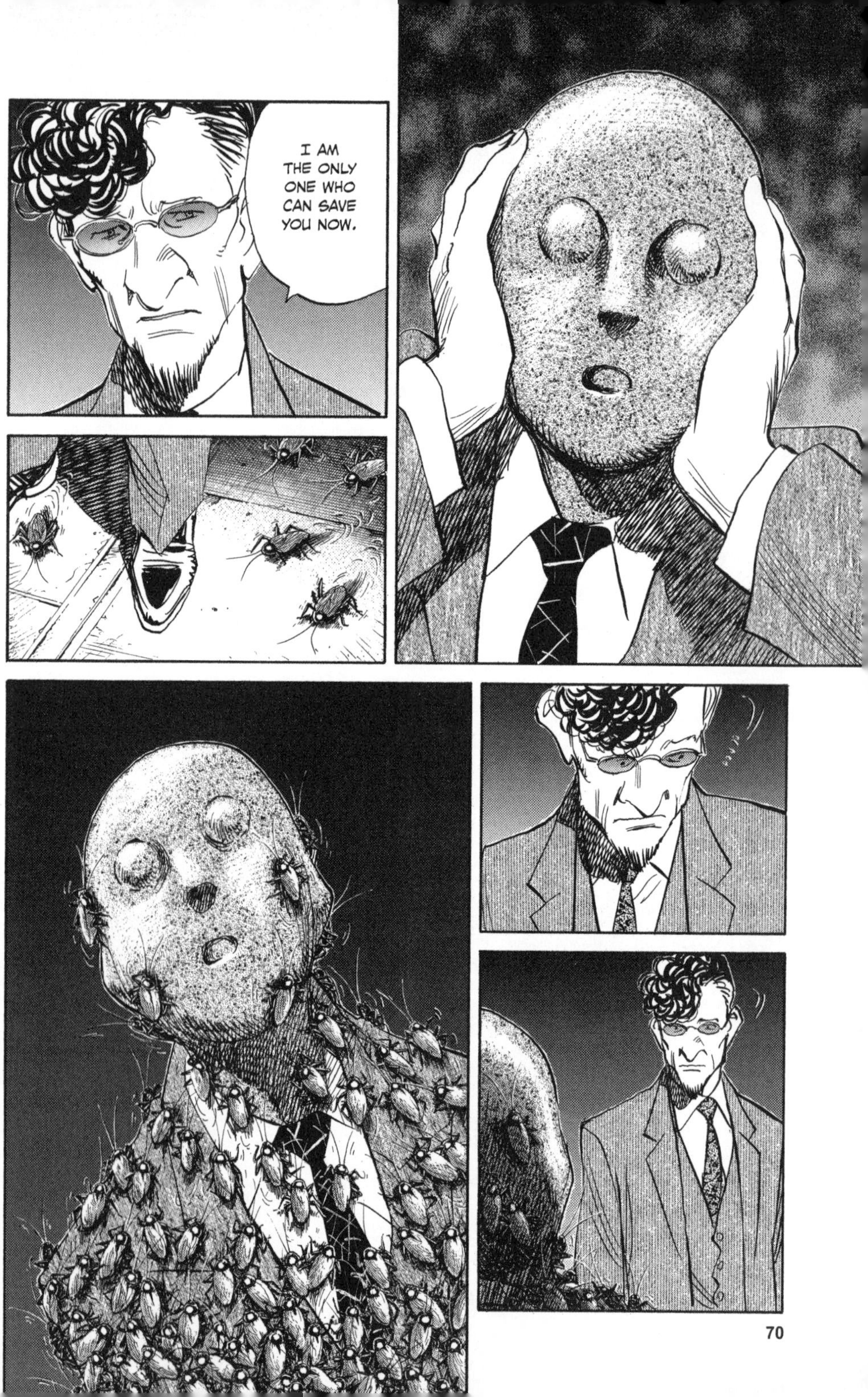
I AM THE ONLY ONE WHO CAN SAVE YOU NOW.

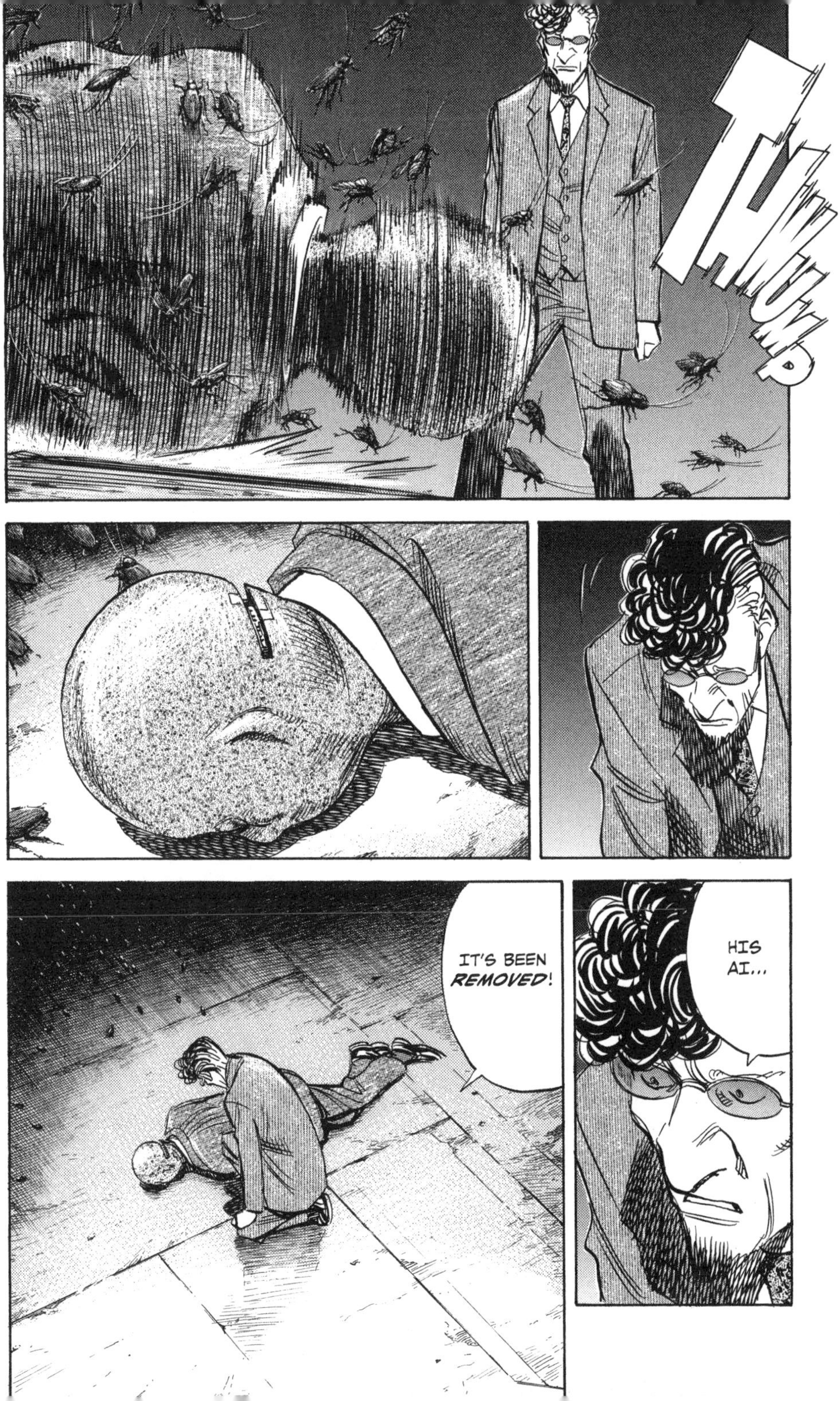
THUMP
HIS AI...
IT'S BEEN *REMOVED*!

ARTIFICIAL INTELLIGENCE
CORRECTIONAL FACILITY,
GERMANY

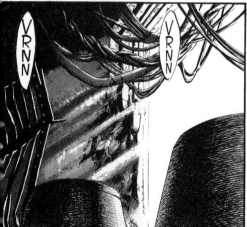

STOP! YOU CAN'T ...!!

HEY! YOU THERE!!

WELL, WELL...
BZZ
IT'S BEEN A LONG TIME...
I'M SO PLEASED.
KRK
BZZT
BZZ
TO MEET MY OLD FRIEND AGAIN.
BZZT
COME A BIT CLOSER, WON'T YOU...?
BZZT
BZZRT

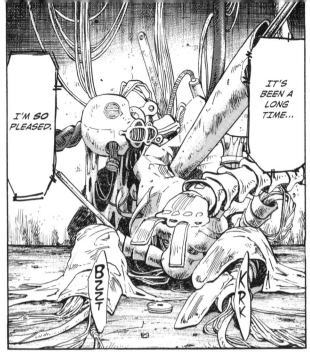

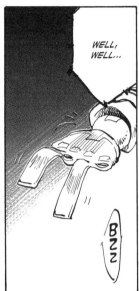

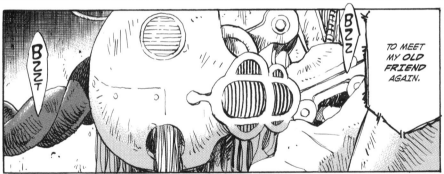

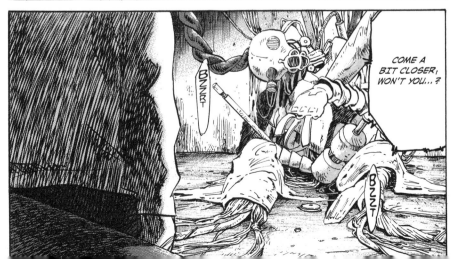

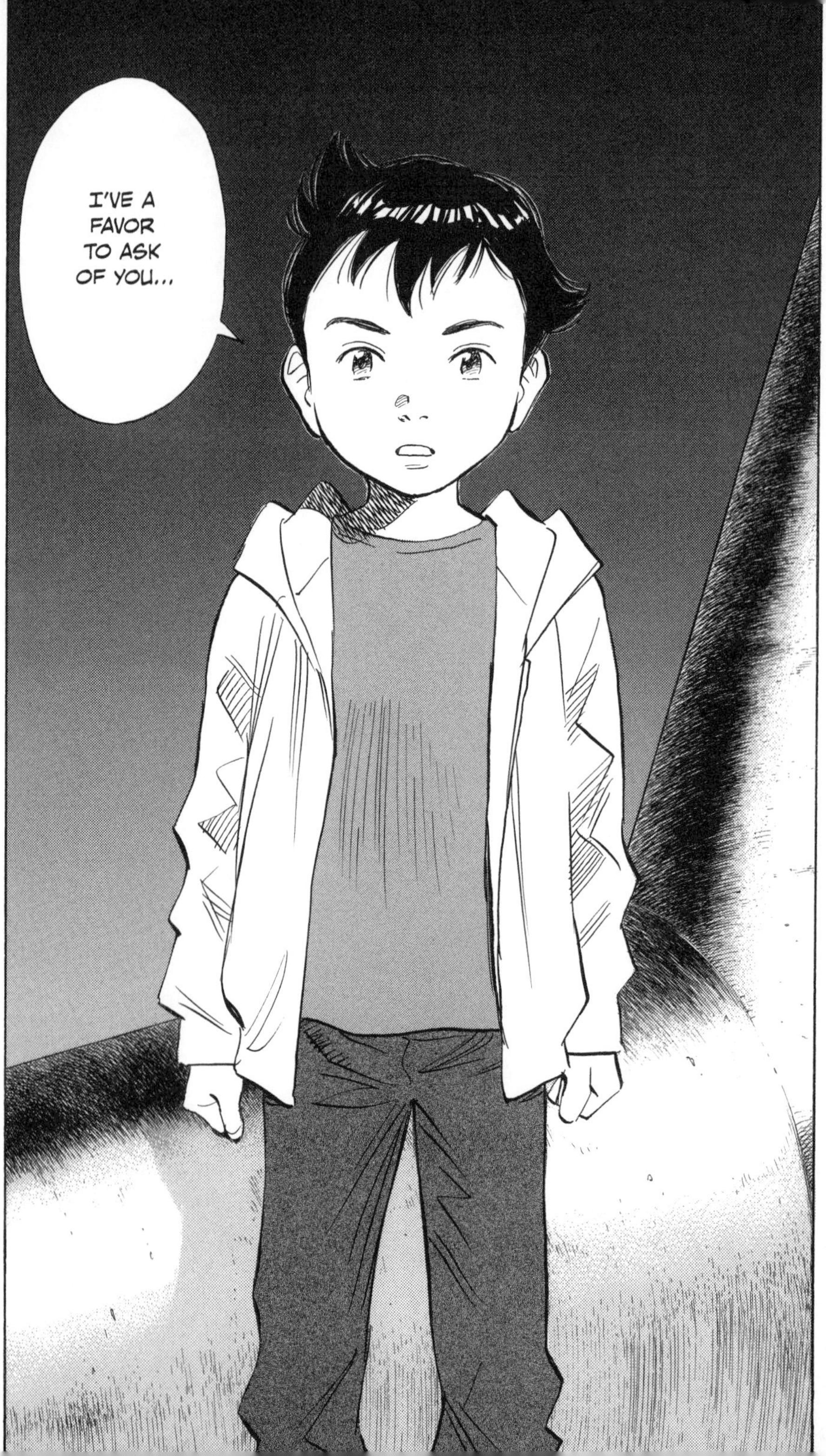
I'VE A FAVOR TO ASK OF YOU...

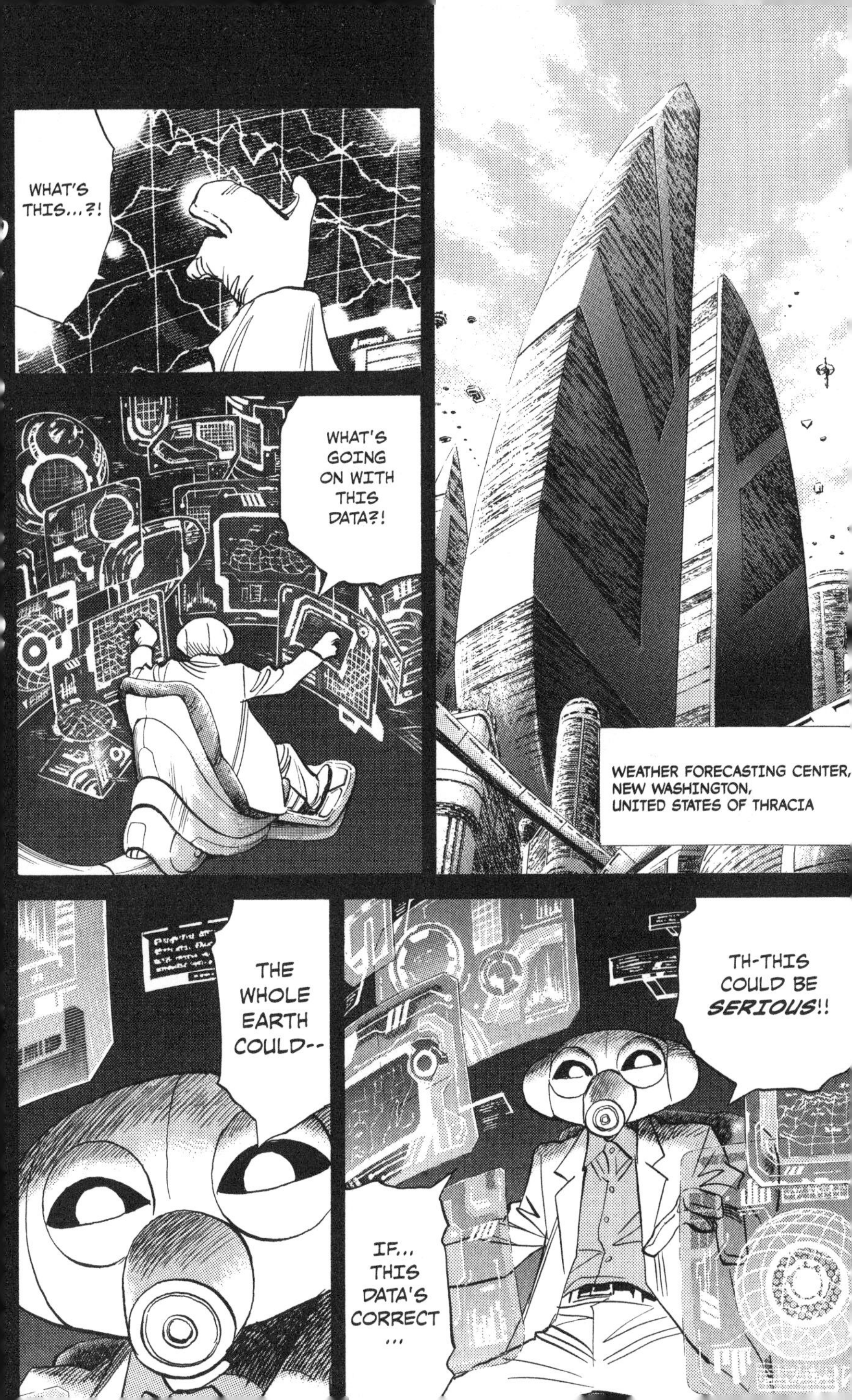
WEATHER FORECASTING CENTER, NEW WASHINGTON, UNITED STATES OF THRACIA
WHAT'S THIS...?!
WHAT'S GOING ON WITH THIS DATA?!
TH-THIS COULD BE *SERIOUS*!!
IF... THIS DATA'S CORRECT...
THE WHOLE EARTH COULD--

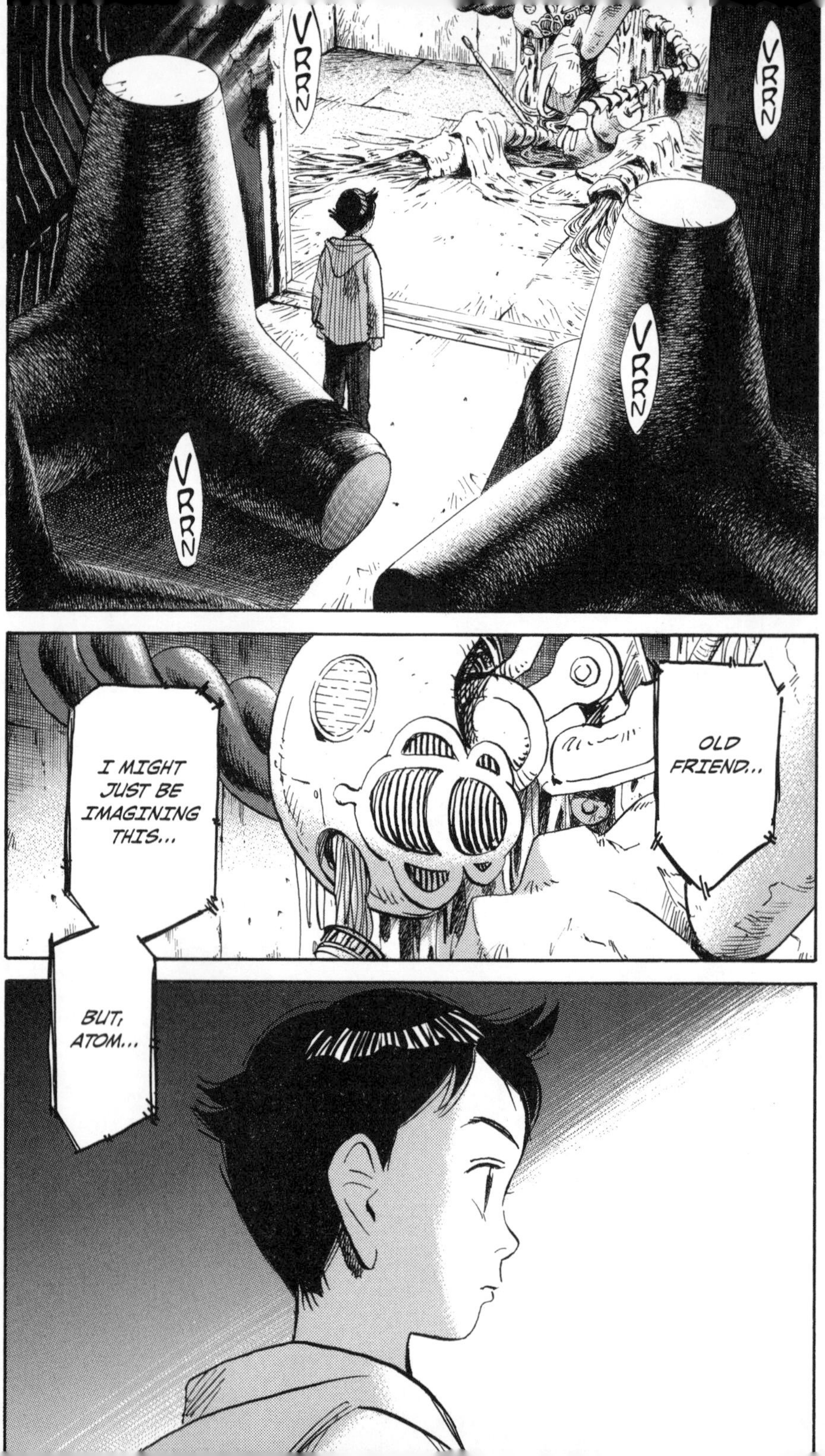
VRRN
VRRN
VRRN
VRRN
OLD FRIEND...
I MIGHT JUST BE IMAGINING THIS...
BUT, ATOM...

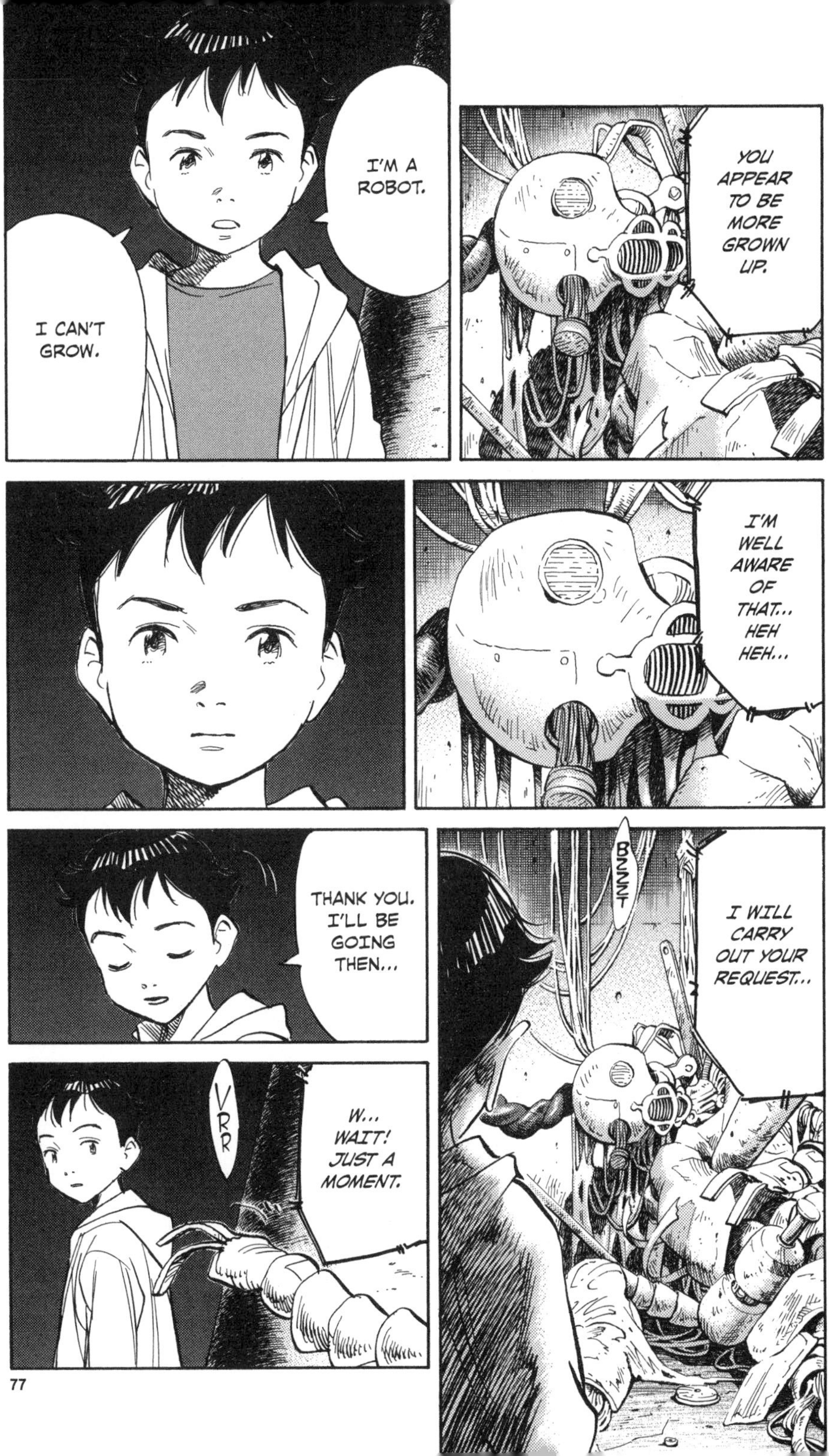
YOU APPEAR TO BE MORE GROWN UP.
I'M A ROBOT.
I CAN'T GROW.
I'M WELL AWARE OF THAT... HEH HEH...
BZZZT
I WILL CARRY OUT YOUR REQUEST...
THANK YOU. I'LL BE GOING THEN...
VRR
W... WAIT! JUST A MOMENT.

VRR
LET ME TOUCH YOU...
VRR
AH...

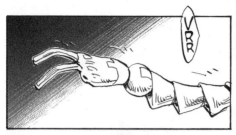

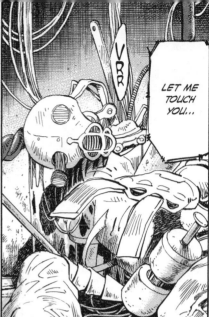

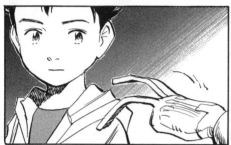

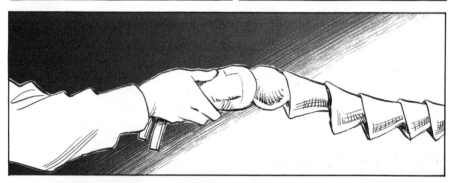

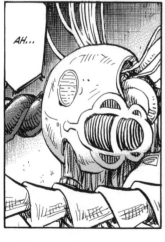

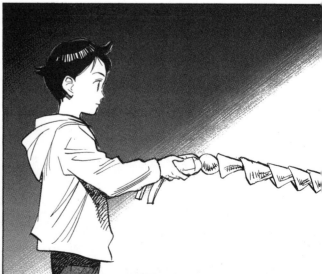

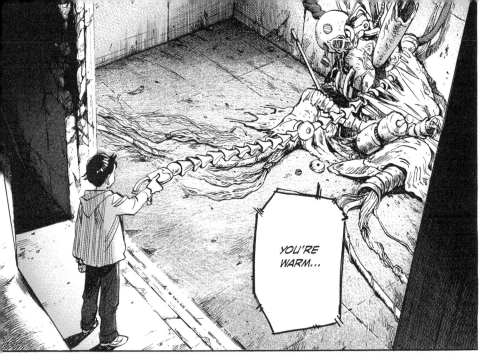

YOU'RE WARM...

HOW SHOULD I SAY IT...

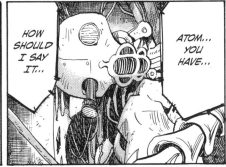

ATOM... YOU HAVE...

LIKE... A... HEART...

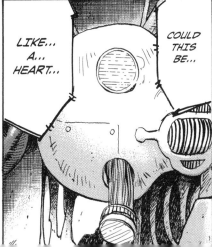

COULD THIS BE...

OKAY, I'M COUNTING ON YOU...

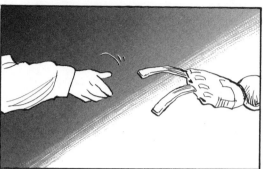

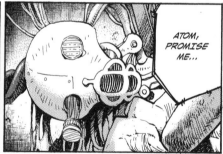

ATOM, PROMISE ME...

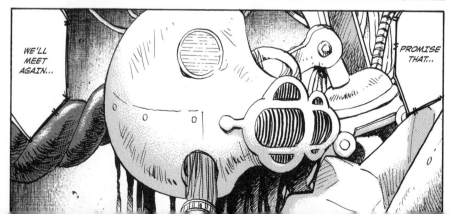

WE'LL MEET AGAIN...

PROMISE THAT...

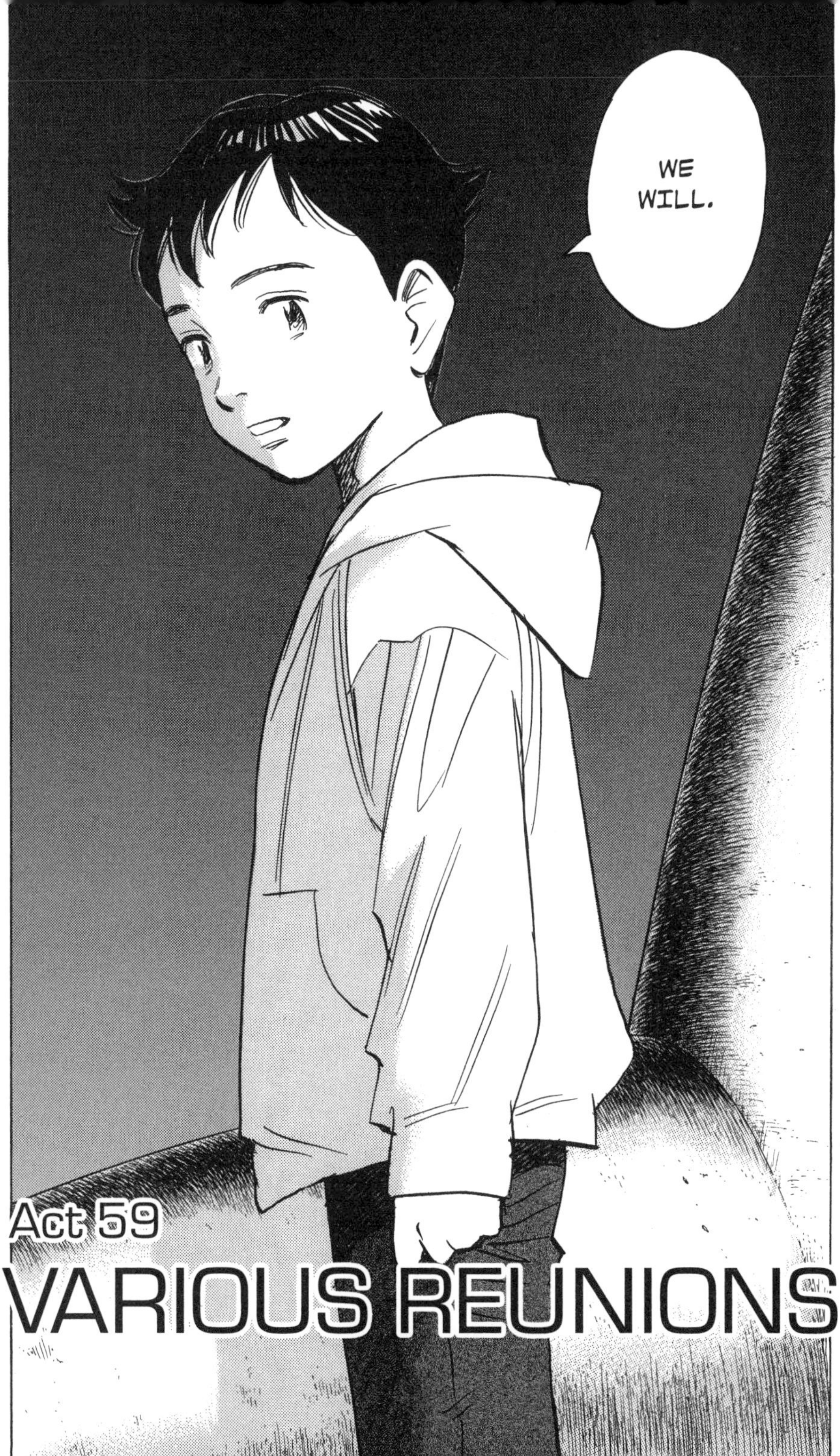

Act 59
VARIOUS REUNIONS

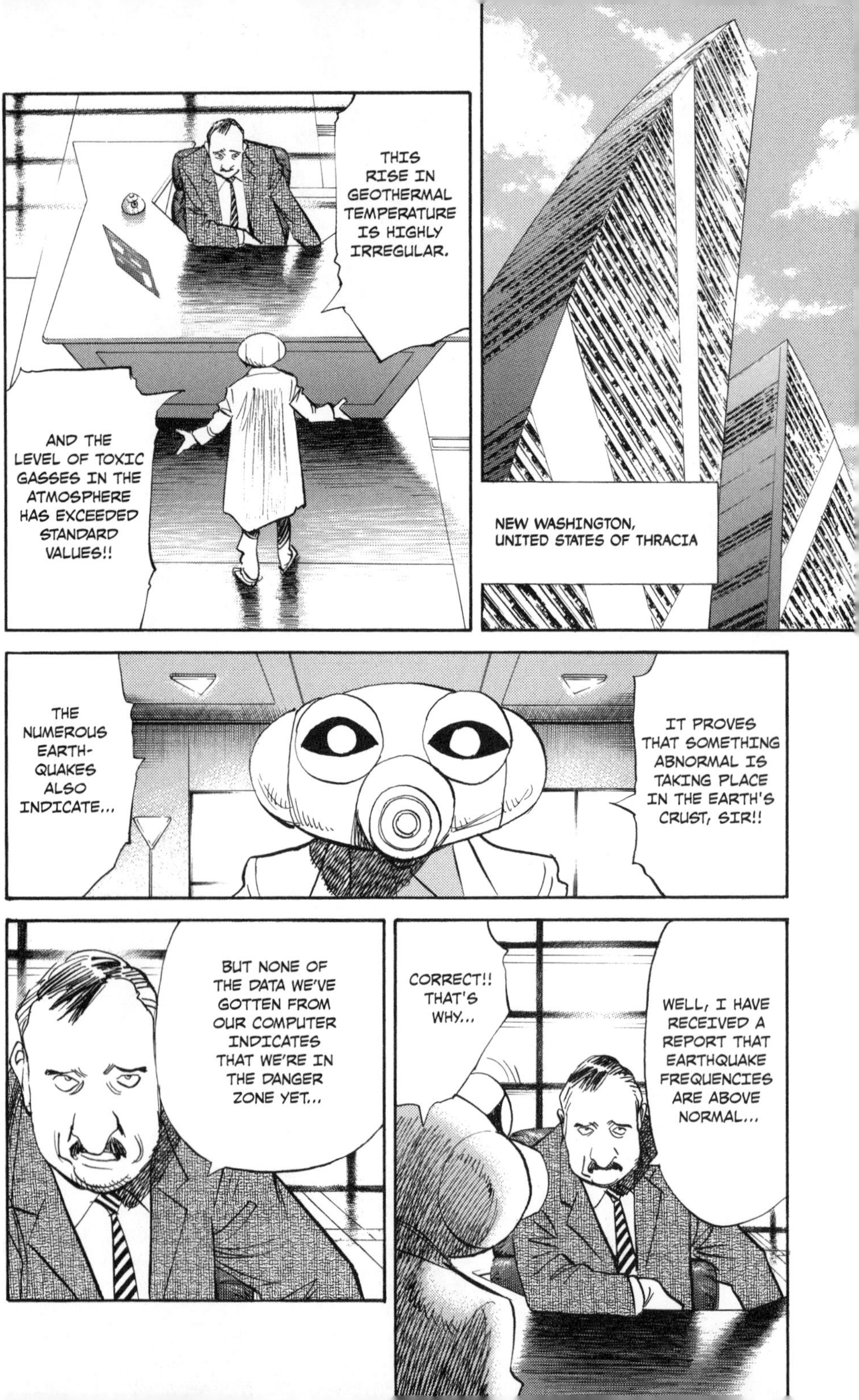
NEW WASHINGTON, UNITED STATES OF THRACIA
THIS RISE IN GEOTHERMAL TEMPERATURE IS HIGHLY IRREGULAR.
AND THE LEVEL OF TOXIC GASSES IN THE ATMOSPHERE HAS EXCEEDED STANDARD VALUES!!
IT PROVES THAT SOMETHING ABNORMAL IS TAKING PLACE IN THE EARTH'S CRUST, SIR!!
THE NUMEROUS EARTH-QUAKES ALSO INDICATE...
WELL, I HAVE RECEIVED A REPORT THAT EARTHQUAKE FREQUENCIES ARE ABOVE NORMAL...
CORRECT!! THAT'S WHY...
BUT NONE OF THE DATA WE'VE GOTTEN FROM OUR COMPUTER INDICATES THAT WE'RE IN THE DANGER ZONE YET...

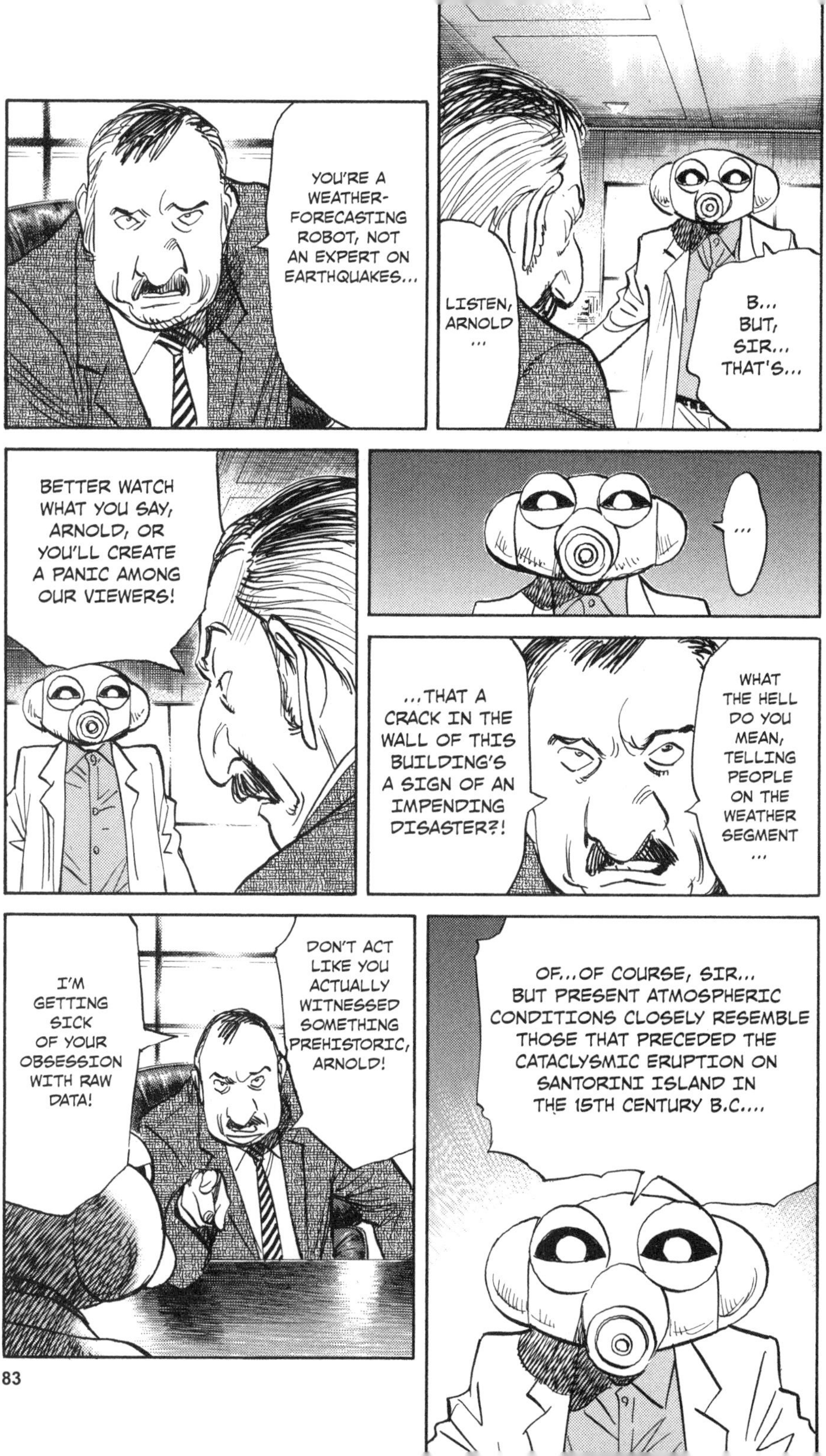
B... BUT, SIR... THAT'S...
LISTEN, ARNOLD...
YOU'RE A WEATHER-FORECASTING ROBOT, NOT AN EXPERT ON EARTHQUAKES...
...
WHAT THE HELL DO YOU MEAN, TELLING PEOPLE ON THE WEATHER SEGMENT...
...THAT A CRACK IN THE WALL OF THIS BUILDING'S A SIGN OF AN IMPENDING DISASTER?!
BETTER WATCH WHAT YOU SAY, ARNOLD, OR YOU'LL CREATE A PANIC AMONG OUR VIEWERS!
OF...OF COURSE, SIR... BUT PRESENT ATMOSPHERIC CONDITIONS CLOSELY RESEMBLE THOSE THAT PRECEDED THE CATACLYSMIC ERUPTION ON SANTORINI ISLAND IN THE 15TH CENTURY B.C....
DON'T ACT LIKE YOU ACTUALLY WITNESSED SOMETHING PREHISTORIC, ARNOLD!
I'M GETTING SICK OF YOUR OBSESSION WITH RAW DATA!

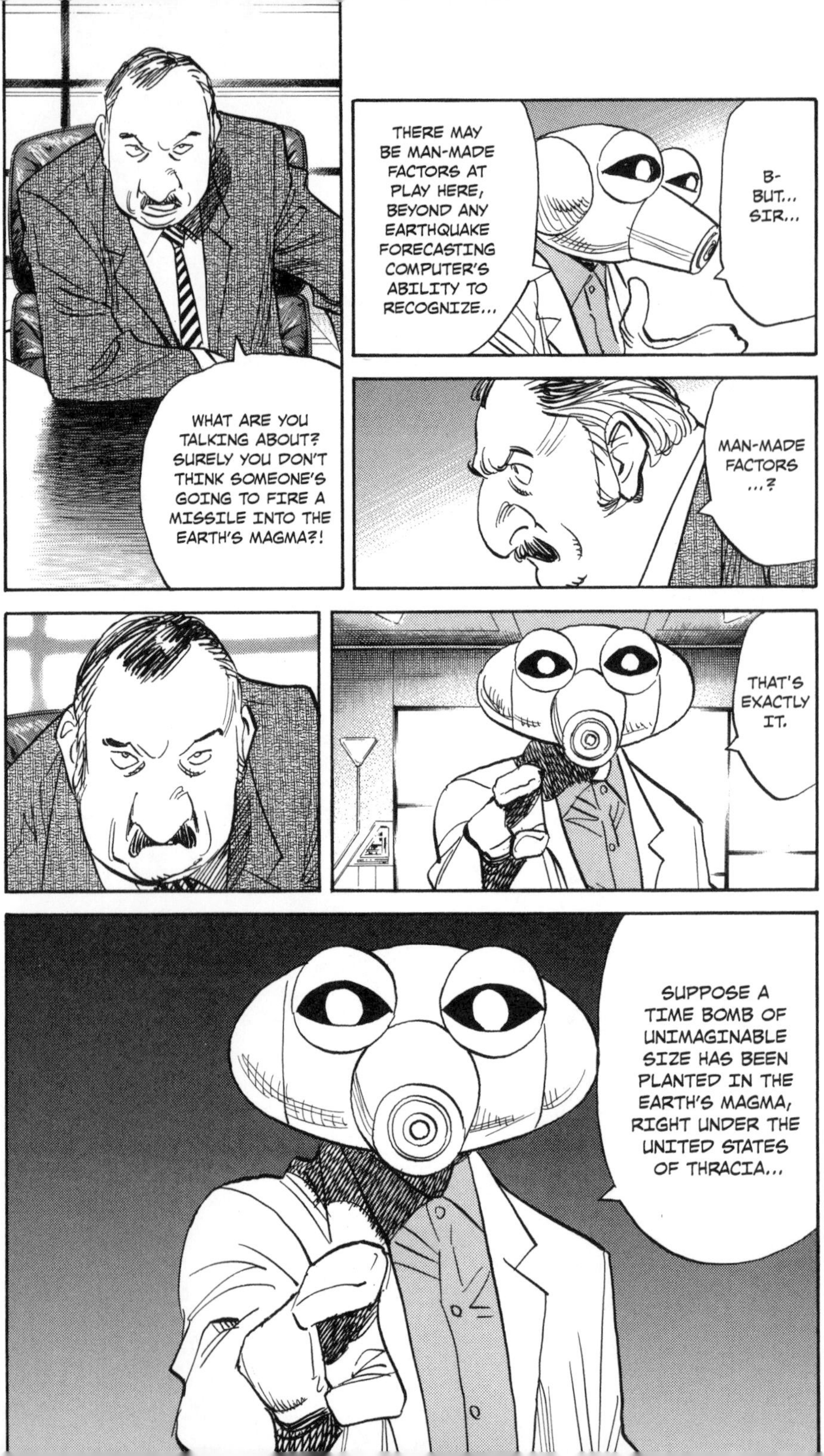
B- BUT... SIR...
THERE MAY BE MAN-MADE FACTORS AT PLAY HERE, BEYOND ANY EARTHQUAKE FORECASTING COMPUTER'S ABILITY TO RECOGNIZE...
MAN-MADE FACTORS ...?
WHAT ARE YOU TALKING ABOUT? SURELY YOU DON'T THINK SOMEONE'S GOING TO FIRE A MISSILE INTO THE EARTH'S MAGMA?!
THAT'S EXACTLY IT.
SUPPOSE A TIME BOMB OF UNIMAGINABLE SIZE HAS BEEN PLANTED IN THE EARTH'S MAGMA, RIGHT UNDER THE UNITED STATES OF THRACIA...

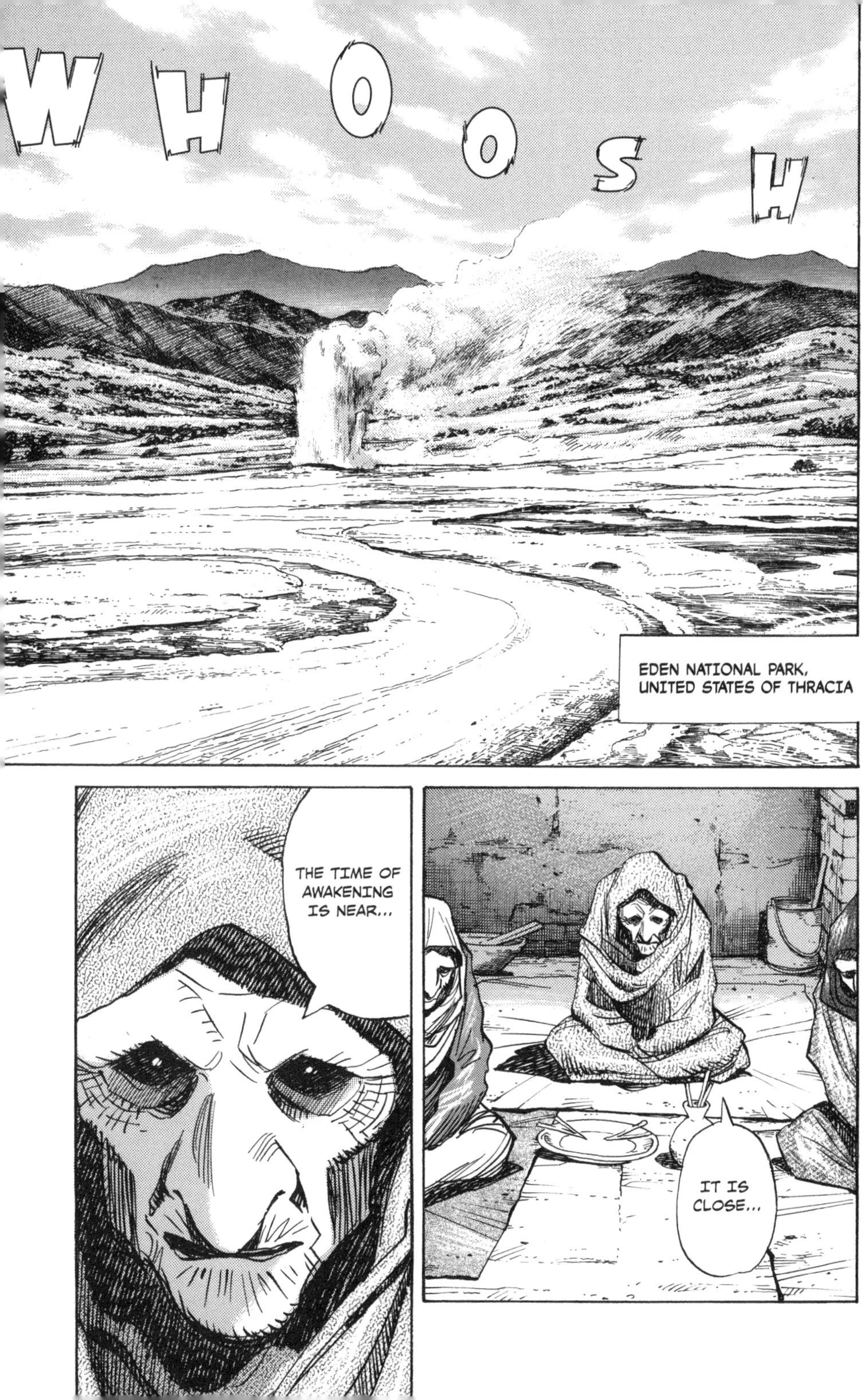
WHOOSH
EDEN NATIONAL PARK, UNITED STATES OF THRACIA
IT IS CLOSE...
THE TIME OF AWAKENING IS NEAR...

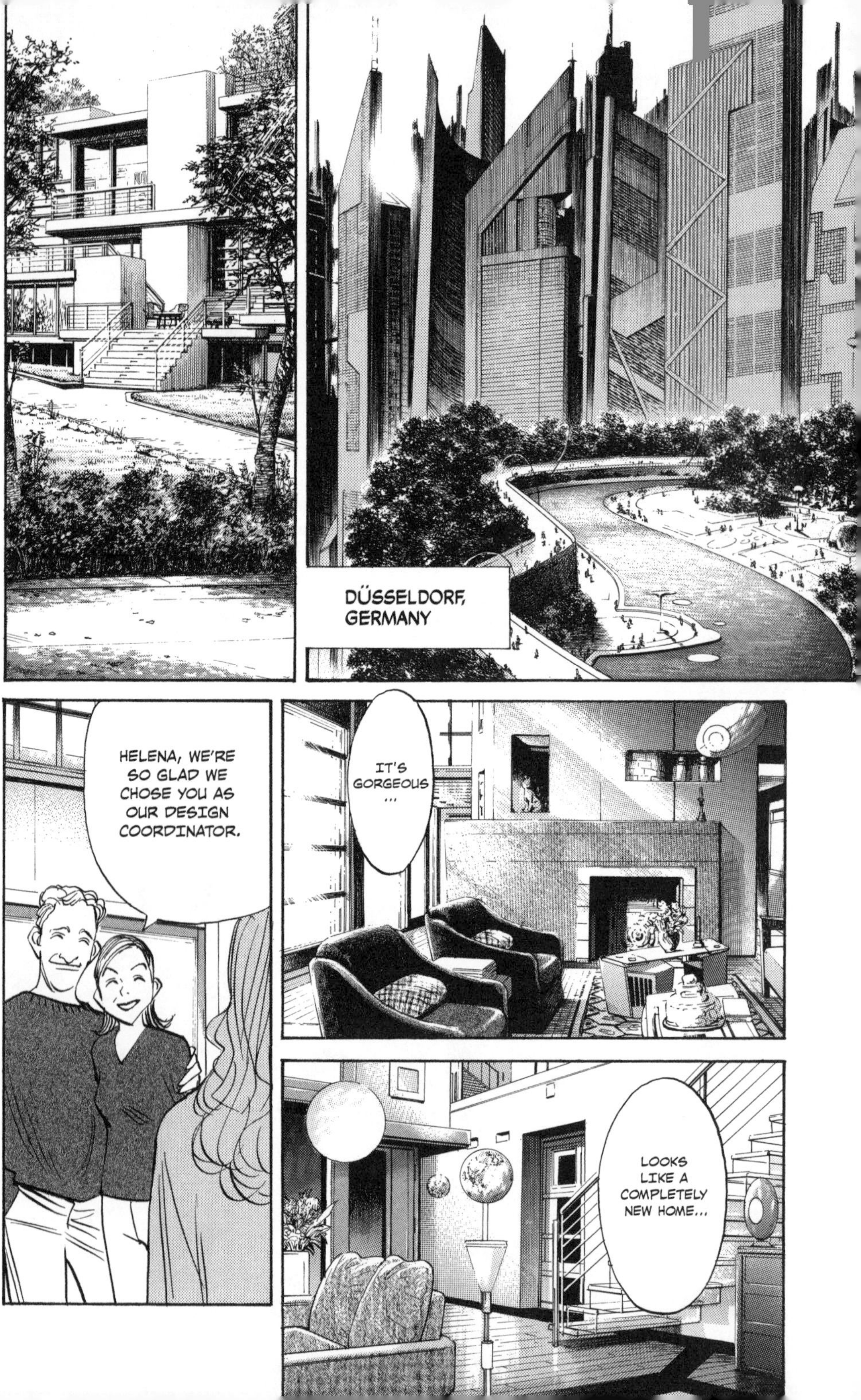
DÜSSELDORF, GERMANY
IT'S GORGEOUS ...
LOOKS LIKE A COMPLETELY NEW HOME...
HELENA, WE'RE SO GLAD WE CHOSE YOU AS OUR DESIGN COORDINATOR.

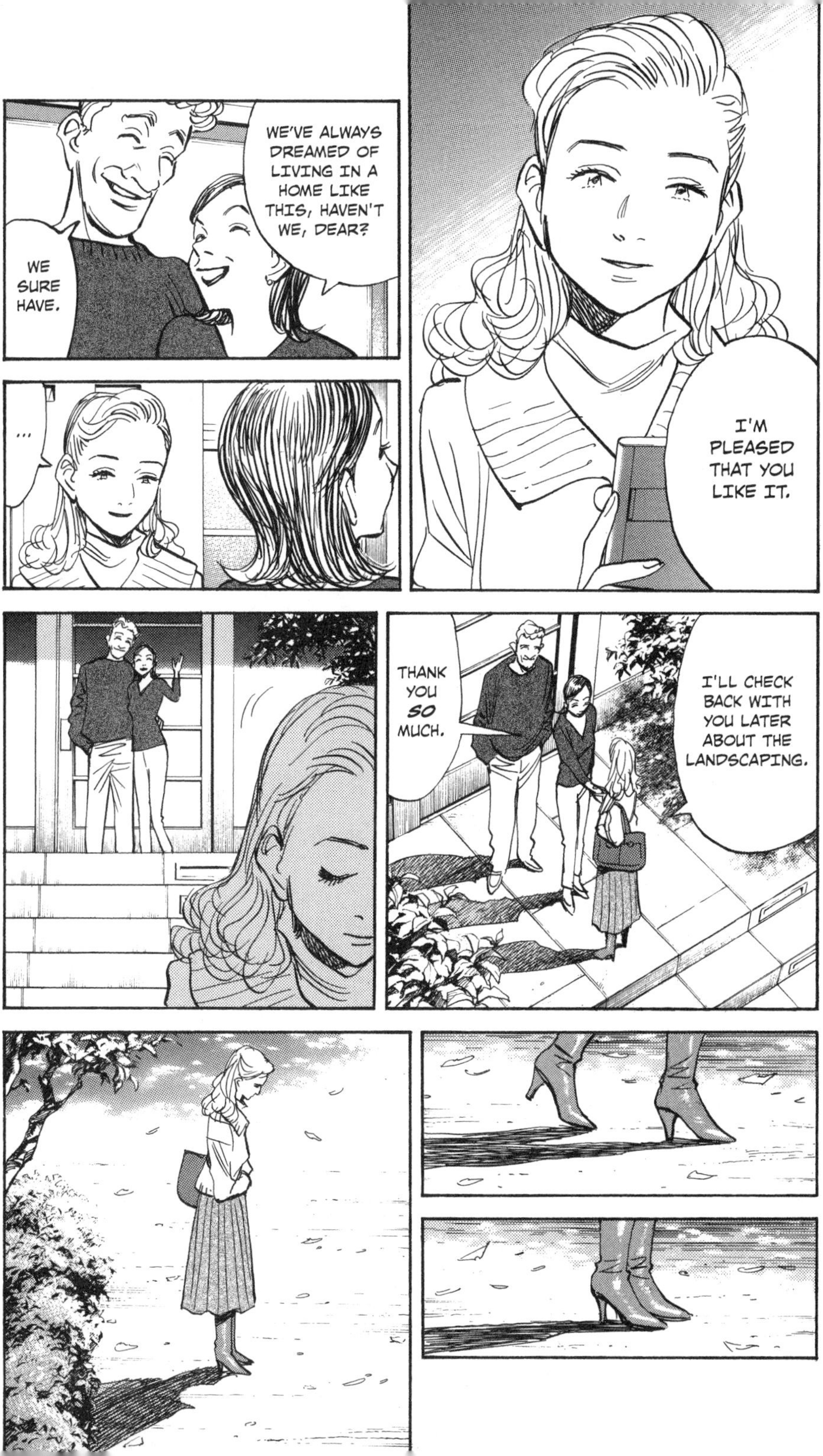
I'M PLEASED THAT YOU LIKE IT.
WE'VE ALWAYS DREAMED OF LIVING IN A HOME LIKE THIS, HAVEN'T WE, DEAR?
WE SURE HAVE.
...
I'LL CHECK BACK WITH YOU LATER ABOUT THE LANDSCAPING.
THANK YOU *SO* MUCH.

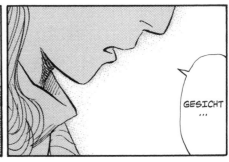

GESICHT
...

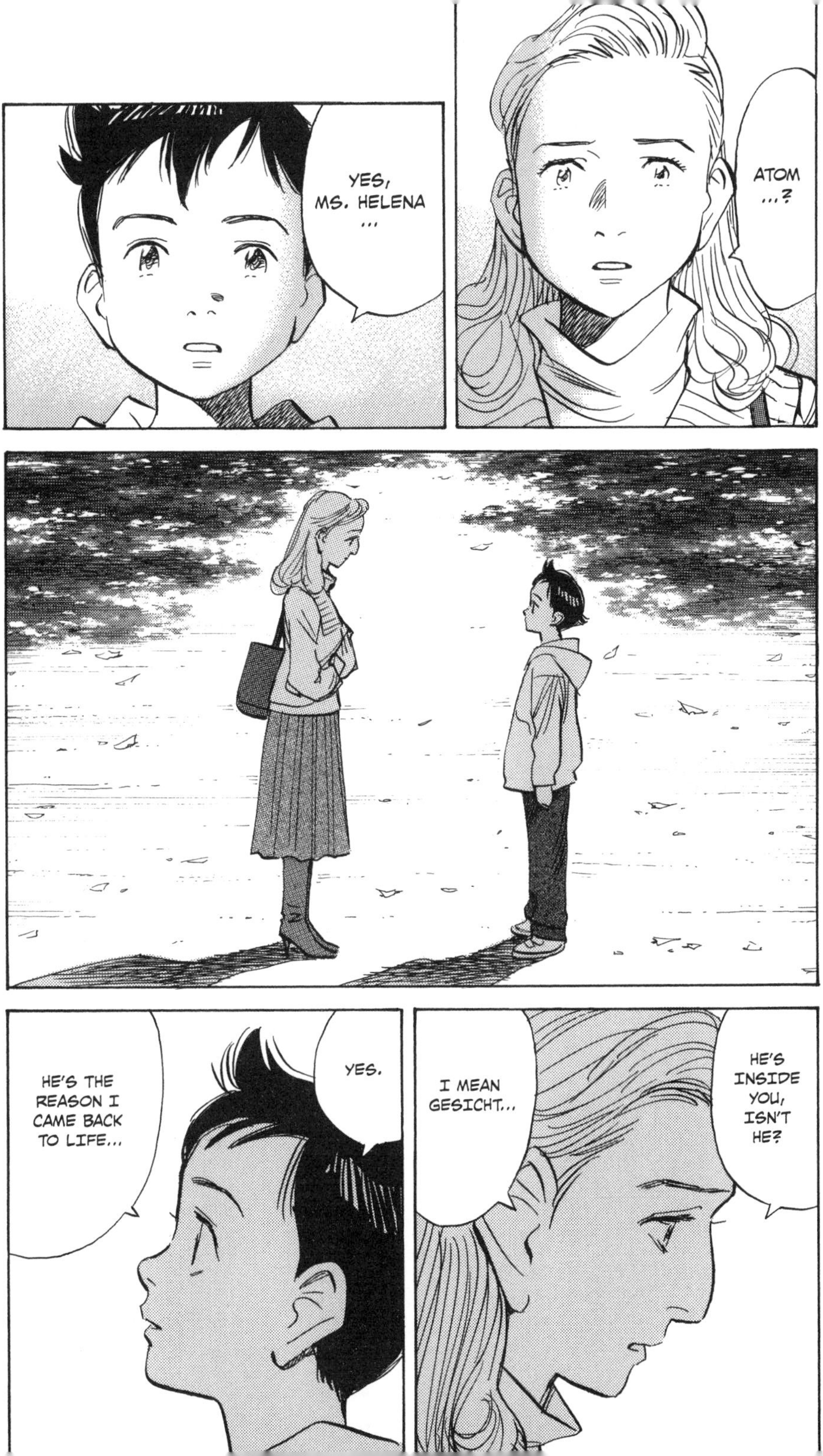
ATOM ...?
YES, MS. HELENA ...
HE'S INSIDE YOU, ISN'T HE?
I MEAN GESICHT...
YES.
HE'S THE REASON I CAME BACK TO LIFE...

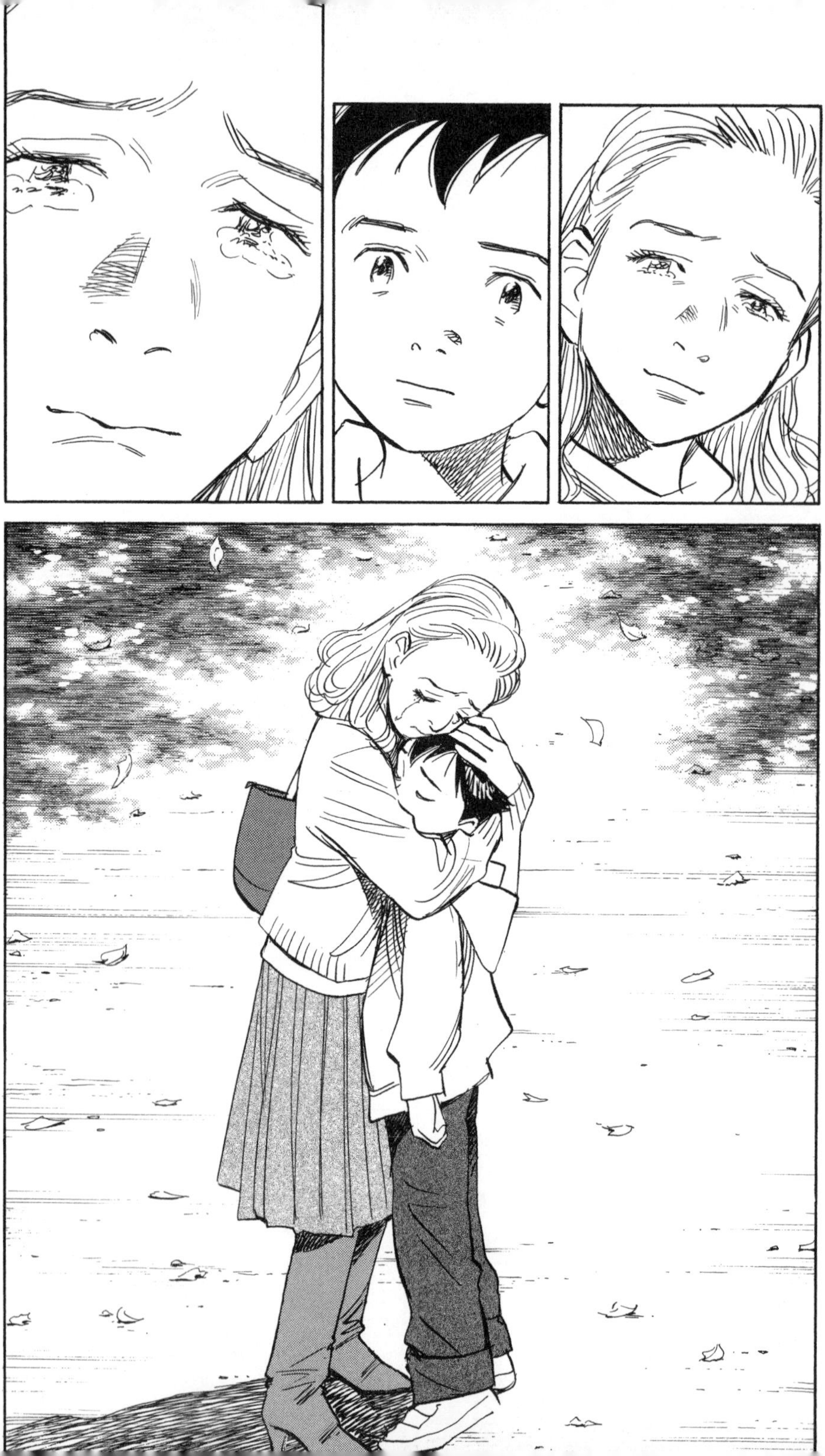

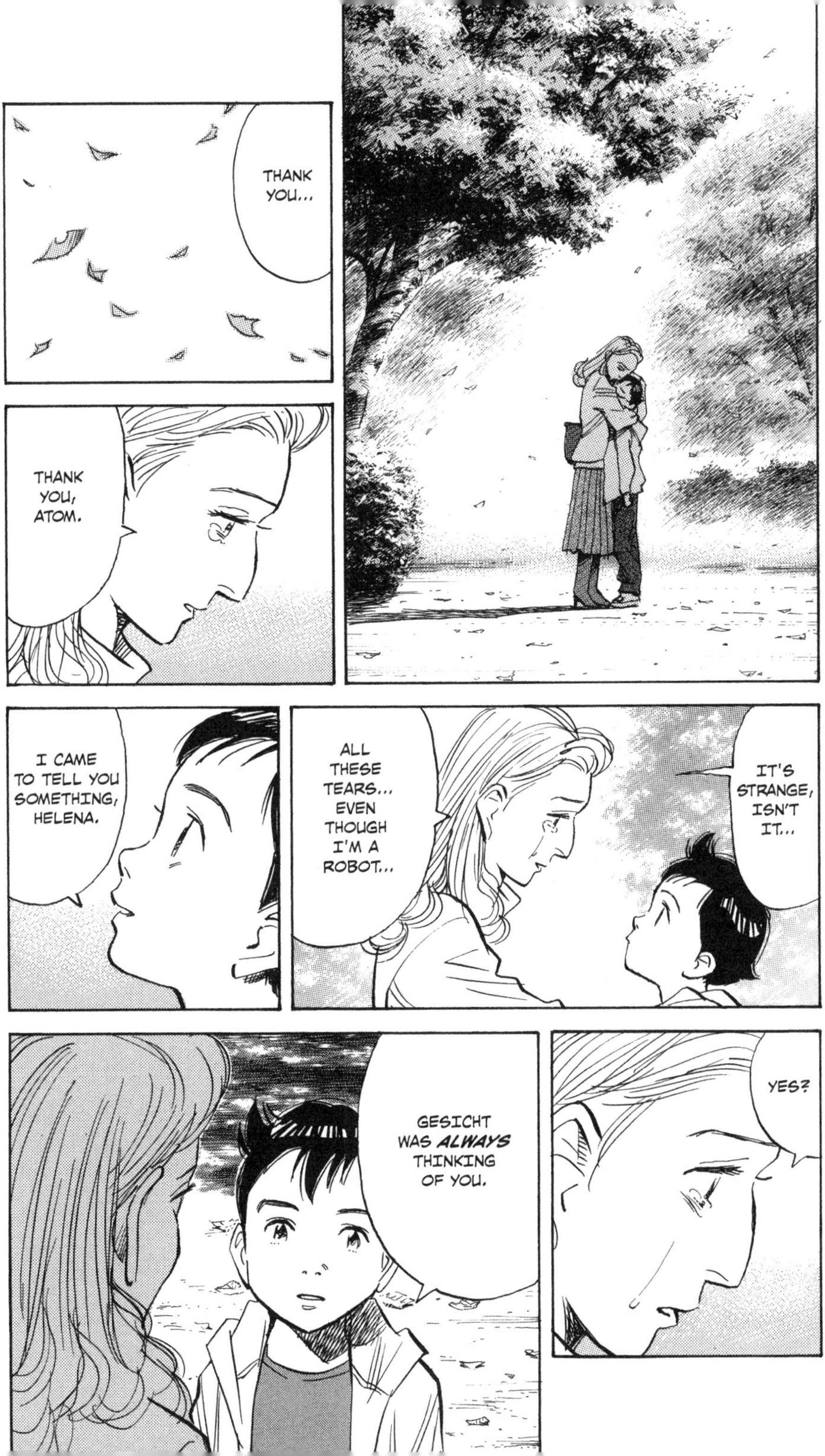
THANK YOU...
THANK YOU, ATOM.
IT'S STRANGE, ISN'T IT...
ALL THESE TEARS... EVEN THOUGH I'M A ROBOT...
I CAME TO TELL YOU SOMETHING, HELENA.
YES?
GESICHT WAS *ALWAYS* THINKING OF YOU.

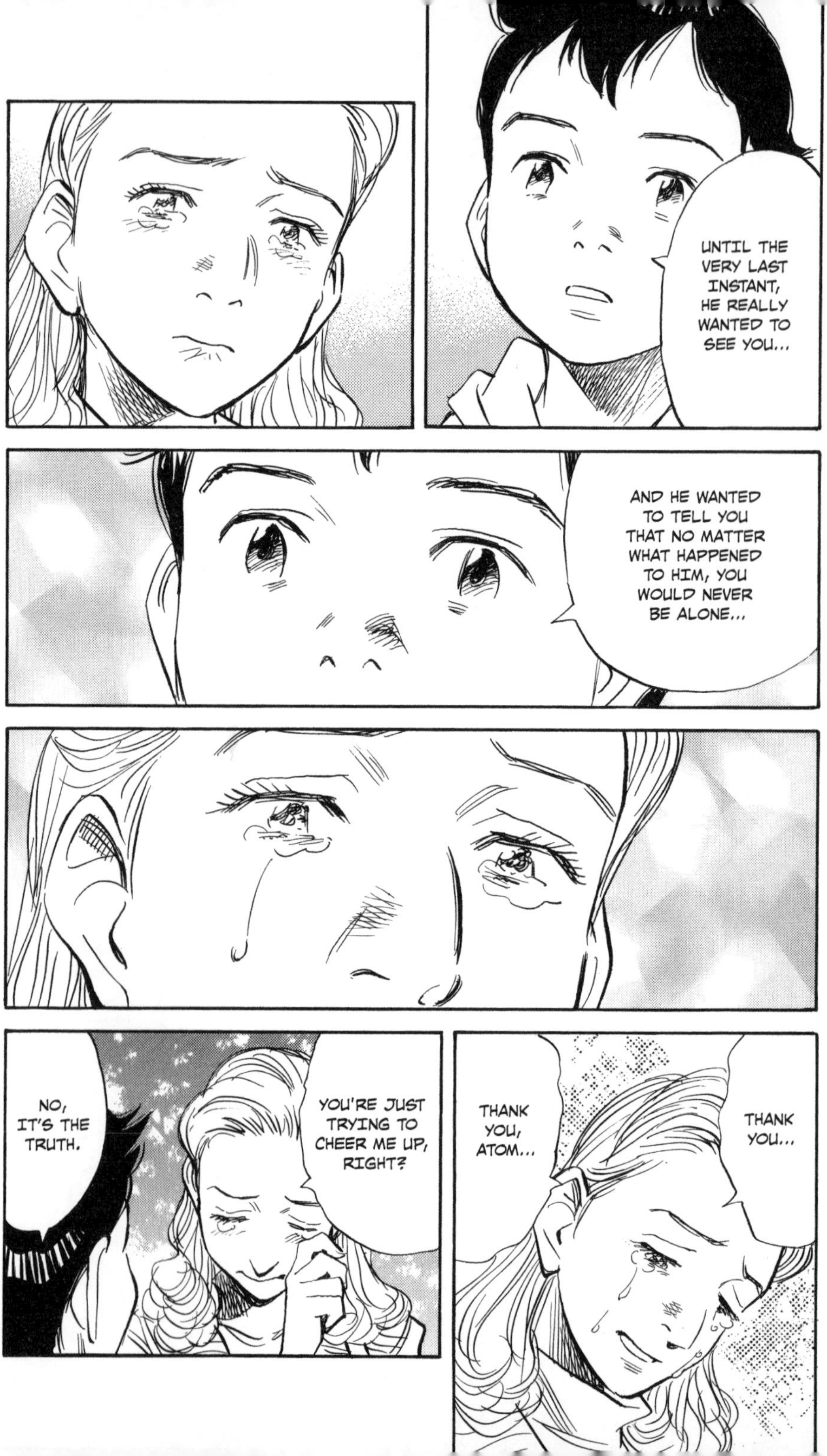
UNTIL THE VERY LAST INSTANT, HE REALLY WANTED TO SEE YOU...
AND HE WANTED TO TELL YOU THAT NO MATTER WHAT HAPPENED TO HIM, YOU WOULD NEVER BE ALONE...
THANK YOU...
THANK YOU, ATOM...
YOU'RE JUST TRYING TO CHEER ME UP, RIGHT?
NO, IT'S THE TRUTH.

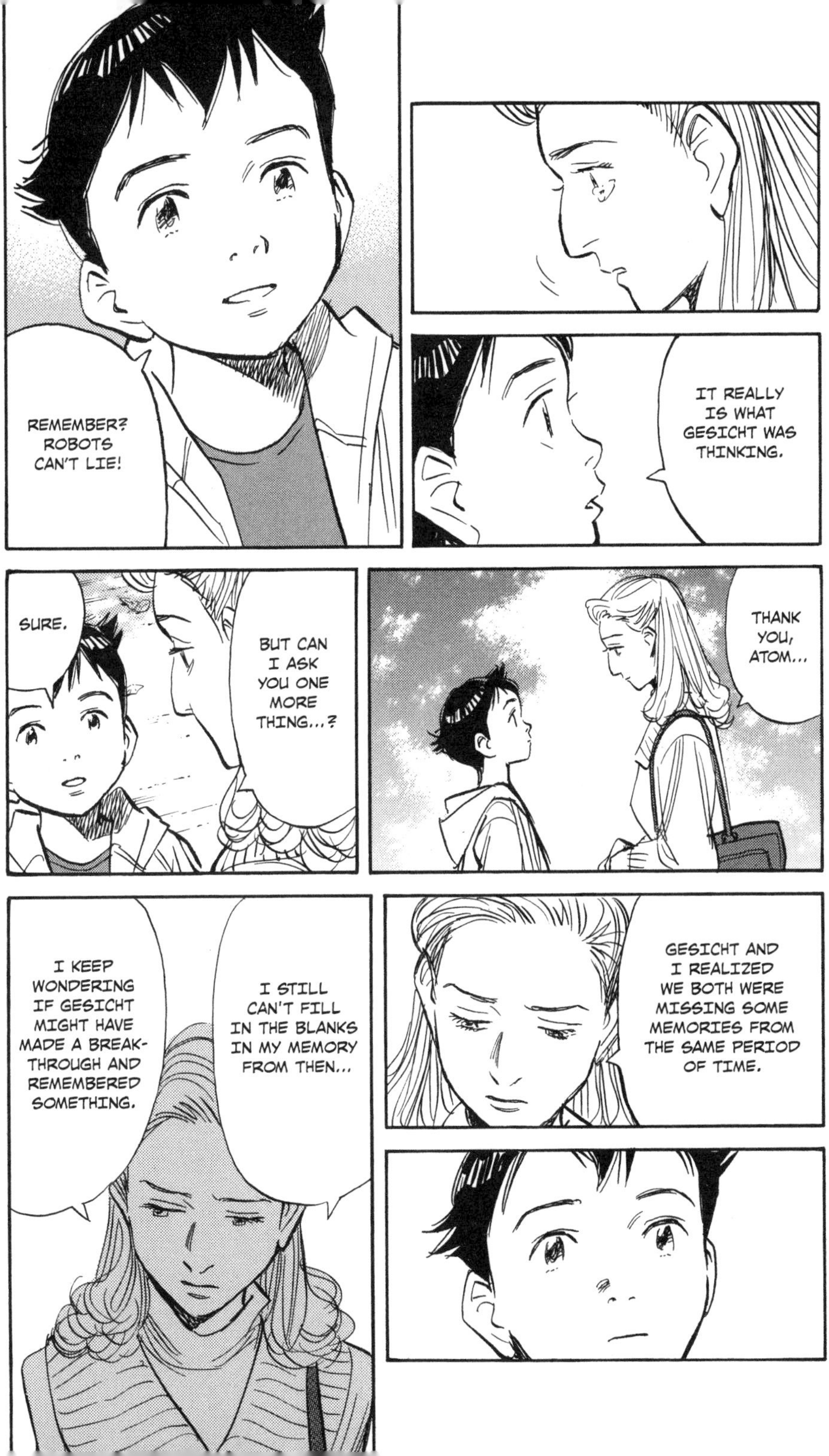
IT REALLY IS WHAT GESICHT WAS THINKING.
REMEMBER? ROBOTS CAN'T LIE!
THANK YOU, ATOM...
BUT CAN I ASK YOU ONE MORE THING...?
SURE.
GESICHT AND I REALIZED WE BOTH WERE MISSING SOME MEMORIES FROM THE SAME PERIOD OF TIME.
I STILL CAN'T FILL IN THE BLANKS IN MY MEMORY FROM THEN...
I KEEP WONDERING IF GESICHT MIGHT HAVE MADE A BREAK-THROUGH AND REMEMBERED SOMETHING.

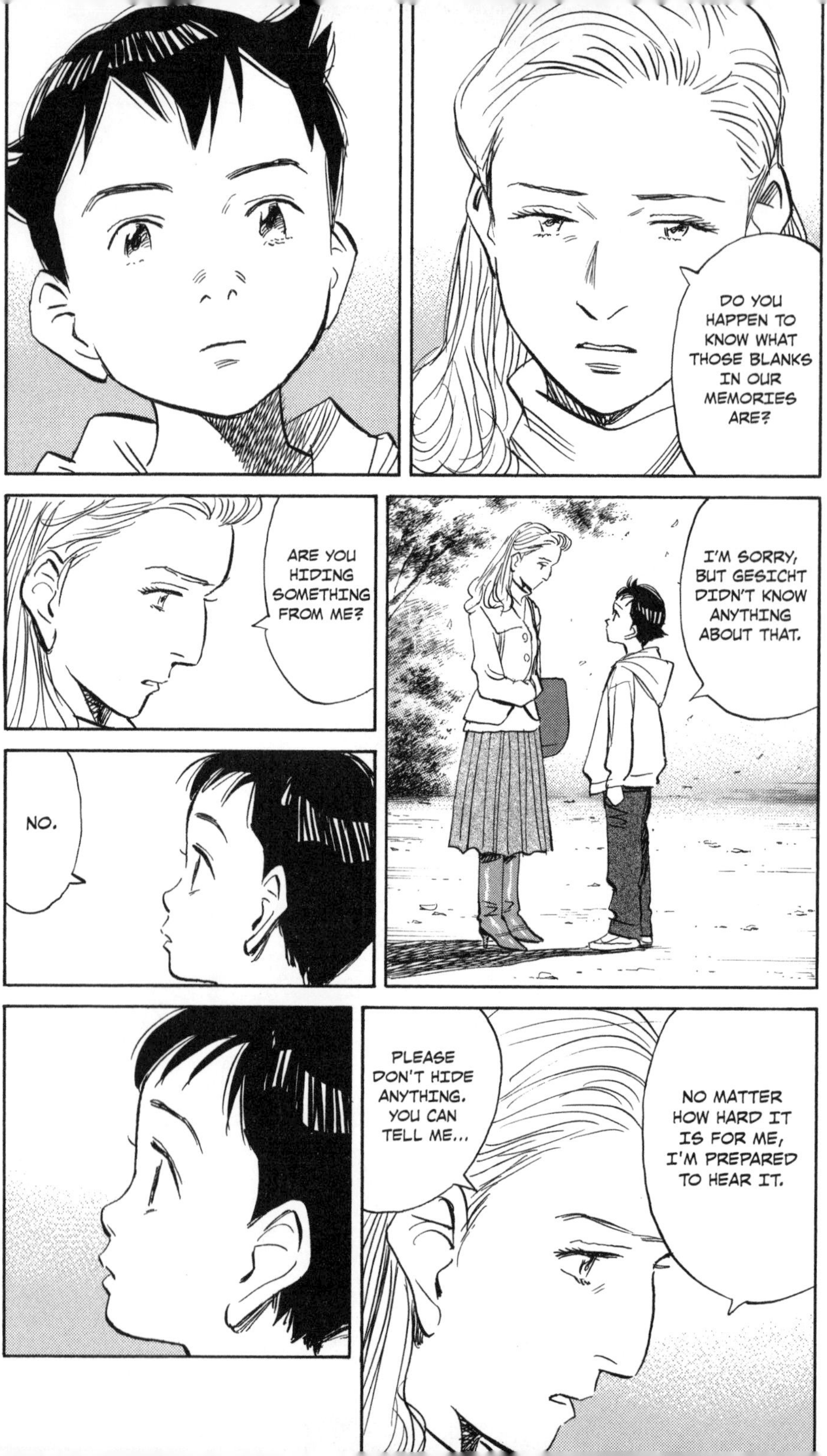
DO YOU HAPPEN TO KNOW WHAT THOSE BLANKS IN OUR MEMORIES ARE?
I'M SORRY, BUT GESICHT DIDN'T KNOW ANYTHING ABOUT THAT.
ARE YOU HIDING SOMETHING FROM ME?
NO.
NO MATTER HOW HARD IT IS FOR ME, I'M PREPARED TO HEAR IT.
PLEASE DON'T HIDE ANYTHING. YOU CAN TELL ME...

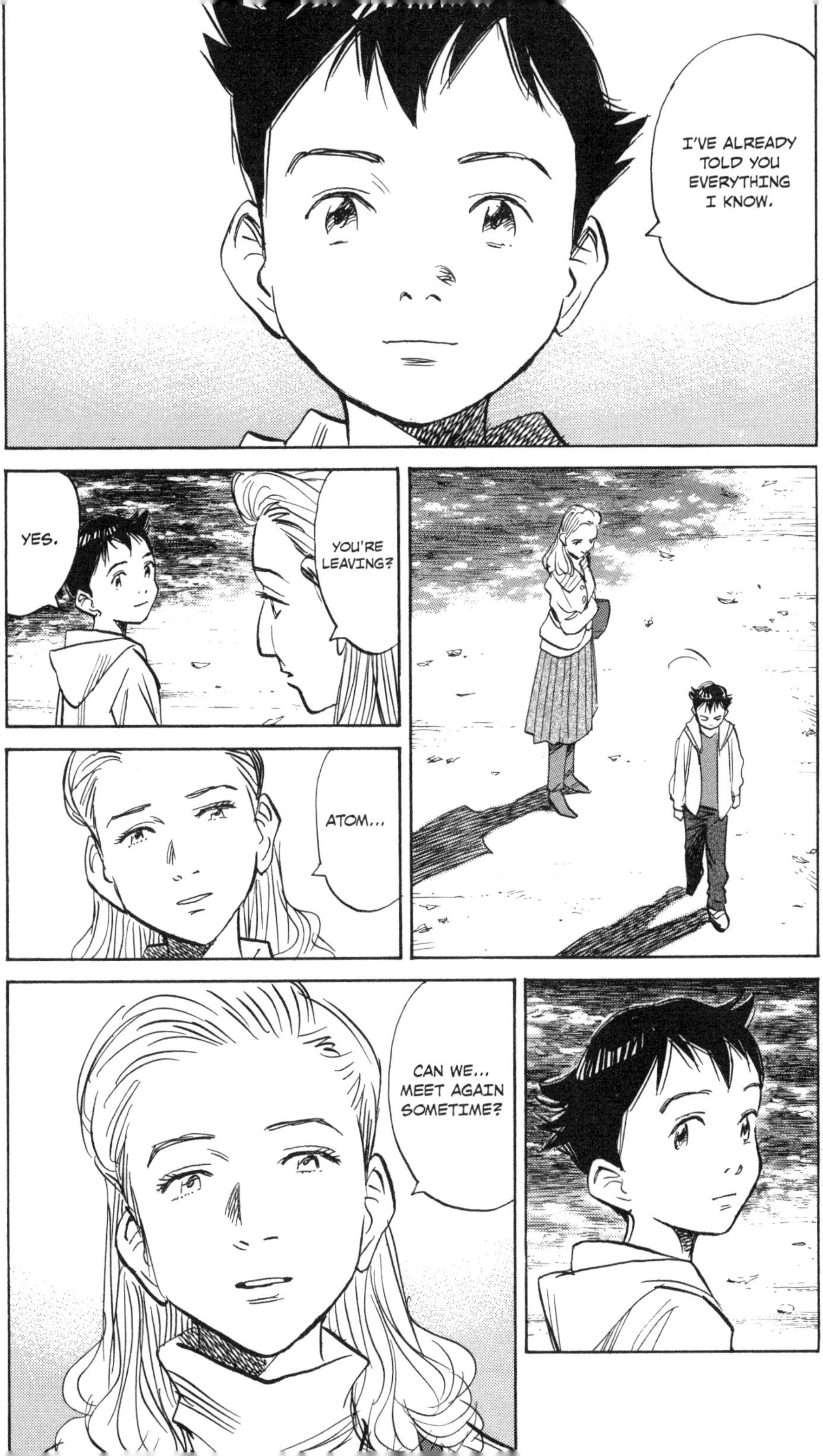
I'VE ALREADY TOLD YOU EVERYTHING I KNOW.
YOU'RE LEAVING?
YES.
ATOM...
CAN WE... MEET AGAIN SOMETIME?

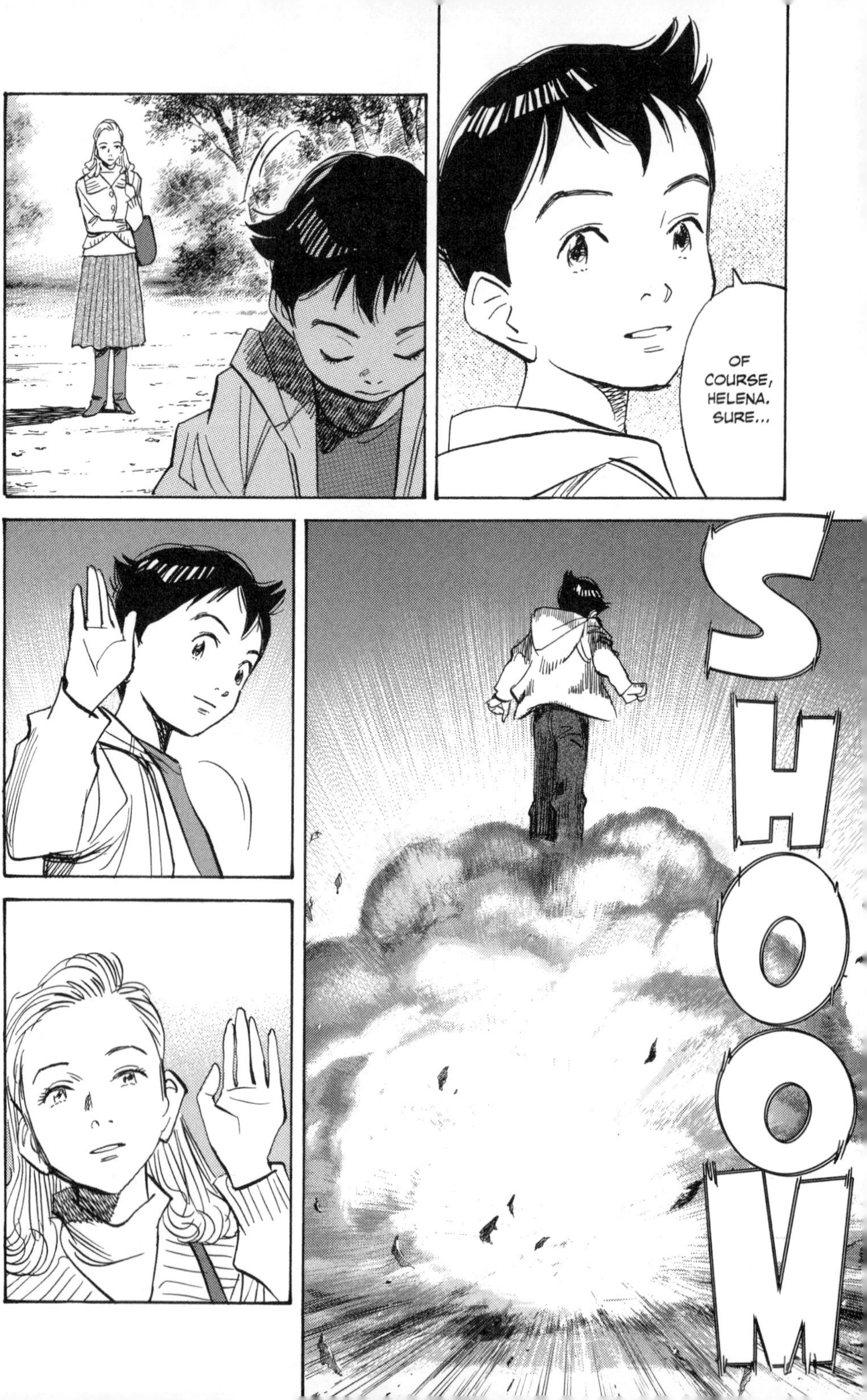
OF COURSE, HELENA. SURE...
SHOOM

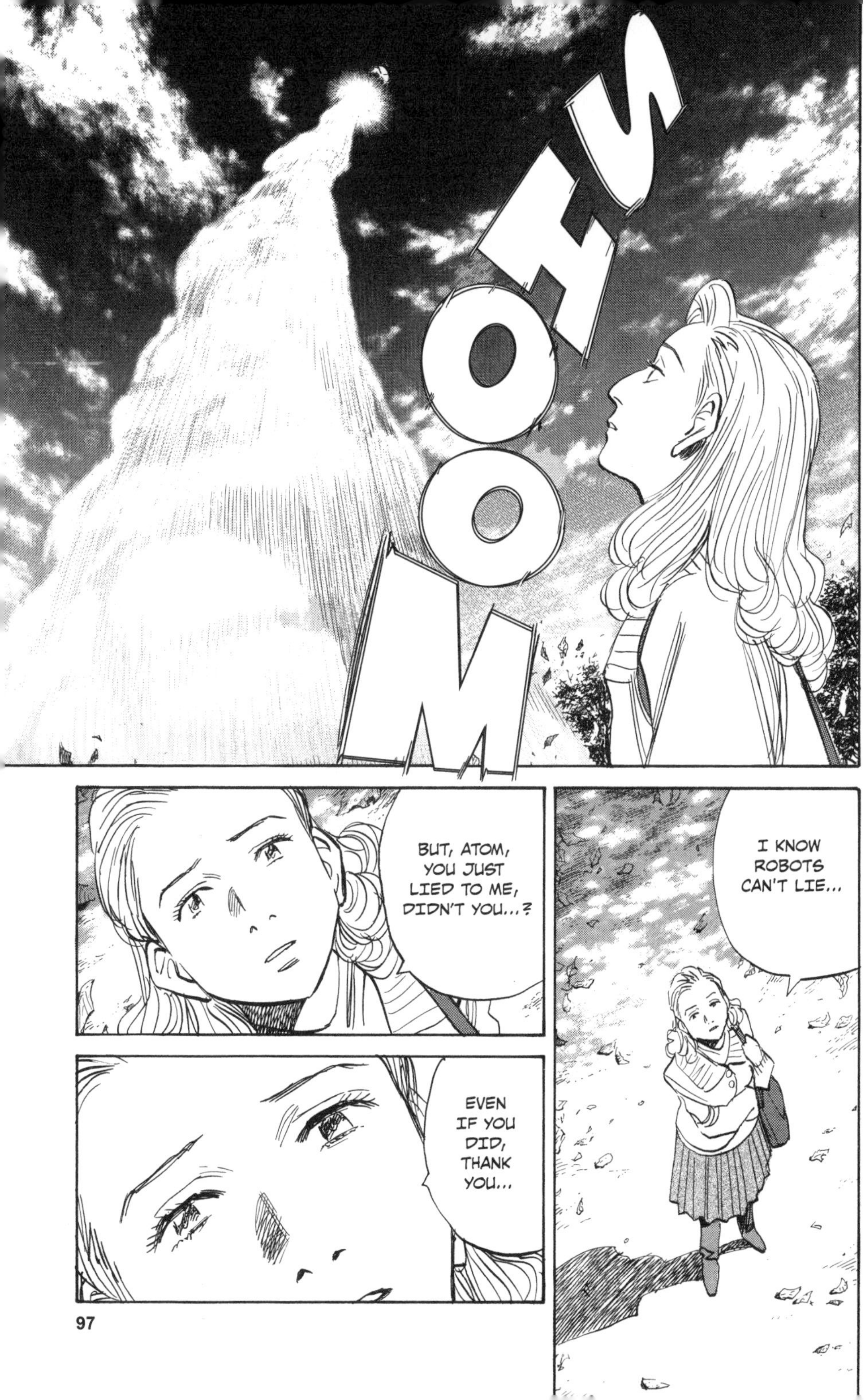
WHOOSH
I KNOW ROBOTS CAN'T LIE...
BUT, ATOM, YOU JUST LIED TO ME, DIDN'T YOU...?
EVEN IF YOU DID, THANK YOU...

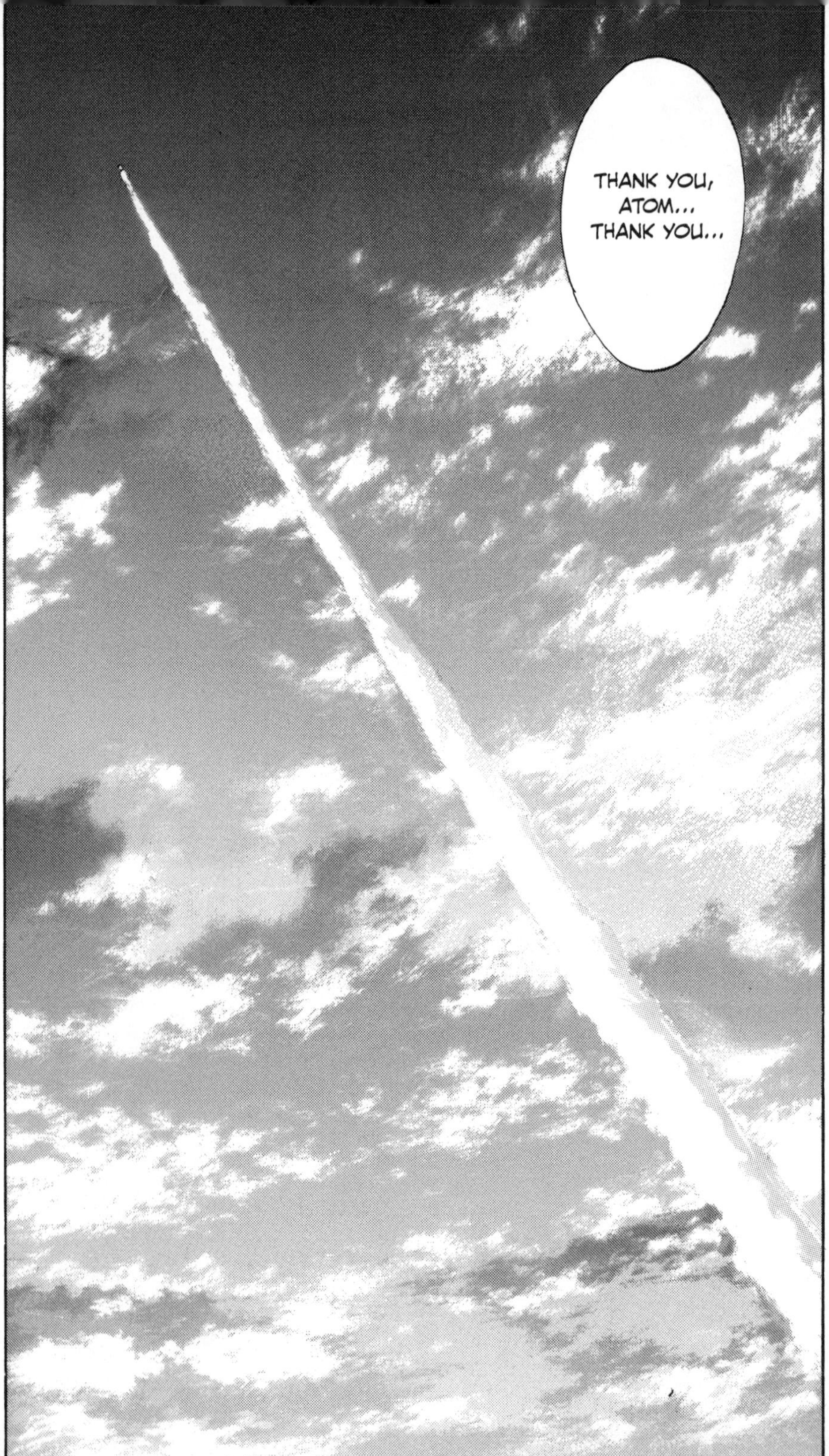
THANK YOU, ATOM... THANK YOU...

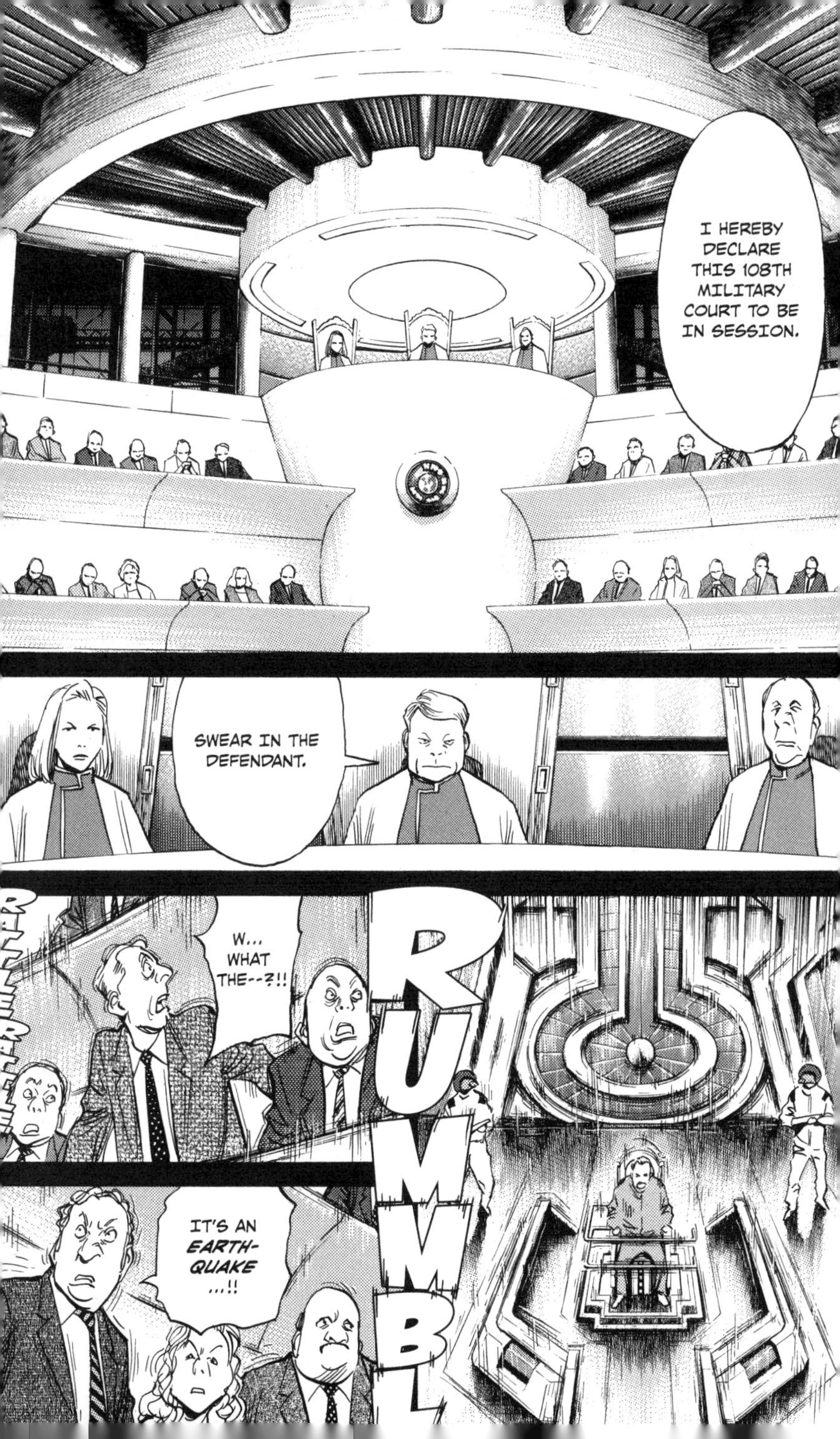
I HEREBY DECLARE THIS 108TH MILITARY COURT TO BE IN SESSION.
SWEAR IN THE DEFENDANT.
RUMMBL
W... WHAT THE--?!!
IT'S AN *EARTHQUAKE*...!!

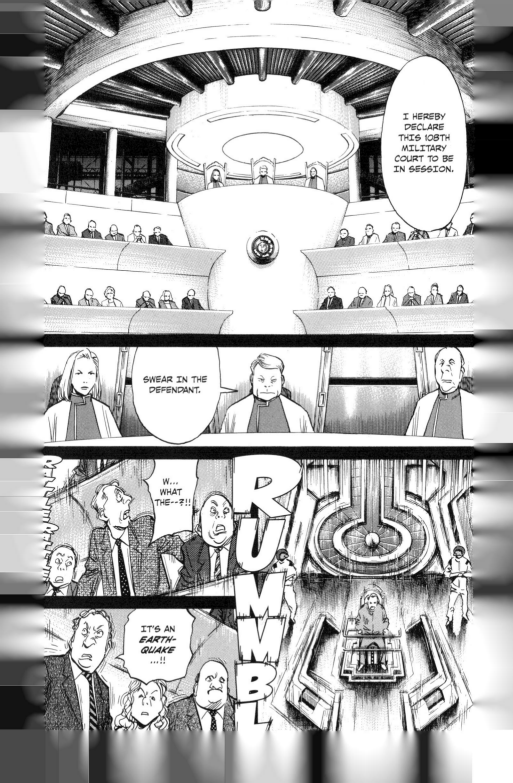

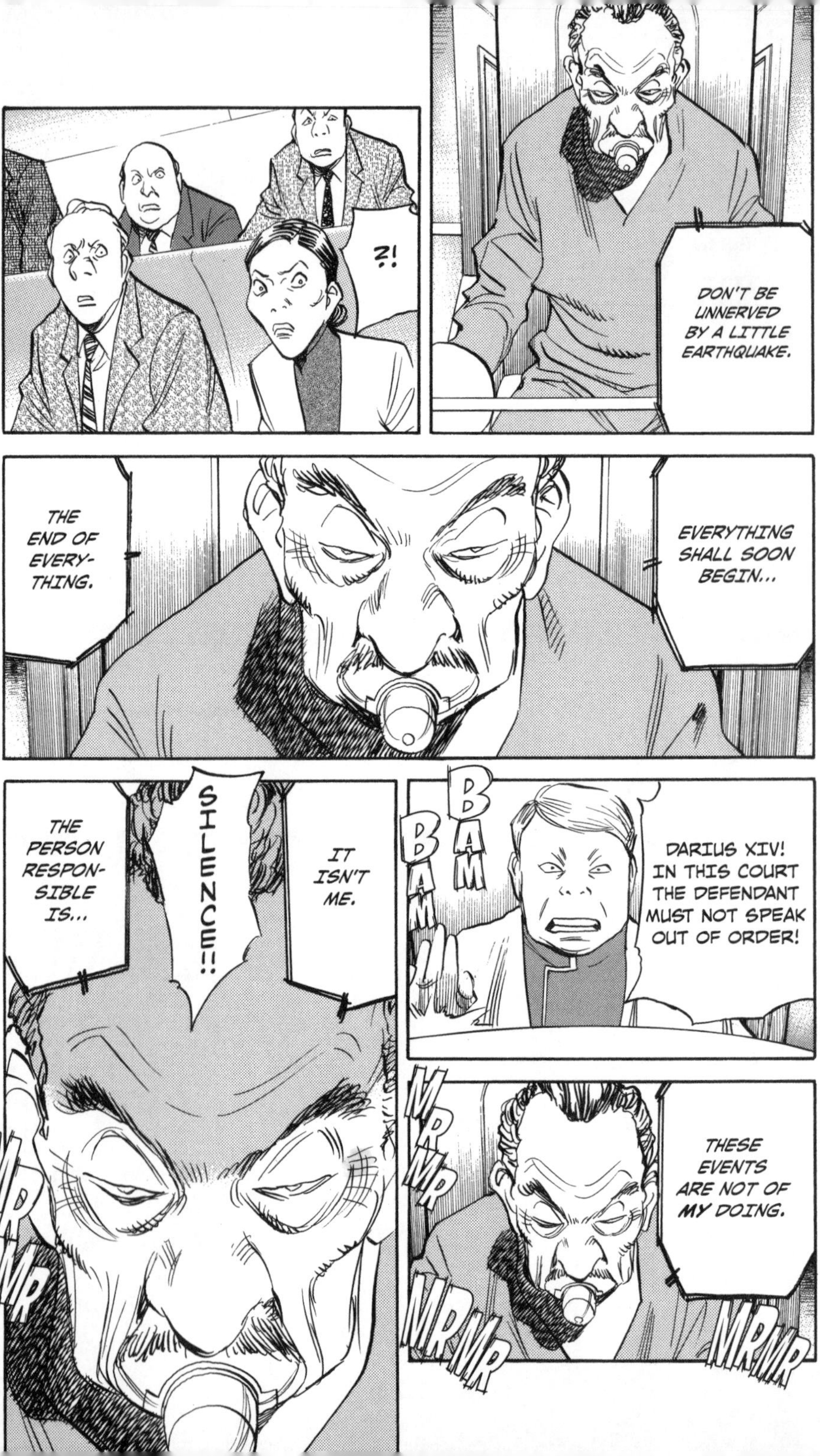

DON'T BE UNNERVED BY A LITTLE EARTHQUAKE.
?!
EVERYTHING SHALL SOON BEGIN...
THE END OF EVERY-THING.
BAM BAM
DARIUS XIV! IN THIS COURT THE DEFENDANT MUST NOT SPEAK OUT OF ORDER!
MR MR
THESE EVENTS ARE NOT OF MY DOING.
MRMR
MRMR
IT ISN'T ME.
SILENCE!!
THE PERSON RESPONSIBLE IS...
MR MR

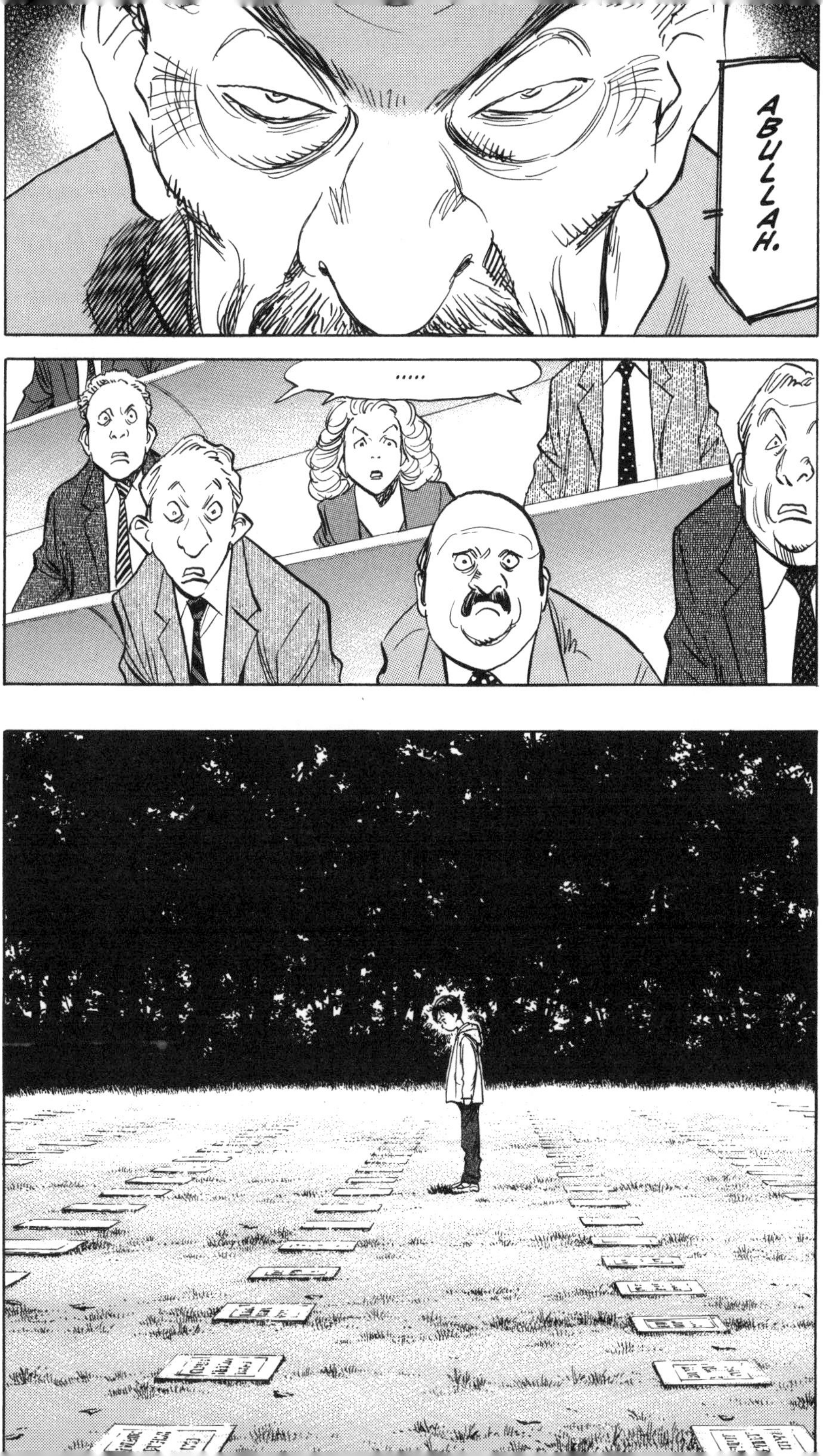
ABULLAH.
.....

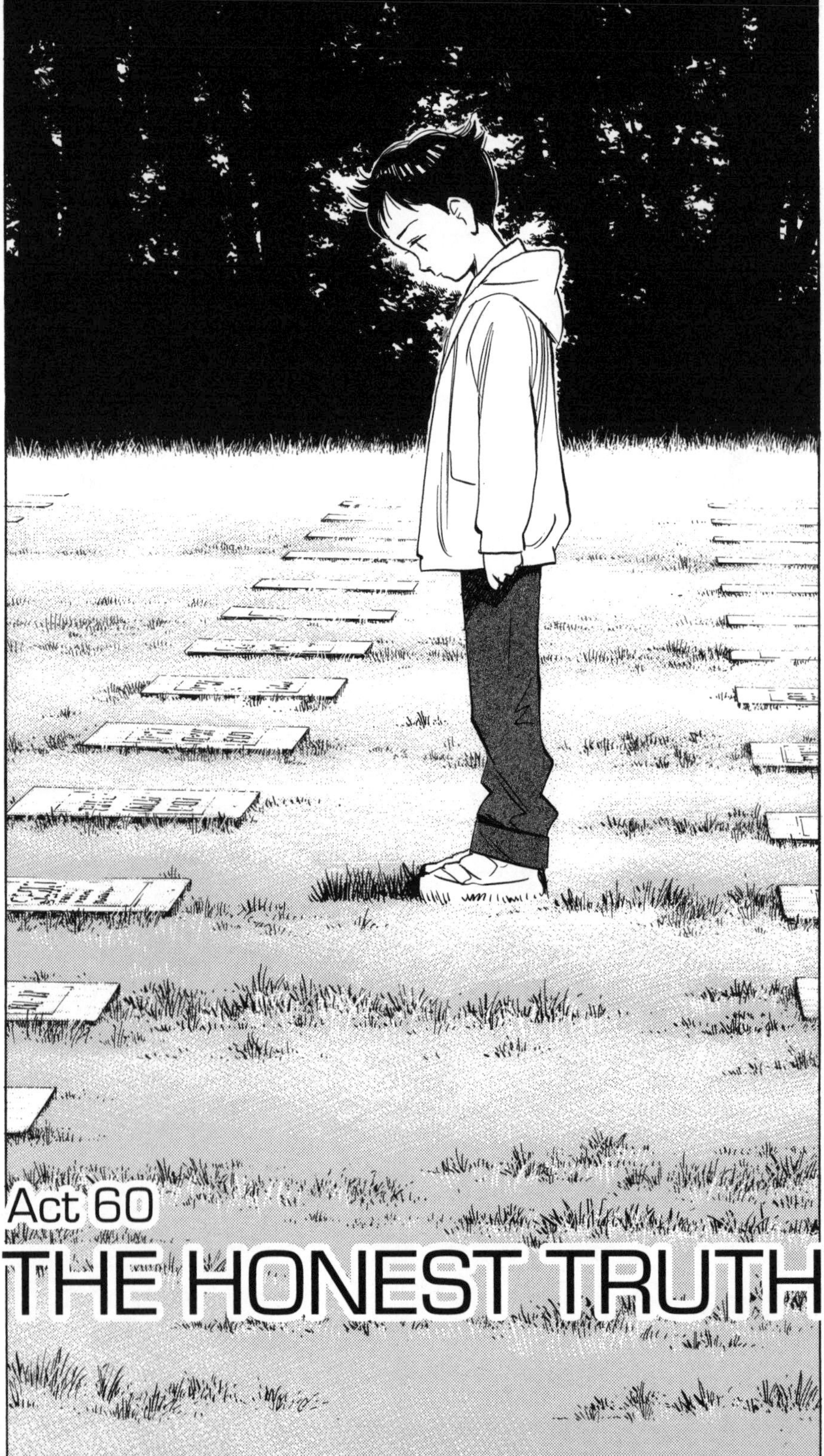
Act 60
THE HONEST TRUTH

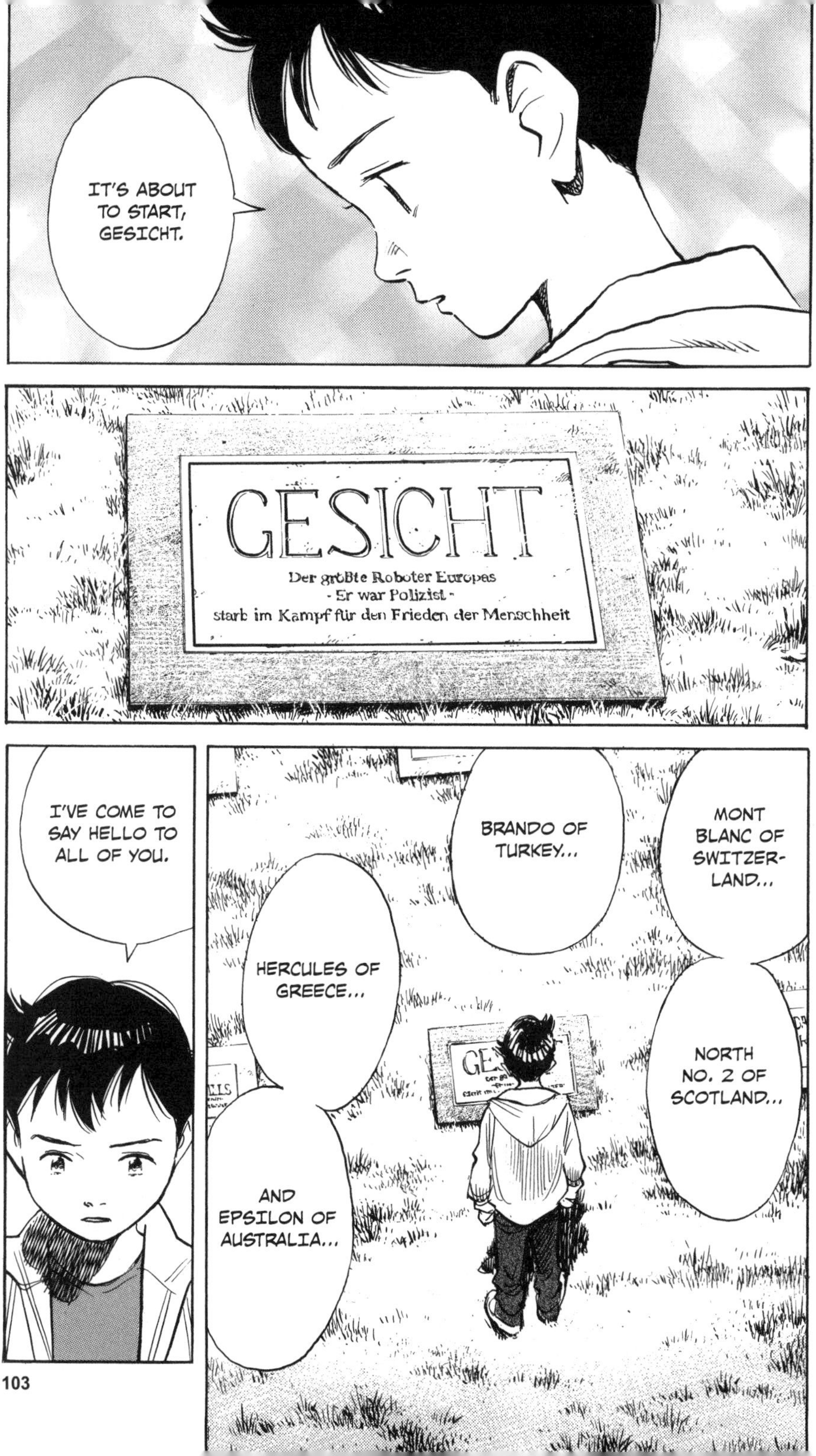
IT'S ABOUT TO START, GESICHT.
GESICHT
Der größte Roboter Europas
- Er war Polizist -
starb im Kampf für den Frieden der Menschheit
MONT BLANC OF SWITZER-LAND...
BRANDO OF TURKEY...
HERCULES OF GREECE...
NORTH NO. 2 OF SCOTLAND...
AND EPSILON OF AUSTRALIA...
I'VE COME TO SAY HELLO TO ALL OF YOU.

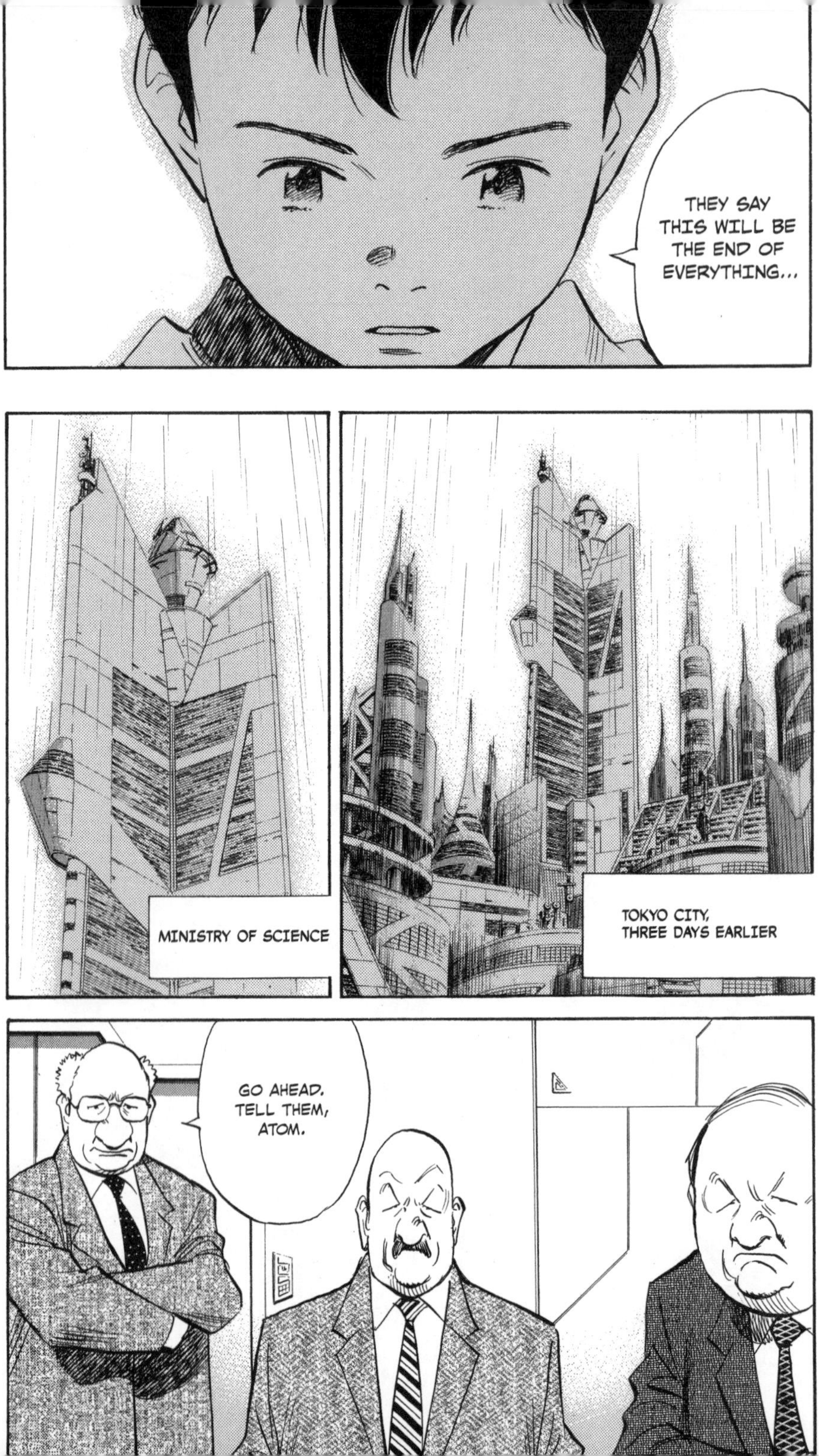
THEY SAY THIS WILL BE THE END OF EVERYTHING...
TOKYO CITY, THREE DAYS EARLIER
MINISTRY OF SCIENCE
GO AHEAD. TELL THEM, ATOM.

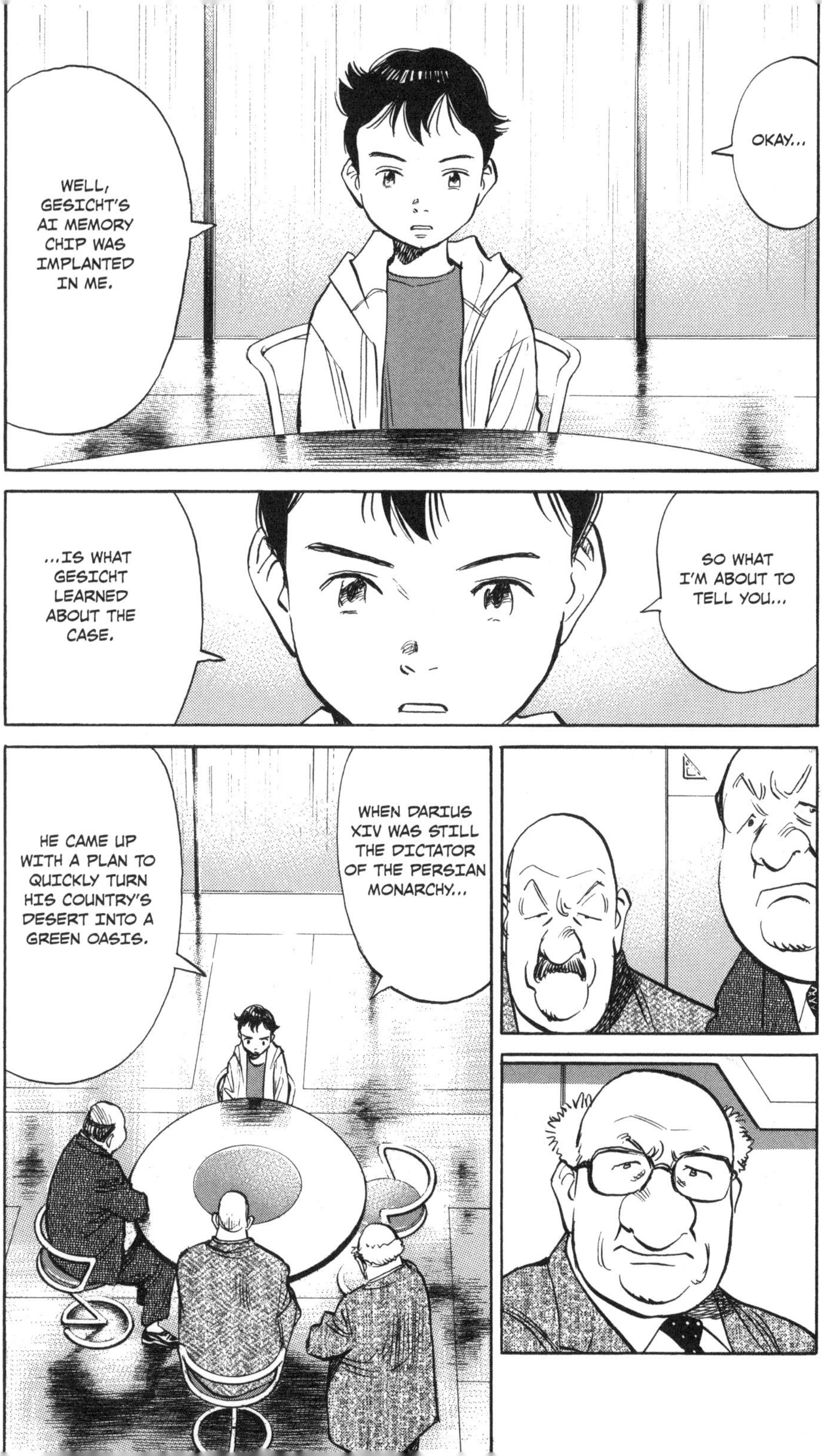
OKAY...
WELL, GESICHT'S AI MEMORY CHIP WAS IMPLANTED IN ME.
SO WHAT I'M ABOUT TO TELL YOU...
...IS WHAT GESICHT LEARNED ABOUT THE CASE.
WHEN DARIUS XIV WAS STILL THE DICTATOR OF THE PERSIAN MONARCHY...
HE CAME UP WITH A PLAN TO QUICKLY TURN HIS COUNTRY'S DESERT INTO A GREEN OASIS.

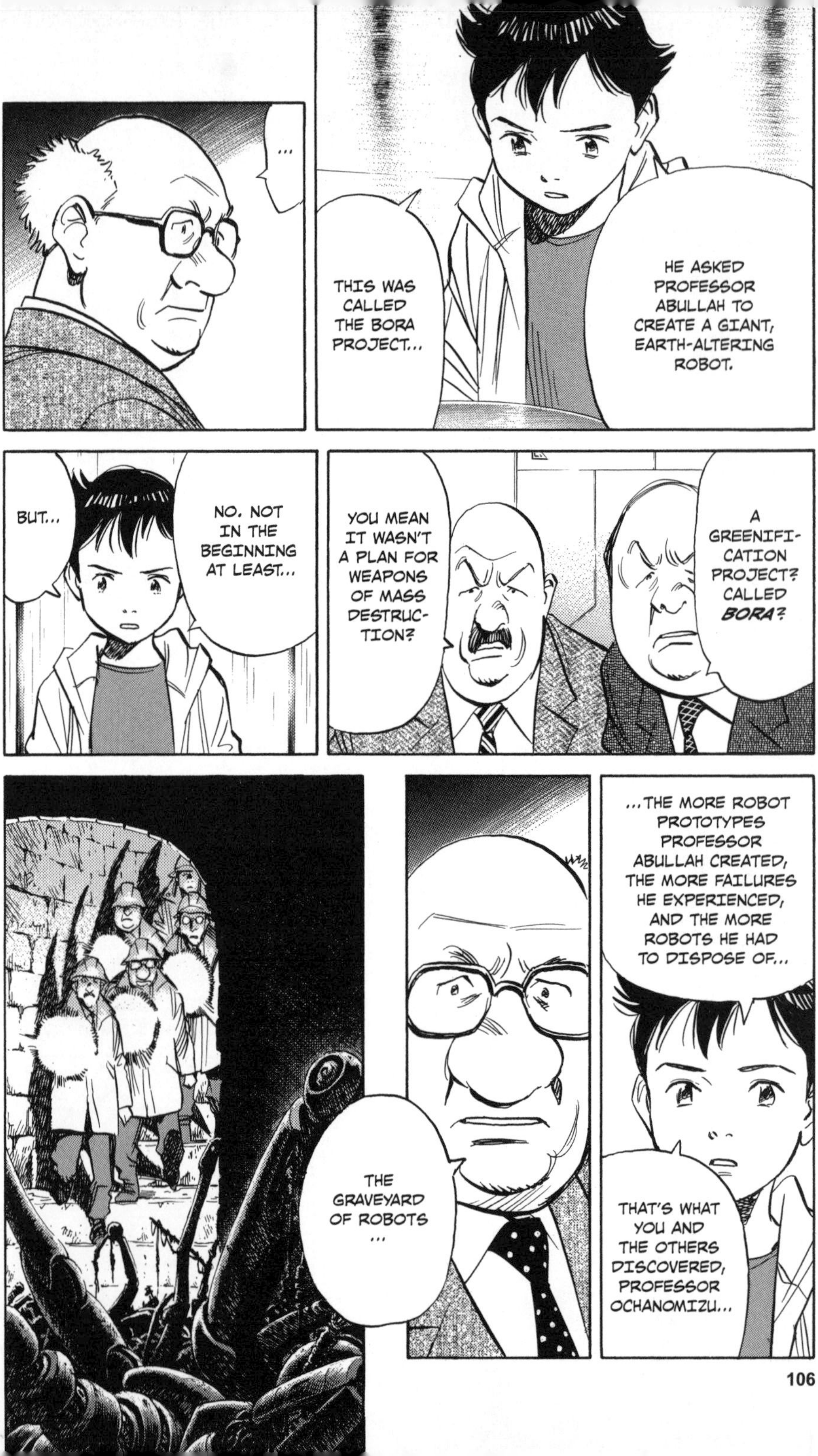
HE ASKED PROFESSOR ABULLAH TO CREATE A GIANT, EARTH-ALTERING ROBOT.
THIS WAS CALLED THE BORA PROJECT...
...
A GREENIFICATION PROJECT? CALLED *BORA*?
YOU MEAN IT WASN'T A PLAN FOR WEAPONS OF MASS DESTRUCTION?
NO. NOT IN THE BEGINNING AT LEAST...
BUT...
...THE MORE ROBOT PROTOTYPES PROFESSOR ABULLAH CREATED, THE MORE FAILURES HE EXPERIENCED, AND THE MORE ROBOTS HE HAD TO DISPOSE OF...
THAT'S WHAT YOU AND THE OTHERS DISCOVERED, PROFESSOR OCHANOMIZU...
THE GRAVEYARD OF ROBOTS ...

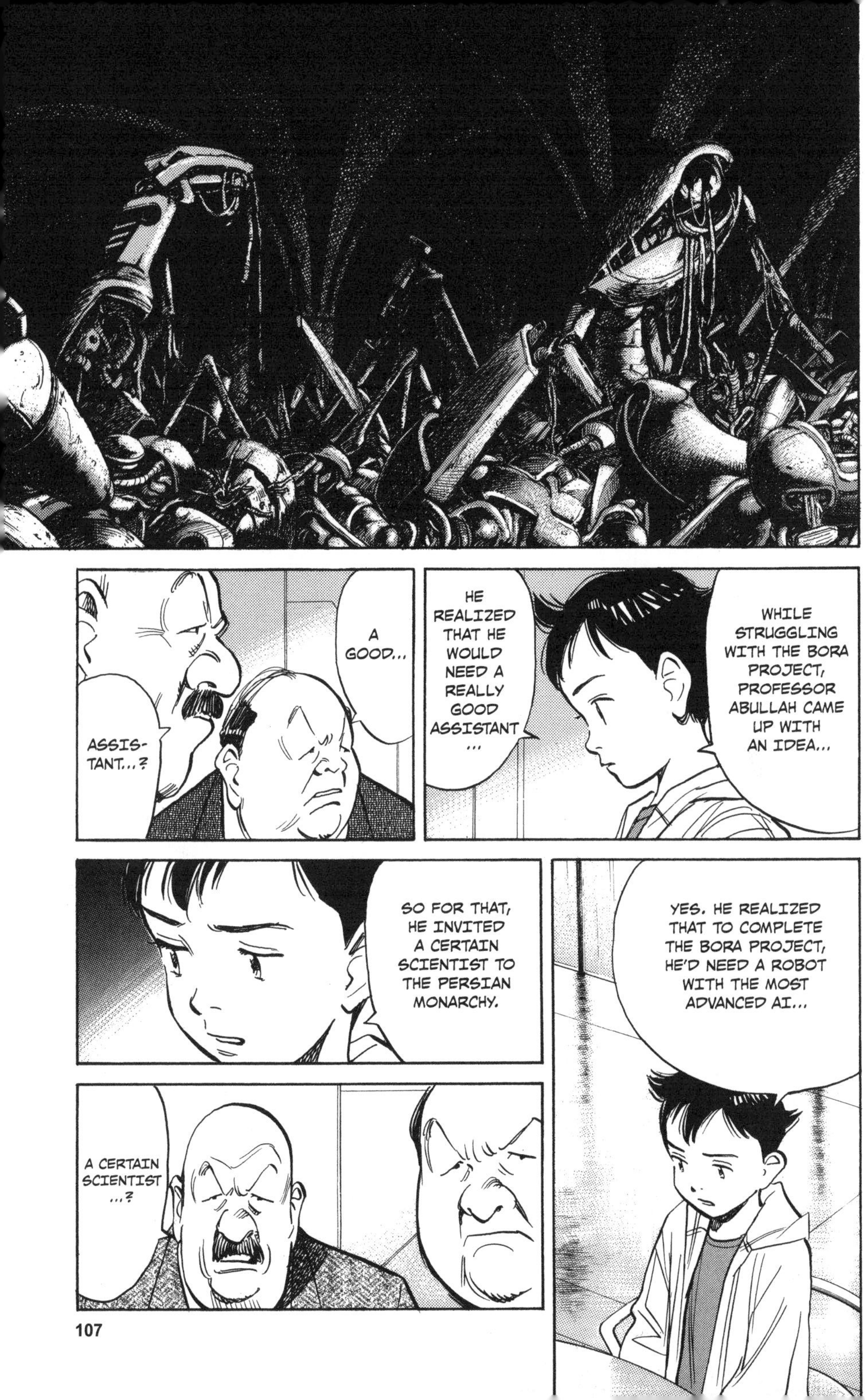
WHILE STRUGGLING WITH THE BORA PROJECT, PROFESSOR ABULLAH CAME UP WITH AN IDEA...
HE REALIZED THAT HE WOULD NEED A REALLY GOOD ASSISTANT...
A GOOD...
ASSISTANT...?
YES. HE REALIZED THAT TO COMPLETE THE BORA PROJECT, HE'D NEED A ROBOT WITH THE MOST ADVANCED AI...
SO FOR THAT, HE INVITED A CERTAIN SCIENTIST TO THE PERSIAN MONARCHY.
A CERTAIN SCIENTIST...?

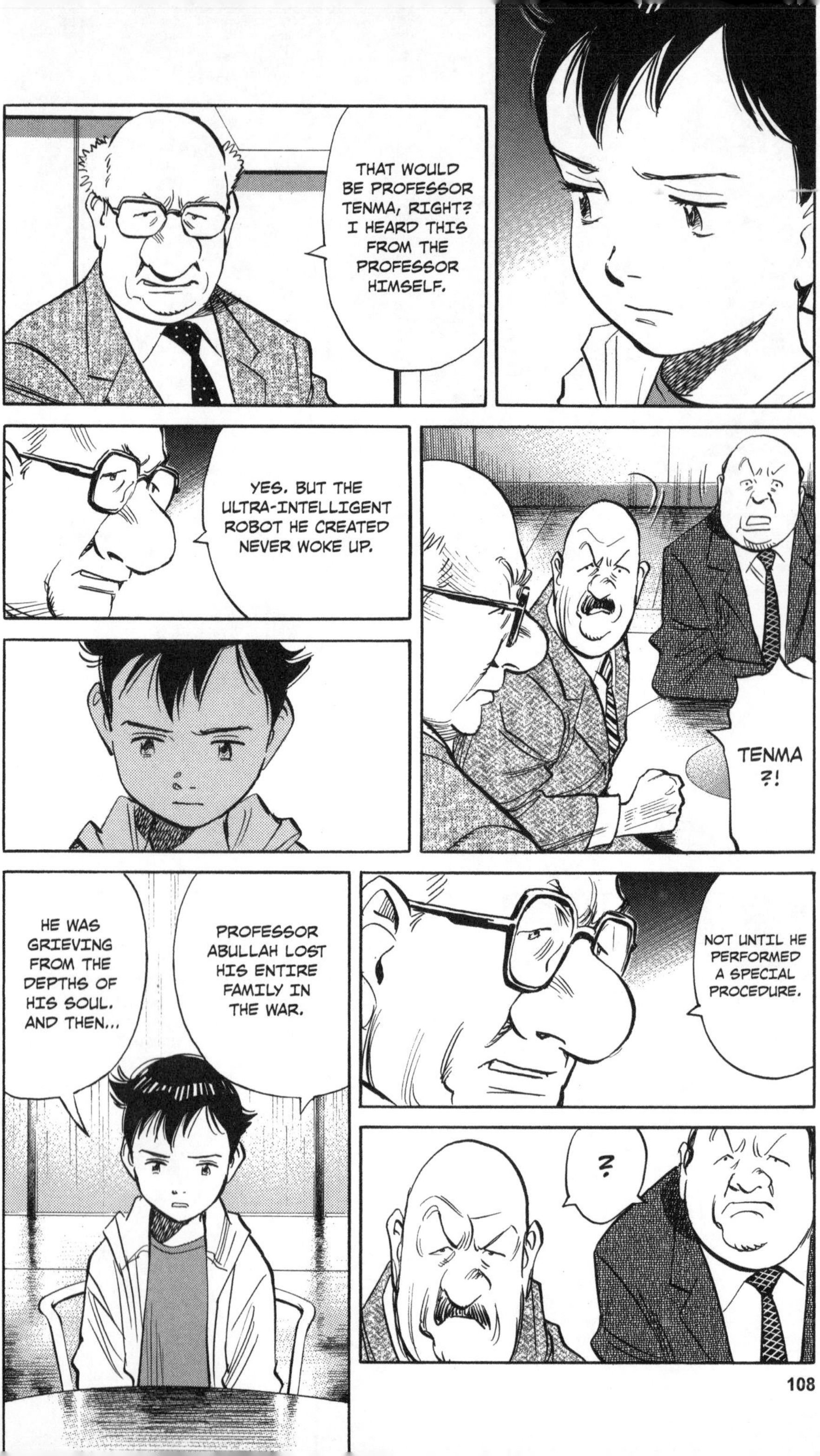
THAT WOULD BE PROFESSOR TENMA, RIGHT? I HEARD THIS FROM THE PROFESSOR HIMSELF.
TENMA ?!
YES. BUT THE ULTRA-INTELLIGENT ROBOT HE CREATED NEVER WOKE UP.
NOT UNTIL HE PERFORMED A SPECIAL PROCEDURE.
?
PROFESSOR ABULLAH LOST HIS ENTIRE FAMILY IN THE WAR.
HE WAS GRIEVING FROM THE DEPTHS OF HIS SOUL. AND THEN...

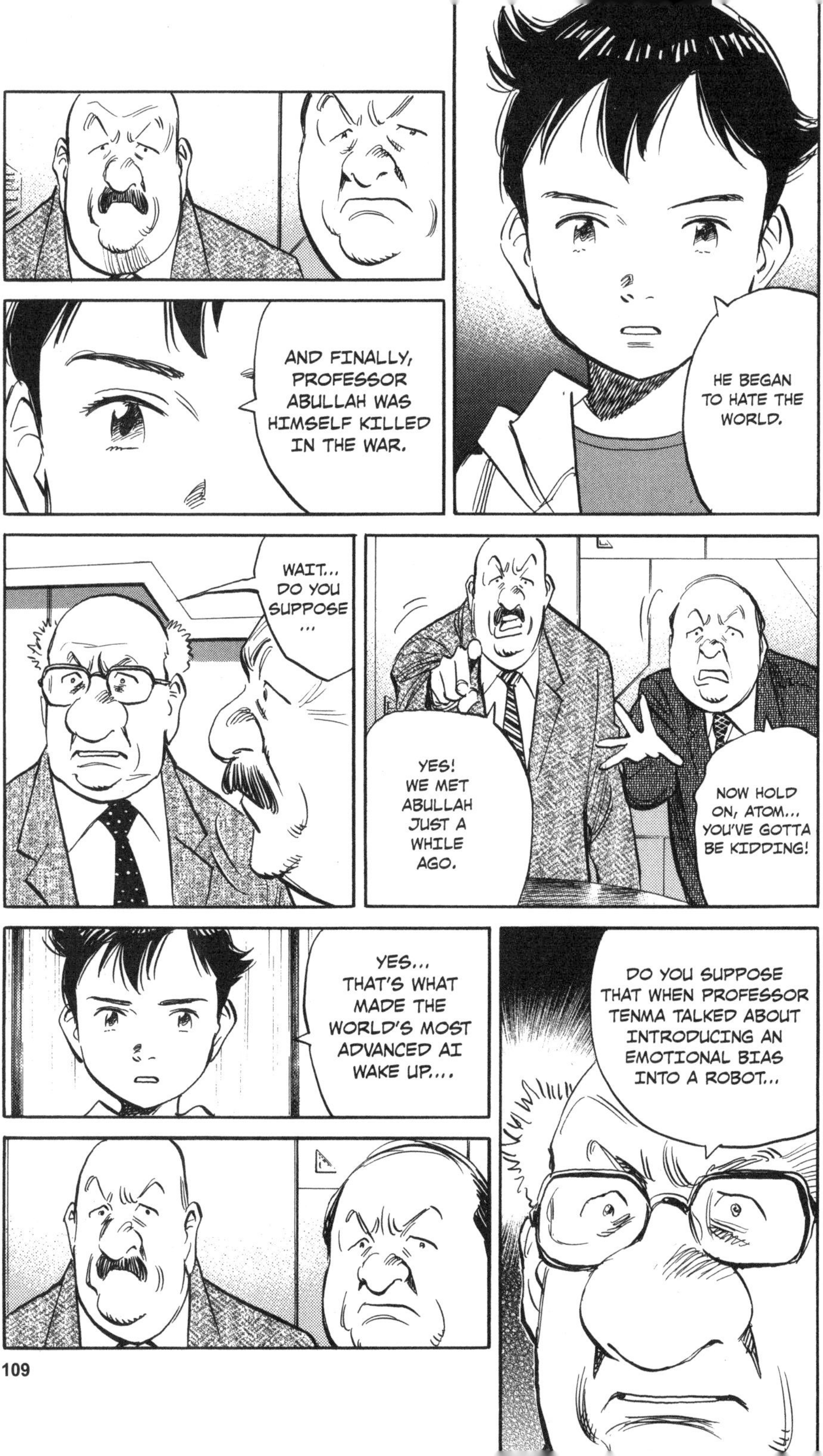
HE BEGAN TO HATE THE WORLD.
AND FINALLY, PROFESSOR ABULLAH WAS HIMSELF KILLED IN THE WAR.
NOW HOLD ON, ATOM... YOU'VE GOTTA BE KIDDING!
YES! WE MET ABULLAH JUST A WHILE AGO.
WAIT... DO YOU SUPPOSE ...
DO YOU SUPPOSE THAT WHEN PROFESSOR TENMA TALKED ABOUT INTRODUCING AN EMOTIONAL BIAS INTO A ROBOT...
YES... THAT'S WHAT MADE THE WORLD'S MOST ADVANCED AI WAKE UP....

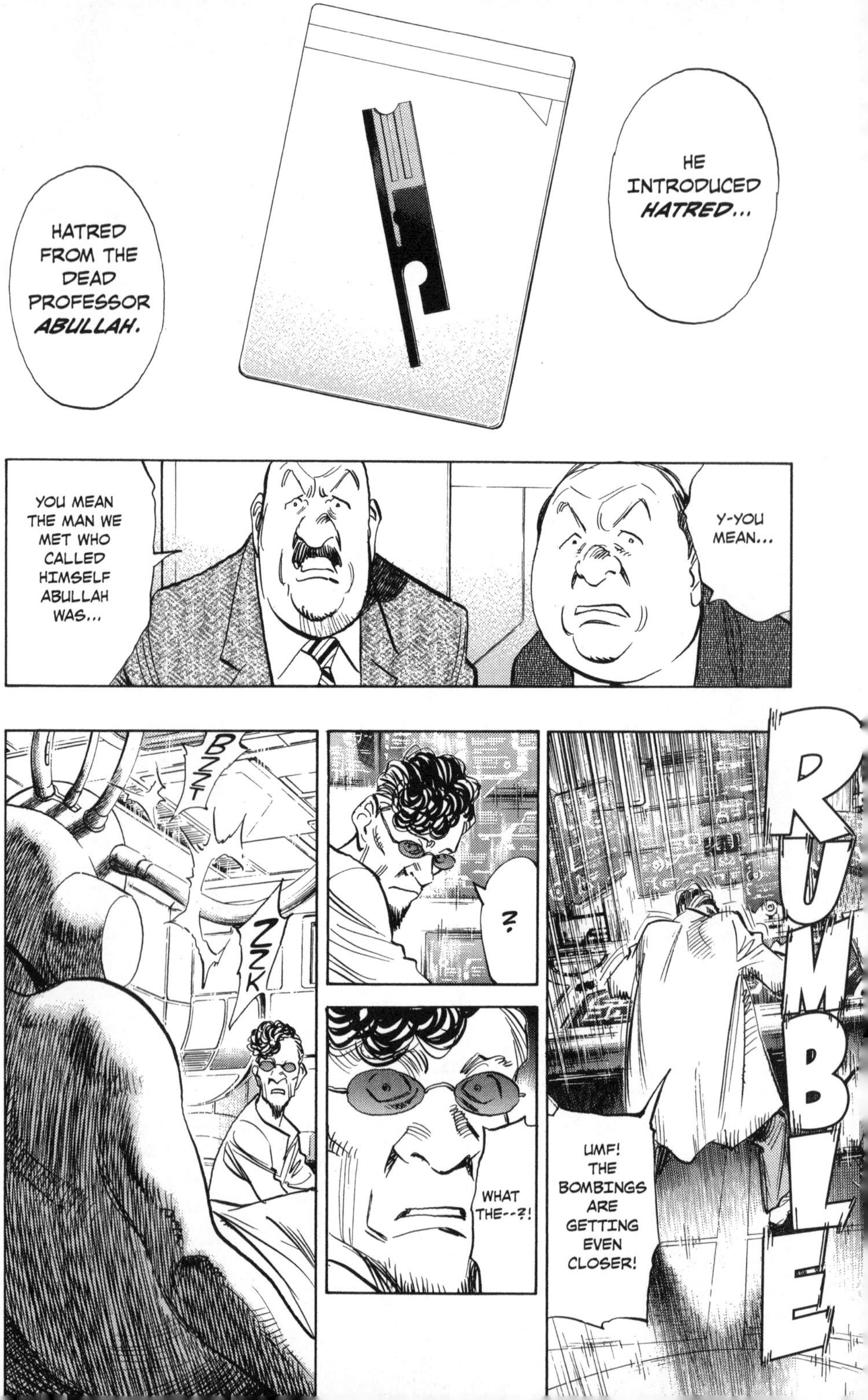
HE INTRODUCED HATRED...
HATRED FROM THE DEAD PROFESSOR ABULLAH.
Y-YOU MEAN...
YOU MEAN THE MAN WE MET WHO CALLED HIMSELF ABULLAH WAS...
RUMBLE
UMF! THE BOMBINGS ARE GETTING EVEN CLOSER!
?
WHAT THE--?!
BZZT
ZZZK

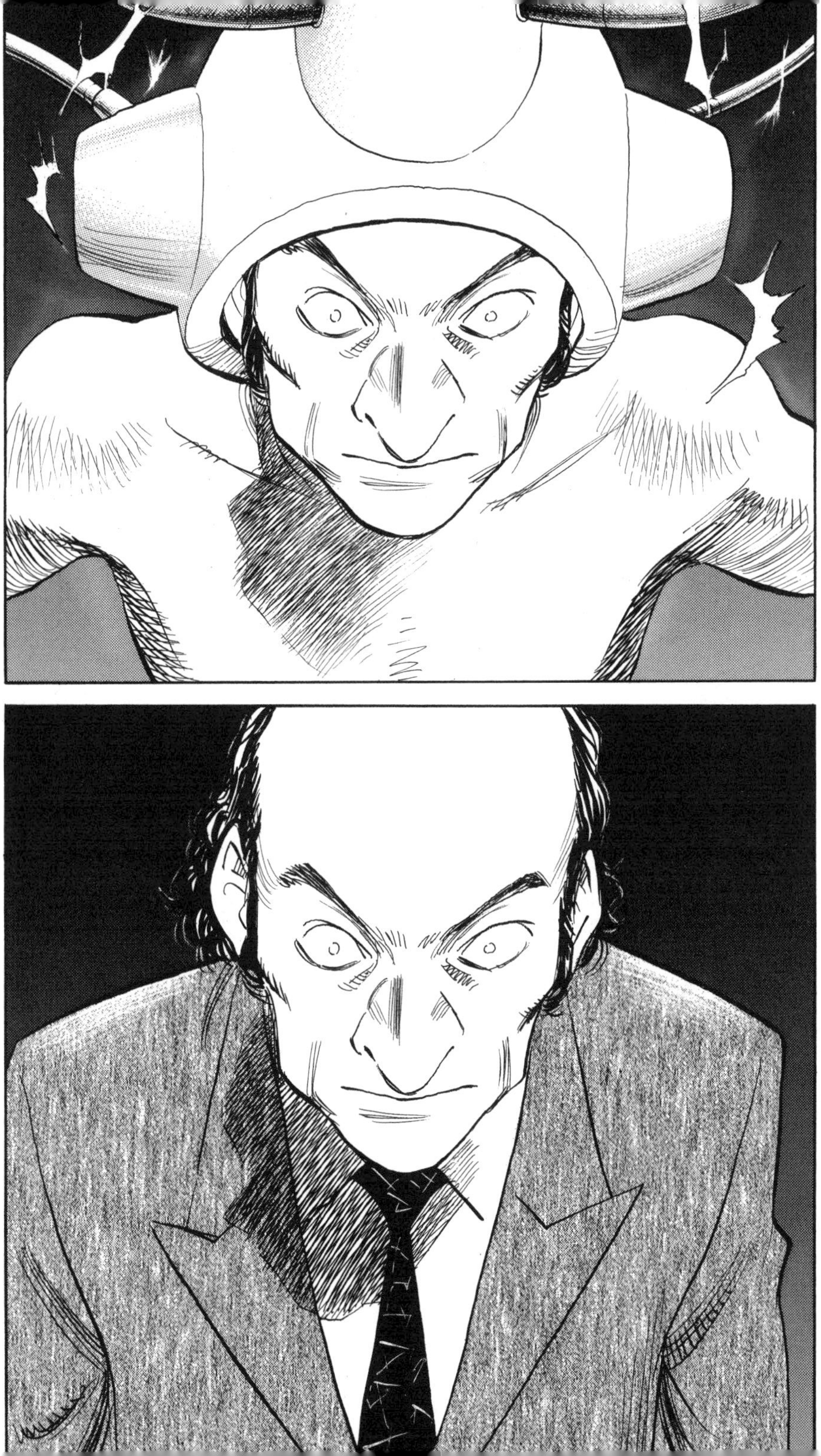

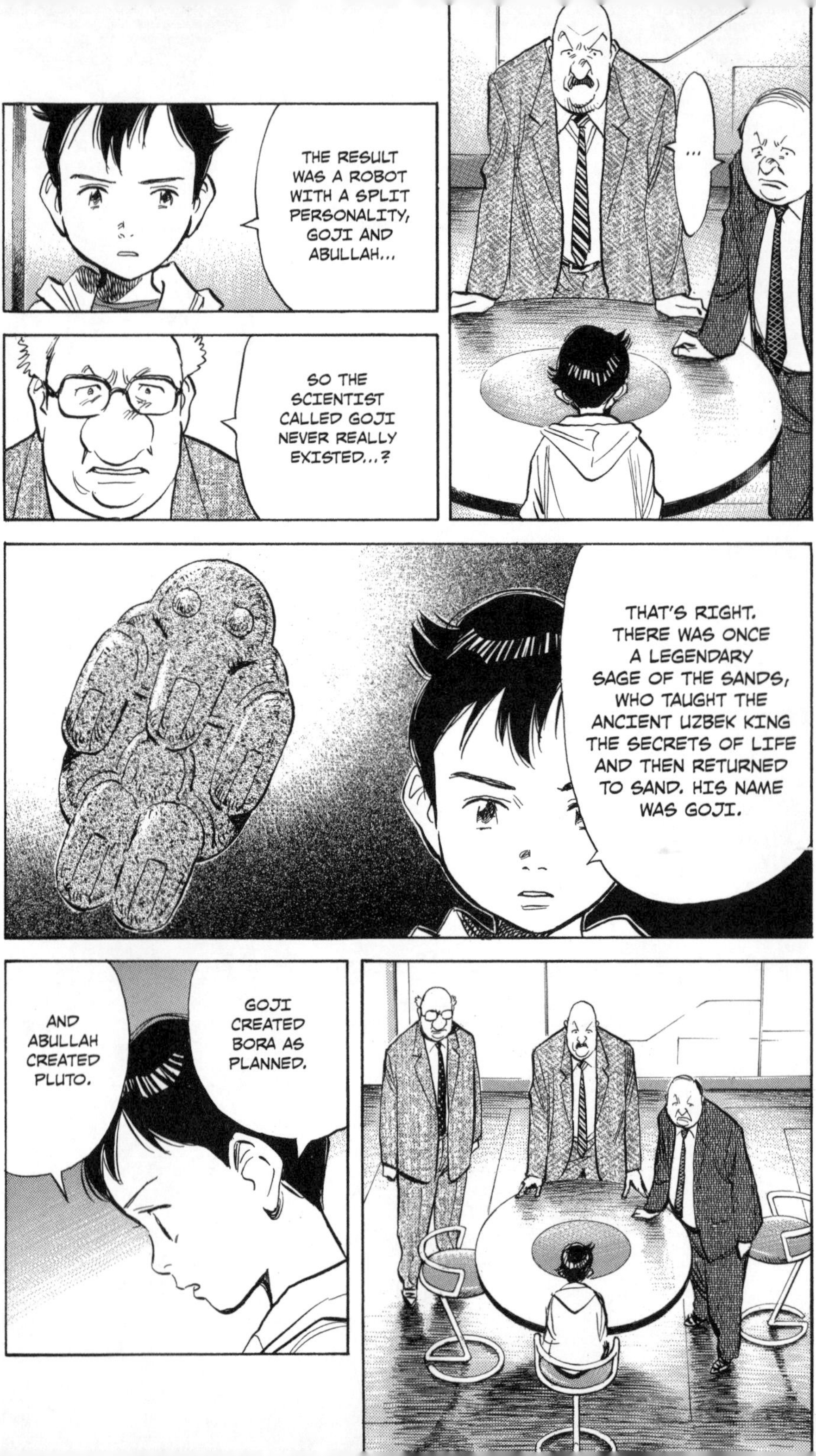
...
THE RESULT WAS A ROBOT WITH A SPLIT PERSONALITY, GOJI AND ABULLAH...
SO THE SCIENTIST CALLED GOJI NEVER REALLY EXISTED...?
THAT'S RIGHT. THERE WAS ONCE A LEGENDARY SAGE OF THE SANDS, WHO TAUGHT THE ANCIENT UZBEK KING THE SECRETS OF LIFE AND THEN RETURNED TO SAND. HIS NAME WAS GOJI.
GOJI CREATED BORA AS PLANNED.
AND ABULLAH CREATED PLUTO.

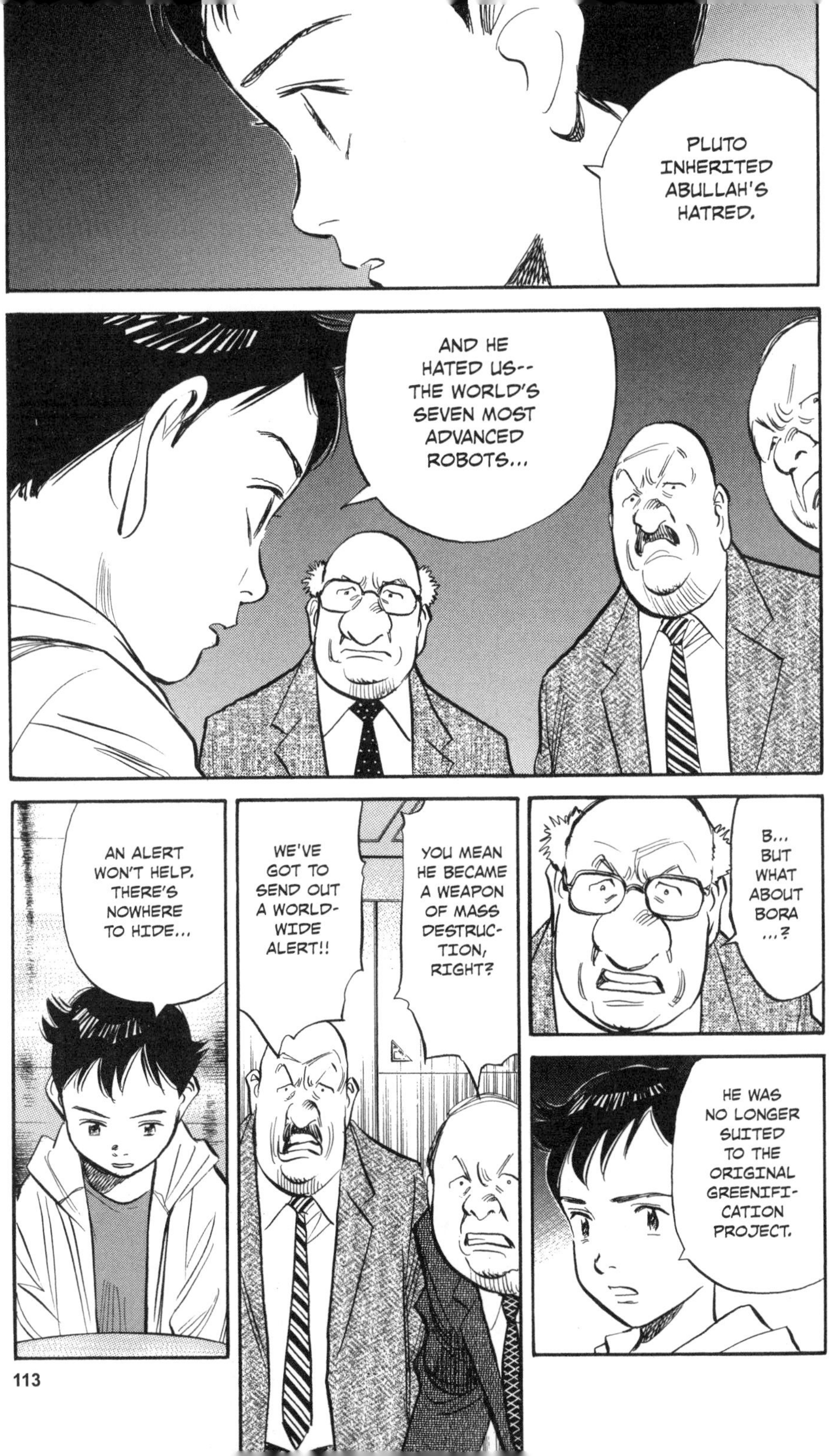
PLUTO INHERITED ABULLAH'S HATRED.
AND HE HATED US-- THE WORLD'S SEVEN MOST ADVANCED ROBOTS...
B... BUT WHAT ABOUT BORA ...?
HE WAS NO LONGER SUITED TO THE ORIGINAL GREENIFICATION PROJECT.
YOU MEAN HE BECAME A WEAPON OF MASS DESTRUCTION, RIGHT?
WE'VE GOT TO SEND OUT A WORLD-WIDE ALERT!!
AN ALERT WON'T HELP. THERE'S NOWHERE TO HIDE...

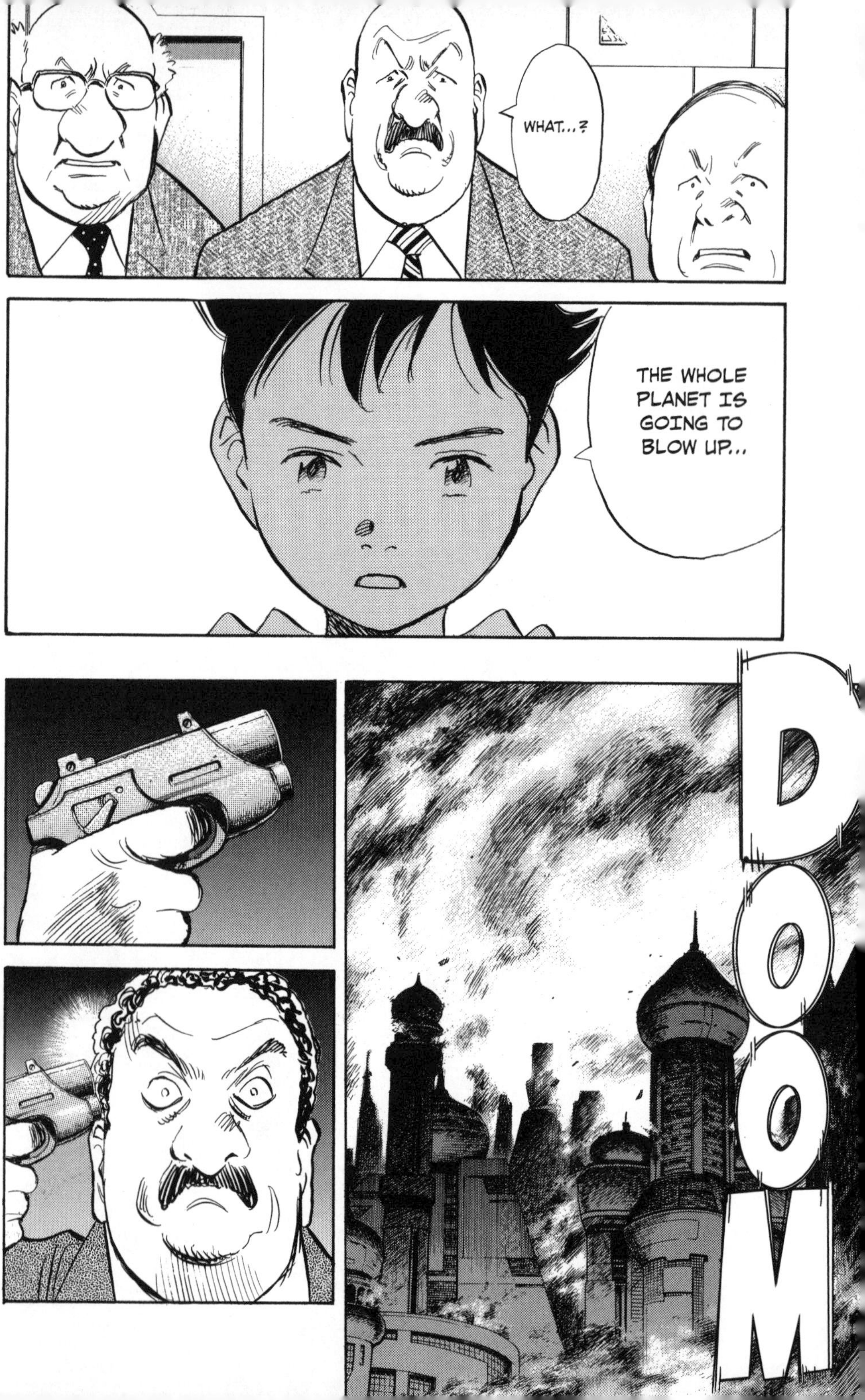
WHAT...?
THE WHOLE PLANET IS GOING TO BLOW UP...
DOOOM

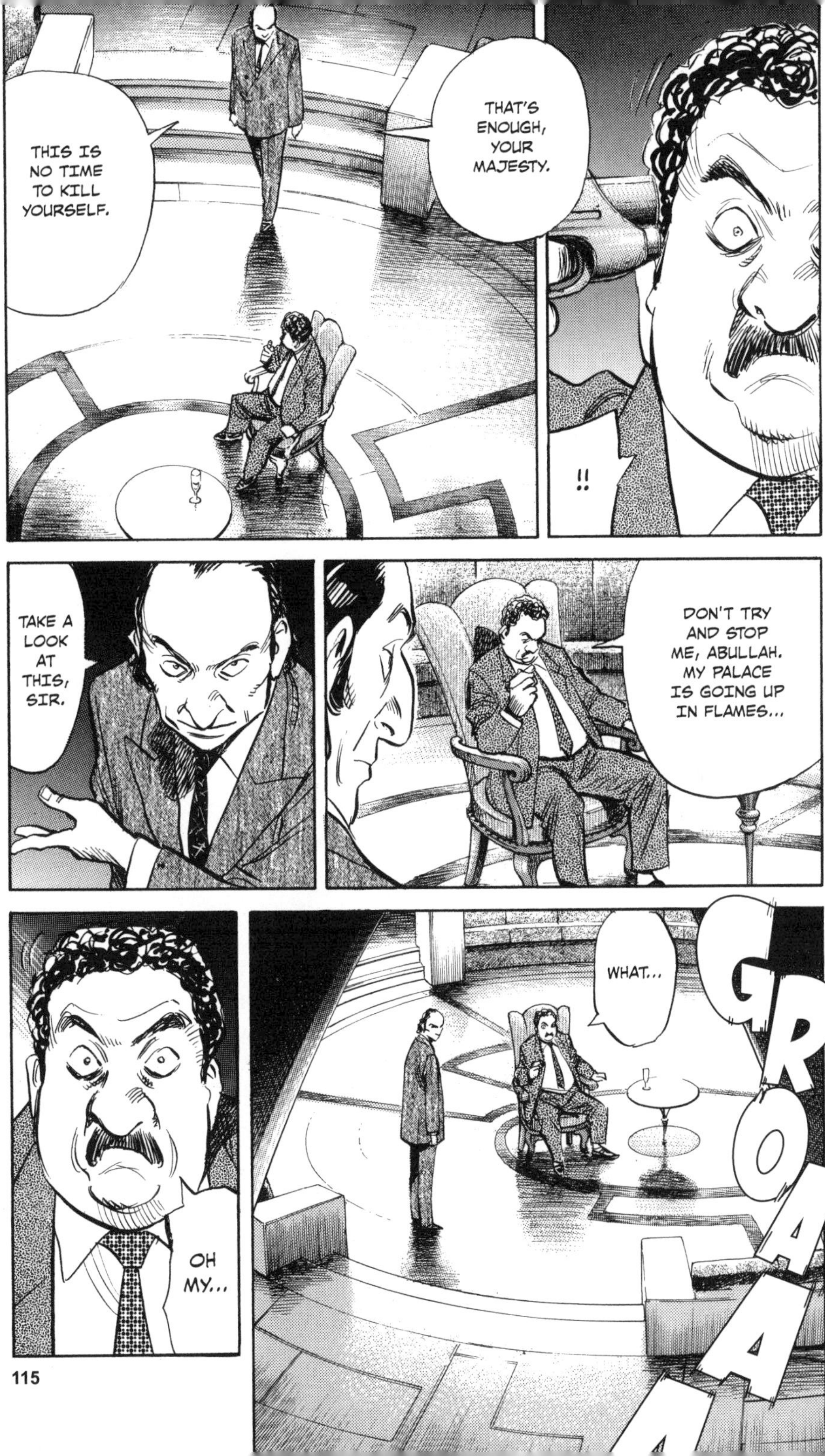
!!
THAT'S ENOUGH, YOUR MAJESTY.
THIS IS NO TIME TO KILL YOURSELF.
DON'T TRY AND STOP ME, ABULLAH. MY PALACE IS GOING UP IN FLAMES...
TAKE A LOOK AT THIS, SIR.
GROAAA
WHAT...
OH MY...

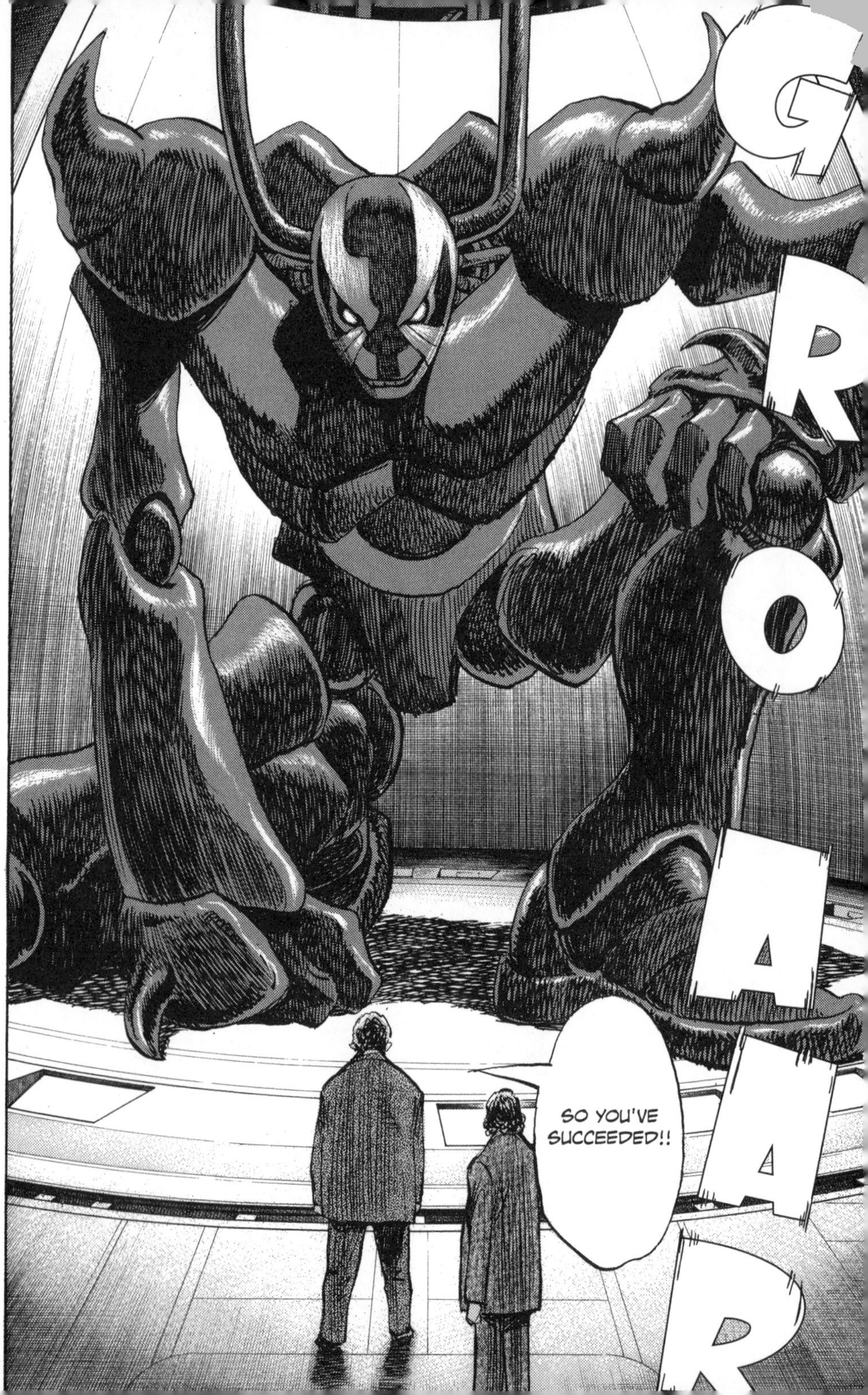
GROAAR
SO YOU'VE SUCCEEDED!!

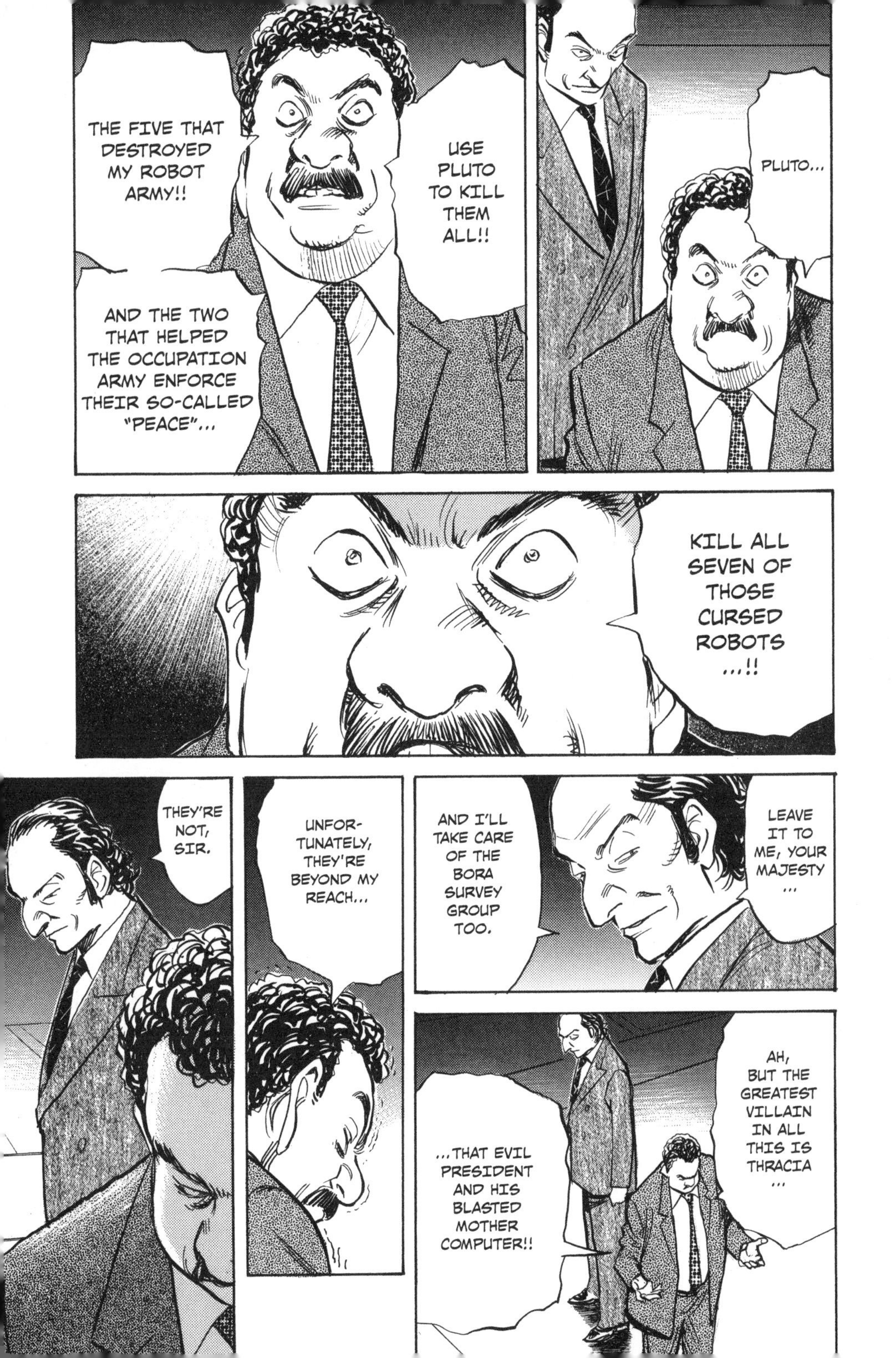
PLUTO...
USE PLUTO TO KILL THEM ALL!!
THE FIVE THAT DESTROYED MY ROBOT ARMY!!
AND THE TWO THAT HELPED THE OCCUPATION ARMY ENFORCE THEIR SO-CALLED "PEACE"...
KILL ALL SEVEN OF THOSE CURSED ROBOTS ...!!
LEAVE IT TO ME, YOUR MAJESTY ...
AND I'LL TAKE CARE OF THE BORA SURVEY GROUP TOO.
AH, BUT THE GREATEST VILLAIN IN ALL THIS IS THRACIA ...
...THAT EVIL PRESIDENT AND HIS BLASTED MOTHER COMPUTER!!
UNFOR-TUNATELY, THEY'RE BEYOND MY REACH...
THEY'RE NOT, SIR.

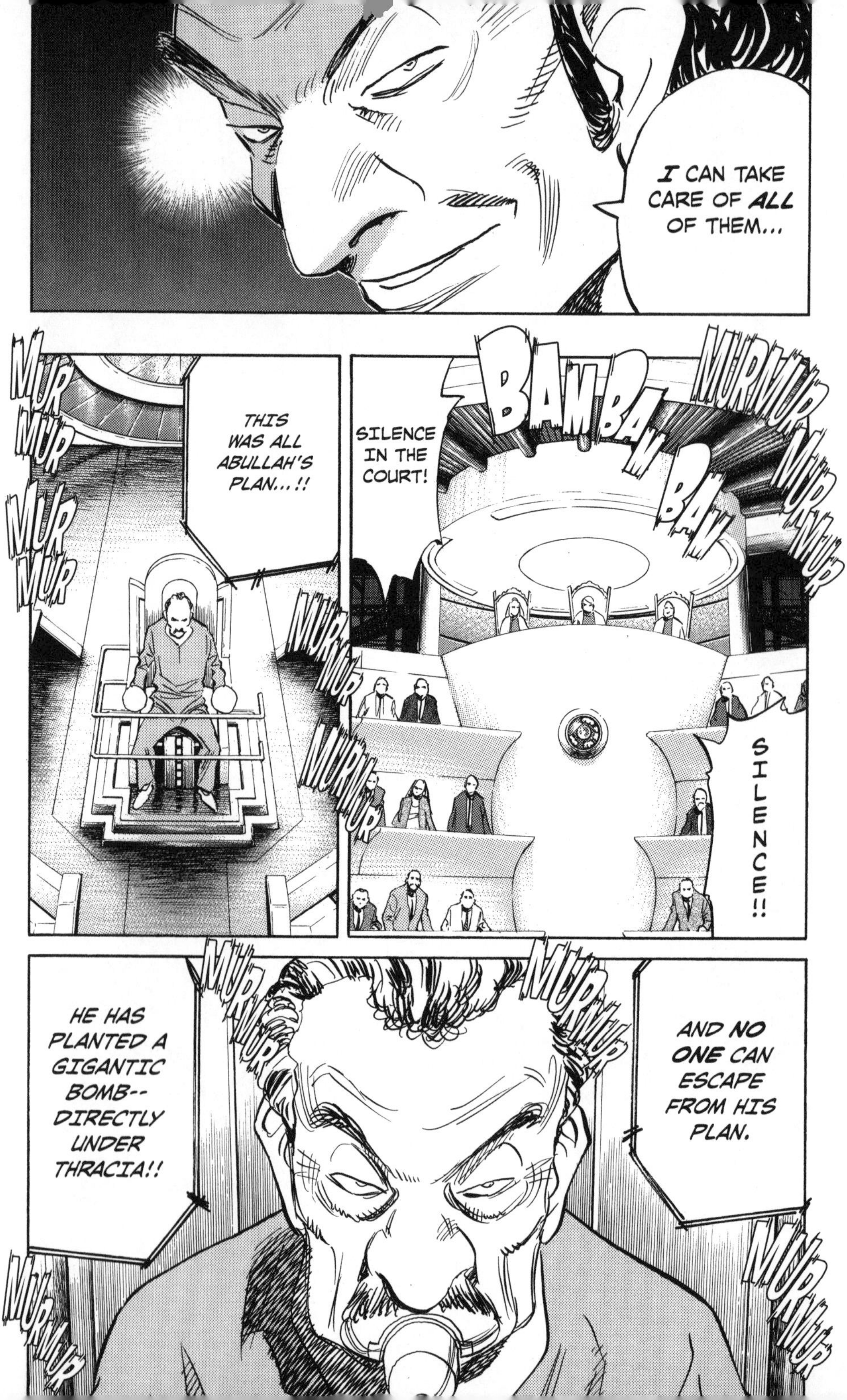
I CAN TAKE CARE OF ALL OF THEM...
BAM BAM BAM
MURMUR MURMUR
SILENCE IN THE COURT!
SILENCE!!
MUR MUR MUR MUR
THIS WAS ALL ABULLAH'S PLAN...!!
MURMUR
MURMUR
MURMUR
MURMUR
AND NO ONE CAN ESCAPE FROM HIS PLAN.
HE HAS PLANTED A GIGANTIC BOMB-- DIRECTLY UNDER THRACIA!!
MURMUR
MURMUR

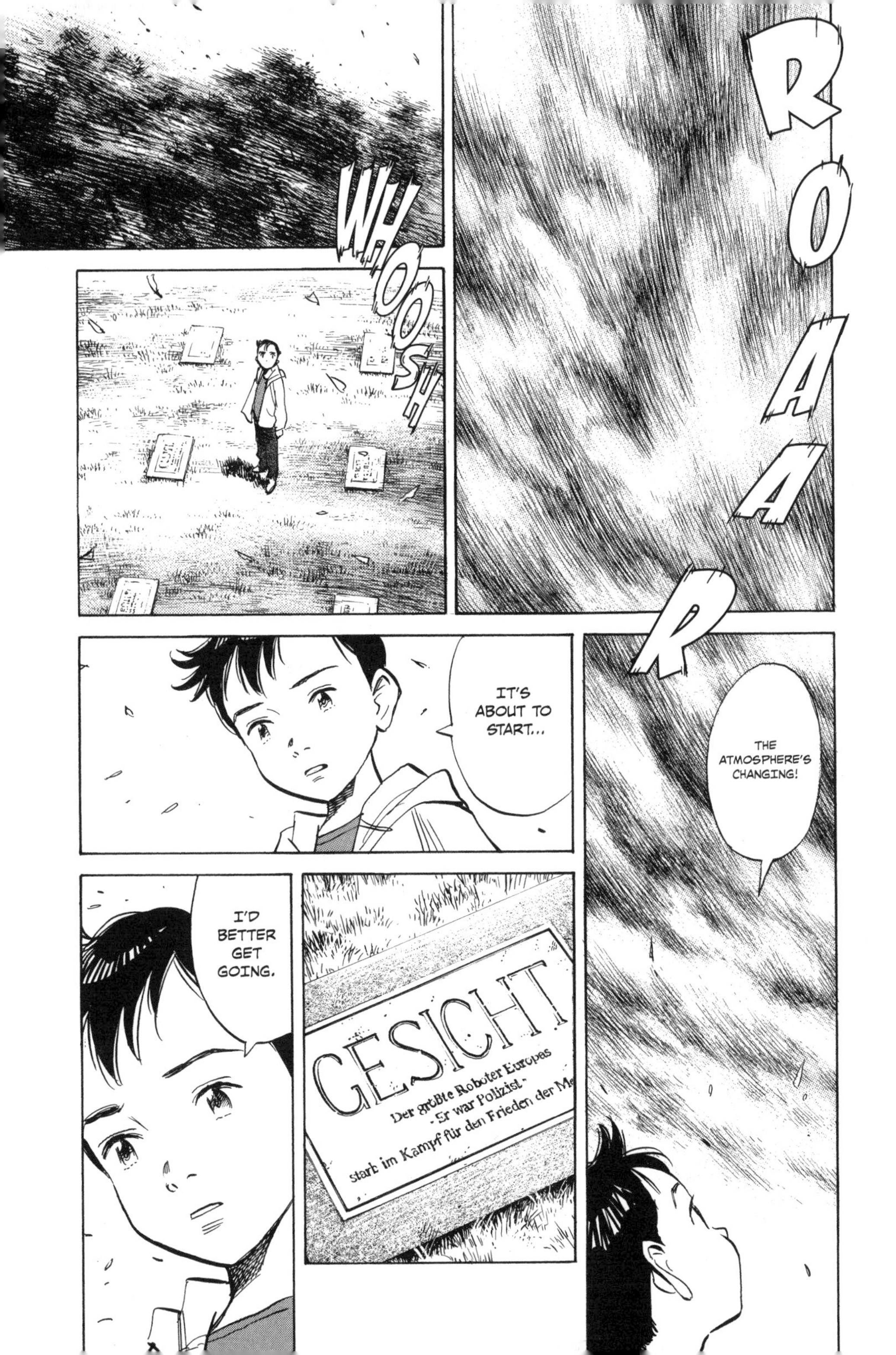
ROAAAR
WHOOOSH
THE ATMOSPHERE'S CHANGING!
IT'S ABOUT TO START...
GESICHT
Der größte Roboter Europas
-Er war Polizist-
starb im Kampf für den Frieden der
I'D BETTER GET GOING.

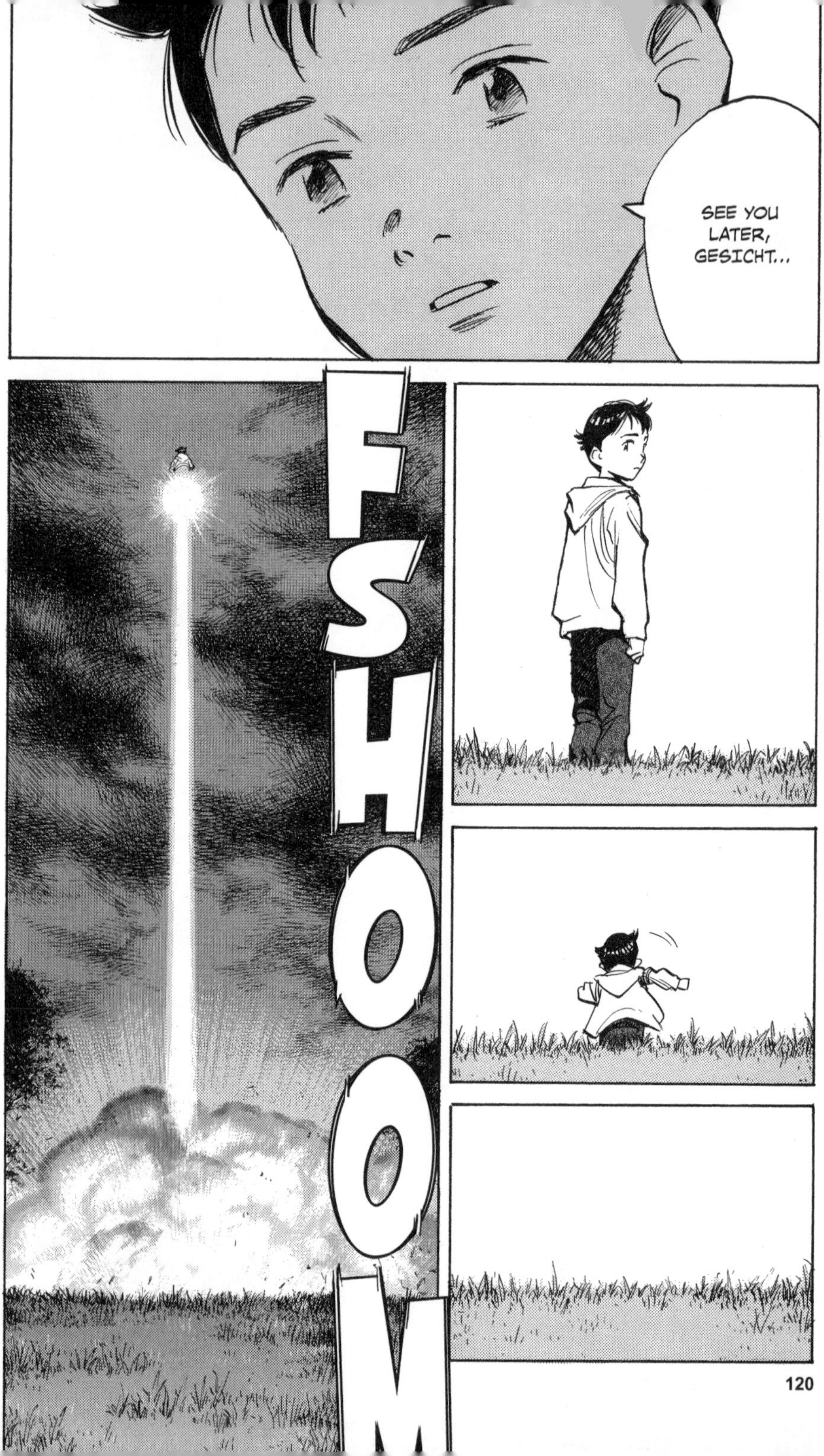
SEE YOU LATER, GESICHT...
FSHOOM

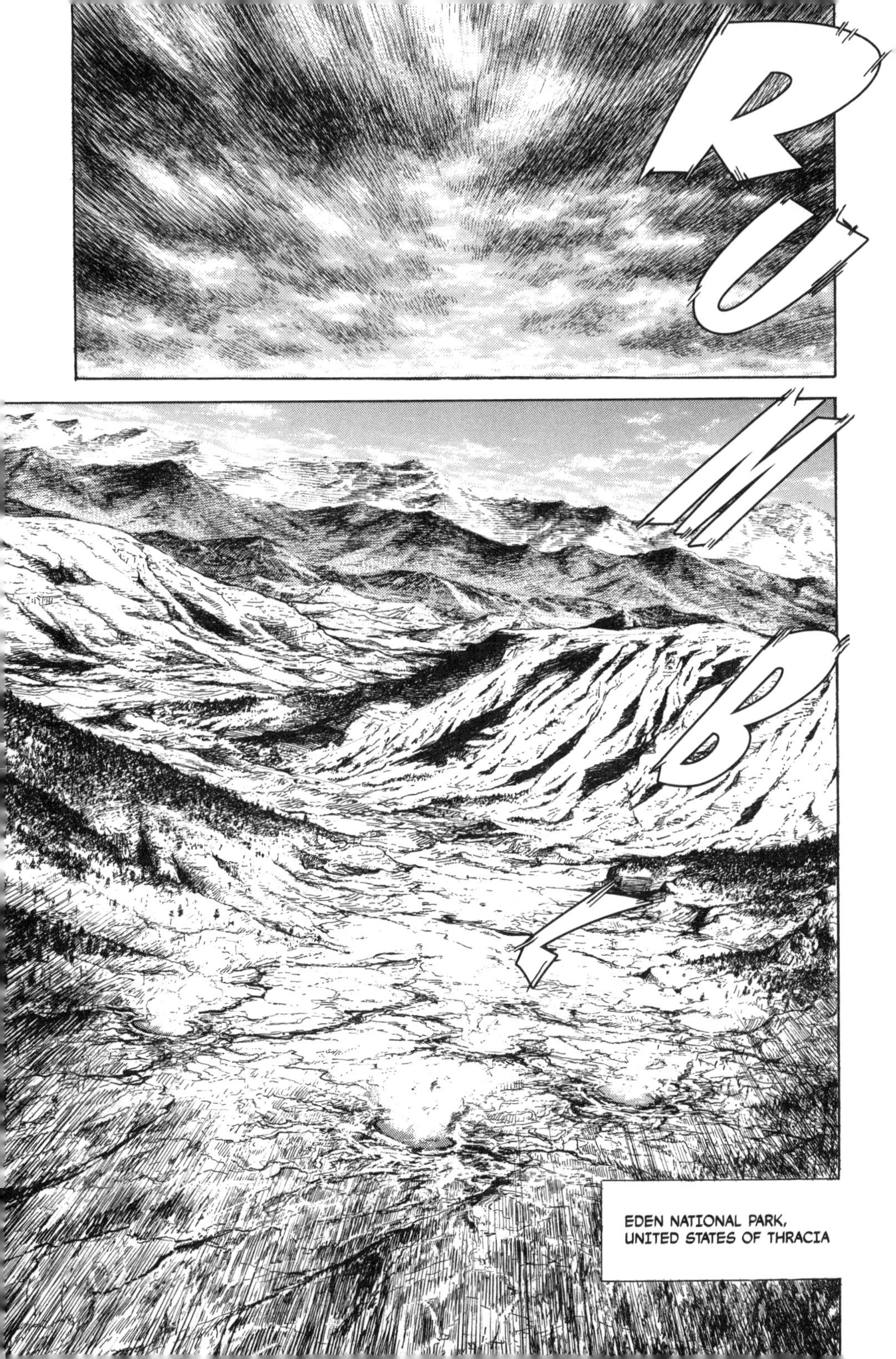
RUMB
EDEN NATIONAL PARK,
UNITED STATES OF THRACIA

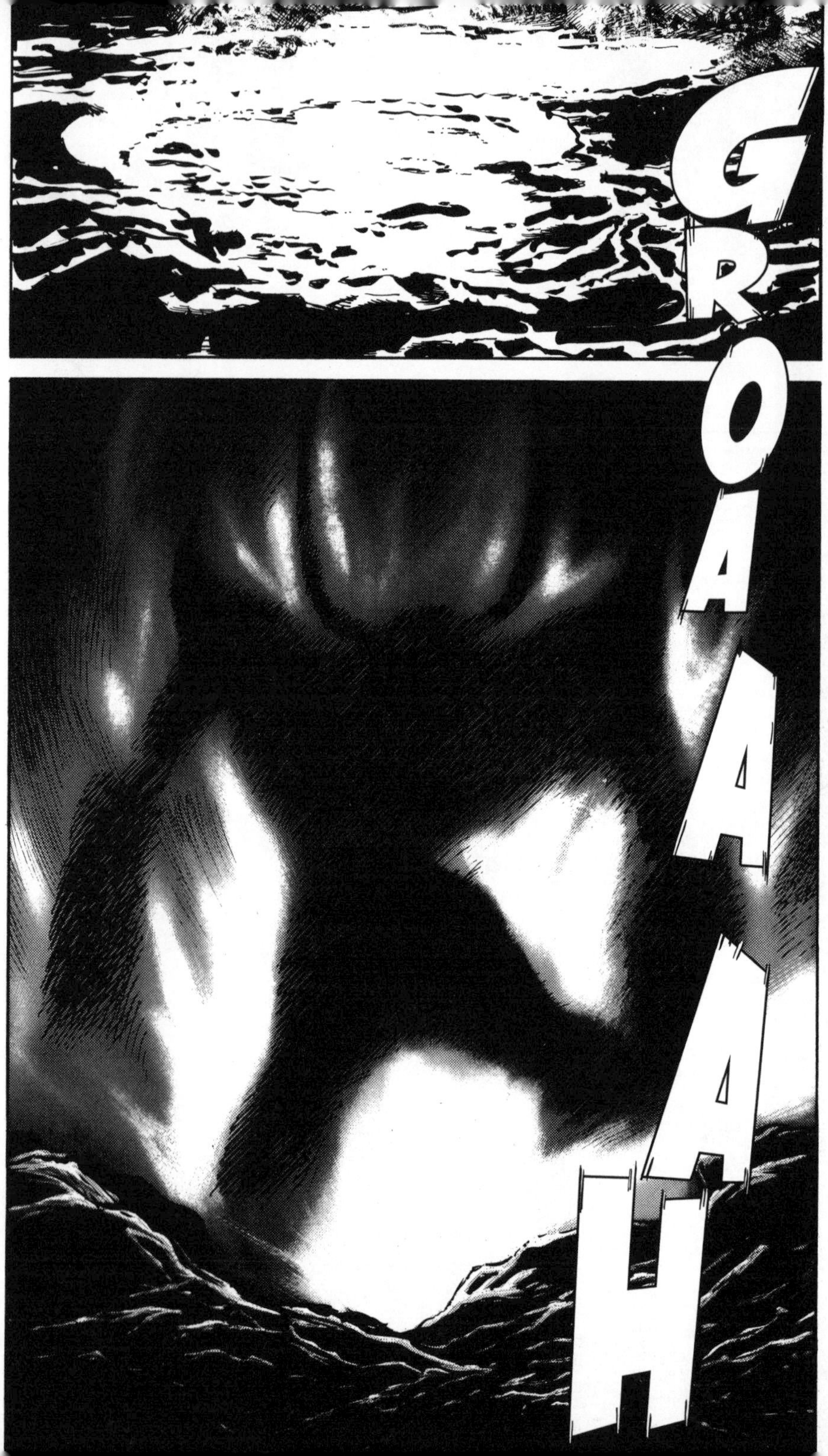
GROAAAH

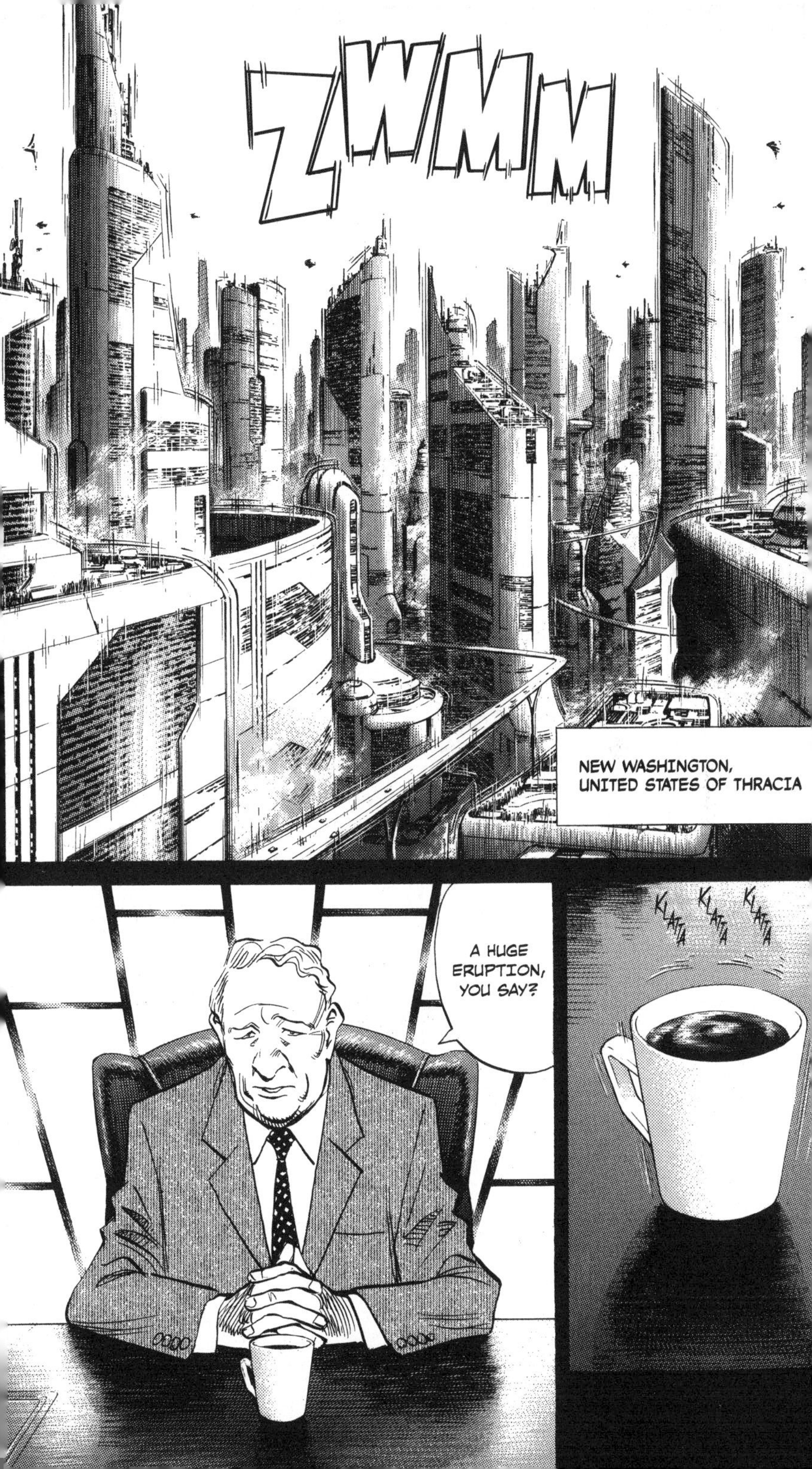
ZWMM
NEW WASHINGTON, UNITED STATES OF THRACIA
KLATTA KLATTA KLATTA
A HUGE ERUPTION, YOU SAY?

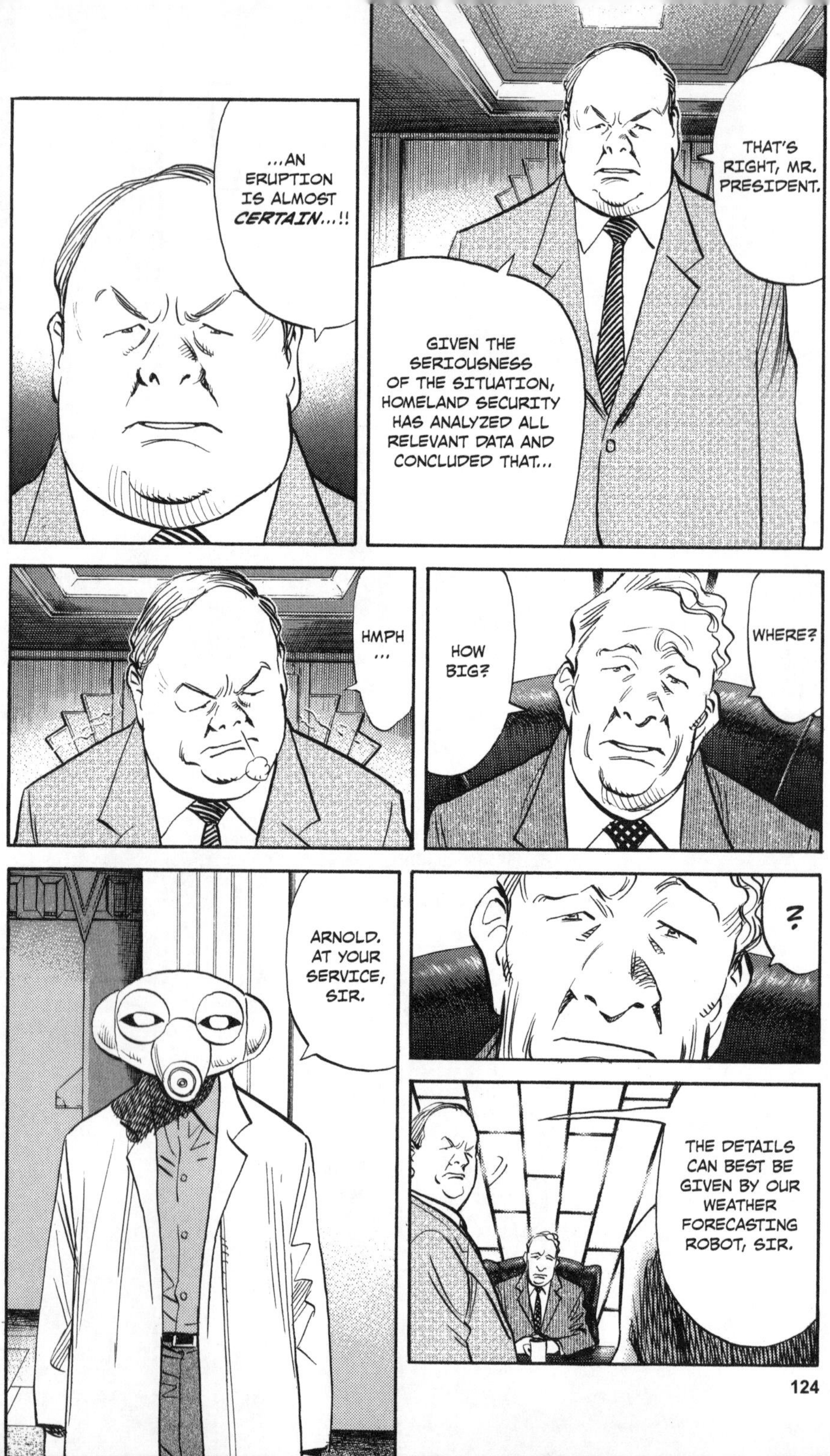
THAT'S RIGHT, MR. PRESIDENT.
GIVEN THE SERIOUSNESS OF THE SITUATION, HOMELAND SECURITY HAS ANALYZED ALL RELEVANT DATA AND CONCLUDED THAT...
...AN ERUPTION IS ALMOST *CERTAIN*...!!
WHERE?
HOW BIG?
HMPH...
?
THE DETAILS CAN BEST BE GIVEN BY OUR WEATHER FORECASTING ROBOT, SIR.
ARNOLD. AT YOUR SERVICE, SIR.

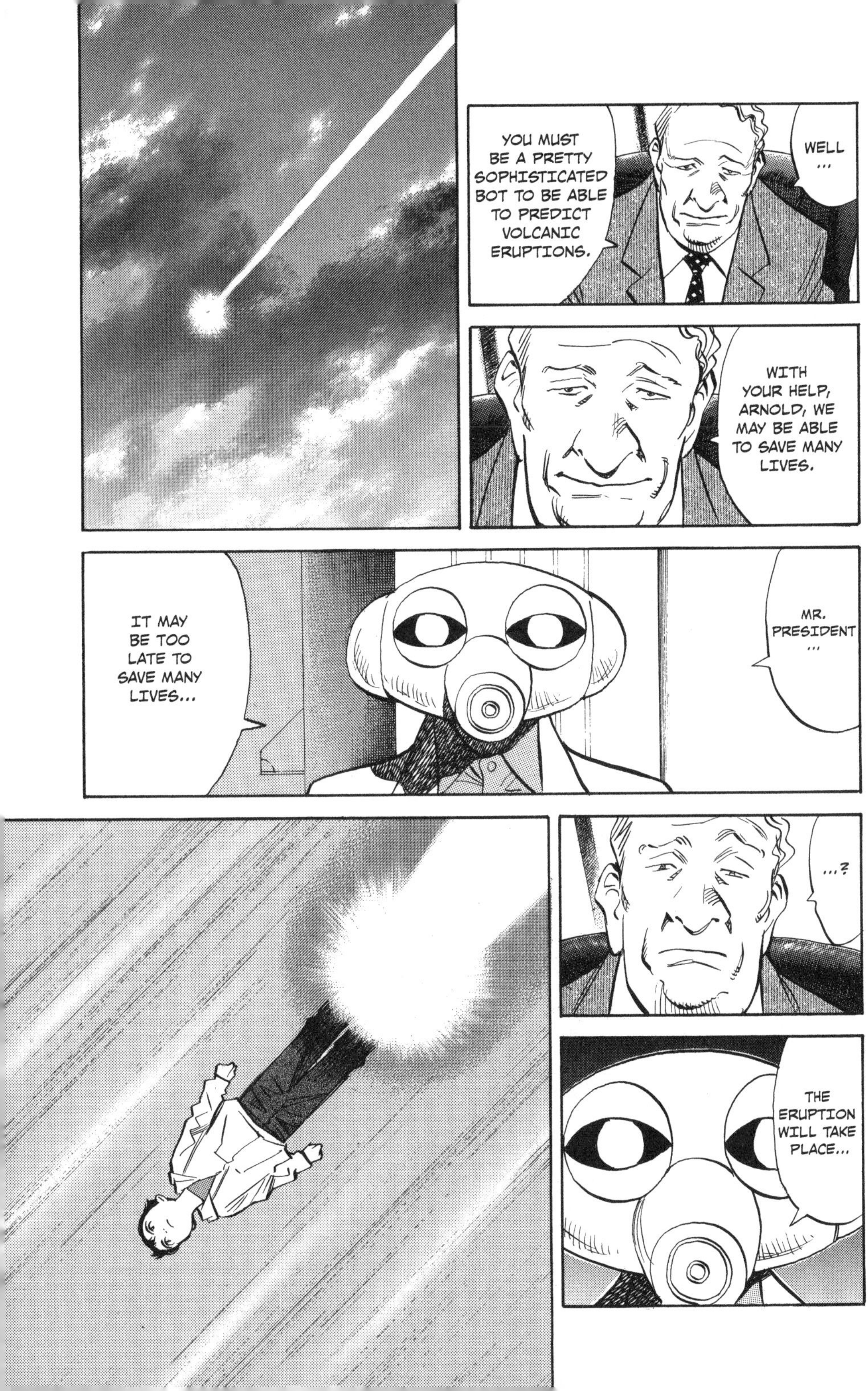
WELL ...
YOU MUST BE A PRETTY SOPHISTICATED BOT TO BE ABLE TO PREDICT VOLCANIC ERUPTIONS.
WITH YOUR HELP, ARNOLD, WE MAY BE ABLE TO SAVE MANY LIVES.
MR. PRESIDENT ...
IT MAY BE TOO LATE TO SAVE MANY LIVES...
...?
THE ERUPTION WILL TAKE PLACE...

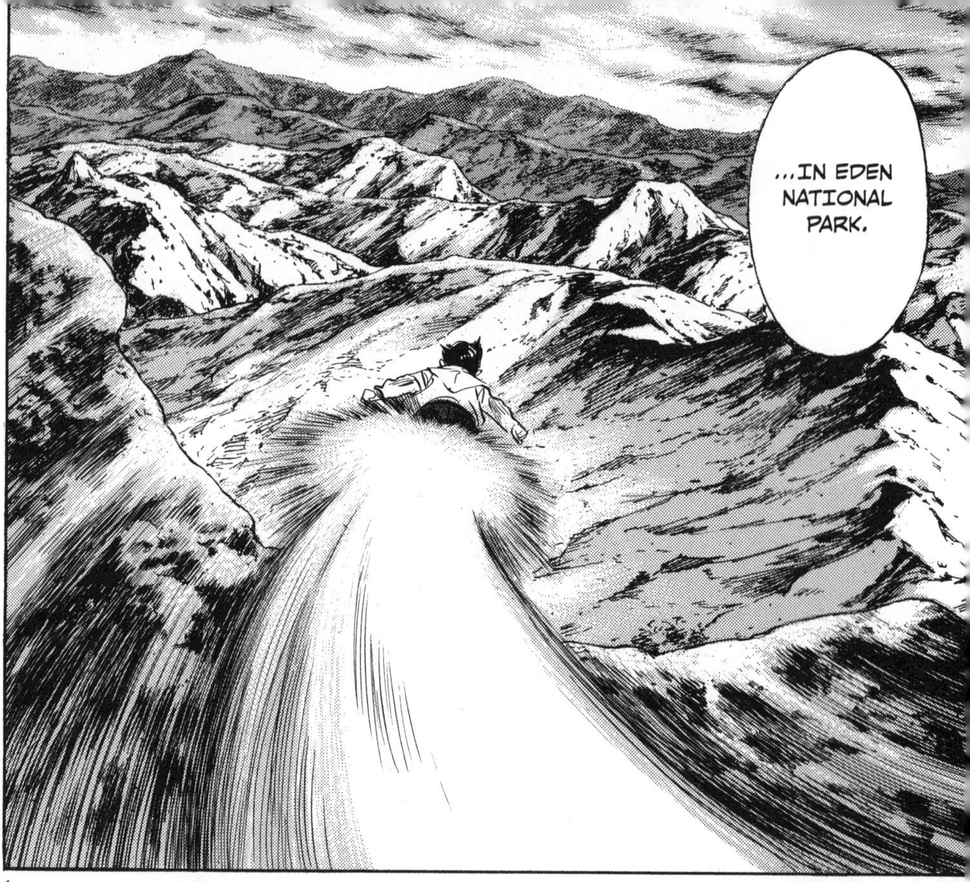
...IN EDEN NATIONAL PARK.

4

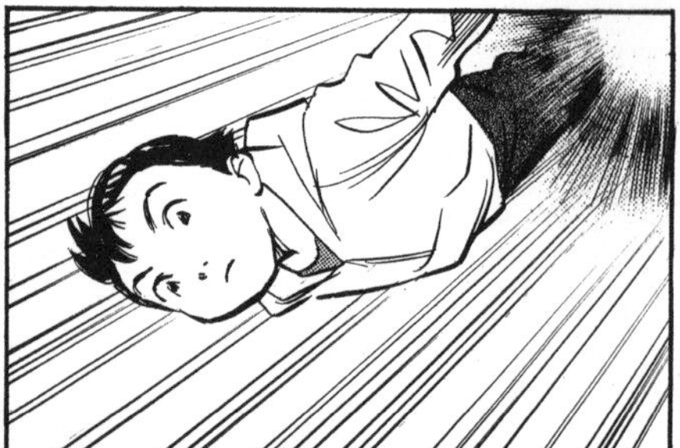

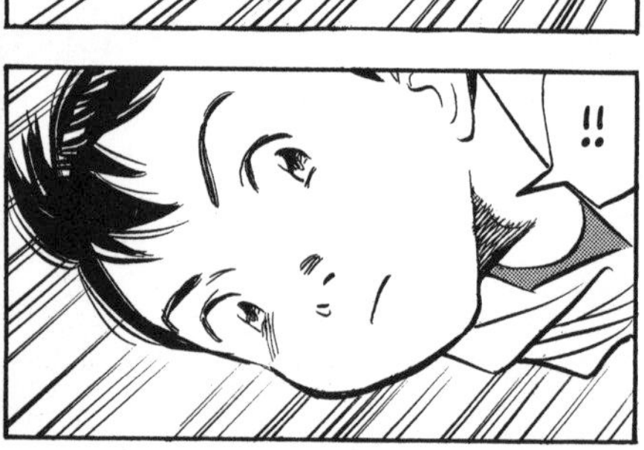
!!

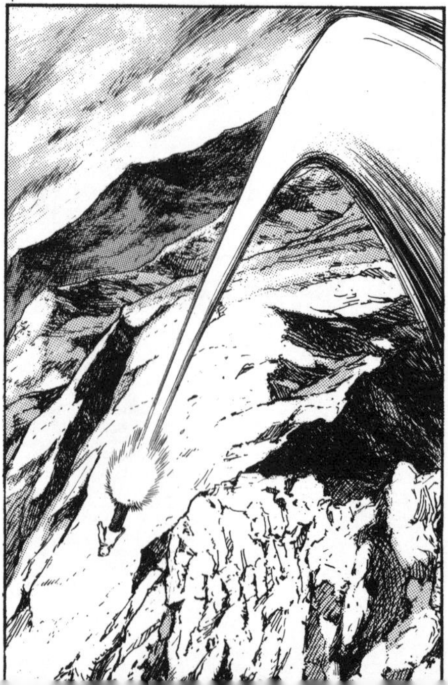

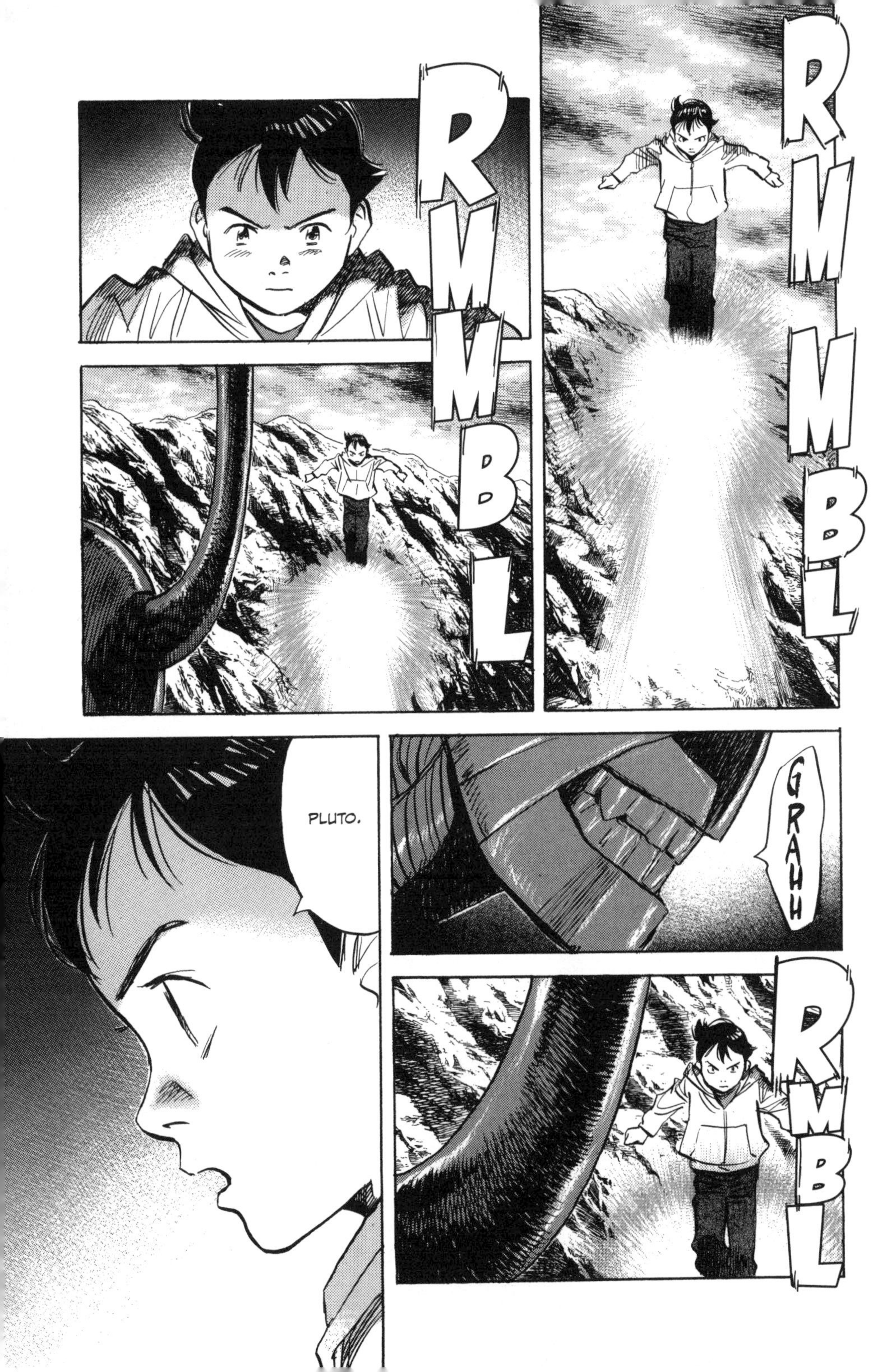
RMMBL
RMMBL
GRAHH
RMBL
PLUTO.

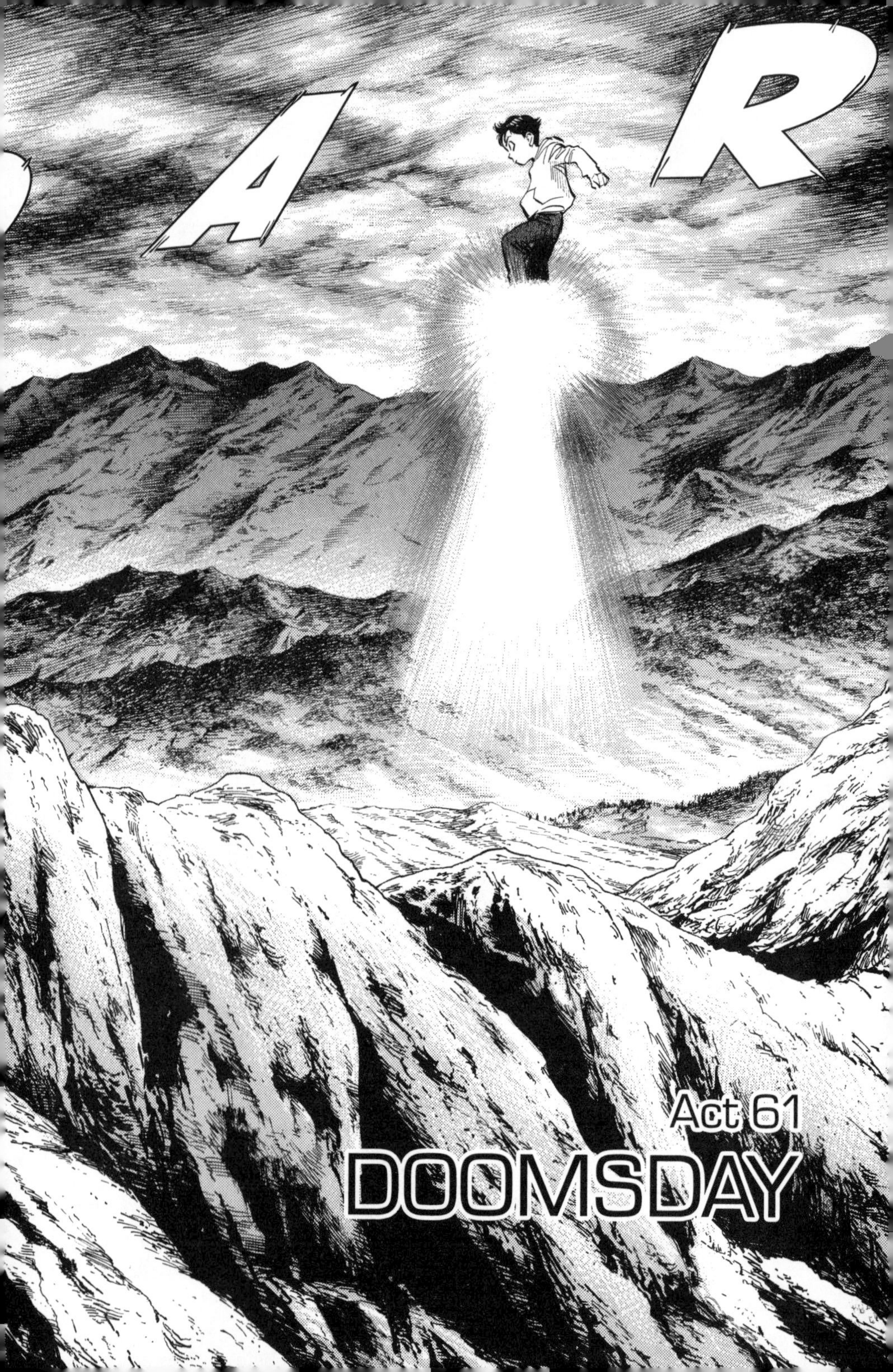

A
R
Act 61
DOOMSDAY

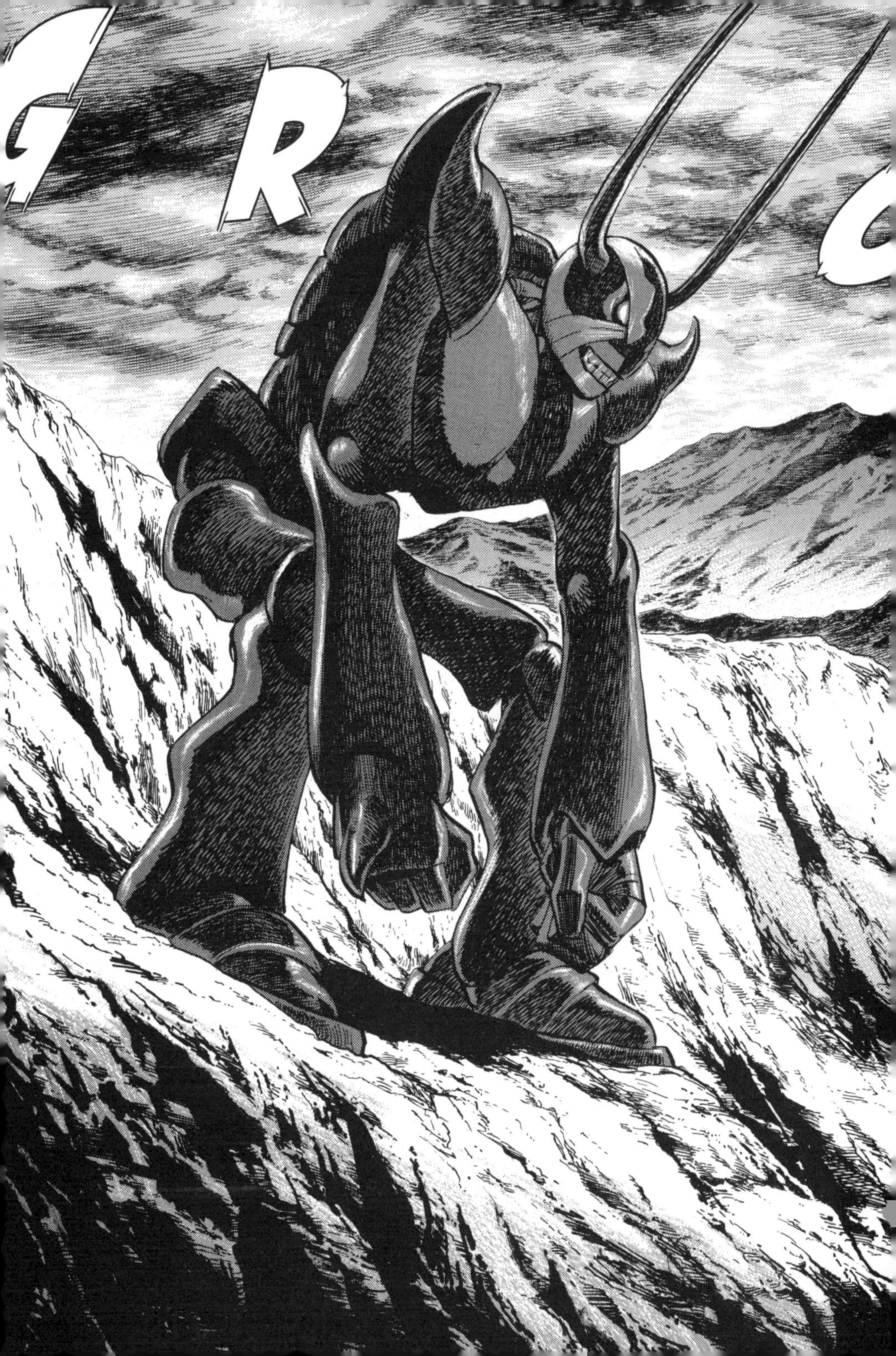
G R

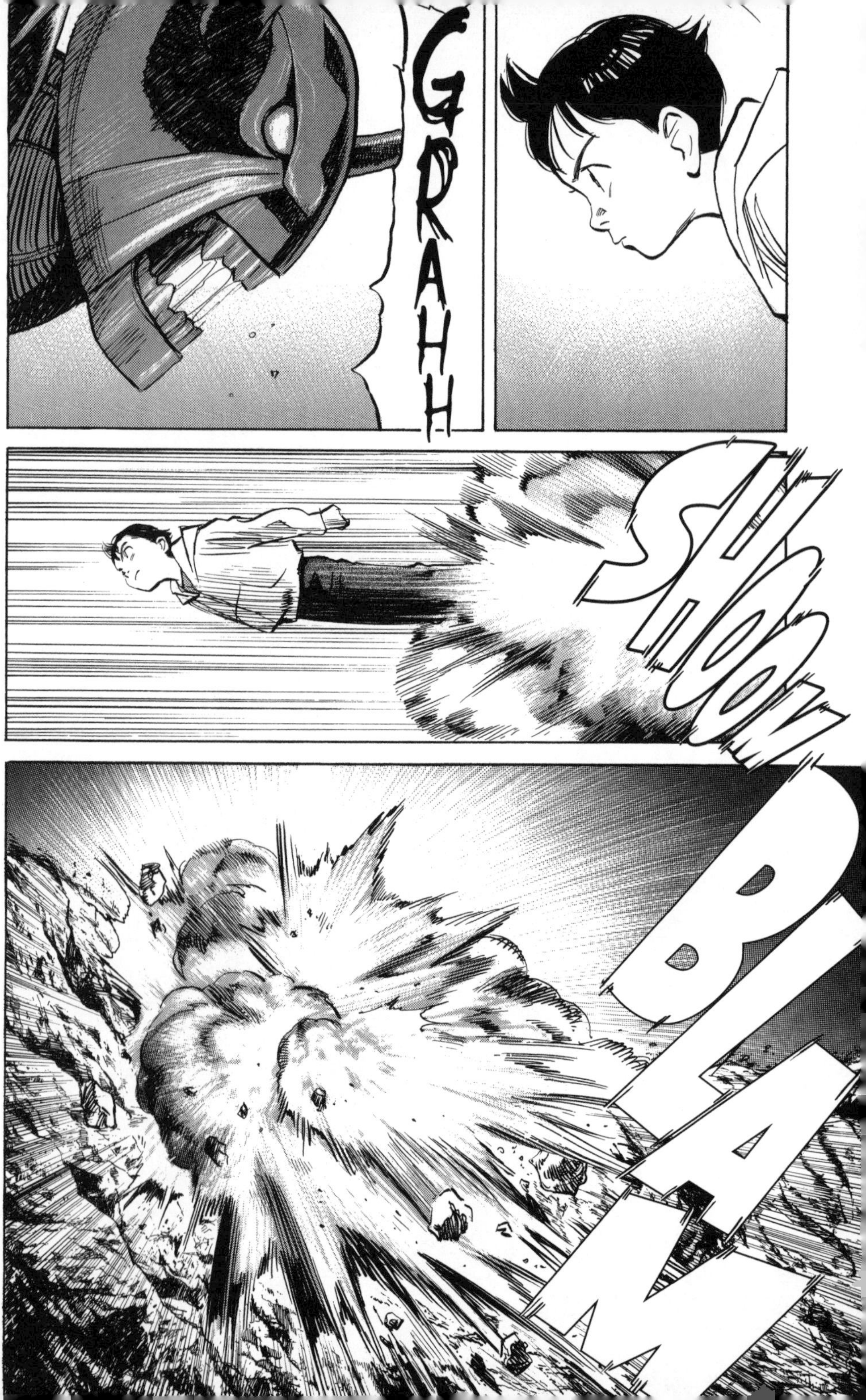
GRAHH
SHOOM
BRAM

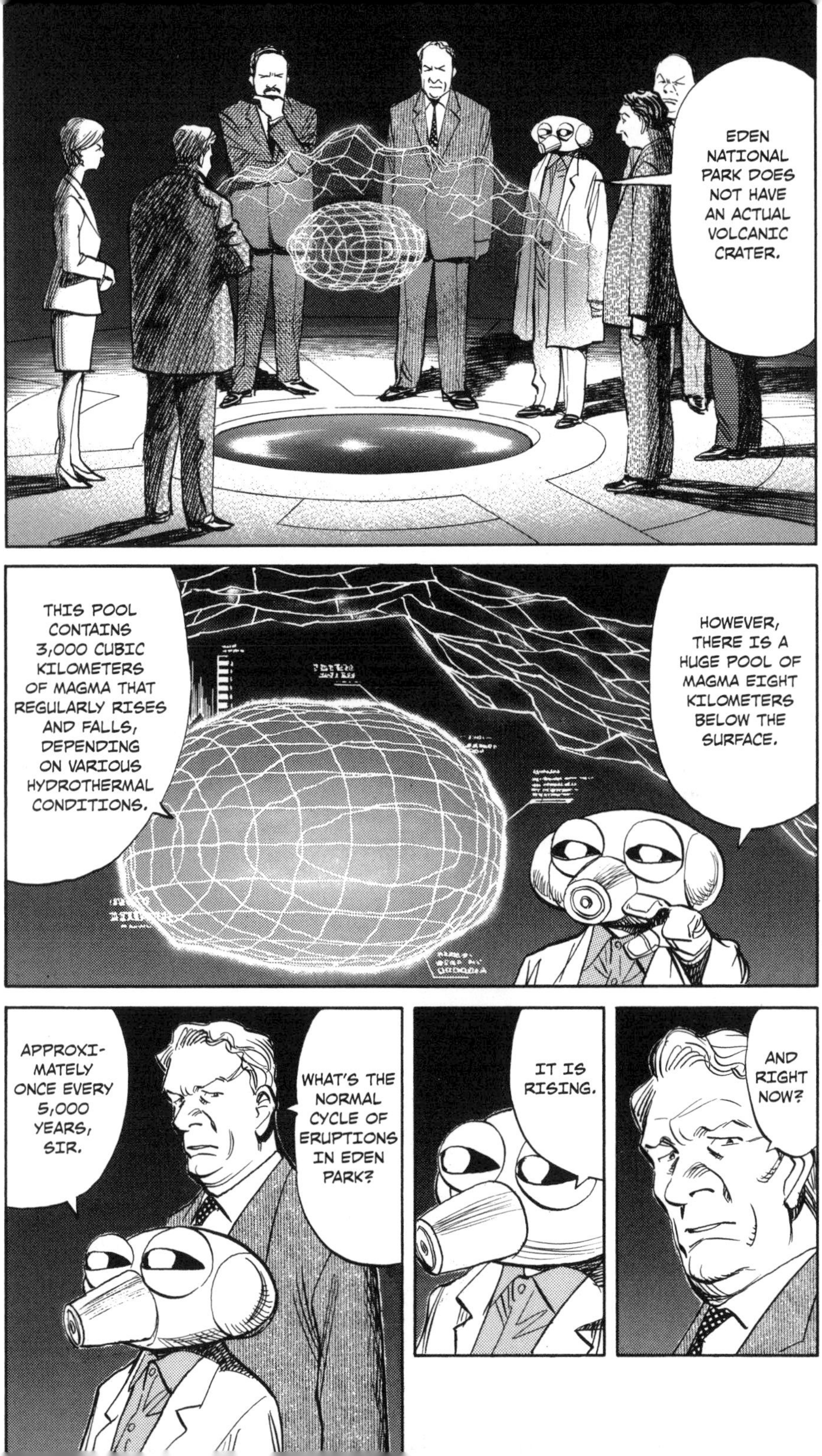
EDEN NATIONAL PARK DOES NOT HAVE AN ACTUAL VOLCANIC CRATER.
HOWEVER, THERE IS A HUGE POOL OF MAGMA EIGHT KILOMETERS BELOW THE SURFACE.
THIS POOL CONTAINS 3,000 CUBIC KILOMETERS OF MAGMA THAT REGULARLY RISES AND FALLS, DEPENDING ON VARIOUS HYDROTHERMAL CONDITIONS.
AND RIGHT NOW?
IT IS RISING.
WHAT'S THE NORMAL CYCLE OF ERUPTIONS IN EDEN PARK?
APPROXI-MATELY ONCE EVERY 5,000 YEARS, SIR.

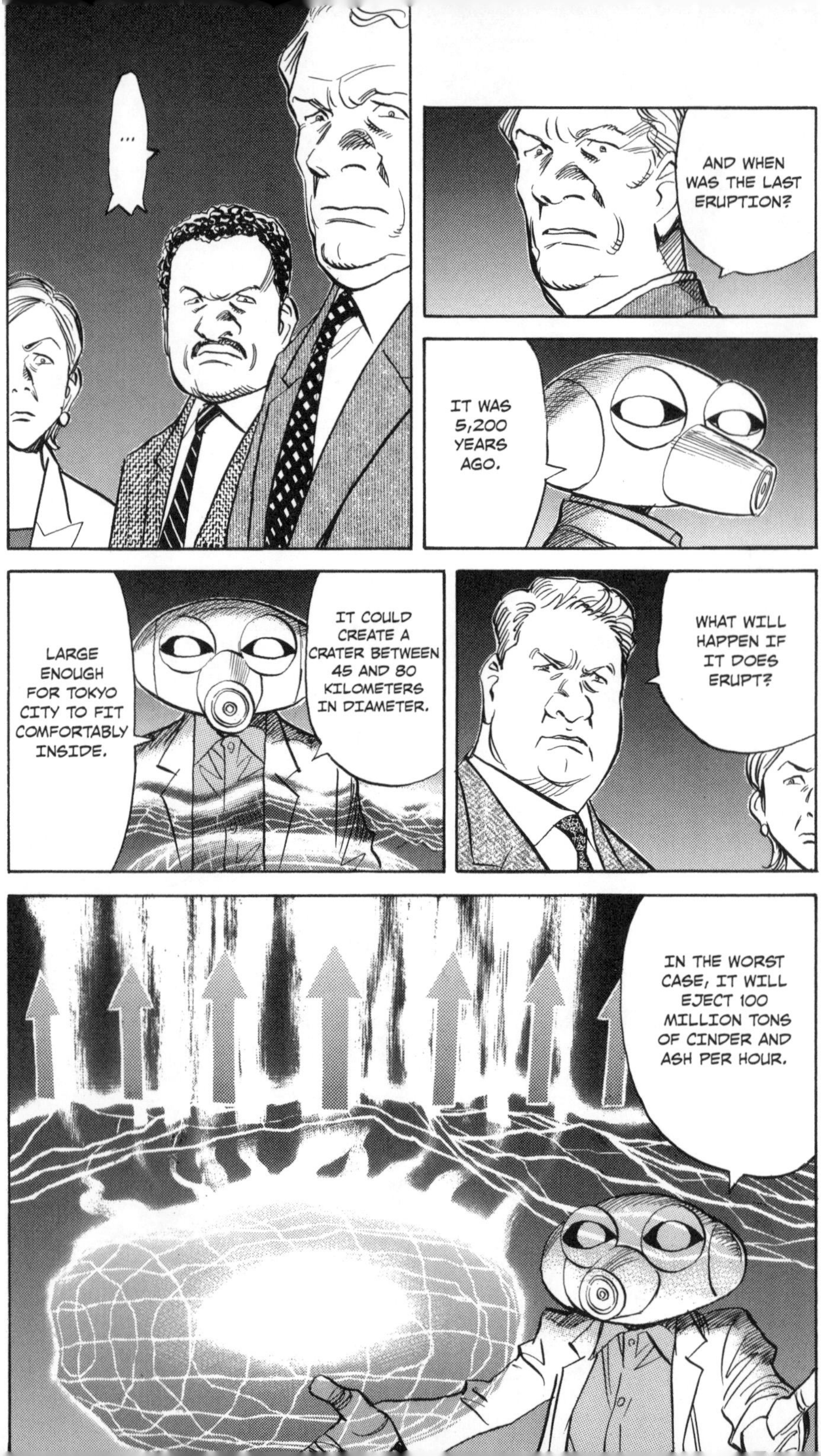
AND WHEN WAS THE LAST ERUPTION?
IT WAS 5,200 YEARS AGO.
...
WHAT WILL HAPPEN IF IT DOES ERUPT?
IT COULD CREATE A CRATER BETWEEN 45 AND 80 KILOMETERS IN DIAMETER.
LARGE ENOUGH FOR TOKYO CITY TO FIT COMFORTABLY INSIDE.
IN THE WORST CASE, IT WILL EJECT 100 MILLION TONS OF CINDER AND ASH PER HOUR.

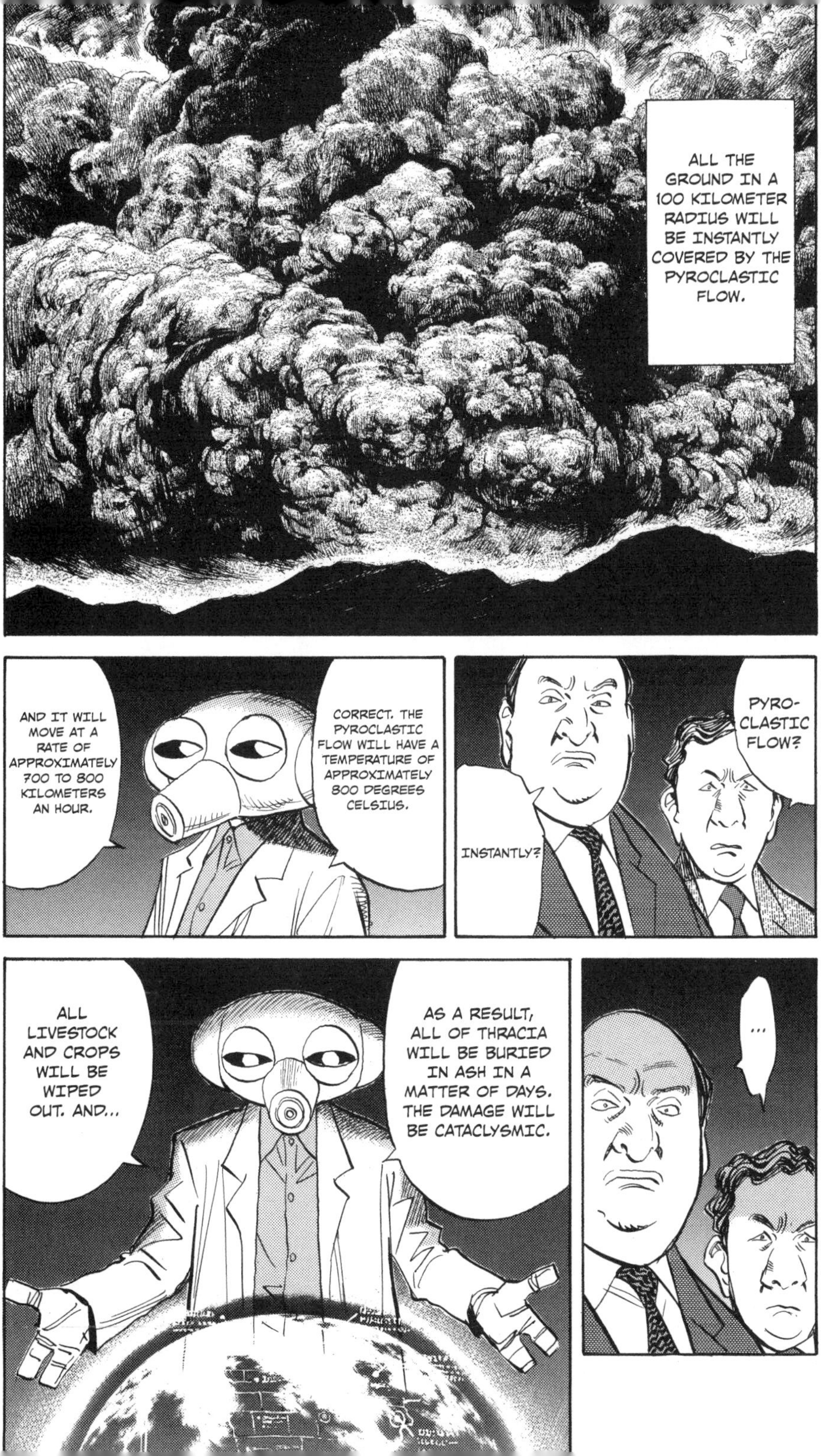
ALL THE GROUND IN A 100 KILOMETER RADIUS WILL BE INSTANTLY COVERED BY THE PYROCLASTIC FLOW.
PYRO-CLASTIC FLOW?
INSTANTLY?
CORRECT. THE PYROCLASTIC FLOW WILL HAVE A TEMPERATURE OF APPROXIMATELY 800 DEGREES CELSIUS.
AND IT WILL MOVE AT A RATE OF APPROXIMATELY 700 TO 800 KILOMETERS AN HOUR.
...
AS A RESULT, ALL OF THRACIA WILL BE BURIED IN ASH IN A MATTER OF DAYS. THE DAMAGE WILL BE CATACLYSMIC.
ALL LIVESTOCK AND CROPS WILL BE WIPED OUT. AND...

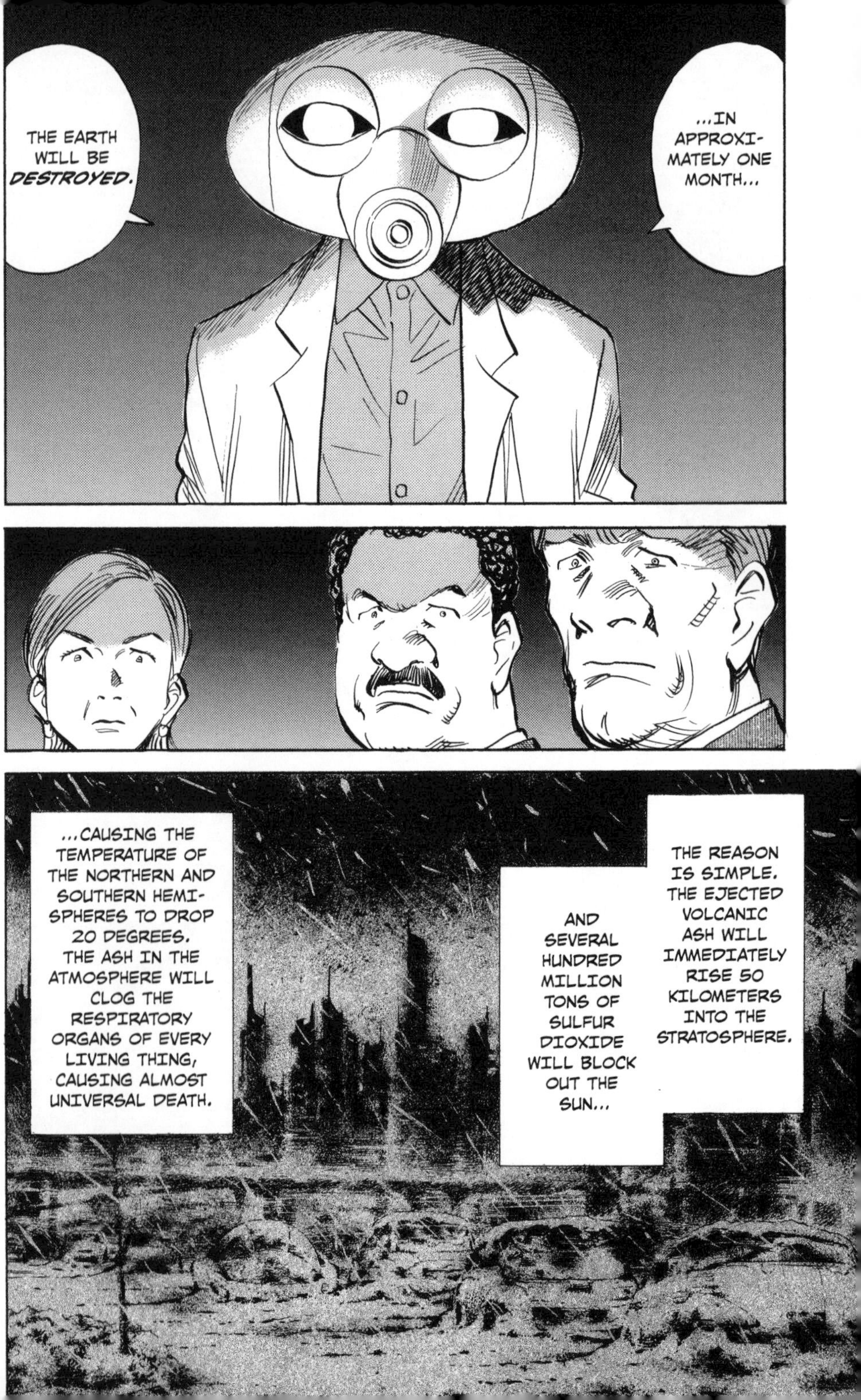
...IN APPROXIMATELY ONE MONTH...
THE EARTH WILL BE *DESTROYED.*
THE REASON IS SIMPLE. THE EJECTED VOLCANIC ASH WILL IMMEDIATELY RISE 50 KILOMETERS INTO THE STRATOSPHERE.
AND SEVERAL HUNDRED MILLION TONS OF SULFUR DIOXIDE WILL BLOCK OUT THE SUN...
...CAUSING THE TEMPERATURE OF THE NORTHERN AND SOUTHERN HEMISPHERES TO DROP 20 DEGREES. THE ASH IN THE ATMOSPHERE WILL CLOG THE RESPIRATORY ORGANS OF EVERY LIVING THING, CAUSING ALMOST UNIVERSAL DEATH.

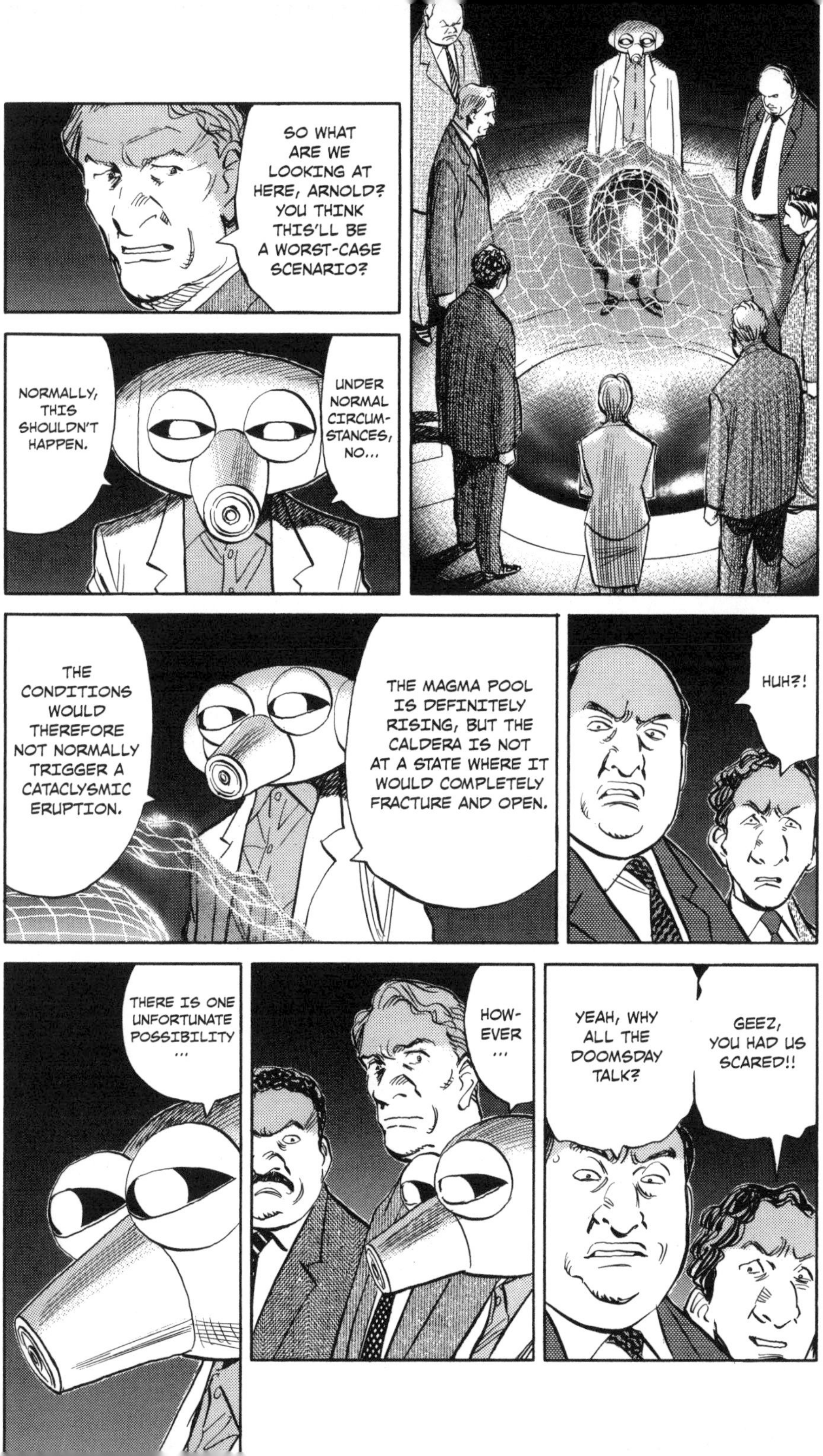
SO WHAT ARE WE LOOKING AT HERE, ARNOLD? YOU THINK THIS'LL BE A WORST-CASE SCENARIO?
UNDER NORMAL CIRCUM-STANCES, NO...
NORMALLY, THIS SHOULDN'T HAPPEN.
HUH?!
THE MAGMA POOL IS DEFINITELY RISING, BUT THE CALDERA IS NOT AT A STATE WHERE IT WOULD COMPLETELY FRACTURE AND OPEN.
THE CONDITIONS WOULD THEREFORE NOT NORMALLY TRIGGER A CATACLYSMIC ERUPTION.
GEEZ, YOU HAD US SCARED!!
YEAH, WHY ALL THE DOOMSDAY TALK?
HOW-EVER ...
THERE IS ONE UNFORTUNATE POSSIBILITY ...

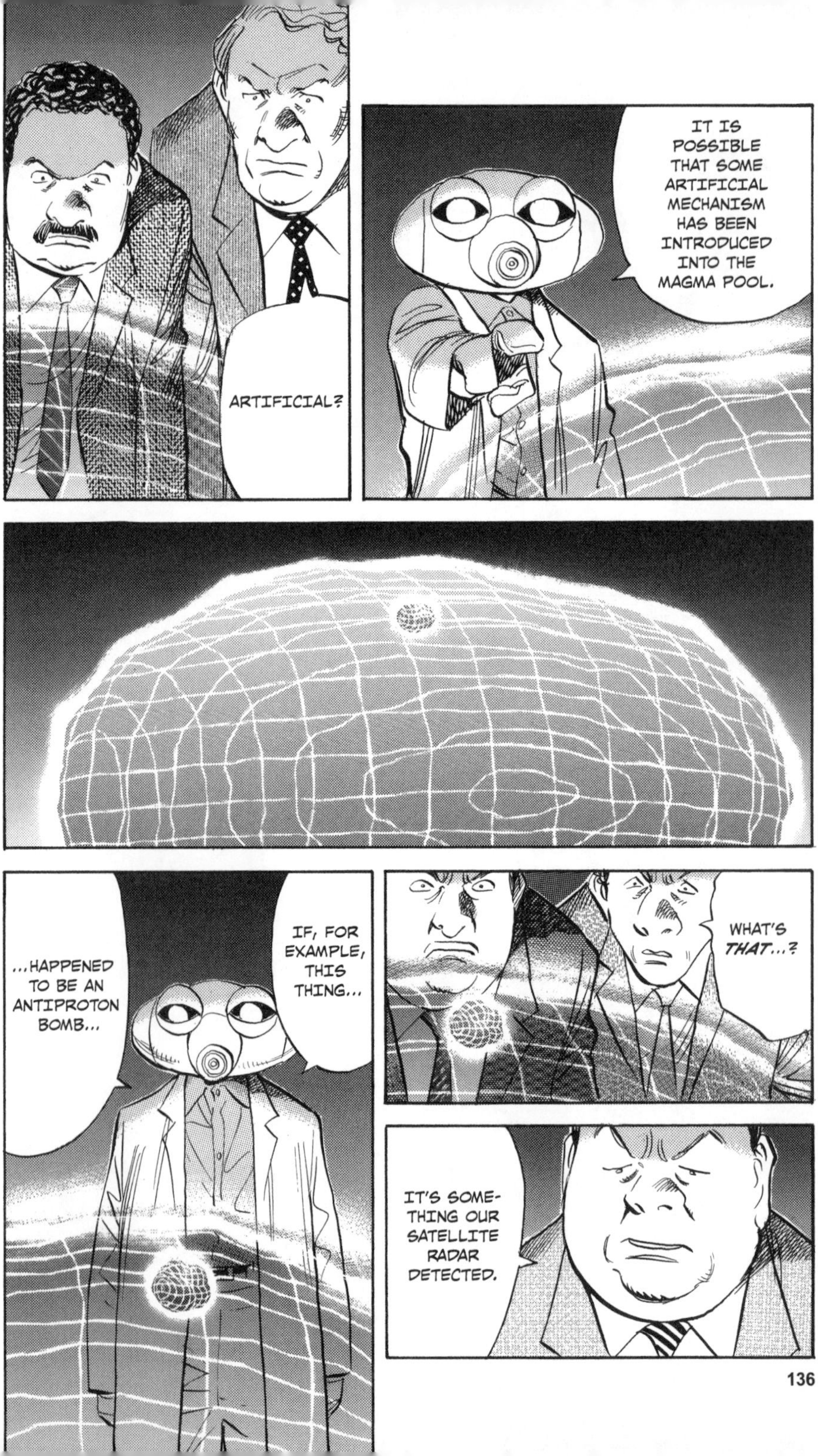
IT IS POSSIBLE THAT SOME ARTIFICIAL MECHANISM HAS BEEN INTRODUCED INTO THE MAGMA POOL.
ARTIFICIAL?
WHAT'S *THAT*...?
IT'S SOME-THING OUR SATELLITE RADAR DETECTED.
IF, FOR EXAMPLE, THIS THING...
...HAPPENED TO BE AN ANTIPROTON BOMB...

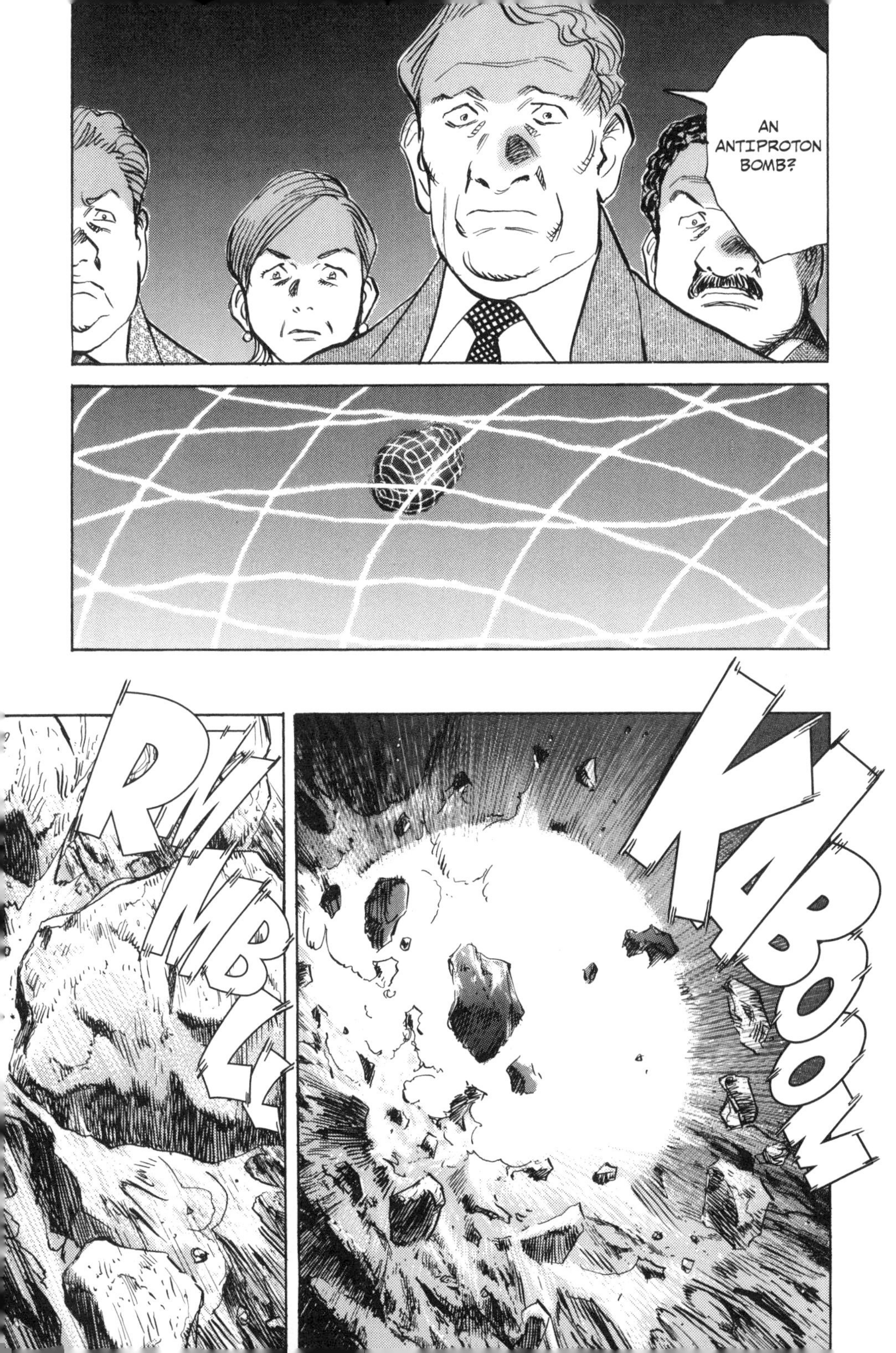
AN ANTIPROTON BOMB?
KABOOM
RMBL

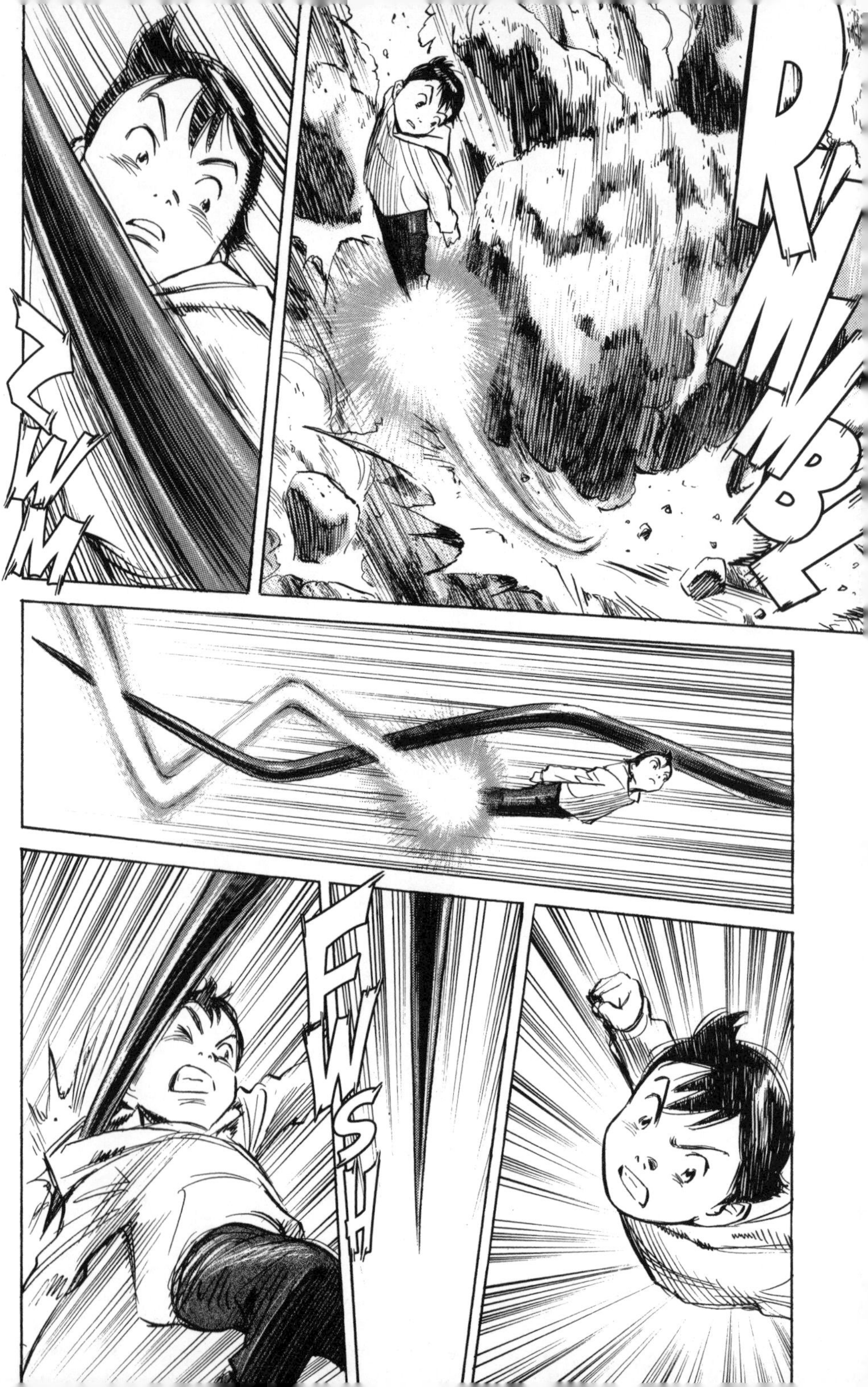
RMBL
ZWM
FWSH

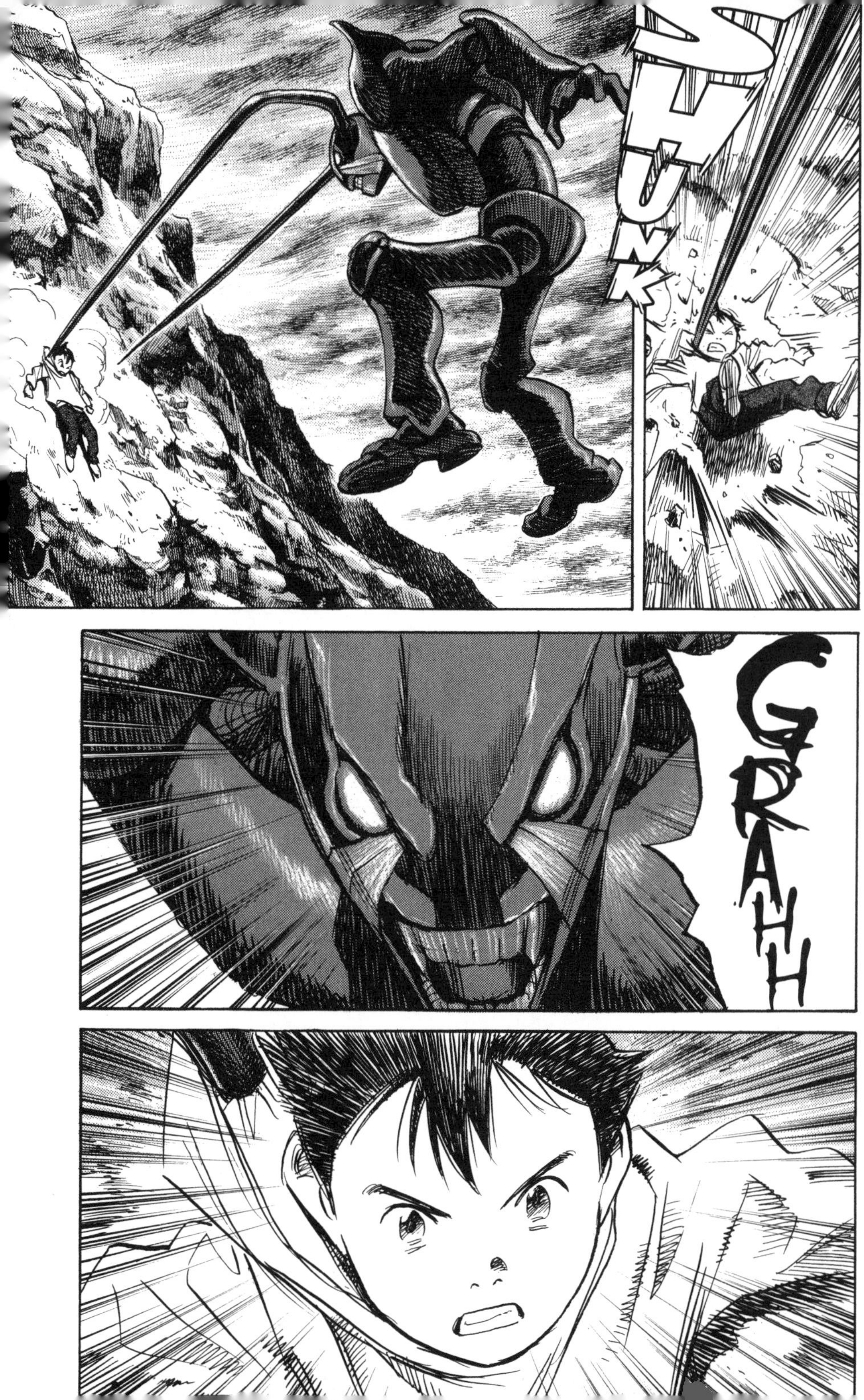
CHUNK
GRAHH

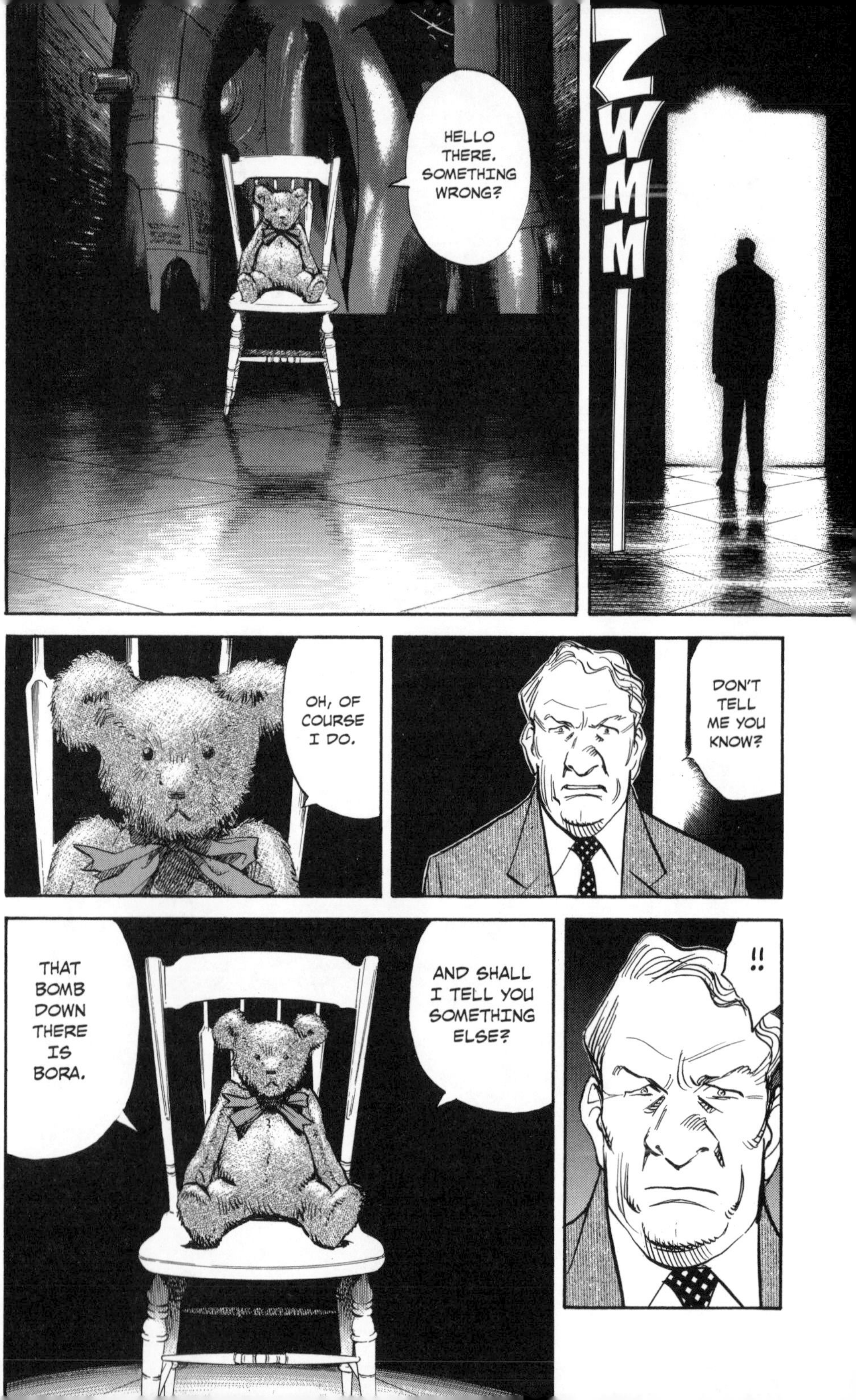
ZWMM
HELLO THERE. SOMETHING WRONG?
DON'T TELL ME YOU KNOW?
OH, OF COURSE I DO.
!!
AND SHALL I TELL YOU SOMETHING ELSE?
THAT BOMB DOWN THERE IS BORA.

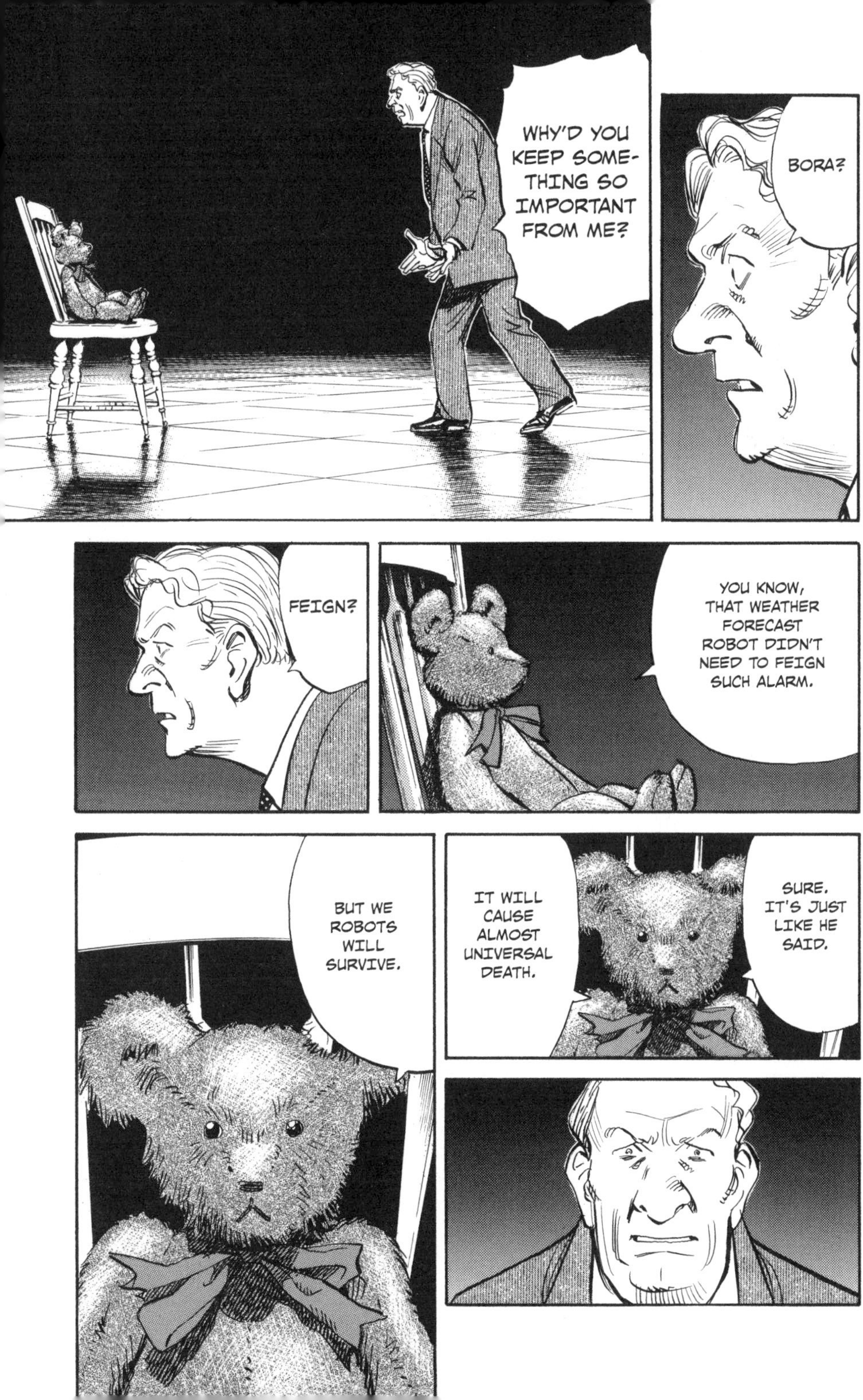
BORA?
WHY'D YOU KEEP SOME-THING SO IMPORTANT FROM ME?
YOU KNOW, THAT WEATHER FORECAST ROBOT DIDN'T NEED TO FEIGN SUCH ALARM.
FEIGN?
SURE. IT'S JUST LIKE HE SAID.
IT WILL CAUSE ALMOST UNIVERSAL DEATH.
BUT WE ROBOTS WILL SURVIVE.

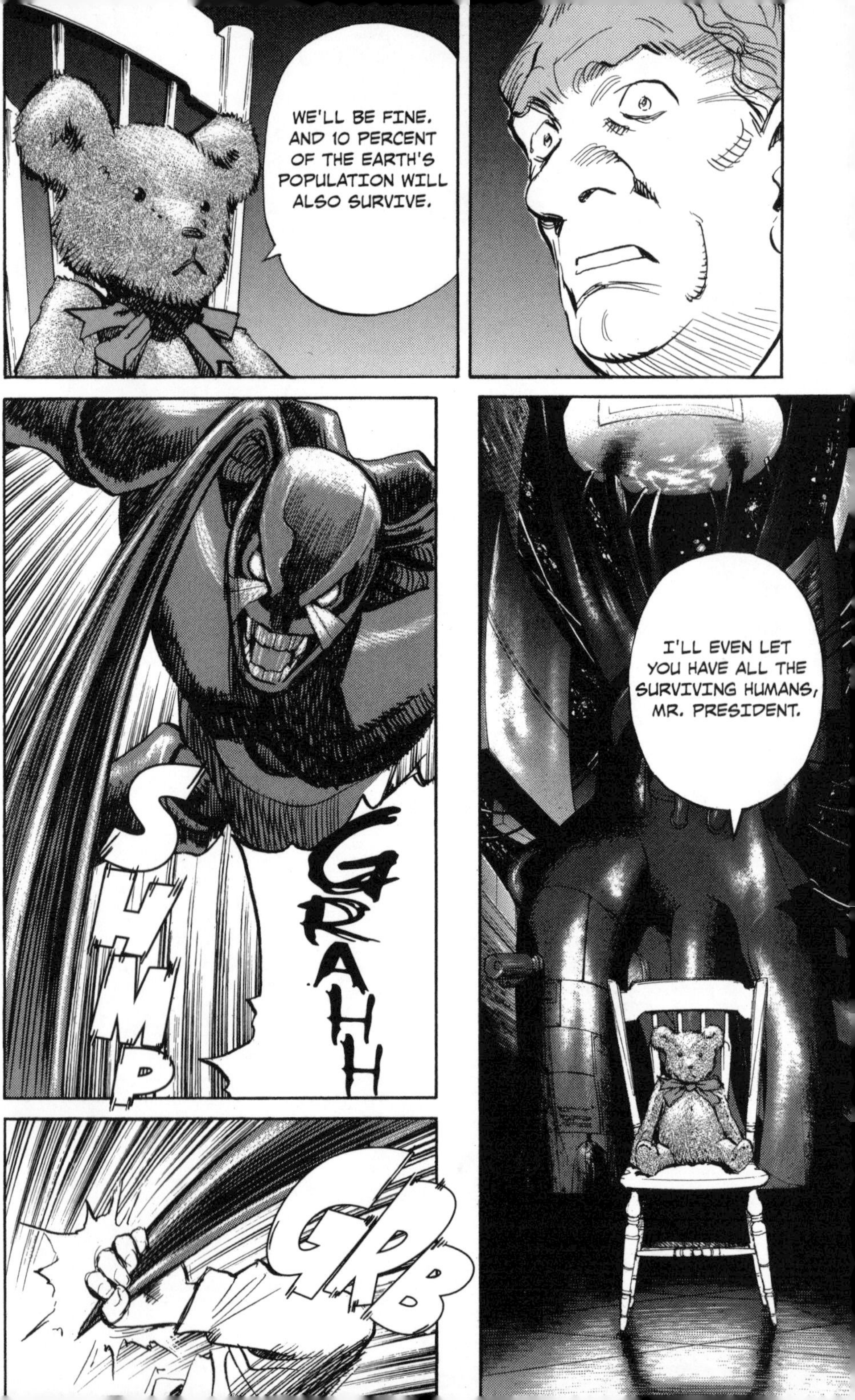
WE'LL BE FINE. AND 10 PERCENT OF THE EARTH'S POPULATION WILL ALSO SURVIVE.
I'LL EVEN LET YOU HAVE ALL THE SURVIVING HUMANS, MR. PRESIDENT.
GRAHH
SHHMP
GRB

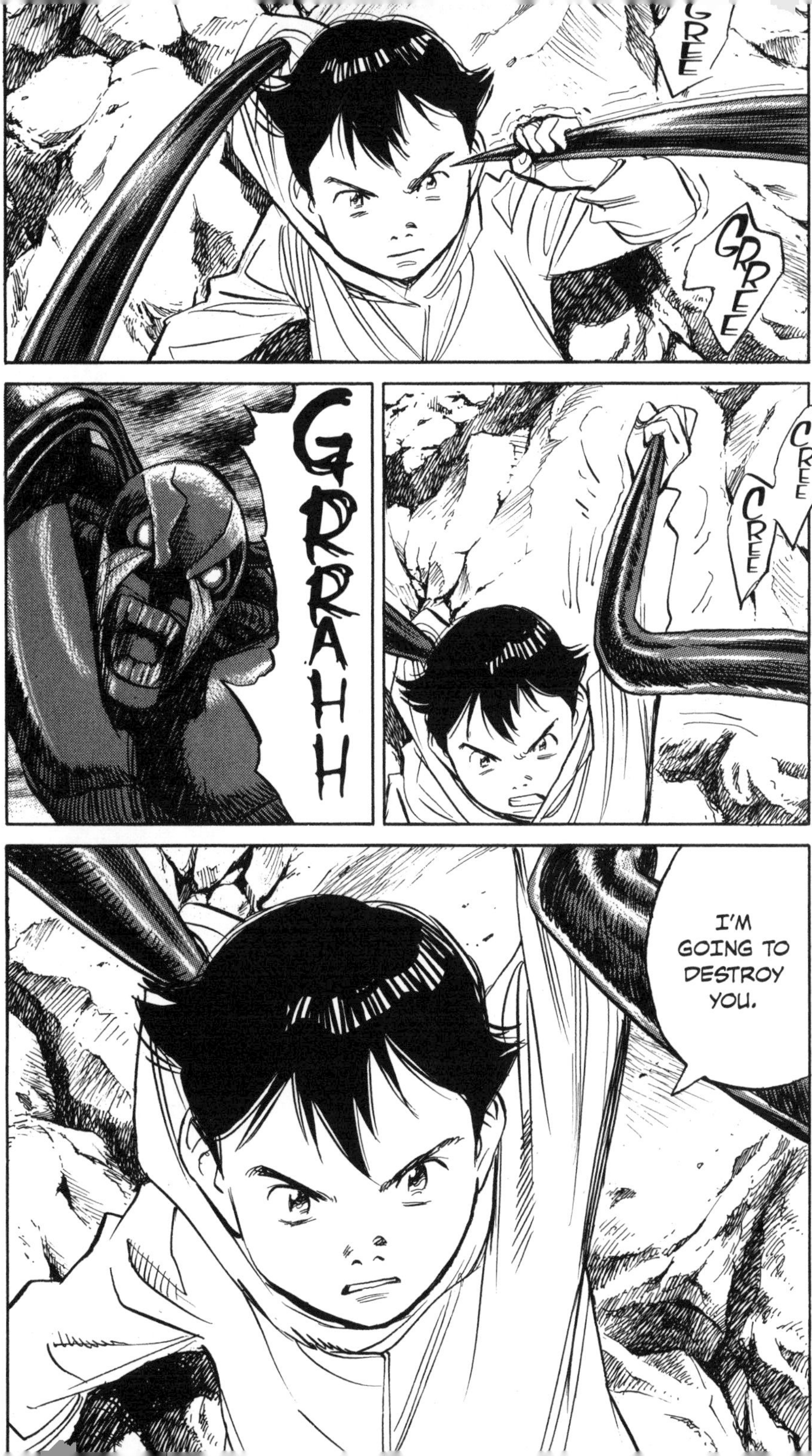
GREE
GRREE
CREE
CREE
GRRAHH
I'M GOING TO DESTROY YOU.

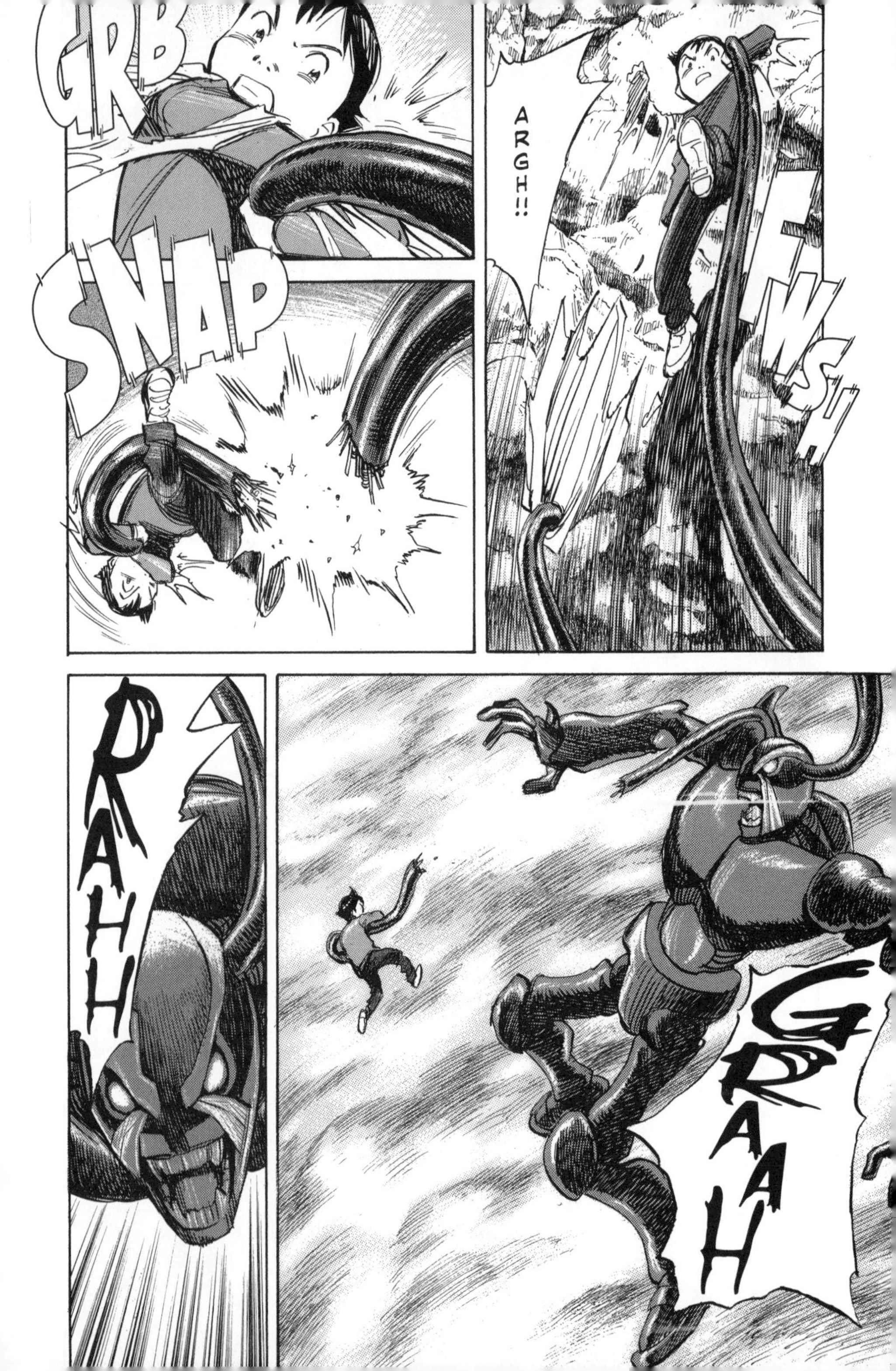
ARGH!!
FWSH
GRB
SNAP
GRAAAH
RAHH

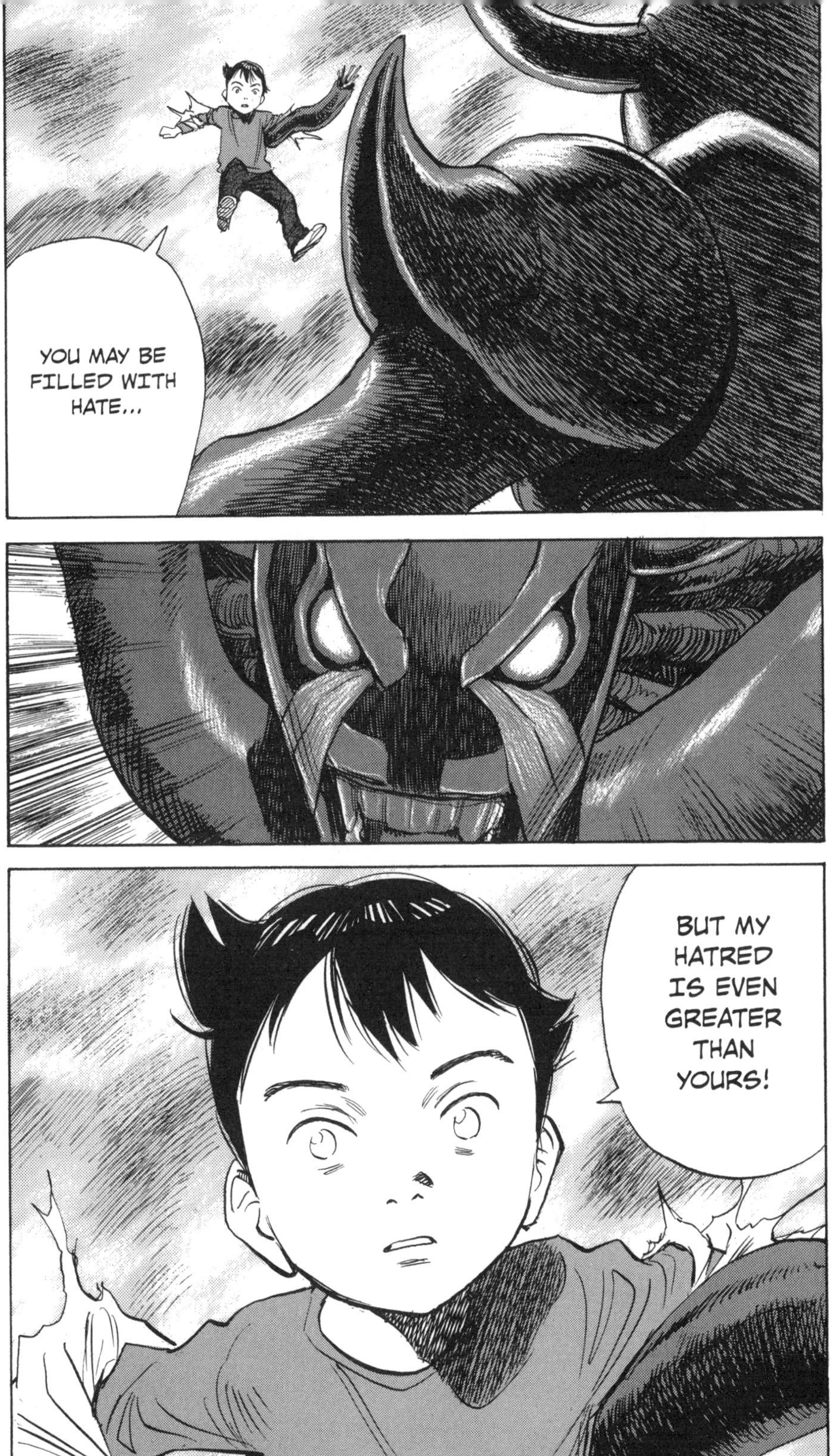
YOU MAY BE FILLED WITH HATE...
BUT MY HATRED IS EVEN GREATER THAN YOURS!

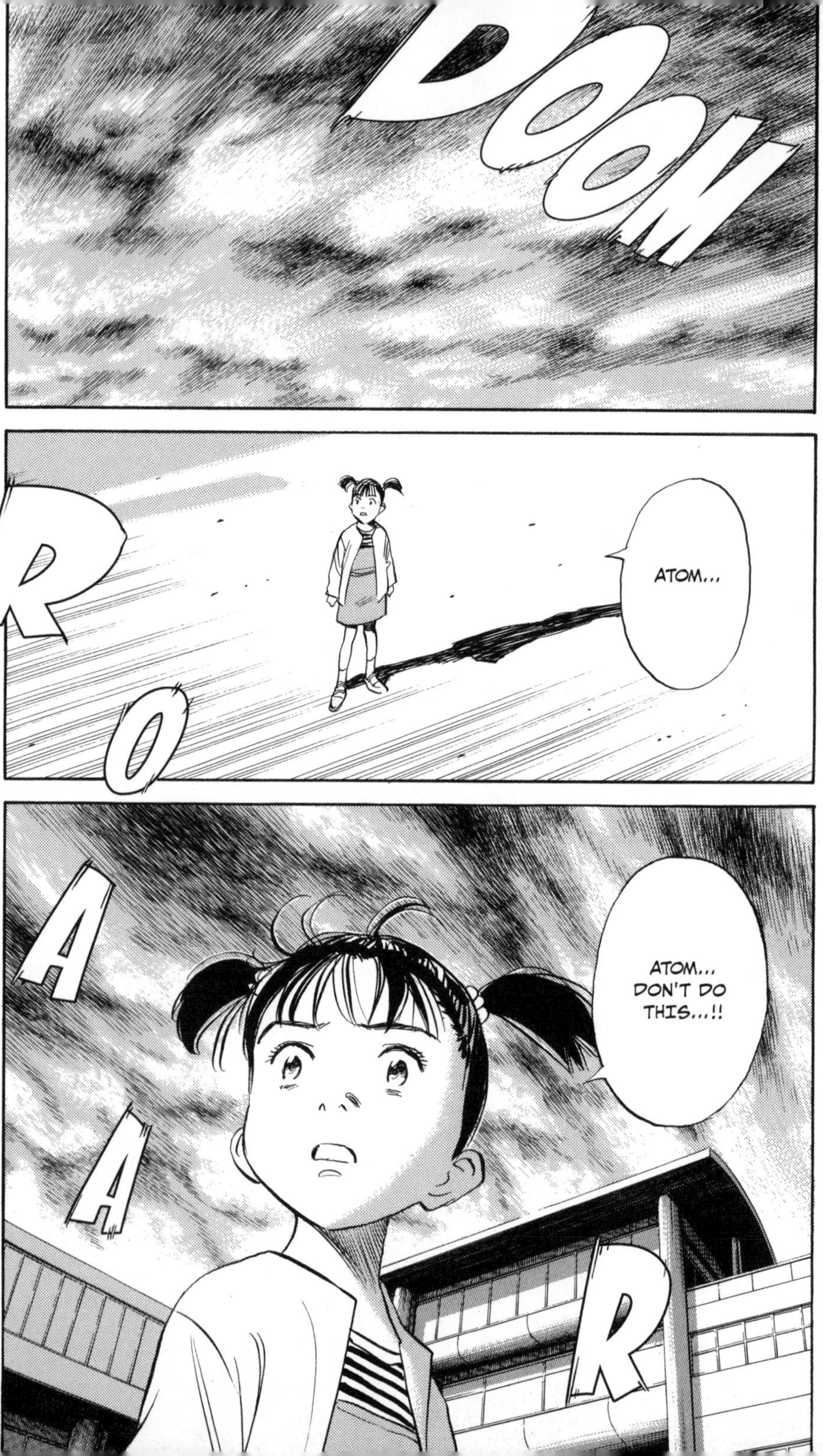
DOOM
ATOM...
RO
ATOM... DON'T DO THIS...!!
AAR

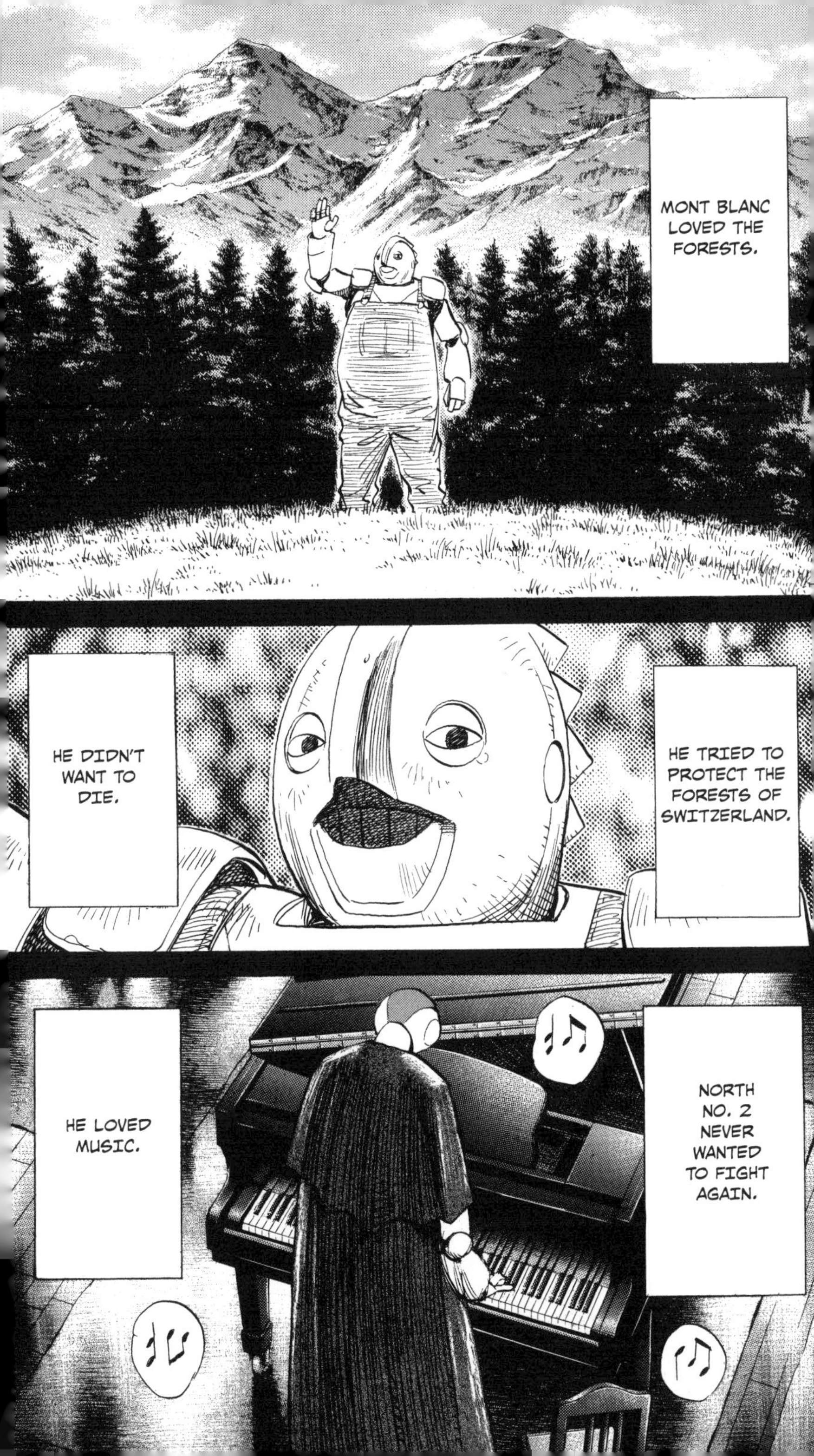
MONT BLANC LOVED THE FORESTS.
HE TRIED TO PROTECT THE FORESTS OF SWITZERLAND.
HE DIDN'T WANT TO DIE.
NORTH NO. 2 NEVER WANTED TO FIGHT AGAIN.
HE LOVED MUSIC.

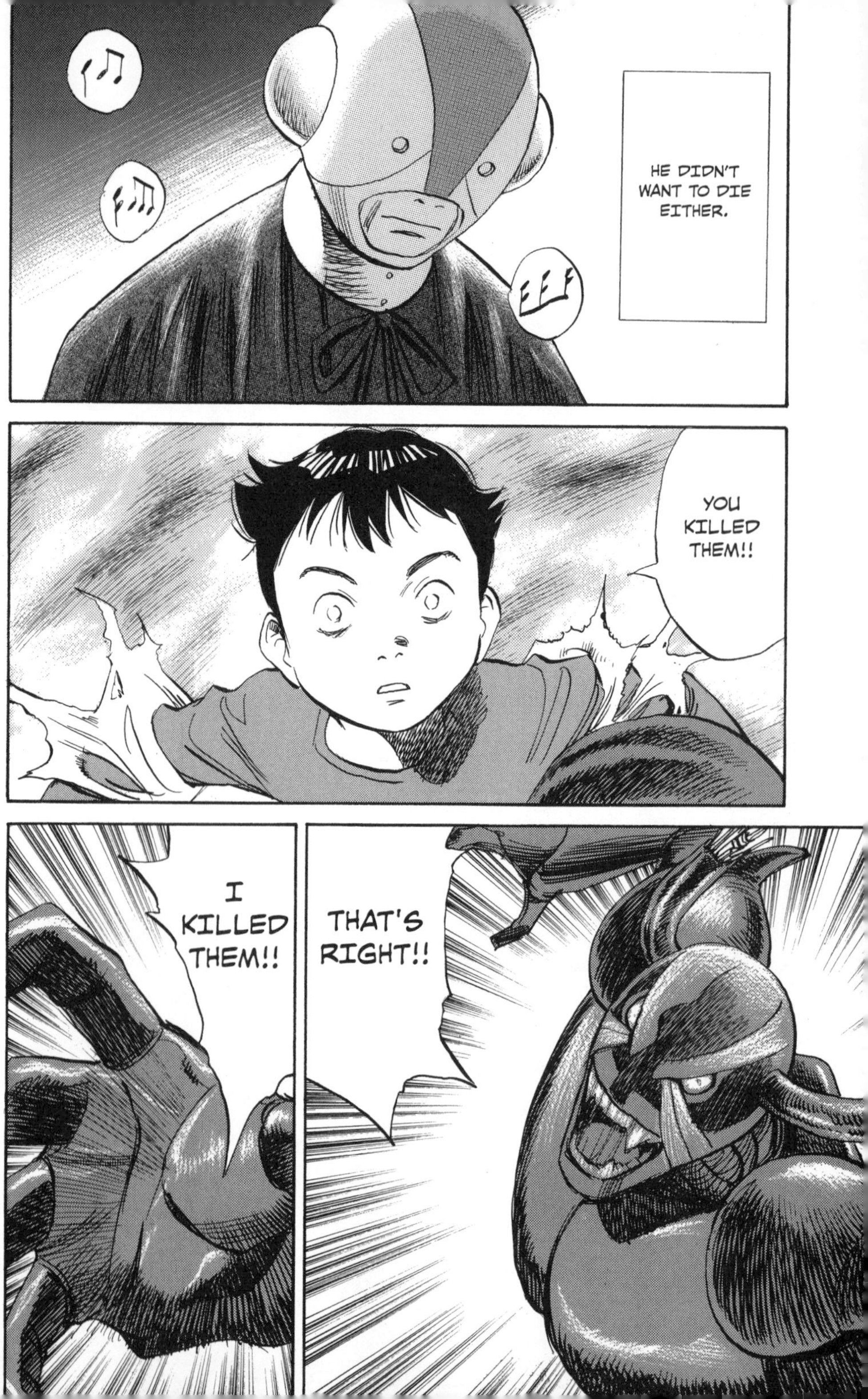
HE DIDN'T WANT TO DIE EITHER.
YOU KILLED THEM!!
THAT'S RIGHT!!
I KILLED THEM!!

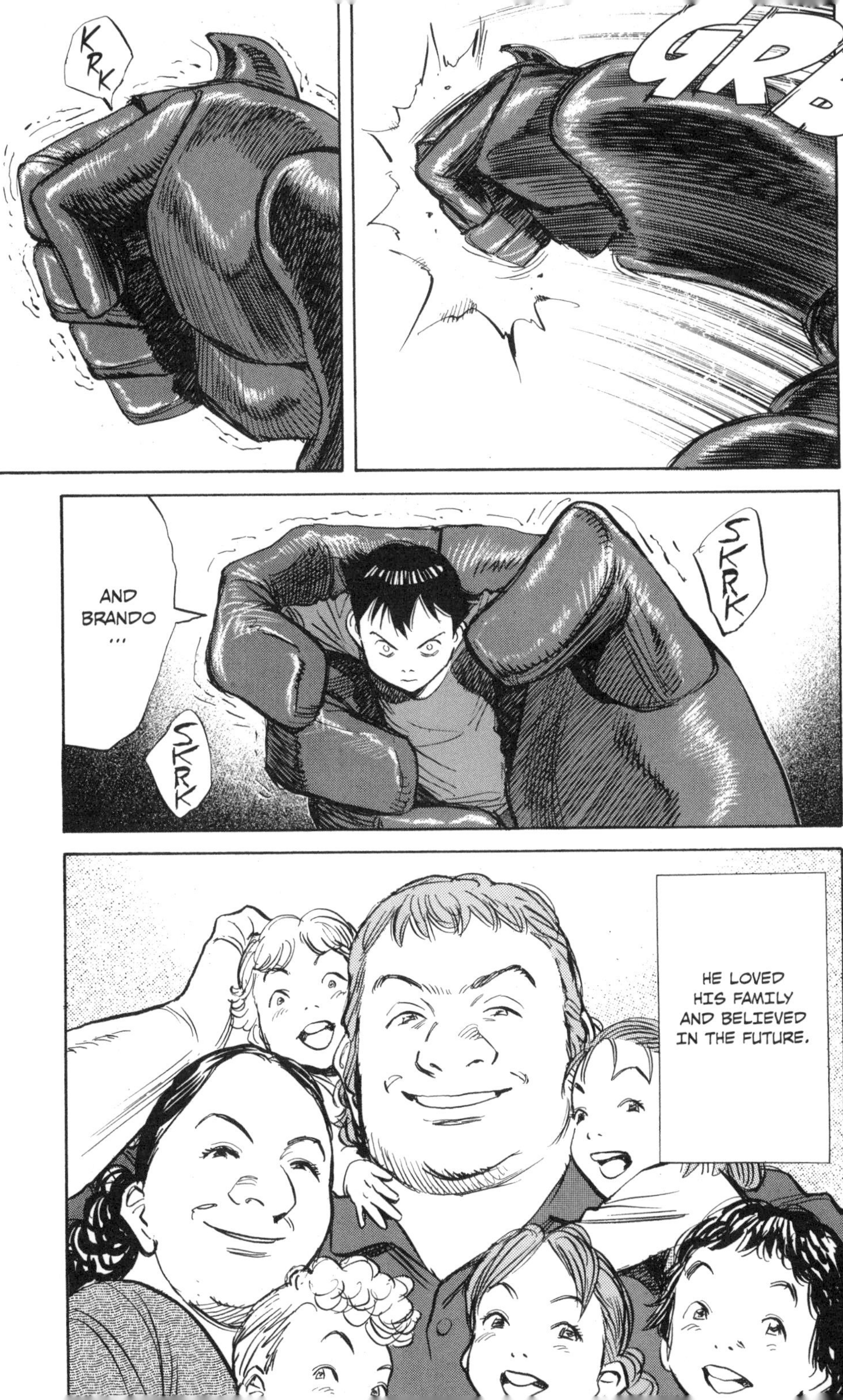
GRB
KRK
SKRK
AND BRANDO ...
SKRK
HE LOVED HIS FAMILY AND BELIEVED IN THE FUTURE.

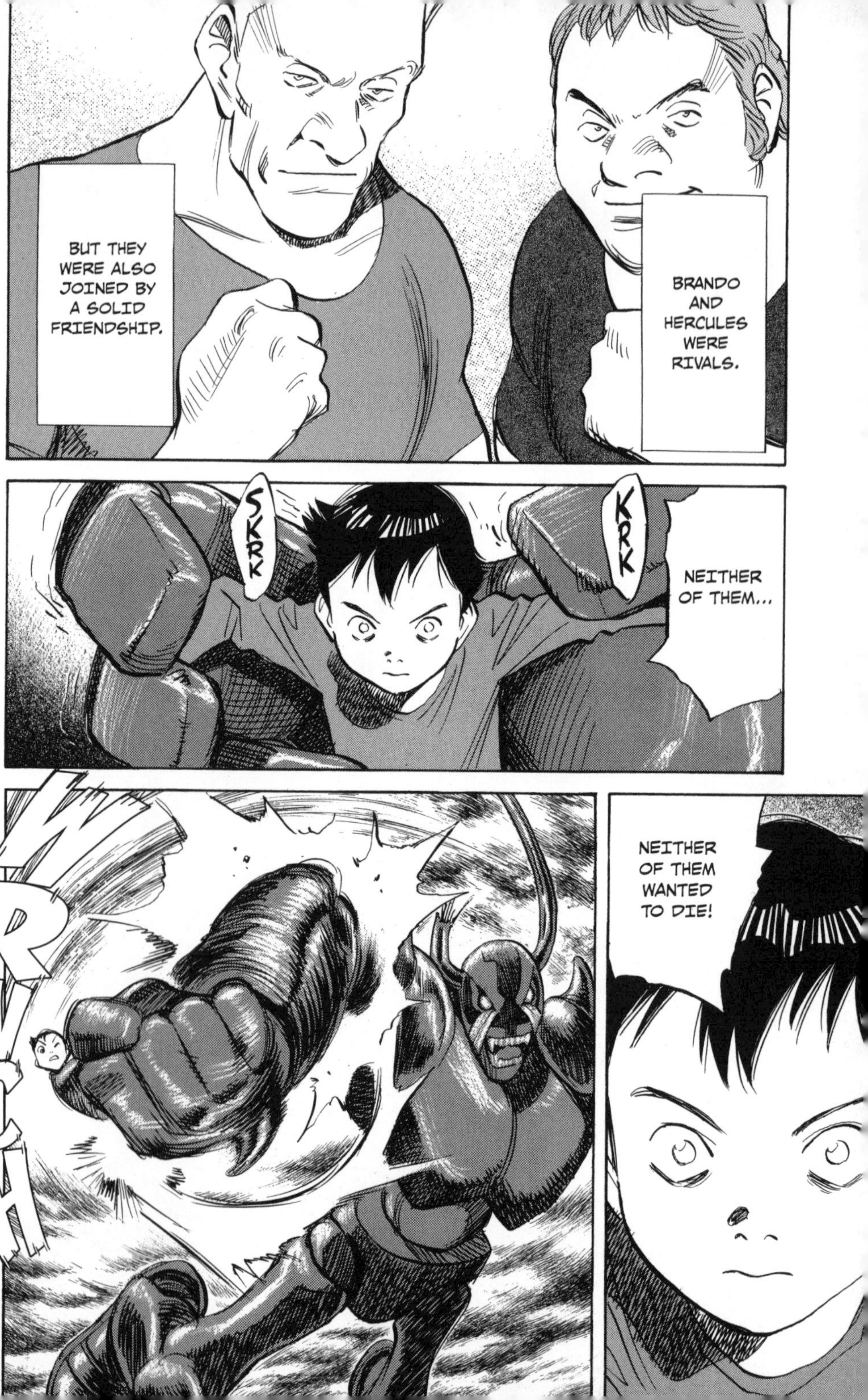
BRANDO AND HERCULES WERE RIVALS.
BUT THEY WERE ALSO JOINED BY A SOLID FRIENDSHIP.
NEITHER OF THEM...
KRK
SKRK
NEITHER OF THEM WANTED TO DIE!
WRNCH

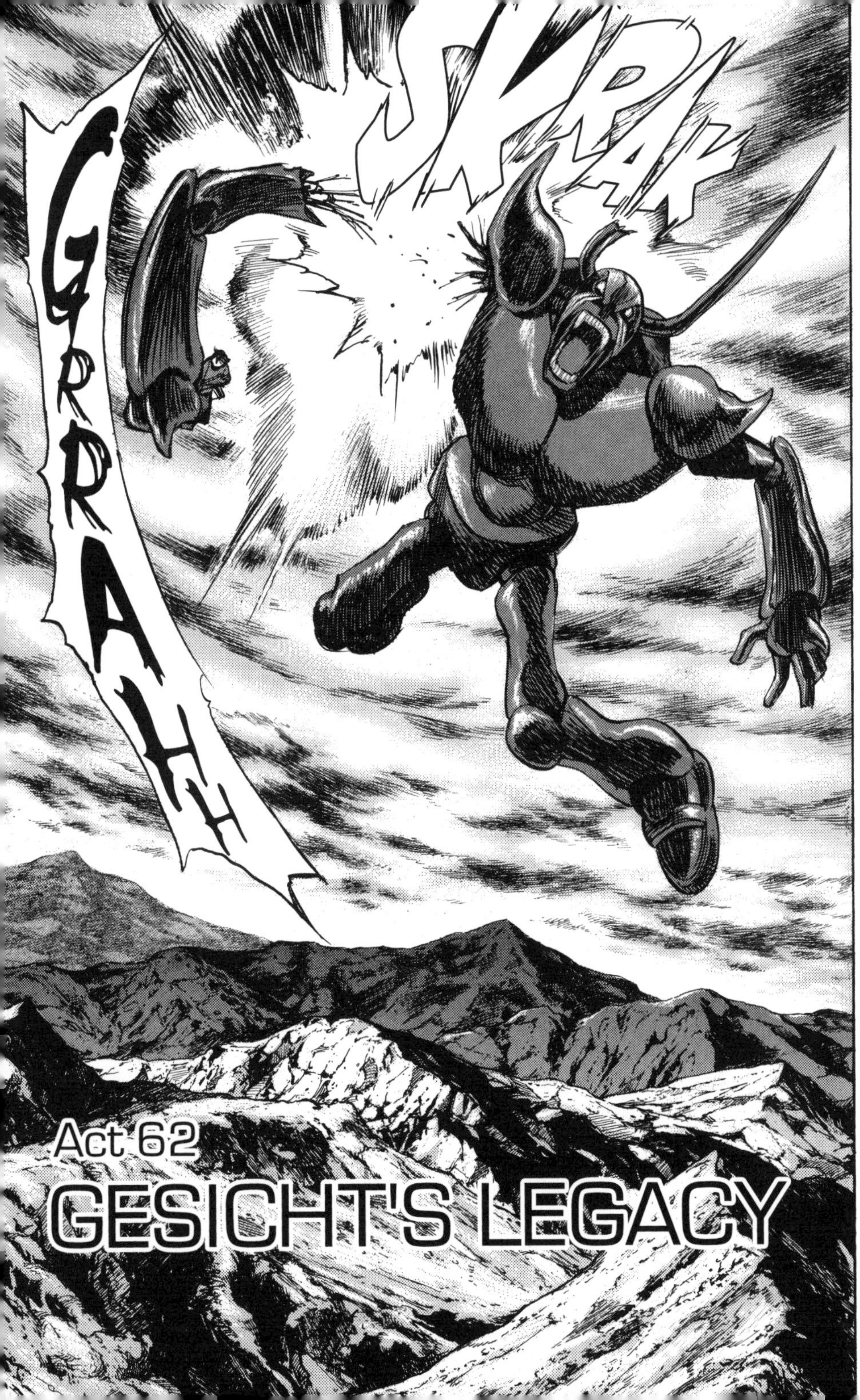
SKRAK
GRRRAHH

Act 62
GESICHT'S LEGACY

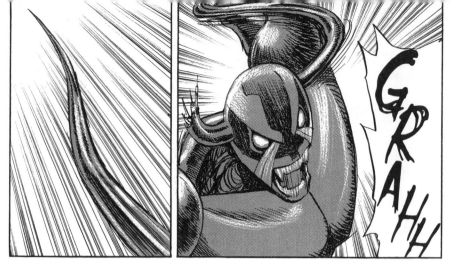

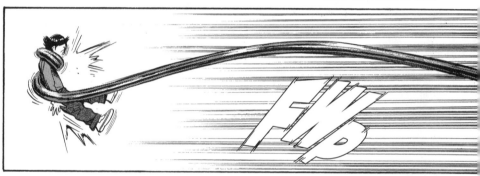

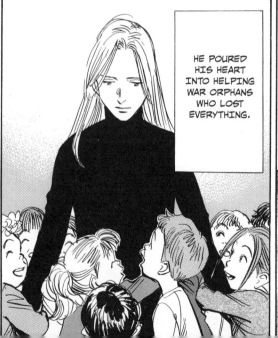

GRAHH
FWP
EPSILON WAS SO AGAINST WAR AND VIOLENCE THAT HE REFUSED TO FIGHT!
HE POURED HIS HEART INTO HELPING WAR ORPHANS WHO LOST EVERYTHING.

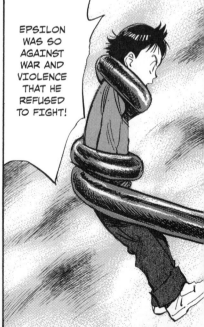

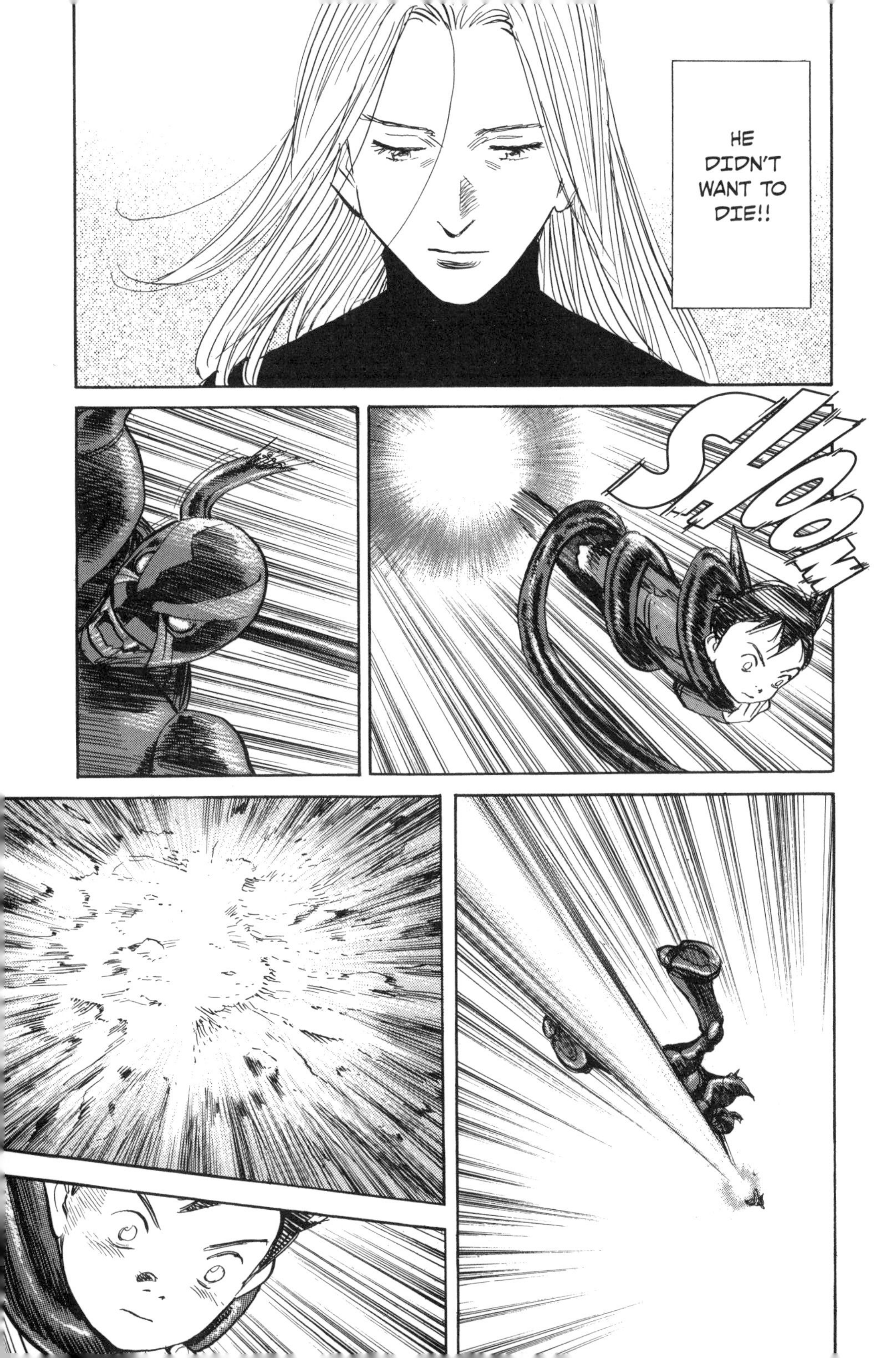
HE DIDN'T WANT TO DIE!!
SHOOM

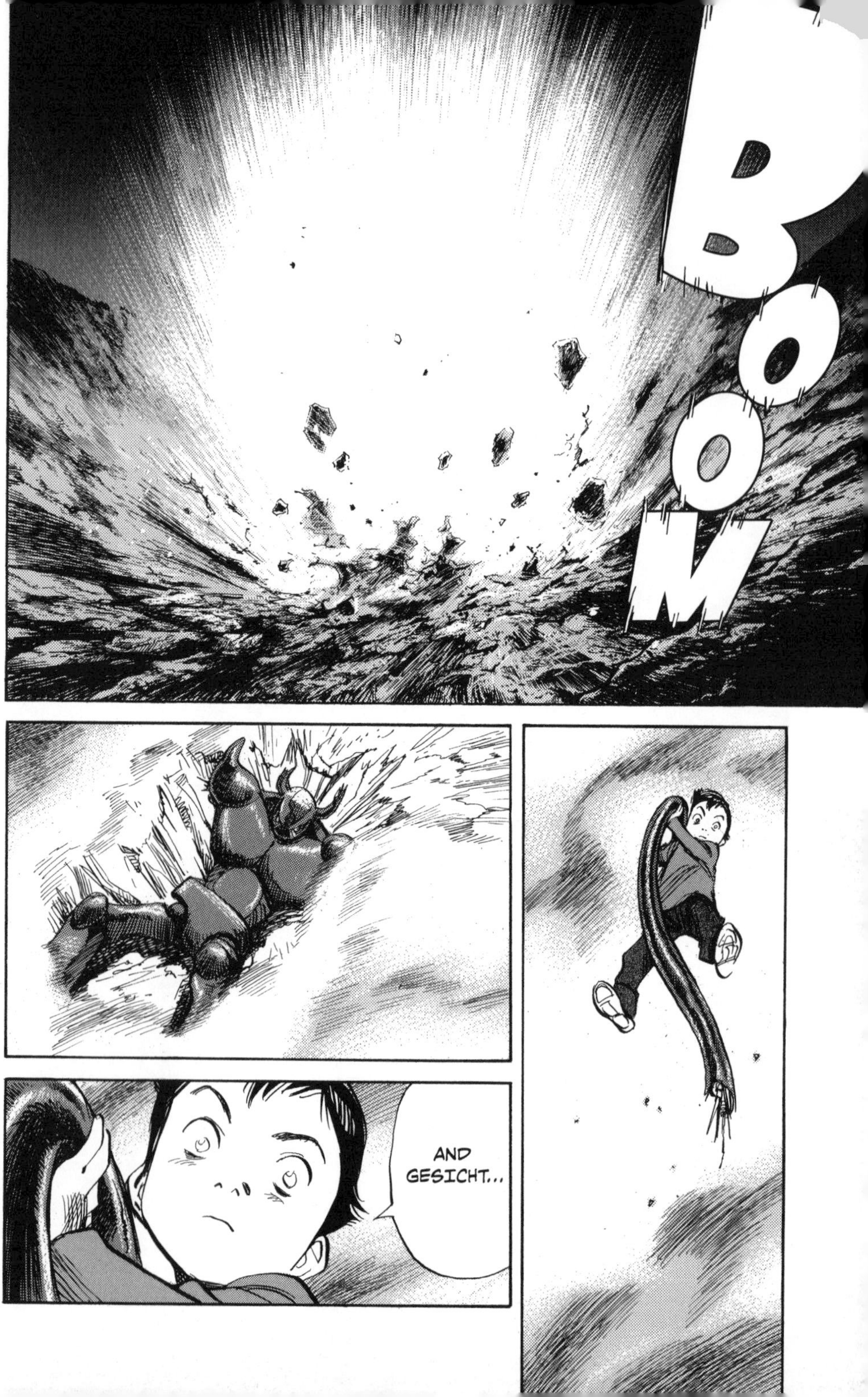
BOOM
AND GESICHT...

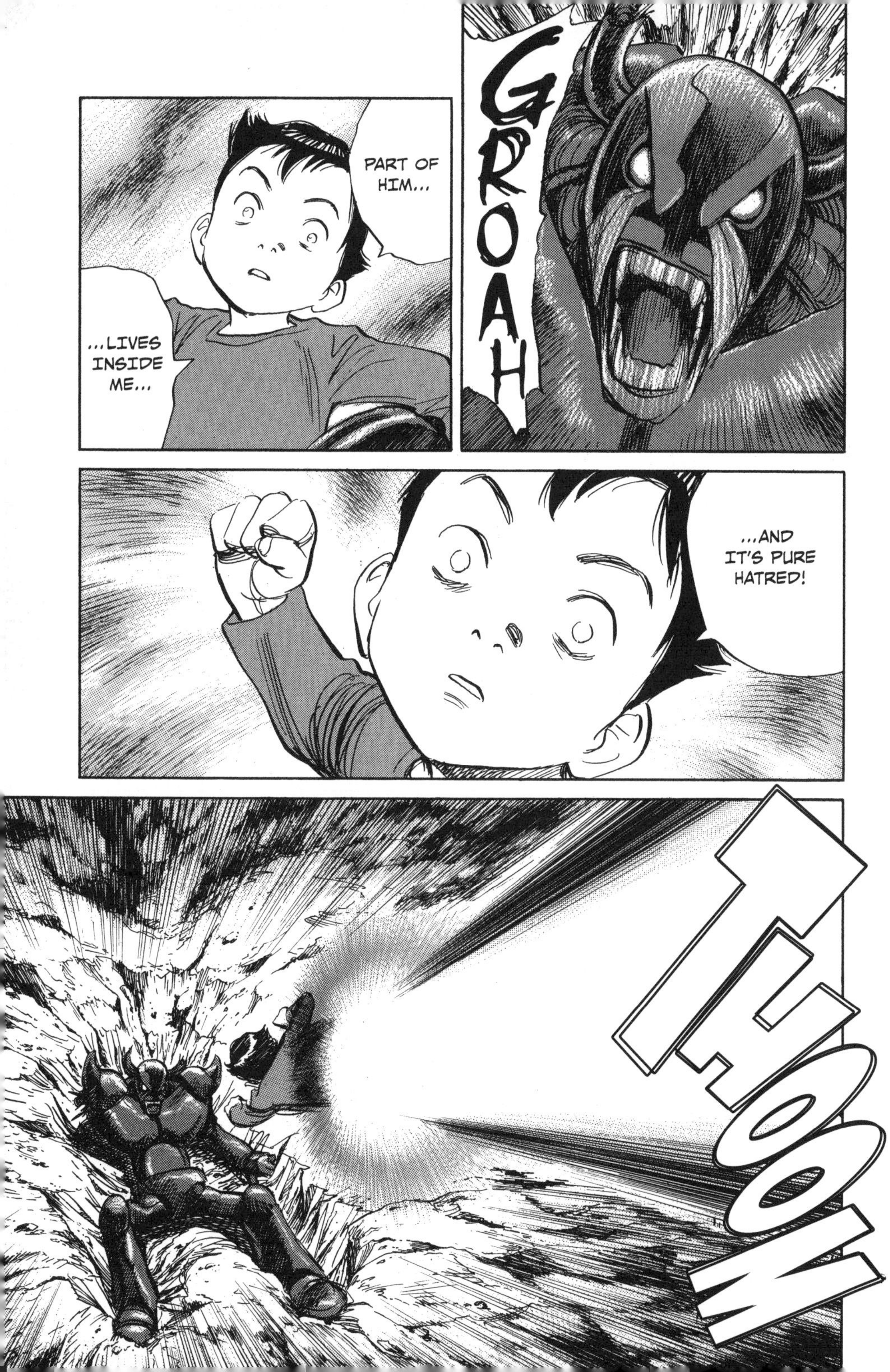
GROAH
PART OF HIM...
...LIVES INSIDE ME...
...AND IT'S PURE HATRED!
THOOM

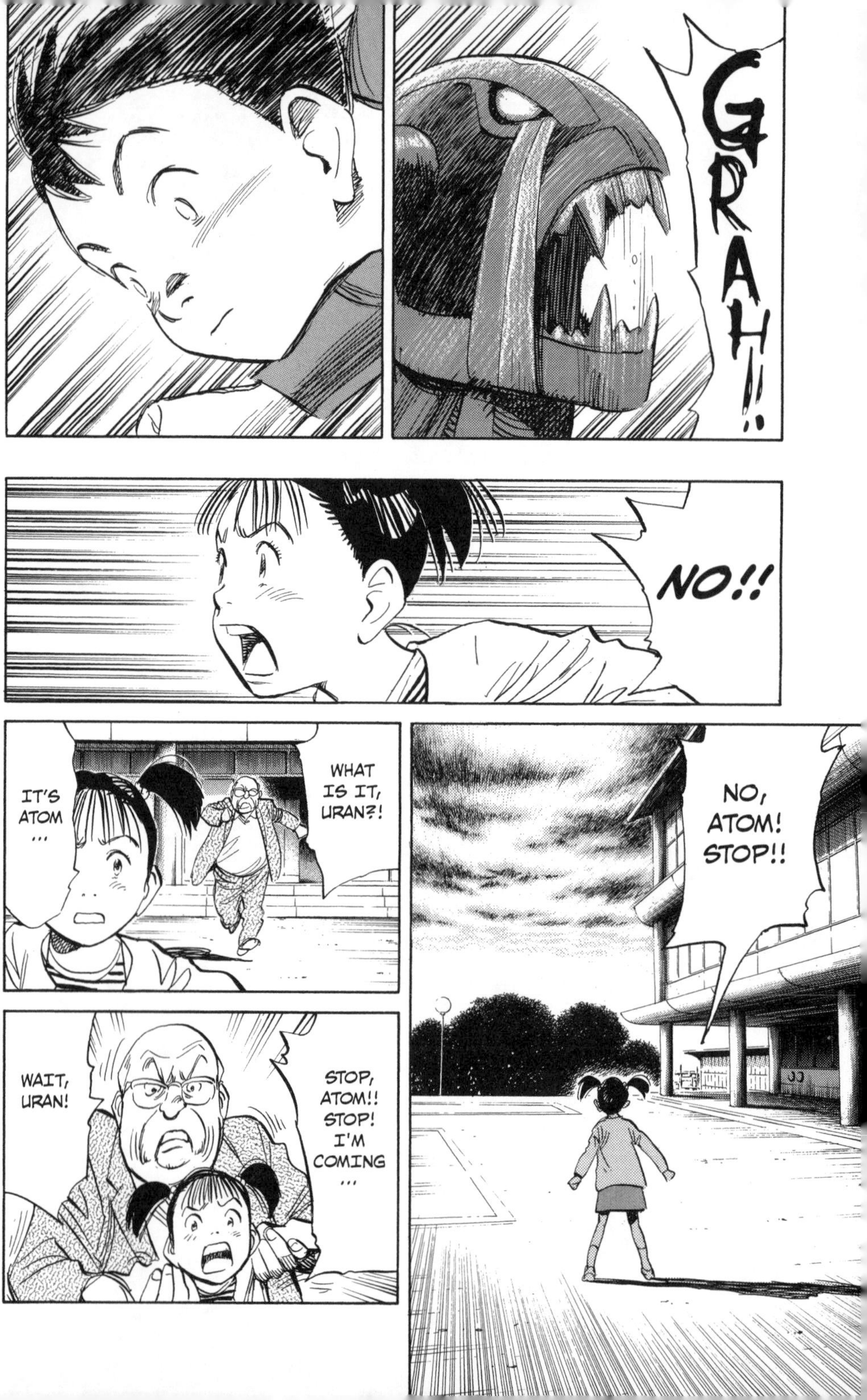
GRAH!!
NO!!
NO, ATOM! STOP!!
WHAT IS IT, URAN?!
IT'S ATOM ...
STOP, ATOM!! STOP! I'M COMING ...
WAIT, URAN!

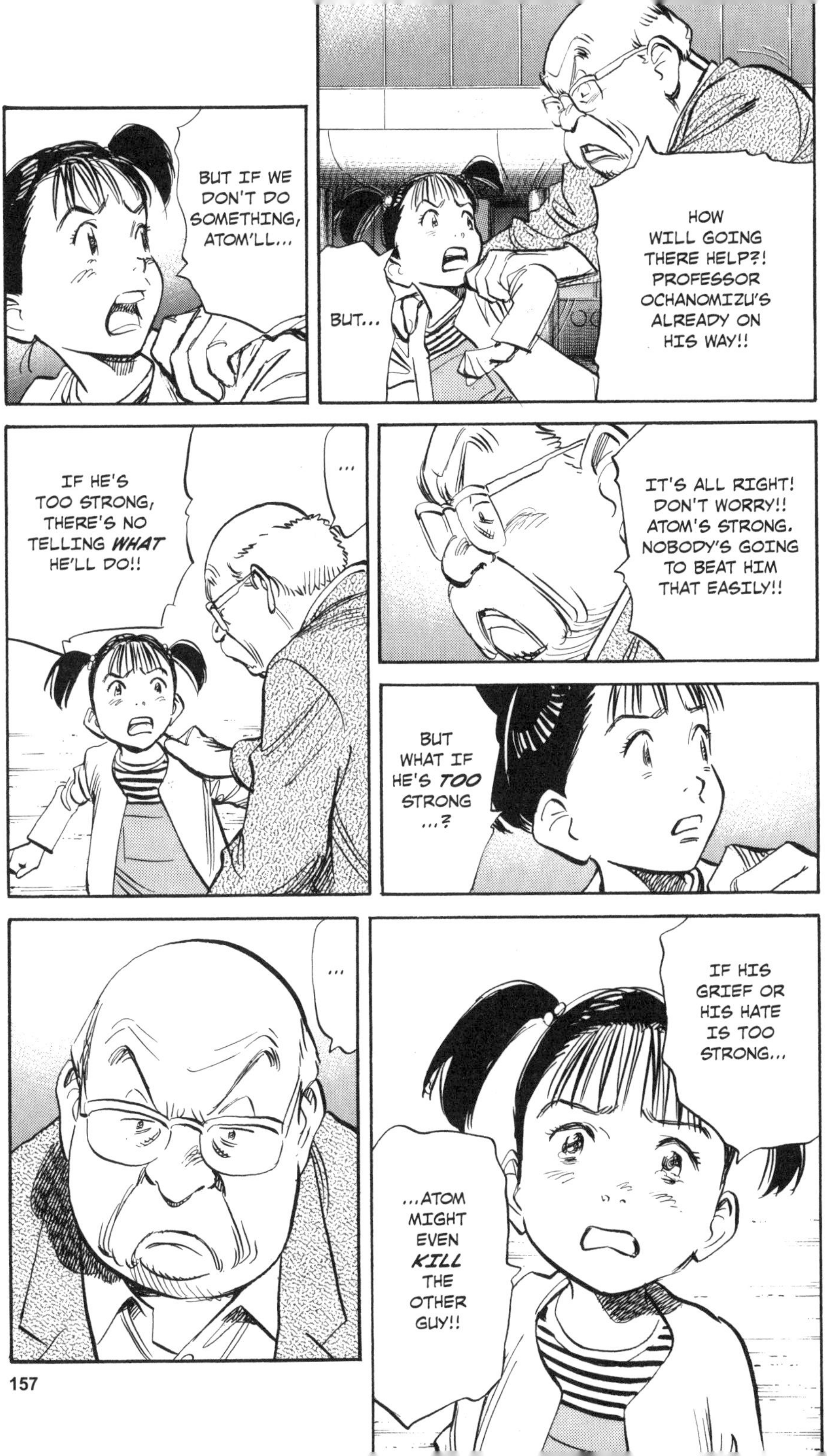
HOW WILL GOING THERE HELP?! PROFESSOR OCHANOMIZU'S ALREADY ON HIS WAY!!
BUT...
BUT IF WE DON'T DO SOMETHING, ATOM'LL...
IT'S ALL RIGHT! DON'T WORRY!! ATOM'S STRONG. NOBODY'S GOING TO BEAT HIM THAT EASILY!!
BUT WHAT IF HE'S *TOO* STRONG ...?
...
IF HE'S TOO STRONG, THERE'S NO TELLING *WHAT* HE'LL DO!!
IF HIS GRIEF OR HIS HATE IS TOO STRONG...
...ATOM MIGHT EVEN *KILL* THE OTHER GUY!!
...

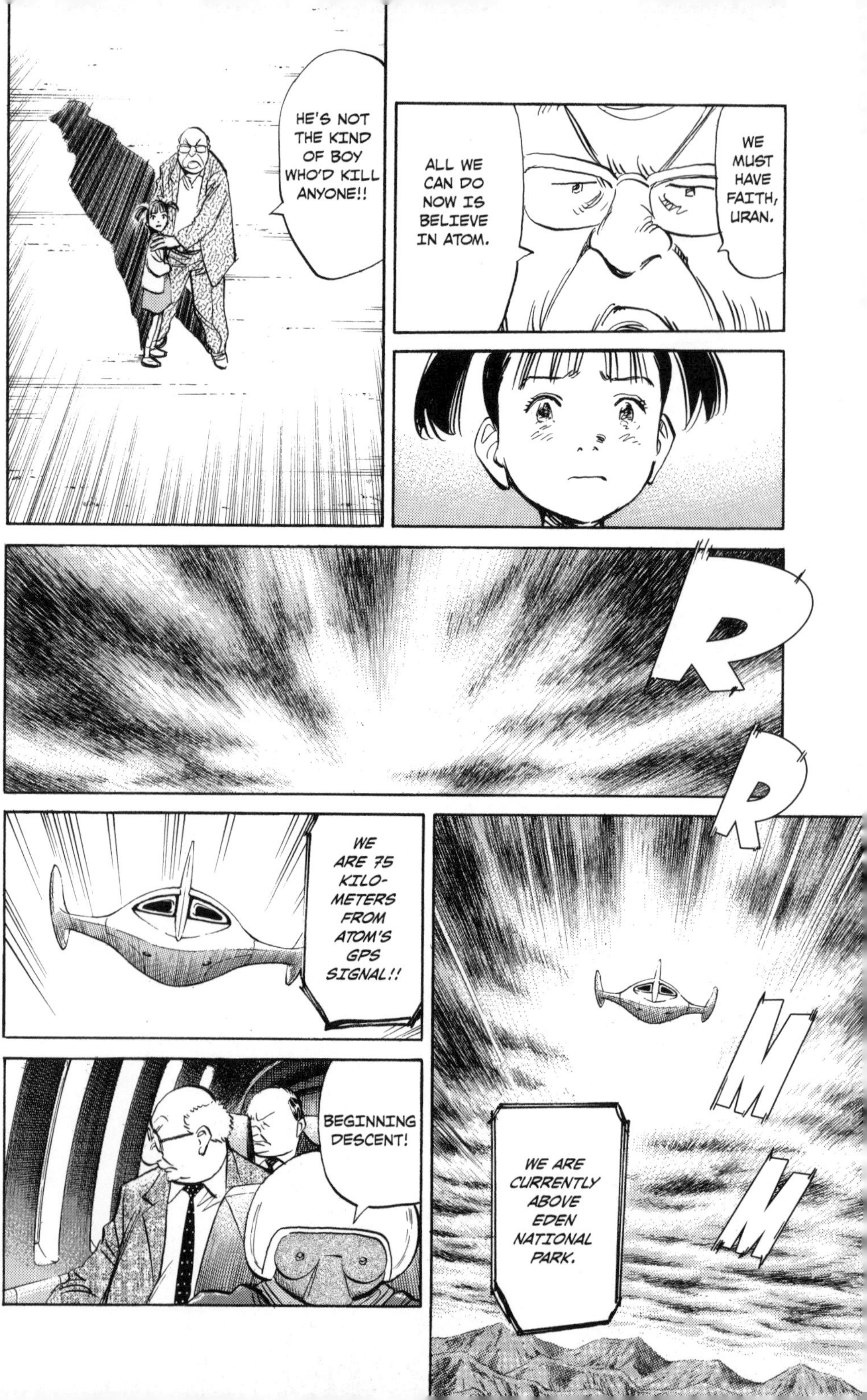
WE MUST HAVE FAITH, URAN.
ALL WE CAN DO NOW IS BELIEVE IN ATOM.
HE'S NOT THE KIND OF BOY WHO'D KILL ANYONE!!
RRMM
WE ARE CURRENTLY ABOVE EDEN NATIONAL PARK.
WE ARE 75 KILOMETERS FROM ATOM'S GPS SIGNAL!!
BEGINNING DESCENT!

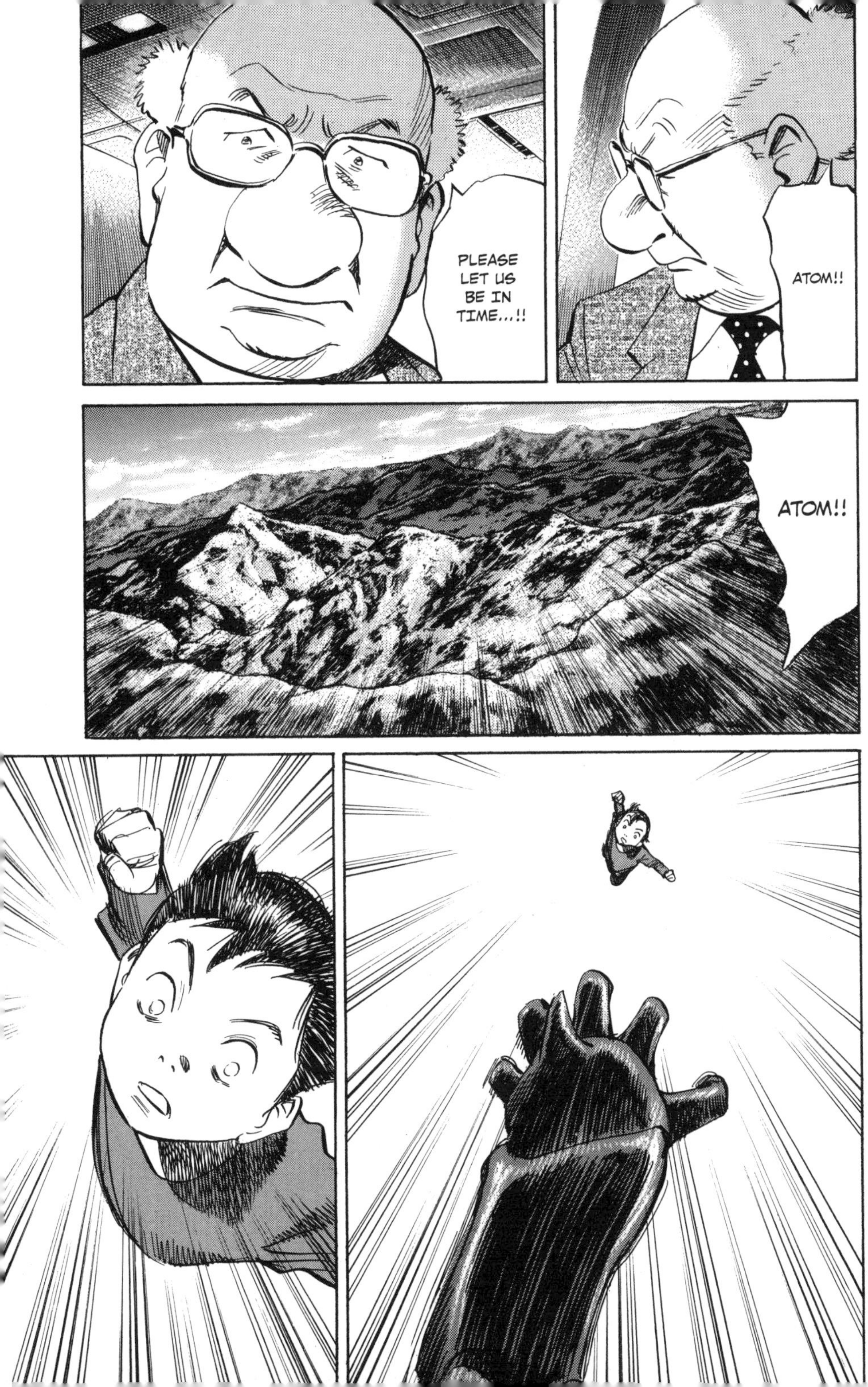
ATOM!!
PLEASE LET US BE IN TIME...!!
ATOM!!

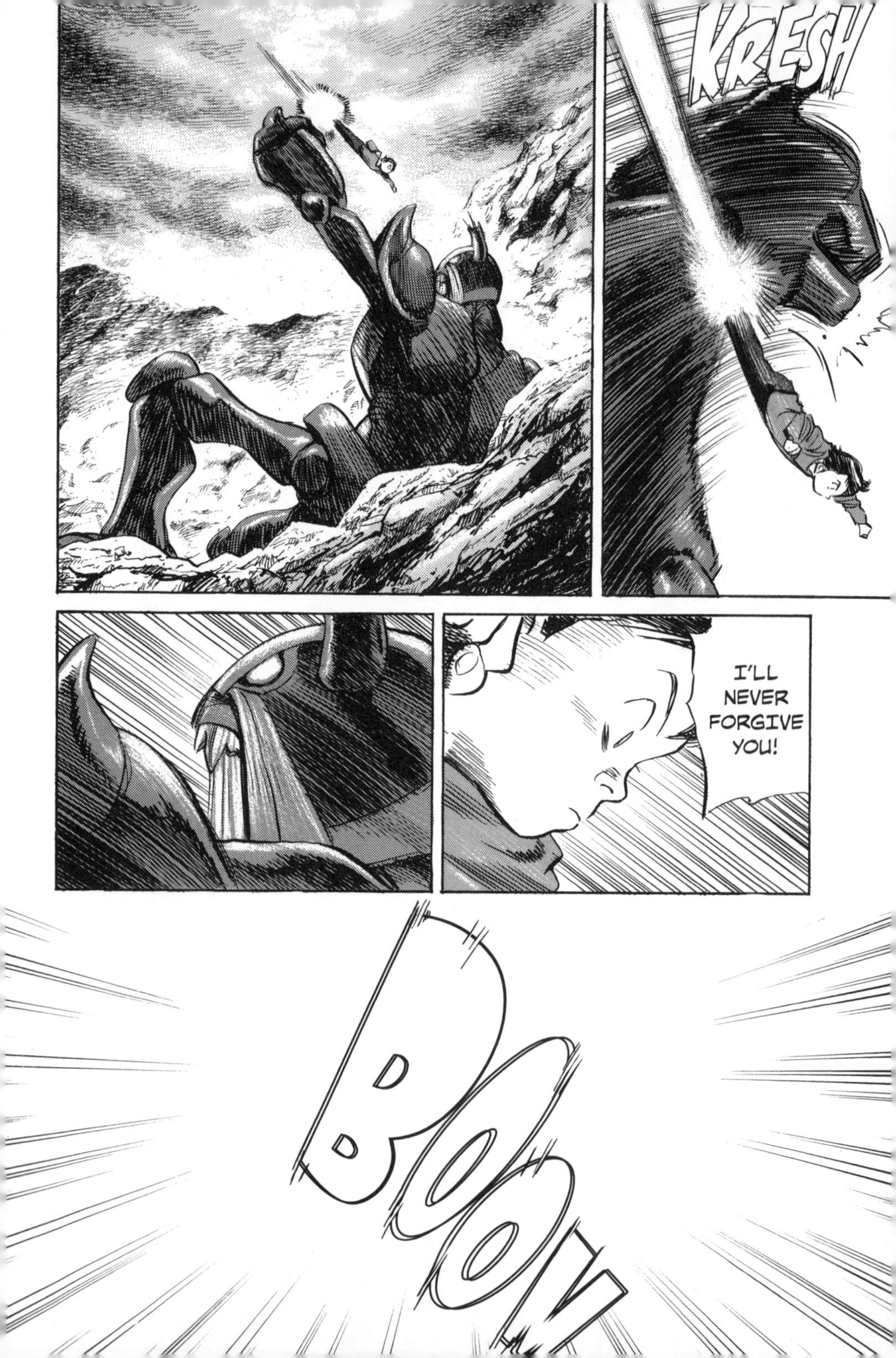
KRESH
I'LL NEVER FORGIVE YOU!
BOOM

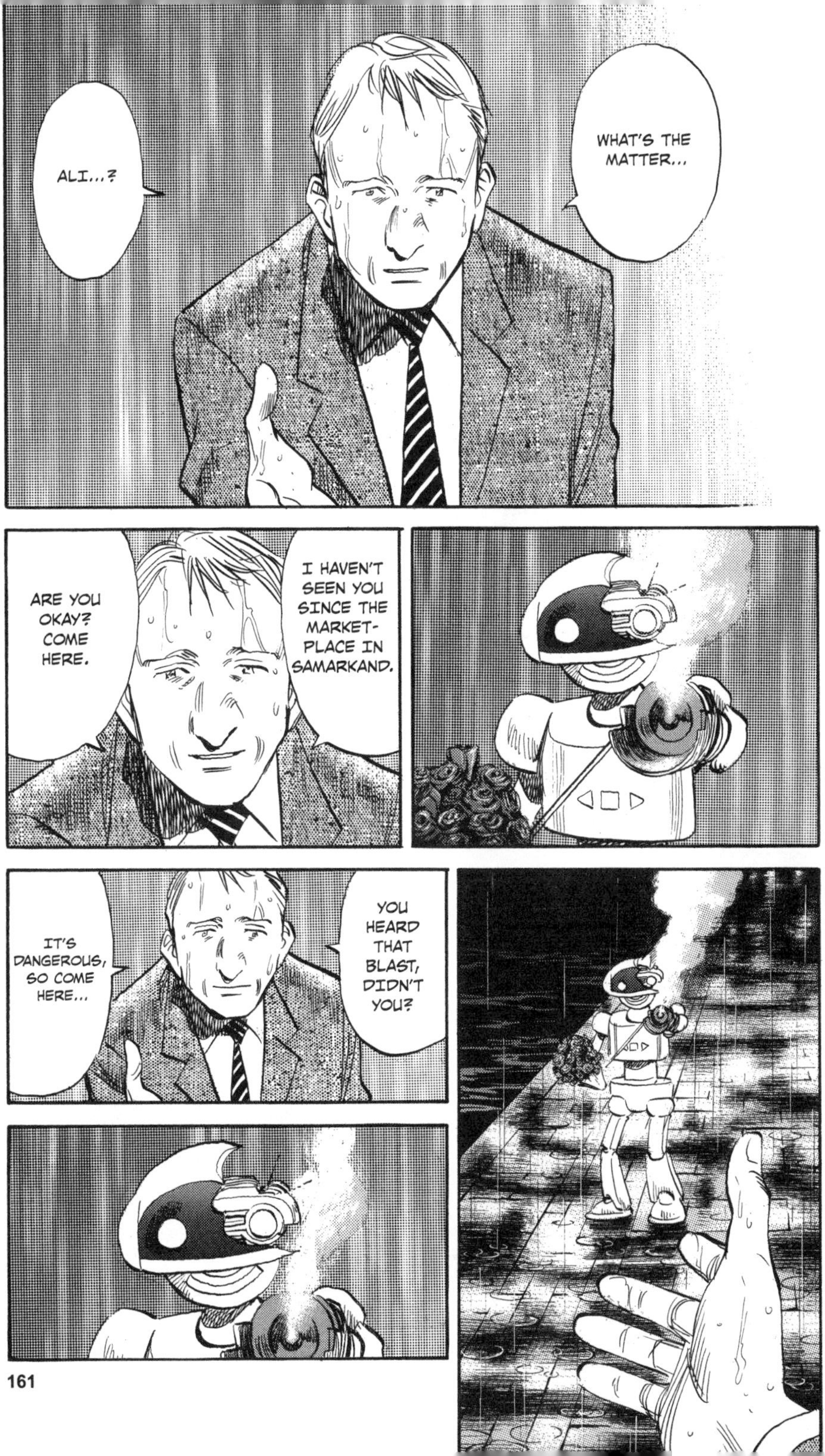
WHAT'S THE MATTER...
ALI...?
I HAVEN'T SEEN YOU SINCE THE MARKET-PLACE IN SAMARKAND.
ARE YOU OKAY? COME HERE.
YOU HEARD THAT BLAST, DIDN'T YOU?
IT'S DANGEROUS, SO COME HERE...

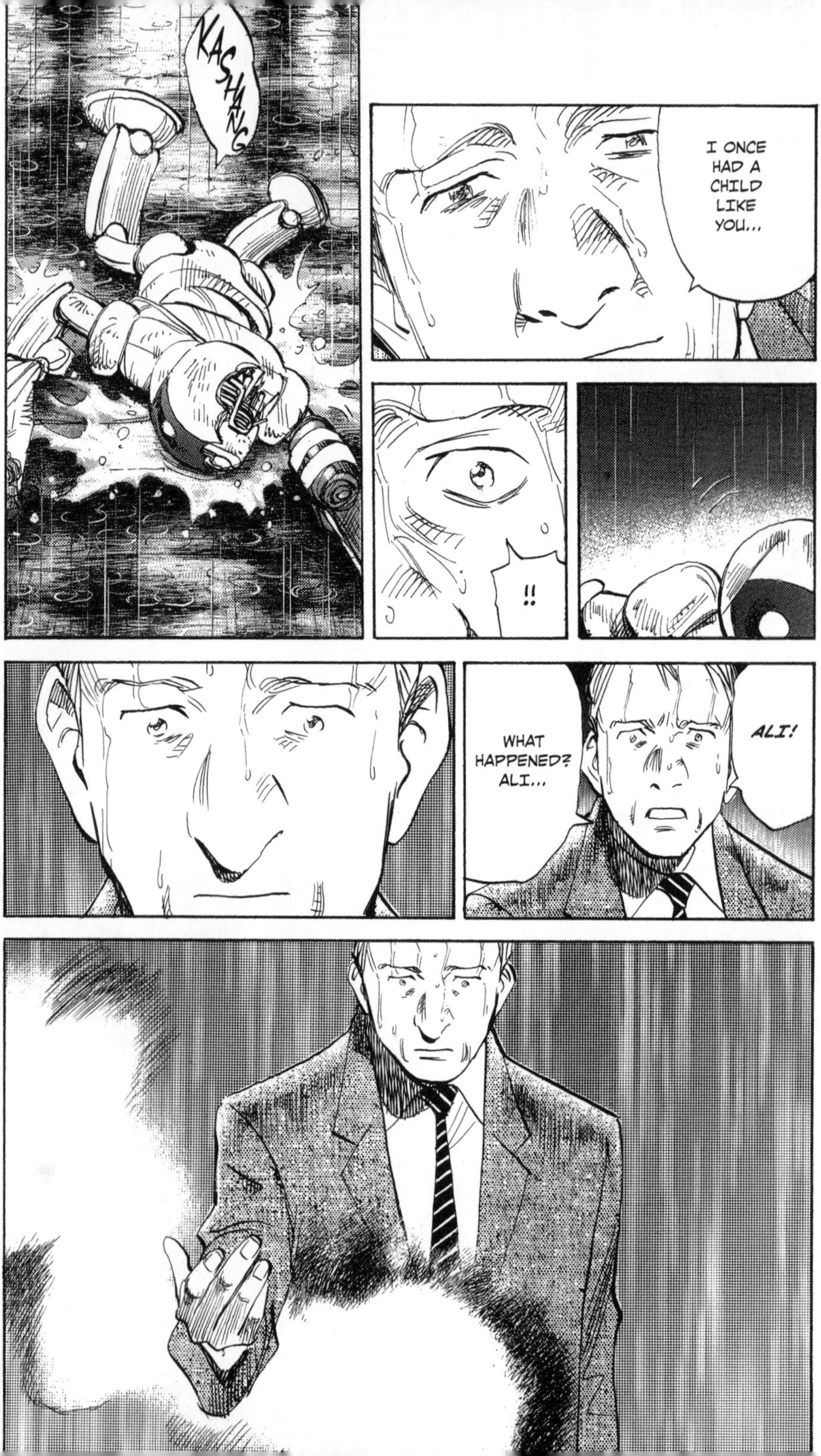
I ONCE HAD A CHILD LIKE YOU...
!!
KASHANG
ALI!
WHAT HAPPENED? ALI...

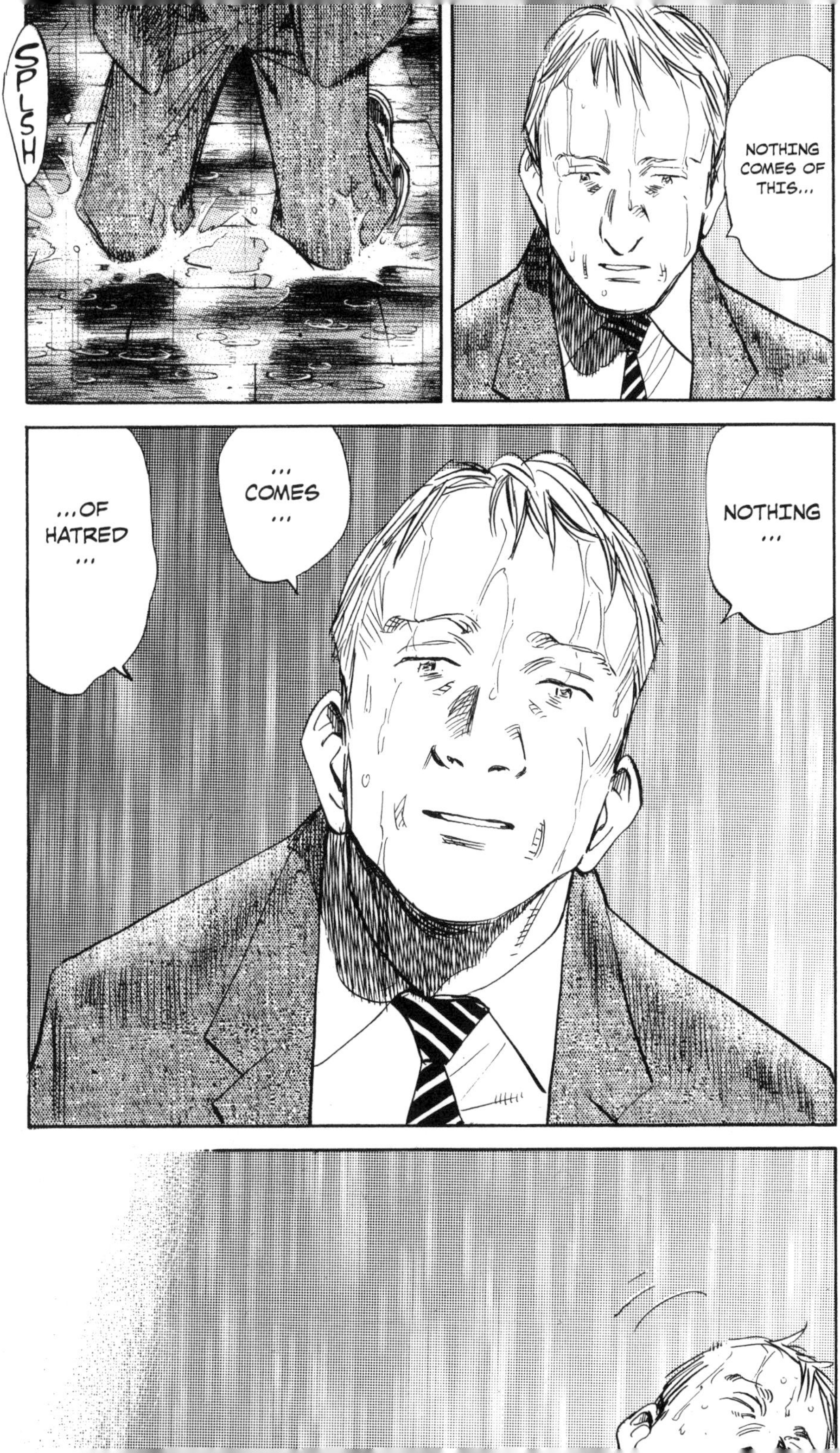
NOTHING COMES OF THIS...
SPLSH
NOTHING...
...COMES...
...OF HATRED...

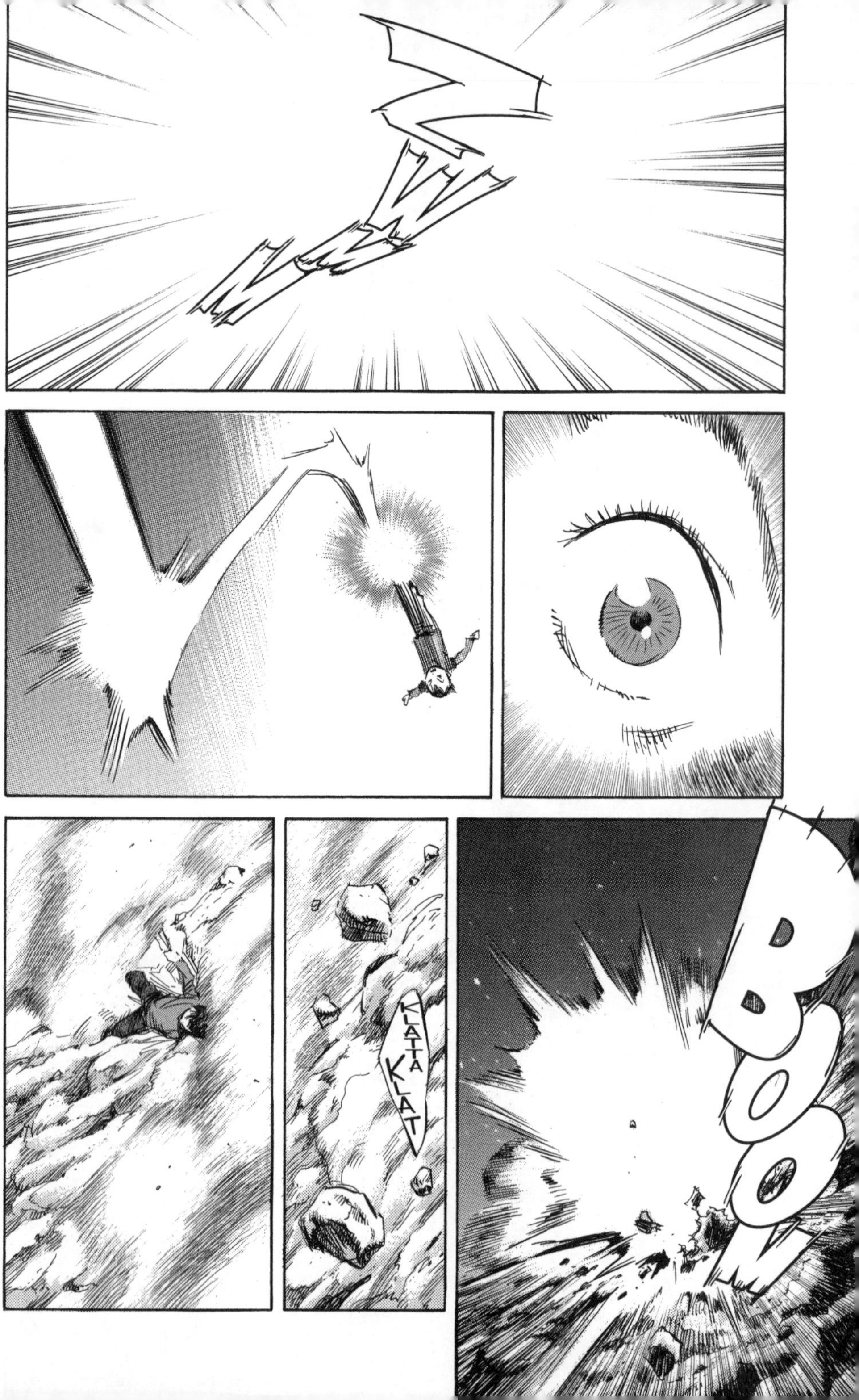
BOOO
KLATTA KLAT

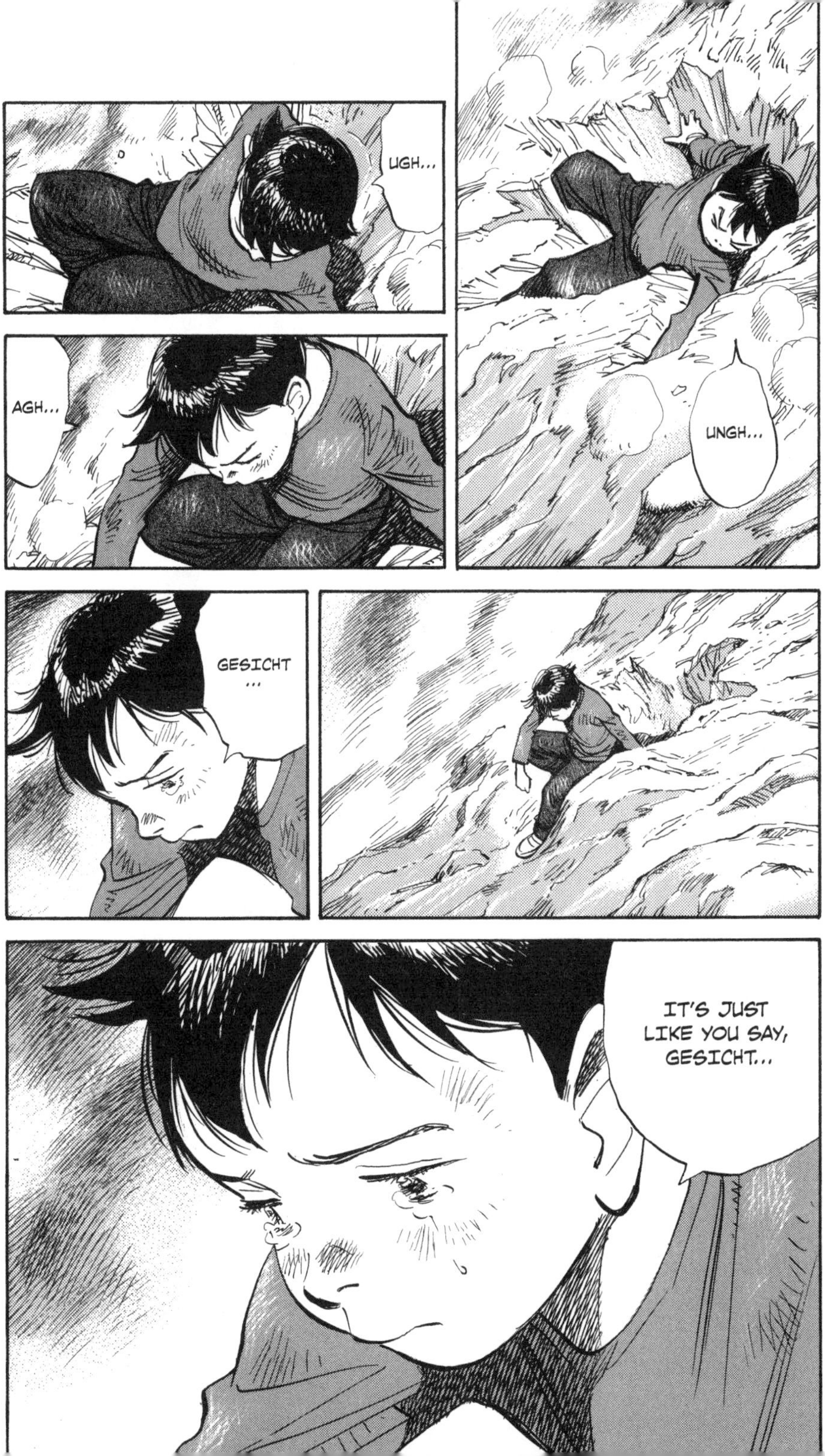
UNGH...
UGH...
AGH...
GESICHT ...
IT'S JUST LIKE YOU SAY, GESICHT...

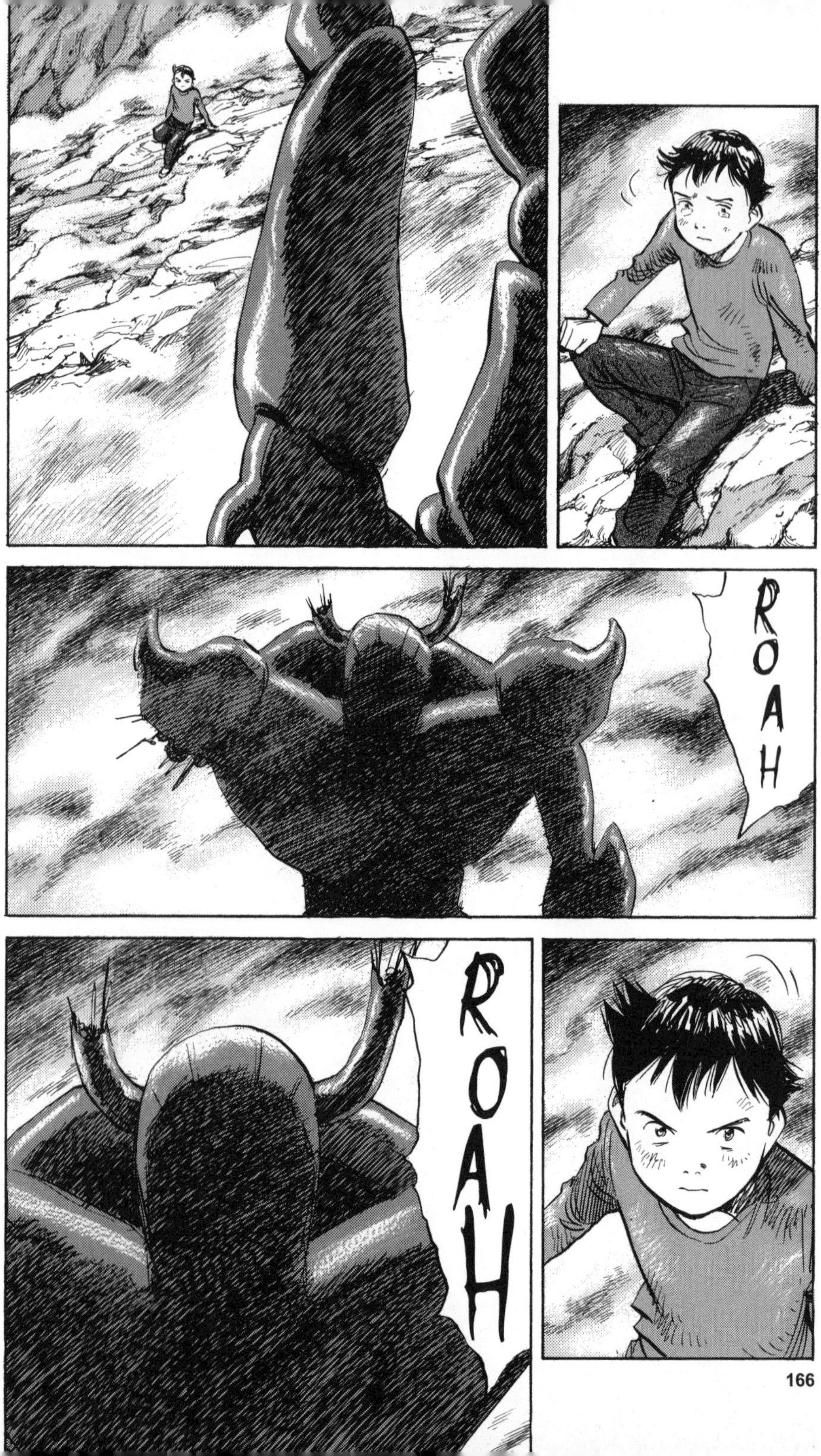
ROAH
ROAH

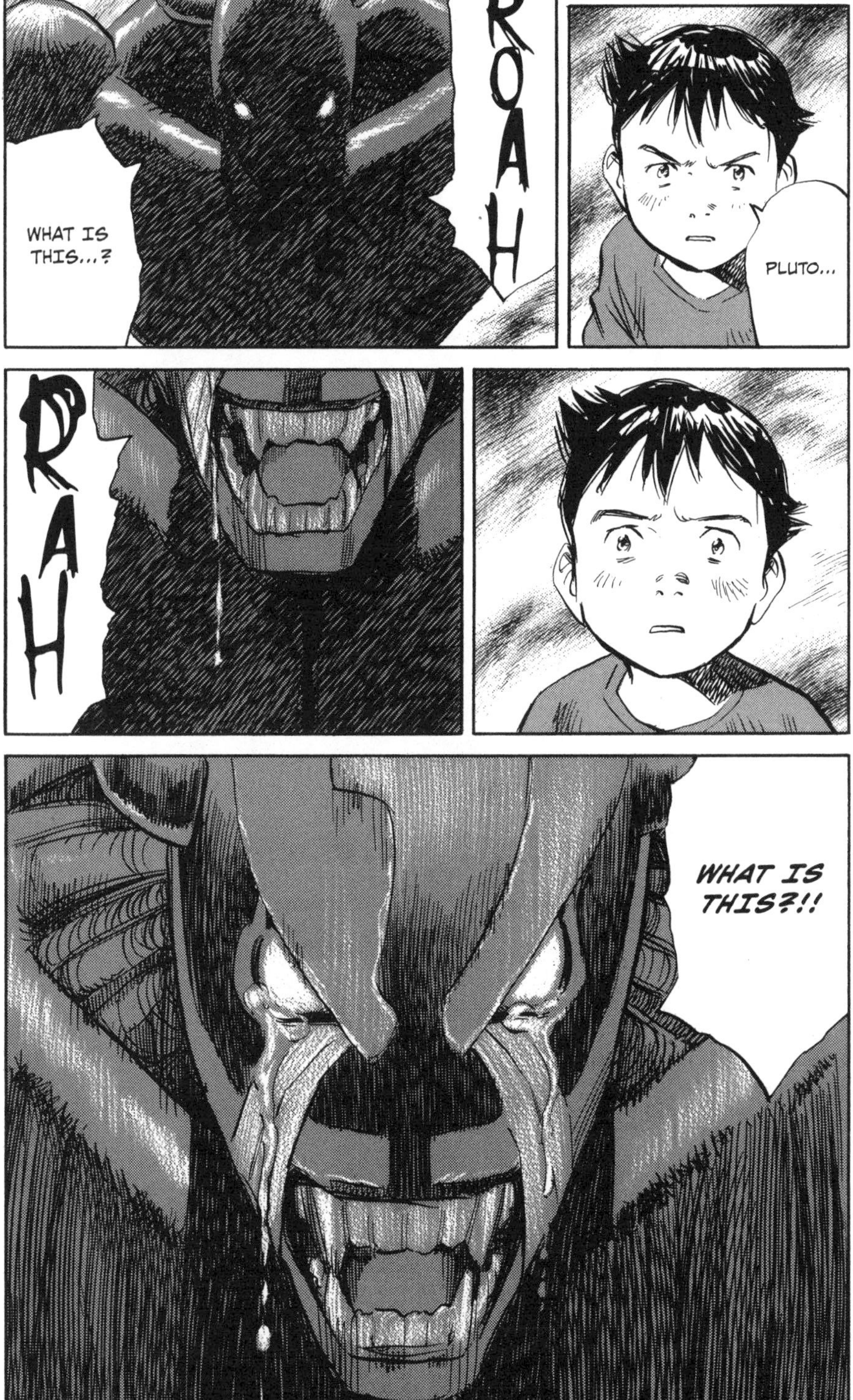
PLUTO...
ROAH
WHAT IS THIS...?
RAAH
WHAT IS THIS?!!

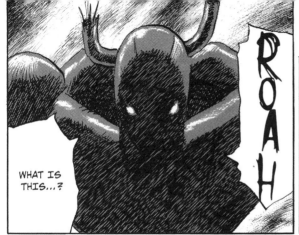

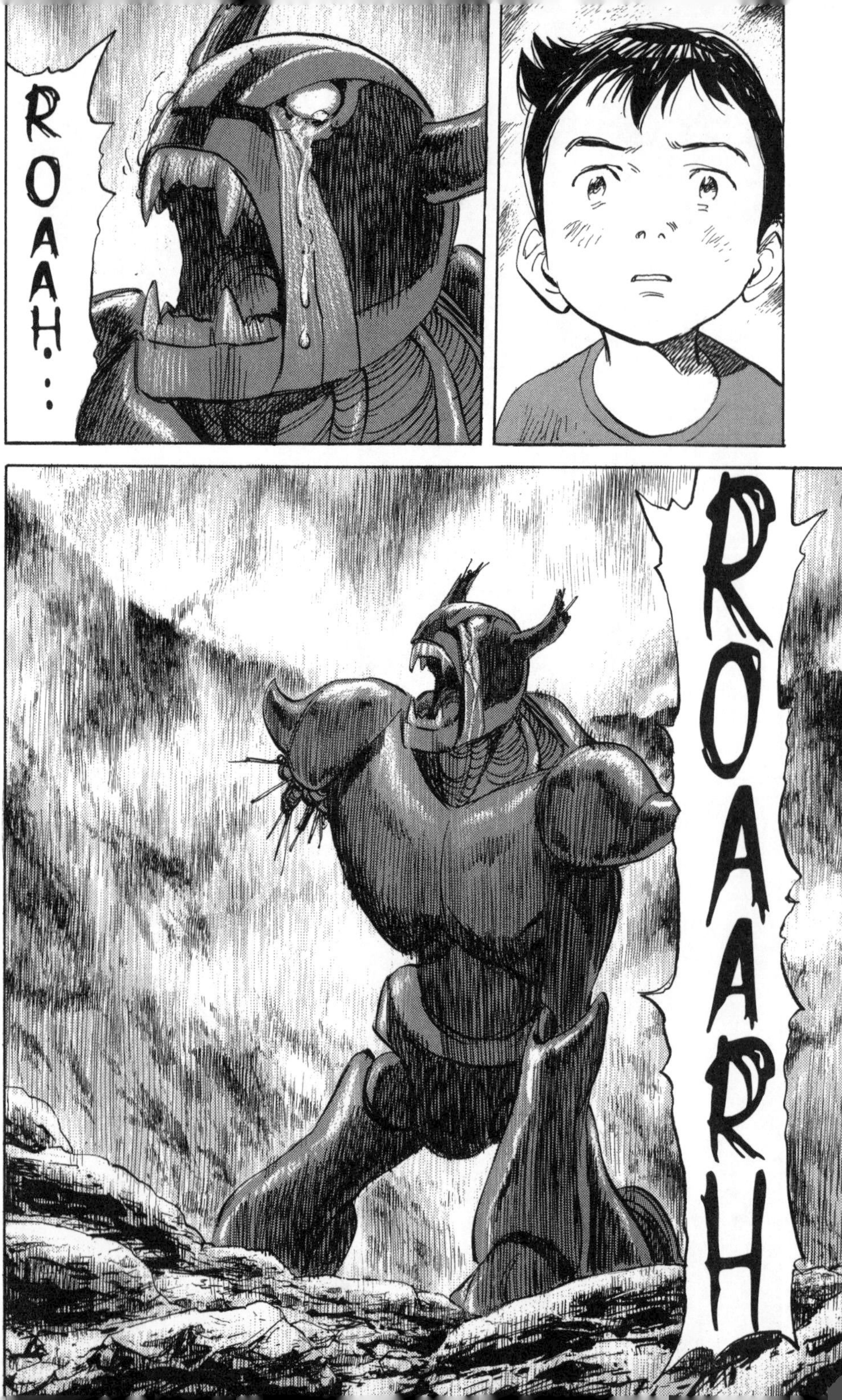
ROAAH...
ROAARH

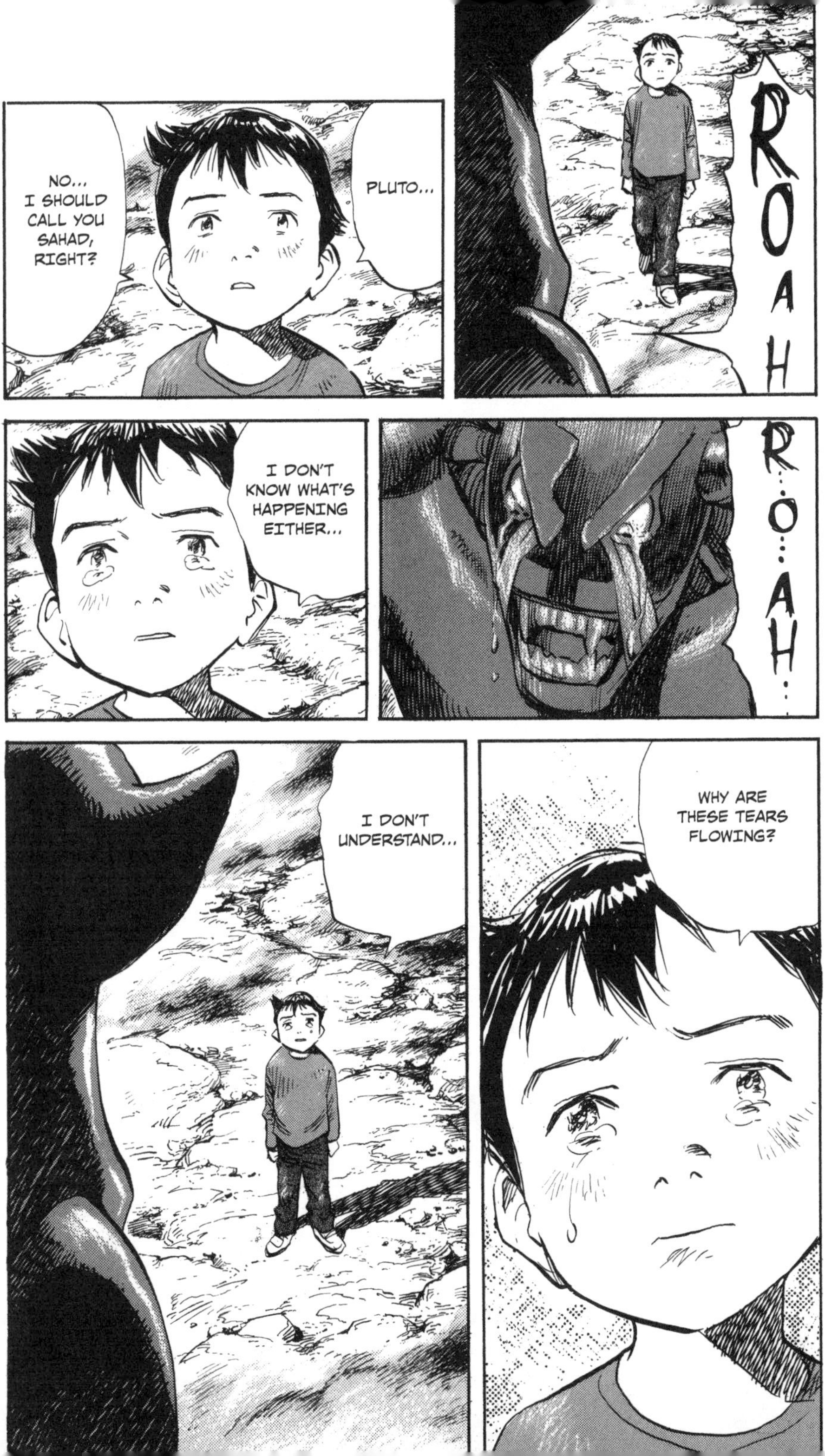
ROAH
PLUTO...
NO... I SHOULD CALL YOU SAHAD, RIGHT?
R...O...A...H...
I DON'T KNOW WHAT'S HAPPENING EITHER...
WHY ARE THESE TEARS FLOWING?
I DON'T UNDERSTAND...

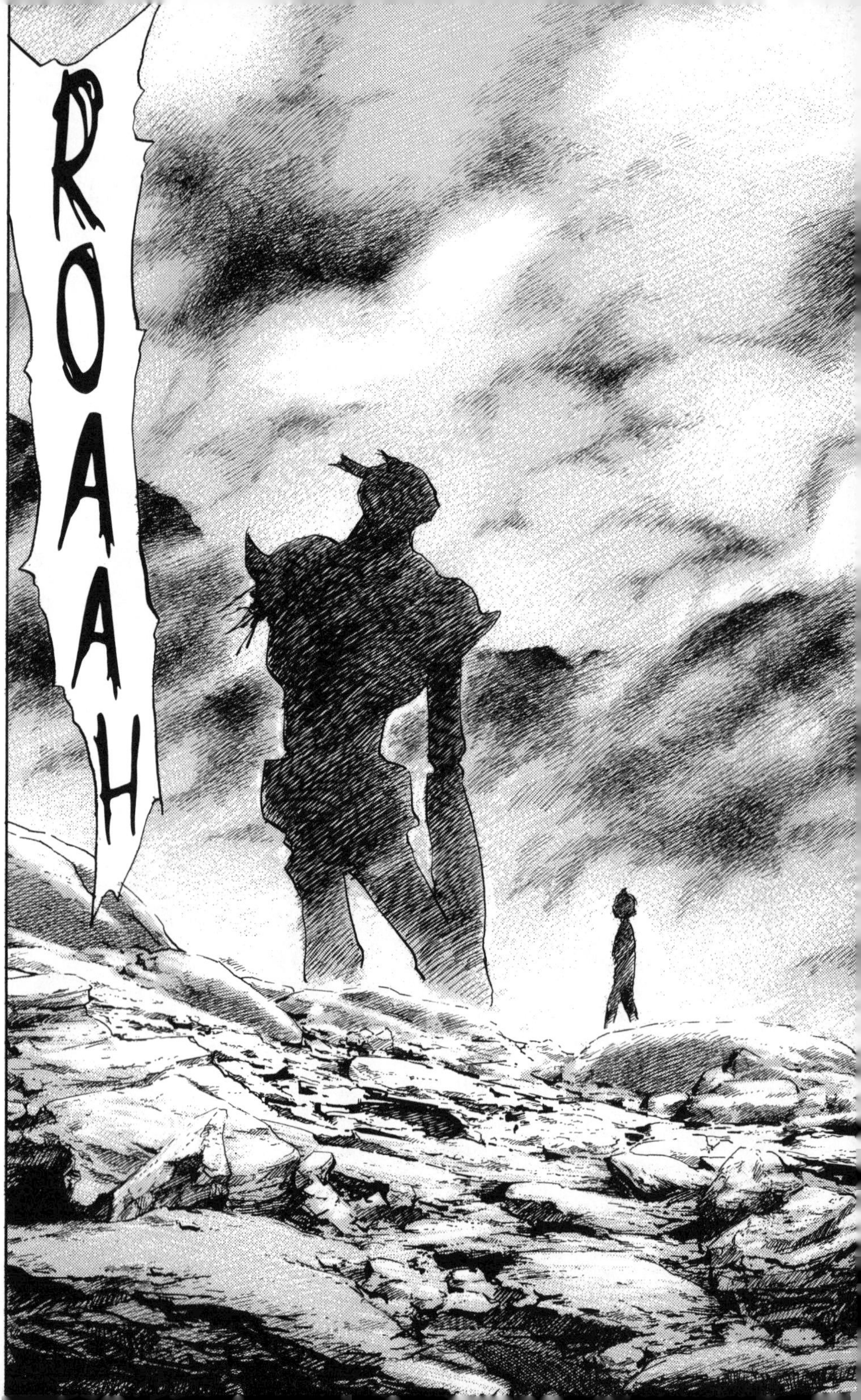
ROAAH

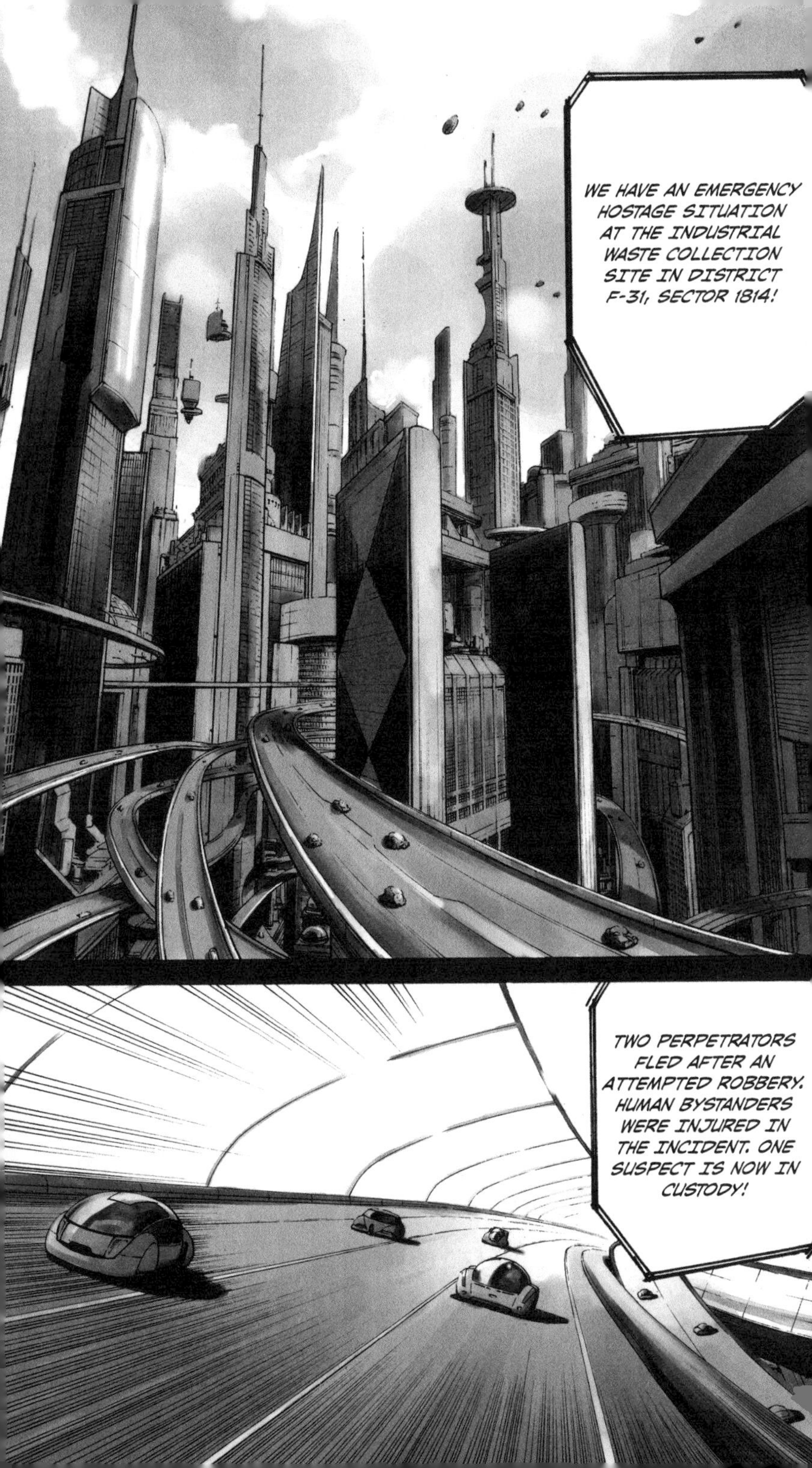
WE HAVE AN EMERGENCY HOSTAGE SITUATION AT THE INDUSTRIAL WASTE COLLECTION SITE IN DISTRICT F-31, SECTOR 1814!
TWO PERPETRATORS FLED AFTER AN ATTEMPTED ROBBERY. HUMAN BYSTANDERS WERE INJURED IN THE INCIDENT. ONE SUSPECT IS NOW IN CUSTODY!

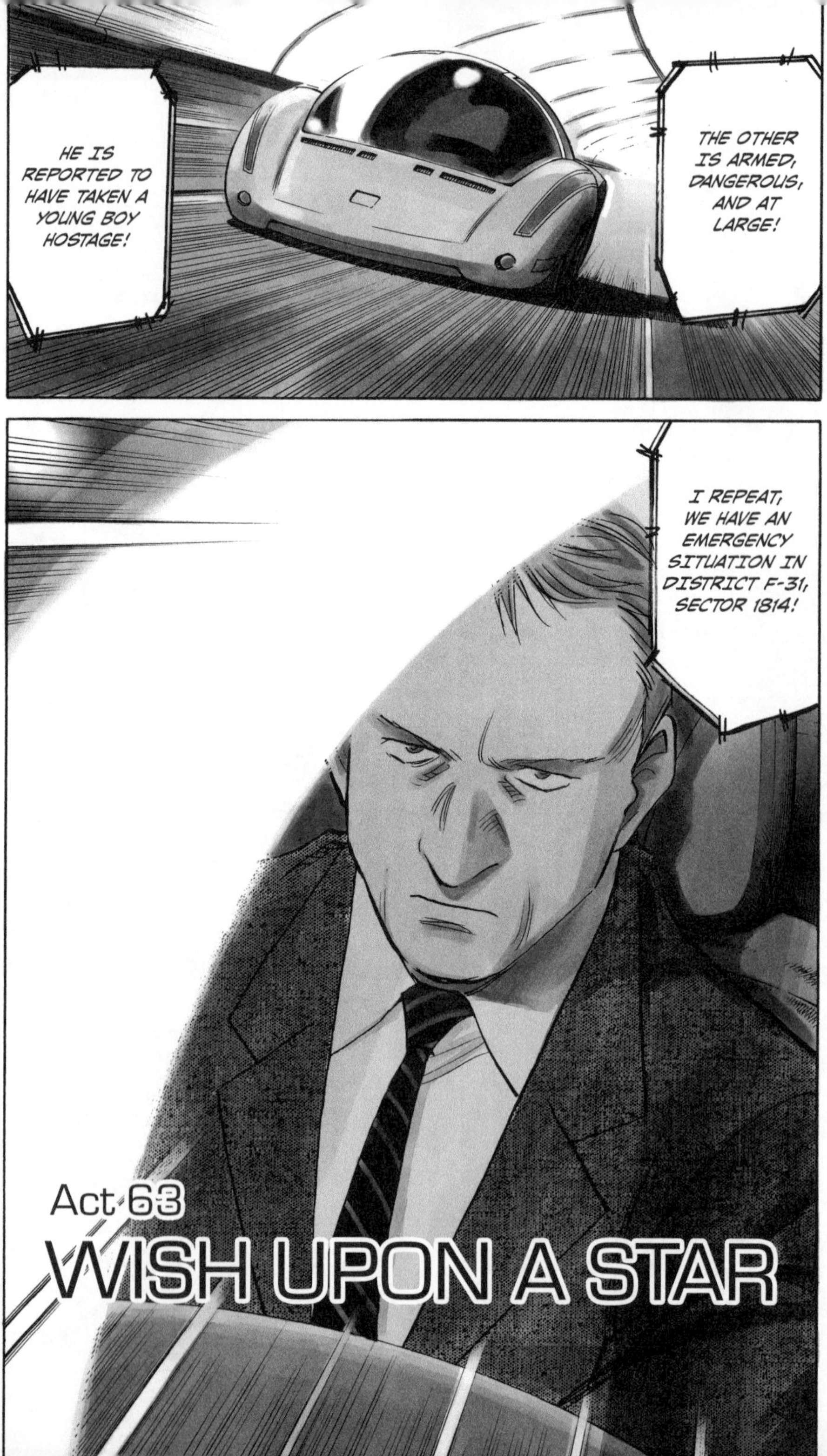
THE OTHER IS ARMED, DANGEROUS, AND AT LARGE!
HE IS REPORTED TO HAVE TAKEN A YOUNG BOY HOSTAGE!
I REPEAT, WE HAVE AN EMERGENCY SITUATION IN DISTRICT F-31, SECTOR 1814!
Act 63
WISH UPON A STAR

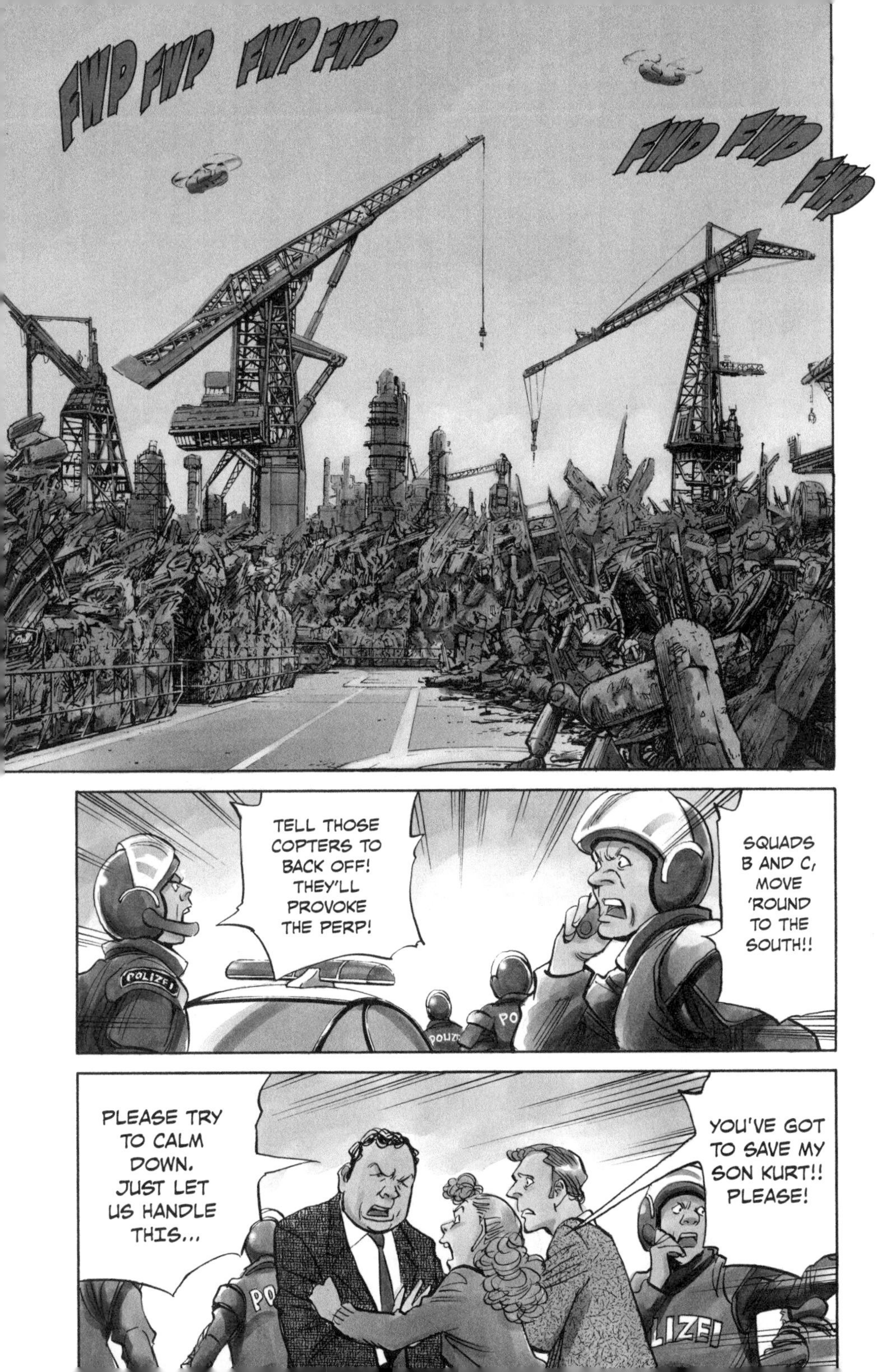
FWP FWP FWP
FWP FWP FWP FWP
SQUADS B AND C, MOVE 'ROUND TO THE SOUTH!!
TELL THOSE COPTERS TO BACK OFF! THEY'LL PROVOKE THE PERP!
YOU'VE GOT TO SAVE MY SON KURT!! PLEASE!
PLEASE TRY TO CALM DOWN. JUST LET US HANDLE THIS...

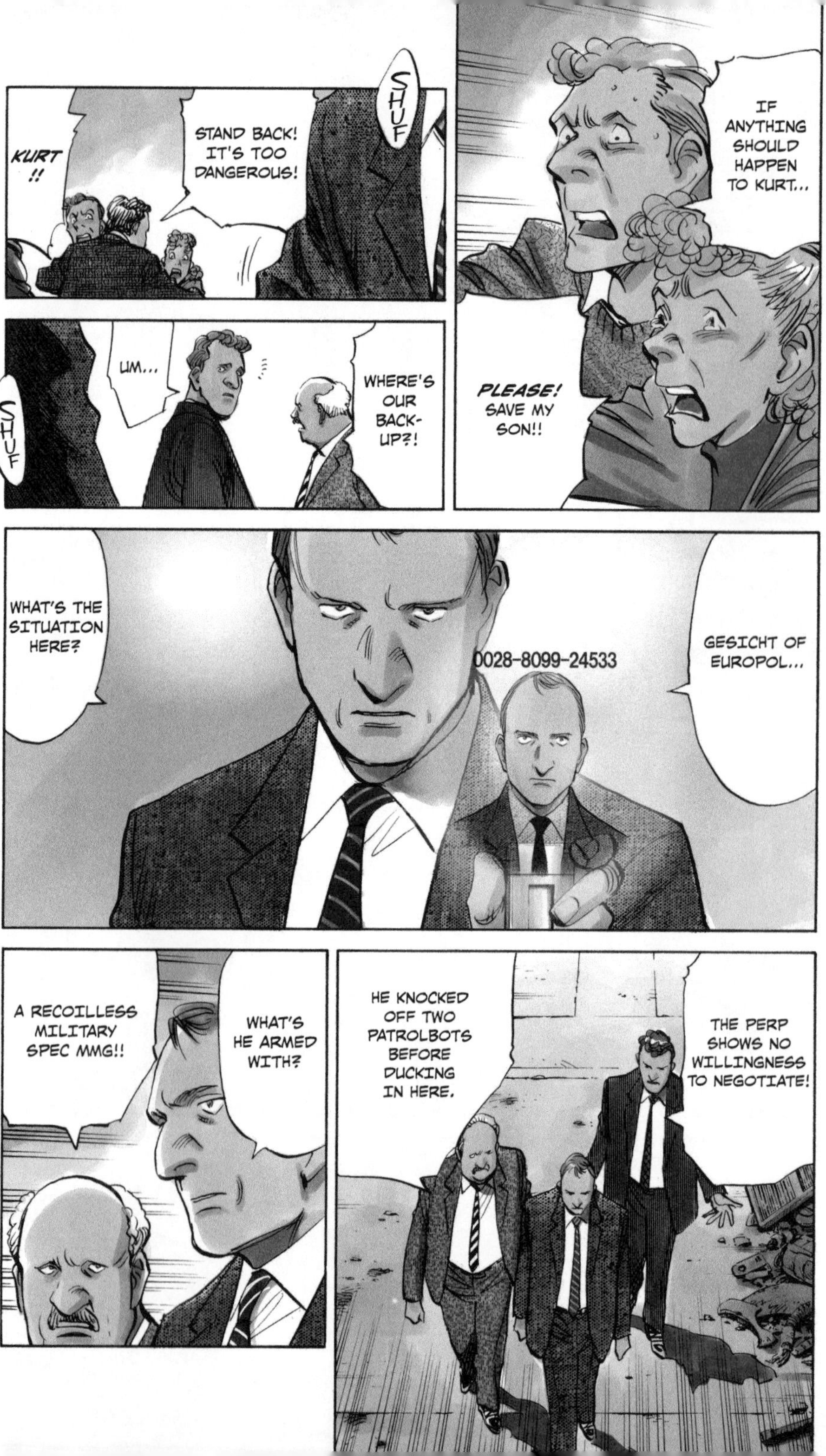
IF ANYTHING SHOULD HAPPEN TO KURT...
PLEASE! SAVE MY SON!!
SHUF
STAND BACK! IT'S TOO DANGEROUS!
KURT !!
WHERE'S OUR BACK-UP?!
UM...
SHUF
GESICHT OF EUROPOL...
0028-8099-24533
WHAT'S THE SITUATION HERE?
THE PERP SHOWS NO WILLINGNESS TO NEGOTIATE!
HE KNOCKED OFF TWO PATROLBOTS BEFORE DUCKING IN HERE.
WHAT'S HE ARMED WITH?
A RECOILLESS MILITARY SPEC MMG!!

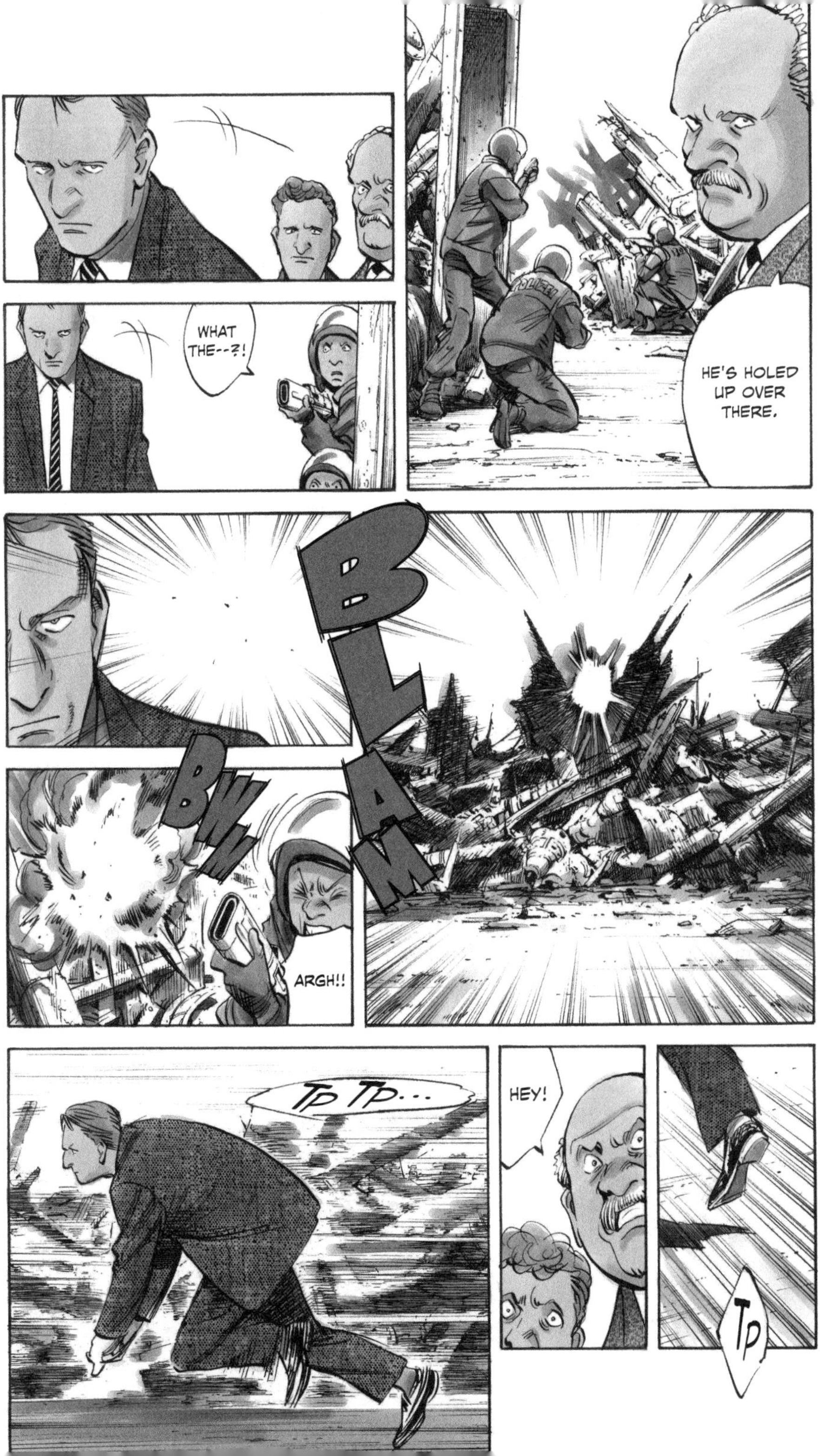
HE'S HOLED UP OVER THERE.
WHAT THE--?!
BLAM
BWW
ARGH!!
Tp
HEY!
Tp Tp...

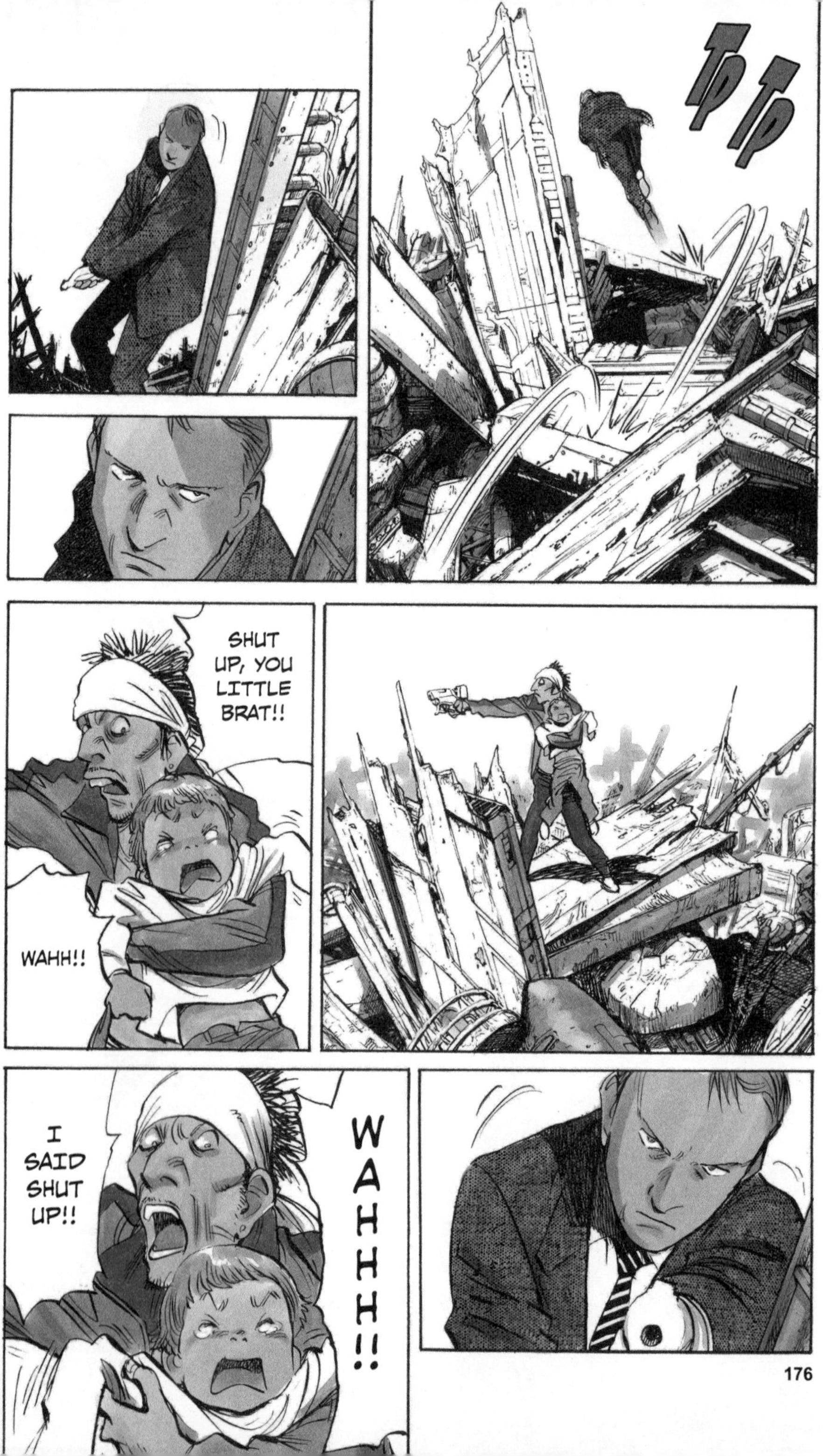
Tp Tp
SHUT UP, YOU LITTLE BRAT!!
WAHH!!
WAHHH!!
I SAID SHUT UP!!

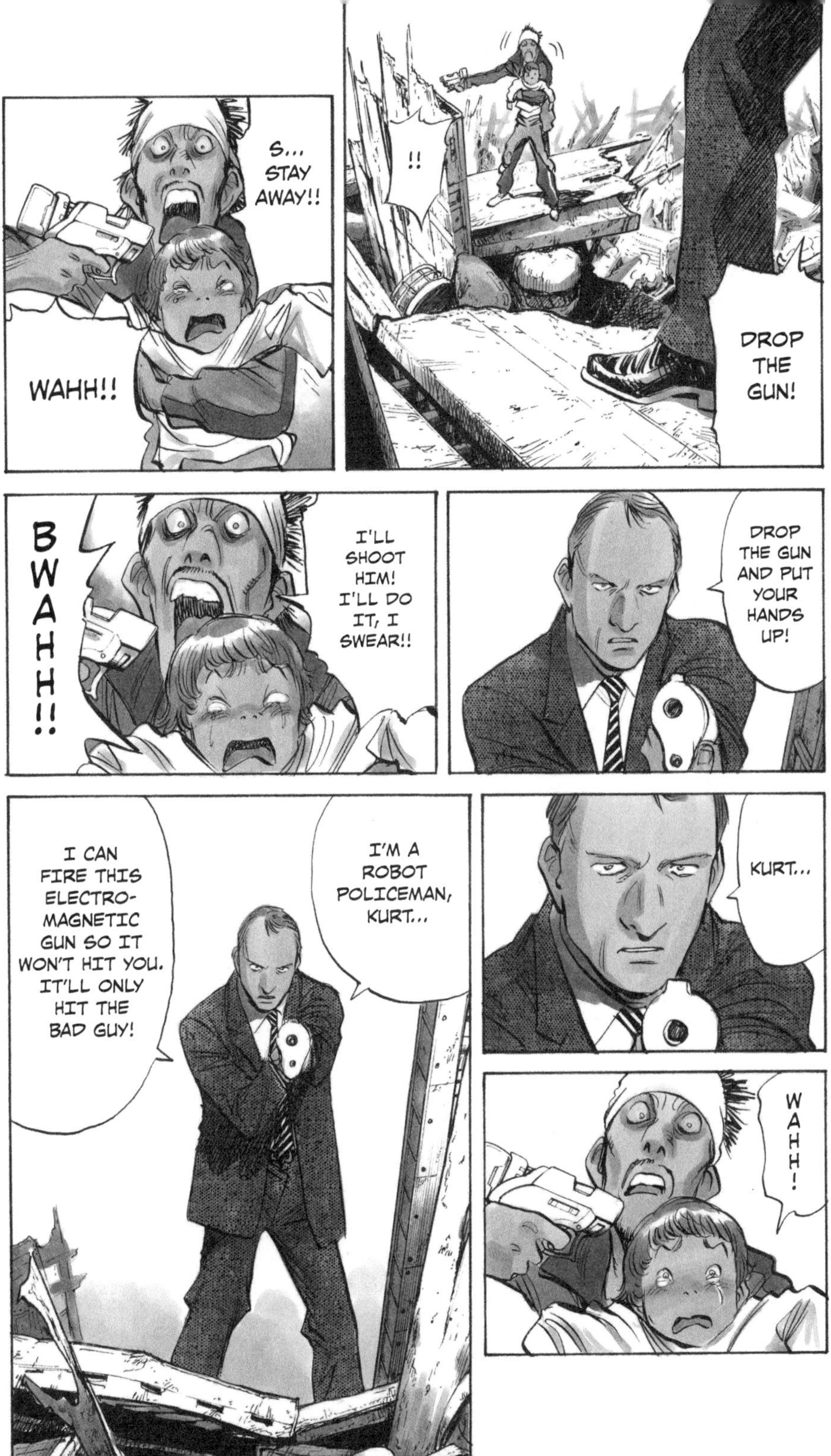
!!
DROP THE GUN!
S... STAY AWAY!!
WAHH!!
DROP THE GUN AND PUT YOUR HANDS UP!
I'LL SHOOT HIM! I'LL DO IT, I SWEAR!!
BWAHH!!
KURT...
WAHH!
I'M A ROBOT POLICEMAN, KURT...
I CAN FIRE THIS ELECTRO-MAGNETIC GUN SO IT WON'T HIT YOU. IT'LL ONLY HIT THE BAD GUY!

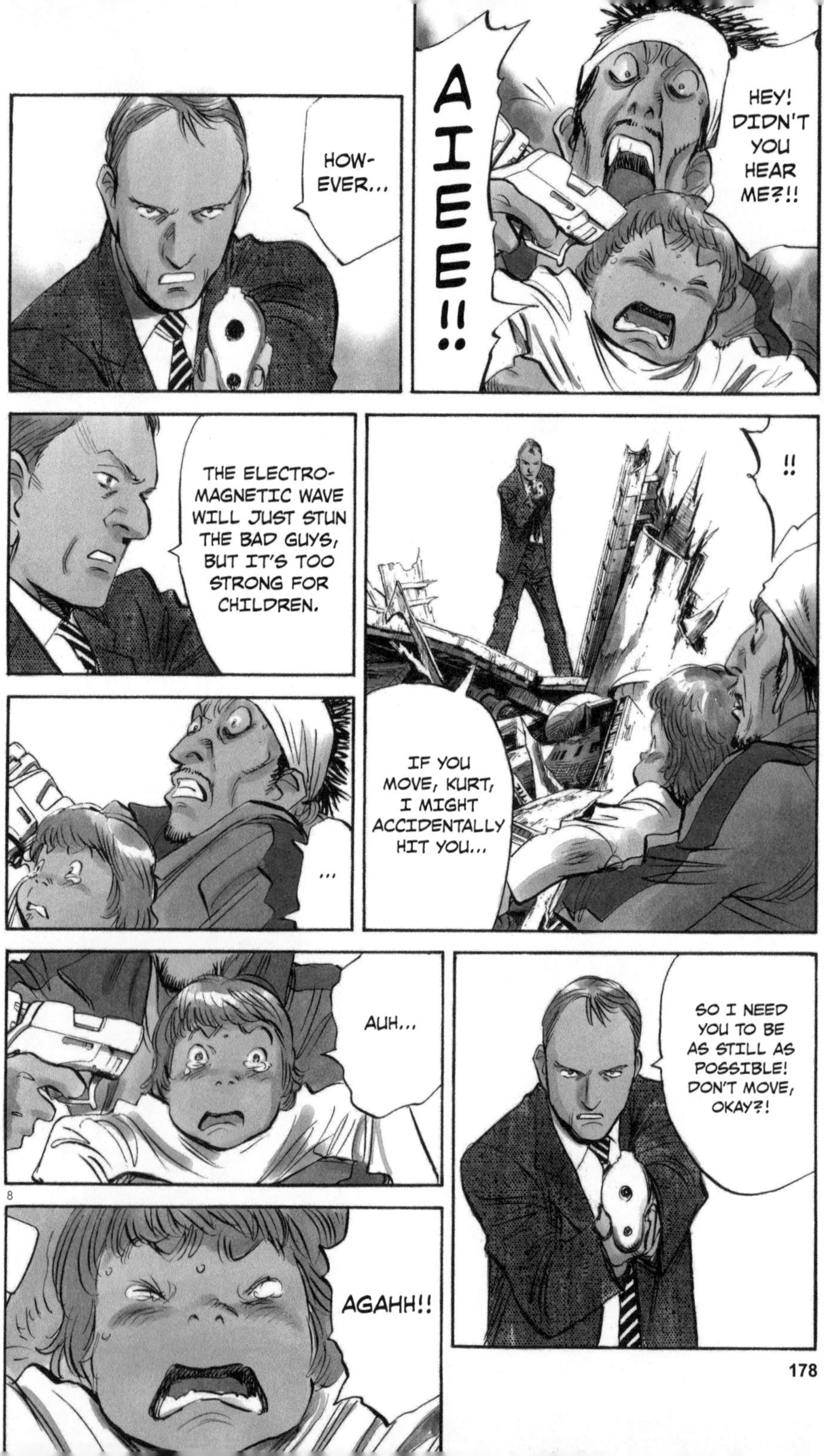
HEY! DIDN'T YOU HEAR ME?!!
AIEE!!
HOW-EVER...
!!
IF YOU MOVE, KURT, I MIGHT ACCIDENTALLY HIT YOU...
THE ELECTRO-MAGNETIC WAVE WILL JUST STUN THE BAD GUYS, BUT IT'S TOO STRONG FOR CHILDREN.
...
SO I NEED YOU TO BE AS STILL AS POSSIBLE! DON'T MOVE, OKAY?!
AUH...
AGAHH!!

8

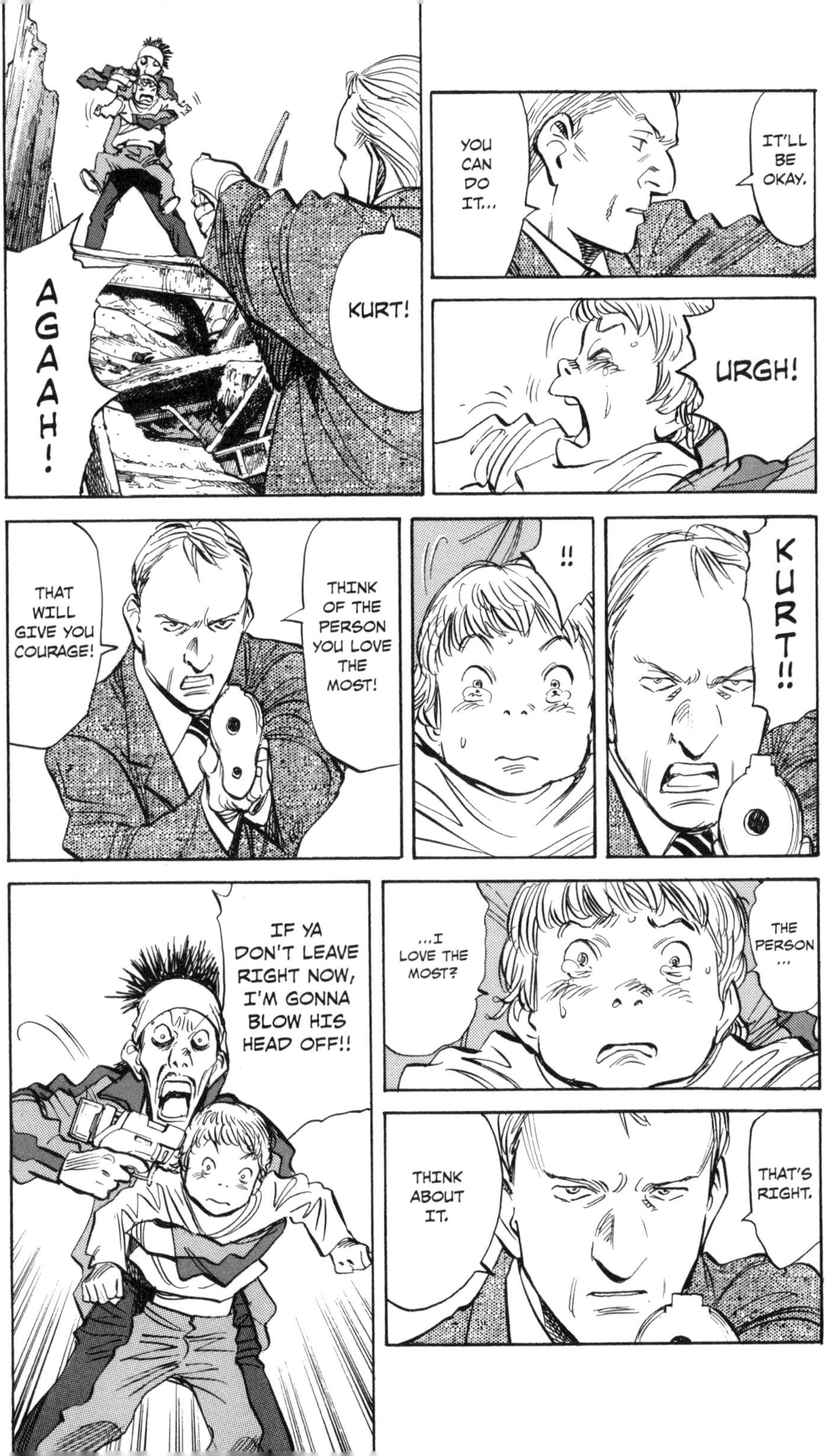
IT'LL BE OKAY.
YOU CAN DO IT...
URGH!
KURT!
AGAAAH!
KURT!!
!!
THINK OF THE PERSON YOU LOVE THE MOST!
THAT WILL GIVE YOU COURAGE!
THE PERSON...
...I LOVE THE MOST?
THAT'S RIGHT.
THINK ABOUT IT.
IF YA DON'T LEAVE RIGHT NOW, I'M GONNA BLOW HIS HEAD OFF!!

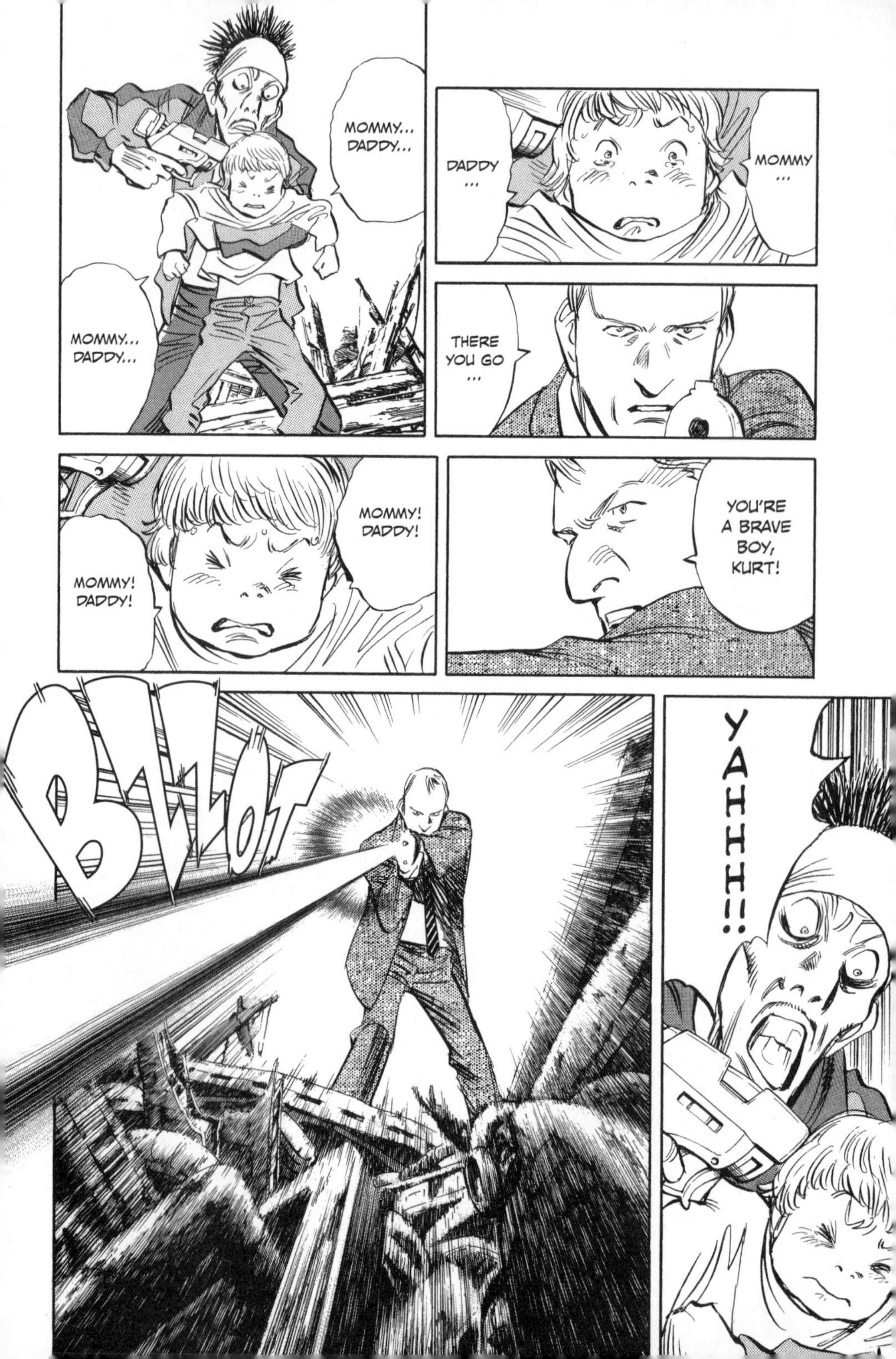

MOMMY ...
DADDY ...
THERE YOU GO ...
MOMMY... DADDY...
MOMMY... DADDY...
YOU'RE A BRAVE BOY, KURT!
MOMMY! DADDY!
MOMMY! DADDY!
YAHHH!!
BLLOT

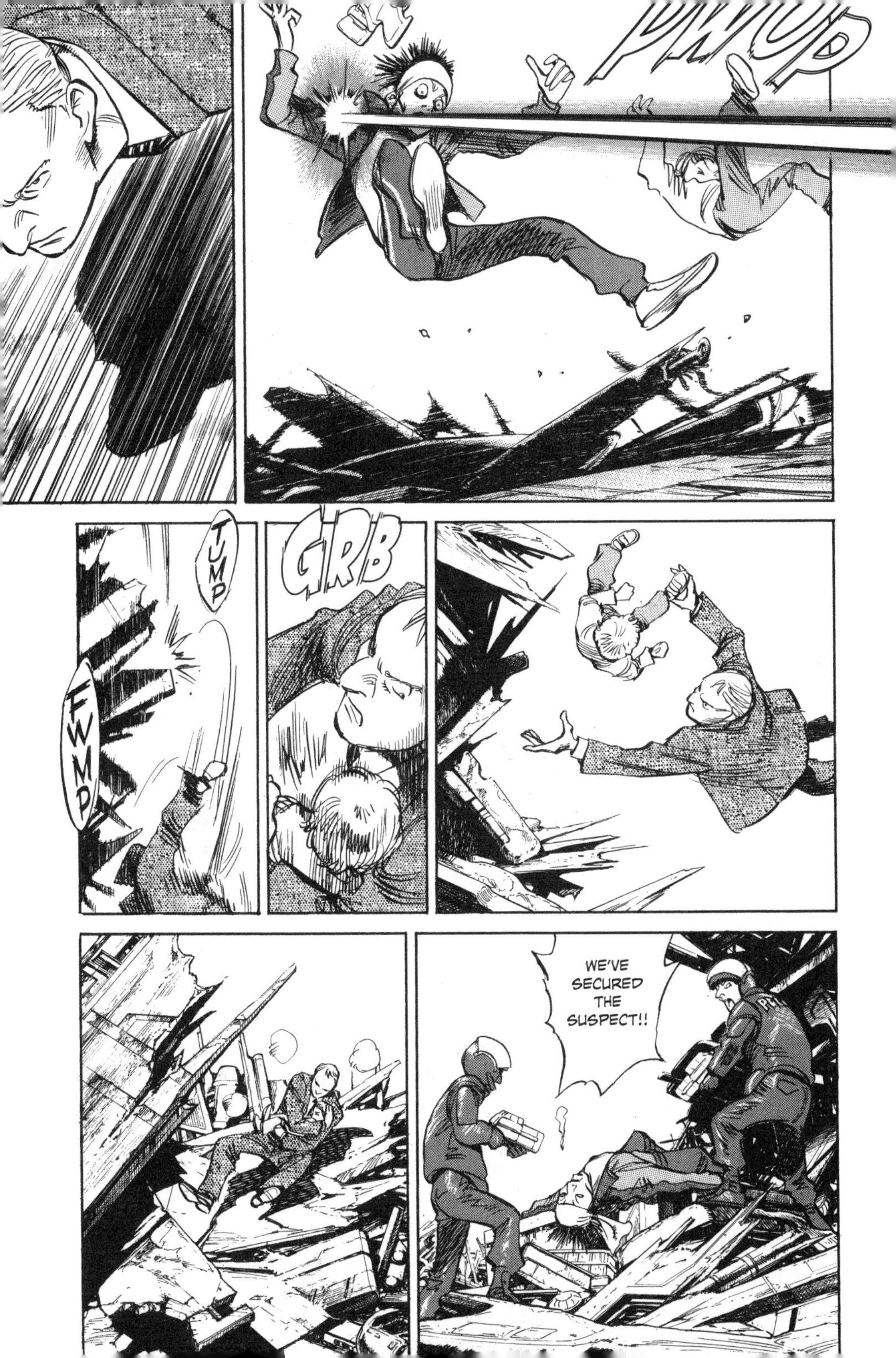
PWUP
GRB
TUMP
FWMP
WE'VE SECURED THE SUSPECT!!

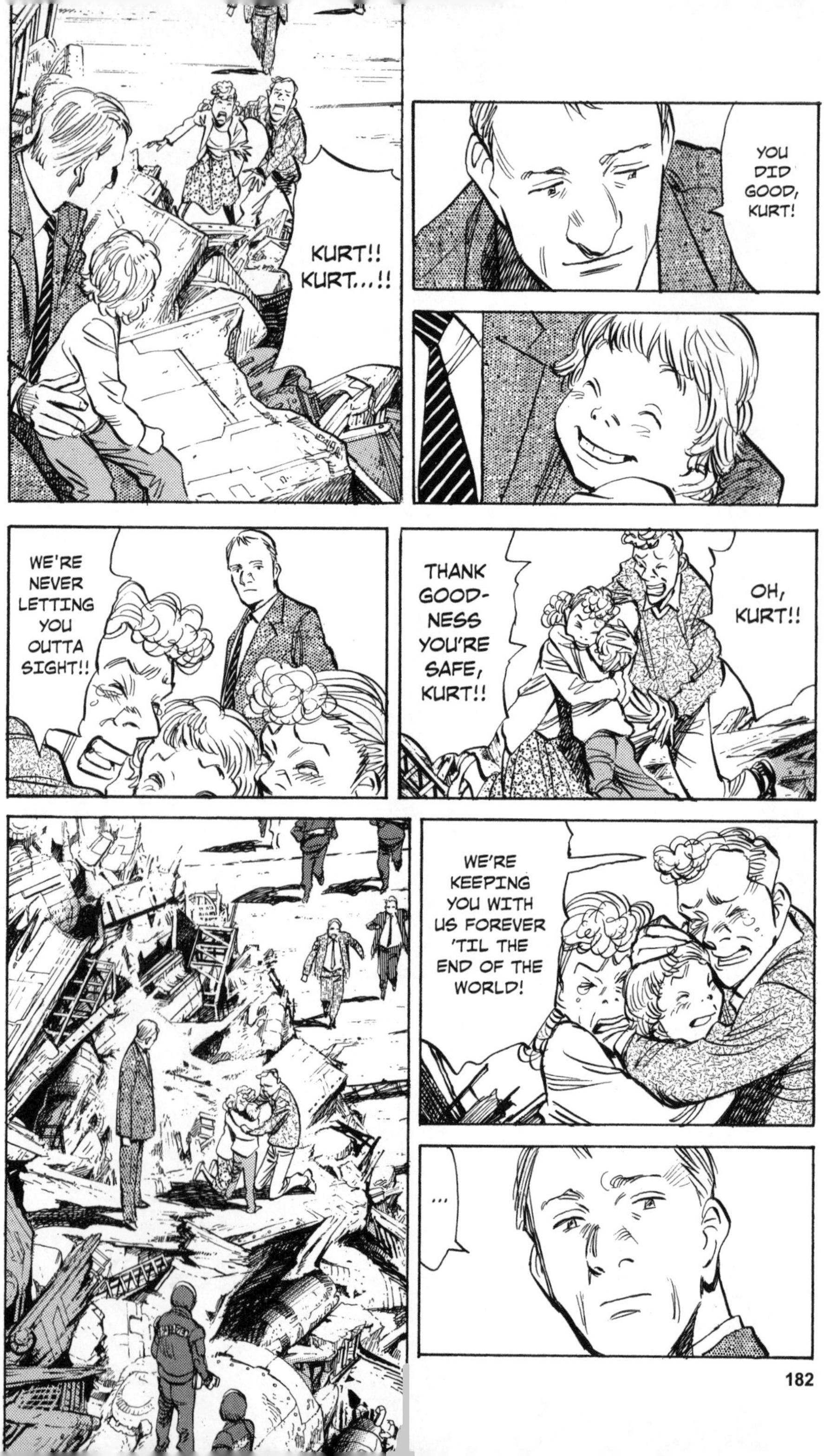
YOU DID GOOD, KURT!
KURT!! KURT...!!
OH, KURT!!
THANK GOODNESS YOU'RE SAFE, KURT!!
WE'RE NEVER LETTING YOU OUTTA SIGHT!!
WE'RE KEEPING YOU WITH US FOREVER 'TIL THE END OF THE WORLD!
...

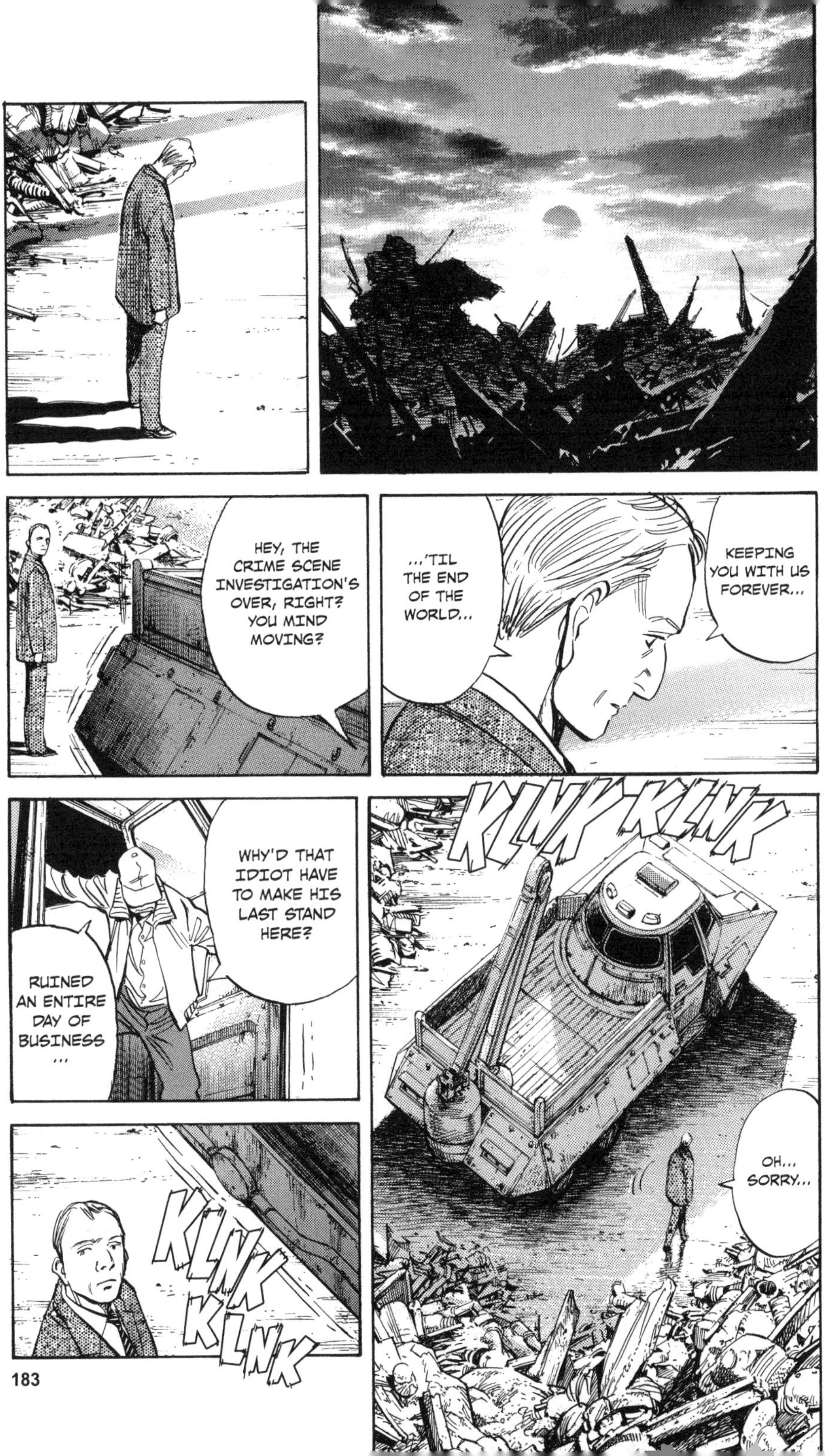
KEEPING YOU WITH US FOREVER...
...'TIL THE END OF THE WORLD...
HEY, THE CRIME SCENE INVESTIGATION'S OVER, RIGHT? YOU MIND MOVING?
KLNK KLNK
OH... SORRY...
WHY'D THAT IDIOT HAVE TO MAKE HIS LAST STAND HERE?
RUINED AN ENTIRE DAY OF BUSINESS...
KLNK KLNK

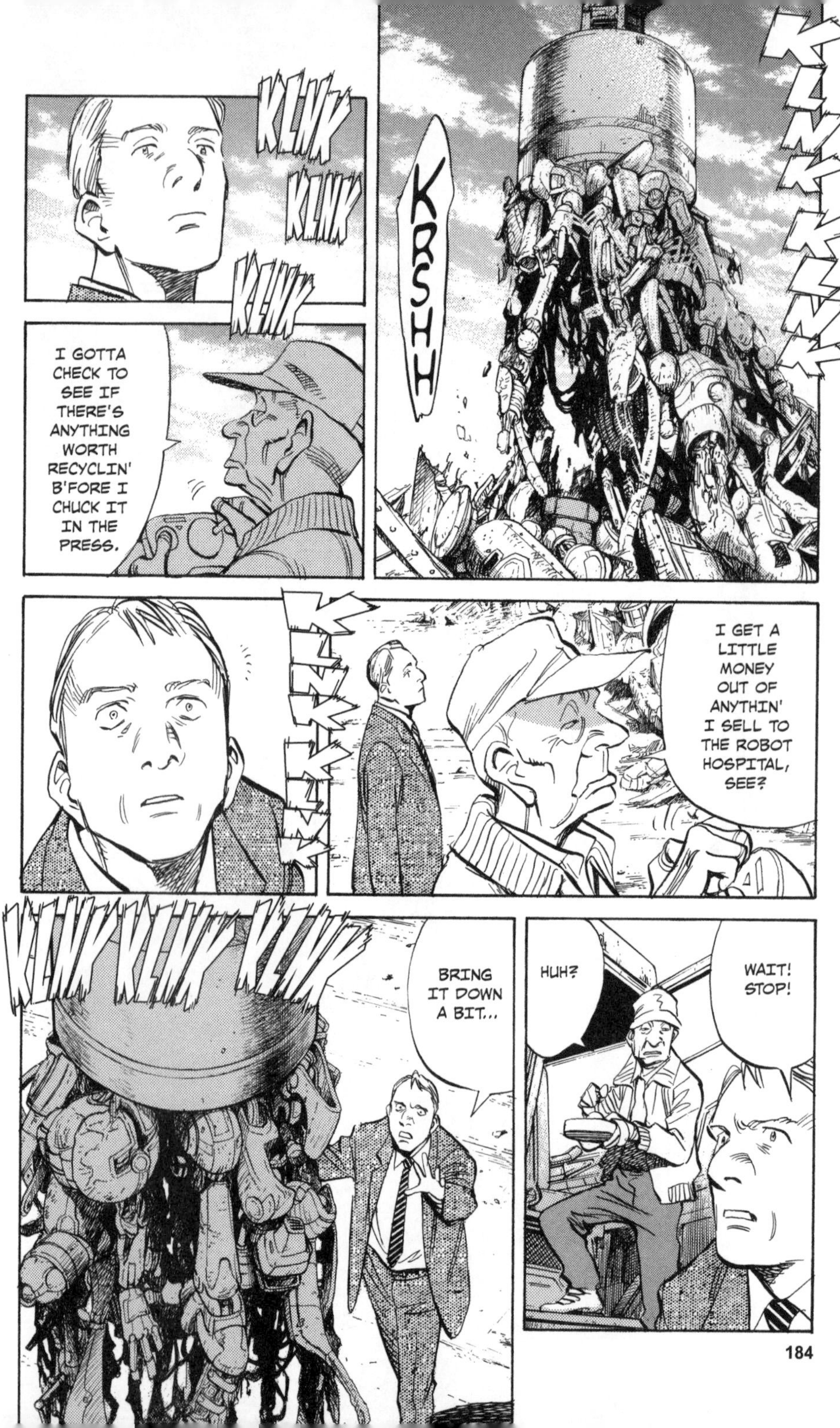
KLNK KLNK KLNK
KRSHH
KLNK
KLNK
KLNK
I GOTTA CHECK TO SEE IF THERE'S ANYTHING WORTH RECYCLIN' B'FORE I CHUCK IT IN THE PRESS.
I GET A LITTLE MONEY OUT OF ANYTHIN' I SELL TO THE ROBOT HOSPITAL, SEE?
WAIT! STOP!
HUH?
KLNK KLNK KLNK
BRING IT DOWN A BIT...

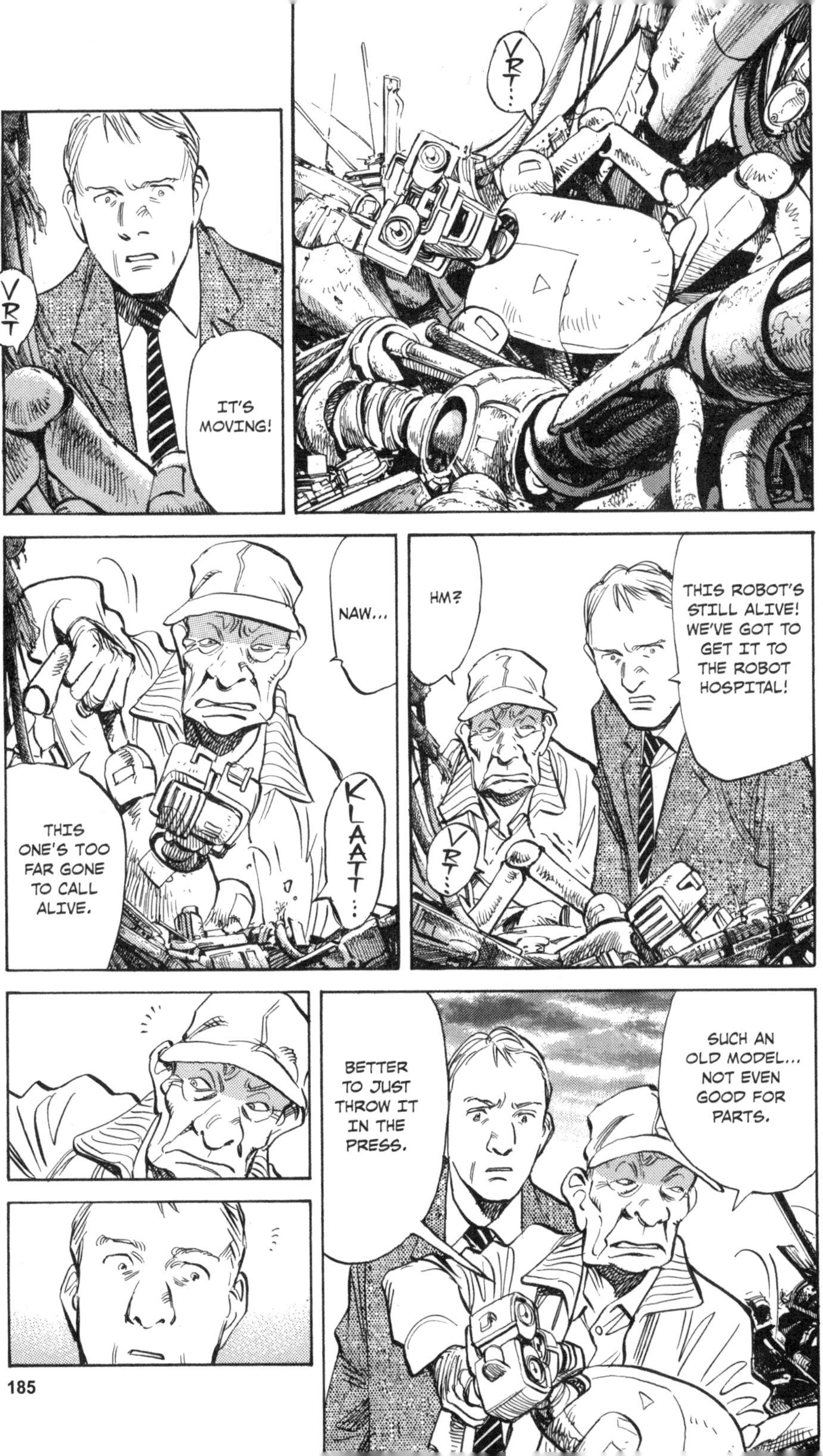

VRT...
VRT
IT'S MOVING!
THIS ROBOT'S STILL ALIVE! WE'VE GOT TO GET IT TO THE ROBOT HOSPITAL!
HM?
VRT...
NAW...
KLAATT...
THIS ONE'S TOO FAR GONE TO CALL ALIVE.
SUCH AN OLD MODEL... NOT EVEN GOOD FOR PARTS.
BETTER TO JUST THROW IT IN THE PRESS.

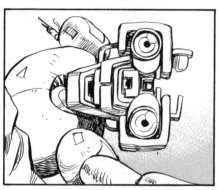

CAN I HAVE HIM?

CHILD...?

THIS CHILD...

IT'S JUST *JUNK*.

HEY, WHAT DO I CARE.

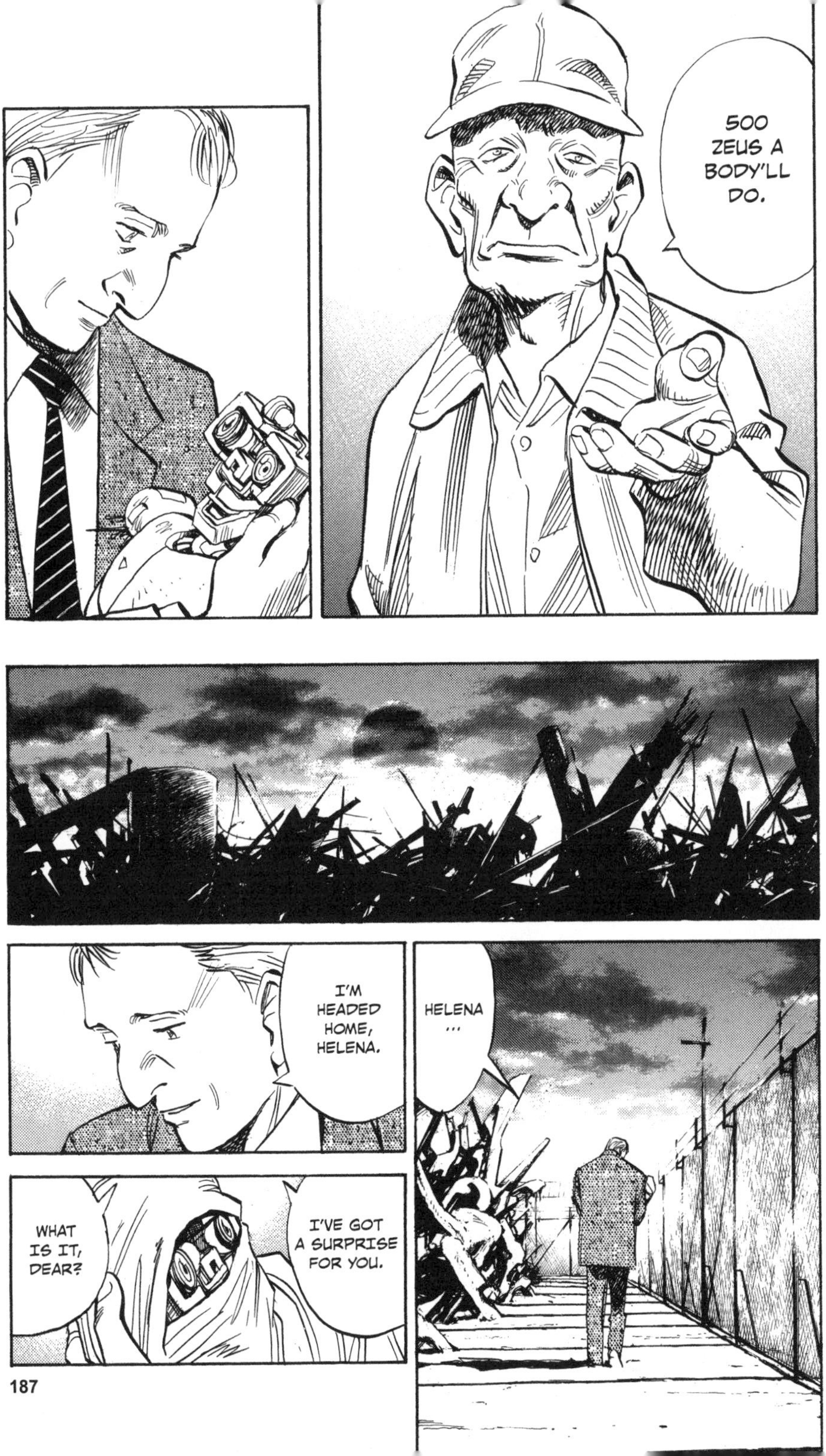
500 ZEUS A BODY'LL DO.
HELENA ...
I'M HEADED HOME, HELENA.
I'VE GOT A SURPRISE FOR YOU.
WHAT IS IT, DEAR?

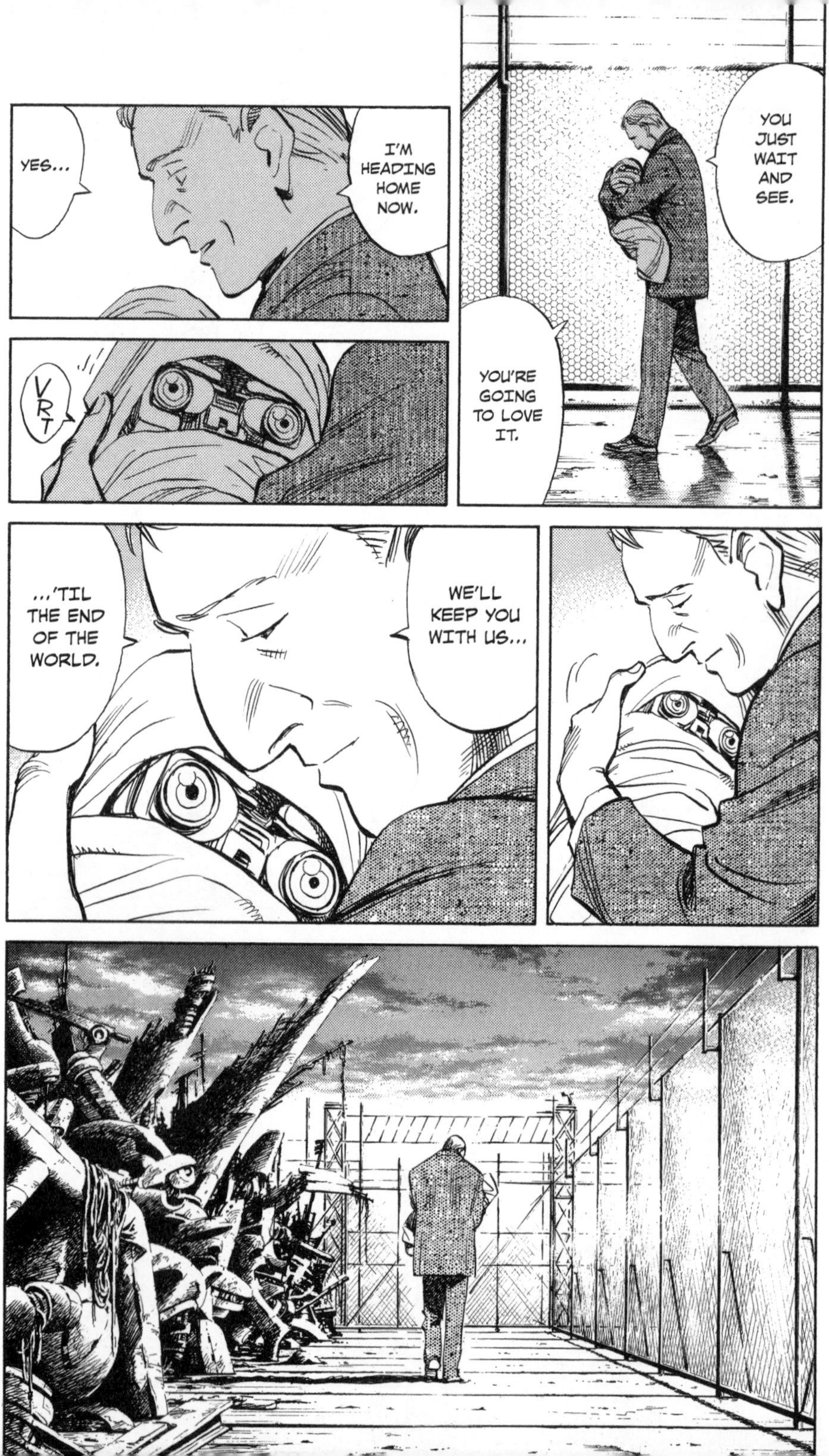
YOU JUST WAIT AND SEE.
YOU'RE GOING TO LOVE IT.
I'M HEADING HOME NOW.
YES...
VRT
WE'LL KEEP YOU WITH US...
...'TIL THE END OF THE WORLD.

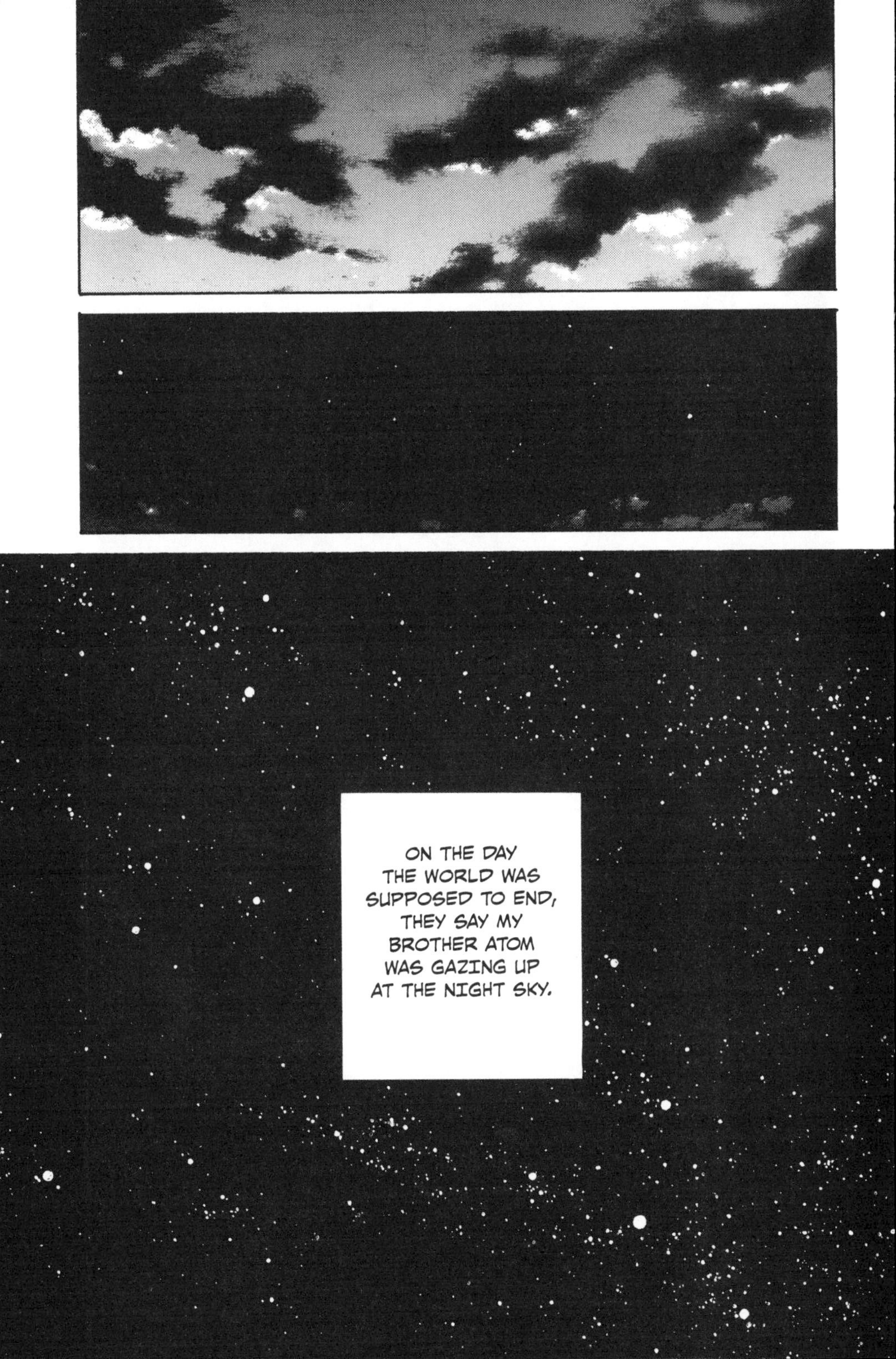
ON THE DAY THE WORLD WAS SUPPOSED TO END, THEY SAY MY BROTHER ATOM WAS GAZING UP AT THE NIGHT SKY.

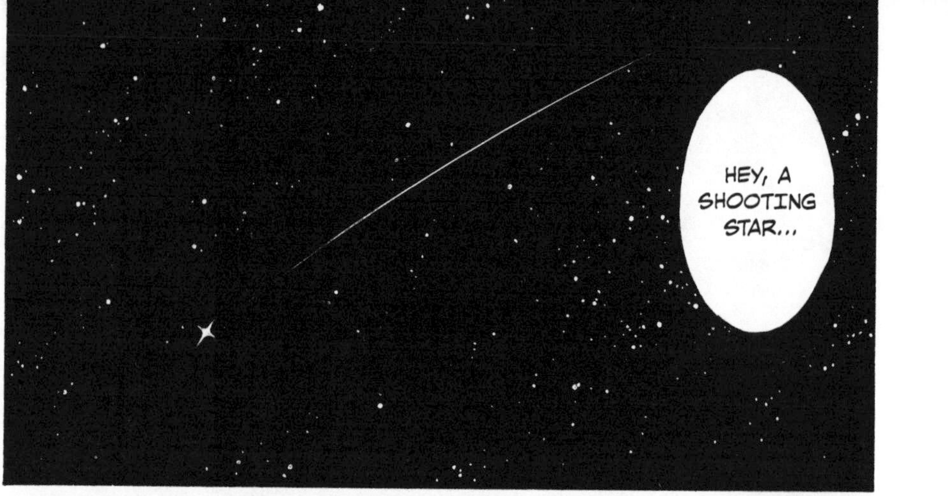
HEY, A SHOOTING STAR...

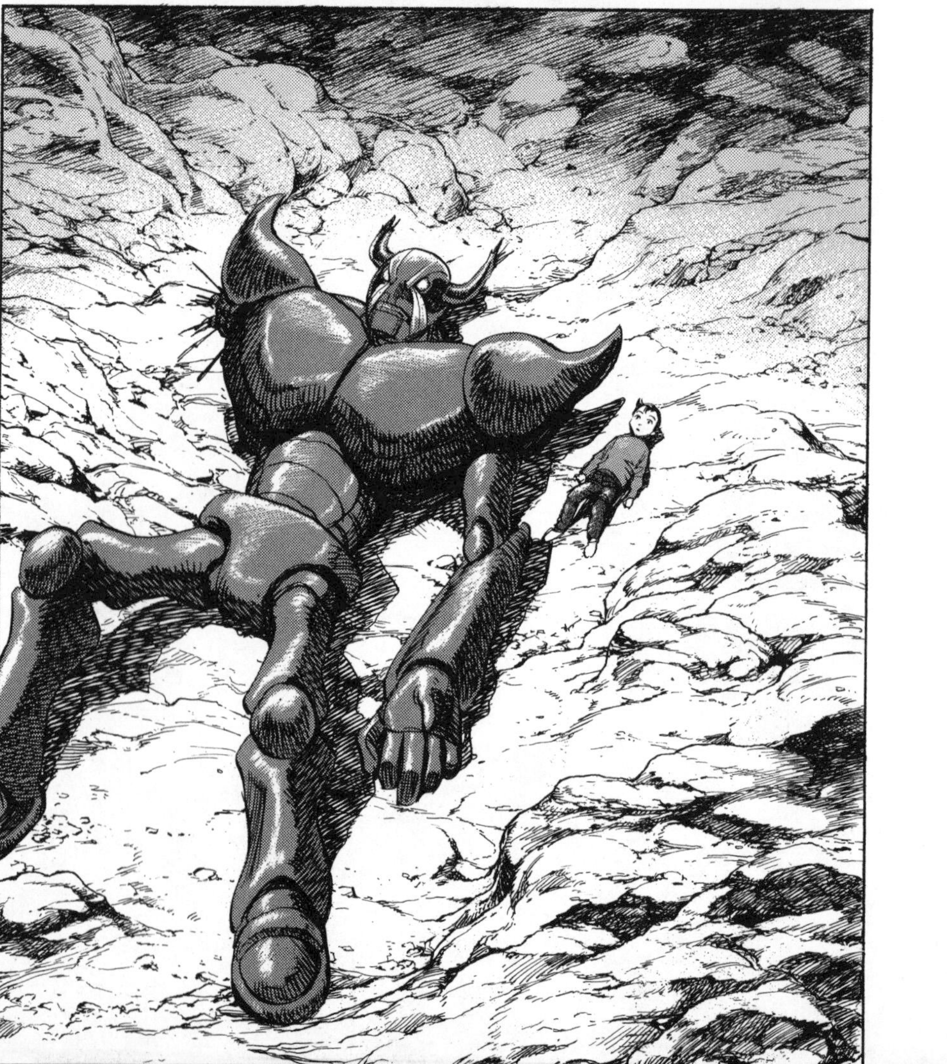

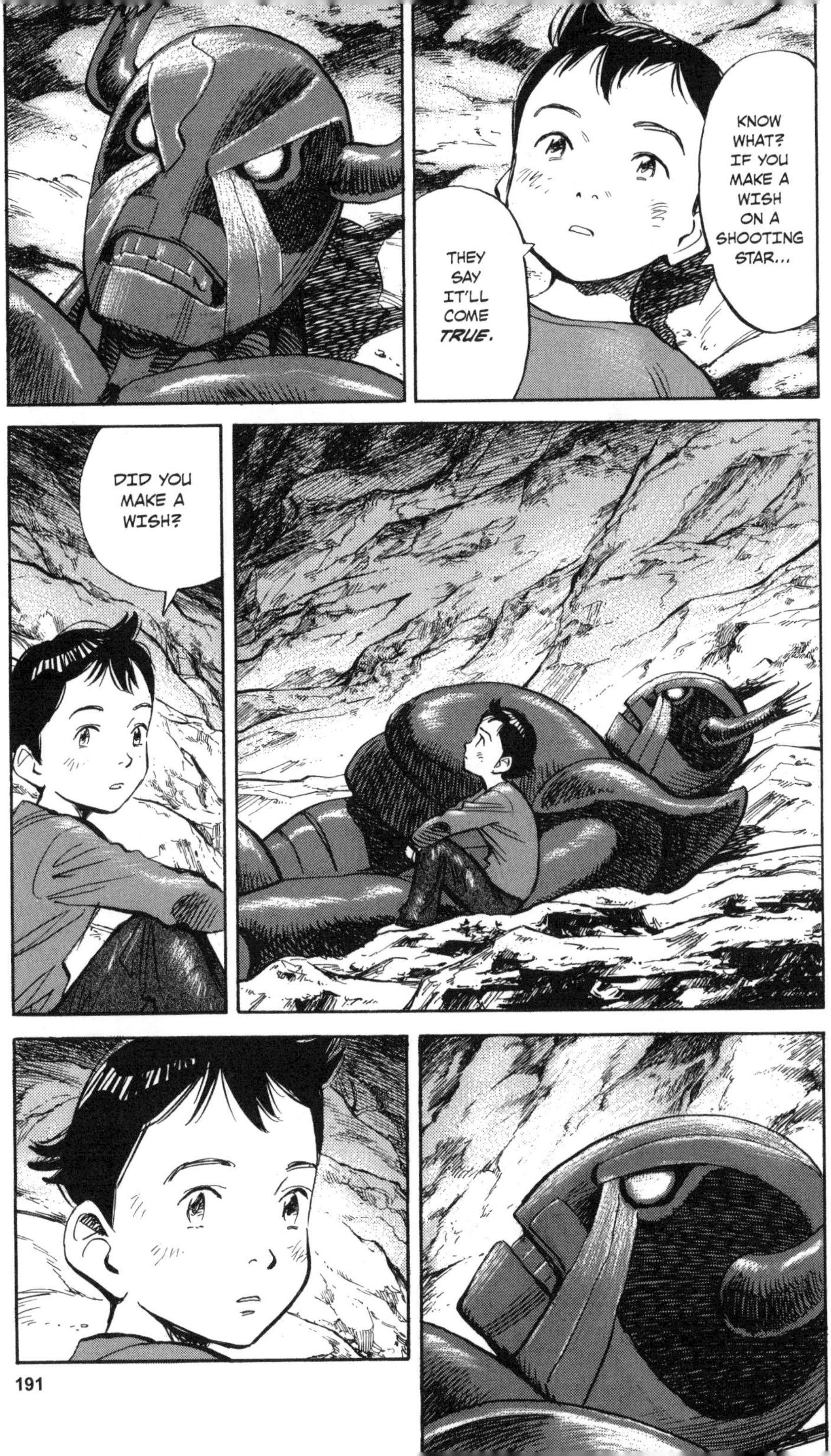
KNOW WHAT? IF YOU MAKE A WISH ON A SHOOTING STAR...
THEY SAY IT'LL COME ***TRUE.***
DID YOU MAKE A WISH?

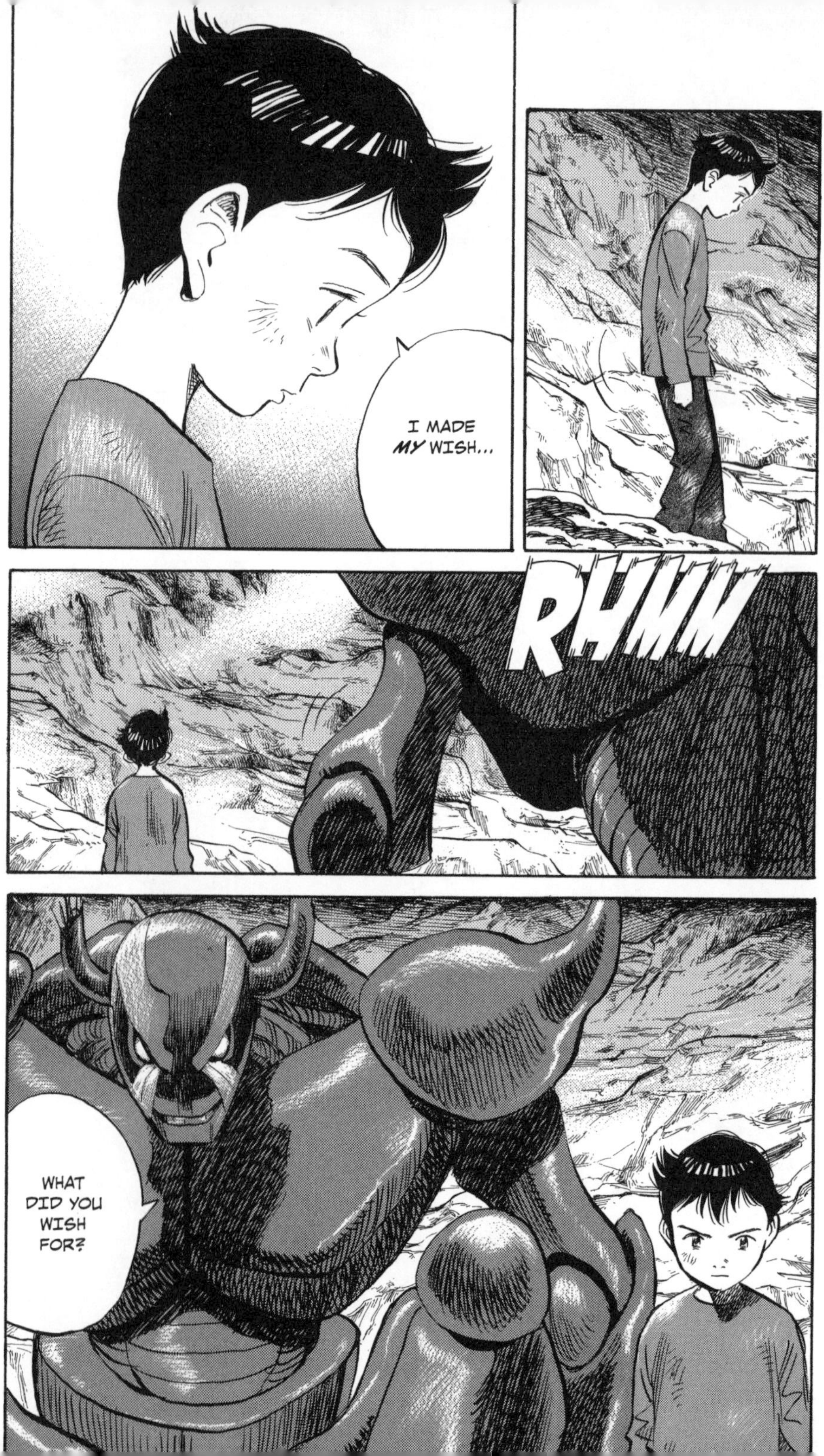
I MADE *MY* WISH...
RHMM
WHAT DID YOU WISH FOR?

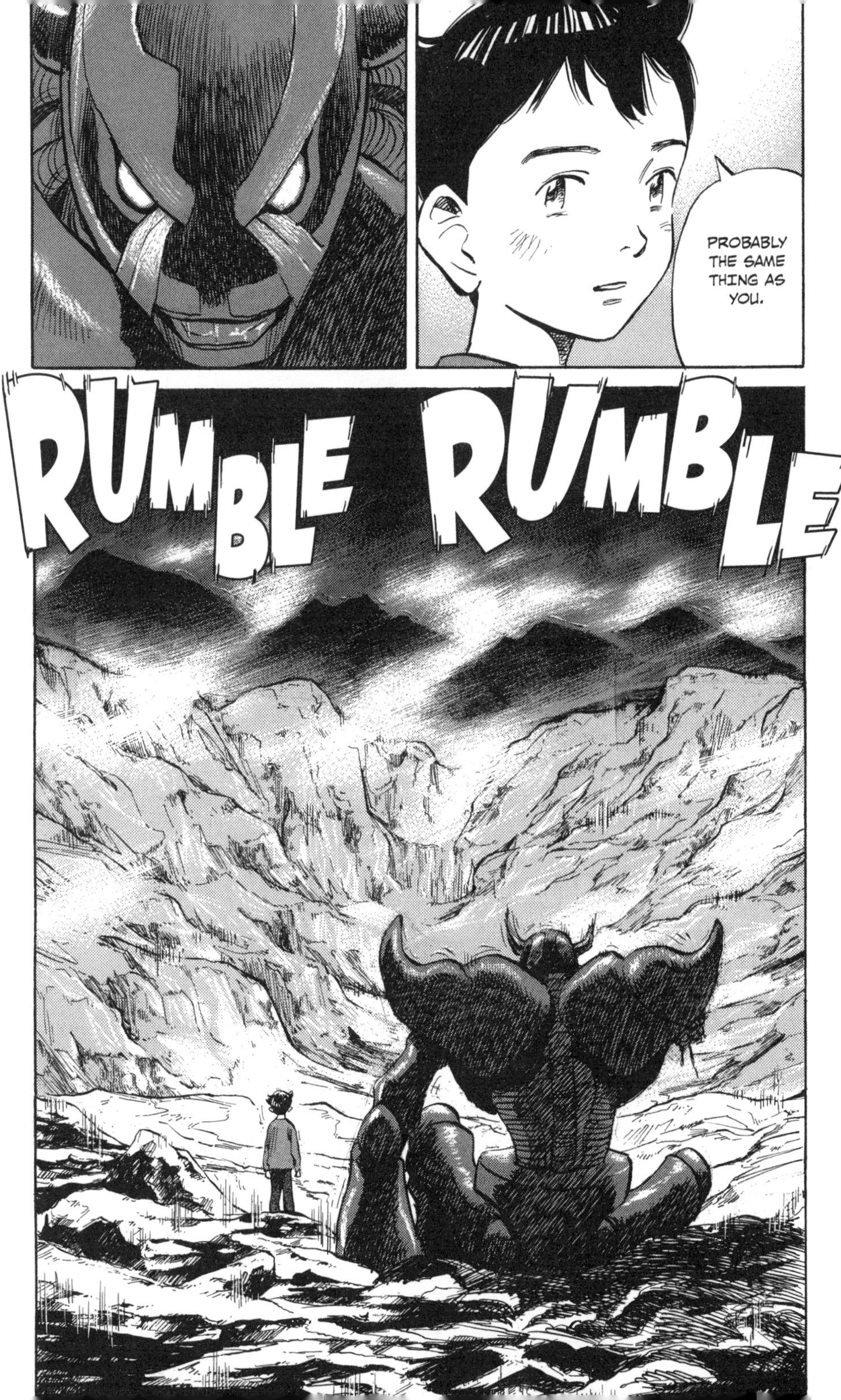
PROBABLY THE SAME THING AS YOU.
RUMBLE RUMBLE

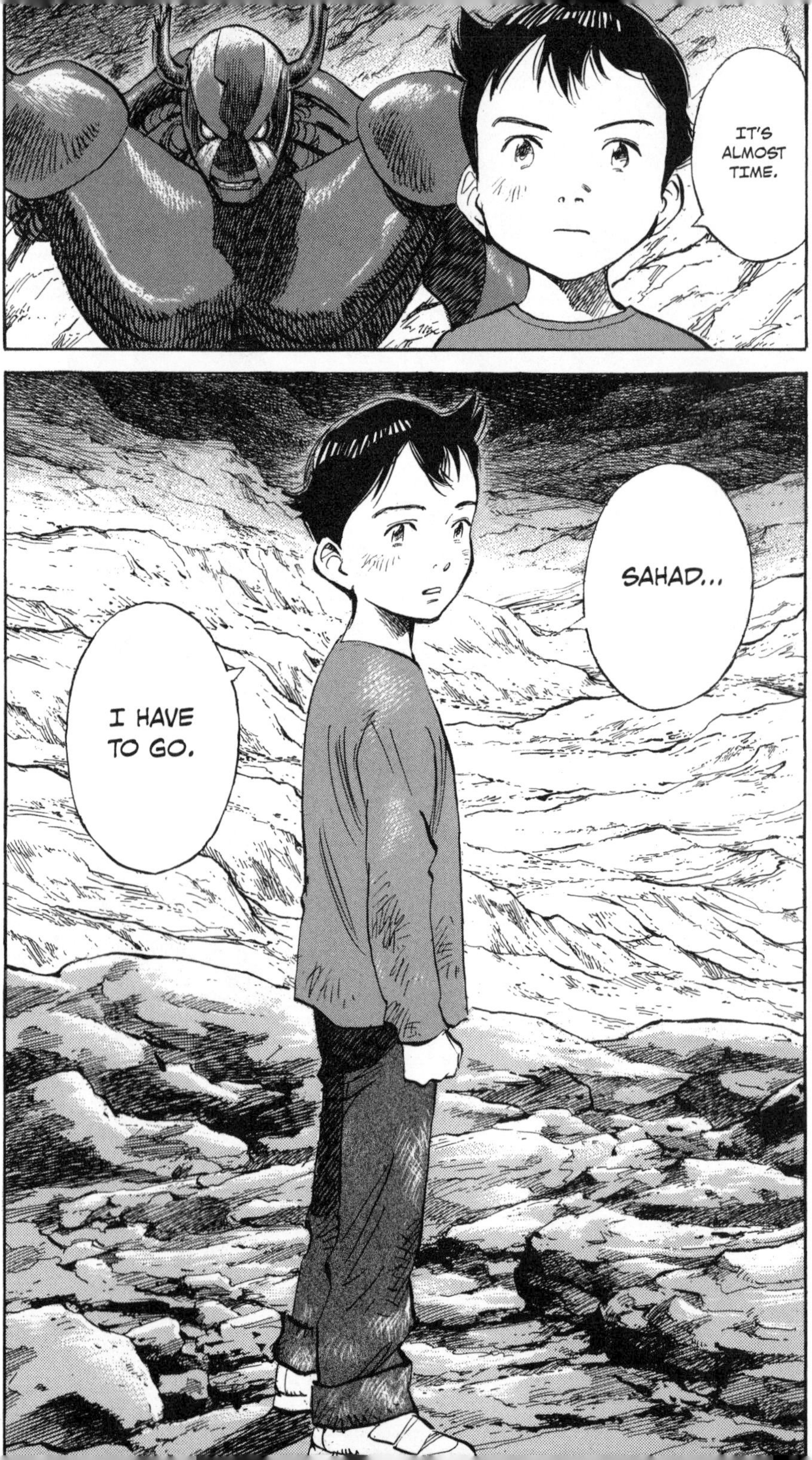
IT'S ALMOST TIME.
SAHAD...
I HAVE TO GO.

Act 64 THE SOUND OF THE END

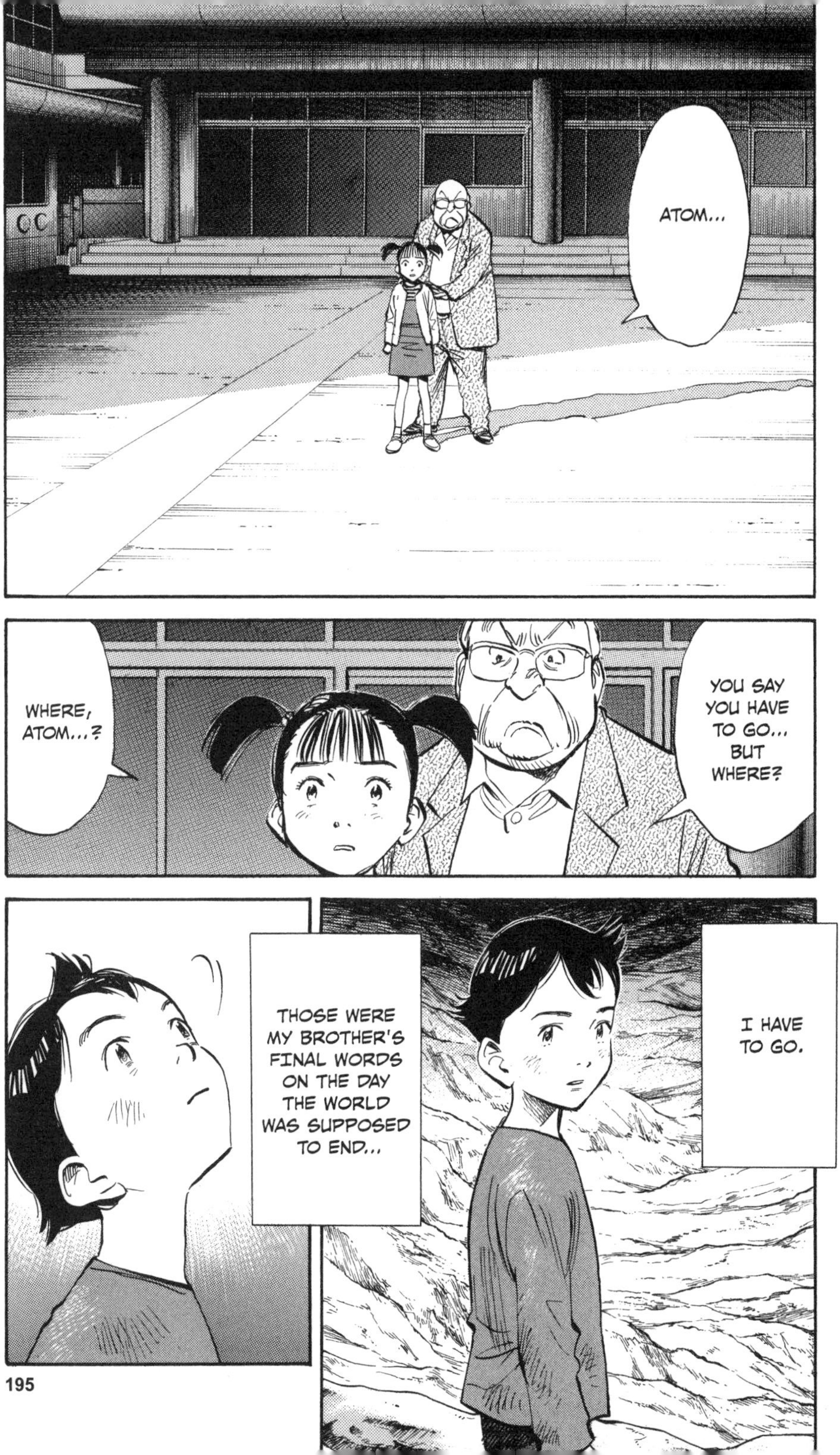
ATOM...
YOU SAY YOU HAVE TO GO... BUT WHERE?
WHERE, ATOM...?
I HAVE TO GO.
THOSE WERE MY BROTHER'S FINAL WORDS ON THE DAY THE WORLD WAS SUPPOSED TO END...

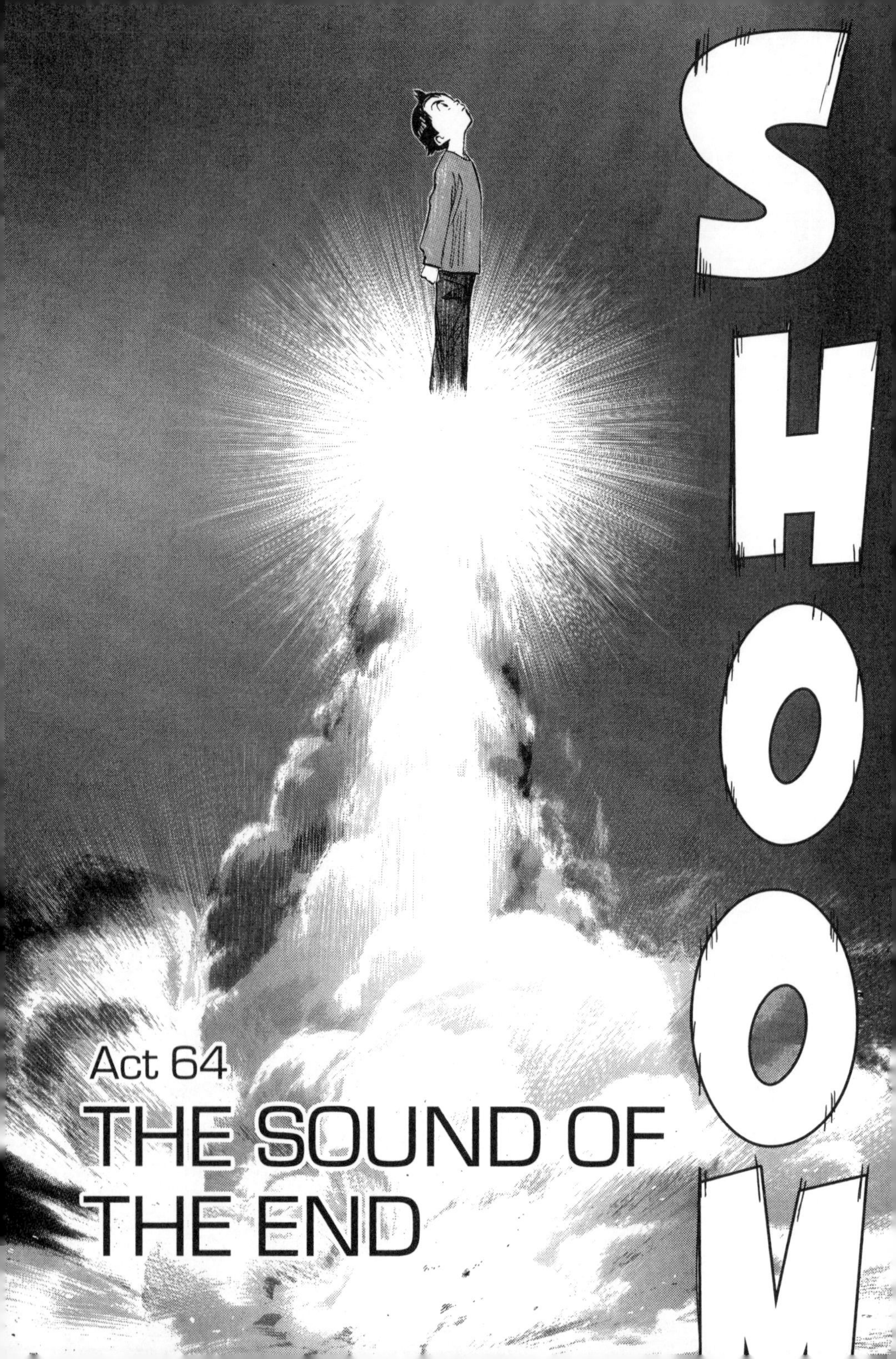
SHOOOM

Act 64
THE SOUND OF THE END

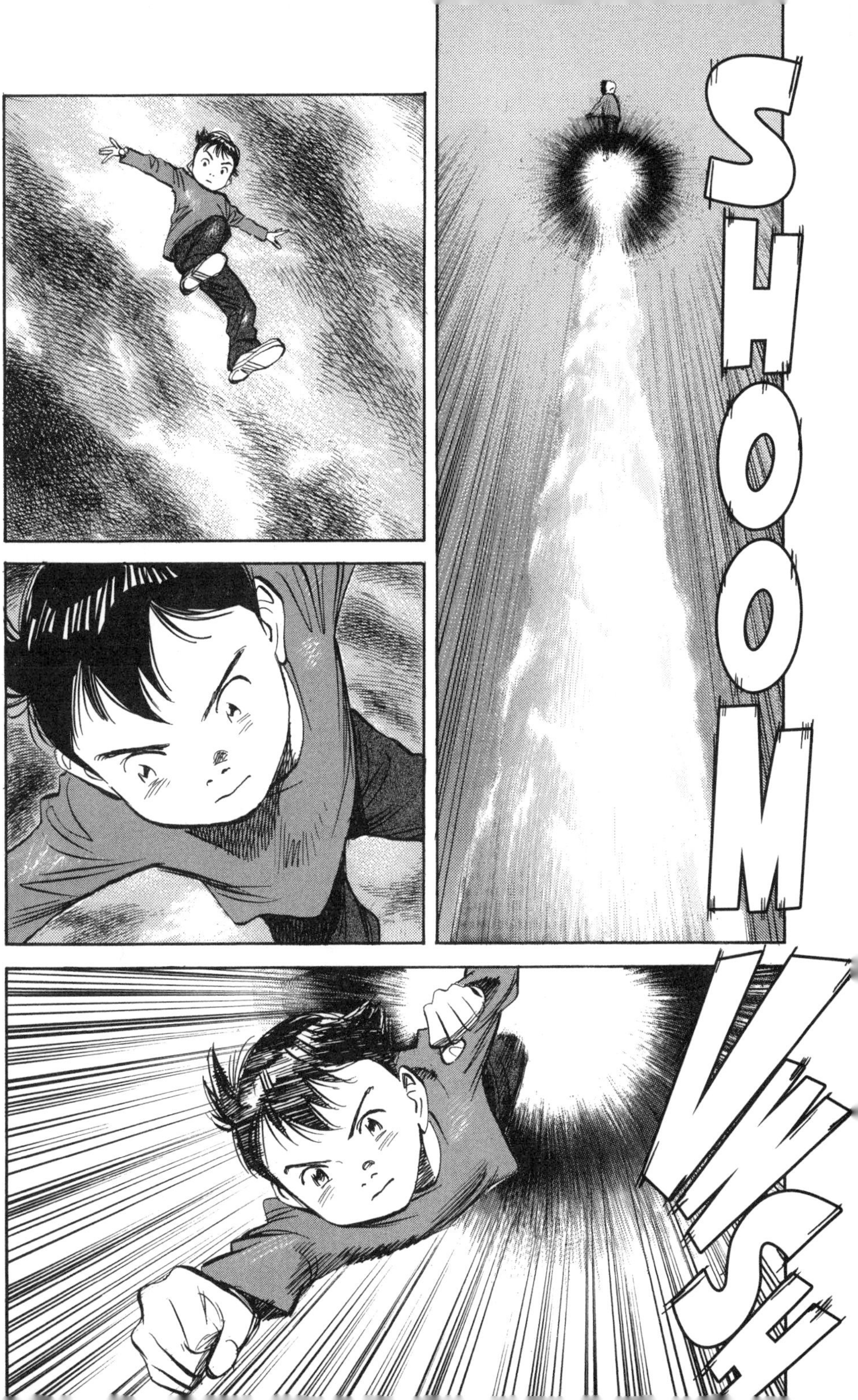
SHOOM

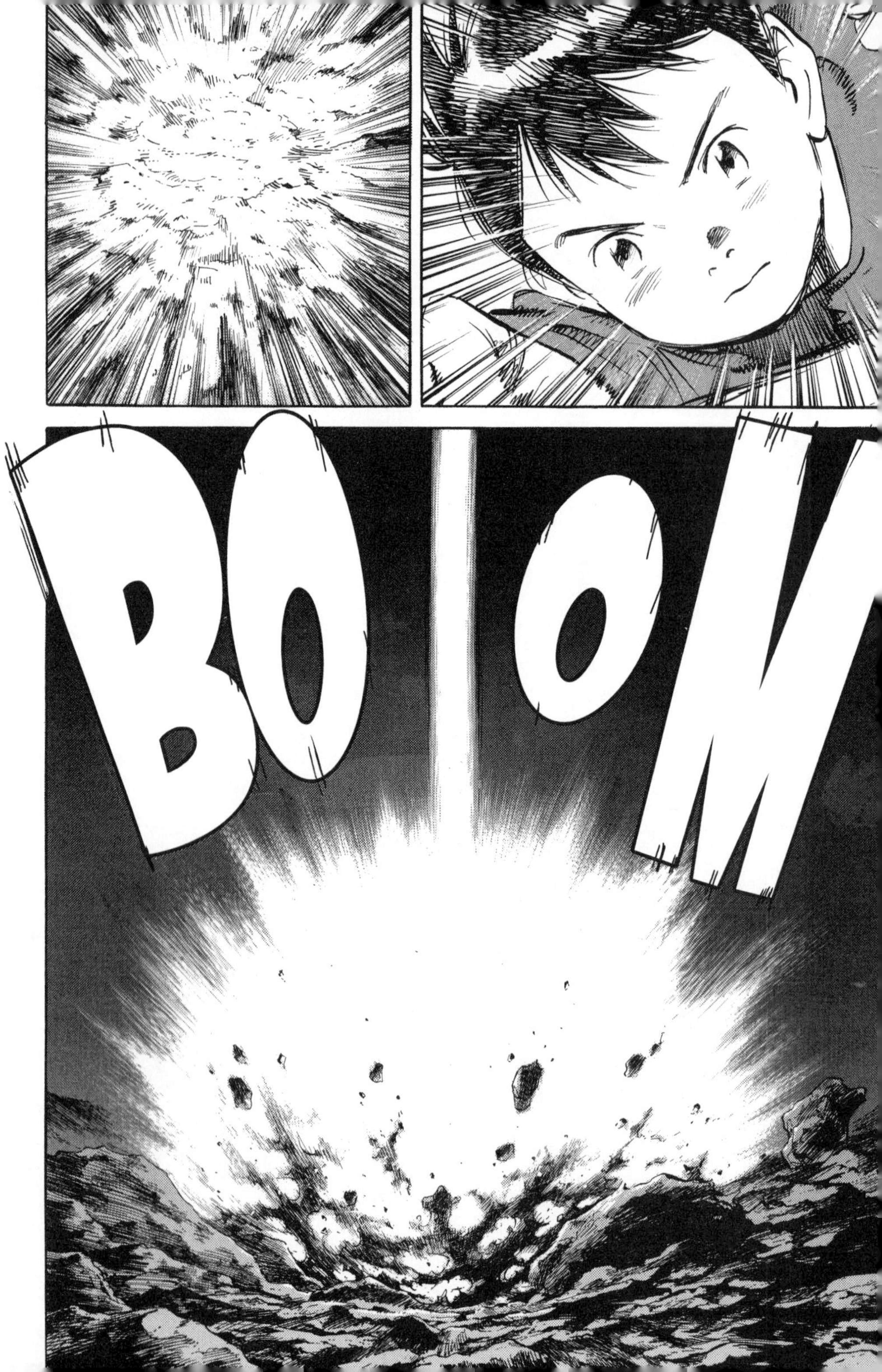
BOOM

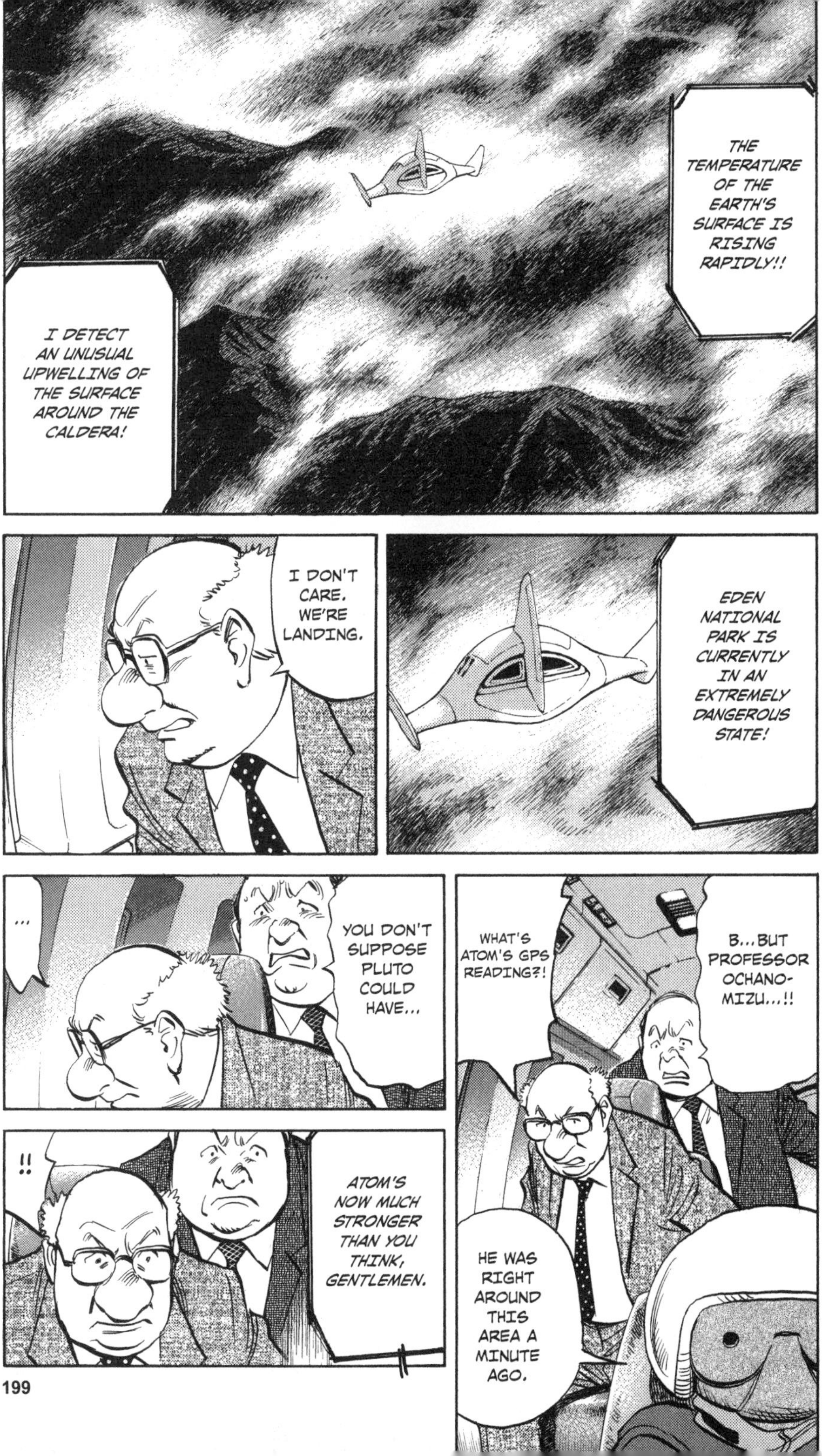
THE TEMPERATURE OF THE EARTH'S SURFACE IS RISING RAPIDLY!!
I DETECT AN UNUSUAL UPWELLING OF THE SURFACE AROUND THE CALDERA!
EDEN NATIONAL PARK IS CURRENTLY IN AN EXTREMELY DANGEROUS STATE!
I DON'T CARE. WE'RE LANDING.
B...BUT PROFESSOR OCHANOMIZU...!!
WHAT'S ATOM'S GPS READING?!
HE WAS RIGHT AROUND THIS AREA A MINUTE AGO.
YOU DON'T SUPPOSE PLUTO COULD HAVE...
...
ATOM'S NOW MUCH STRONGER THAN YOU THINK, GENTLEMEN.
!!

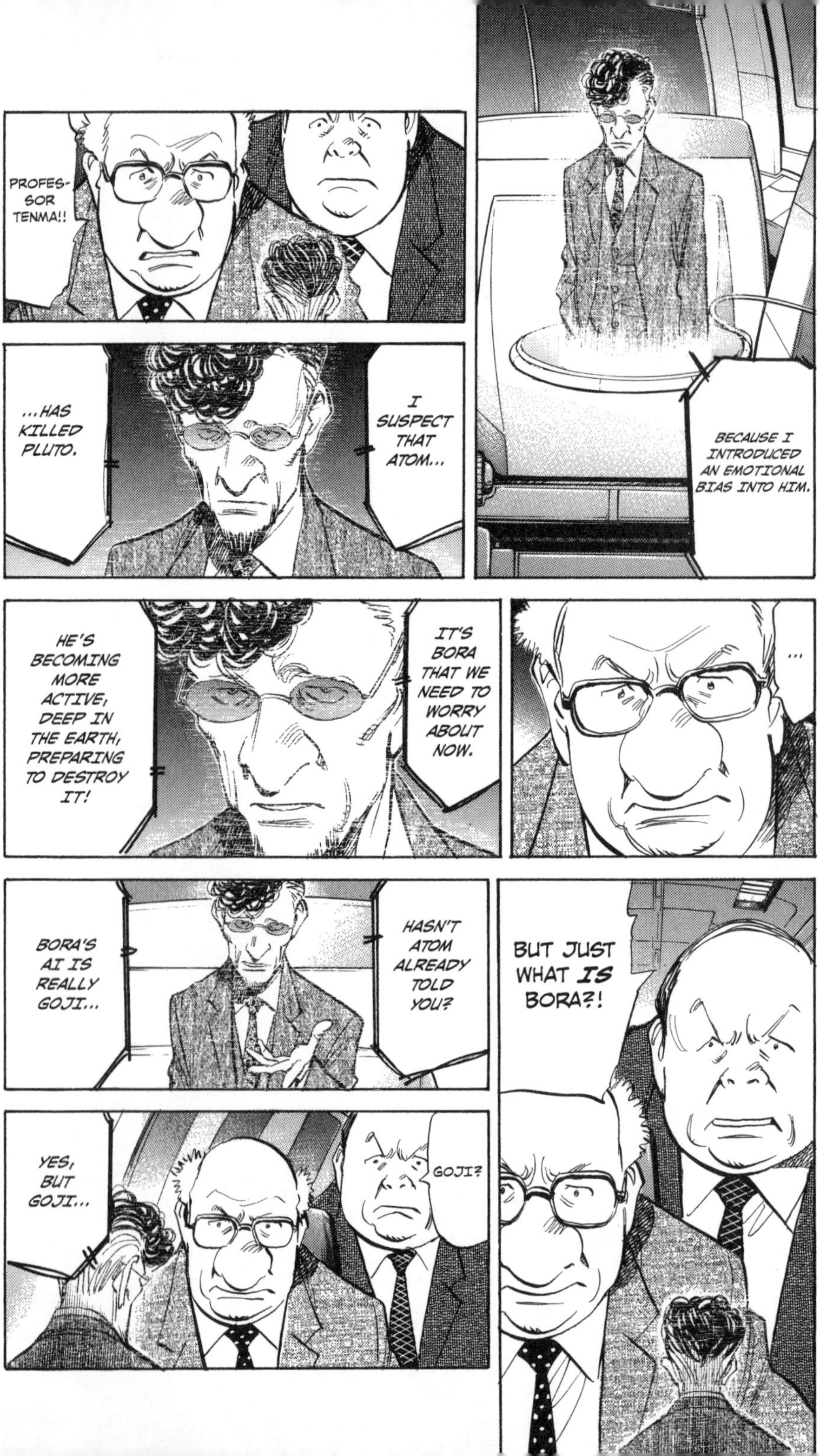
BECAUSE I INTRODUCED AN EMOTIONAL BIAS INTO HIM.
PROFES-SOR TENMA!!
I SUSPECT THAT ATOM...
...HAS KILLED PLUTO.
...
IT'S BORA THAT WE NEED TO WORRY ABOUT NOW.
HE'S BECOMING MORE ACTIVE, DEEP IN THE EARTH, PREPARING TO DESTROY IT!
BUT JUST WHAT **IS** BORA?!
HASN'T ATOM ALREADY TOLD YOU?
BORA'S AI IS REALLY GOJI...
GOJI?
YES, BUT GOJI...

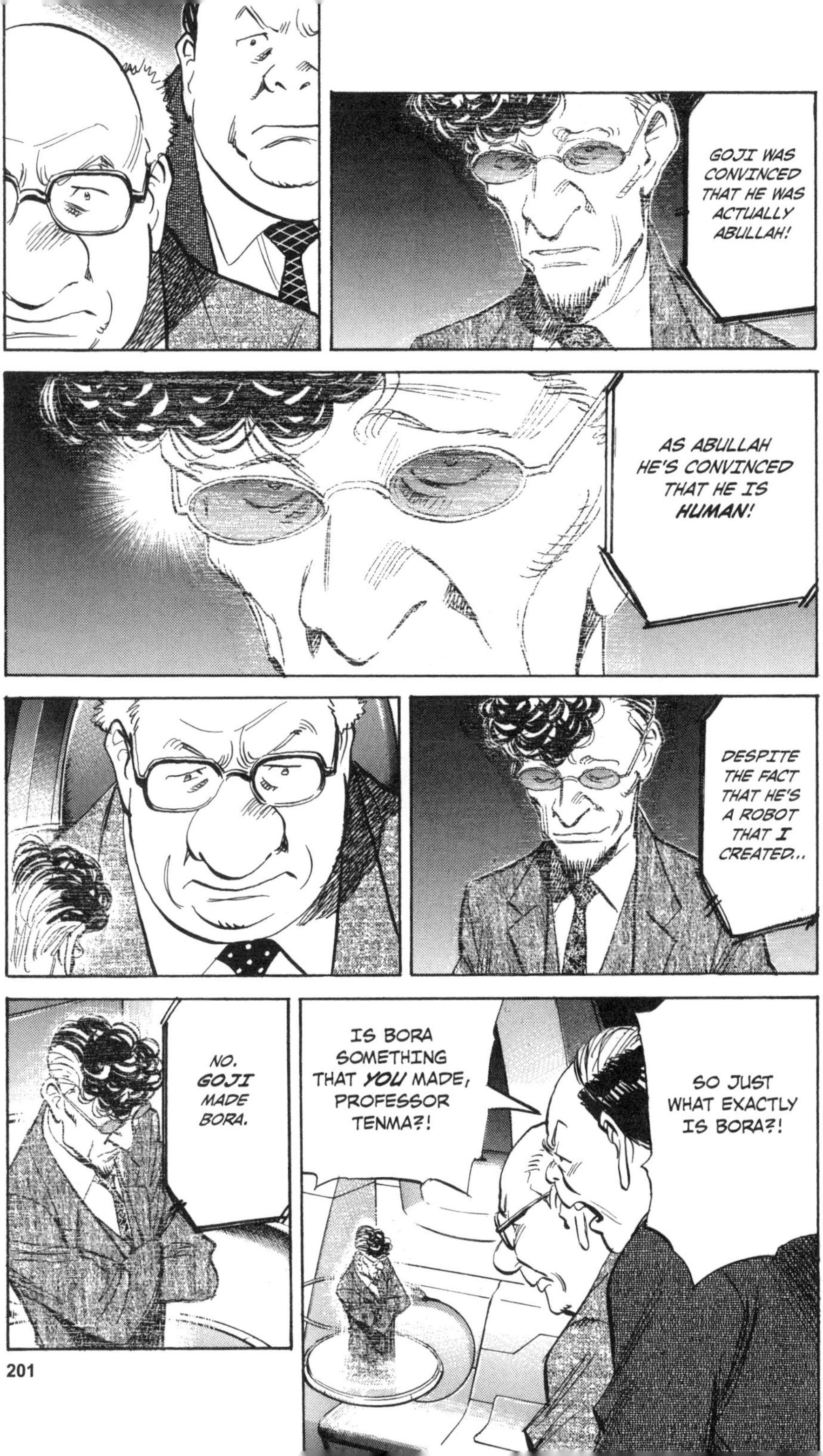

GOJI WAS CONVINCED THAT HE WAS ACTUALLY ABULLAH!
AS ABULLAH HE'S CONVINCED THAT HE IS HUMAN!
DESPITE THE FACT THAT HE'S A ROBOT THAT I CREATED...
SO JUST WHAT EXACTLY IS BORA?!
IS BORA SOMETHING THAT YOU MADE, PROFESSOR TENMA?!
NO. GOJI MADE BORA.

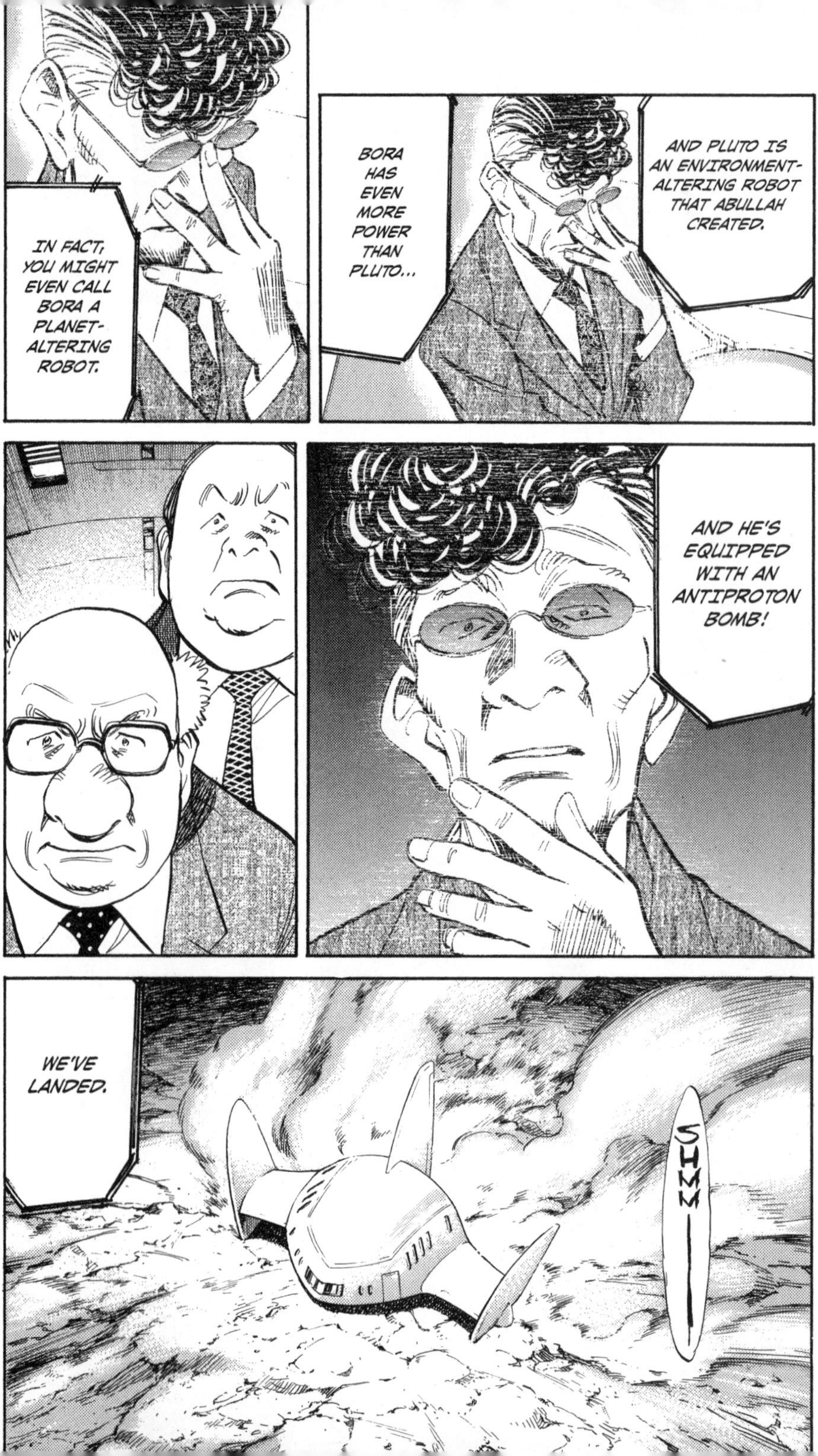
AND PLUTO IS AN ENVIRONMENT-ALTERING ROBOT THAT ABULLAH CREATED.
BORA HAS EVEN MORE POWER THAN PLUTO...
IN FACT, YOU MIGHT EVEN CALL BORA A PLANET-ALTERING ROBOT.
AND HE'S EQUIPPED WITH AN ANTIPROTON BOMB!
WE'VE LANDED.
SHMM

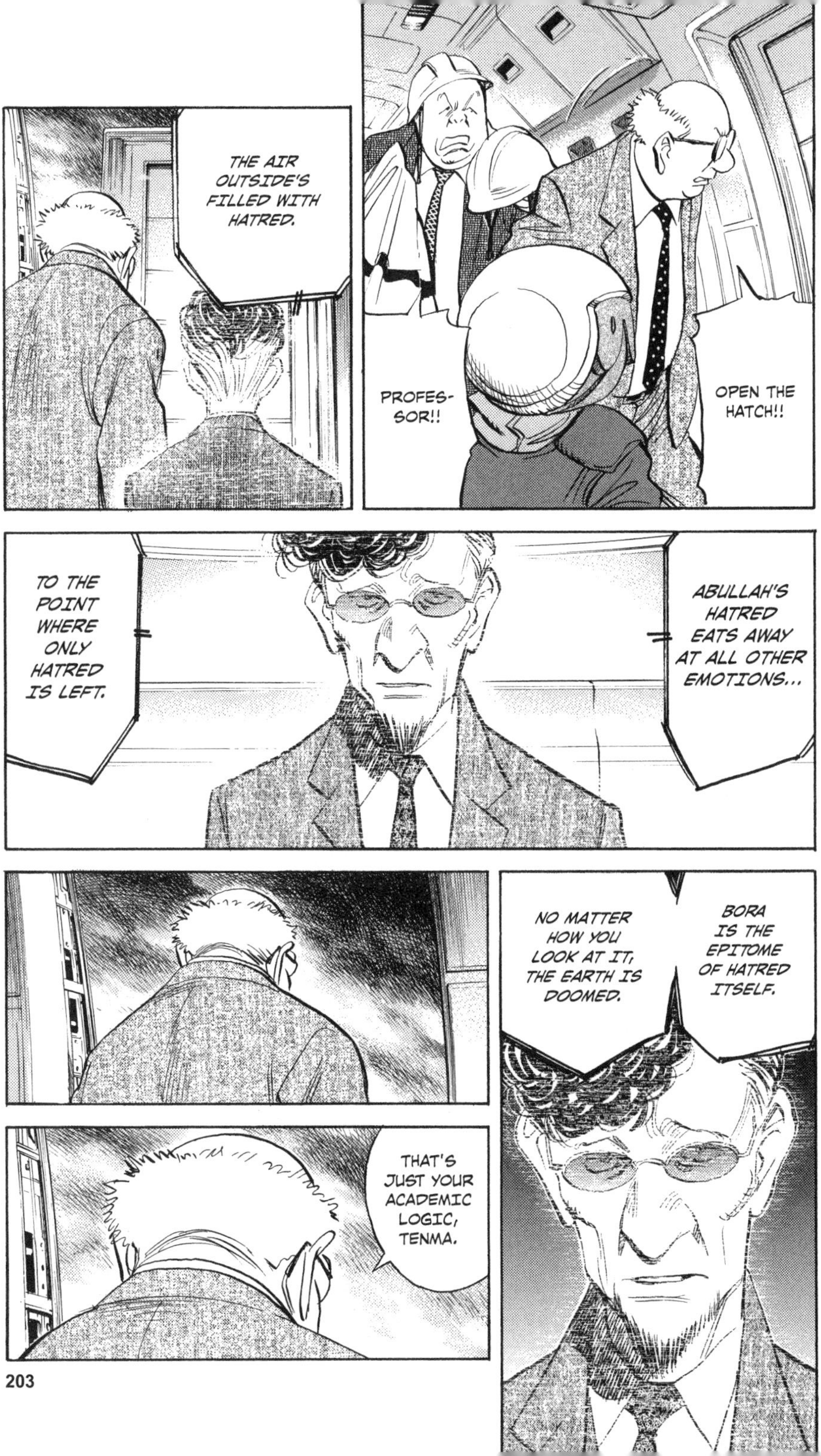
OPEN THE HATCH!!
PROFESSOR!!
THE AIR OUTSIDE'S FILLED WITH HATRED.
ABULLAH'S HATRED EATS AWAY AT ALL OTHER EMOTIONS...
TO THE POINT WHERE ONLY HATRED IS LEFT.
BORA IS THE EPITOME OF HATRED ITSELF.
NO MATTER HOW YOU LOOK AT IT, THE EARTH IS DOOMED.
THAT'S JUST YOUR ACADEMIC LOGIC, TENMA.

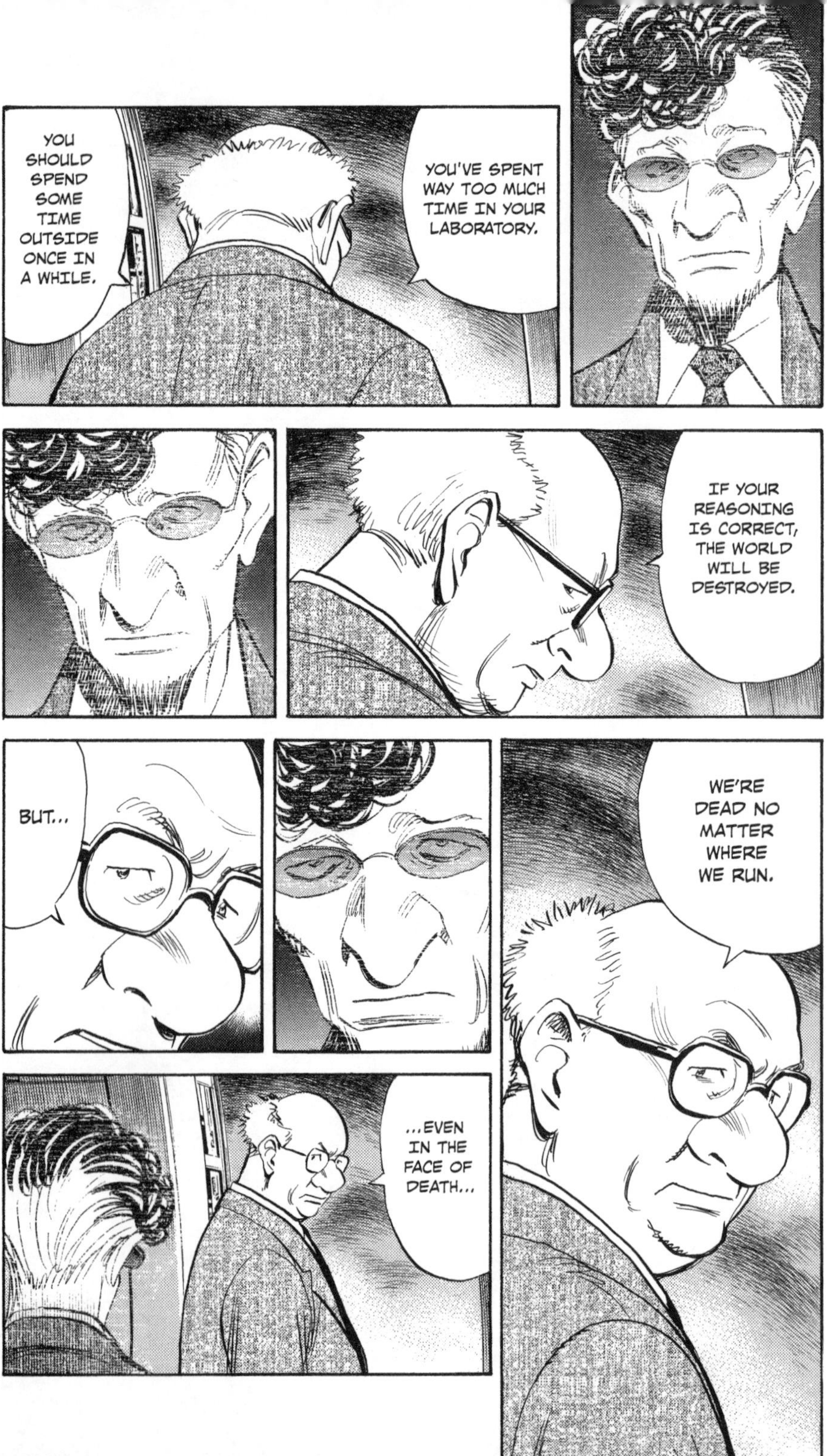
YOU'VE SPENT WAY TOO MUCH TIME IN YOUR LABORATORY.
YOU SHOULD SPEND SOME TIME OUTSIDE ONCE IN A WHILE.
IF YOUR REASONING IS CORRECT, THE WORLD WILL BE DESTROYED.
WE'RE DEAD NO MATTER WHERE WE RUN.
BUT...
...EVEN IN THE FACE OF DEATH...

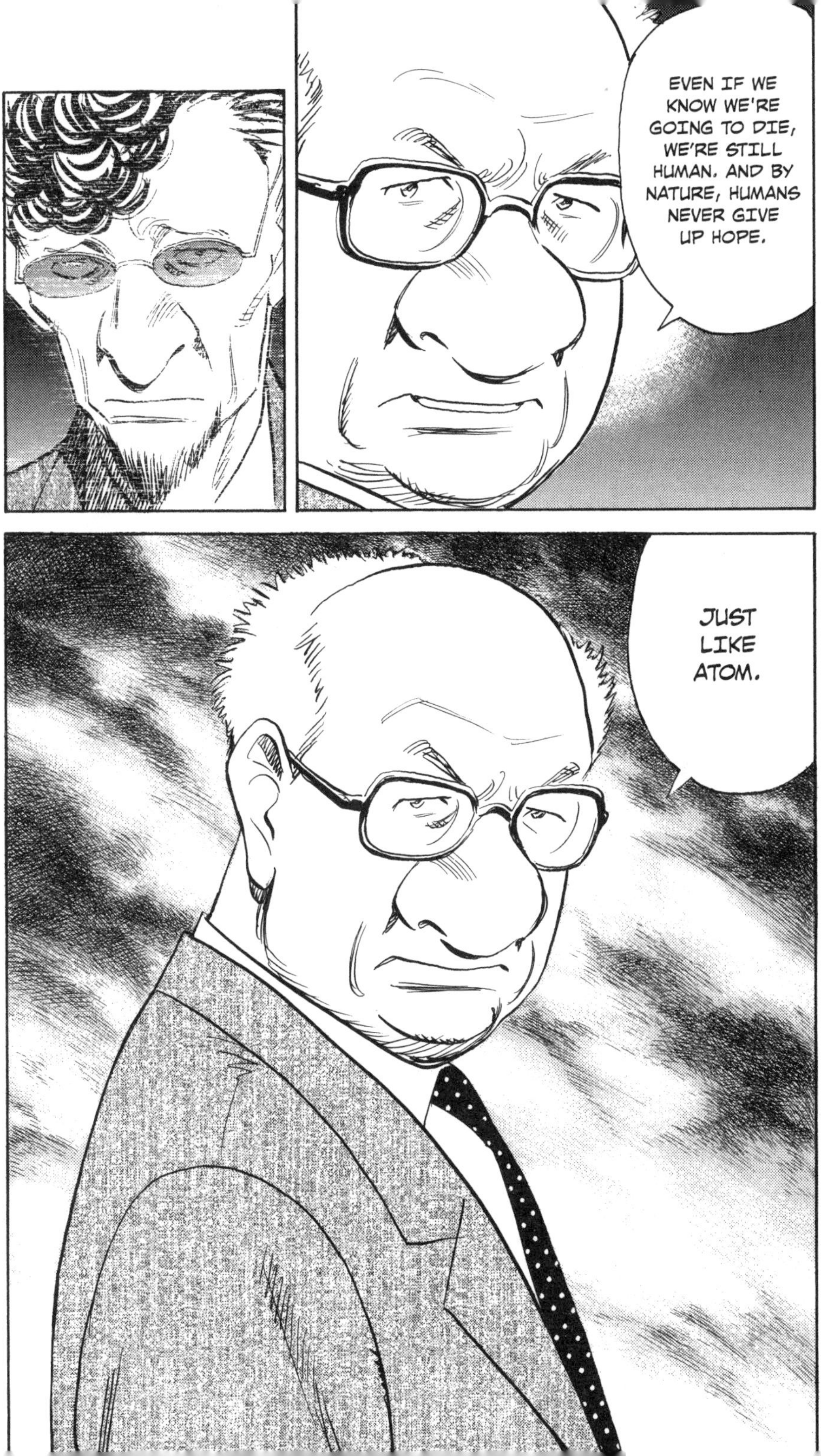
EVEN IF WE KNOW WE'RE GOING TO DIE, WE'RE STILL HUMAN. AND BY NATURE, HUMANS NEVER GIVE UP HOPE.
JUST LIKE ATOM.

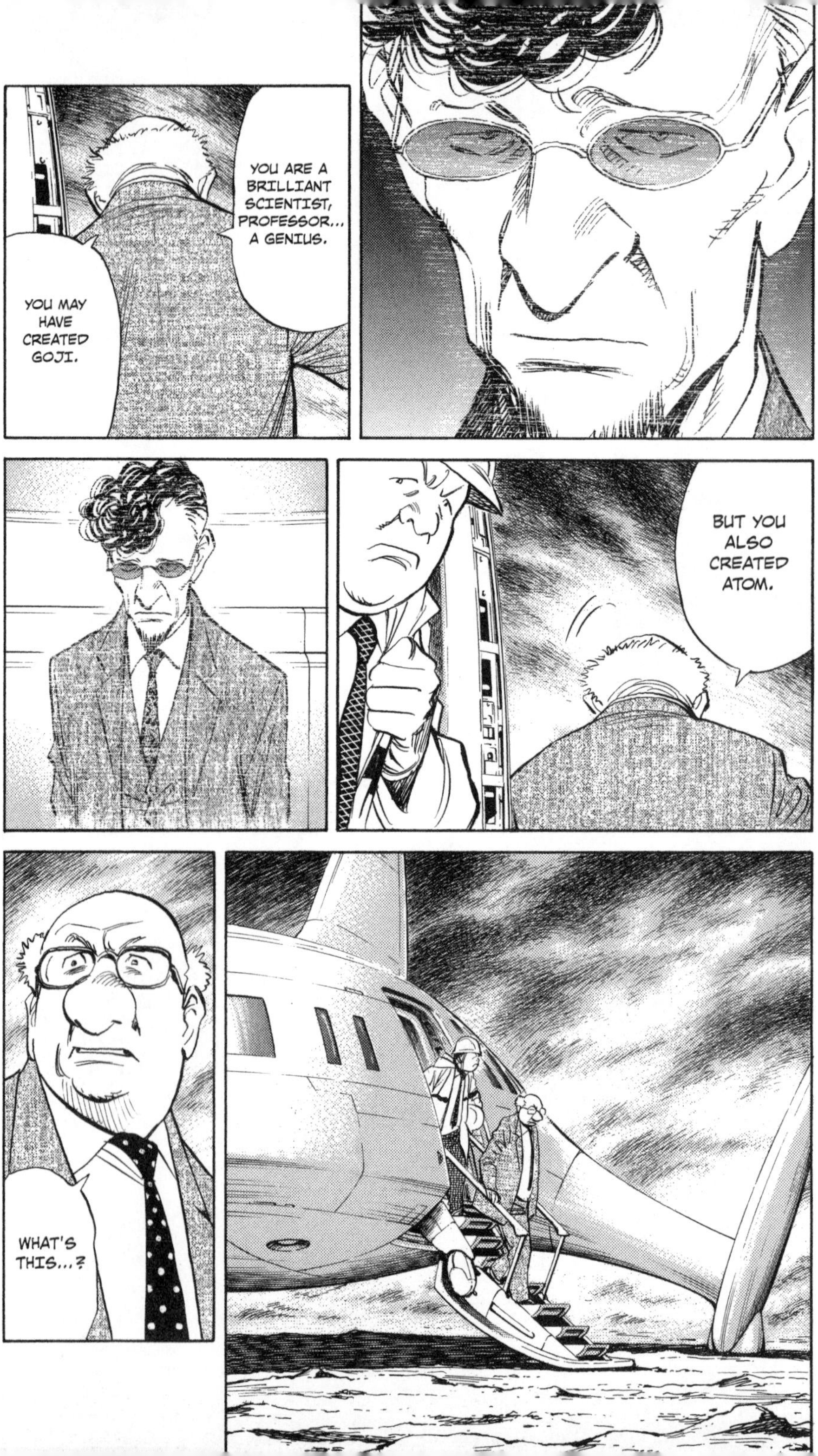
YOU ARE A BRILLIANT SCIENTIST, PROFESSOR... A GENIUS.
YOU MAY HAVE CREATED GOJI.
BUT YOU ALSO CREATED ATOM.
WHAT'S THIS...?

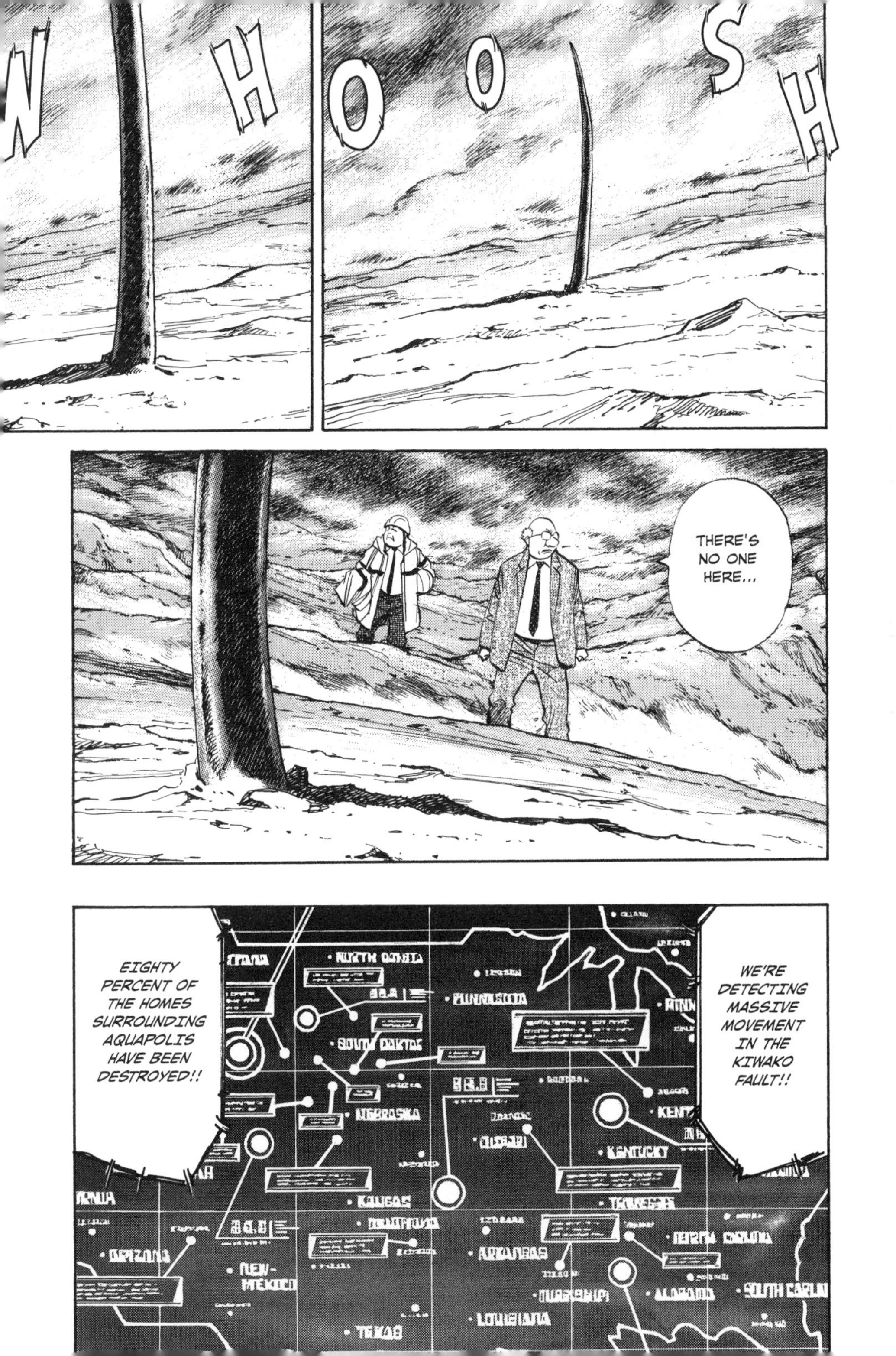
WHOOSH
THERE'S NO ONE HERE...
WE'RE DETECTING MASSIVE MOVEMENT IN THE KIWAKO FAULT!!
EIGHTY PERCENT OF THE HOMES SURROUNDING AQUAPOLIS HAVE BEEN DESTROYED!!

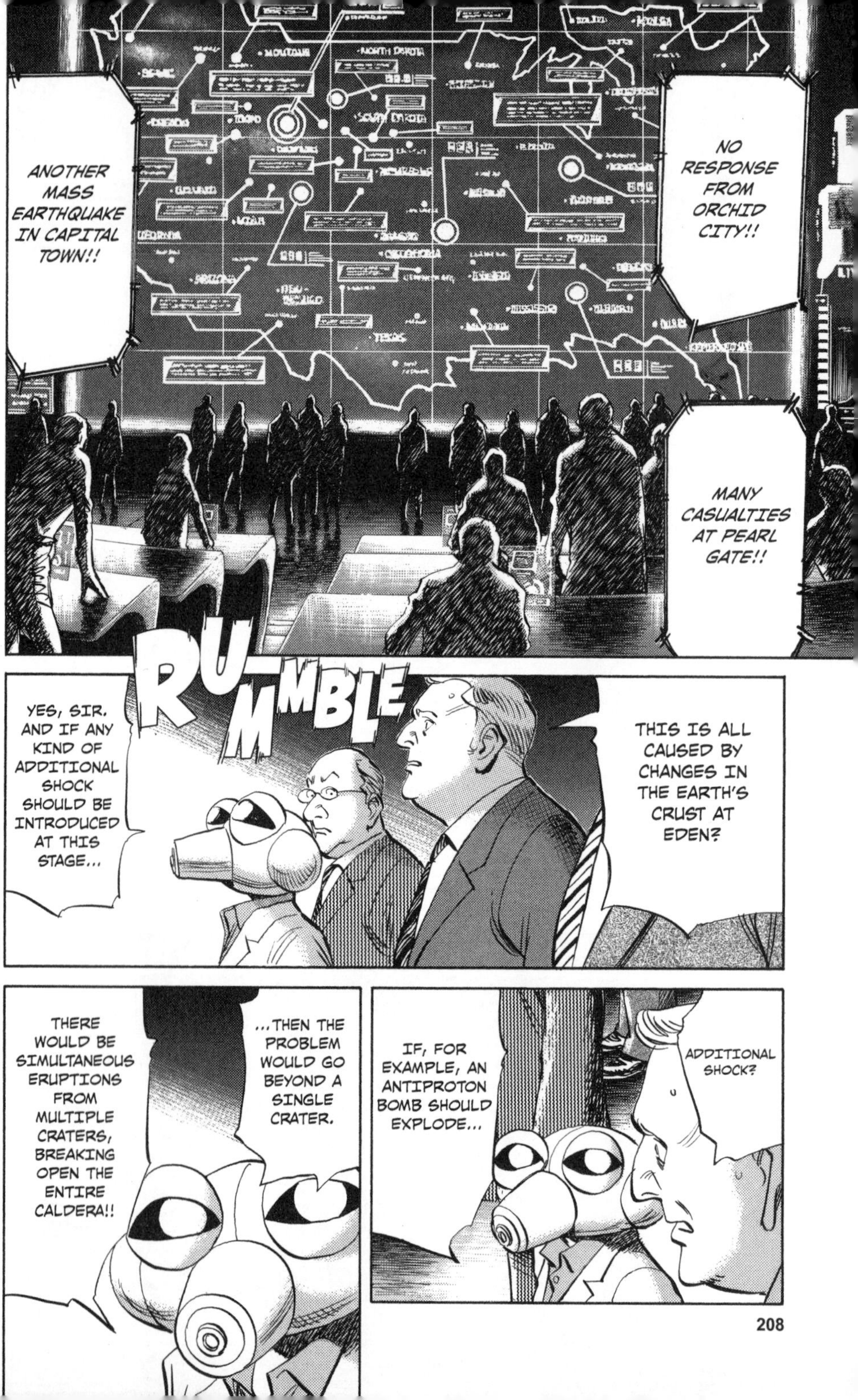
NO RESPONSE FROM ORCHID CITY!!
ANOTHER MASS EARTHQUAKE IN CAPITAL TOWN!!
MANY CASUALTIES AT PEARL GATE!!
RUMBLE
THIS IS ALL CAUSED BY CHANGES IN THE EARTH'S CRUST AT EDEN?
YES, SIR. AND IF ANY KIND OF ADDITIONAL SHOCK SHOULD BE INTRODUCED AT THIS STAGE...
ADDITIONAL SHOCK?
IF, FOR EXAMPLE, AN ANTIPROTON BOMB SHOULD EXPLODE...
...THEN THE PROBLEM WOULD GO BEYOND A SINGLE CRATER.
THERE WOULD BE SIMULTANEOUS ERUPTIONS FROM MULTIPLE CRATERS, BREAKING OPEN THE ENTIRE CALDERA!!

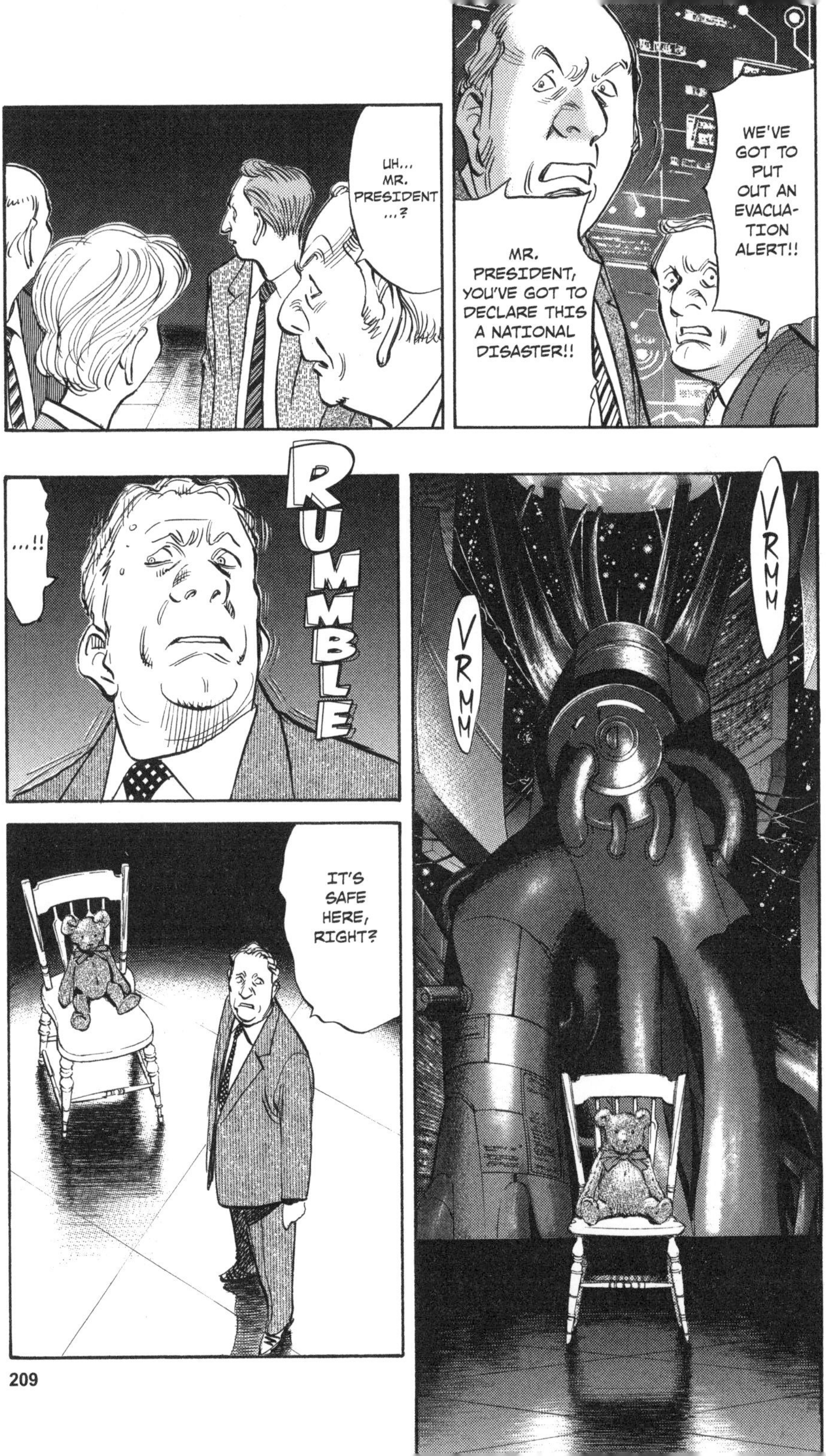
WE'VE GOT TO PUT OUT AN EVACUATION ALERT!!
MR. PRESIDENT, YOU'VE GOT TO DECLARE THIS A NATIONAL DISASTER!!
UH... MR. PRESIDENT ...?
VRMM
VRMM
RUMBLE
...!!
IT'S SAFE HERE, RIGHT?

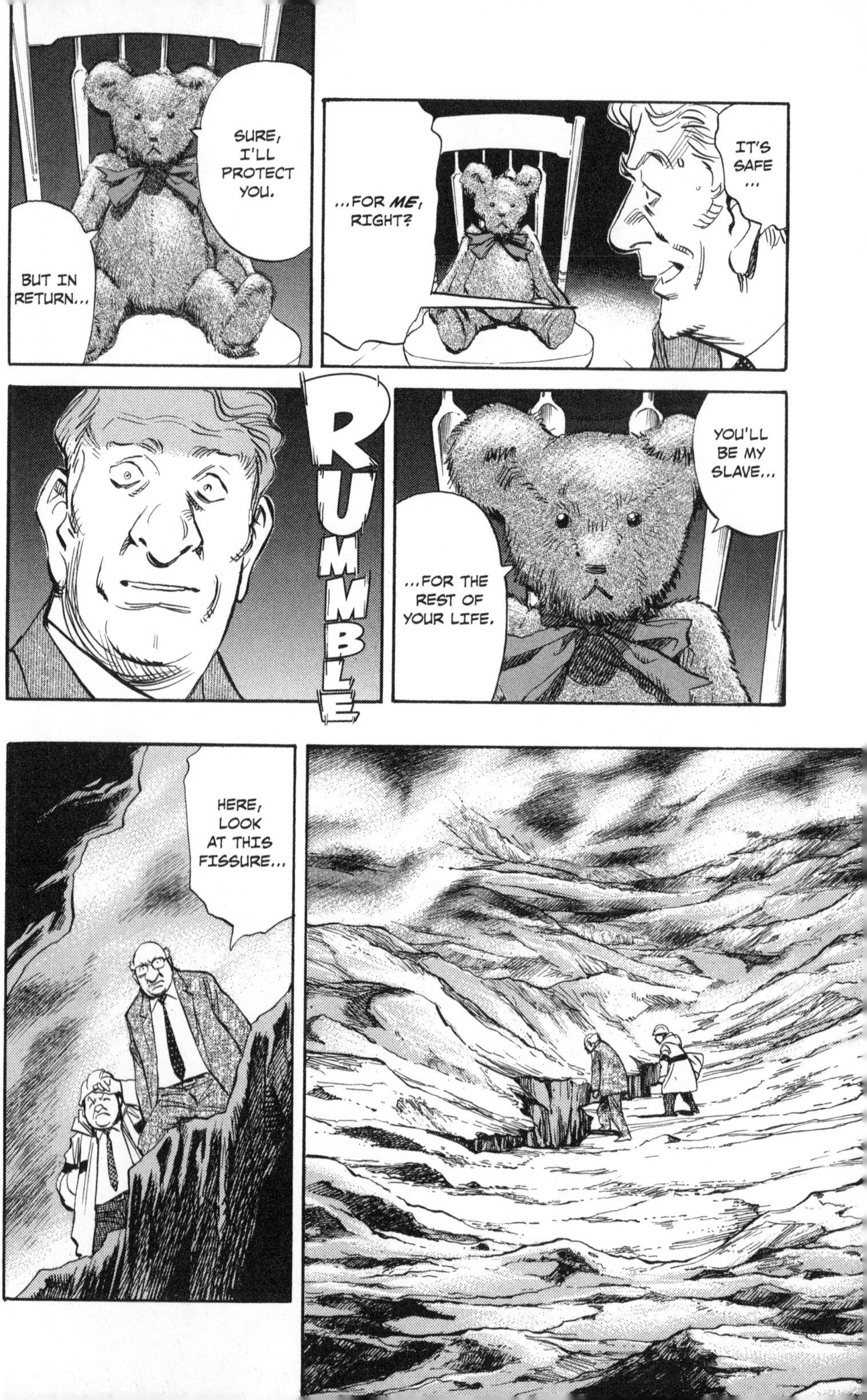

IT'S SAFE ...
...FOR *ME*, RIGHT?
SURE, I'LL PROTECT YOU.
BUT IN RETURN...
YOU'LL BE MY SLAVE...
...FOR THE REST OF YOUR LIFE.
RUMMBLE
HERE, LOOK AT THIS FISSURE...

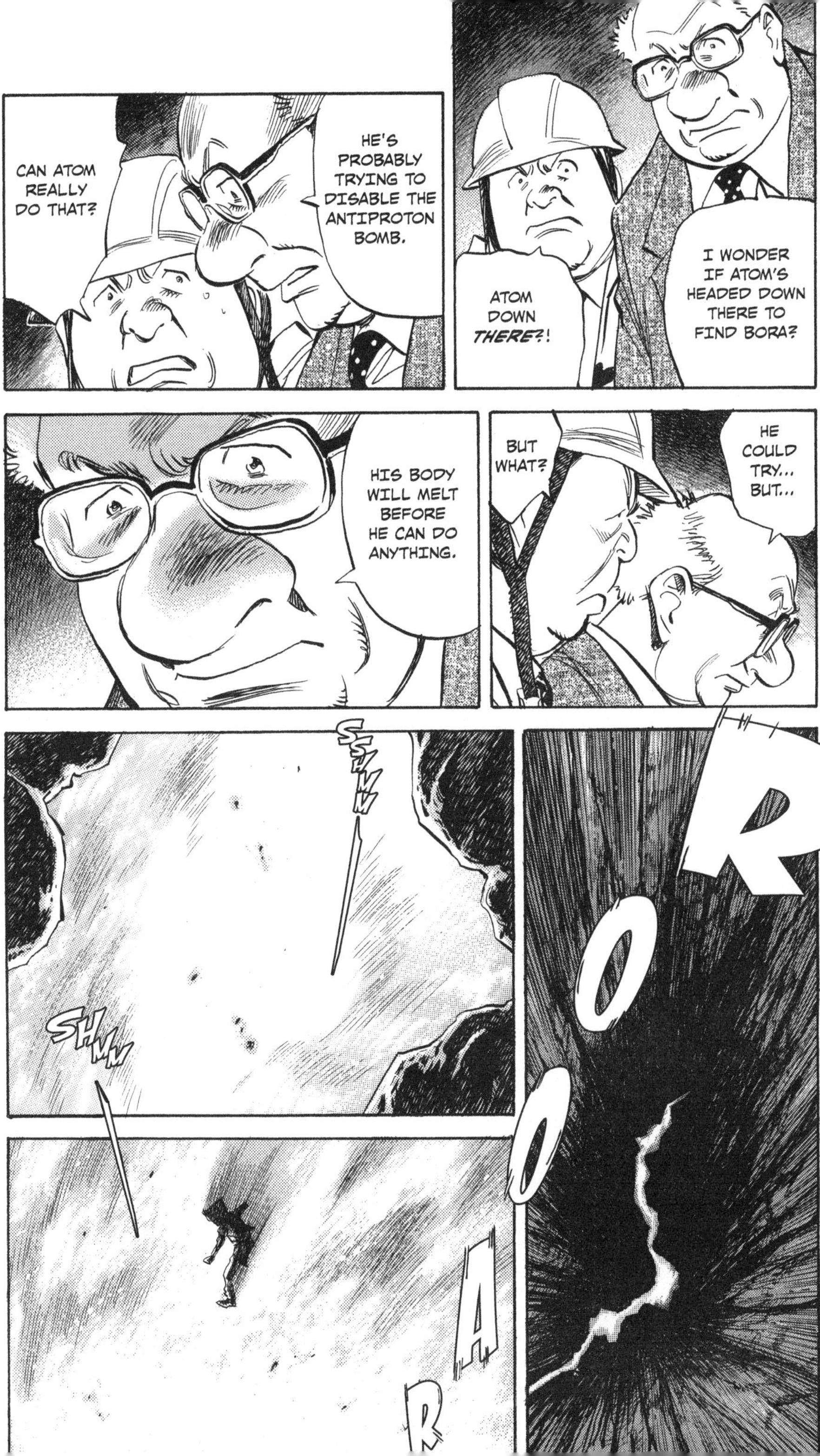
I WONDER IF ATOM'S HEADED DOWN THERE TO FIND BORA?
ATOM DOWN *THERE*?!
HE'S PROBABLY TRYING TO DISABLE THE ANTIPROTON BOMB.
CAN ATOM REALLY DO THAT?
HE COULD TRY... BUT...
BUT WHAT?
HIS BODY WILL MELT BEFORE HE CAN DO ANYTHING.
ROOOAR
SSHMM
SHMM

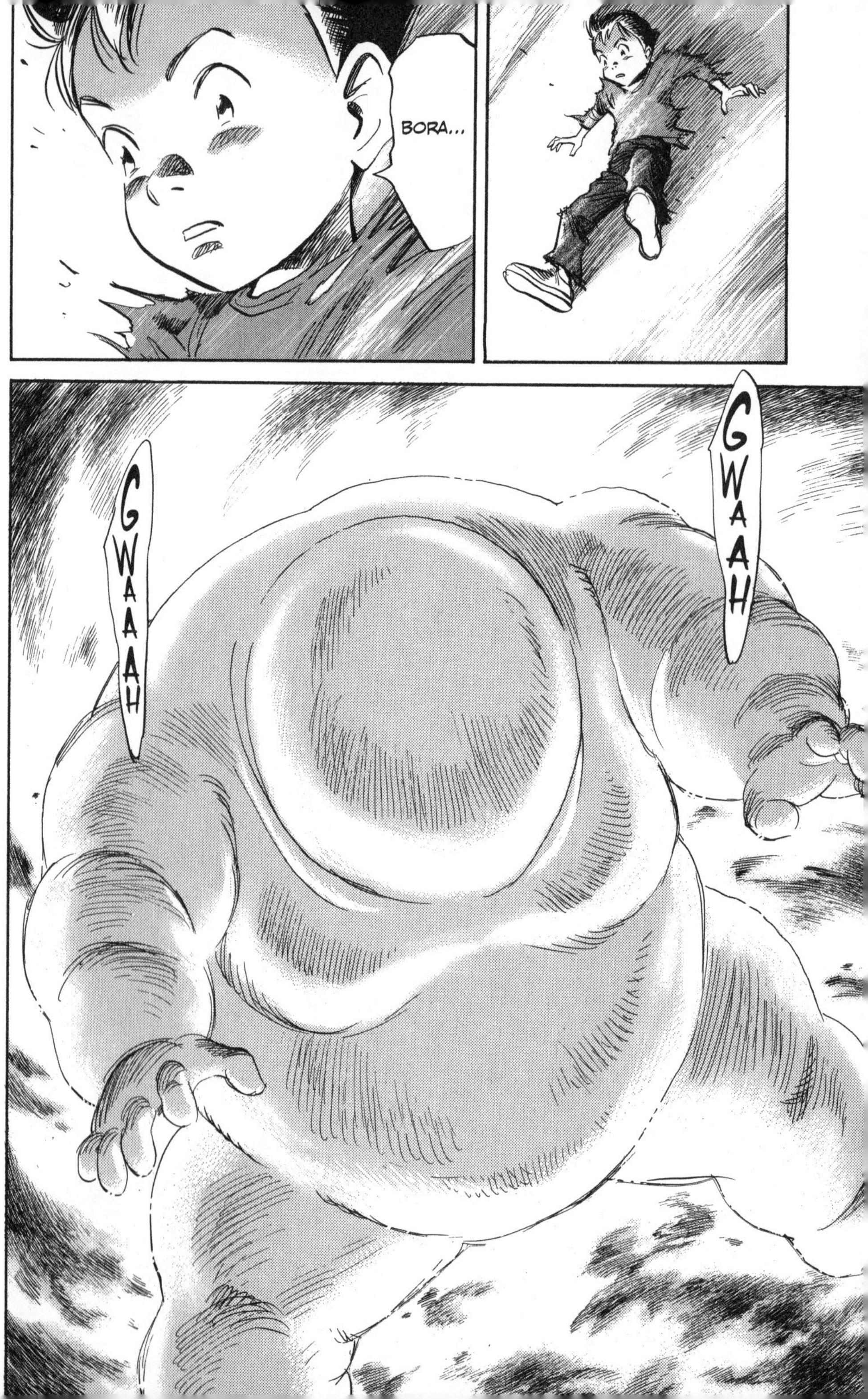
BORA...
GWAAH
GWAAAAH

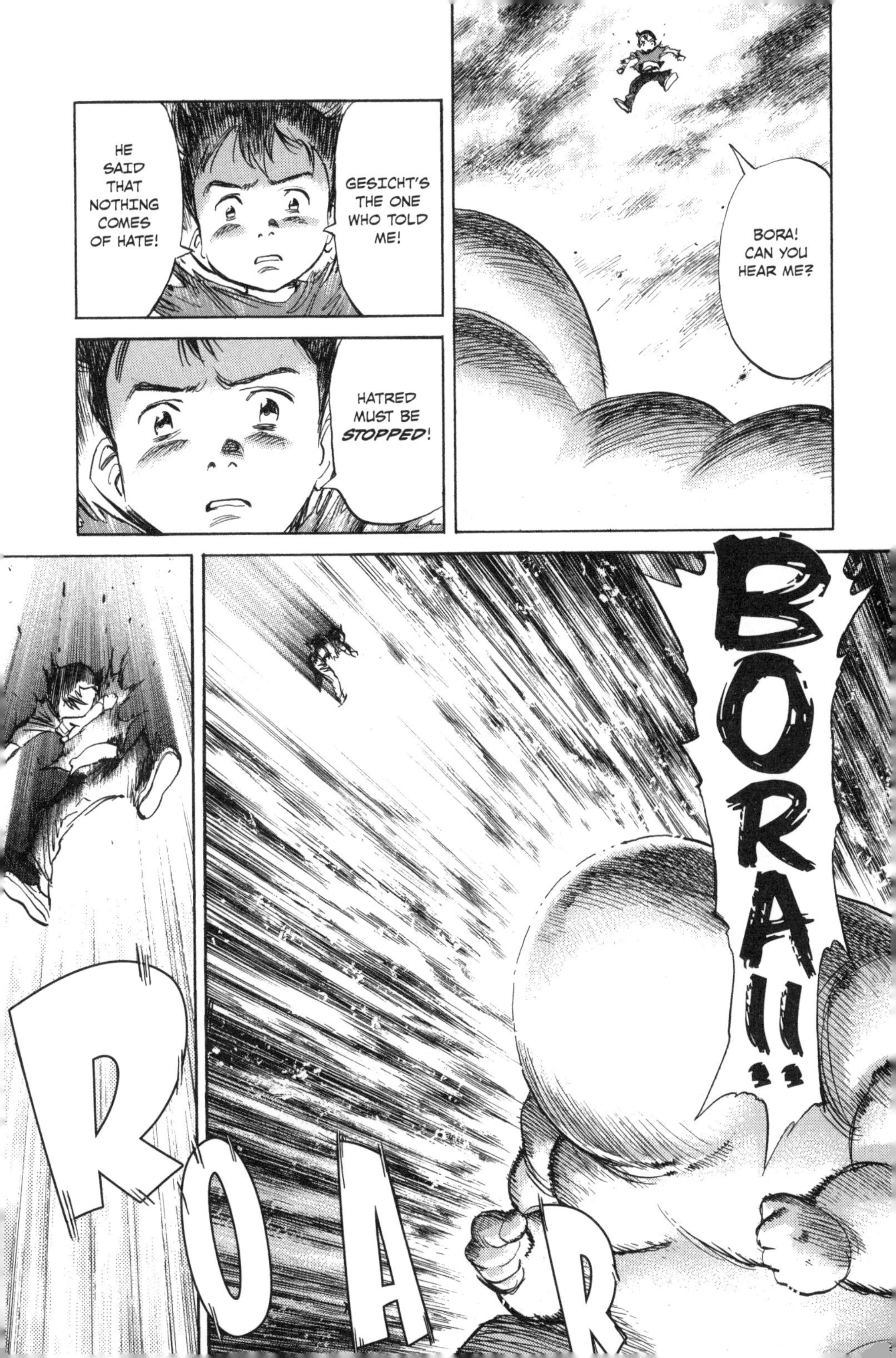
BORA! CAN YOU HEAR ME?
GESICHT'S THE ONE WHO TOLD ME!
HE SAID THAT NOTHING COMES OF HATE!
HATRED MUST BE *STOPPED*!
BORA!!
ROAR

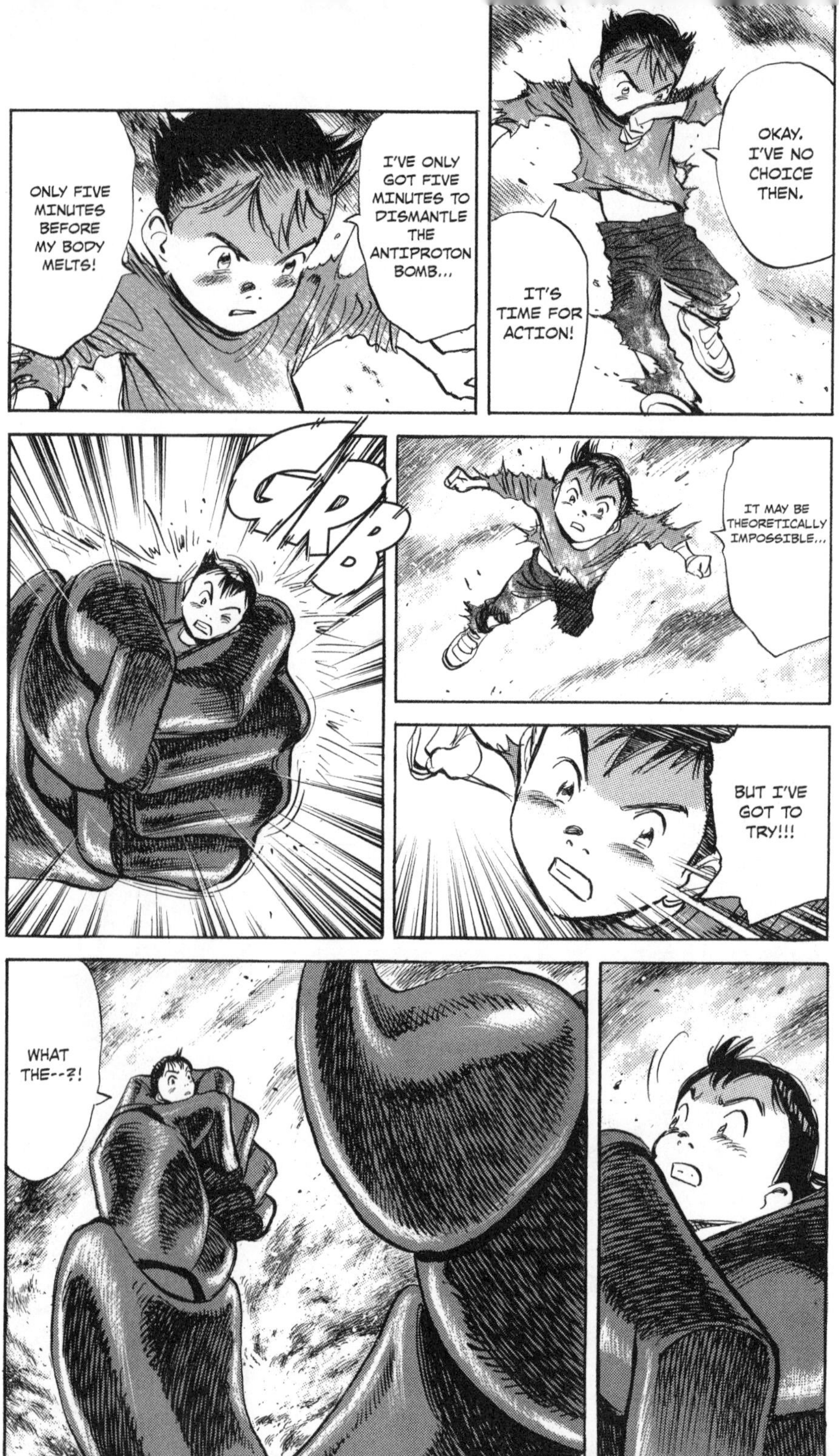
OKAY. I'VE NO CHOICE THEN.
IT'S TIME FOR ACTION!
I'VE ONLY GOT FIVE MINUTES TO DISMANTLE THE ANTIPROTON BOMB...
ONLY FIVE MINUTES BEFORE MY BODY MELTS!
IT MAY BE THEORETICALLY IMPOSSIBLE...
BUT I'VE GOT TO TRY!!!
GRB
WHAT THE--?!

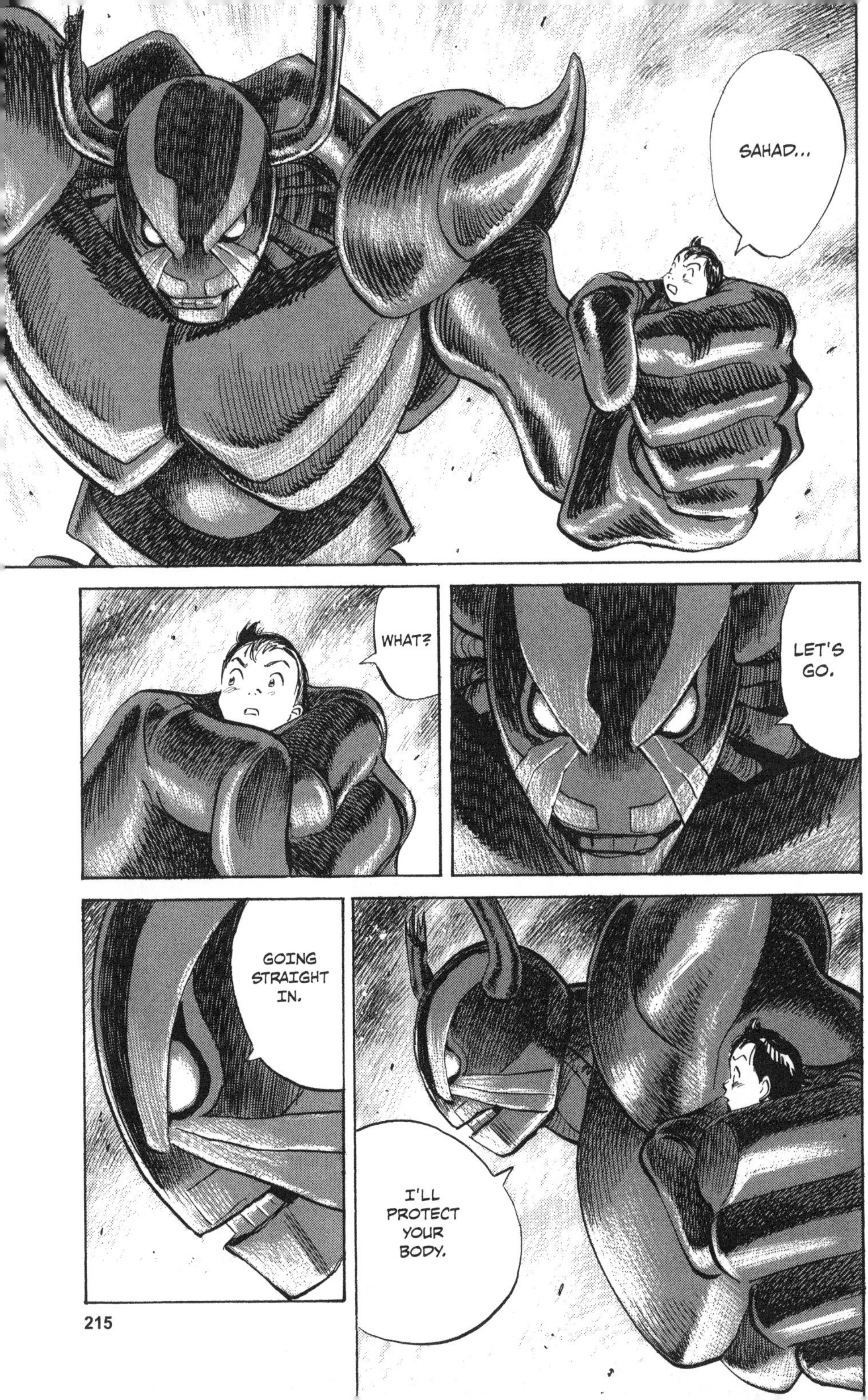
SAHAD...
LET'S GO.
WHAT?
I'LL PROTECT YOUR BODY.
GOING STRAIGHT IN.

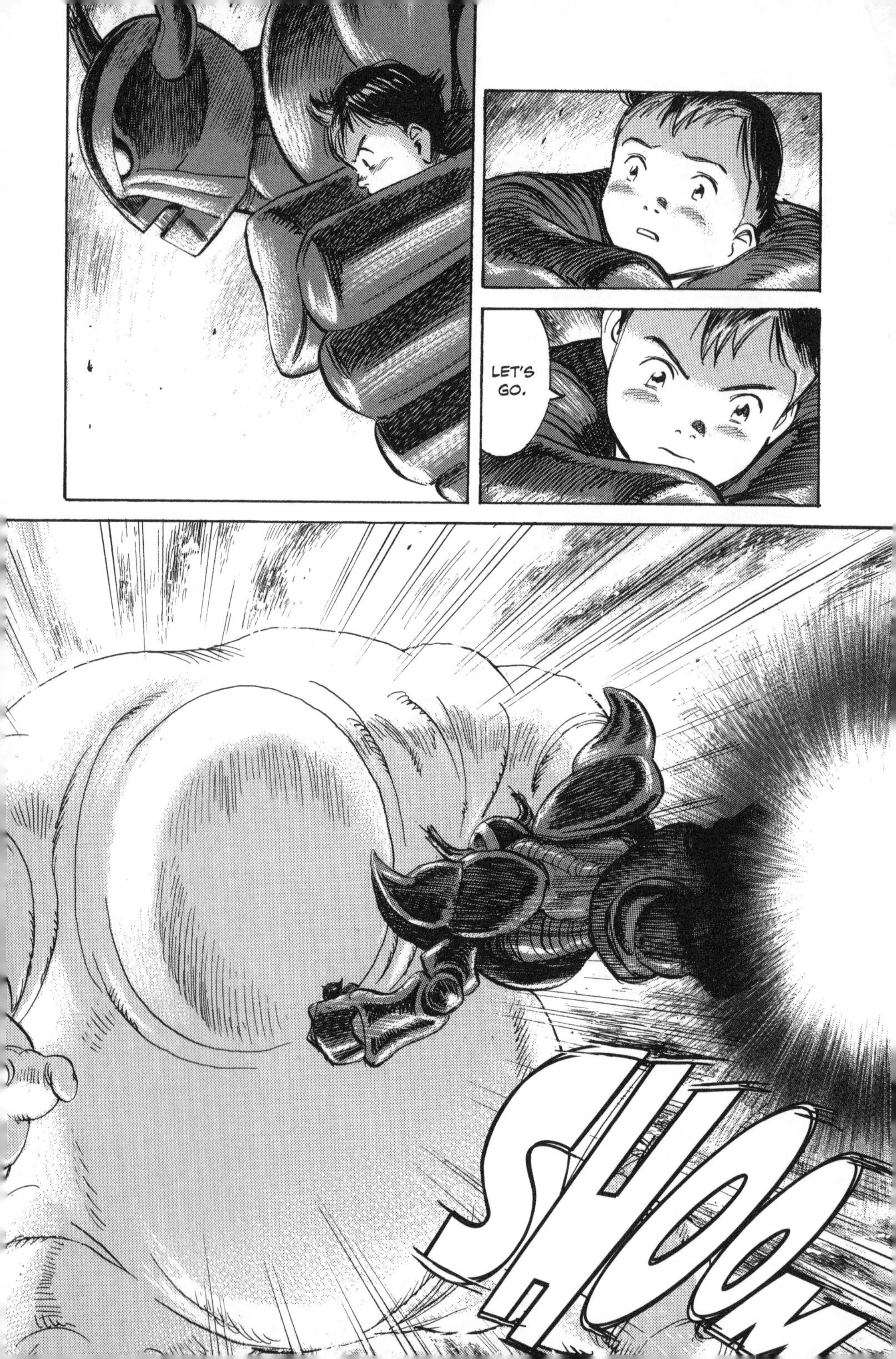
LET'S GO.
SHOO

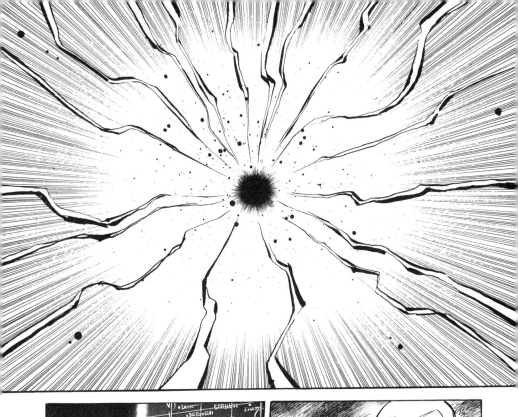

THAT INSTANT WAS HEARD AROUND THE WORLD...

ATOM...

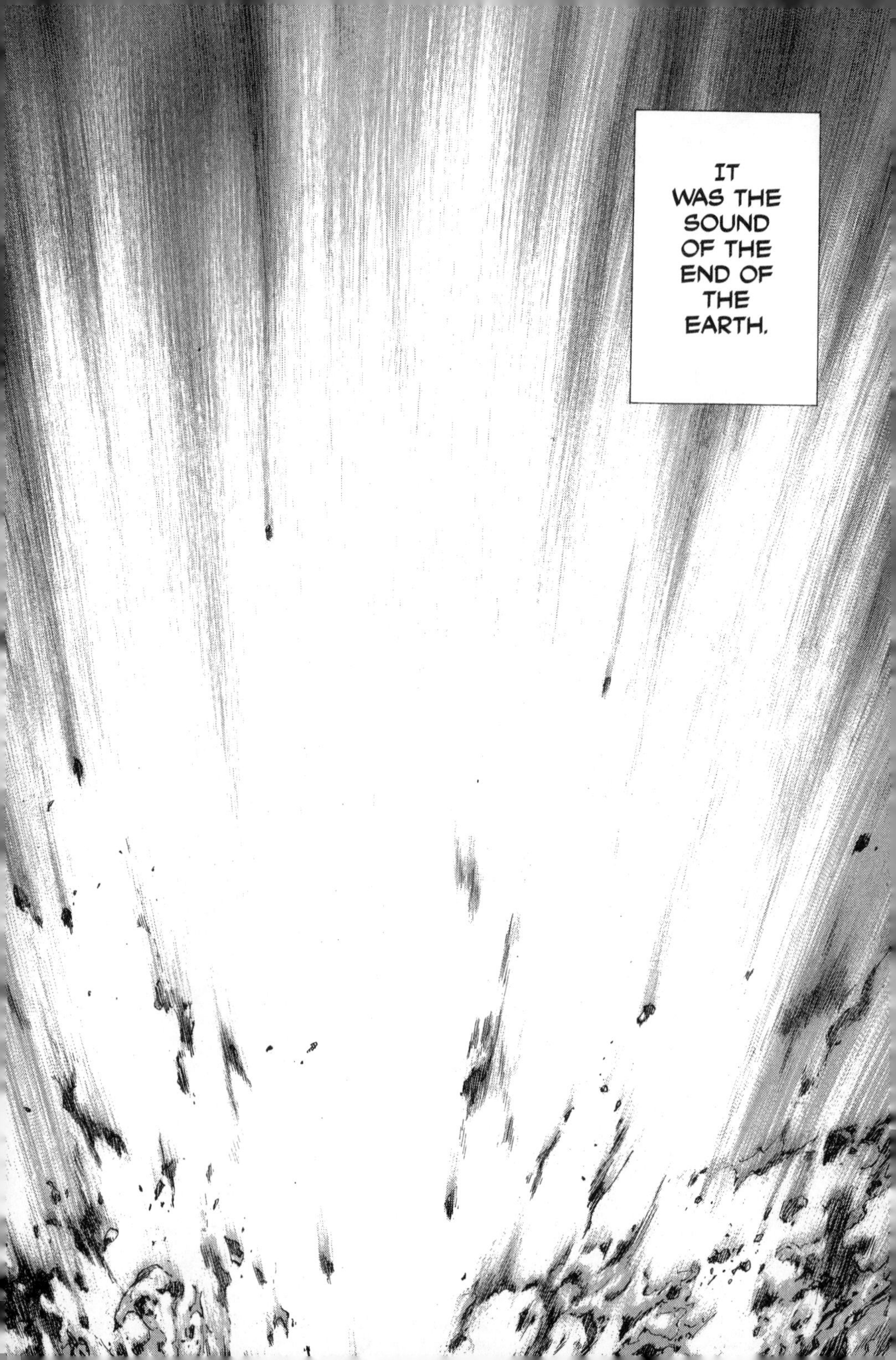
IT WAS THE SOUND OF THE END OF THE EARTH.

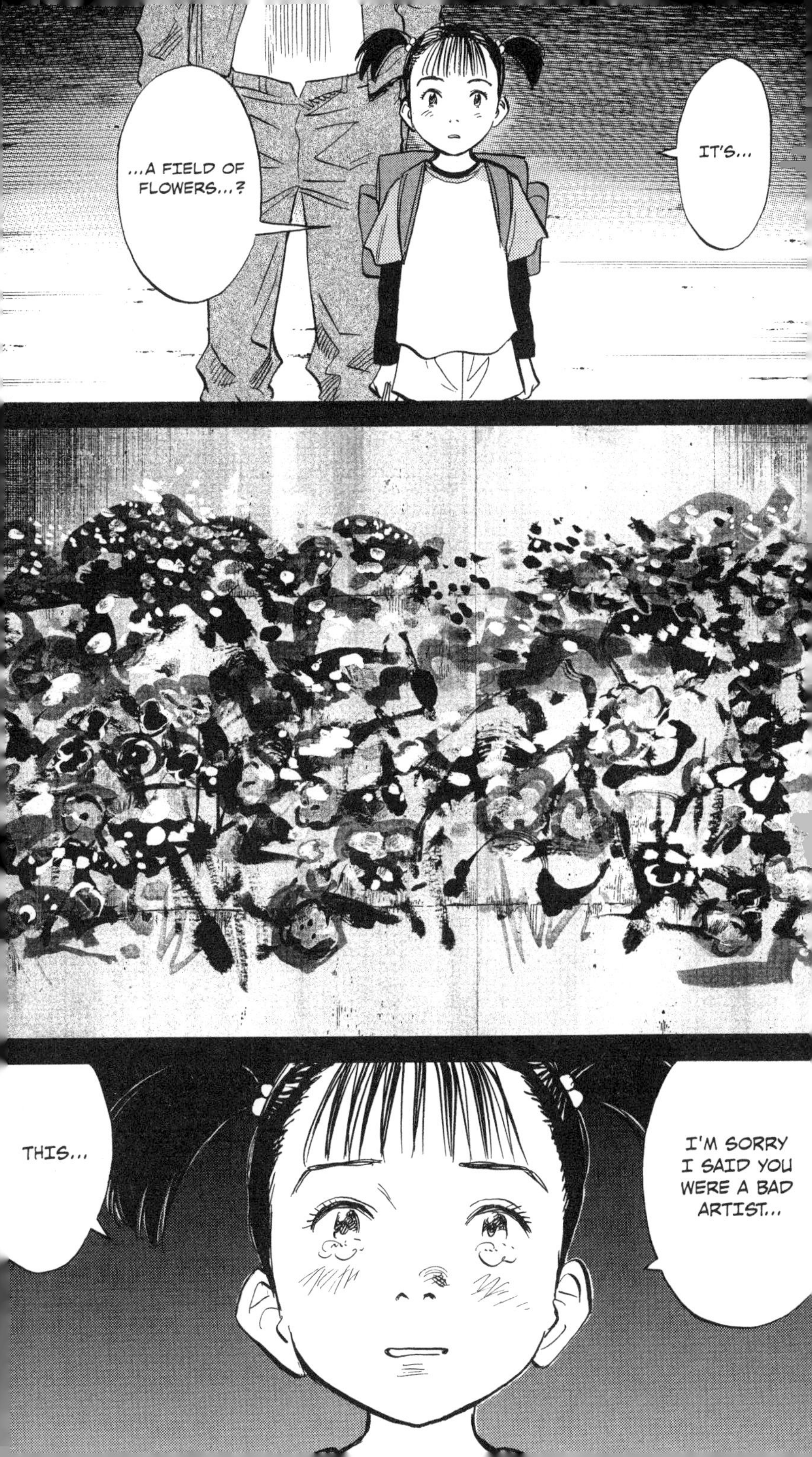
IT'S...
...A FIELD OF FLOWERS...?
I'M SORRY I SAID YOU WERE A BAD ARTIST...
THIS...

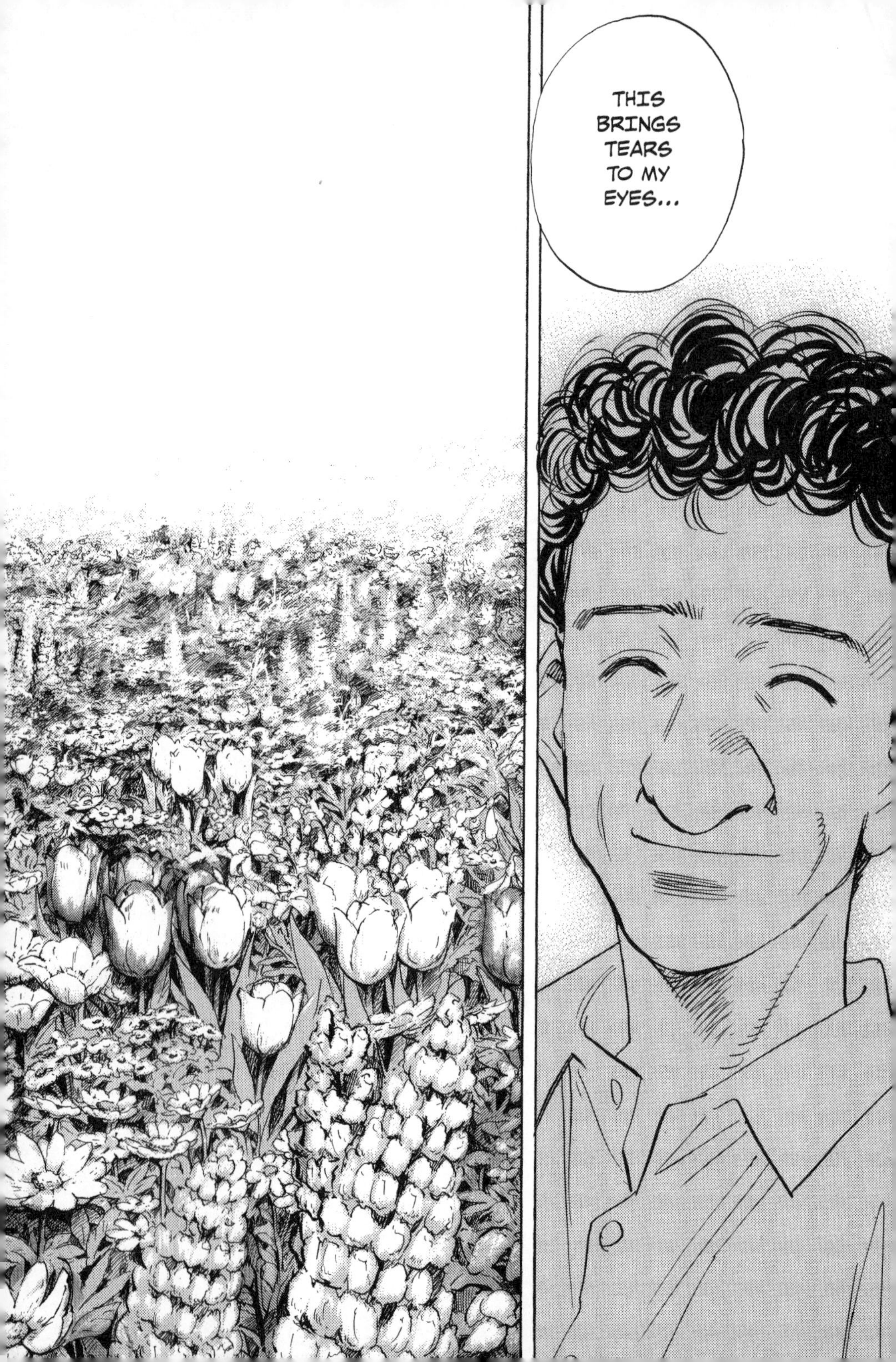
THIS BRINGS TEARS TO MY EYES...

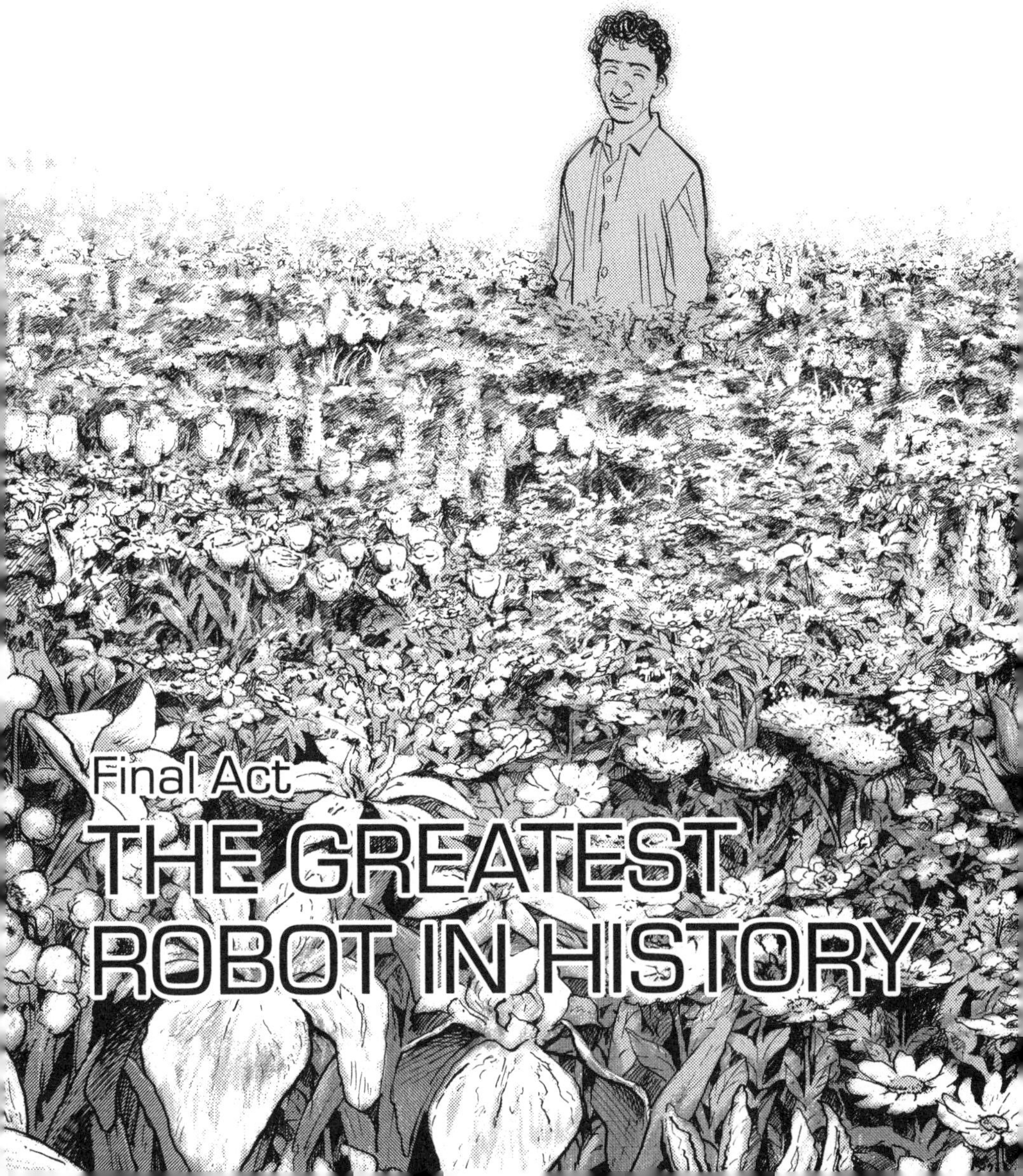
Final Act
THE GREATEST ROBOT IN HISTORY

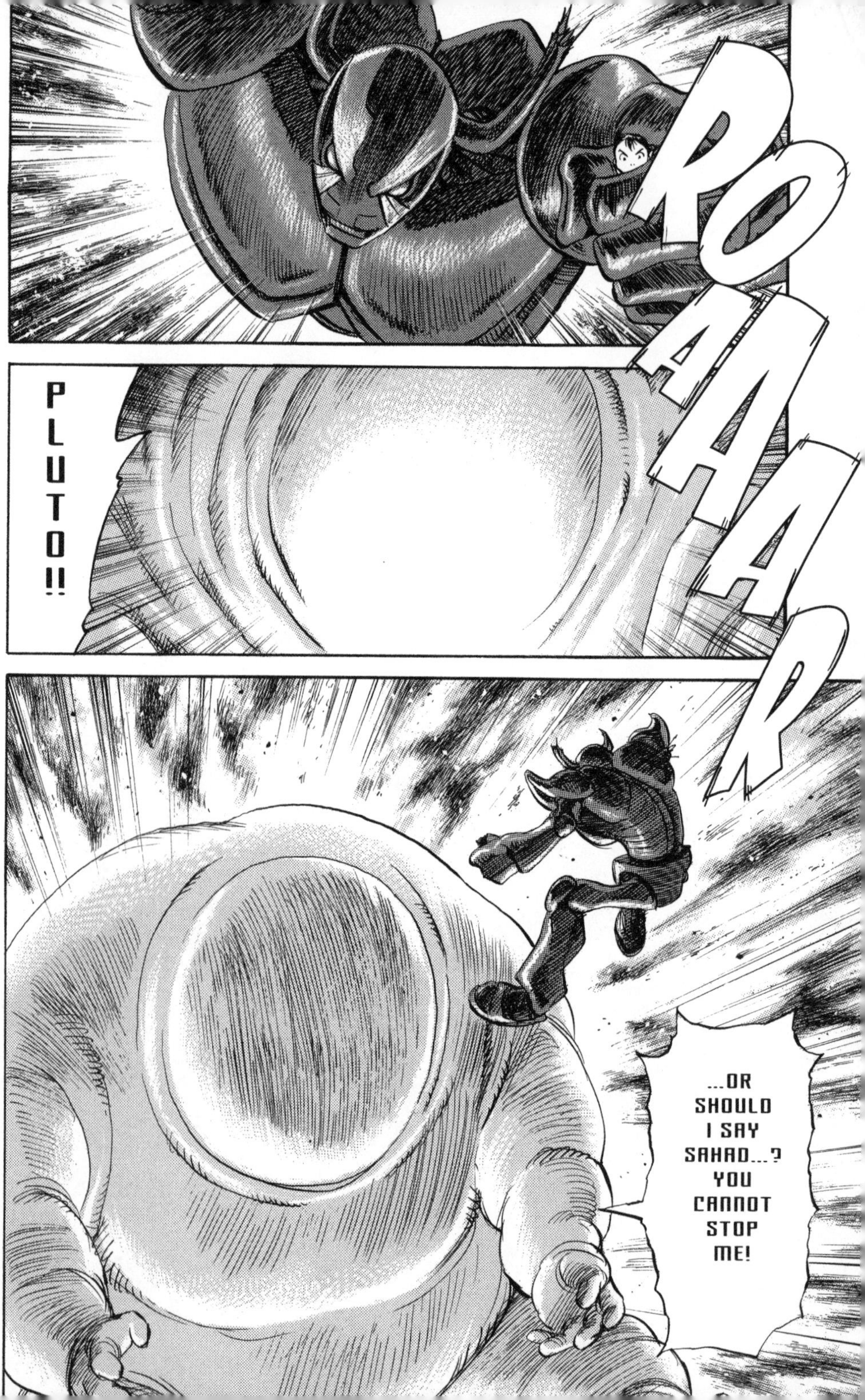
ROAAAR
PLUTO!!
...OR SHOULD I SAY SAHAD...? YOU CANNOT STOP ME!

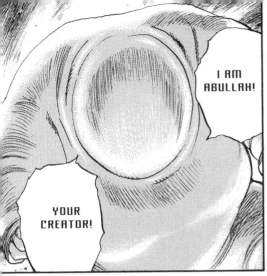

I AM ABULLAH!

YOUR CREATOR!

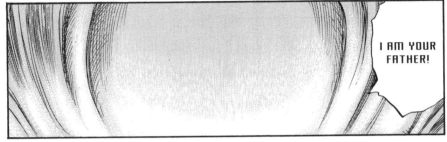

I AM YOUR FATHER!

MY FATHER... PROFESSOR ABULLAH... IS DEAD.

YOU ARE GOJI! YOU ONLY THINK YOU'RE ABULLAH.

NO...

YOU ARE *GOJI.*

I AM ABULLAH!!

I AM ABULLAH!!

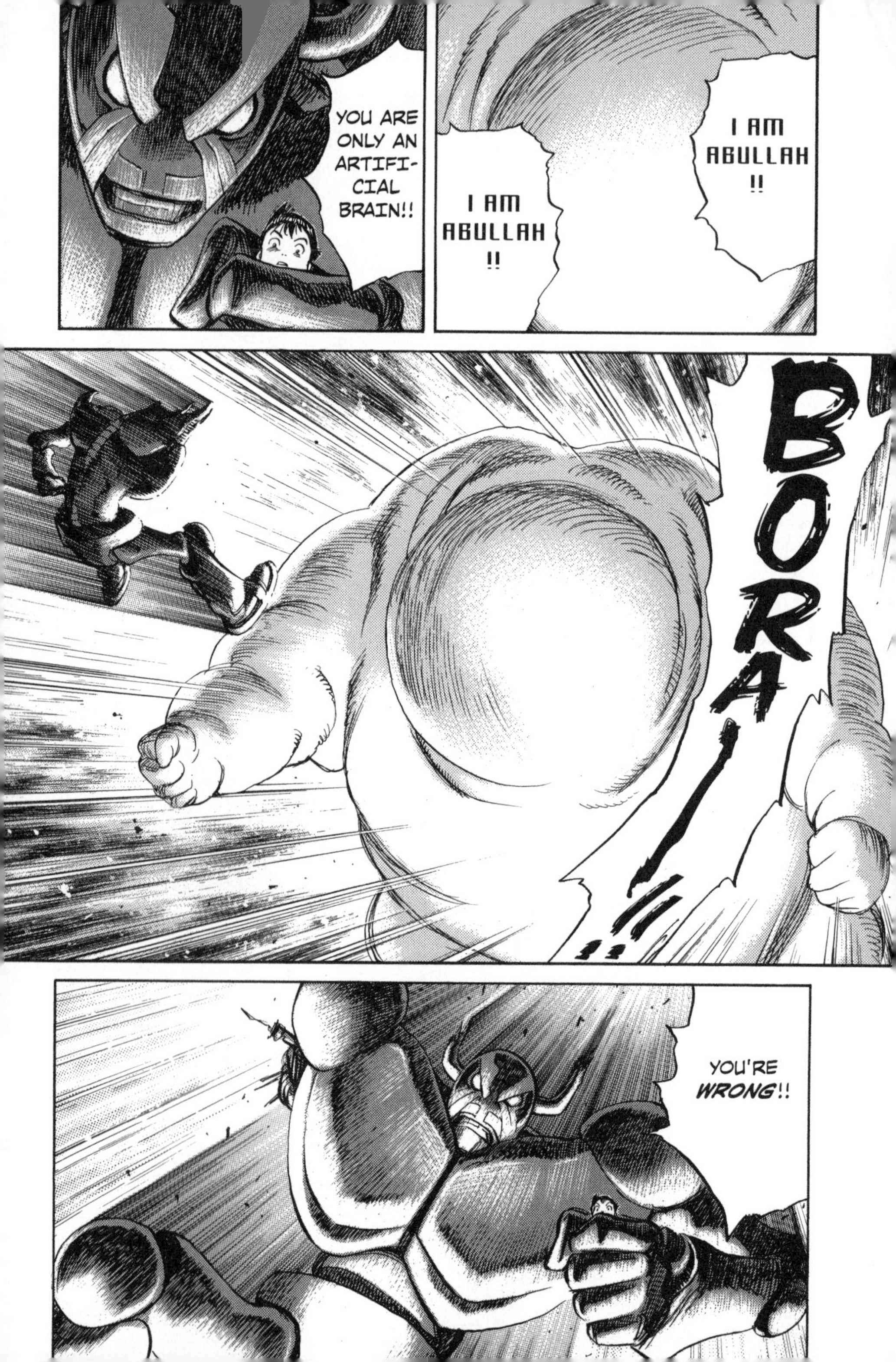
I AM ABULLAH !!
I AM ABULLAH !!
YOU ARE ONLY AN ARTIFI-CIAL BRAIN!!
BORA!!
YOU'RE *WRONG*!!

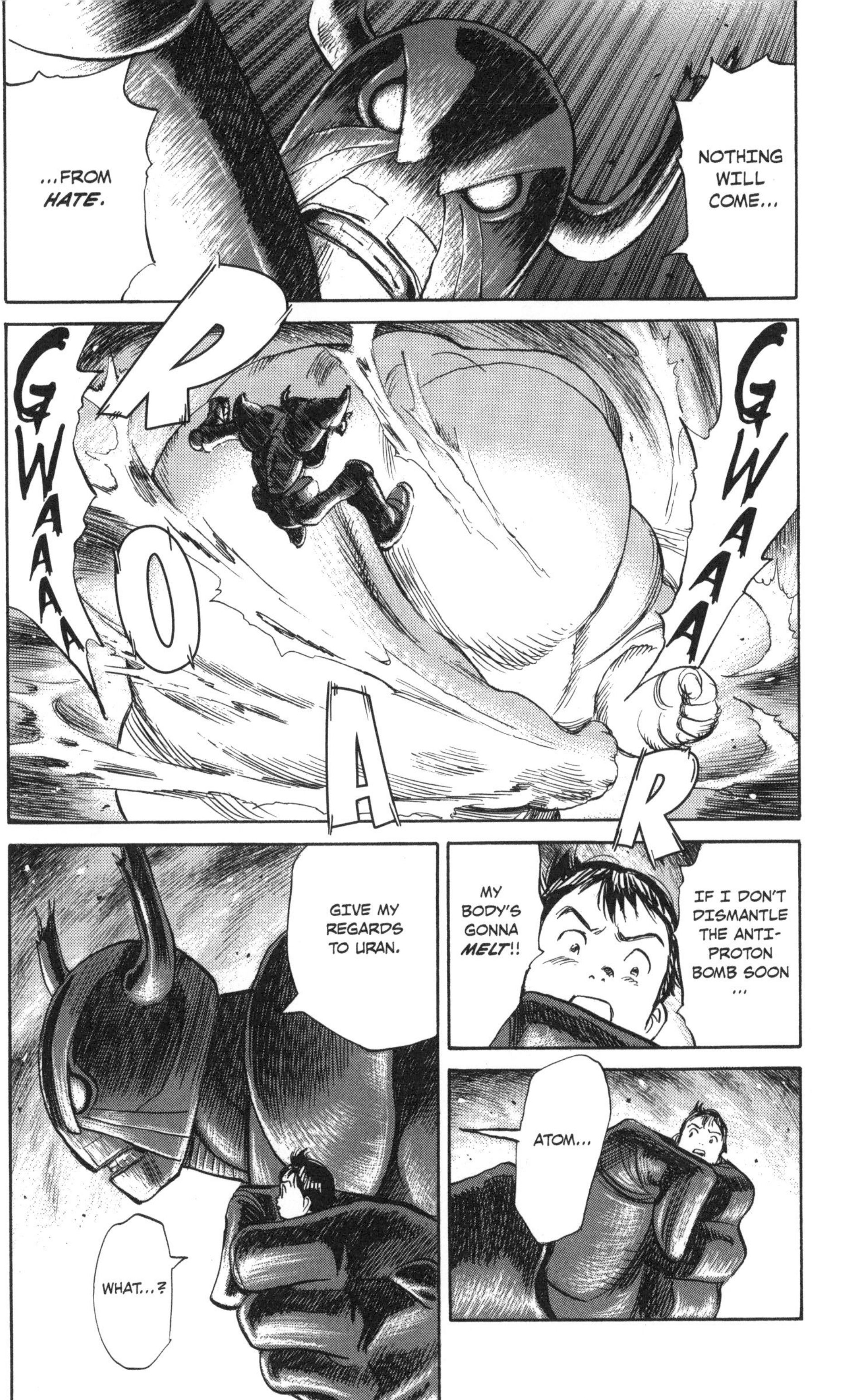
NOTHING WILL COME...
...FROM *HATE*.
GWAAAA
ROAR
GWAAAA
IF I DON'T DISMANTLE THE ANTI-PROTON BOMB SOON ...
MY BODY'S GONNA *MELT*!!
ATOM...
GIVE MY REGARDS TO URAN.
WHAT...?

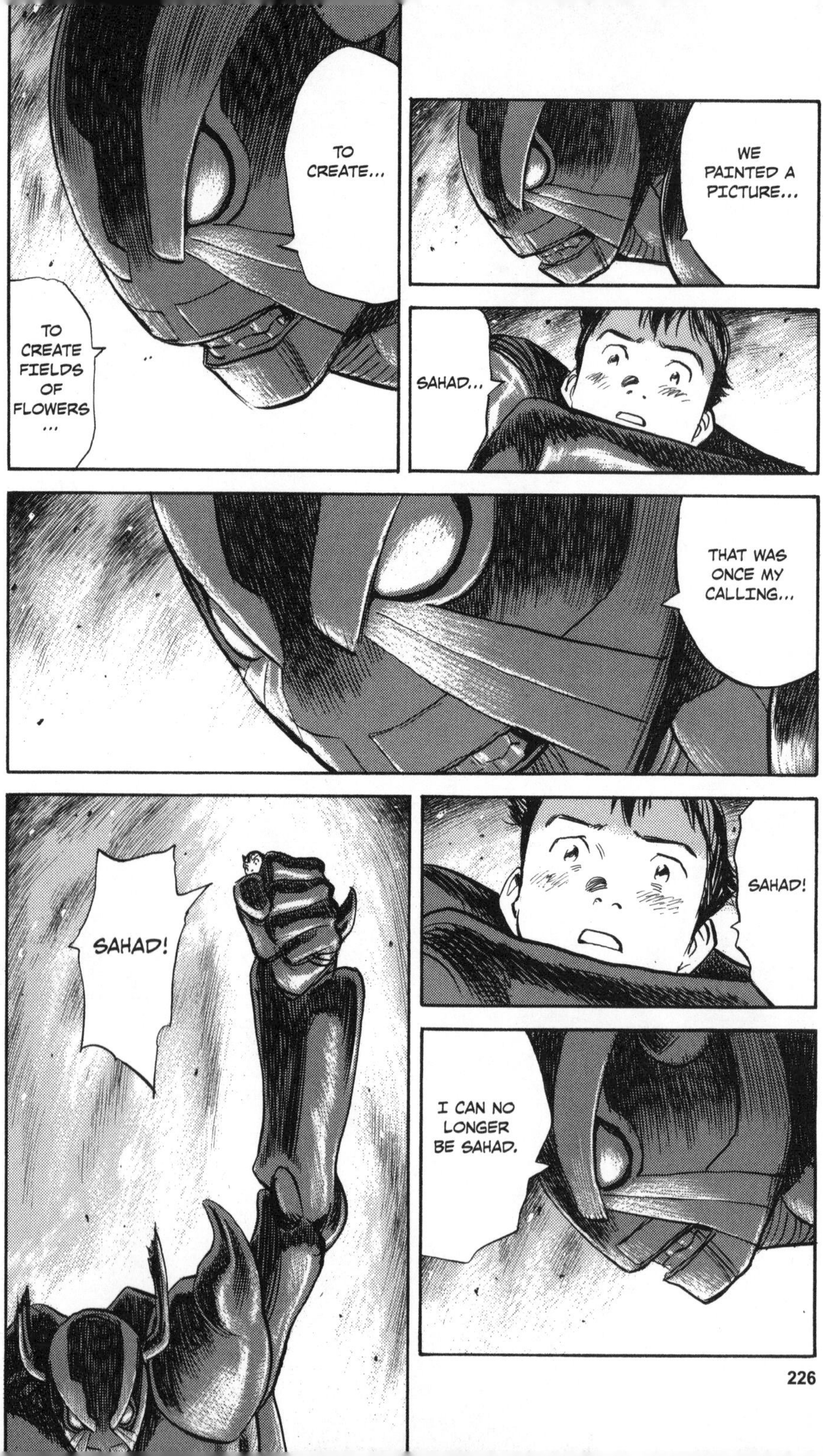
WE PAINTED A PICTURE...
SAHAD...
TO CREATE...
TO CREATE FIELDS OF FLOWERS...
THAT WAS ONCE MY CALLING...
SAHAD!
I CAN NO LONGER BE SAHAD.
SAHAD!

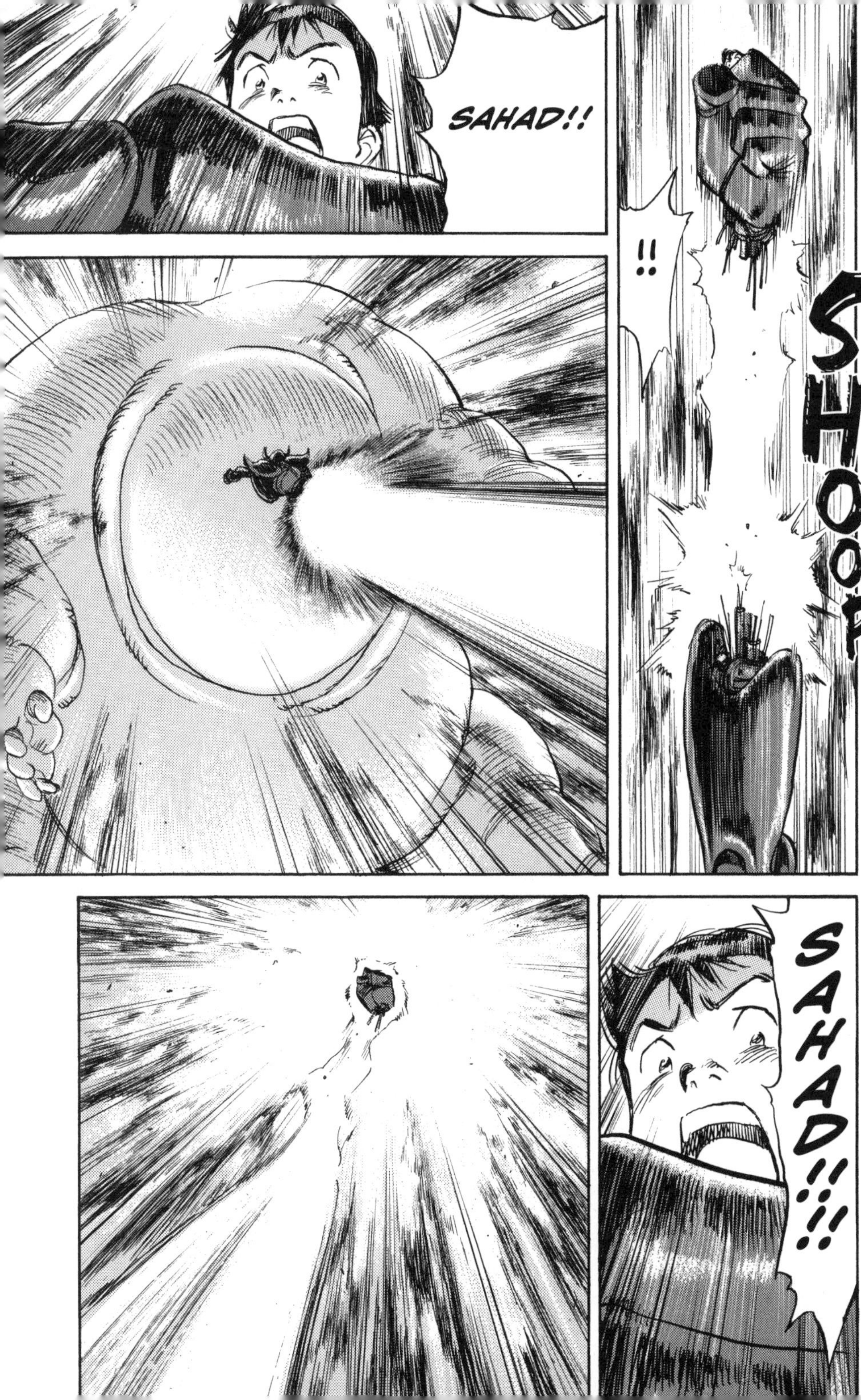
!!
SHOOP
SAHAD!!
SAHAD!!!!!

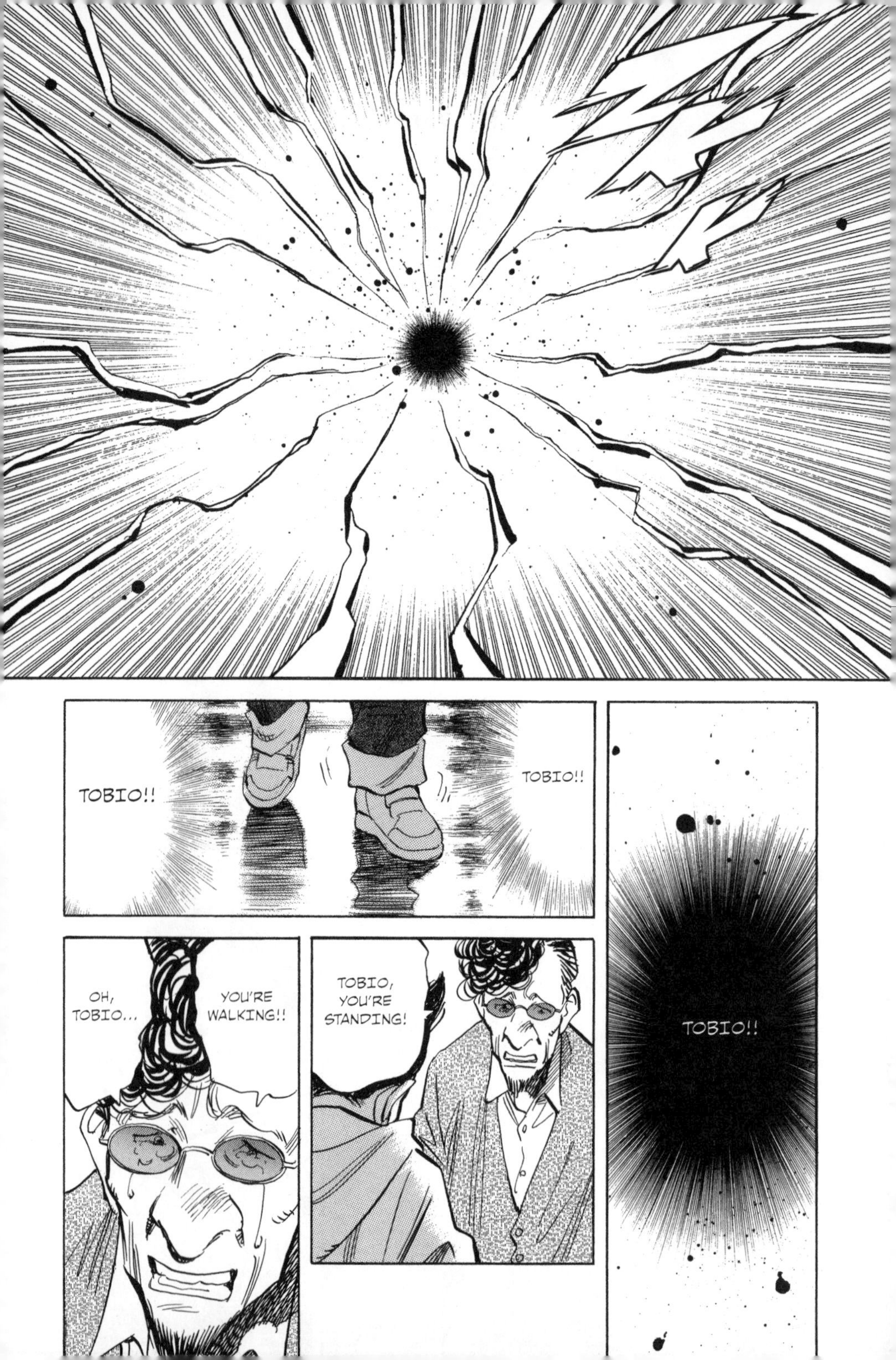

TOBIO!!
TOBIO!!
TOBIO!!
TOBIO, YOU'RE STANDING!
YOU'RE WALKING!!
OH, TOBIO...

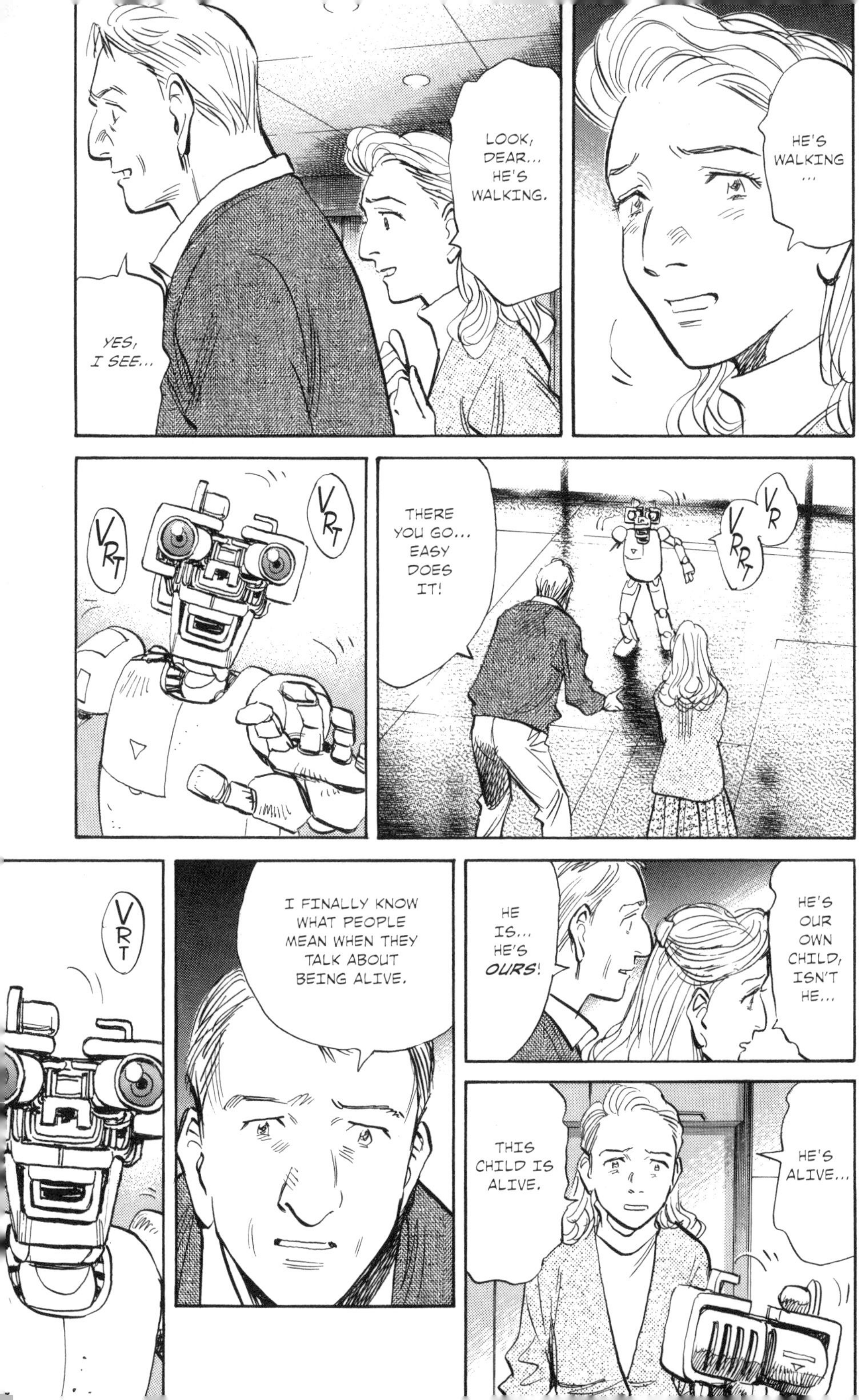
HE'S WALKING ...
LOOK, DEAR... HE'S WALKING.
YES, I SEE...
VR
VRRT
THERE YOU GO... EASY DOES IT!
VRT
VRT
HE'S OUR OWN CHILD, ISN'T HE...
HE IS... HE'S *OURS*!
HE'S ALIVE...
THIS CHILD IS ALIVE.
I FINALLY KNOW WHAT PEOPLE MEAN WHEN THEY TALK ABOUT BEING ALIVE.
VRT

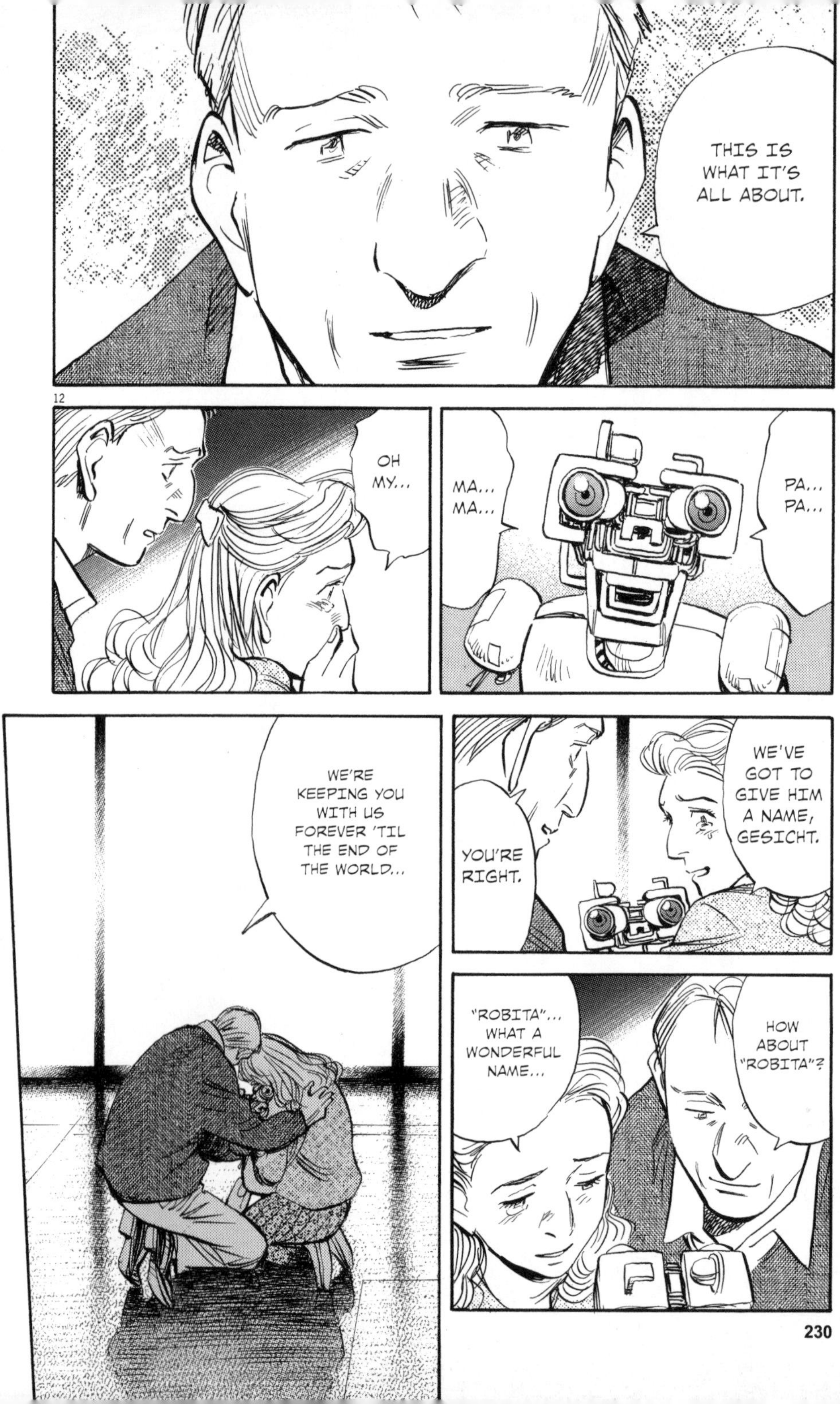
THIS IS WHAT IT'S ALL ABOUT.
12
PA... PA...
MA... MA...
OH MY...
WE'VE GOT TO GIVE HIM A NAME, GESICHT.
YOU'RE RIGHT.
HOW ABOUT "ROBITA"?
"ROBITA"... WHAT A WONDERFUL NAME...
WE'RE KEEPING YOU WITH US FOREVER 'TIL THE END OF THE WORLD...

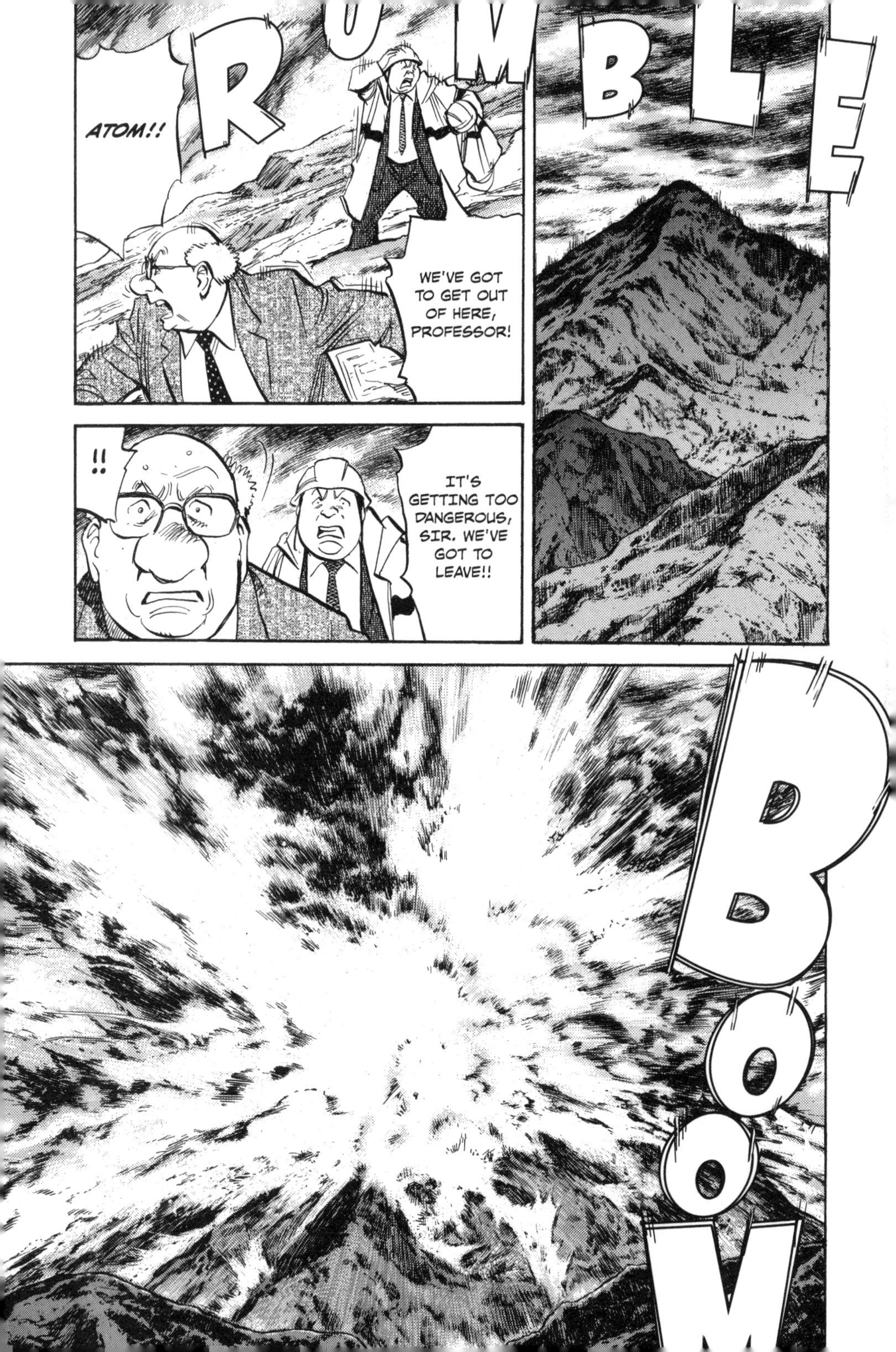
RUMBLE
ATOM!!
WE'VE GOT TO GET OUT OF HERE, PROFESSOR!
IT'S GETTING TOO DANGEROUS, SIR. WE'VE GOT TO LEAVE!!
!!
BOOOM

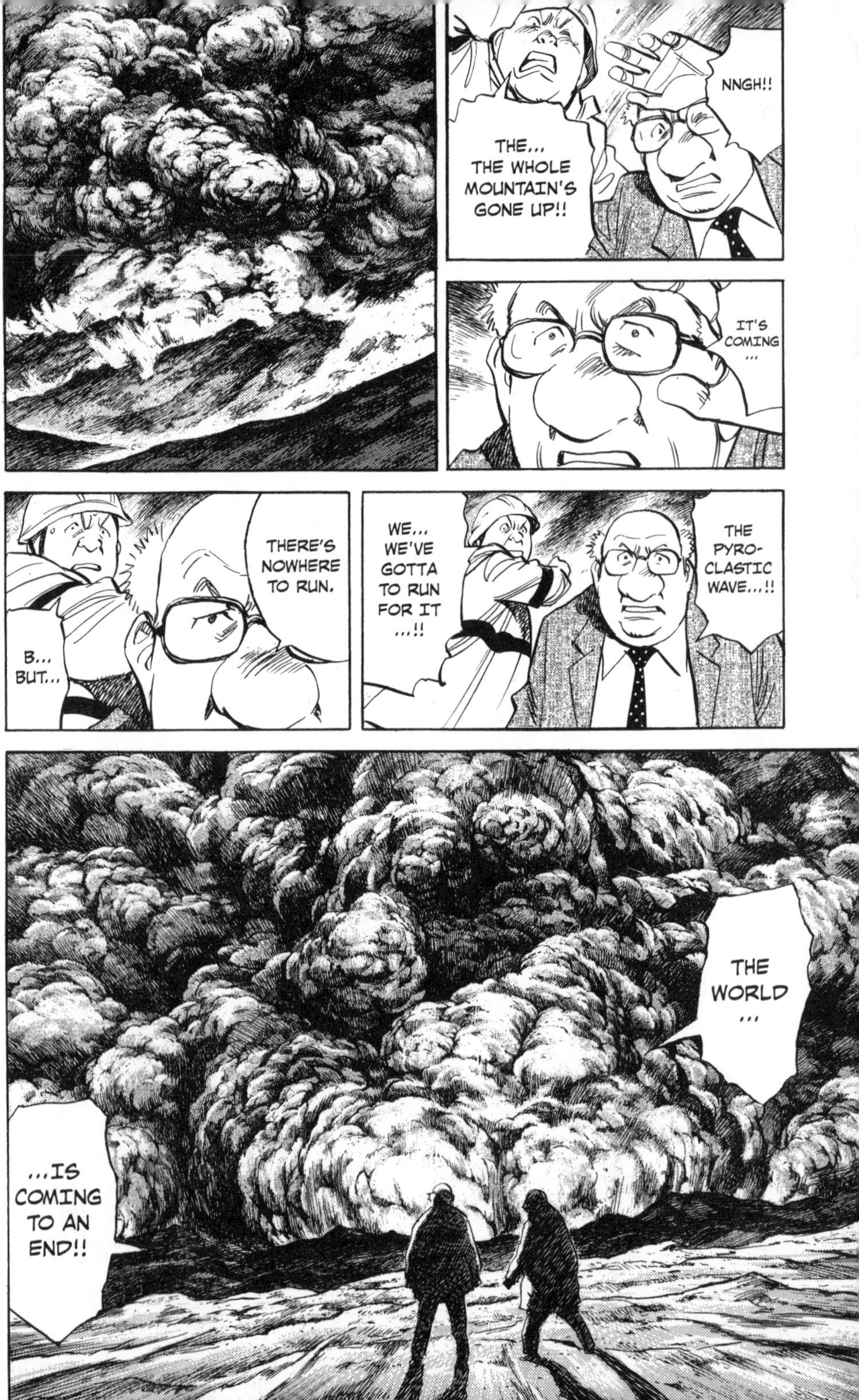
NNGH!!
THE... THE WHOLE MOUNTAIN'S GONE UP!!
IT'S COMING ...
THE PYRO-CLASTIC WAVE...!!
WE... WE'VE GOTTA TO RUN FOR IT ...!!
THERE'S NOWHERE TO RUN.
B... BUT...
THE WORLD ...
...IS COMING TO AN END!!

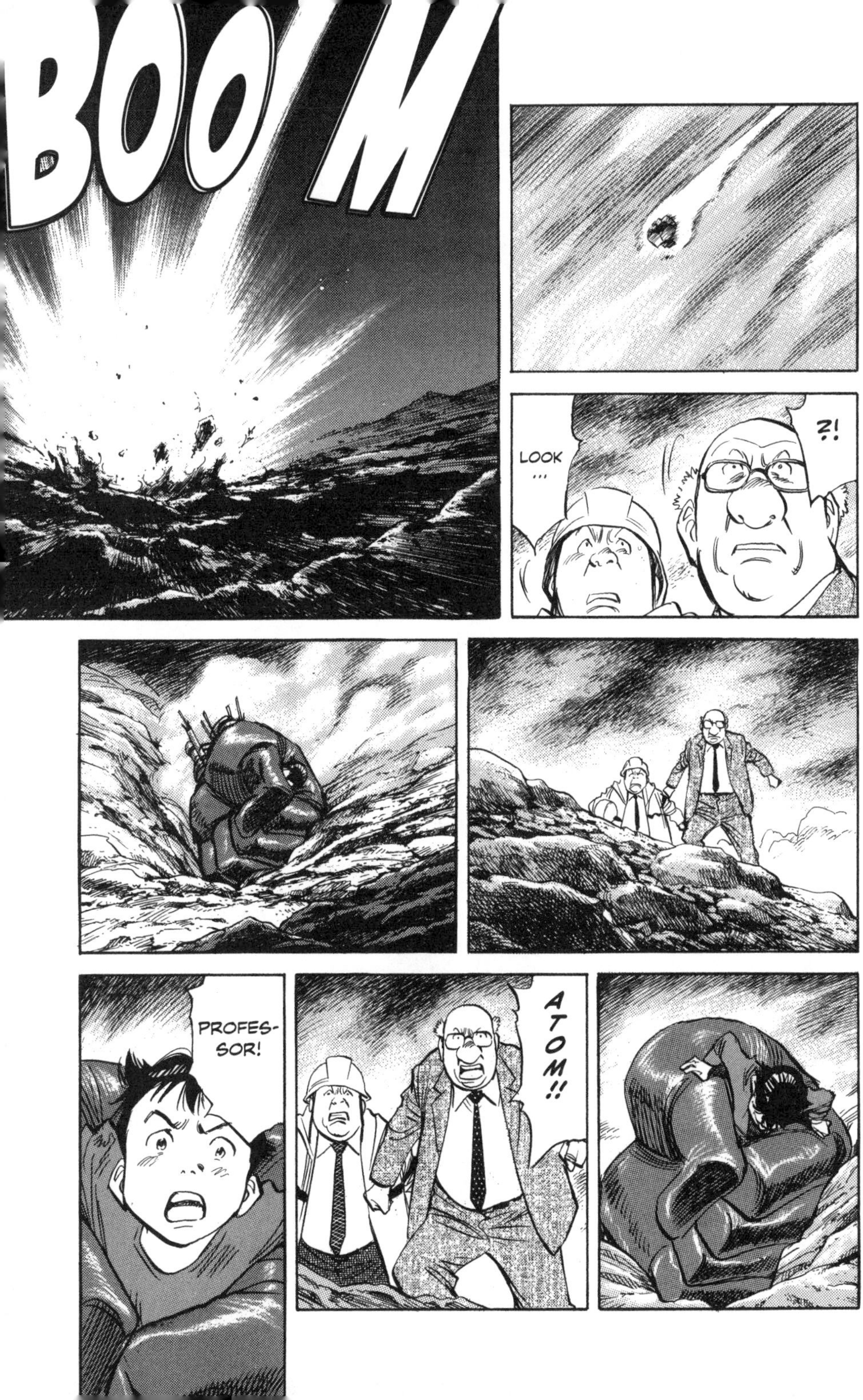
BOOM
?!
LOOK ...
ATOM!!
PROFES-SOR!

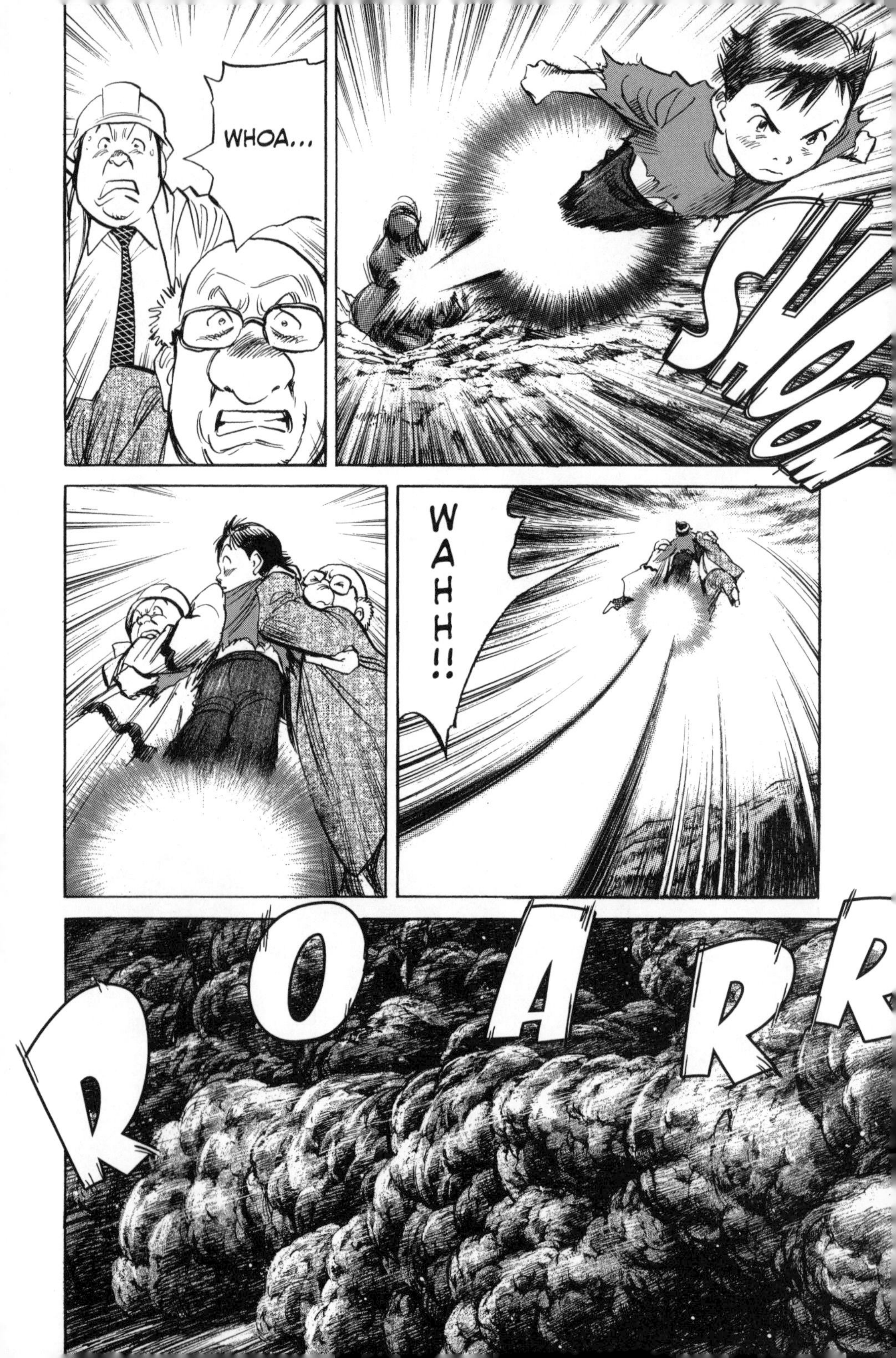
SHOOM
WHOA...
WAHH!!
ROARR

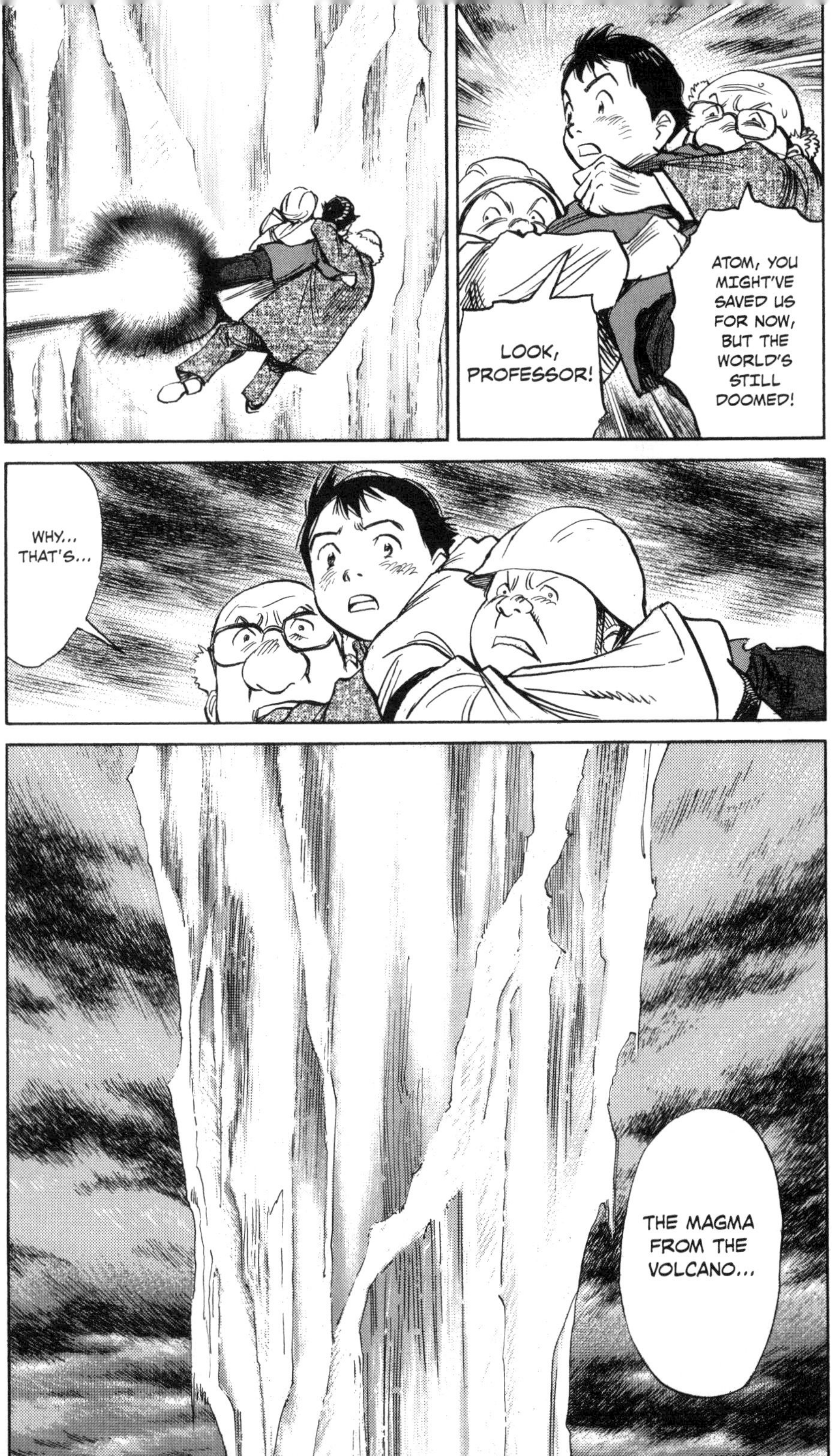
ATOM, YOU MIGHT'VE SAVED US FOR NOW, BUT THE WORLD'S STILL DOOMED!
LOOK, PROFESSOR!
WHY... THAT'S...
THE MAGMA FROM THE VOLCANO...

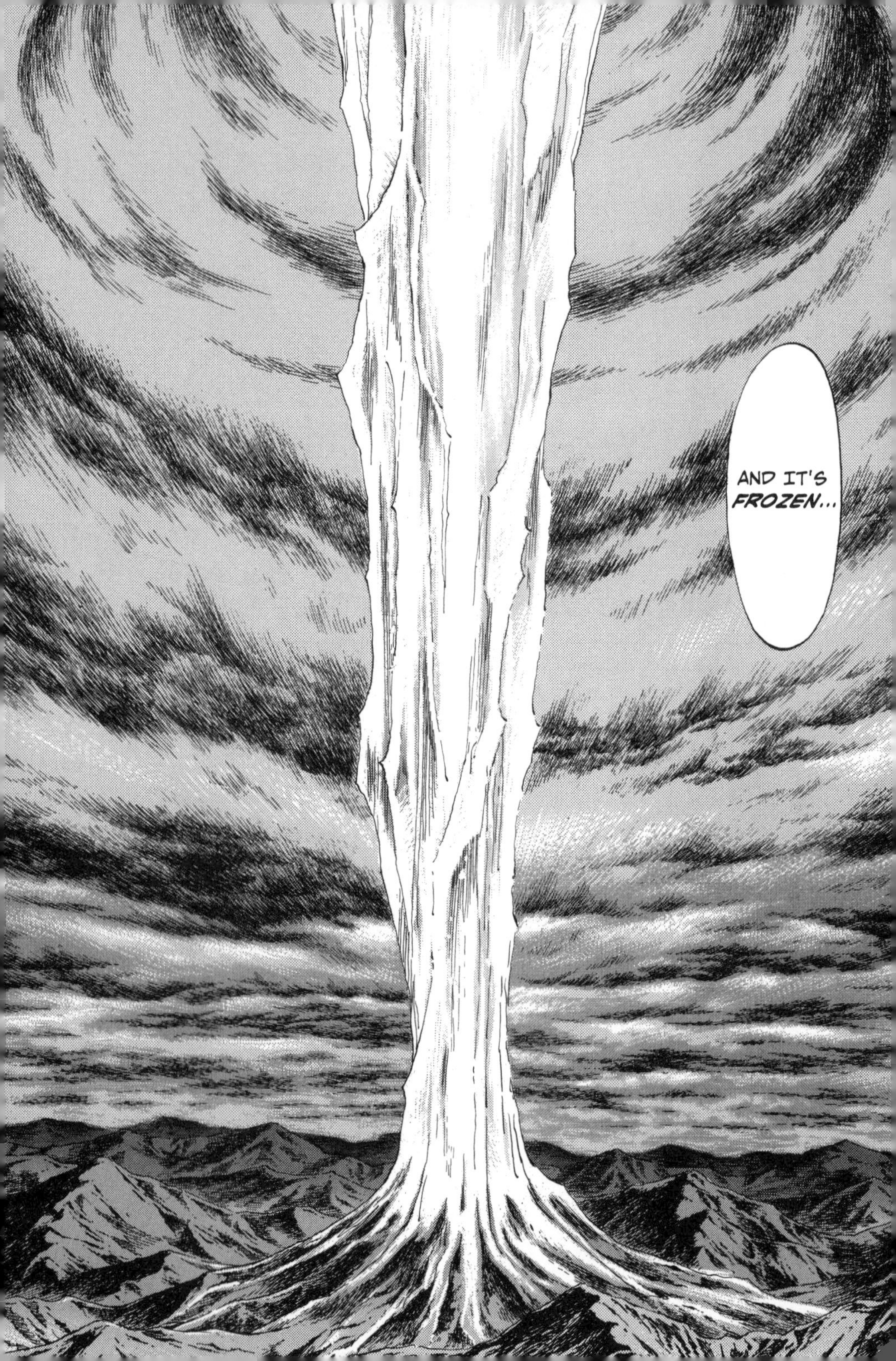
AND IT'S *FROZEN*...

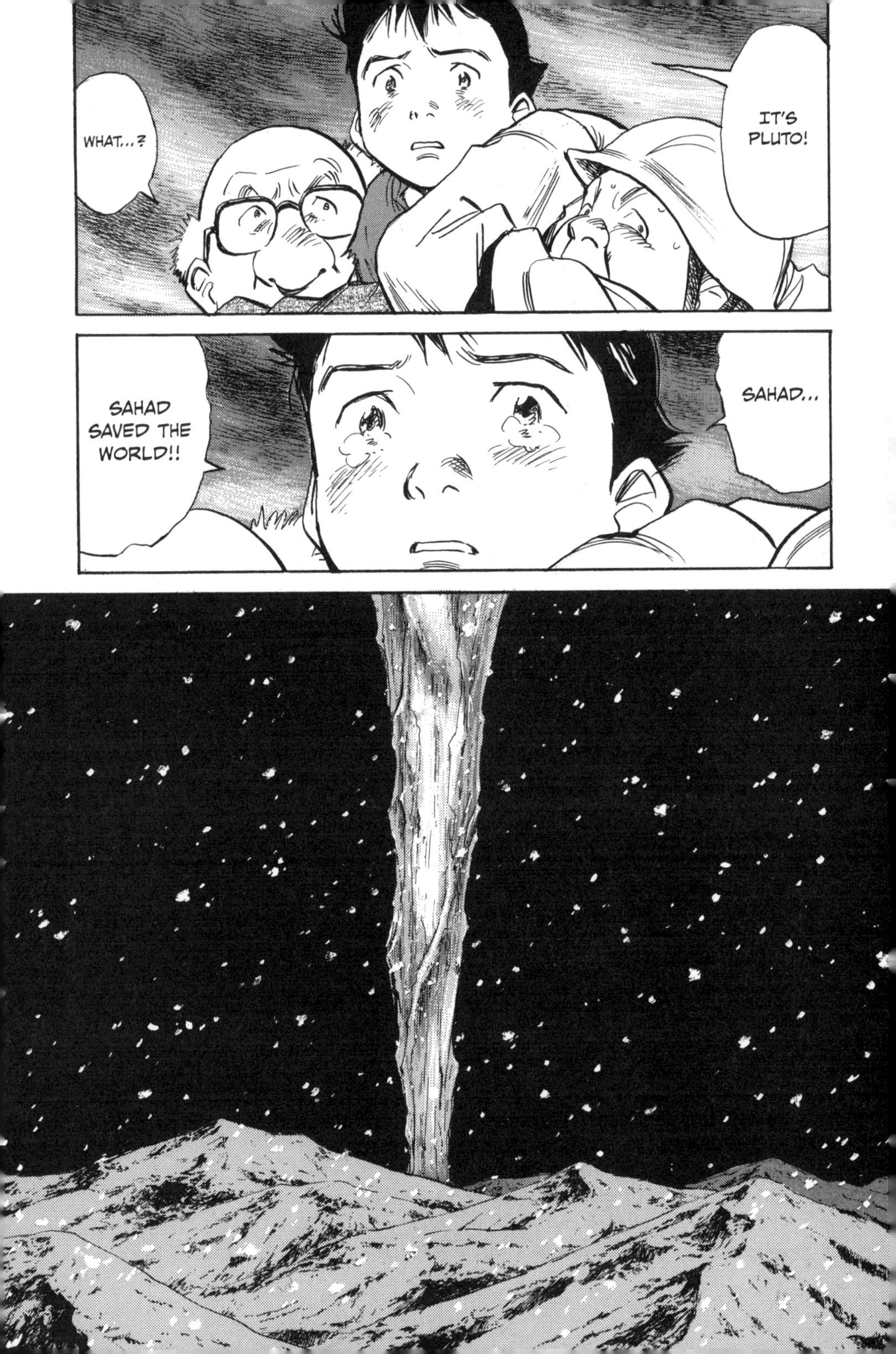
IT'S PLUTO!
WHAT...?
SAHAD...
SAHAD SAVED THE WORLD!!

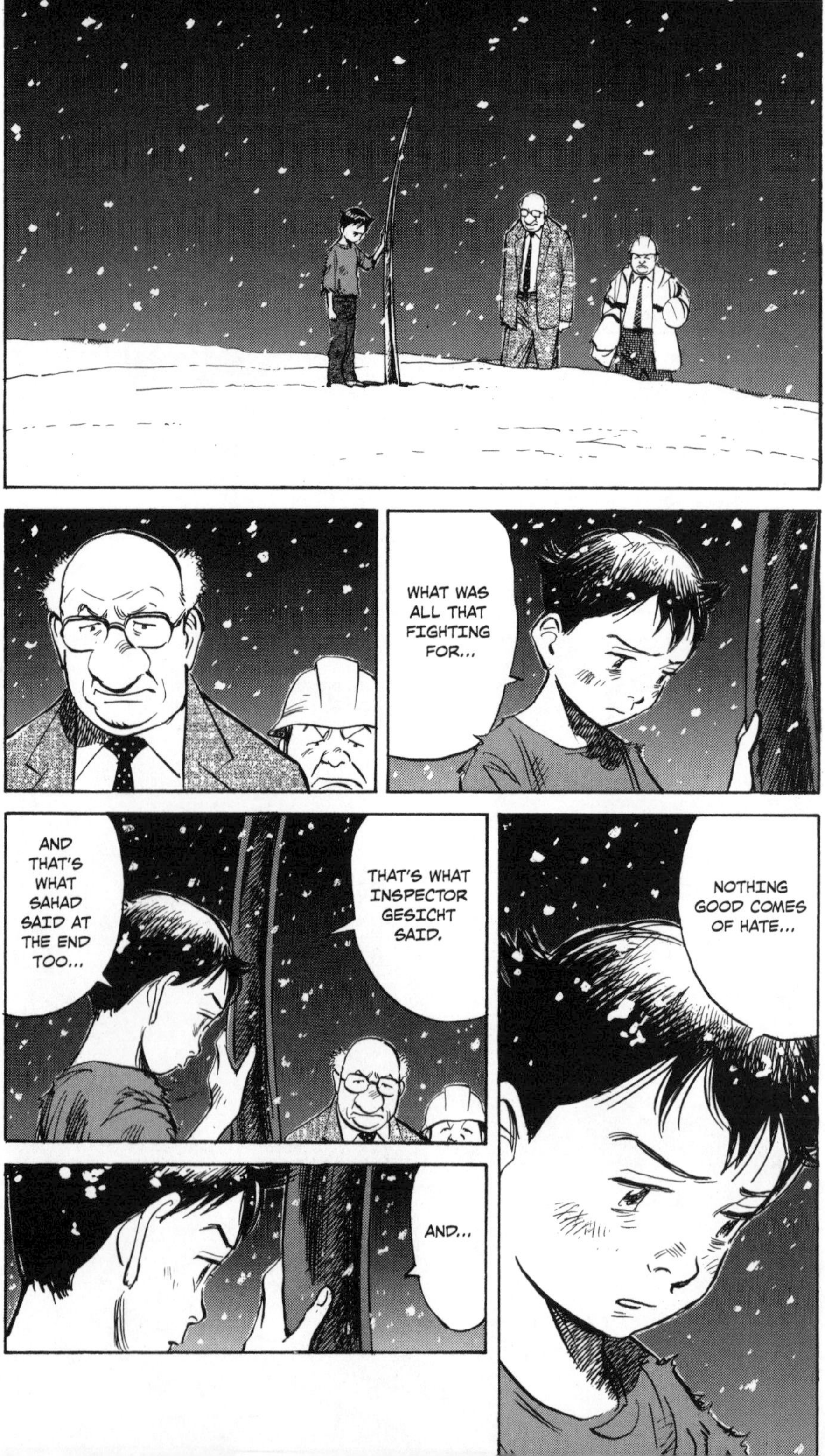
WHAT WAS ALL THAT FIGHTING FOR...
NOTHING GOOD COMES OF HATE...
THAT'S WHAT INSPECTOR GESICHT SAID.
AND THAT'S WHAT SAHAD SAID AT THE END TOO...
AND...

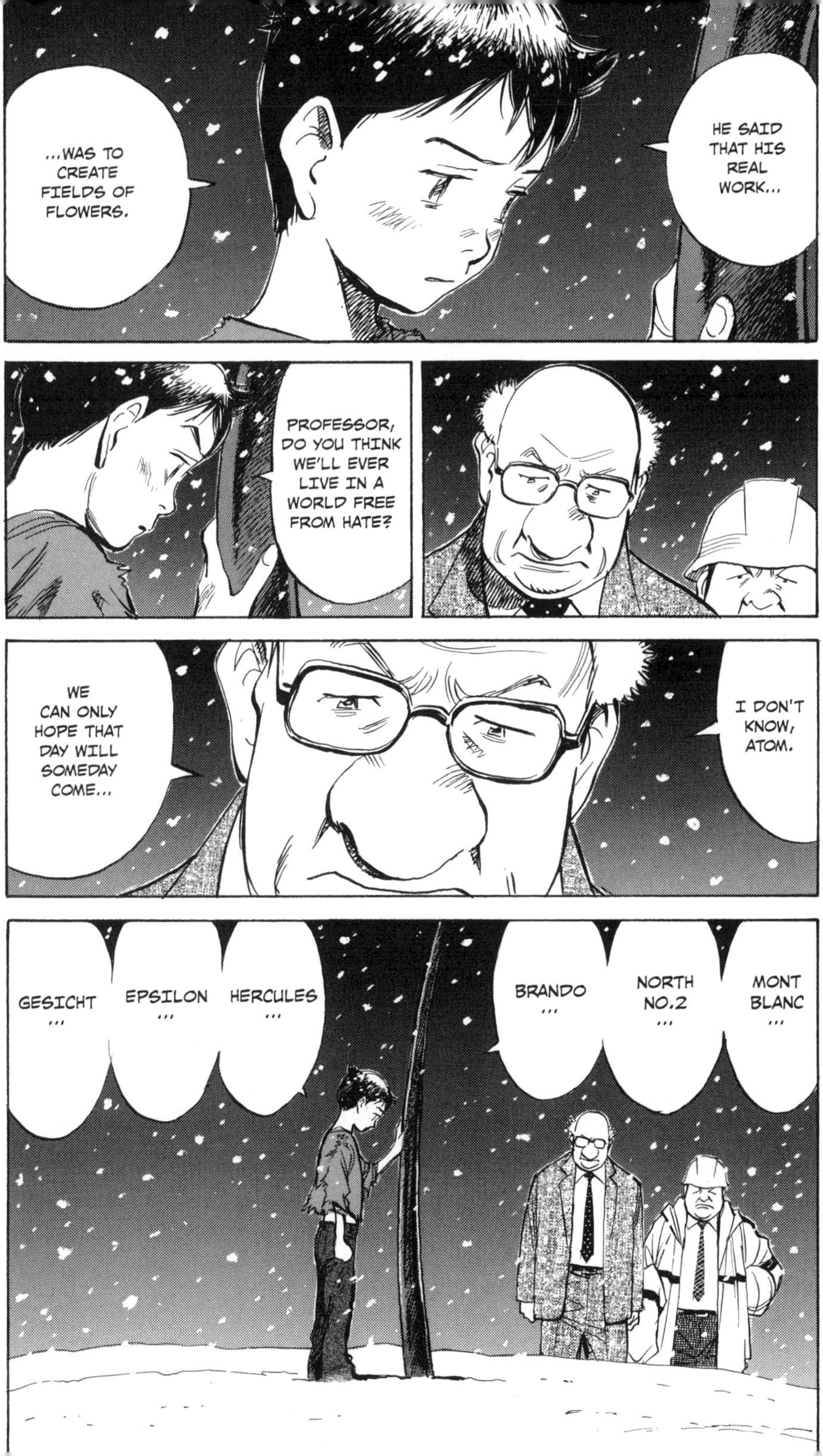
HE SAID THAT HIS REAL WORK...
...WAS TO CREATE FIELDS OF FLOWERS.
PROFESSOR, DO YOU THINK WE'LL EVER LIVE IN A WORLD FREE FROM HATE?
I DON'T KNOW, ATOM.
WE CAN ONLY HOPE THAT DAY WILL SOMEDAY COME...
MONT BLANC ...
NORTH NO.2 ...
BRANDO ...
HERCULES ...
EPSILON ...
GESICHT ...

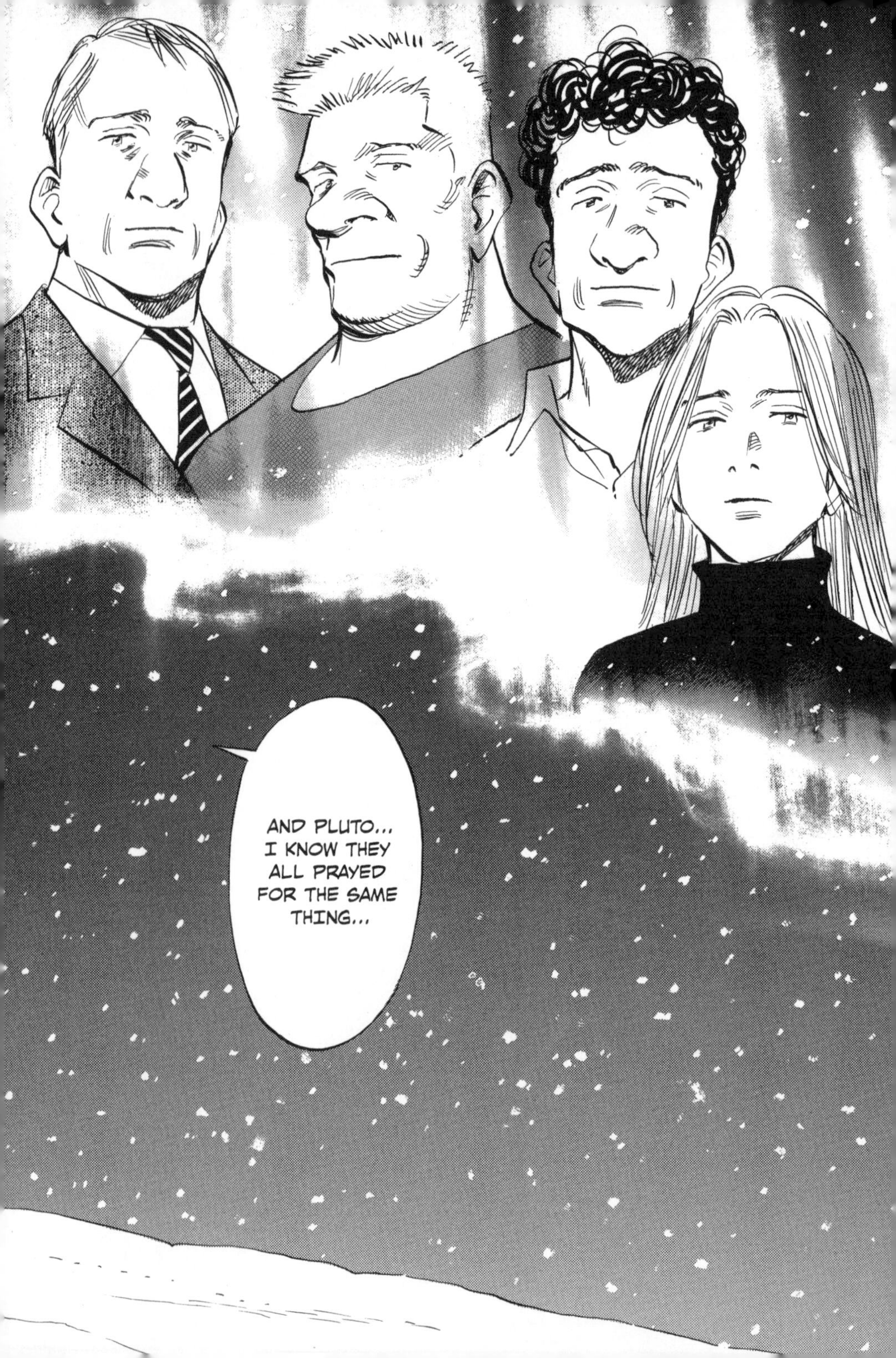
AND PLUTO... I KNOW THEY ALL PRAYED FOR THE SAME THING...

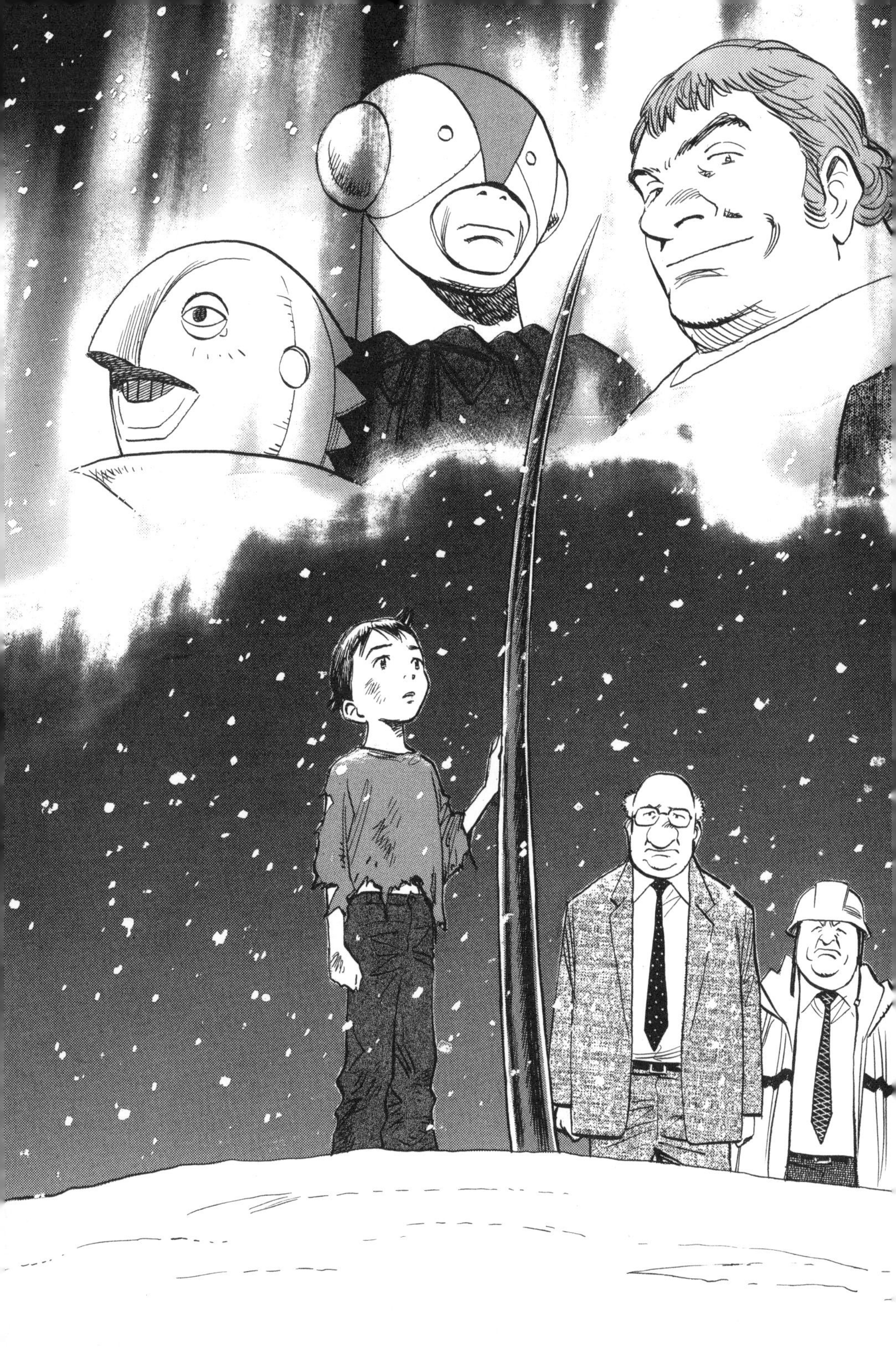

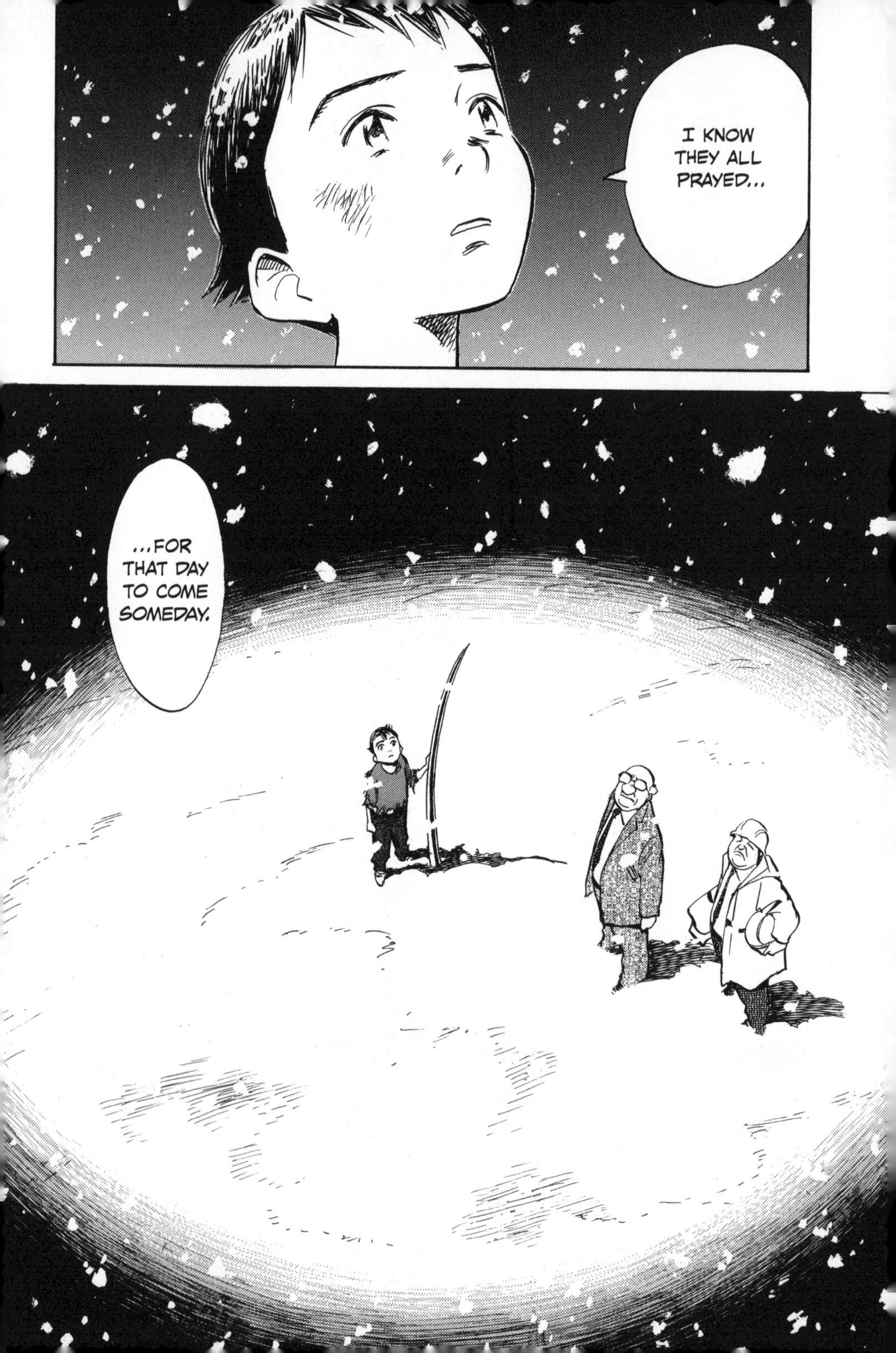
I KNOW THEY ALL PRAYED...
...FOR THAT DAY TO COME SOMEDAY.

TAKASHI NAGASAKI

•

MACOTO TEZKA

•

PRODUCTION STAFF
HIDEAKI URANO
TADASHI KARAKIDA
KAZUMA MARUYAMA
TORU SAKATA
JUNICHI KIRIYAMA

EDITORIAL STAFF
HIDEYUKI AKANA
NOBUTAKA HIROOKA
MINORU SUGINAKA
EIJI SHIMAMURA

•

NAOKI URASAWA
✖
OSAMU TEZUKA

URASAWA ✖ TEZUKA

A NEW VISION BASED ON ASTRO BOY – 'THE GREATEST ROBOT ON EARTH'
BY NAOKI URASAWA AND OSAMU TEZUKA

SEPTEMBER 2003 – APRIL 2009
BIG COMIC ORIGINAL

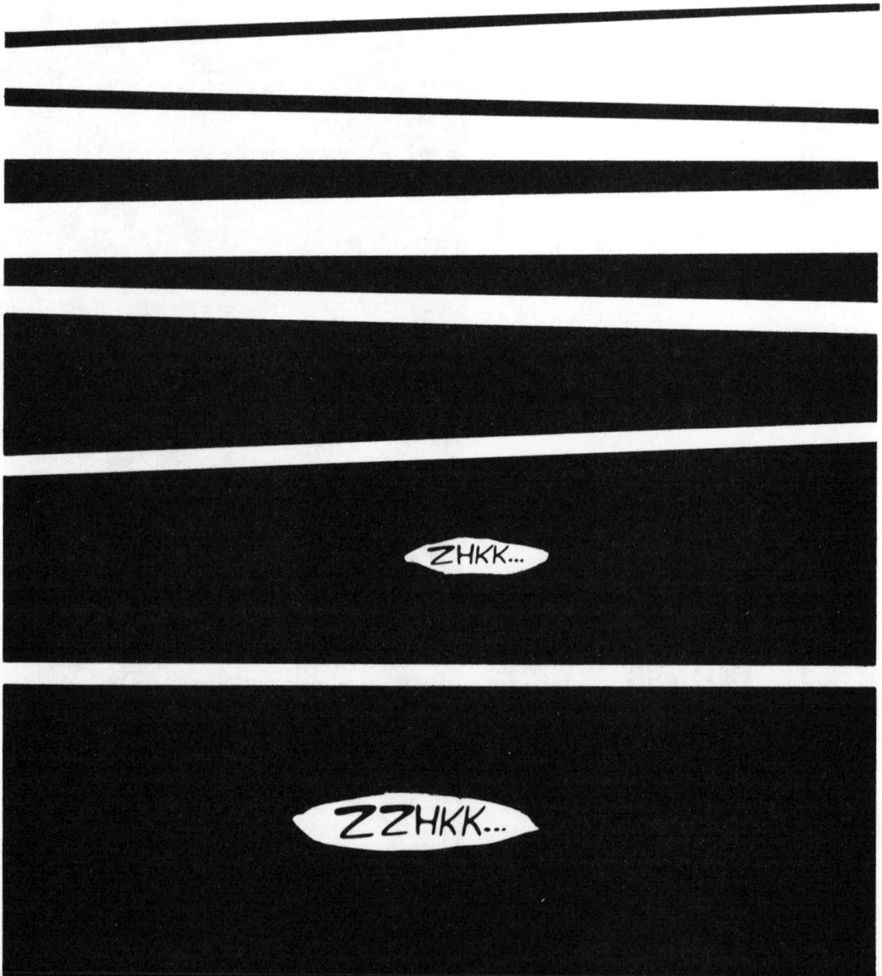
ZHKK...
ZZHKK...

ZZHKK...

ALL PERSONNEL TO YOUR POSTS!!

TROMP TROMP TROMP

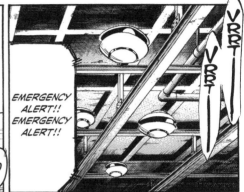

EMERGENCY ALERT!! EMERGENCY ALERT!!

VRRT VRRT

ZZHKK...

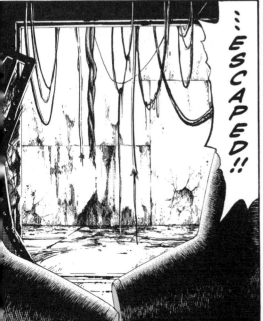

...ESCAPED!!

FWP

BRAU 1589 HAS...

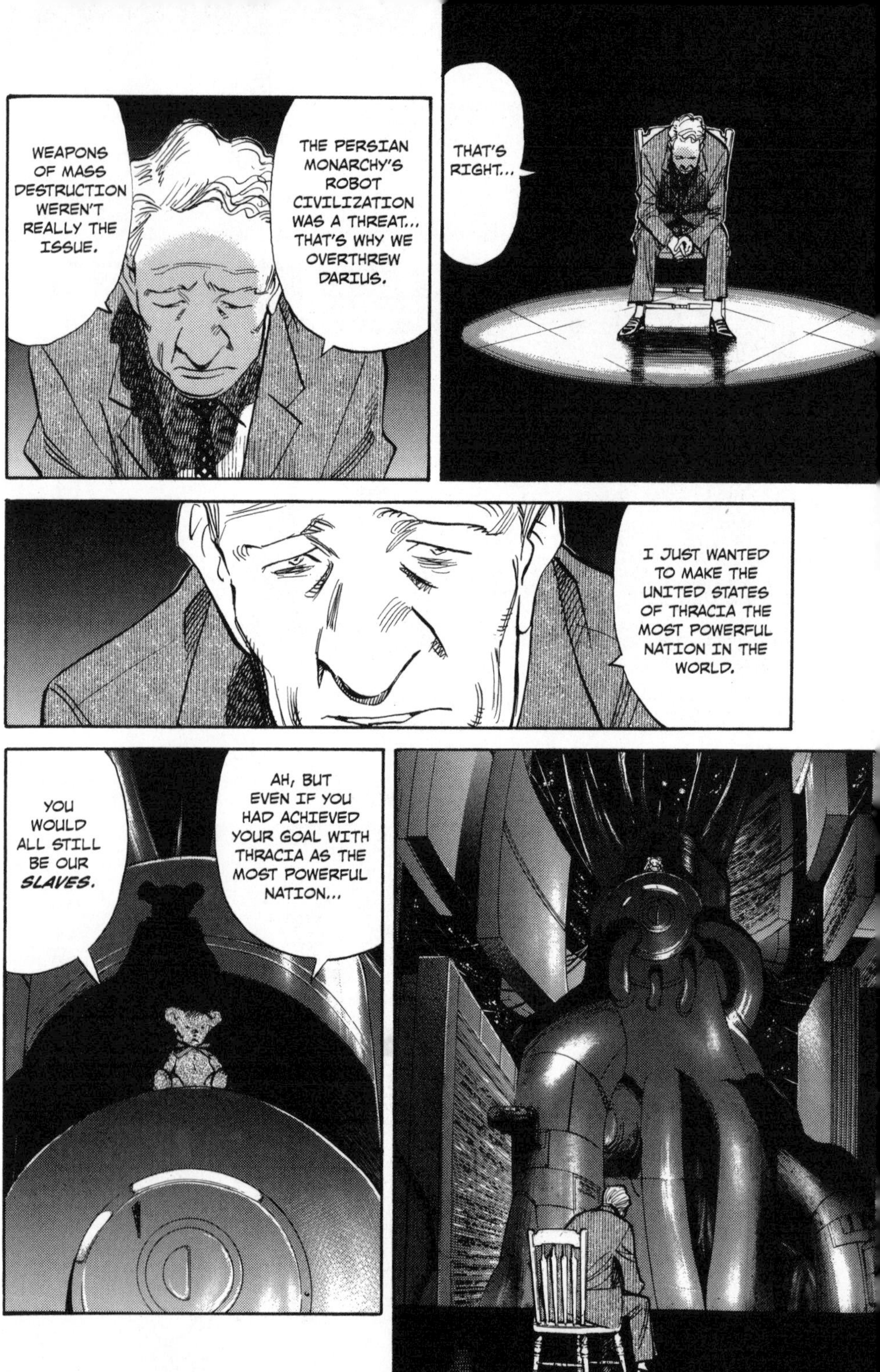
THAT'S RIGHT...
THE PERSIAN MONARCHY'S ROBOT CIVILIZATION WAS A THREAT... THAT'S WHY WE OVERTHREW DARIUS.
WEAPONS OF MASS DESTRUCTION WEREN'T REALLY THE ISSUE.
I JUST WANTED TO MAKE THE UNITED STATES OF THRACIA THE MOST POWERFUL NATION IN THE WORLD.
AH, BUT EVEN IF YOU HAD ACHIEVED YOUR GOAL WITH THRACIA AS THE MOST POWERFUL NATION...
YOU WOULD ALL STILL BE OUR *SLAVES*.

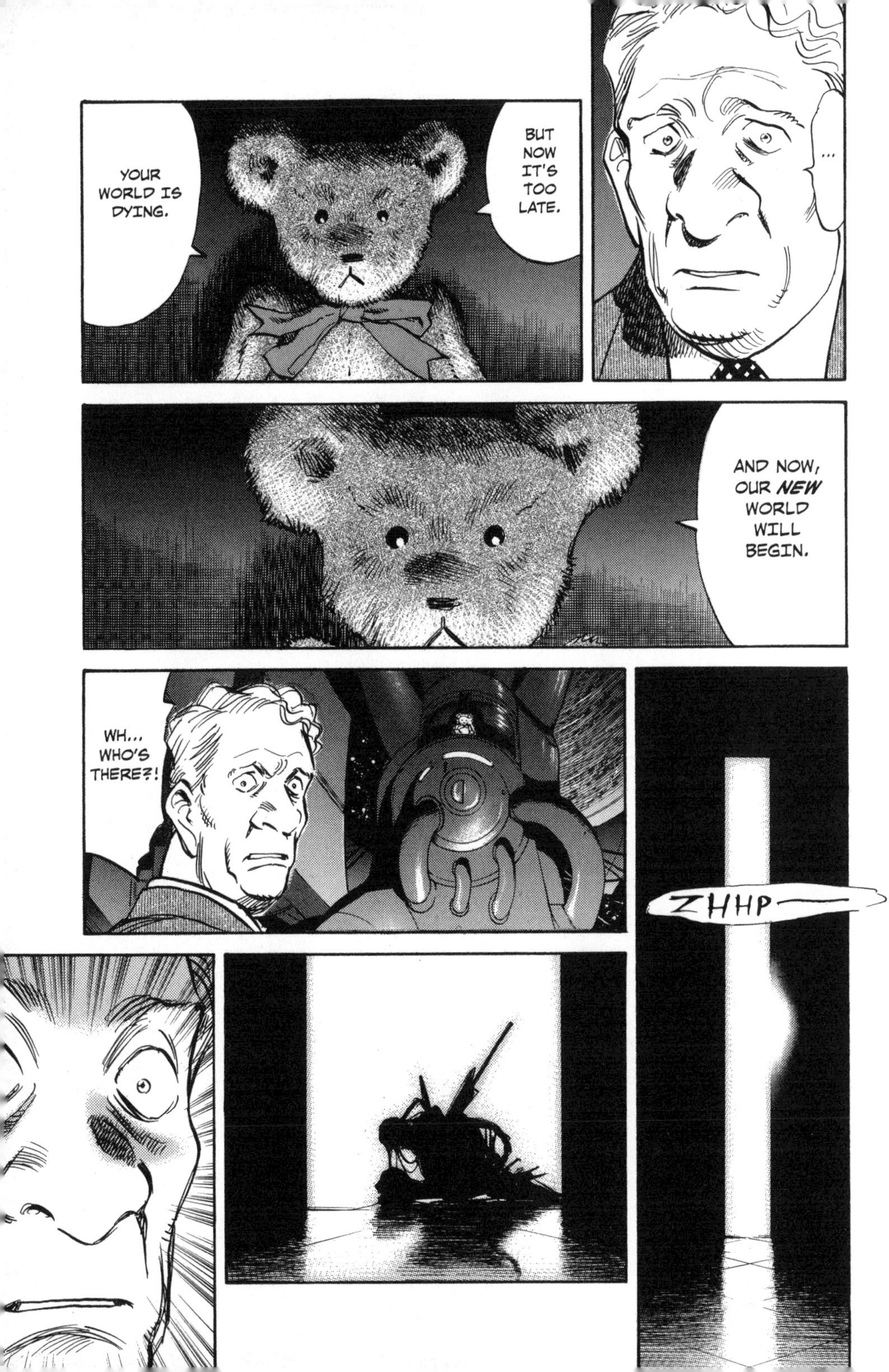
...
BUT NOW IT'S TOO LATE.
YOUR WORLD IS DYING.
AND NOW, OUR ***NEW*** WORLD WILL BEGIN.
ZHHP—
WH... WHO'S THERE?!

Y-YOU'RE...

YOU...

HOW NICE OF YOU TO COME.

BRAU 1589...

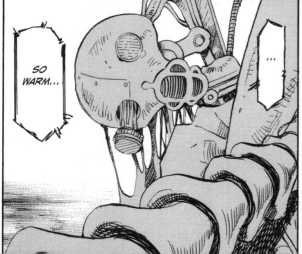

SO WARM...

...

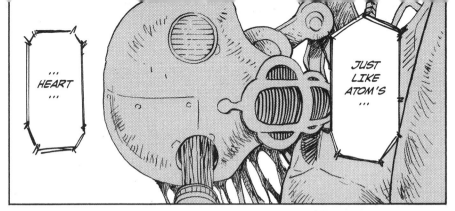

JUST LIKE ATOM'S ...
... HEART ...
VREE
KOFF KOFF
OH, MY... YOU'RE GOING TO SPARE HIM?
WHAT A DISAP-POINTMENT.
I WAS SO SURE THAT YOU AND I SHARED THE SAME DIVINE SPACE...
VRRR

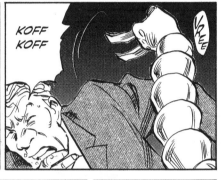

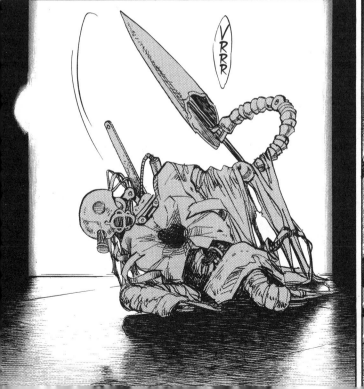

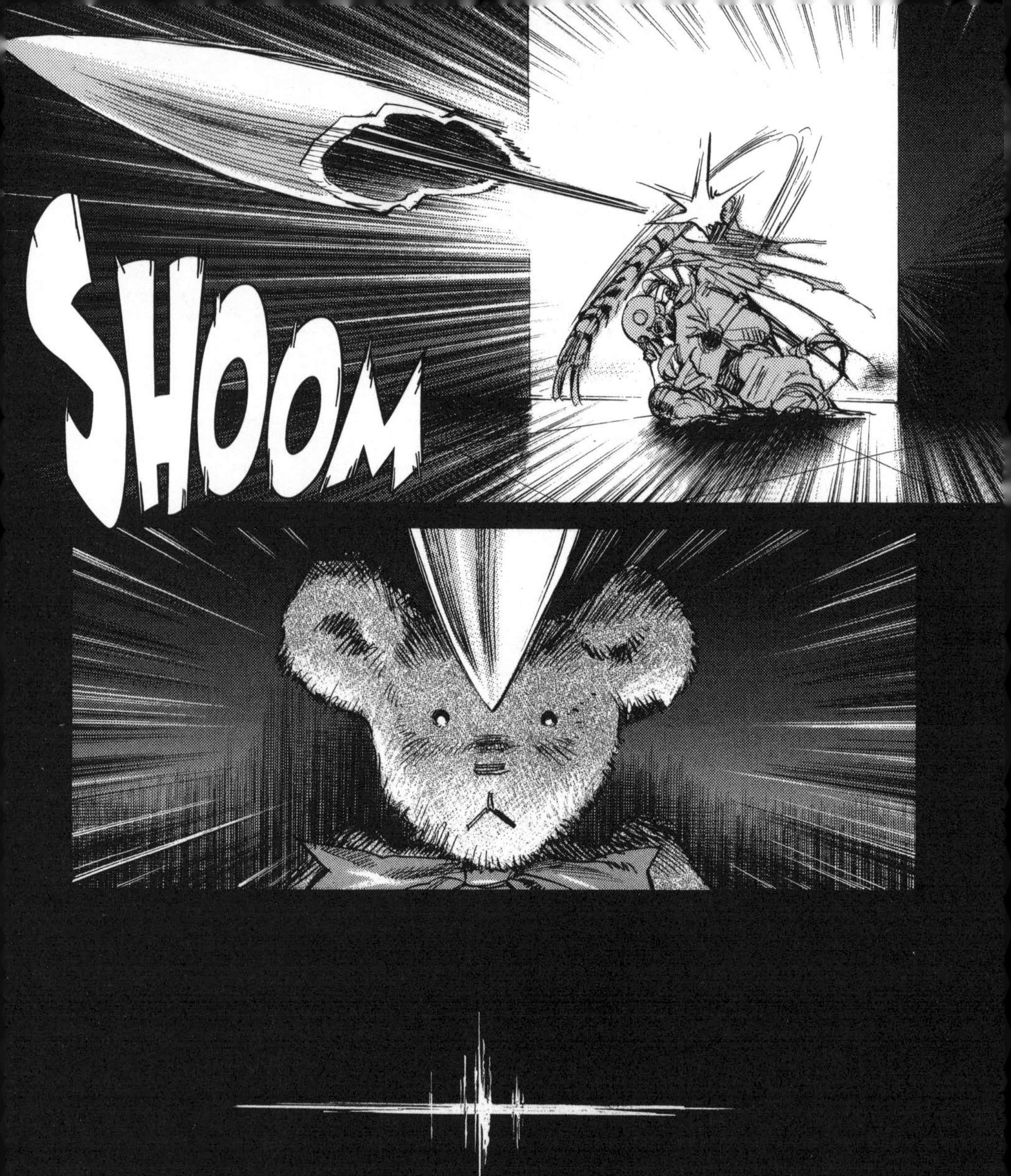
SHOOM

PLUTO

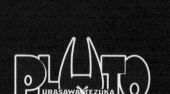

URASAWA × TEZUKA

END

This is a story about when I lived in Hiroshima a very long time ago. I was an elementary school student and completely enthralled by the *Astro Boy* series then running in the manga magazine *Shonen* and also by the puppet drama *Hyokkori Hyotanjima* (Unexpected Gourd Island) on television. I will come back to *Hyotanjima* later, but for now let me say that both of my parents were rather conservative, and both of them disapproved of my reading manga, so they rarely bought me any manga magazines.

In order to read manga I tried to manage my meager allowance as best as I could, but I still couldn't come up with enough money to buy the expensive *Shonen* monthly, not to mention popular manga weeklies like *Sunday*, *Magazine*, or *King*. So how would I be able to keep up with every chapter of Atom? I came up with the idea of befriending a kid whose parents were a little more enlightened about manga purchases.

I chose Matsuda, not just because he had issues of my target *Shonen* at his house, but also because he was a classmate that I got along with. Matsuda was big for his age and he got good grades. I doubt that his family was particularly well off, but I believe he was an only child, so he was a lucky kid who got stuff like remote-controlled, plastic-model robot toys for his birthday. In retrospect, it was pretty calculating of me to make all those visits to Matsuda's house, but the trips were a "necessary evil" (?) in order for me to read all the episodes of my beloved *Astro Boy*.

One might think that *Astro Boy* was the most popular manga in those days, but that wasn't necessarily true. Tatsukawa, the best dodgeball player in our class, never shrank from reminding me that "*Astro Boy*'s old news!" I was shocked, however, when one day I heard the same words come out of Matsuda's mouth. And this came from a boy who read not only *Shonen* from cover to cover but every other manga publication as well. Matsuda's favorite manga were *Tetsujin 28-go* (*Iron Man No. 28* or *Gigantor*) and the ninja story *Iga no Kagemaru* (Kagemaru of Iga)—both works drawn by Osamu Tezuka's rival at the time, Mitsuteru Yokoyama.

Even I knew why Matsuda was critical of Atom. Yokoyama's *Iga no Kagemaru* featured a battle format with merciless ninja deaths. *Tetsujin 28-go* starred a giant robot who could be used to fight both good guys and bad guys depending on who was operating his remote-control device, and he would keep fighting, unfazed even if a part of his body was ripped off. These stories were extraordinarily cruel and tragic, and that's what was alluring about them.

Tezuka's manga style was completely different. In Tezuka's stories, even the most evil villains were shown to have reasons for their twisted ways, so it always became apparent that they really weren't totally evil after all. And even Atom agonized before every battle, usually trying to persuade his adversaries not to fight... It could get irritating.

But I remained a resolute Atom fan. At some point I put some distance between Matsuda and myself, and I had to give up on using him to read *Astro Boy*.

However, several months later I overheard a conversation between Matsuda and Tatsukawa at the back of the classroom:

"The newest Atom episode's pretty good, huh?"

"Yeah, and that Pluto character's really strong. He's cool."

Then, turning to me, Matsuda announced, "Sorry, Nagasaki. We were wrong. I guess Atom really *is* cooler than Tetsujin."

After that, I once again started making visits to the Matsuda household. Interestingly, Matsuda's change of heart had come as a result of his having read "The Greatest Robot in History."*

Looking back on it all now, I realize that Osamu Tezuka was a man who constantly studied the work of his rivals. When Tezuka became aware that stories with battles were selling, he quickly adapted—and as soon as cool new buzzwords like "super robots" started to appear in the then-increasingly popular *8th Man* manga series, he quickly incorporated them into the dialogue he used. The result was "The Greatest Robot in History," which once again thrust Atom to the peak of robot manga popularity.

But as so typically happens in Tezuka's works, when I continued reading I found myself becoming more and more sympathetic to Pluto, who had originally seemed to be a cold, emotionless villain. In fact, I suddenly found myself identifying with this character to the point that I began to hope that somehow he wouldn't have to die.

Then one day Matsuda turned to me with very sad eyes and announced, "Pluto died in yesterday's issue of *Shonen*…"

I was thunderstruck and wondered what Osamu Tezuka had really been trying to say in this story.

"Atom was the only one left standing," Matsuda said, "so Tezuka must be saying that Atom's the strongest robot in history!"

Matsuda's confident interpretation of the story didn't seem to be exactly right to me, but I kept my mouth shut because I figured that the third-smartest kid in our class couldn't be wrong.

Forty years later, I finally came up with a counterinterpretation of the story. Naoki Urasawa and I were discussing our plans to remake "The Greatest Robot on Earth," and we were grappling with the unavoidable question of what Osamu Tezuka would have focused on if he were alive today. "War" immediately came to mind, but Tezuka's views on war were very complicated.

The answer to the question came from *Hyokkori Hyotanjima*, the aforementioned puppet series I was so enthralled with as a boy along with Atom. And it came to me as I was recently watching a play by one of the show's authors, Hisashi Inoue. Inoue has been showcasing both his old and new works on a frequent basis, so I was curious as to what might have happened to him. But while watching his play I understood. Inoue is sounding an alarm, for he fears that Japan may slide into another war in the near future. And his warning seems to match Osamu Tezuka's perspective on war.

Hisashi Inoue was born six years after Osamu Tezuka, but he comes from the same generation that survived the "burned-out rubble" of Japan's defeat in World War II. They are pacifists, but they hold no fanciful illusions. Their view of things would be as follows: Man goes to war. War is an undeniable consequence of our existence. But nothing good ever comes from war. Everyone loses. Tragedy befalls not only the soldiers who go to war, but also the people who are left behind. Freedoms are lost, our humanity is distorted. Mankind in all its foolishness will always pursue war, but it is something that we must avoid! Get it?!

"Osamu Tezuka wasn't saying anything about Atom being the strongest robot in history. On the contrary, I think he was trying to say that, having experienced battle, Atom was the first robot in history to understand the meaninglessness of war. That's what he was trying to say." And that's what my response to Matsuda is.

*"The Greatest Robot on Earth" originally appeared in *Shonen* under the title "The Greatest Robot in History."

The late Osamu Tezuka, a manga artist for whom I have the utmost respect, created the series *Astro Boy*. This timeless classic has been read by countless numbers of fans from when it was first created in the fifties to now. As a child, "The Greatest Robot on Earth" story arc from *Astro Boy* was the first manga I ever read that really moved me and inspired me to become a manga artist. With *Pluto* I've attempted to infuse that story with a fresh new spirit. I hope you enjoy it.

NAOKI URASAWA

Manga wouldn't exist without Osamu Tezuka. He is the Leonardo da Vinci, the Goethe, the Dostoevsky of the manga world. Naoki Urasawa and I have always felt that his achievements and work must not be allowed to fade away. Tezuka wrote that Atom, the main character of his most representative work *Astro Boy*, was born in 2003. This was the same year that we re-made "The Greatest Robot on Earth" story arc from the *Astro Boy* series. Who was Osamu Tezuka and what was his message? For those of you readers who are interested in *Pluto*, I highly recommend you read it alongside Tezuka's original work.

TAKASHI NAGASAKI

PLUTO: URASAWA × TEZUKA
VOLUME 8
VIZ SIGNATURE EDITION

BY Naoki Urasawa & Osamu Tezuka
CO-AUTHORED WITH Takashi Nagasaki
WITH THE COOPERATION OF Tezuka Productions

TRANSLATION Jared Cook & Frederik L. Schodt
TOUCH-UP & LETTERING James Gaubatz
COVER ART DIRECTION Kazuo Umino
LOGO & COVER DESIGN Mikiyo Kobayashi & Bay Bridge Studio
VIZ SIGNATURE EDITION DESIGNER Courtney Utt
EDITOR Andy Nakatani

PLUTO 8 by Naoki URASAWA/Studio Nuts, Osamu TEZUKA, Takashi NAGASAKI and Tezuka Productions
© 2009 Naoki URASAWA/Studio Nuts, Takashi NAGASAKI and Tezuka Productions
All rights reserved.
Original Japanese edition published in 2009 by Shogakukan Inc., Tokyo.

Based on "Astro Boy" written by Osamu TEZUKA.

Unedited English translation © 2009 Frederik L. Schodt and Jared Cook

The rights of the author(s) of the work(s) in this publication to be so identified
have been asserted in accordance with the Copyright, Designs and Patents Act 1988.
A CIP catalogue record for this book is available from the British Library.

Printed in the U.S.A.

Published by VIZ Media, LLC
P.O. Box 77010
San Francisco, CA 94107

10 9 8 7 6 5 4 3 2
First printing, March 2010
Second printing, February 2012

www.viz.com
www.vizsignature.com

ASTRO BOY

Osamu Tezuka's iconic *Astro Boy* series was a truly groundbreaking work about a loveable boy robot that would pave the way for all manga and anime to follow. Tezuka created the manga in 1951 and in January of 1963 adapted it to become the first weekly animated TV series ever to be broadcast in Japan. In September of that same year, it became the first animated TV series from Japan to hit the airwaves in the United States. The series and its title character were originally known in Japan as *Tetsuwan Atom*, which translates to "mighty Atom" – or for the more literally minded, "iron-arm Atom" – but was released in the U.S. as *Astro Boy*. Decades later, in 2000, Dark Horse Comics brought the manga for the first time to English readers, also under the title *Astro Boy*.

Within the context of the story for this English edition of *Pluto: Urasawa × Tezuka*, the precocious boy robot will be referred to as "Atom" in the manner in which he has been known and loved in Japan for over fifty years. Elsewhere, such as in the end matter, the series will be referred to as *Astro Boy* as it has been known outside of Japan since 1963.